REVIEW OF RESEARCH IN EDUCATION

Review of Research in Education is published on behalf of the American Educational Research Association by SAGE Publications, Thousand Oaks, CA 91320. Copyright © 2008 by the American Educational Research Association. All rights reserved. No portion of the contents may be reproduced in any form without written permission from the publisher. POSTMASTER: Send address changes to AERA Membership Department, 1430 K St., Suite 1200, Washington, DC 20005.

Member Information: American Educational Research Association (AERA) member inquiries, member renewal requests, changes of address, and membership subscription inquiries should be addressed to the AERA Membership Department, 1230 17th St., NW, Washington, DC 20036-3078; fax 202-775-1824. AERA annual membership dues are $120 (Regular and Affiliate Members), $100 (International Affiliates), and $35 (Graduate and Undergraduate Student Affiliates). **Claims:** Claims for undelivered copies must be made no later than six months following month of publication. Beyond six months and at the request of the American Educational Research Association, the publisher will supply missing copies when losses have been sustained in transit and when the reserve stock permits.

Subscription Information: All non-member subscription inquiries, orders, back-issue requests, claims, and renewals should be addressed to Sage Publications, 2455 Teller Road, Thousand Oaks, CA 91320; telephone (800) 818-SAGE (7243) and (805) 499-0721; fax: (805) 375-1700; e-mail: journals@sagepub.com; http://www.sagepublications.com. **Subscription Price:** Institutions: $141; Individuals: $50. For all customers outside the Americas, please visit http://www.sagepub.co.uk/customercare.nav for information. **Claims:** Claims for undelivered copies must be made no later than six months following month of publication. The publisher will supply missing copies when losses have been sustained in transit and when the reserve stock will permit.

Abstracting and Indexing: This journal is abstracted or indexed in Current Contents: Social & Behavioral Sciences, ERIC (Education Resources Information Center), Scopus, and Social Sciences Citation Index (Web of Science).

Copyright Permission: Permission requests to photocopy or otherwise reproduce copyrighted material owned by the American Educational Research Association should be submitted by accessing the Copyright Clearance Center's Rightslink® service through the journal's website at http://rre.aera.net. Permission may also be requested by contacting the Copyright Clearance Center via its website at http://www.copyright.com, or via e-mail at info@copyright.com.

Advertising and Reprints: Current advertising rates and specifications may be obtained by contacting the advertising coordinator in the Thousand Oaks office at (805) 410-7763 or by sending an e-mail to advertising@sagepub.com. To order reprints, please e-mail reprint@sagepub.com.

Change of Address: Six weeks' advance notice must be given when notifying of change of address. Please send old address label along with the new address to ensure proper identification. Please specify name of journal.

International Standard Serial Number ISSN 0091-732X
International Standard Book Number ISBN 978-1-4129-6433-3 (Vol. 32, 2008, paper)
Manufactured in the United States of America. First printing, February 2008.
Copyright © 2008 by the American Educational Research Association. All rights reserved.

REVIEW OF RESEARCH IN EDUCATION

What Counts as Knowledge in Educational Settings: Disciplinary Knowledge, Assessment, and Curriculum

Volume 32, 2008

Gregory J. Kelly, Editor
The Pennsylvania State University

Allan Luke, Editor
Queensland University of Technology

Judith Green, Editor
University of California, Santa Barbara

American Educational
Research Association

SAGE

Review of Research in Education
What Counts as Knowledge in Educational Settings: Disciplinary Knowledge, Assessment, and Curriculum
Volume 32

EDITORS

JUDITH GREEN
University of California, Santa Barbara

GREGORY J. KELLY
The Pennsylvania State University

ALLAN LUKE
Queensland University of Technology

AMERICAN EDUCATIONAL RESEARCH ASSOCIATION
TEL: 202-238-3200 FAX: 202-238-3250
http://www.aera.net/pubs

FELICE J. LEVINE
Executive Director

BARBARA LEITHAM
Publications Coordinator

Contents

Introduction
What Counts as Knowledge in Educational Settings: Disciplinary Knowledge, Assessment, and Curriculum

GREGORY J. KELLY
The Pennsylvania State University
ALLAN LUKE
Queensland University of Technology
JUDITH GREEN
University of California, Santa Barbara

At this historical moment, knowledge itself is in transition. The digitalization of the human archive has created new objects of science and experience; it has created new sciences and reorganized the relationships between long-standing disciplines and fields of inquiry; and it has created new cultural representations and industries. Complex histories and ethnographies of knowledge production show that universities, school systems, governments, and corporations are in transition, developing new systems for the generation, systematization, surveillance, and management of knowledge. The new knowledge bases are being shaped by, and are shaping, current international debates on issues of access to knowledge as well as intellectual, artistic, and industrial property. At the center of these debates are questions about how knowledge is made, who will control these directions, and who should have access to what kind of knowledge, in all of its traditional and emergent forms, from books to websites to mass media and the arts.

In part, abetted and deterred by the new technological media and a dynamic, fluid world of the 21st century (Bauman & Vecchi, 2004), the knowledge claims of communities of learners who historically have stood at the margins of the mainstream have been placed on the table alongside, and at times in contrast to, "official" school knowledge (e.g., Nasir, Hand, & Taylor, 2008 [this volume]). This includes the knowledges and knowledge-making practices of cultural and linguistic minorities, women, and socioeconomically marginalized communities. There is recognition across this volume of the emergence and significance of alternative approaches to knowledge that merit

Review of Research in Education
February 2008, Vol. 32, pp. vii–x
DOI: 10.3102/0091732X07311063
© 2008 AERA. http://rre.aera.net

consideration in the formation of curriculum. Additionally, there is a growing recognition that we are educating current students for jobs, pathways, and life worlds that are still in formation—and some that have yet to come into existence. This challenges long-standing curriculum directions that have their roots in modernist traditions where the boundaries of knowledge were assumed to be known and the skills needed for future learning and work taken as identifiable and quantifiable.

It is timely and relevant, then, that we revisit the question of what should count as knowledge and, by extension, whose knowledge counts. Our aim here is to move research and educational policy-research-practice dialogues back to foundational questions about what counts as knowledge and whose knowledge counts in an historical context where much of the policy debate has been preoccupied with issues of reform of institutional structure and instructional method. In many of these current debates between media and politicians, policymakers and researchers, disciplinary experts and educationists, questions about knowledge, or rather, knowledges, have been taken as given: that there is a corpus of "basic skills," core knowledges or competencies that have self-evident educational value; or the assumption that there is a corpus of canonical disciplinary and cultural knowledge, received wisdom, that is beyond criticism and is "essential" for cultural literacy, citizenship, national identity, and so forth. These assumptions have, in turn, been translated into key criteria, standards, and benchmarks for legal-juridical, technical-scientific, and ethical-moral assessments of school efficiency in the production of educational "outcomes." Yet what might count as an educational *outcome*, however constrained by the scientific, institutional, and political economic contexts, has been preempted in the current policy climate by a narrow focus on what is readily measurable, that is, on knowledge constructs and domains readily amenable to standardized achievement testing (Au, 2007).

This volume of *Review of Research in Education* brings together a group of international scholars who are asking questions about the nature of academic disciplines, knowledge and pedagogy, curriculum and assessment. Authors were asked to (re)examine what counts as knowledge across disciplinary areas as they reviewed their respective fields and to consider future research directions. The authors (re)examined knowledge and explored implications for learning and teaching in the arts, English, foreign languages, history, literacy, mathematics, and science. Additional chapters examine knowledge and pedagogy beyond specific disciplinary frameworks to consider teacher professional learning, assessing knowledge for English-language learners, and the sociology of the curriculum. Throughout this volume the chapters speak to issues related to learning, teaching, and critical access to residual and emergent traditions. The authors also consider the cultural, linguistic, and social class diversities of the institutional settings where knowledge and pedagogy meet. As the chapters demonstrate, these diversities pose opportunities and challenges for education.

Across the chapters, the authors document ways that specific social groups, including discipline-based groups, create specialized discourse, signs and symbols, ways of representing knowledge, and ways of thinking and inquiring that come to count as knowledge in these groups over time. They also offer cogent critiques of current versions of what Michael Apple (1993) termed "official knowledge." We view each of the chapters as characterizing ways that specialized knowledge was, and is, created for specific purposes and entered into educational settings through actions taken by members of various groups, disciplines, and societies. These knowledges, as demonstrated by current research and theories presented, are constructed by members through discourse and interaction and develop institutional histories through social practices as they are reinvoked and reinvented over time. Accordingly, knowledge in education is constructed, and knowledge of concepts and practices serves as a tool for learning and building capacity for problem solving, identity, and affiliation. Thus, as is argued across the chapters, learning disciplinary knowledge entails more than acquiring basic skills or bits of received knowledge. It also involves developing identity and affiliation, critical epistemic stance, and dispositions as learners participate in the discourse and actions of a collective social field. From this perspective, knowledge is not held in archives and texts, but is constructed through ways of speaking, writing, and acting. Thus, knowledge is continually tested, contested, and reconstructed through the emerging genres of academic knowledge in education.

Throughout the volume, therefore, authors argue that although there are demonstrable reasons for considering the value of thinking about knowledge through disciplinary frameworks, there needs to be full acknowledgement that the boundaries and practices of academic disciplines are fluid and negotiated. Across the ways of knowing characterized in the various chapters (e.g., the arts, science, history, languages, English), knowledge claims, evaluation of knowledge claims, and the criteria for the evaluation of knowledge claims change over time. Importantly, these changes in knowledge claims, evaluation, and criteria occur through specific actions taken by individuals and by groups through concerted activity. In this way, *what counts* as knowledge, who has access to such knowledge, and whose knowledge counts are interactionally accomplished and are potentially subject to questioning, critique, and change—depending, of course, on the rules and regularities of the institutional, political, and economic fields where knowledge is constructed. Knowledge is not held in the "official" curriculum, although such curriculum supports and constrains the possibility of access to particular types of knowledge for all students.

The responses of our various contributors cover a broad spectrum. All begin from a recognition of the historical, cultural, political, and social forces that affect the selection, shaping, transmission, and construction of knowledge in school settings. All begin from a recognition that school subjects and "school knowledge" are built and shaped according to different criteria than disciplinary traditional knowledge per se. Furthermore, many show that disciplinary knowledge beyond schooling does not map directly to the construction of school subjects (Deng & Luke, 2007)—there is no discipline of "science"; history is often taught in the U.S. context, for example, as "social studies"; art in complex and connected cultural contexts does not necessarily parallel art in school. At the same time, each field discussed here—from arts to history to English to language study to science to mathematics—is formed and shaped in relation to concomitant changes and shifts in relevant disciplinary fields. Yet across these chapters, there is a more sophisticated understanding of what counts as discipline and the related issues of what counts as disciplinary discourses, practices, and techniques: as tied to institutional, material, and ideological interests; as contested; as situated within both microethnographic and macrosocial and cultural contexts; as having multiple perspectives; and as in an historical transition in a period of trans-disciplinary, interdisciplinary problem solving and major paradigm shifts.

The critical reviews here return us to Pierre Bourdieu's (1990) key insight that disciplines constitute complex social fields whereby "systems of objectification"—epistemological frameworks for naming and understanding the world—are themselves produced by complex political economies, institutional cultures, and relationships of power. The continually contested nature of curriculum in schooling represented in different chapters demonstrates how changes are the results of dialectic debate (Kelly, 2006). The contributors address questions about how and in what ways educational actors in particular institutional contexts are reframing knowledge and how they are defining and (re)formulating what counts as knowledge for teachers, students, teacher educators, and researchers.

REFERENCES

Apple, M. W. (1993). *Official knowledge: Democratic education in a conservative age.* London: Routledge.

Au, W. (2007). High-stakes testing and curricular control: A qualitative metasynthesis. *Educational Researcher, 36,* 258–267.

Bauman, Z., & Vecchi, B. (2004). *Identity: Conversations with Benedetto Vecchi.* Cambridge, UK: Polity.

Bourdieu, P. (1990). *The logic of practice* (R. Nice, Trans.). Cambridge, UK: Polity.

Deng, Z., & Luke, A. (2007). Subject matter: Defining and theorizing school subjects. In M. Connolly, M. F. He, & J. Phillion (Eds.), *Sage handbook of curriculum and instruction.* Thousand Oaks, CA: Sage.

Kelly, G. J. (2006). Epistemology and educational research. In J. Green, G. Camilli, & P. Elmore (Eds.), *Handbook of complementary methods in education research* (pp. 33–55). Mahwah, NJ: Lawrence Erlbaum.

Nasir, N. S., Hand, V., & Taylor, E. V. (2008). Culture and mathematics in school: Boundaries between "cultural" and "domain" knowledge in the mathematics classroom and beyond. *Review of Research in Education, 32,* pp. 187–40.

Chapter 1

From Constructivism to Realism in the Sociology of the Curriculum

MICHAEL YOUNG

Institute of Education, University of London and University of Bath

Education is . . . a living struggle, a replica on a small scale of the conflicting purposes and tendencies which rage in society at large.

Karl Mannheim, 1936

INTRODUCTION[1]

What is educationally worthwhile knowledge, and what are (and what should be) the significant differences between curriculum or school knowledge and the everyday, commonsense knowledge that people acquire at home, in the community and in the workplace? Until the 1970s, answers to these questions were either taken for granted by both sociologists of education[2] and curriculum researchers as being part of existing educational systems or seen as issues to be left to philosophy. Education was seen as a good thing; the only big issues for sociology were distributional—in particular, the persistence, in all forms of selective education, of social class inequalities (Jencks, 1975). Why was progress to upper secondary and higher education limited to the few, and how could these persistent inequalities, found in all systems of mass education, be explained and reduced or overcome? The *what* of education, the knowledge that students did or did not acquire, was not questioned, at least by sociologists.[3] It was taken for granted that school and nonschool knowledge were different; they had always been so. Only rarely in the past, and invariably around religious issues, did the content of the knowledge that was included in the curriculum become part of educational debates, let alone those involving the wider public.

Review of Research in Education
February 2008, Vol. 32, pp. 1–28
DOI: 10.3102/0091732X07308969
© 2008 AERA. http://rre.aera.net

With the publication of *Knowledge and Control* (Young, 1971) in England and Michael Apple's (1979) *Ideology and the Curriculum* in the United States, this situation began to change, at least among those involved in educational studies. What became known as the "new sociology of education" and "critical curriculum studies" that these books led to questioned the traditional separation of school and nonschool knowledge and argued that the curriculum and its selection and structuring of knowledge need not and indeed should not be taken as given. The curriculum, these books argued, had to be understood in terms of questions of power, politics, and ideology, both within and beyond schools. More significantly, in showing how questions about knowledge and the curriculum could be seen as "political," the new sociology of education offered (or at least claimed to offer) tools for teachers and educational researchers to challenge existing curricula and to develop more democratic forms reflecting wider and not just elite needs and interests. It was not surprising that such developments generated opposition as well as support, both within university education departments and beyond; some of the most basic assumptions of modern societies were being called into question. Studying sociology of education in the 1970s was, as many teachers said at the time, a literally mind-changing experience.

Looking back to this period, more than 30 years later, when the basic assumptions of this sociological approach to the curriculum have undergone much sustained criticism, it is worth remembering the initial vision of democratic control that was symbolized by the idea that the curriculum was not something given but a social and political construct reflecting particular sets of interests, beliefs, and values. As is indicated by a recent book (Weis, McCarthy, & Dimitriades, 2006) that reflects on the influence of Michael Apple's work in the United States and globally, the political vision and the sense of possibilities that inspired the early sociology of the curriculum still capture the imagination of many educators. That said, it is not clear that the congratulatory tone of Lois Weis and her colleagues' (2006) book can really be justified. First, although the critical vision that they endorse may live on, it no longer is directly involved in teacher education or with educational policy, at least in the United Kingdom; both appear to have been able to disregard it. This lack of influence undoubtedly reflects the explicit move to the Right that began in the Reagan and Thatcher years and continued, despite changes of government in both countries, through the 1990s (Young, 2004). However, I shall argue that the lack of influence on curriculum policy of both the English tradition of the new sociology that I was associated with and the American tradition of critical curriculum studies also reflected real problems with their assumptions about knowledge and the curriculum. Visions are important, for without them (as is all too evident in much contemporary political debate in the United Kingdom), we would have no basis for envisaging alternatives. However, on their own, they are not enough, at least if they claim to be based on social science. They can easily become dogmas and, as a result, largely immune to debate and criticism.

Like the other social sciences, the sociology of education is in an ambiguous position as an intellectual field. It makes claims to have theories that *explain* educational problems with sufficient grounds, both conceptual and empirical, to be taken seriously by policy-makers and teachers. On the other hand, as Jeffrey Alexander (1995) once argued about sociology in general, theories in the social sciences are never just explanations; they always involve visions about the possibilities of something better. Inequalities are such an endemic feature of all educational systems that it is easy for critiques of existing structures to take precedence over the difficult and less overtly political task of searching for and testing theories. This is what many of us involved in the new sociology of education were inclined to do the 1970s, and this is what many of the authors writing in Lois Weis et al.'s (2006) collection still seem to be doing more than 30 years later. As social scientists, we can, I am sure, and without losing our visions or our politics, do better.

A shift from vision to theory, however, imposes constraints on our thinking as sociologists that were often dismissed by the new sociology of education in the 1970s with what now seems an excess of naivety and wishful thinking. I want to sug-gest two of these constraints—I will call them realities or truths[4]—which any soci-ology of the curriculum cannot, I now think, avoid. The first is that schooling, or formal education more broadly, involves the transmission of knowledge from one generation to another. This has to be a premise of the sociology of education, not, as it was in the 1970s, something to be debated or even opposed and resisted.[5] The second truth disregarded by the new sociology of education was that although the knowledge transmitted in curricula changes over time and is not a given or beyond question, it imposes constraints on curricular options that it is the task of the soci-ology of education to identify. In contrast, the new sociology of education treated curriculum knowledge as a socially constructed reality like any other. It followed that if knowledge structures such as subjects or disciplines appeared to be barriers to greater equality, they could always be changed. The problem, which I shall return to, is not just a theoretical one. This oversociological view of knowledge led to an over-politicized and instrumental view of the curriculum as something that could always be changed if political purposes changed.[6] In concentrating on the link between the social construction of the knowledge structures of the curriculum and the politics of changing them (Young & Whitty, 1976), sociologists of education were led away from identifying the social basis of the knowledge structures themselves. As Basil Bernstein would have expressed it, in his aphoristic way, there was too much focus on the purposes to be relayed by schooling and not enough focus on the relay itself.

In reflecting on the sociology of the curriculum as it has developed since the early 1970s, I am not in this chapter going to trace the many stages of the debates about different varieties of phenomenology, Marxism, feminism, and the more recent post-modern critiques; they have been well analyzed elsewhere (Ladwig, 1996; Moore & Muller, 1999). I want instead to develop two ideas that have until recently been neglected but that, I will argue, are central to the future of the sociology of the curricu-lum; they are the *structural differentiation* and *institutionality* of knowledge in the curriculum. Both ideas have long been at the center of sociological theory—particularly, that strand that traces its origins back to the French sociologist Emile Durkheim (Lukes, 1972; Young & Muller, 2007). However, they were given little attention in the early days of the sociology of the curriculum or when, as in the 1980s, it became more diversified and increasingly involved with the identity politics of gender and race.[7] The idea of the structural differentiation between fields of knowledge within the curriculum, between theoretical and practical knowledge, and between curricular and everyday knowledge was resisted and even dismissed by the new sociology of education; it was seen as masking the reality of the power relations underlying all such structures. The possibility that such knowledge structures might actually be conditions for learning and the creation of new knowledge seemed to stand in the way of the commitment to a more inclusive and participatory curriculum. Likewise, the idea that the curriculum might have an institutional form that was not just a product of the day-to-day realities of classroom life or the sectoral interests of teachers was avoided for somewhat similar reasons.[8] The idea of the curriculum as a social "institution" that is independent of the activities of teachers and pupils was assumed to have only conservative meanings. As a result, the possibility that an institution, such as the curriculum, or a subject, such as history or physics, might represent a necessary condition for the acquisition of some types of knowledge was avoided.

There have been two strands of sociological research on the curriculum that have taken the themes of institutionality and the structural differentiation of knowledge seriously. However, for the reasons I have suggested, they were never directly a part of the critical curriculum studies or new sociology of education movements. The first strand was the "neoinstitutionalism" associated with the work initiated by John Meyer (1992) and his colleagues at Stanford; I shall refer to their work in a later section, "The Curriculum as a Social Institution." The second strand is the work of Basil Bernstein and those who have developed his ideas (Moore, Arnot, Beck, & Daniels, 2004; Morais, Neves, Davies, & Daniels, 2001; Muller, Davies, & Morais, 2004). Bernstein has been associated by some with the new sociology of education,[9] and he certainly inspired many of us associated with it to focus on the curriculum (Young, 2007a). However, from very early in the 1970s, he developed his own quite distinctive approach to the curriculum with its roots in a sophisticated interpretation of Durkheim's ideas; it had little in common with the radical social constructivism of the new sociology of education (Moore, 2004). As early as 1971, in his well-known paper *On the Classification and Framing of Educational Knowledge*, Bernstein identified knowledge differentiation as a key issue for the sociology of the curriculum (Bernstein, 1971b). His link with critical curriculum studies was also complex. His work is often referred to by critical curriculum theorists such as Michael Apple. However, if one contrasts the recent collection edited by Lois Weis and her colleagues (2006) and the books based on the series of Bernstein research symposia (Moore et al., 2004; Morais et al., 2001; Muller et al., 2004), it is clear that those drawing explicitly on Bernstein's work have developed it in a very different direction to critical curriculum studies. Before discussing these two strands of research in more detail, the next section considers the broader question of how the sociology of the curriculum might address its most fundamental issue, the question of knowledge, and why I give such importance to the structural differentiation of knowledge in my approach to the curriculum.

AN APPROACH TO KNOWLEDGE AND THE CURRICULUM

Thinking about the role of knowledge in education has to begin, I suggest, not with knowledge itself nor with questioning how we produce and acquire it; both imply a separation of knowledge from its social origins—the relationship that the sociology of knowledge has always tried to recover. We must begin with reflecting on our relationship with the world of which we are a part and the symbols that we develop in perceiving and making sense of it (Cassirer, 2000).[10] It is the symbolic nature of our relationship to the world that enables us to have knowledge that we can rely on; and it is that relationship that distinguishes us as human beings, who create and acquire knowledge and use it to transform the world, from animals, who can only adapt to the world as they find it. It is for that reason that Durkheim and Vygotsky, among others, put education, which both saw as the active acquisition of knowledge, at the center of their ideas about society and human development. How else, they asked, other than through learning (and teaching), could we become social and in the process construct, maintain, and change societies? (Young, 2003, 2007a)

Aby Warburg, a colleague of the German philosopher Ernst Cassirer, summed up the point I want to make when she wrote,

The conscious creation of distance between oneself and the external world may be called the fundamental act of civilization. (as cited in Habermas, 2001, p. 7)

Viewing knowledge as an expression of the symbolic relationship between us and the world necessarily constrains the range of social (and educational) possibilities open to us at any particular time. First, it limits the ways in which we can construct the world. Our concepts and theories have a history and a structure that we have to take account of; they vary over time and across cultures, but they are not infinitely variable. Second, the world (both natural and social) of which we have knowledge is itself structured and not arbitrary, even if we can never be absolutely certain what those structures are. This approach to knowledge shares with the new sociology of education of the 1970s, and the writings of those such as Berger and Luckman (1967) that it drew on, the idea that the structures of our knowledge are social in origin—that they are not either divinely inspired, inherent in our minds, or in a world external to us. The disciplines, subjects, and fields though which we acquire and produce knowledge have been created historically by men and women acting collectively. However, the sociology of knowledge that is argued for in this chapter differs sharply from the constructivism of the new sociology of education in its view of the nature of those structures and their relationship to the world. Although social and therefore not beyond history, knowledge structures (and therefore curricula) face both learners and teachers as real constraints and cannot, as some of us once thought, be "constructed away" by political or pedagogic action (Young & Muller, 2007). In this sense, philosophers such as Pring (1972) and science educators such as Jevons (1972) were right, and I (Young, 1974) and other "new sociologists" were wrong when at the time we set no limits, at least explicitly, on the possibilities of constructing the world differently. These limits, too, are themselves social in origin, albeit in a very specific ways (Collins, 1998).

To what extent do the knowledge structures of the curriculum represent barriers to be overcome in the process of creating a fairer and more inclusive system? Or are they, at least to some extent, the "epistemological" price we pay for a better understanding of the world? These are major questions for the sociology of education. It has been through coming to recognize their importance that I have been led to adopt what I refer to in this chapter as a form of "social realism"[11] and to rethink my earlier idea that knowledge in education can be viewed as a social construct, like any other social phenomenon.

Addressing these issues and especially taking account of the fact that, despite (or perhaps because of!) avoiding the epistemological questions, the new sociology of education inspired and continues to inspire researchers and teachers and raises some fundamental questions about the role of sociology in educational studies.[12] First, the question of knowledge is a uniquely difficult issue and one that, I now recognize, the new sociology of education dealt with superficially at best. This difficulty may partly explain the reluctance of many educational researchers to engage in "knowledge" or epistemological issues. It may also be because questions about knowledge take one into the long philosophical tradition that can be traced back from Plato and Aristotle to Kant, Hegel, and Popper. However, a more practical reason may be that questions about knowledge in education always take us back to some of our most basic assumptions about what it is to be educated. It is, I suggest, not possible to think more than superficially about education without considering what it is we want students to learn and why. Education is never just a process. Furthermore, for those of us who teach, at any level, there is always a tension between the real difficulties that students face in learning something new and the basis of one's confidence as a teacher in saying that despite such difficulties, certain things are worth learning, that a subject or field is worth studying, not because they are or will be useful, but, as the rather misleading phrase expresses it, "education can be for its own sake."[13] Second, questions about knowledge in education involve issues that overlap with a number of quite distinct specialist literatures (for example, not only epistemology and the sociology of knowledge and educational policy and practice but the wide range of subject knowledges associated with the curriculum). Prior to the emergence of the sociology of the curriculum, specialists in these literatures had few if any connections, and it was possible to specialize in one and be quite ignorant of the others. It is therefore not surprising that many curriculum researchers have put questions about knowledge aside as best left to other specialists.

Reaching the conclusion that questions about knowledge in education could not just be set aside did not arise for me, at least initially, from any theoretical principle but from my experience throughout the 1990s of working on curriculum policies for postschool and vocational education (Young, 2007a).[14] I kept coming up against the differences between the types of knowledge that could be acquired in workplaces and those acquired in colleges and schools and that both teachers and their students were expected to "integrate" them in the vocational curriculum. I found it impossible even to begin to provide answers to how the integration of college-based and work-based knowledge should be approached without a theory of knowledge that distinguishes different types of knowledge and their different purposes and conditions for acquisition. A particularly problematic issue faced by vocational teachers arises when governments try to base the vocational curriculum on statements of outcomes or standards (Young & Gamble, 2006). How do you develop a curriculum from a set of standards that are abstracted from any institutional context in which knowledge is developed and used? We are dealing, I came to believe, with a fundamental incompatibility between acquiring skills and demonstrating competence on one hand and acquiring knowledge on the other (Allais, 2003; Weelahan, in press; Young, 2004). I found that there was no research that addressed the issues faced by vocational teachers, only statements of standards or competence that at best could be the basis for assessment, certainly not pedagogy. To find a way forward, I needed a theory of knowledge and was led back to Durkheim's sociology of knowledge and Vygotsky's distinction between "theoretical" and "everyday" concepts (Young, 2003, 2007b). It was from Durkheim, and especially the lectures on sociology and pragmatism (Durkheim, 1983) that he gave to trainee teachers, that I learned that questions about knowledge could be practical and everyday and need not be abstract and philosophical. His sociology of knowledge was an attempt to give meaning to this idea.

In the 1970s, the new sociology of education restated the argument already implicit in Durkheim's work that the sociology of education needed a social theory of knowledge. However, it was almost as if the assertion of the sociality of knowledge was enough. Inevitably this led to a problem that I, like most of those involved in the sociology of education at the time, failed to recognize. Asserting the sociality of knowledge can easily slip into a form of reductionism. For some, of course, this was part of its appeal. If knowledge can be reduced to the interests or standpoints of knowers, all kinds of new political possibilities appear to be open.[15] However, this reductionism[16] means that questions about the curriculum lose their specificity and become almost synonymous with any phenomenon where the power to make decisions is unevenly distributed. A tendency to lose what is specific to the curriculum—how and what knowledge is acquired and how it should be paced, sequenced, and assessed—was the trap that the new sociology of education and critical curriculum studies often fell into and is perhaps why their substantive research record (Whitty, 2006) is, with some exceptions (Goodson, 1998), not extensive.

The alternative to reductionism that retains the insights of the sociology of knowledge follows from two of Durkheim's much neglected ideas. One is the distinction that he makes between knowledge and experience (Durkheim, 1983). This distinction can be traced back to the separation between the "sacred" and the "profane" orders of meaning that he identified in the aboriginal societies that he studied (Durkheim, 1912/1995; Durkheim & Mauss, 1970). It is this separation that underpins the idea that knowledge and experience are structurally differentiated—in other words, they are based on different forms of social organization, in all societies. It is this idea that informs Bernstein's (1971a) curriculum theory that I will discuss in a later section, "Knowledge Differentiation and the Sociology of the Curriculum." However, the idea is not without its problems (Muller, 2000; Young, 2003). It can easily become the basis for the total separation of the two and lead back to the kind of asocial idealism associated with Kant and the neo-Kantians that Durkheim set out to replace. On the other hand, without an analytical separation of knowledge from experience, it is difficult to see how we can find principled grounds for making the school–nonschool knowledge distinction that is crucial to any theory of the curriculum.

Durkheim's second insight that many traditions in the sociology of knowledge fail to grasp (Durkheim, 1983),[17] was that recognizing the social basis of knowledge does not imply that all knowledge is biased and therefore can never be objective. For Durkheim, as Collins (1998) and others have pointed out, the social basis of knowledge is the condition for its objectivity and why we can rely on it. Durkheim (1983) argued that it is our social being as humans that grounds the very possibility of our having objective knowledge about the world. However, such a position can easily slip from providing grounds for the authority of knowledge and, of course, of the teacher to being a license for authoritarianism and the imposition of particular worldviews. One of the tasks of the sociology of the curriculum is to develop Durkheim's idea and specify the forms of social organization that underlie different types of knowledge and their forms of objectivity.[18]

Michael Gibbons and his colleagues (1994) offer an interesting way of conceptualizing different forms of knowledge organization. They argue that a new mode of knowledge production—Mode 2 (or transdisciplinary knowledge), which is context driven, problem focused, and interdisciplinary—is replacing the traditional (Mode 1, or disciplinary) mode, which is academic, investigator initiated, and discipline based.[19] In their book, Gibbons and his colleagues are primarily concerned with the management problems facing universities when faced with multiple sources of funding; they largely avoid epistemological or pedagogic questions. By arguing that the mode of knowledge production in universities has to change to respond to changing economic circumstances, they adopt what Durkheim (1983) described as a form of "logical utilitarianism," which assumes that knowledge is validated by its uses. For Durkheim, uses, which are always a posteriori, can never be reliable grounds for the objectivity of knowledge. Johann Muller and I (Young & Muller, 2007) spell out Durkheim's argument that knowledge is both a priori and social.

With these general principles in mind about how the sociology of education might rethink the question of knowledge, the next section turns more explicitly to the new sociology of education and the closely related field of critical curriculum studies.

KNOWLEDGE AND THE CURRICULUM IN THE NEW SOCIOLOGY OF EDUCATION

Like many researchers working in the field of curriculum studies, I was excited by Michael Apple's (1979) book *Ideology and Curriculum* when it was first published more than 25 years ago. It resonated with, and in certain ways extended, the attempts of a number of us in the United Kingdom (e.g., Whitty & Young, 1977; Young & Whitty, 1976) to use the sociology of knowledge to develop a critical approach to the curriculum. Finding some of our ideas being picked up with such enthusiasm in the United States made us feel part of a global movement and not just a national debate. Writing after the publication of Bowles and Gintis's (1976) influential Marxist critique of American schooling, Apple was able to demonstrate the nonneutrality of the curriculum and how the everyday practices of teachers in classrooms expressed and even mirrored the unequal power relations of capitalist societies. Furthermore, he was not trapped in Bowles and Gintis's overeconomistic and deterministic version of Marxism. Inspired by the work of Paul Willis (1977) and the ideas of the Italian Marxist Antonio Gramsci (1971), Apple's later books argued that dominant power relations in education were always, even if not consciously, resisted and therefore always had to be "achieved" by those in power. More recently, his analysis of the project of "conservative modernization" (Apple, 2006) has reminded the educational research community that innovation is by no means always progressive. At the same time and against the trend of the times, he has retained the political optimism of his earlier work by drawing on a range of examples of local resistance. However, despite the merits of the critical curriculum studies tradition that he initiated, its lack of any explicit theory of knowledge leads to a number of problems. First, it has been difficult for these more "politicized" approaches to the curriculum to do more than critique existing curriculum models, and second, we are left with an absence of substantive curriculum analyses or alternatives. I think those of us in the United Kingdom, the United States, and elsewhere who, since the 1970s, have drawn on the sociology of education to develop a critical approach to educational studies must address the unintended consequences of our overpoliticization of the curriculum. In other words, we have to reexamine what we mean by being "critical" in curriculum studies and whether it is possible to have a coherent concept of criticality without an explicit theory of knowledge (Moore, 2007). Critical curriculum studies displays how subordinate groups are discriminated against. However, without a theory of knowledge, it has no basis for suggesting what a system that discriminated less against subordinate groups might look like. Nor can it argue convincingly that doing away with or even modifying the characteristic features of the current system—its subjects, its pedagogic hierarchies, its external examinations, and its textbooks—would make discrimination and inequality less rather than more likely. This is not to defend these characteristics as being beyond criticism but to suggest that although they may perpetuate inequalities, the issue about knowledge organization and sequencing that they address remains an issue for any modern curriculum.

The mistake that I certainly made in the 1970s and 1980s was to imagine that demonstrating the power relations underlying the existing curriculum could be the basis for creating one that was more democratic. It has not happened, and in some ways, it can be argued that public education has gone backward in the past 25 years. A good example in England is the recent proposal to give more emphasis to student choice in the secondary curriculum by providing a range of "vocational" options for students at 14 and older. Because many educational researchers have a theory of access but not a theory of knowledge, there is hardly a debate about the consequences of creating such choices when many students may lack the cultural resources to make them. Without an explicit concept of knowledge acquisition, policies that give priority to widening participation and student choice could well be the basis for new, albeit less visible, inequalities (Weelahan, in press; Young, in press).

We have to ask what went wrong—not just with the policies of successive governments in different countries but with our theory. Many sociologists of education in the 1970s and 1980s were attracted by Bourdieu and Passeron's (1977) evocative conceptualization of pedagogy as "symbolic violence." What we neglected were the problems posed by Bourdieu's less heralded claim that culture is arbitrary and therefore that any form of cultural transmission, in imposing itself as if it were not arbitrary, is "violent" (Nash, 1990). It is significant that Bourdieu (2004) himself tried, in my view not very successfully, to address this problem in relation to the sociology of science in his last book. If all culture is arbitrary and all pedagogies are forms of symbolic violence and therefore to be struggled against, the logical conclusion is that each generation has to reinvent knowledge anew and therefore, like animals, be limited to survival (but with a much more limited range of instinctive capacities to draw on). The argument made here is not to deny that the curriculum may be experienced as external and even threatening by some young learners; we are, after all, born into the world with capacities but no culture. My point is that the discontinuity between the culture of any curriculum and that of pupils represents the fundamental pedagogic problem that teachers always face.[20] Furthermore, this discontinuity will be most acute for those most disadvantaged by their social circumstances. The question for the sociology of education becomes not to just to critique the imposed (or even violent) nature of the curriculum but to ask what kinds of knowledge should be the basis of the curriculum and how can they be made accessible to the majority of students. Only with a theory of the differentiation of knowledge can we begin to address such questions.

The second assumption of my argument is that the knowledge that takes people beyond their experience has historically been expressed largely in disciplinary or subject forms. Critical curriculum theory has focused on the dominant relations between knowledge and power and the inequalities that have been embodied historically in the disciplinary and subject basis of school curricula. It has neglected the extent to which the knowledge from which the disadvantaged are disproportionately excluded—the social sciences, the natural sciences, history and literature, foreign languages, mathematics, and technological subjects such as engineering—is not just the "knowledge of the powerful," which it has for too long been, but it is also, in an important sense, "knowledge itself." As a result, critical curriculum theory can expose neoliberalism's endorsement of choice and markets and how they inevitably disadvantage children from poor families, but it has no basis for offering an alternative.[21]

Before discussing the theoretical basis for an alternative knowledge-based approach to the curriculum, the next section of the chapter tackles the second crucial aspect of the curriculum largely neglected by the new sociology of education: its institutional form. By this, I mean the argument that the curriculum is not just a product of the practices of teachers and pupils or even of government policies but a social institution that needs to be understood independently of the individual actions of teachers and curriculum policymakers. The findings of research on the curriculum as a global institution provide important links to the theory of knowledge differentiation developed in the later section, "Knowledge Differentiation and the Sociology of the Curriculum."

THE CURRICULUM AS A SOCIAL INSTITUTION

In a series of studies, "neoinstitutional" sociologists (e.g., Meyer, 1992, and Baker & LeTendre, 2005) have charted the progressive democratization and modernization of the curriculum as a global phenomenon. There are two elements in their analysis that I want to refer to. One is the idea of the "institutionality" of the curriculum itself, and the second is their evidence for a growing and global emphasis in the curriculum on relevance, student choice, and responding to the needs of the individual learner or child. These trends are revealed across a range of curriculum subjects on which they have data. They argue that the striking similarities across what are in other ways very different national educational systems are indicative that schooling, and specifically, the school curriculum, is an institution that expresses an increasingly global culture that is largely independent of national policies. The statistical data from international surveys that they rely on have limitations that they are aware of. However, this does not detract from the power of the data as evidence of global similarities and the challenge it provides for theories that seek to explain curriculum changes in terms of teachers' practice or the priorities of national governments. There are interesting parallels in their argument with Durkheim's (1952) famous study of suicide. Durkheim used official statistics to argue that although suicide is self-evidently the most individual act that is possible, rates of suicide are social facts that vary systematically in relation to structural features of societies, such as their degree and form of integration. The parallel with Durkheim in the studies by Meyer and his colleagues is that they show that the curriculum, perhaps the most nationally distinctive of educational policies, appears, using their cross-national statistical data, as the product of internationalizing or global forces. Dale (2000) criticizes their "global culture" thesis as being too descriptive and not explanatory and argues that their data need to be located in the contradictions of global capitalism rather than in their somewhat ill-defined concept of global culture. However, he does not challenge the structure of Meyer's argument about the curriculum as a global, modernizing institution. There are two more specific issues that this research raises for curriculum policymakers and the sociology of the curriculum. One arises from their hypothesis that national policies have had, at best, a weak causal role in the development of the curriculum. If they are right, this suggests a way of making sense of the frequent failures of nationally led curriculum reforms—a good example here is the case of vocational education in England (Keep, 2006).

The second issue that I want to give attention to is their finding that there is a growing tendency across the countries that they studied for the amount of "technical" or subject-specific content of curriculum programs to be reduced.[22] These findings that the priorities of schooling appear to be changing from a focus on the acquisition knowledge that students are unlikely to have access to at home to a focus on the role of schools in the broad "socialization" of young people as future citizens can be interpreted in a number of ways. Some would, of course, argue that this is a change in form rather than purpose and that mass schooling has always been primarily about the socialization of future citizens; critical curriculum studies and the new sociology of education have frequently adopted a critical version of this argument (Young, in press). The finding about the content reduction of the curriculum appears, at least superficially, at odds with the influential knowledge economy and information economy arguments of researchers such as Bell (1973) and Castells (1996), who argue that more and more jobs are becoming knowledge based. However, whereas the latter are referring to the expansion of research-based knowledge, which is largely acquired in the university, the statistics drawn on by the neoinstitutionalists refer to mass schooling and include the many students who will never reach university. This tension points to two problems hardly yet studied by sociologists of education. One is the emergence of new divisions within the emerging knowledge economies, between the "knowledge haves" and the "knowledge have-nots." The second problem is whether the reduction in content implies a new curriculum model in which the processes of thinking take precedence over what the thinking is about. Whether this implication of a shift from content to process points to "up-skilling" through the development of new intellectual skills or to "down-skilling" because any intellectual development is inescapably linked to content remains another important but neglected research question for the sociology of education. More than 30 years ago, Braverman (1976), in a postscript to his book *Labour and Monopoly Capital*, commented on how the evacuation of content within the school curriculum for the lowest social classes in each cohort was following the more general "deskilling" of work. One possible implication of the neoinstitutionalist findings is that the process identified by Braverman may be extending upward, albeit masked as a public issue by the growing number of students gaining some form of school-leaving certificate and going on to higher education.

Bernstein's (2000) analysis of the structuring of educational knowledge, which is discussed in the next section, suggests a way that the implications of the content reduction of the curriculum identified by Meyer (1992) might be explored. If the extension of a global culture is a despecifying or dedifferentiating process—in other words, if knowledge fields, occupational fields, and specialist sectors such as education are becoming more similar—then in Bernstein's terms, the curriculum is responding to external political and economic forces rather than to the internal conditions for knowledge acquisition. We may be seeing a dedifferentiation of the curriculum as the primary institution for the acquisition of specialized knowledge, at least for some sections of each age cohort. There is evidence from the neoinstitutional research that this dedifferentiation is both an internal process (the pattern appears to be similar across different subjects) and an external process (the pattern is common across different national systems). Despite the global evidence for this trend, it has generated little public anxiety, at least in this country, when governments can also point to evidence of widening participation, longer periods of full-time study, and higher proportions of each cohort achieving higher grades and progressing to university. In raising this issue, I am not making the well-known, politically conservative argument that "more means worse." The possibility remains, however, that the expansion of mass schooling is being paralleled by the dedifferentiation of the curriculum. In responding to government pressures, schools strive to involve an ever-widening proportion of each cohort, often without the necessary pedagogic resources to be successful, especially with students who find knowledge acquisition difficult. This process may be exacerbated by the internationalization of education policy, the role of international organizations, and the increasing emphasis on "league tables" and international comparisons. Governments may feel forced to find shortcuts to scoring higher on international comparisons, regardless of the longer-term consequences in terms of what knowledge students are acquiring.

KNOWLEDGE DIFFERENTIATION AND THE SOCIOLOGY OF THE CURRICULUM

In 1971, *Knowledge and Control* (Young, 1971) proposed a reorientation of the sociology of education toward questions of knowledge and the curriculum and away from its previous focus on the distribution of educational opportunities. This was a belated recognition of Durkheim's (1956) insight that it is the process of *cultural transmission* that lies at the heart of the role of formal education in modern societies. It followed, as mentioned earlier, that a key issue for sociologists was the discontinuity between the culture of the curriculum or school knowledge and the culture that different groups of students acquire in their homes, peer groups, and communities and bring to school. The social-class basis of this cultural discontinuity was first analyzed by Bernstein (1971a) in his research on language codes and by Bourdieu and Passeron (1977) with their concept of cultural capital. However, research in the sociology of education at the time was split between a focus on the social factors influencing the differential attainment of children from different social classes, which paid little attention to the curriculum, and the new sociology of education, which pointed toward the socially distributing effects of the school curriculum without a similar attention to cultural discontinuity between home and school. However, if it is accepted that knowledge transmission is a key role of schools, then the curriculum must assume that some types of knowledge are more worthwhile than others, and their differences must form the basis for the differences between school or curriculum knowledge and nonschool knowledge. If the school tries to modify its curriculum in favor of the culture of the pupils who come to the school, then it is failing in its role as an agent of cultural transmission. It was in reflecting on these issues that I was led to focus on the question of knowledge differentiation and to make a distinction between two ideas, *knowledge of the powerful* and *powerful knowledge*. *Knowledge of the powerful* is defined by who gets the knowledge in a society and has its roots in Marx's (1964) well-known dictum that the ruling ideas at any time are the ideas of the ruling class. It is understandable that many sociological critiques of school knowledge that have drawn, however loosely, on Marxist ideas have equated school knowledge and the curriculum with the idea of *knowledge of the powerful*. It was, for example, the upper classes in England in the early 19th century that gave up their private tutors and sent their children to the public (fee-charging) schools to acquire *powerful knowledge* (as well as, of course, to acquire powerful friends). However, the fact that some knowledge is *knowledge of the powerful*, or "high-status" knowledge, as I once expressed it (Young, 1971, 1998), tells us nothing about the knowledge itself. To explore the differentiation of knowledge in the curriculum, we need another concept that I want to refer to as *powerful knowledge*. This refers not to the backgrounds of those who have most access to knowledge or who give it legitimacy, although both are important issues. *Powerful knowledge* refers to what the knowledge can do or what intellectual power it gives to those who have access to it. *Powerful knowledge* provides more reliable explanations and new ways of thinking about the world and acquiring it and can provide learners with a language for engaging in political, moral, and other kinds of debates. Accessing *powerful knowledge* is, if not always consciously, what parents hope their children will achieve in making sacrifices to keep them at school; they hope that their children will acquire knowledge that is not available to them at home. In modern societies, *powerful knowledge* is, increasingly, specialized knowledge; and schooling, from this perspective, is about providing access to the specialized knowledge that is embodied in different knowledge domains. It follows that the key curriculum questions will be concerned with

(a) the differences between different forms of specialist knowledge and the relations between them,
(b) how this specialist knowledge differs from the knowledge people acquire in everyday life,
(c) how specialist and everyday knowledge relate to each other, and
(d) how specialist knowledge is "pedagogized" (in other words, how it is paced, selected, and sequenced in the curriculum for different groups of learners).

It is these differences and how they are expressed in different knowledge domains that the idea of knowledge being structurally differentiated refers to. Underlying these differences, however, is a more basic difference between two types of knowledge. One is the *context-dependent* (or everyday, commonsense) knowledge that people develop in the course of their everyday lives. Context-dependent knowledge can be practical, such as knowing how to repair a mechanical or electrical fault or how to find a route on a map. It can also be procedural, as in sets of regulations for health and safety or manuals for operating machines (Gamble, 2006). Context-dependent knowledge is acquired during the course of growing up; it enables the individual to cope in the world that he or she is a part of. It deals with particulars that arise in everyday life but provides no reliable basis for moving beyond those particulars. The second type of knowledge is *context-independent* knowledge.[23] This is the conceptual knowledge that is not tied to particular cases and therefore provides a basis for generalizations and making claims to universality. Unlike context-dependent knowledge, it provides a reliable basis for moving beyond particulars and therefore beyond one's experience. It refers to knowledge that is codified, tested, and elaborated by specialist communities and is typically, but not solely, associated with the sciences and technology. My hypothesis is that context-independent knowledge cannot, except in special cases, be acquired in homes and communities; its acquisition requires curriculum structures located in schools and the support of teachers with the specialist knowledge and links with universities that enable them to select, pace, and sequence contents. These are the conditions for the transmission of what I earlier referred to as *powerful knowledge*.

Inevitably, schools are not always successful in enabling pupils to acquire *powerful knowledge*. It is also true that schools are more successful with some pupils than with others. The success of pupils is partly dependent on the pedagogic and subject knowledge of teachers and partly on the culture that pupils bring to school. Elite cultures that are less constrained by the material exigencies of life are, not surprisingly, more congruent with the conditions for acquiring context-independent knowledge than disadvantaged and subordinate cultures. The distributional consequences of a curriculum based on context-independent knowledge mean that schools have to take the knowledge base of the curriculum very seriously, even when this appears to go against the immediate demands of pupils (and sometimes of their parents). Teachers have to ask the question, "Is this curriculum a means by which pupils can acquire *powerful knowledge?*" For children from disadvantaged homes, active participation in school may be the only opportunity that they have to acquire *powerful knowledge* and be able to move, intellectually at least, beyond their local and the particular circumstances. It does them no service to construct a curriculum around their experience (context-dependent knowledge) on the grounds that everyone's experience is equally valid, at least for them; if schools do no more than validate the experience of pupils, they can only leave them there.

The idea of school and nonschool knowledge as structurally differentiated provides a principled basis for the sociology of the curriculum. It is not, however, adequate on its own as the basis for a theory of pedagogy. Teachers have to develop ways of enabling pupils to move beyond the nonschool knowledge that they bring to school in a process that can be described as the "recontextualization" of both school and nonschool knowledge. There is not the space to develop this point here.[24]

The most sustained and original attempt to conceptualize the differentiation between school and nonschool knowledge is that developed by the English sociologist Basil Bernstein (1971a, 2000). His distinctive insight was to emphasize the key role of boundaries between types of knowledge (or knowledge domains) in how learner identities are established. Bernstein argued that only through engaging with boundaries can learners move beyond their experience and acquire new knowledge. He saw boundaries as social and not fixed and as both a condition for the acquisition of knowledge and an expression of the power relations that are necessarily involved in pedagogy.

Bernstein (1971a) began by conceptualizing how knowledge boundaries vary in terms of two dimensions. First, he distinguished between the classification and the framing of knowledge; second, he argued that both classification and framing can vary on a continuum between strong and weak forms. *Classification* refers to the insulation between knowledge domains, for example, between physics and chemistry and history and geography. The classification of knowledge is strong when domains are highly insulated from each other (as in the case of physics and history) and weak when there are low levels of insulation between domains (as between history and geography in the humanities or social studies and between physics and chemistry in general science programs). In contrast, *framing* refers to the boundaries between knowledge domains and nonschool knowledge. Framing of knowledge in the curriculum can also be strong, when school and nonschool knowledge are highly insulated from each other, or weak, when the boundaries between school and nonschool knowledge are blurred, as in the case of many programs in adult education and some curricula designed for less able pupils where the knowledge that pupils bring to school is emphasized. He used these distinctions to compare curriculum models and to explore their different implications for teachers and learners.

In his later work, Bernstein (2000) moved from a focus on the relations between domains to the structure of the domains themselves by introducing a distinction between vertical and horizontal *knowledge structures*. This distinction refers to the way that different domains of knowledge embody different ideas of how knowledge progresses. Whereas in vertical knowledge structures (typically the natural sciences), knowledge progresses by moving toward higher levels of abstraction (for example, from Newton's laws of gravity to Einstein's theory of relativity), in horizontal knowledge structures (such as the social sciences and humanities), knowledge progresses by developing new languages and new concepts that pose new problems (an example is how the symbolic interactionism of the Chicago School, [e.g., the work of Everett Hughes, Howard S. Becker, and their successors] raised sociological questions that were quite beyond the scope of the structural functionalism of Talcott Parsons and Neil Smelser). Bernstein's second crucial argument was to make the link between knowledge structures, boundaries, and learner identities. His hypothesis was that strong boundaries between knowledge domains and between school and nonschool knowledge play a critical role in establishing learner identities and are a key condition for learners to progress. In developing his theory, he challenged many of the arguments of progressive educationalists.

There are, however, a number of other important features of the way Bernstein (1971a, 2000) developed the idea of knowledge boundaries, all of which can be traced back to Durkheim (Moore, 2004). First, boundaries refer to relations between contents, not the knowledge contents themselves. Bernstein did not see the specific contents of different subject syllabi as the topic for sociological analysis. Instead, he was concerned with the relationships between the contents of different subjects and between them and other subjects. It was in the *form* of boundary relationships that he saw the sources of innovation and resistance to it. Second, although strong boundaries have traditionally been expressed in disciplines and subjects, from Bernstein's perspective, this is a historical fact, not an argument that they are unchangeable. The disciplines and subjects with which we have become familiar in most systems of mass schooling are not necessarily the only form that strong boundaries can take. Third, he argued that strong boundaries between contents will have distributional consequences; in other words, they will be associated with certain inequalities of outcomes. Fourth, whether innovation is associated with creating new knowledge (in the university) or extending the acquisition of *powerful knowledge* to new groups of learners, it will involve crossing boundaries and calling into question the identities of both students and teachers. The latter implications of Bernstein's analysis make clear the extent to which he was aware that his work had its own political implications, even if he did not himself develop them.

This section has argued that a key concept for the sociology of the curriculum must be knowledge differentiation[25] and that it suggests a quite new agenda for the sociology of education. First, it involves identifying the conditions for learners to acquire *powerful knowledge* in terms of both the internal structures of schools, such as subject divisions, and their external structures, such as the boundaries between schools and professional and academic "knowledge-producing communities," between schools and local communities, and between schools and the state. Second, the sociology of education will need to explore the different networks and associations that specialist teachers are involved in with university-based and other specialists; it is these associations that will provide the contexts for the ongoing selection, sequencing, pacing, and interrelating of knowledge in different domains. Third, sociologists of education will need to address the tension between the essentially conservative role of schools as institutions with responsibility for knowledge transmission and the pressures on them to become flexible and respond to fast-changing global pressures. The key research issue will be distinguishing between forms of resistance to change that preserve the conditions for acquiring *powerful knowledge* and those forms primarily concerned with the preservation of particular professional interests and privileges (*knowledge of the powerful*). A good example of where this tension might be explored is when students are allowed to construct their own curriculum from within a bank of modules and, potentially at least, undermine the selection, sequencing, and pacing of knowledge that are the conditions for learning a subject. Radical educators and some sociologists of education have in the past tended to assume that to become more democratic, schools must become more responsive to external pressures, in particular, pressures from the labor movement. Such developments, however, could undermine the specialist knowledge of teachers and treat schools as no more than another site of politics; this takes us back to the tension between differentiation and dedifferentiation that I referred to earlier in this chapter.

The evidence of the neoinstitutional research discussed in the previous section suggested that dedifferentiation may be leading to a weakening of the boundaries between school and nonschool knowledge. I have drawn on Basil Bernstein's (1971a, 2000) work on the differentiation of curriculum knowledge to suggest that to follow this path may be to deny the conditions for acquiring *powerful knowledge* to the very pupils who are already disadvantaged by their social circumstances. Resolving this tension between external political pressures on schools for dedifferentiation and the arguments from the sociology of knowledge that differentiation of school from nonschool knowledge may be a condition for the acquisition and production of knowledge offers a powerful new agenda for the sociology of education.

CONCLUSIONS

The explicit theme of this chapter has been the question of knowledge in educa-tion and, more particularly, the importance of the differentiation of knowledge as a starting point for the sociology of the curriculum. The chapter has also had two sub-themes: change and difference. First, I have argued that if the sociology of education is to make its potential contribution to curriculum debates, it must *change* its approach to knowledge. Second, I have contrasted the sociology of the curriculum of the 1970s and 1980s, which opposed an emphasis on the specificity of curricula differences as masking wider social differences, with the position taken in this chap-ter, that certain knowledge *differences* need defending on both educational and soci-ological grounds. It can be argued that I am documenting little more than a familiar story in the cyclical history of ideas, when one extreme, social constructivism, is replaced by another, social realism. My response to this challenge is twofold. First, this chapter is frankly autobiographical and I am assuming that my experience of searching for a more reliable sociology of the curriculum is unlikely to be unique and that a self-conscious recognition of past mistakes may have some value for others strug-gling with similar issues.[26] Second, the debates between what I have referred to as social constructivism and social realism have a long history and indeed have a partly cyclical character (Berlin, 1991). However, this does not mean, either, that we should not return to them. They are part of the social condition; the issues that these debates address will shape our analyses, whether we like it or not. As social scientists, we have a responsibility to make them explicit in the new contexts in which we find ourselves. Our ideas, theories, and concepts, like those of earlier generations of sociologists, have to be seen in their historical context; they are never developed in isolation but always in opposition to other ideas, even when no explicit reference is made to what they are opposing. Unless a concept such as social realism is seen in a relational way, it, as much as social constructivism, can become a new dogma. The social realist approach to knowledge is not a replacement for the earlier social constructivism; it is a critique of the earlier ideas and tries to encompass and goes beyond them.

I have traced the issue of knowledge in the sociology of education historically and biographically. I began with the hopes that I and others involved in the new sociol-ogy of education in the 1970s had for the emancipatory potential of bringing the soci-ology of knowledge into educational studies. These hopes were doubtless as much a product of the radical climate of the time, when, in a way that it is easy now to forget, all things seemed possible, as of a "new" and more rigorous sociology. We took ideas, often eclectically, from bodies of knowledge as diverse as phenomenology, cultural anthropology, and Marxism when they appeared to point to the fragility of what was given and the possibility of change. As I have written about elsewhere with Johan Muller (Young & Muller, 2007), this largely "unbounded" epistemological radicalism itself contributed to the undoing of the project of the new sociology of education.

Through a focus on the more traditional sociological themes of institutionality and the structural differentiation of knowledge, the sections of this chapter titled "The Curriculum as Social Institution" and "Knowledge Differentiation and the Sociology of the Curriculum" attempted to rescue the sociology of the curriculum from its own earlier weaknesses and learn from its mistakes without, as it were, "throwing out the baby (of the sociology of knowledge) with the bathwater (oversimplistic social constructivism)." A weakness of the new approach that I have proposed is that despite its promise, it lacks empirical substantiation. Empirical work is more difficult if one is trying at the same time to tackle basic epistemological issues. However, that is only a partial excuse. One encouraging outcome of writing this chapter for me has been identifying possible links between the sometimes overabstract ideas associated with a social realist approach to the curriculum and the hard-nosed empiricism of the neoinstitutionalist research discussed in "The Curriculum as Social Institution" section.[27]

I want to conclude this chapter by stepping back[28] and then looking forward. In conceptualizing the problem of knowledge in the sociology of the curriculum, I have drawn on a series of dichotomies, some taken from Durkheim (1912/1995), such as the sacred and the profane; some from Bernstein (1971a, 2000), such as vertical and horizontal knowledge structures; some not associated with one particular theorist, such as school–nonschool and context-dependent/context-independent types of knowledge; my own distinction between *knowledge of the powerful* and *powerful knowledge;* and the familiar distinction between social constructivism and social realism. This dichotomizing raises a number of questions. For example, does it oversimplify the issues? Do the dichotomies adequately capture social reality of knowledge and its acquisition? Surely, no knowledge is entirely context independent or vertical? Does the social realist approach to knowledge take us beyond the typical conservative view of knowledge as something given and to be adapted to, at least for all except those at the leading edge of research? These are all serious questions that cannot be ignored. I have the space here to deal with only some of them.

Robert Moore and I began to move beyond dichotomies in an earlier article, which I have recently revised for republication (Moore & Young, 2001; Young, 2007a, chap. 2). Elaborating slightly on our original ideas, it is possible to reformulate the social constructivist–social realist dichotomy as a fourfold typology.[29] They are as follows:

1. The conservative traditionalists. In England, this stance on knowledge has been associated with the elitist convictions of 19th-century liberal educators such as Cardinal Newman (1996) and Matthew Arnold (1960). In the early 20th century, their ideas were developed by the poet and literary critic T. S. Eliot (1963), among others. This traditionalist view of knowledge was given a more prescriptive curriculum form in the 1960s and 1970s by the English philosophers of education Paul Hirst and Richard Peters (Peters & Hirst, 1970) and in the United States by Phenix (1964). Hirst and Peters argued that the principles of school knowledge were given by tradition and saw the role of philosophers as guardians of that tradition. Two decades later, the former came to reject this position in favor of a "practice-oriented" approach (Hirst, 1993).

There are two quite distinct ways in which traditionalist ideas about knowledge are expressed in contemporary writing about education. One is by those taking an explicitly conservative stance, such as the ex–chief inspector of schools Chris Woodhead (2002). The second is less easy to be precise about. It refers to the way that contemporary educational researchers, especially educational psychologists, do not feel it necessary to problematize the question of knowledge in their approach to curriculum and pedagogy. By neglecting the question, they are necessarily drawn back to the assumption that it is "given."

2. The technocratic (or pragmatic) instrumentalists. This stance toward education was first identified by Raymond Williams (1961) when he referred to the "industrial trainers." However, in the past 40 years, an instrumental approach to education has broadened from industrial training to become a much broader aspect of government policies (Moore & Young, 2001). It is a widely shared view of education, first espoused by the Reagan and Thatcher governments as part of their neoliberal approach to the economy and by the Labour governments that succeeded them. It is also implicit in Gibbons et al.'s (1994) Mode 2 knowledge discussed earlier and, as Muller (2001) has argued, in the tradition of progressive education inspired by Dewey.

3. The postmodernists. Postmodernists such as Usher and Edwards (1994) critique the first two positions on the basis of rejecting the distinction between knowledge and experience. I include critical curriculum theory and critical pedagogy in this category. However they are often themselves critical of postmodernism on political grounds, they also reject the idea of knowledge differentiation.

4. The social realists. A social realist approach is the position adopted in this chapter. It is analytically distinct from (1), (2), and (3) in a number of senses. First, it does not treat any knowledge as given as is the case with the conservative traditionalists but has an explicit social theory of knowledge and its differentiation. Second, it treats knowledge as a distinct social category separate from experience, separate from the political and economic uses of knowledge, and separate from the pedagogic problems faced by teachers with different groups of learners.[30] It aims to link the social differentiation of knowledge (and its acquisition) with answers to questions as to why some types of knowledge are more powerful than others. In both his early (1971a) and later (2000) work, Bernstein laid the basis for analyzing this process of differentiation. In recognizing the powerful and determining role of knowledge-producing communities, such as those associated with specialist disciplines and professions, my argument can appear conservative in the sense highlighted by the new sociology of education that I mentioned earlier in the chapter. However, by providing criteria by which a curriculum can be evaluated in terms of whether it provides the conditions for the acquisition of *powerful knowledge*, it goes beyond any taken-for-granted or traditional conservatism.

Let us turn to the further question, Do such typologies oversimplify? My answer is yes but that we have no alternative. In the social sciences, they are the only types of concept that we have; they are our unique conceptual resources. The problem with all sociological concepts is that because their empirical referents are invariably weak, they easily become descriptors and stop being treated analytically. Max Weber (1948a, 1948b) was one of the first to point out the dangers in treating concepts (he referred to them as ideal types) descriptively and not seeing them in relation to each other. They do not tell us definitively how the world is; they identify trends and enable us to ask questions and propose hypotheses about the world. For example, Bernstein's (2000) concept of vertical and horizontal knowledge structures is one of the ways that we have of exploring the possible implications of different forms of curricular organization and of explaining why, for example, students will learn little mathematics or science from a curriculum that relies largely on "street" or everyday examples of number use (Dowling, 1998). Much of the empirical work in the sociology of the curriculum that might or might not lend support to the hypotheses suggested in this chapter remains to be done. My argument is that despite their limitations, without dichotomies such as Bernstein's that suggest structural differences between school and nonschool knowledge, we cannot even begin.

A final point: It can be argued that Durkheim's and Bernstein's concepts that I have discussed in this chapter are too static and do not take into account how the curriculum and social reality more generally are constantly changing. This, I think, is only true if the concepts are presented descriptively and independently of any empirical substantiation. One example of how both diachronic and synchronic approaches can be combined, is by Bernstein's account of changes in higher education and professional curricula in terms of three types of knowledge relations: singular, regional, and generic (Beck & Young, 2005; Bernstein, 2000). His insight suggests that these changes represent examples of progressively weaker boundaries between professional and nonprofessional knowledge and poses questions about the conditions for professionalism in a context where these boundaries are under challenge. In the social sciences, we are always dealing with a tension between our attempts to find order by drawing on the stability of our concepts and the changes in reality. It is the concepts that provide us with our criteria for identifying whether a change is more than a mere difference. Any more overarching theory of change tends to become what Gellner (1992) referred to as "providentialism." For Gellner, providentialism referred to the (to him) untenable claims made by Hegel (for reason) and by Marx (for the proletariat) that each was "the future." Gellner substitutes for providentialism what he refers to as "the great asymmetry" of industrialization and the idea that "some ways of producing knowledge are simply better than others" (Moore, 2007, p. 39). It is an asymmetry for Gellner because no society will willingly deindustrialize and return to a life of medieval poverty any more than physicists will go back to agreeing that the sun goes around the earth. If we apply Gellner's idea of the great asymmetry to the sociology of the curriculum, it means that we cannot go back to a time before the 1970s when the curriculum was a given. The sociality of the curriculum will mean that its assumptions will always, at least potentially, be open for debate, albeit within the limits that we are more aware today than we were 30 years ago. That, at least, is the progress that was achieved by the new sociology of education. On the other hand, Gellner's great asymmetry means that we do have *powerful knowledge,* and it must set limits on how we construct the curriculum, even if the characteristics of those limits and how they shape the sequencing, selecting, and pacing of curricula need much more research.

NOTES

[1]Parts of this chapter draw on sections of the introduction to Young (2007a) and on Young (in press).

[2]This chapter is written from the perspective of a sociologist of education working in the United Kingdom. I am aware that the sociology of the curriculum embraces a much wider field within educational studies than I have been able to consider here. I have treated the "new sociology of education" (but now, of course, no longer new) that was first developed in the United Kingdom and the "critical curriculum studies" that emerged in the United States and other Anglophone countries as bodies of work with largely common purposes, despite their different origins and somewhat different trajectories of development. I have not, within the time and space available, been able to go much beyond English and American developments. This does not imply that I do think there has not been important work elsewhere, especially within Anglophone countries (for example, in Australia, New Zealand, and South Africa). It does imply my reluctance to comment on bodies of work with which I have only limited familiarity. However, as I have found in lecturing in China, Japan, Brazil, and other European countries, the issues about knowledge and the curriculum that this chapter is concerned with engage scholars in many countries and frequently transcend national boundaries.

[3]An early exception in the United States that did not receive the recognition it deserved was Philip Wexler's (1976) *The Sociology of Education: Beyond Inequality.* Wexler went on to make one of the sharpest critiques of the new sociology of education (Wexler, 1990). However, in arguing that sociology of education should be replaced by a much broader social analysis, his critique got lost in the relativism that has characterized so much of cultural studies.

[4]The way that I am using the words *reality* and *truth* follows philosophers such as Gellner (1992), B. Williams (2002), and Blackburn (2006). For Gellner, for example, unlike postmodernists and pragmatists such as Rorty, truth is a premise of rational debates, not a topic for them. To put it another way, truth is both an ontological reality and a regulatory ideal without which the sciences (and here I include the social sciences), and society as we understand it, would not be possible. At least since the mid-19th century, and notwithstanding the romanticism of "deschooling" theorists such as Illich (1971) and Reimer (1971), the ontological reality or truth about education is that it involves institutions such as schools, colleges, and universities transmitting knowledge to each successive generation.

[5]I do not, of course, mean that there is no need for debates about the form or content of cultural transmission or about the dangers of applying one-way mechanical metaphors to the idea of cultural transmission.

[6]Ironically, although the new sociology of education, especially in those strands informed by Marxism, was critical of neoliberal reforms, the license that it gives to an instrumental view of the curriculum unintentionally gives such reforms a tacit support.

[7]This does not mean that issues concerning race and gender are unimportant for the sociology of the curriculum or vice versa (Gilborn & Youdell, 2000; Youdell, 2006). It is to make the point that a focus on the different axes of diversity and inequality, if unrelated to the question of knowledge, leads to forms of contextualism (Young, 2004) with all their relativistic implications. A focus on diversity in the absence of a theory of knowledge involves, as Moore (2004) has expressed it, a shift in analytical focus from knowledge to knowers in the sociology of education. As a consequence, the specificity of the curriculum as a condition for knowledge acquisition is lost.

[8]This underplaying (and sometimes rejection) of the institutionality of the curriculum is a specific example of a much wider trend of what became known as the "practice turn" in the social sciences. Some notion of the curriculum as an institution reappeared in the Marxist strands of the new sociology of education; however, this was associated with an overinstrumentalist concept of knowledge as a tool of wider political purposes.

[9]Not unreasonably, as one of his most influential papers was included in my book *Knowledge and Control*, which was subtitled *New Directions for the Sociology of Education* (Young, 1971).

[10]The idea of a symbolic relationship with the world was also taken up by Vygotsky and his followers with their concept of mediation (Wertsch, 1991).

[11]I am using the term *social realist* as it relates to the idea that knowledge is structurally differentiated from experience in ways that are beyond the perceptions and actions of individuals. I develop this idea later, drawing on Durkheim and the more recent work of Collins, Moore, and Muller, which are referred to elsewhere in this chapter.

[12]I am increasingly convinced that it is crucial for sociologists to maintain a distance between their political and intellectual stances. This is what I understand Max Weber (1948a, 1948b) to mean when he made the distinction between "value freedom" and "value relevance" in social research.

[13]I do not mean this in the naïve sense that is defended by liberal educators that learning has nothing to do with careers, jobs, or winning prizes but in the sense that understanding something difficult is intrinsically satisfying and worthwhile.

[14]During the decade of the 1990s, I had virtually nothing to do with the sociology of education either as a teacher or a researcher.

[15]At the time, my colleague Geoff Whitty (1974) aptly referred to this view as "naïve possibilitarianism."

[16]I use the term *reductionism* to refer to the sociological assumption that questions about knowledge can "reduced" to questions about knowers—their backgrounds and personal interests.

[17]An outstanding exception is, of course, Randall Collins's (1998) remarkable book, *A Sociology of Philosophies*.

[18]It was to tackle this question that my colleague Johan Muller and I turned to the work of Ernst Cassirer (2000; Young & Muller, 2007) and how he differentiates between types of objectivity.

[19]The distinctions that Gibbons and his colleagues make have been the subject of much debate within the sociology of science (e.g., Fuller, 2000). However, although the issues raised are important for the sociology of the curriculum, I do not have the space to explore them in this chapter.

[20]This discontinuity was expressed by Alexander (1995) in epistemological terms. In an earlier article, Rob Moore and I (Moore & Young, 2001) linked the fundamental pedagogic dilemma facing teachers with the epistemological problem facing social scientists that was identified by Alexander.

[21]Greg Kelly pointed out to me that there are parallels between my analysis and the argument developed by Strike (1989) in a book that I regret not having come across in preparing this chapter.

[22]In the United Kingdom, at least, this reduction of content tends to be justified as part of a wider attempt to make the curriculum more "meaningful" to a wider range of pupils and therefore to increase participation. One recent example is the proposal in England to reduce the subject content of school science and replace it with opportunities to debate science-related issues such as the environment and HIV/AIDS. Few would question the importance of such debates' having a role in the curriculum. However, whether they would lead to a greater depth of understanding when the scientific knowledge base of pupils is reduced seems highly doubtful.

[23]The idea of context-independent knowledge is a slight misnomer. It refers to knowledge that is bounded by specific kinds of contexts—for example, specialist academic or professional communities. However, the knowledge generated in those communities is not tied to them; it is this relative independence that gives this knowledge its generalizing capacities.

[24]See Barnett (2006) for an exploration of what he refers to as the "double de-contextualisation" problems faced by vocational teachers.

[25]In beginning with a theory of why types of knowledge differ and not just the fact of differences, the concept of knowledge differentiation is quite distinct from (and a critique of) the superficially similar descriptive idea that there are different types of knowledge.

[26]In writing this conclusion, I was reminded of the Polish Marxist Rosa Luxemburg (1919/2004), who argued that the working-class movement could always learn more from its defeats than from its successes. In commenting on the Russian Revolution, she wrote,

The leadership has failed. Even so, the leadership can and must be recreated from the masses. . . . [They] have developed this "defeat" into one of the historical defeats which are the pride and strength of international socialism. And that is why the future victory will bloom from this "defeat." (p. 536)

A similar observation, I suggest, might apply, albeit in less apocalyptic terms, to the sociology of the curriculum!

[27]I am grateful here to David Baker (Pennsylvania State University), a referee of my earlier draft. The recent article by Baker and his colleagues (Baker, Thorne, Eslinger, & Blair, 2007) suggests a challenging new way of addressing some of the questions that I have been concerned with here.

[28]I making these final comments, I am grateful to Bill Green (Charles Sturt University, Australia) for the questions that he raised in commenting on an earlier draft of this chapter.

[29]Another potentially fruitful approach that is not pursued here is to see dichotomies as fractal relations in which differences reappear at different levels of analysis (Abbott, 2001; Moore & Muller, 2002).

[30]The key implications of the diverse needs of learners are, from a social realist position, not that the knowledge content of the curriculum must be reduced but that the pacing, sequencing, and length of the program needs reconsideration.

ACKNOWLEDGMENTS

I am most grateful to Ian Hextall and Johan Muller for their support in reading earlier drafts of this chapter. I should also like to thank my referees, David Baker and Bill Green, and my editors, Judith Green, Greg Kelly, and Allan Luke, for their helpful and constructive suggestions.

REFERENCES

Abbott, A. (2001). *The chaos of disciplines*. Chicago: University of Chicago Press.

Alexander, J. C. (1995). *Fin de siècle social theory: Relativism, reduction and the problem of reason*. London: Verso.

Allais, S. (2003). The national qualifications framework in South Africa: A democratic project trapped in a neo-liberal paradigm? *Journal of Education and Work, 16*(3), 305-323.

Apple, M. (1979). *Ideology and curriculum*. London: Routledge/Kegan Paul.

Apple, M. (2006). *Educating the "right" way: Markets, standards, God, and inequality* (2nd ed.). London and New York: Routledge.

Arnold, M. (1960). *Arnold on education*. Cambridge, UK: Cambridge University Press.

Baker, D., & LeTendre, G. (2005). *National differences, global similarities: World culture and the future of schooling*. Stanford, CA: Stanford University Press.

Baker, D. P., Thorne, S., Eslinger, P., & Blair, C. (2007). *Cognition, culture, and institutions: Affinities within the social construction of reality*. Unpublished manuscript, Pennsylvania State University, University Park.

Barnett, M. (2006). Vocational knowledge and vocational pedagogy. In M. Young & J. Gamble (Eds.), *Knowledge, qualifications and the curriculum for South African further education* (pp. 143-157). Pretoria, South Africa: Human Sciences Research Council.

Beck, J., & Young, M. (2005). The assault on the professions and the restructuring of academic and professional identities: A Bernsteinian analysis. *British Journal of Sociology of Education, 26*(2), 183–198.

Bell, D. (1973). *The coming of the post-industrial society*. New York: Basic Books.

Berger, P., & Luckman, T. (1967). *The social construction of reality*. London: Penguin.

Berlin, I. (1991). *The crooked timber of humanity: Chapters in the history of ideas*. New York: Random House.

Bernstein, B. (1971a). *Class, codes and control* (Vol. 1). London: Routledge/Kegan Paul.

Bernstein, B. (1971b). On the classification and framing of educational knowledge. In M. Young (Ed.), *Knowledge and control: New directions for the sociology of education* (pp. 47–69). London: Collier-Macmillan.

Bernstein, B. (2000). *Pedagogy, symbolic control and identity: Theory, research, critique* (2nd ed.). Oxford, UK: Rowman & Littlefield.

Blackburn, S. (2006). *Truth: A guide for the perplexed*. London: Penguin.

Bourdieu, P. (2004). *Science of science and reflexivity*. Cambridge, UK: Polity.

Bourdieu, P., & Passeron, J.-C. (1977). *Reproduction in education, society and culture*. London: Sage.

Bowles, S., & Gintis, H. (1976). *Schooling in capitalist America*. New York: Basic Books.

Braverman, H. (1976). *Labour and monopoly capital*. New York: Monthly Review Press.

Cassirer, E. (2000). *The logic of the cultural sciences: Five studies* (S. G. Lofts, Trans.) New Haven, CT: Yale University Press.

Castells, M. (1996). *The information age: Economy, society and culture*. Oxford, UK: Blackwell.

Collins, R. (1998). *The sociology of philosophies: A global theory of intellectual change*. Cambridge, MA: Belknap.

Dale, R. (2000). Globalization and education: Demonstrating a "common world educational culture" or locating a "globally structured educational agenda?" *Educational Theory, 50*(4), 427–448.

Dowling, P. (1998). *The sociology of mathematics education*. London: Falmer.

Durkheim, E. (1952). *Suicide: A study in sociology*. London: Routledge/Kegan Paul.

Durkheim, E. (1956). *Education and sociology*. Glencoe, IL: Free Press.

Durkheim, E. (1983). *Pragmatism and sociology* (J. C. Whitehouse & J. B. Alcock, Trans., with an introduction by F. Cuvillier). Cambridge, UK: Cambridge University Press.

Durkheim, E. (1995). *The elementary forms of religious life* (K. Fields, Trans.). New York: Free Press. (Original work published 1912)

Durkheim, E., & Mauss, M. (1970). *Primitive classifications*. Chicago: University of Chicago Press.

Eliot, T. S. (1963). *Notes towards the definition of culture*. London: Faber.

Fuller, S. (2000). *The governance of science: Ideology and the future of the open society*. Maidenhead, UK: Open University Press.

Gamble, J. (2006). What kind of knowledge for the vocational curriculum? In M. Young & J. Gamble (Eds.), *Knowledge, qualifications and the curriculum for South African further education* (pp. 87-104). Pretoria, South Africa: Human Sciences Research Council.

Gellner, E. (1992). *Post modernism, reason and religion*. London: Routledge.

Gibbons, M., Limoges, C., Nowotny, H., Schwartzman, S., Scott, P., & Trow, M. (1994). *The new production of knowledge*. London: Sage.

Gilborn, D., & Youdell, D. (2000). *Rationing education: Policy, practice, reform and equity*. Maidenhead, UK: Open University Press.

Goodson, I. V. (1998). *Subject knowledge: Readings for the study of school subjects*. Brighton, UK: Falmer.

Gramsci, A. (1971). *Selections from the prison notebooks*. London: Lawrence and Wishart.

Habermas, J. (2001). *The liberating power of symbols: Philosophical essays* (P. Dews, Trans.). Cambridge, MA: MIT Press.

Hirst, P. (1993). The foundations of the national curriculum: Why subjects? In P. O'Hear & J. White (Eds.,) *Assessing the national curriculum* (pp. 31–18). London: Paul Chapman.

Illich, I. (1971). *Deschooling society*. London: Penguin.

Jencks, C. (1975). *Inequality: A reassessment of the effect of family and schooling in America*. New York: Penguin.

Jevons, F. (1972). The place of science in education. *Physics Education, 7*(7), 430–432.

Keep, E. (2006). State control of the English education and training system: Playing with the biggest train set in the world. *Journal of Vocational Education and Training, 58*(1), 47–65.

Ladwig, J. (1996). *Academic distinctions: Theory and methodology in the sociology of school knowledge*. London: Routledge.

Lukes, S. (1972). *Emile Durkheim: His life and work*. New York: Harper & Row.

Luxemburg, R. (2004) Order reigns in Berlin. In P. Hudis & K. B. Anderson (Eds.)., *The Rosa Luxemberg Reader*. New York. Monthly Review Press. (Original work published 1919).

Mannheim, K. (1936). *Ideology and utopia*. London: Kegan Paul/Trench, Trubner.

Marx, K. (1964). *The German ideology*. London and Moscow: Progress.

Meyer, J. W. (1992). *School knowledge for the masses: World models and national primary curricular categories in the twentieth century*. London: Falmer.

Moore, R. (2004). *Education and society*. London: Polity.

Moore, R. (2007). Going critical: The problem of problematising knowledge in educational theory. *Critical Studies in Education, 48*(1), 25–43.

Moore, R., Arnot, M., Beck, J., & Daniels, H. (Eds.). (2004). *Knowledge, power, and educational reform: Applying the sociology of Basil Bernstein*. Abingdon, UK: Routledge.

Moore, R., & Muller, J. (1999). The discourse of voice and the problem of knowledge and identity in the sociology of education. *British Journal of Sociology of Education, 20*(2), 189–206.

Moore, R., & Muller, J. (2002). The growth of knowledge and the discursive gap. *British Journal of Sociology of Education, 23*(4), 627–637.

Moore, R., & Young, M. (2001). Knowledge and the curriculum in the sociology of education: Towards a re-conceptualisation. *British Journal of Educational Studies, 22*(4), 445–461.

Morais, A., Neves, I., Davies, B., & Daniels, H. (Eds.). (2001). *Towards a sociology of pedagogy: The contribution of Basil Bernstein to research*. New York: Peter Lang.

Muller, J. (2000). *Reclaiming knowledge: Social theory, curriculum and education policy*. London: RoutledgeFalmer.

Muller, J. (2001). Progressivism redux. In M. Young & A. Kraak (Eds.), *Education in retrospect* (pp. 59–73). Pretoria, South Africa: Human Sciences Research Council.

Muller, J., Davies, B., & Morais, A. (Eds.). (2004). *Reading Bernstein, researching Bernstein*. London: RoutledgeFalmer.

Nash, R. (1990). Bourdieu on education and social reproduction. *British Journal of Sociology of Education, 11*(1), 431–447.

Newman, J. H. (1996). *The idea of a university*. New Haven, CT: Yale University Press.

Peters, R., & Hirst, P. (1970). *The logic of education*. London: Routledge/Kegan Paul.

Phenix, P. H. (1964). *Realms of meaning: A philosophy of the curriculum for general education*. New York: McGraw-Hill.

Pring, R. (1972). Knowledge out of control. *Education for Teaching, 89*(2), 19–28.

Reimer, E. (1971). *School is dead*. London: Penguin.

Strike, K. (1989). *Liberal justice and the Marxist critique of education*. New York: Routledge.

Usher, R., & Edwards, R. (1994). *Post modernism and education*. London: Routledge.

Weber, M. (1948a). Politics as a vocation. In H. Gerth & C. W. Mills (Eds.), *Max Weber: Essays in sociology* (pp. 77–128). London: Routledge/Kegan Paul.

Weber, M. (1948b). Science as a vocation. In H. Gerth & C. W. Mills (Eds.), *Max Weber: Essays in sociology* (pp. 129–159). London: Routledge/Kegan Paul.

Weelahan, L. (in press). How competency-based training locks the working class out of powerful knowledge: a modified Bernsteinian analysis. *British Journal of Sociology of Education*.

Weis, L., McCarthy, C., & Dimitriades, G. (Eds.). (2006). *Ideology, curriculum, and the new sociology of education: Revisiting the work of Michael Apple*. New York and London: Routledge.

Wertsch, J. (1991). *Voices of the mind: A sociocultural approach to mediated action*. Cambridge, MA: Harvard University Press.

Wexler, P. (1976). *The sociology of education: Beyond equality*. Indianapolis, IN: Bobbs-Merrill.

Wexler, P. (1990). *Social analysis of education: After the new sociology*. London: Routledge.

Whitty, G. (1974). Sociology and the possibility of radical educational change. In M. Flude & J. Ahier (Eds.), *Educability, schools and ideology* (pp. 112–138). London: Croom Helm.

Whitty, G. (2006). Preface. In L. Weis, C. McCarthy, & G. Dimitriades, G. (Eds.), *Ideology, curriculum, and the new sociology of education: Revisiting the work of Michael Apple* (preface). New York and London: Routledge.

Whitty, G., & Young, M. (Eds.). (1977). *Society, state and schooling*. Brighton, UK: Falmer.

Williams, B. (2002). *Truth and truthfulness: An essay in genealogy*. Princeton, NJ: Princeton University Press.

Williams, R. (1961). *The long revolution*. London: Chatto and Windus.

Willis, P. (1977). *Learning to labour*. Aldershot, UK: Saxon House.

Woodhead, C. (2002). *Class war: The state of British education*. London: Little, Brown.

Youdell, D. (2006). *Impossible bodies, impossible selves: Exclusions and student subjectivities*. Guildford, UK: Springer.

Young, M. (Ed.). (1971). *Knowledge and control: New directions for the sociology of education*. London: Collier Macmillan.

Young, M. (1974). *Notes for a sociology of science education* (Vol. 1, pp. 51–60). Leeds, UK: University of Leeds, Studies in Science Education.

Young, M. (1998). *The curriculum of the future*. London: Falmer.

Young, M. (2003). Durkheim, Vygotsky and the curriculum of the future. *London Review of Education, 1*(2), 100–119.

Young, M. (2004). An old problem in a new context: Rethinking the relationship between sociology and educational policy. *International Studies in Sociology of Education, 14*(1), 3–20.

Young, M. (2007a). *Bringing knowledge back in.* London: Routledge.

Young, M. (2007b). Durkheim and Vygotsky's theories of knowledge and their implications for critical educational theory. *Critical Studies in Education, 1*(1), 46-63.

Young, M. (in press). What are schools for? In H. Daniels, H. Lauder, & J. Porter (Eds.), *The Routledge companion to education.* London: Routledge.

Young, M., & Gamble, J. (2006). (Eds.). *Knowledge, qualifications and the curriculum for South African further education.* Pretoria, South Africa: Human Sciences Research Council.

Young, M., & Muller, J. (2007). Truth and truthfulness in the sociology of educational knowledge. *Theory and Research in Education, 5*(2), 173–201.

Young, M., & Whitty, G. (Eds.). (1976). *Explorations in the politics of school knowledge.* Driffield, UK: Nafferton.

Chapter 2

The Arts and Education: Knowledge Generation, Pedagogy, and the Discourse of Learning

VIVIAN L. GADSDEN
University of Pennsylvania

Within the past 20 years, the arts have gained increasing prominence in educational discourses as well as public arenas. At the same time that traditional genres of art (e.g., music, visual art, and performance) are being taught as part of school curricula, the study of the arts in education has taken on new venues in supporting learning and teaching through technology and multimedia (Carey, 2005; Eisner, 2002; Flood, Heath, & Lapp, 2005). These new foci are especially critical in bridging the local and the global, and in linking cultures and worlds across age, time, and space that in earlier periods in history would have been virtually impossible to connect. Moreover, they portend opportunities for enhancing learning and improving pedagogy and practice (Bresler, 2001; Bresler & Ardichivili, 2002). They call attention to the ways in which these opportunities are constructed across place and culturally diverse groups, how knowledge (and what counts as knowledge) is defined and shaped within and outside of formal classrooms, and the ways in which reciprocal relationships across different settings are (re)formed and sustained. In short, they prompt us to examine critically how patterns of practice in areas outside of the arts are supported through the arts. They urge us to take up questions about the role the arts play in linking students' knowledge outside the classroom with the knowledge gained through the official curriculum and, in turn, about how such knowledge contributes to the formation of student and teacher identities.

This chapter focuses on the arts within a social–cultural–contextual framework, examining their role as a (re)source in educational theory, research, and practice. Rather than highlighting individual disciplines within the field, typically referred to as "the arts," the chapter is concerned with the changing nature of the arts and what counts as the arts.[1] The chapter has a six-part structure that begins with an overview of issues that are central to redefining the relationship of the arts and education. This is followed

Review of Research in Education
February 2008, Vol. 32, pp. 29–61
DOI: 10.3102/0091732X07309691
© 2008 AERA. http://rre.aera.net

by a discussion of power, culture, and engagement, which is, in turn, followed by a discussion of epistemological considerations. The next section focuses on arts learning and dispositions, followed by a section that describes research issues in arts learning, including challenges in and to current conceptualizations of the arts. The chapter concludes with a focus on ways of expanding the role of arts education in schools and other learning and teaching communities.

SHIFTING DEFINITIONS AND REFERENCES TO THE ARTS

It is not surprising that definitions and references to the arts have shifted in the past 20 years, particularly at the beginning of what Gardner (1989) described as the "renaissance of interest in education in the arts" (p. 71) and the emergence of initiatives created by the National Endowment for the Arts and the Arts Education Partnership (www.aep-arts.org). What was described once as art education has been revised to focus on *arts education*, denoting the multiplicity of art genres; *art learning*, denoting the intersections of cognitive and social dimensions of students' engagement, creativity, and imagination; *arts in education*, denoting the centrality of art as both precipitator and repository of learning, teaching, and schooling; and *the arts and education*, denoting the reciprocal and interactional relationship that exists between the two areas of inquiry.

This conceptual and semantic shift is important for several reasons. First, what has been described as arts education has a historical life in education and schooling that extends beyond what the recent attention might suggest (Dewey, 1934; Eisner, 1982, 1994; Smith, 1872). Art courses were either discrete offerings in schools, or a focus on art was integrated into courses such as literacy, math, and science. The scope and substance of the integration continue to vary sufficiently enough so as to make a systematic analysis of whether and how the arts are experienced in classrooms difficult, though not impossible (Bransford & Schwartz, 1999; Kalin & Kind, 2006; Larson & Walker, 2006).

Efforts at such integration are perhaps most evident in early childhood programs, which have long focused on children's grasp of aesthetics (Schirrmacher, 2002; Thompson, 2006). Yet early childhood teachers, not unlike teachers of higher grades, differ, sometimes significantly, in how they interpret the developmental needs of children, in what they prepare as stimulating activities for children, and in the degree to which they infuse the arts into other foundational areas of learning, (i.e., literacy, math, and science), using content and approaches that promote children's dispositions for the arts.

Variability in how the arts are understood, how knowledge of the arts is gained, and how pedagogical approaches are crafted is not limited to early childhood (Bresler, DeStefano, Feldman, & Garg, 2000). It may be seen as a source of concern or a source of possibility, depending on the lens one brings to the task. In this chapter, it is seen as a source of possibility that the field holds for creating rich and expansive conceptualizations of learning and teaching art. It has the potential to contribute to textured analyses of the processes by which knowledge of the arts, art forms, and art media are generated and used and the social contexts in which participation in the arts takes place.

Second, a casual observer of education in the United States might well argue that although the idea of arts education is embraced, it does not own a space in American schooling—that we have not taken up the affordances and possibilities of the arts in education. Eisner (1997) a decade ago provided a poignant picture of the place that the teaching of art held in American elementary and secondary schools. He notes that in Grades 1 through 6, "on the average less than one-half hour is devoted to the teaching of art each week . . . less than three percent of school time per week" (p. 61). Despite the apparent infusion of new programs designed to enhance the arts in schools since Eisner's writing, for example, those inspired by efforts such as the Arts Education Partnership, the arts occupy a precarious and uncertain position in schools and school systems, and empirical research on the arts is relatively limited compared to other areas of inquiry.

Third, references to the arts in education denote a shift in epistemological grounding. At one and the same time, there is movement toward expansive and multilayered ways of thinking, centered in cultural and social practices and diversity of visual texts and art forms, and there is movement away from codifying the arts into discrete categories (Alim & Baugh, 2007; Dartnall, 2002; Flood, Heath, & Lapp, 2005; Greene, 2000; Hull & Nelson, 2005). These new references highlight the organic nature of the arts, challenge simplistic notions of product and process, and promote a view in which the varied substance and enactments of the arts are studied and understood in relationship to where and how they are situated in the human experience and in individuals' experiences as members of cultural and social collectives (Begoray, 2001). In describing the varied substance of the arts, Dewey (1934) noted that our reference to activities that are typically considered art (e.g., singing, acting, and dancing) actually reflect art in the conduct of the activities and that the product of art is not the work of art.

Dewey's (1934) argument is central to understanding the importance of the three ways of referencing the arts and education presented earlier and visible in current discourses, that is, the focus on the arts in education, education in the arts, or art and education. These different ways of conceptualizing the relationship between education and the arts point to the plurality of art experiences. They remove the adjectival status of the arts (e.g., art education) in schooling, teaching, and learning and assign the arts equal status to education. Those advocating this perspective see this linking process as setting a tone that encourages learners to be co-constructors of a dynamic education rather than recipients of schooling and shapers of knowledge rather than recipients of knowledge shaped primarily by forces external to them (Gee & Green, 1998). Moreover, they embrace a kind of public engagement that gives equal weight to art experiences and human experiences of both those who create and those who live in the settings where such experiences are created, that is, of artists and audiences (e.g., students and/or community members).

Fourth, current discourses that focus on educational contexts where oppression and marginalization have been the order of the day for children, their families, and the schools and communities that support and house them argue that the experiences that inform and are informed by the arts and the creativity they potentially nurture become paramount. This public engagement takes on a new urgency, when diverse communities of learners—often with few financial resources and victimized by acts of injustice and violence—are invited into conversations about what counts as knowledge and become enactors of a new experience of learning, teaching, and schooling. In this way, the arts act as a venue for social justice and a platform for those often invisible in traditional classroom settings (Cochran-Smith, 1995; Ladson-Billings, 1994, 2006; Lee, 2007).

A common theme in the work that has been described in this section is the need to (re)frame research and pedagogy to focus on understanding the possibilities for learning and teaching in the arts. Understanding the arts is predicated on understanding cultural and social contexts that shape and sustain them (Gadsden, 2003): the processes of learning, teaching, and seeing the world that are valued in these contexts (Green & Dixon, 2003); the relationships that exist in them and their relative nature to the arts, art forms, and interactions; the products that emerge from them; and the sense of self, possibility, and learning that is experienced in and through them (Ballengee-Morris & Stuhr, 2001). The arts in this instance are both representative of social institutions and social life (Rostvall & West, 2006a) and unique in their representations (Efland, 1990). They offer a lens into historical and contemporary issues while, at once and through interpretation, challenging such issues, on the basis of the generational moment—that is, practices, beliefs, and structures that are associated with a specific set of circumstances, age, and sociopolitical activities.

The Arts, Policy and Research Contexts: A Further Framing of the Issues

Despite the shifts described in the previous section and greater attention to the arts by researchers and teachers, the arts in education reside in a relatively small space in educational policy, which acknowledges the importance of the arts but has not matched, until recently, this acknowledgement with funding. The incongruence (i.e., between public appreciation and lack of funding support) raises questions about what constitutes academic achievement and the value of the arts to students' academic achievement and educational success. Academic achievement is increasingly defined in relationship to students' gaining proficiency in specific "skills," for example, reading, writing, and arithmetic. In such cases, the unfolding of thinking processes often appears secondary to the act of producing "the right answer" and ultimately an outcome. There is no doubt that developing these abilities is foundational and fundamental to learning in school and encompasses essential knowledge and skills that contribute to students' intellect, purpose, and thriving in the world. Hence, the choice should not be supporting students' foundational abilities versus supporting students' imagination, artistry, and learning of art.

The situation of policy support for the arts and education may be likened to discussions about multiculturalism and education. On one hand, academic and political commentaries refer to the increasing cultural, ethnic, and social diversity in the United States and in American schools; on the other, educational and social policies and public practices often demonstrate a striking lack of urgency to address diversity in the United States or abroad. The two areas—the arts and multicultural-ism—are also similar in that neither has a corpus of empirical work that shows a causal relationship to students' achievement or that can be measured in ways that have come to define achievement. If such a relationship could be established, both areas of inquiry would likely assume a more tenable place in policy plans and would increase the range of research studies. Such a proposition is inherently problematic, however, if the only relationship sought is a causal relationship or one that demon-strates a clear case of transfer. Any failure to find such a direct relationship puts the arts in the untenable position of being labeled soft, inexact, emotional, and inaccu-rate—in other words, unscientific.

In this era of high-stakes testing, policies that are single-minded or one-dimensional in determining measurable change, accountability, and standards are likely to disad-vantage the arts. These policies are especially important at this moment of increased efforts at the federal level and in selected states (Ruppert & Nelson, 2006). In 2007, the Arts in Education program at the U.S. Department of Education was funded at $35.3 million; the U.S. Congressional Arts Caucus has called for an increase in fund-ing, to $53 million, in 2008. In the absence of such support, the result will be an increasingly wide gulf between the study and practice of the arts in education and poli-cies that seek uniformity. As the gap widens, school programs focused on the arts may be reduced or eliminated completely.

In posing the question, What can education learn from the arts about the practice of education? and in noting the current emphasis on research that meets the standard of science, Eisner (2002) proposes a way of reenvisioning the issue of research, accountability, and evidence. He points to the ways in which science and the arts have been constructed as oppositional. He similarly describes the tensions between science and the arts, emanating in part from psychology's influence, on the study of the arts, and the lower status to which the arts have been relegated over time:

> Science and art became estranged. Science was considered dependable; the artistic process was not. Sci-ence was cognitive; the arts were emotional. Science was teachable; the arts were matters of preference. Science was useful; the arts were ornamental. . . . One relied on art when there was no science to provide guidance. Art was a fallback position. (p. 6)

As Eisner (2002) implies, the arts must be studied not as a contrast to science or as a failure to be scientific but as a primary area of inquiry that draws on a range of conceptual frameworks. Although the arts and art forms adhere to a kind of precision and require systematicity, they do not readily submit to the accepted scientific order expected in many other fields (Dartnall, 2002; Eisner & Powell, 2002; Rauscher et al., 1997). However, it is not too dramatic to suggest that not offering students the opportunity to experience a broad array of thinking, social, and emotional dispositions through art—to reorder their habits of mind—is to deny them the full experience of learning and deny teachers the full opportunity to understand the breadth of possible knowledge.

Although the body of empirical research on the arts is relatively small, the number of conceptual and theoretical analyses, dating back to Dewey, as well as instructional and curricula discussions has increased with time, as have the forms of creativity that have come to be included in the arts. However, the lack of empirical work is both the subject and object of concerns and raises a range of questions about the arts: What is the nature of the empirical work that should be conducted? What are the questions that must be framed? What are the contexts to be studied and with what approaches? What interpretive lenses will emerge, and with what accuracy? What are the other ways (e.g., approaches, continua) that we can use to learn about, chart, and understand change? To the degree that questions are posed about the effects of the arts on student achievement, they may need to be reconceptualized and rewritten to ask what constitutes a well-educated student, a successful learning and teaching experience, successful schooling, or educational success. In other words, what are the broad and nuanced learning and teaching opportunities that prepare students to think broadly while honing in on the foundational abilities of reading, writing, and arithmetic and the thinking, social, and emotional dispositions that allow for learning?

By dispositions, I am referring to the tendencies toward different patterns of behavior. Lewis (1997) argues that dispositions are intrinsic to the entity but that they are subject to the laws of nature (Mellor, 1974; Molnar, 1999; Ryle, 1949). Educational philosophers (e.g., Ennis, 1962, 1994) and educational researchers (e.g., Facione, Facione, & Giancarlo, 2000; Facione, Sanchez, & Facione, 1994) have focused on thinking dispositions as a special subset of human dispositions, arguing that thinking dispositions require time and space for reflection. Salomon (1994) describes dispositions as a cluster of preferences, attitudes, and intentions, complemented by a set of capabilities that allow preferences to become realized in a particular way. In much the same way, Facione et al. (1994) refer to such dispositions as being represented in a core of attitudes for schools, intellectual virtues, and habits of mind. One example of how these interpretations of disposition is being enacted can be found in Art-Works, part of Harvard's *Project Zero*. In this project, four dispositions are highlighted: (a) the disposition to explore diverse perspectives; (b) the disposition to find, pose, and explore problems; (c) the disposition to reason and evaluate, and (d) the disposition to find and explore metaphorical relationships. (See www.pz.harvard.edu/Research/Artwks.tm)

Last, any focus on the arts must consider the ways in which questions of difference, diversity, and change are imagined. That is, how are issues related to ethnic background, class, culture, gender, and sexual orientation are woven into the fabric of academic and public discourses, and how are the everyday issues of racial discrimination and exclusion in a national perspective examined and addressed. These issues are used often to make the case for the infusion of the arts in curricula and the increase of arts programs. The emphasis on them and the students, families, and communities affected by them is not misplaced, as researchers and educators alike seek ways to enhance the experience and engagement of students who are marginalized in multiple ways in schools and society. It speaks as well to the limitations of existing paradigms to engage students whose experiences differ from dominant practices and whose knowledge, understanding, and interpretation of art and the arts may similarly differ. Arts education and the experience of the arts in learning and teaching, not unlike learning and teaching science, math, reading, and writing, are inextricably tied to the identities that learners and teachers assume and imagine are possible. Where policy fails to attend to these issues, the role of research becomes more critical.

POWER, CULTURE, AND ENGAGEMENT IN THE ARTS

The study of the arts encompasses a range of genres, foci, and methodological approaches that are used to examine academic achievement and school engagement. As stated in the section on shifting definitions, academic achievement is more than the collection of individual learning of foundational skills. Rather, it is the collective of experiences to which students are exposed, through "reflective shaping of media: paint, clay, musical sound or written words, bodies in movement" (Greene, 2001, p. 1) as well as those who work to engage students in and out of classrooms. The arts represent a broad expanse of work, ways of doing, talents, and knowledge that can be nurtured by institutions and promoted by those in them. Mostly, however, the arts are reflective of a freedom to imagine—to place oneself in the center of a work as observer and actor. In other words, they allow individuals to place themselves in the skin of another; to experience others' reality and culture; to sit in another space; to transport themselves across time, space, era in history, and context; and to see the world from a different vantage point.

Several nagging questions emerge when we consider how the arts might be nurtured (for those who believe that the arts cannot be taught) or taught in classrooms and what we know about how they are taught: Are some arts and art forms more valuable than others to promote expression and reflection and to engage students in learning, for example, painting, film, dance, music, or photography? Greene (1997) suggests that if the experience includes creative or expressive adventures in any of the art forms, understanding and the ability to notice and to respond can only be enhanced. Although most of us are inclined to accept this powerful statement, the on-the-ground realities of what is valued in society, how it comes to be valued, and for whom it is valued raise questions about whose art counts. References to high and low art, for example, denote a hierarchy or assessment of the cognitive value of an art form and a kind of art. Some art may be seen as unique for the sake of art whereas other forms of art may be labeled as utilitarian. This assessment may result in certain art forms being used and valued in mainstream curricula and others excluded or certain arts experiences provided for some children and different arts experiences for other children.

Whether one chooses one approach versus another may be indicative of the chooser's awareness of and breadth of exposure to diverse genres and groups and the valuing assigned to both by teachers, schools, and other social institutions. Such choices appear in everyday life as well as research. For example, I recently attended commencement exercises at a prestigious, progressive, private middle school. Throughout the ceremony, the music teacher played several popular songs. An African American parent leaned over to me and pointed out that none of the songs had been written or performed by people of color. Both disappointed and frustrated, the parent noted that the music teacher had consistently demonstrated a remarkable lack of sensitivity to the diversity of the students. We were left wondering, What does the teacher understand about diversity, the cultures of the students, and their relationship with the arts? What exposure had the students had to different art forms, what discussions ensued, and what was the scope of their exposure?

This kind of questioning is not unlike the questioning that led to research projects such as talent development (Boykin & Bailey, 2000; Jordan & Plank, 1998; Madhere & MacIver, 1996; McPartland, Legters, Jordan, & McDill, 1996) and Project Zero (e.g., Perkins, Tishman, Ritchhart, Donis, & Andrade, 2000; Tishman, Perkins, & Jay, 1995). Research on talent development at the Center for Research on the Education of Students Placed at Risk is developed around the idea that schools and classrooms have yet to understand and build on the abilities, artistry, and talents that students from diverse backgrounds bring to the classroom. Attempting to use talent, broadly defined, as a basis for understanding how to engage students in classroom activities, research on talent development questions whether and how schools are prepared to welcome the early signs of talent in students whose learning and artistry fall into different hierarchies of tradition, genres, and acceptance or who represent different ethnic backgrounds. are In other words, what are the values assigned to different genres and to students who appear to be more readily engaged in one versus another? (Greene, 2001)

It has been a failure of schools and those in other institutions designed to support schools to think broadly about diversity and practices that perpetuate the dual identities that many students of color experience, irrespective of social class, in schools. Two examples come to mind. First, many prestigious institutions of higher education have allowed students of color, mostly students of African descent, to hold alternative commencements in addition to the formal university commencement exercises. In these alternative commencement exercises, not only are the students more visible but they also take opportunities to express their own artistic preferences—found in their choices of music and performances—and to reflect on their art, their histories, their ways of seeing the world, and their negotiations between and across their different worlds. Through these exercises, the students attempt to demonstrate publicly and personally (through the planning and preparation of the activities) their cultural power in settings where such power appears to be ignored. Second, similar responses may be found in work that commits to community action research. Mercado and Santamaria (2005) identified the arts as one of four areas that Latino community members identified as important to the education of their children. In a volume edited by Pedraza and Rivera (2005), Mercado and Santamaria address the inherent complexity of addressing the issue of the arts as well as teacher preparation and related issues for those who are new to speaking English and those who have lived in multilingual, multidialectal communities.

The question of power—who has it and how it is used—is as embedded in discussions of the arts as any other area of inquiry, particularly, multiculturalism in education. In describing visions of arts education, Eisner (1994, 1999, 2002), as do others (e.g., Messaris & Moriarty, 2005), focuses on visual art, using it as a framework to discuss how to engage students in an appreciation for the diversity of the arts and the diversity of artists. As he notes, in American society, money and position make a difference, and the powerful control which images will be shown. As he also suggests, many art forms are being regarded as texts to be read, where students bring a critical eye to the messages conveyed and the values communicated. In this way, each person—representing diverse racial, gender, class, cultural, political, and social experience—exerts power in framing new discourses. Eisner (2002) appropriately refers to the ways that a critical reading of visual text is a way of protecting personal rights but also a way of "determining whose interests are being served by the images that surround us" (p. 29).

Again, it is worth pointing to the similarities between the criticisms of the arts and the criticisms of multiculturalism in education as "soft" and unscientific. Neither responds well to standardization, neither has standard curricula, neither results in instructional efficiency, neither is affirmed through measurable outcomes, both are conceptualized and taught differently than other content areas in classrooms, both ask teachers to consider knowledge and issues that are unfamiliar and uncomfortable, and both are best studied in social contexts. Increasingly, theory in multiculturalism focuses on how educational and societal practices, including various forms of racial discrimination, evolve and are translated into structural barriers (Zuberi, 2001). As is true for multiculturalism in education, fundamental to the expansion of theory and pedagogy in the arts is the notion that educational institutions and educators themselves must support students in transforming existing practices for academic achievement, cultural understanding, social equality, and social justice.

What is the nature of interaction and engagement needed in classrooms to promote imagination, thinking, and learning in the arts? What values and ways of chronicling learning, teaching, and experience matter? What are the curricular, pedagogical, and practical issues that we can address through research? Several documents (e.g., Deasy, 2002; Fiske, 1999) have been written about programs that have strong arts components. Many examples can be found in early childhood education, where programs often include an aesthetics component, described typically in terms of its goal to enhance young children's awareness and appreciation of beauty and the merging of the cognitive and affective (Bradley & Szegda, 2006; Schirrmacher, 2002; Welch, 2006). The Reggio Emilia schools, started by parents of the villages around the area of the same name in Italy after World War II, are regaled for their focus on the arts (Cadwell, 2003; Clemens, 1999; Glassman & Whaley, 2000; Katz, 1990; New, 1993) and for their ability to draw on what we know about sensory stimulation, to promote creative expression, and to build on social, contextual, and cognitive factors in teaching.

Other early childhood programs, such as those using the Montessori method, place considerable emphasis on the arts in instruction. Still other programs, such as Head Start (see Fantuzzo, Gadsden, & McDermott, 2007; Gadsden, Frye, & Wasik, 2005), are attempting to integrate into a single program of teaching and learning cognitive and social-emotional curricula, with the arts—child art and art created for children—as an embedded dimension of the curriculum. Fantuzzo et al. (2007), for example, have initiated such a project in which literacy, math, and social-emotional development are arts based, designed in collaboration with teachers and teaching assistants, and situated in contextual learning and learning communities. Using experimental and qualitative methods, the study holds promise in demonstrating the success of both the research approach and the collaborative context. Such projects are examples of efforts that make the arts a seamless part of learning and teaching.

Bresler (1998) provides a glimpse of the experiences of arts specialists in schools and outlines the ways that different purposes for the arts are approached:

(1) "Child art," meaning original compositions created by children in dance, drama, visual art, and music; (2) "fine art," meaning classical works in the different arts media created by established artists; and (3) "art for children," meaning art created by adults specifically for children. (p. 3)

She found child art to be the most prevalent in using the visual arts, secondarily in dance and drama when they were taught. However, she did not find child art in music instruction. In addition, she found that when the arts were taught by arts specialists, the specialists typically focused on the elements of a specific form of art, whereas classroom teachers focused on themes associated with holidays, seasons, and special events, not unlike the tendency for teachers to focus on costumes, holidays, and related events when they address multicultural issues. Bresler's observations of the different types of knowledge and expertise that arts specialists bring should be not a surprise but confirmation. On the other hand, data on the activities that classroom teachers use suggest a need for observations that can yield information about classroom practices and teacher knowledge and inquiry, particularly on topics about which teachers are not particularly knowledgeable.

As Bresler (1998) suggests, teachers make the many choices because resources are not available and inquiry is not supported, not because they are unable to create more provocative, sustainable instruction. She similarly argues that school art functions in contexts that are neither artistic nor elitist and points to the slow, painful rise of school art during the past century. Writing that the "contemporary reality of school arts is tinged with the bare necessities of educational settings" (p. 8), she describes interactions with principals and administrators who, when asked about the importance of the arts in their schools, responded that the arts existed primarily to comply with union requirements of release time for classroom teachers. In no way should we think that most principals take this position; however, the comments of the principals to whom Bresler spoke indicate a clear subset of views.

The problem here is a policy problem. We have no way of knowing how these principals would respond if policies governing their districts and schools took greater measure to demonstrate the significance of the arts to students' learning and to teaching and commitment to improving them. Bresler (1998) notes this problem and asserts the need for more targeted instruction in teacher education programs—instruction that focuses on the three genres of school art and that prepares teachers to address them. She writes that policies should reconcile the constraints of arts education in school contexts, recognizing the interplay between "artistic notion and pluralistic community values and desires" (p. 11).

Hull and Nelson (2005) present a core of compelling arguments in an article on multimodality—speech, writing, image, gesture, and sound. Although it is not described in terms of the arts, I include it here because of its focus on literacy and performance and because of the complexity of the work that emerged from youth in an out-of-school program as they created a kind of textual art. The process through which the work was achieved privileges the diversity of language and literacies. The article is a masterful example of the weaving of different genres of thought and draws on different art forms. Noting that visual methods have made their way into the social sciences, the authors point to the fact that literacy studies until recently have "eschew[ed] the pictorial in favor of the verbal" (p. 232). The research study is based in a program in Oakland, California, and was started as a center to teach digital storytelling. The multimedia composing consists of images and segments of video combined with background music and a voice-over narrative. The author narrates a personally composed story and an assemblage of visual artifacts, taken from personal collections, the Internet, and other sources.

Through this work, Hull and Nelson (2005) offer a perspective on methodology—their own described as "roughly within the tradition of design experiments, whereby program development is intertwined with continual attempts to assess and improve . . . efforts and document what participants . . . learned" (p. 232). The authors chronicle the purpose, process, and product of engagement; the approaches participants used to gather and use data to tell their stories; the ways in which art was understood and created; and the uses of multimedia and multimodalities. The study provides a good example of innovative research that brings to the forefront the life experiences of learners and their voices and contributes to a curriculum of thought and substance that has application to in-school classroom experiences. Their work raises the question, Is it possible to take these learnings back to formal schools? If yes, with what expectations, trade-offs, and possibilities?

Other researchers on the international front have also focused on multimodality, for example, Rostvall and West (2006b), whose work resulted in a framework to study interaction in music education, and Kenner and Kress (2003), whose work focused on young children in London. In a study that examined young children's engagement in writing and how to respond to varied multimodal experiences, Kenner and Kress found that children gain access to a wider range of communicative resources when they have familiarity with multiple writing systems. Chinese was used as a logographic script, Arabic was used as a non-Roman script, and Spanish was used as a Roman script with differences from the English writing system. The 5- and 6-year-old children in the study possessed a range of multisemiotic resources and were able to switch between and among them as they used multiple visual and actional modes.

In Sweden, Rostvall and West (2006b) have focused on teaching and classroom interactions in music. Instrumental music, they write, engages hundreds of thousands of Swedish children and thousands of music teachers, with every municipality having its own music school for school-age children. The teaching is provided through private lessons primarily. The authors attempted to capture the nature of interaction and the frequency of it, because the role of the music teacher in engaging and sustaining students' engagement was limited if it existed at all. The authors note that student achievement and dropout had traditionally been explained away by attributing both to students' inherent musical aptitude. Using data collected from 12 hours of video recording, they were interested in challenging this explanatory model by examining how different interaction patterns during instrumental music lessons affect students' as well as teachers' opportunities to learn. The results of the analysis are discussed and interpreted from a historical and sociological perspective. The authors also used an institutional perspective as their interpretive framework, with lessons viewed as social encounters and performances in which participants act to create and recreate social orders at different institutional levels, using communication routines of speech, music, and gesture. Findings show that music during the lessons was broken down into separate note symbols as read from the score, rather than the expected musical phrases, rhythms, or melodies. Expressive qualities of music performance were, surprisingly, not addressed at all. Most unsettling, the authors report, was the finding that teachers controlled the interactions and either ignored or ridiculed students' initiative.

These and many other studies (Burkhart, 2006; J. Burton, Horowitz, & Abeles, 1999; Chessin & Chessin, 2006; Strasser & Seplocha, 2007; S. A. Wolf, 2006; Wright, Lindsay, Ellenbogen, & Offord, 2006) reflect the diversity and potential interdisciplinarity possible in examining issues related to teaching and classroom interactions in the arts. However, none was conducted in a public school classroom, raising pedagogical questions; issues of structure, form, and process; questions about the content of classroom instruction; and issues of methodology—how should the arts be studied in classrooms? Last, the proverbial elephant in the room is the question of how, whether, and with what purpose and content are prospective teachers prepared to teach and infuse the arts into their instruction. A fundamental question concerns what teachers and those who prepare teachers count as knowledge and how different epistemological stances matter.

WHAT COUNTS AS KNOWLEDGE: EPISTEMOLOGICAL CONSIDERATIONS

Epistemology may be described as a theory of knowledge. It is included here to connote the expansiveness of emerging theories of knowledge and the need to reconcile new theories with old conceptualizations of the arts. Based on the Greek words *episteme* (knowledge or science) and *logos* (account or explanation), it has more commonly been used to denote how people know what they know and the processes by which they come to know. Extended to current debates in education, it also stimulates questions about who decides what others know, what knowledge counts as important, and how the value of knowledge is determined (Dartnall, 2002). Defined more narrowly, epistemology is the study of knowledge and justified belief. As the study of knowledge, it is concerned with questions such as What are the necessary and sufficient conditions of knowledge? What are its sources? and What is its structure, and what are its limits? As the study of justified belief, epistemology aims to answer questions such as How do we understand the concept of justification? What makes justified beliefs justified? and Is justification internal or external to one's own mind? Understood more broadly, epistemology is about issues having to do with the creation and dissemination of knowledge in particular areas of inquiry.

Epistemology has been primarily concerned with propositional knowledge, that is, knowledge that a certain core of information exists and is true, rather than other forms of knowledge such as applied knowledge (e.g., how to do something). A likely focus for such applied knowledge in education would be teacher education and research on teaching in which pragmatic knowledge may be expected to supersede propositional knowledge. Yet the work of researchers in teacher education and teaching through foci such as teacher inquiry remind us of the significance of epistemology at all levels of research—whether by teachers in classrooms or researchers working with teachers—to examine teachers' own inquiry and the ways students inquire into the world and their learning. In these and other interactions, knowledge of how to do something requires us to unpack assumptions about what constitutes reality for students and is as critical as the content of our teaching. Similarly important is uncovering the process by which emerging and practicing teachers come to know what they know about the content and nature of classroom interactions and the students, families, and communities whom they support.

Epistemology also attempts to raise questions that help us to distinguish true (adequate) knowledge from false (inadequate) knowledge. As Sleeter (2001) suggests, this question translates into issues of scientific methodology. A clear epistemological trend began with a view of knowledge that stressed its absolute, permanent character. The result has been clear focus on normative approaches to identifying the needs and abilities of learners through standards and measures of change. The alternative form is a focus on the social and contextual and acknowledges issues of temporality, relativity, and situation dependence—from a static, passive view of knowledge toward a more adaptive and active one.

This shift raises several questions about the evolution of epistemologies for arts and education, among them, the following:

1. In what ways has the implementation of empiricism in the experimental sciences led to new views of knowledge that encompass the arts?
2. In what sense does proposed knowledge in education and the arts truly correspond to a part of external reality of the institutions in which they are situated to achieve increasing promise and result in negotiated realities?

There are characteristics of the arts in education that cohere with epistemological frames (e.g., Kant, 2001) and that accept the subjectivity of basic concepts, such as space and time, and the impossibility of reaching purely objective representations of things as they are. Two stages of epistemology are relevant to discussions of art. First, pragmatic epistemology constructs knowledge as consisting of models that attempt to represent the environment in such a way so as to maximally simplify problem solving (Klein, 1998; Rand, Tannenbaum, & Feuerstein, 1979). Pragmatic epistemology does not give a clear answer to the question about the source of knowledge or models. There is an implicit assumption that models are built from parts of other models and empirical data on the basis of trial and error, complemented with some heuristics or intuition.

In contrast, constructivism offers a more acceptable frame and assumes that all knowledge is built up from scratch by the subject of knowledge. There are no "givens," neither objective empirical data or facts nor inborn categories or cognitive structures. The idea of a correspondence or reflection of external reality is rejected. Constructivism then may include two component features: individual constructivism, in which an individual attempts to reach coherence among the different pieces of knowledge, deleting from mind and action pieces of knowledge that are inconsistent, and social constructivism, which seeks consensus between different subjects as the ultimate criterion to judge knowledge. "Truth" or "reality" is accorded only to those constructions on which most people of a social group agree (Maturana & Varela, 1987). These constructivist approaches put much more emphasis on the changing and relative character of knowledge. A broader, synthetic outlook is offered by different forms of evolutionary epistemology in which knowledge is constructed by the subject or group of subjects to adapt to their environment in the broad sense; construction is seen as an ongoing process at different levels, biological as well as psychological or social.

Epistemologies that drive the study and practice of the arts have a long history in educational scholarship—from the study of aesthetics and imagination (Greene, 1994) to debates on the cognitive dimensions of art (Catterall, 2002; Eisner, 2002) to discussions about dispositions (Perkins & Tishman, 2001). Recent studies on multimodality, digital literacy, and hip-hop culture have also captivated scholarship not simply as newly recognized art forms but mostly as complex art forms that cannot be situated neatly in categories. In their 2005 article, Hull and Nelson argue that in "this age of digitally afforded multimodality" (p. 224), there are unmistakable signs that what counts as a text and what constitutes reading and writing are changing. They note that rather than privileging a single mode of language, art, and experience, new genres "draw upon a variety of modalities (speech, writing, imagine, gesture, and sound—to create different forms of meaning" (p. 225). The same can be said of the arts in education. What Hull and Nelson, among others, suggest is the need to extend our notions of creativity—to seek a non-atomistic, combinatorial theory of knowledge that can account for the fluidity and flexibility of human thought and learning. The epistemological issues in the arts then may be combined into at least four areas that raise questions about reality and who defines reality, with what knowledge of the reality and tools, and with what interpretive agendas:

1. The arts as a way of human knowing—of imagination, aesthetic knowledge, and translation to practical knowledge;

2. The arts as cultural knowledge and as differential cultural knowledge;
3. The arts as traditional (visual, musical, dance, theater, and aesthetics) and emerging genres (e.g., new modalities, media, and technologies); and
4. Interpretation and performance as fundamental concepts.

Moreover, what counts as art and the arts is an equally and increasingly complex question. How do the arts include performance or engagement with diverse media? The arts in education have taken on a range of meanings, and not everyone concerned with the study of the arts agree on what constitutes the arts. What are the characteristics of the knower of the arts, a learner of the arts, or a classroom that engages students through the arts? What socially constructed sense of the world does the learner, teacher, and researcher bring to the study and teaching of the arts?

ARTS LEARNING AND DISPOSITIONS

In both of the previous sections, the assumption was that the individual has certain dispositions that invite engagement in the arts. In this section, we focus on thinking, social, and emotional dispositions as contexts for arts learning. In considering good thinking as more than cognitive ability and skill, it is equally important to address questions of motivation, social and emotional well-being, and attitudes. We are then able to determine how judgments are made about the value of different issues as people approach thinking, whether and how they make choices about their approach(es), and how they move from a state of superficial interest and thinking to more deepened analysis, including questioning, reflection, and inquiry about nuanced problems and issues.

The concepts of thinking, social, and emotional behaviors take on a more complex and interesting meaning when they are considered as dispositions. It is this idea of dispositionality, of tendencies or inclinations toward patterns of behavior, that allows us to learn more both about the processes of thinking and the interrelationships between thinking, emotional (as part of personality) engagement, and social engagement and about how learners build on and implement learnings in different settings, under different conditions or circumstances, and with different outcomes (i.e., with outcomes being more than a single, correct response or a simple, desired result). Much of this view of dispositionality coheres with ideas about writing and literacy processes, inquiry and reflective practice, and critical thinking and reinforces the significance of questioning, worldviews, values, and uncovering of essential beliefs (Costa & Kallick, 2000). In this way, the discussions are extended beyond notions of metacognition, theory of mind, or habits of mind to identify the goal of learning—to unmask pathways to the goal, expectations and changes in expectations along different pathways, and uses for learning for multiple purposes. Learning for a given task is not finite; rather, it is open, continuous, and complex—salient features of life-long learning, learning across the life cycle, and life-course development (Gadsden, 1999).

In education, thinking is often taken for granted. At the same time, understanding is seen as critical to learning, and critical thinking is seen as a goal of schooling.

However, as Tishman and Andrade (1995) suggest in their writing on thinking dispositions, one can have the ability to think critically and not be disposed to thinking critically. Another less illustrative example focuses on children, adolescents, and college-age students who can read but do not—a long-standing and unresolved question in the study of literacy. Thus, what is necessary is a stronger grasp on how people learn, when, how, and under what conditions they are disposed to learning, uncovering an issue, and engaging in critical analysis.

There are many areas (traditional and contemporary) that the work on dispositions might inform more directly and effectively in the arts and education, five of which include our understanding of (a) persistence—how it develops and is revised with time, the conditions and contexts that foster it, and the factors that militate against it; (b) creativity, its unfolding, and its applications; (c) language, literacy, and math; (d) self-regulation, approaches to learning, and learning behaviors; and (e) students' development of critical reflection and introspection, particularly as these relate to empathy and understanding others. A major area of focus in which this work might be examined is in relationship to different groups of learners—for example, hearing-impaired children or autistic children—and to the act and processes of instruction itself, an area that Frye and Ziv (2005) and others have addressed. Another area of considerable importance is a focus on students' understanding, uncovering, and manipulation of complex issues of access and justice, for example, the kinds of issues that might be addressed in questions of racial privacy, its relationship to ethnic and cultural identity, and discussions of race and racial discrimination; students' aversive racism (McGillicuddy-De Lisi, Daly, & Neal, 2006); and related issues of human experience within a range of literary and scientific genres.

RESEARCH DISCOURSES ON LEARNING AND THE ARTS IN EDUCATION

What do we mean by arts learning? Are we referring to building students' knowledge about different art forms? Are our aims about helping students to think like artists and understand their motivations; the broader realm of the arts, culture, and art work; performance and performative acts; or visual and media texts? Or, are we attempting to address the complex role of arts engagement in children's cognitive development and academic achievement? Eisner's (2002) chapter on visions and versions in arts education addresses some of these issues and highlights some of the prevailing tensions and possibilities in the field, including the quandary about cognition and the impact of the arts on children's academic achievement. A critical analysis by Dartnall (2002) also seeks to reveal connections between creativity and cognition, whereas others, such as Thornton (2002), raise questions about learning in the context of creativity and the degree to which learning speaks to the task, not the process.

The cognitive and social dimensions of learning have been a source of tension but not only in relationship to the arts (see Pellegrino, Chudowsky, & Glaser, 2001). One source of the tension in the arts and education stems from isolation of cognitive and social dimensions and concerns about the lack of strong designs and impact data to determine the efficacy of the arts in classrooms. Another is the result of a tendency for those concerned with these measures to conflate evidence of cognitive change with change in children's academic performance in the foundational areas (see commentary and response by Eisner, 2002, and Catterall, 2002). There are data to suggest that a relationship exists between students' engagement in the arts—as learner and performer—and their engagement in learning and school (Rauscher, 2003). There are also qualitative data that show change in the kind of engagement, for example, students' creation of visual texts and digital renderings and performances as well as their ability and willingness to write about their changing identities, their life experiences, and their neighborhoods and to reconnect with the enterprise of learning (Fisher, 2004, 2006; Vasudevan, 2006).

Haney, Russell, and Bebell (2004) provide an interesting compilation of works in which students' drawings are used to document change and to enact change. Their analysis points to the importance of children's drawings as a medium of research. For example, they note that in times of war and crisis, "children's drawings have frequently been recognized as offering a unique window on events and their meaning" (p. 241). However, as they argue, educational research has generally not paid serious attention to the ways in which children's school art can be used for this purpose. Children's school art also tells us something about the children—who they are, the contexts and issues that are most prominent, and the ways in which learning in the classroom can interrupt potentially debilitating tensions and build on the strengths outside of the classroom (Gadsden, 2006).

In a 2004 report, *The Arts and Education: New Opportunities for Research*, conducted in collaboration with the Arts Education Partnership (2004), the editors note that reliable information is "unavailable about student access to arts instruction, about current and predicted availability of qualified teachers, and about student performance" (p. 28). They examine cognition within the realm of multiple forms of expression but also speak to the importance of studying the arts in relationship to personal and social development, community democracy and civil society, and teaching and learning environments. Among the areas of study that they highlight in relationship to the arts and artistic expression are language and literacy, the arts in young children, and the arts and the transfer of learning. They also note that considerable attention has focused on the arts and the transfer of learning, with some specialists expressing concern that a one-to-one correlation between the arts and academic achievement will make the role of the arts in schools even more vulnerable. For example, as part of their review of 188 reports on the arts, Winner and Hetland (2000) argue that the arts would quickly lose their position if significant academic improvement does not result. They found 275 effect sizes, with three areas having the most reliable causal links: (a) listening to music and spatial-temporal reasoning, (b) learning to play music and spatial reasoning, and (c) classroom drama and verbal skills.

The concerns about narrow views of transfer are addressed, in a particularly poignant way, by Bransford and Schwartz (1999), who write, "A belief in transfer lies at the heart of our educational system" (p. 61). Bransford and Schwartz point to the disenchantment with the transfer literature, for example, work by Lave and Wenger (1991), Greeno (1998), and Wertsch (1998) on situative cognition, as well as questions raised in more traditional analyses of cognition (e.g., Detterman & Sternberg, 1993). Drawing heavily on work by Broudy (1977) on "knowing with," the authors make a case for a focus on "preparation for learning," citing the possibilities that exist for understanding the active nature of transfer and for providing perspectives on the arts and the humanities. They similarly make a case for possibilities of understanding learning by understanding and knowing about the lived experiences of learners, lived experiences that they suggest can be enriched by a study of the arts and the humanities. Bransford and Schwartz's expansion of Broudy's work offers a critical perspective not only on how we study learning but also how we understand change and progress in learning. As they write, "The arts and humanities offer a framework for interpreting experiences and helping people develop a more coherent worldview" (p. 85) and note that "the activities that prepare people for static tests may be different from those that best prepare them for future learning" (p. 93).

In highlighting the value of lived experiences and the potential for the study of the arts and the humanities, Bransford and Schwartz (1999) reinforce anecdotal reports and empirical studies alike that focus on the role of the arts in providing a venue for children in vulnerable situations or at risk for hardship. *The Arts and Education* (Arts Education Partnership, 2004) described earlier also focuses on the need to examine the arts in relationship to social and personal development, for example, arts learning and self-identity, arts learning and persistence and resilience, and arts learning and social skills. The focus on persistence and resilience are of particular interest in relationship to children placed at risk. Although our knowledge of the range of risk, vulnerability, and hardship has increased in education and we are paying more attention to the intersections of child well-being and child welfare, we continue to grapple with questions of how to respond to the needs of children coming from diverse home settings, many of which are unstable, or who are experiencing personal turmoil. Research by L. Burton (2007), on adultification of children, where young children take on the responsibilities and personas of adults in the household, and by Spencer (2006), on resilience among high school youth, are but a couple of poignant studies of how students persist. These and other studies might well beg the question of whether and how the arts contribute to children's persistence and resilience in schooling—willingness and desire to persist in a setting in which many find incongruous with their lives (see also Cauce, Stewart, Rodriguez, Cochran, & Ginzler, 2003; Garmezy, 1993; Rutter, 1996).

If we were designing a study to understand the experience of and measurable change for children in such settings, we may find that many of them, because of their participation in the arts, come to school more often, get better grades, and/or graduate from high school. If we could peel away other possible influences (e.g., life-altering experiences, parent involvement, and academic epiphanies), we would have a measure, though not a precise one, of the effects of the arts on the students' behavior and their achievement. However, what we would mostly have is a measure of a relationship between participation and achievement, but not the nature of the participation, leaving us to determine whether the arts or some other part of the learner's experience may account for change.

One study consistently cited as an example of evidence of the effects of the arts on achievement, and a source of controversy, is Rauscher et al.'s (1997) experimental study on the effects of music on young adults' spatial task performance. The authors found that students' performance on the spatial task improved after listening to Mozart compared with when they were exposed to relaxation music or silence. Work by Rauscher et al. (1997) represents some of the tensions and concerns about an emphasis on the arts in which the sole focus is on transfer of the arts to other cognitive domains. Some argue that the goal of the arts is not to ensure transfer but that inherent to the arts and processes associated with them are a kind of engagement with the environment that prepares children to observe carefully the world around them, make sound decisions, and engage in both abstract and concrete thinking. Moreover, the argument is that the arts play to the imagination and images in ways that are often lost in many current-day academic practices.

NEW KNOWLEDGE BASES FOR TEACHING AND LEARNING

The arts may be offered as individual courses or integrated into foundational courses that allow for learners and teachers to focus on representation. Representation, however, may serve multiple purposes; for example, in reports of fieldwork, researchers represent the renderings of their informants. As in the use of representation in the classroom, the learner is manipulating images and transactions of ideas, beliefs, practices, and ways of seeing the world that may cohere or differ dramatically from those of his or her peers. Learning, then, is both an individual act and a social act that draws on personal experience and social context.

There is agreement that the arts engage multiple skills and abilities rather than a set of discrete skills. They provide young people with authentic learning experiences that engage their minds, hearts, and bodies. Several of the strengths of the arts are described in the 1999 report *Champions of Change* (Fiske, 1999), which lists several shared perspectives emanating from studies conducted by well-known scholars and serves as a good framework to discuss a range of other issues in the study of the arts. The document suggests that the arts reach youth who are not otherwise reached, including those who are disengaged from schools and social institutions in the community and those at risk for hardship and alienation. A significant portion of this work focuses on learners in low-income, minority, oppressed communities—youth who are often labeled hardest to reach (D. P. Wolf, 2000).

The arts for these groups of youth often resemble traditional forms of engagement but are as likely if not more likely to take up new art forms that connect images, texts, music, and technologies in different ways. The activities in which students are engaged may take place in school or, more poignantly, after school in programs held on school sites or in community institutions. Much of this work is to be found in literacy studies that bring to the surface the ways in which youth in difficult situations draw on their realities to demonstrate both problems and possibilities in the environments in which they live, that are friendly to them, and that often make them vulnerable. They are as likely to be located in discussions of popular culture, which has become the luminous example of bridging the global and local and the border crossings of class, race, and gender of youth and youth cultures.

Fisher's work (2004, 2006) on open mike in an Oakland, California, book store points to the opportunities afforded to children and adults through intergenerational activities that present their spoken art. Likewise, her work describing the written texts of high school students in New York City demonstrates the ways in which students, typically marginalized, assert an agentive self and in so doing create a valuable art form. Jocson (in press) examines students' use of digital literacies and the ways in which their sense of self unfolds. A core of emerging scholars, such as Stovall (2006) and Alim (2002), focuses directly on hip-hop and its strength as a medium and mediator for youth at risk. The concept of popular culture, Duncan-Andrade and Morrell (2005) would suggest, is the everyday social experience of marginalized students as they confront, make sense of, and contend with social institutions such as schools, the mass media, corporations, and governments. What these young researchers share is a keen understanding of the issues facing youth, many of them vacillating between multiple worlds similar to the experiences of the researchers. Each situates the issues within social and contextual processes to help us understand the individual and shared needs and possibilities as well as the ways in which they transform life experience into art, taking on, through lyrics and multi-images, institutions that fail them with vengeance and those that support them with skepticism. As Kress (2003) points out, such modal transformations are central in understanding education and learning from a multimodal perspective.

Wissman's (2005) work with high school girls offers another example of literacy engagement that might be considered art. Using photographs, taken by the students over time, and their written and oral interpretations of these pictures, the students created new forms of visual art and text (Eisner, 2002). Wissman (re)presents intersections between and among the literacy practices and strengths of the adolescent girls, diverse cultural and social dimensions of their school and out-of-school lives, and the role of identity formation and revision. In studying the literacy and artistic practices of her students, she enhances, through students' personal expression and academic texts, our understanding of narratives as complex both in their purpose and in the identities they reveal. Drawing on a practitioner-inquiry methodological frame, she positions the issues of the students' self-perceptions and disclosures within the context of their school experiences. She then highlights otherwise understudied issues related to the experiences of girls in this context and makes the issues of their selfhood and their emerging, newly visioned, reshaped identities as part of how we understand and construct the cultural and gendered lives of students—specifically young women of color—in our research questions, studies, and pedagogy. Moreover, her work gives us a new way of seeing their experience (Eisner, 2002).

Brooks (2007) is engaged in similarly compelling work in which she examines the ways that adolescent girls in an urban setting read and interpret "street-lit" or street fiction novels as well as canonized young adult fiction. Here, she demonstrates the ways in which traditional art forms of fiction writing are being modified and how inner-city youth are taking up these works to become engaged in formal school curricula and to sustain their interests. She appropriately denotes both the rise in the focus on street-lit as a form of student engagement and the multiplicity of interpretations and applications that students make. She posits that adolescents examining of different genres is essential to engagement in the concepts, acts, events, and processes of literacy learning. Thus, she seeks to understand how and why students access different genres, how they read them, and how their interactions with them are translated into their experiences as learners within school. Appropriately, she draws from several areas of theory, research, and practice—an important and well-crafted mix of critical areas of inquiry—in an effort to create an expansive conceptual framework.

This and related work, such as Dyson's (2003) *The Brothers and Sisters Learn to Write: Popular Literacies in Childhood and School Cultures*, build on and are distinguished from other recent writings and studies on contemporary literary genres in their clear focus on the ways in which students engage with multiple types of texts for the purposes of meaning making intellectually, academically, and personally. The issues that the research aims to address and the methodological approaches must respond to the increasingly apparent need to consider a range of data collection and analytic venues to understand the complex questions of student access, engagement, and negotiation in literacy. Despite considerable work in the past few years on literacy and various forms of contemporary genres, many of the issues that are raised continue to be contested domains of work, requiring us to expand and revisit our research and assumptions about cultural practices, gendered experiences, and student engagement. The range of this research offers broad perspectives on the ways that students take up through their reading what anthropologists such as Rex (1996) refer to as the tensions between public and private.

Unique across researchers whose work focuses on youth culture and schooling is the reality that schools do not take, have not taken, or have not been able to take advantage of the school setting itself as a place of creativity for new art forms. They are more likely to occur in structured and unstructured community programs (Heath, 2001; Hull & Nelson, 2005), after-school programs (Heath, 2001), and informal gatherings within communities. What is distinctive about the art produced is that it draws from multiple traditions, from Western genres of music and orality to storytelling associated with the Black diaspora. However, although much of this work addresses the needs of youth in low-income, minority homes and families, they are not isolated from the needs and problems facing youth in general. As Heath (2001) notes, there is an institutional gap that is resulting in a range of negative experiences and effects for children in school. Unlike youth of the past, who did not have access to the multimedia and technologies now available, these youth have access to the vagaries of institutional promises, failed efforts, and inequities of access and support.

What the studies on youth also share is the effective use of strong fieldwork, qualitative approaches, and interpretive lenses that privilege the experience that they observe while making public the limitations of the researchers as outsiders to this experience. The data from them demonstrate change in the language, problem solving, writing, and social-emotional lives of students. What the studies lack in large samples they offer in the depth, texture, and step-by-step chronicling of the experience of youth, whom Heath (2001) describes as invisible but whom I have also felt are a kind of academic throwaway. I have been struck, for example, in my own work with children of incarcerated parents, most of whom are children of color and all of whom come from low-income and working-class families, that the same opportunities to engage in the arts available to their imprisoned fathers are not available in the neighborhoods where the children live or in many of the schools that they attend. Programs such as those presented by Heath and Roach (1999), Catterall and Waldorf (2000), D. P. Wolf (2000), and others offer both opportunities for youth to engage in the arts and enhance their cognitive abilities and places of respite for them to reveal themselves through artistry.

A recent volume edited by Hill and Vasudevan (in press) asks a salient question: What is at stake when media texts play a central role in teaching and learning processes? This question could be posed for a range of new ideas, concepts, and practices in education, particularly, those related to students' literacy engagement. However, for media, as a long-standing literary and performance genre, this question takes on and takes up a special poignancy because of the relatively limited ways media have been used in classrooms and by teachers and the (dis)comforts that they create. Such (dis)comforts are as likely as not to result from the new knowledge required of teachers to understand the multiple possibilities of media and media use in classrooms and media's situatedness in new technologies and modalities, whether accessing the evening news through MSNBC, peering into the hip-hop generation, or producing digital media.

In the same volume, authors respond to two other questions. First, the editors ask, What possibilities exist for engaging school learning differently when media and media texts are part of the learning fabric? Jocson (in press), in this volume, skillfully connects traditional ways of engaging students in poetry with state-of-the-art media approaches to expressing self. Hence, she complicates the idea of learning in isolation and the practices associated with teaching by positioning teachers' own learning and ways of seeing the world as a contested and public space for teachers and others to question. In my own pedagogy and work with teachers, I have found the processes of uncovering our own experiences as learners and intentions as teachers to be among the most challenging and enriching activities if we hope to make learning more transparent and the structures in which learning takes place less daunting for students. Jocson's work demonstrates the ways in which media push the boundaries of teacher knowledge to highlight transformations in teachers' learning and the strengths of using digital media to transform. The meticulous nature of her inquiry and the process of using digital media require teachers to wrestle with a range of complex issues in teaching—for example, race, class, gender, culture, sexuality, and difference in general—and difficult social problems—for example, crime, child abuse, policy harassment, homelessness, and poverty; to map these against other real-world problems facing students, families, and communities; and to use them as forays into discourses about and action that promotes social transformation.

Second, Hill and Vasudevan (in press) raise questions about the types of relationships that are enabled and constrained as a consequence of the recognized presence of media and media texts (see also Staples, in press). The salient issue in this question is not simply media and media texts but the inextricability of current foci on media as learning and teaching contexts, texts, and tools to support youth. Meacham (2003), through his work with inner-city youth, using hip-hop as a musical genre and media as a primary venue, raises a similar issue, arguing that any response requires a focus on youth themselves. Through this research, he allows us to coexamine situated learning, students' engagement in school and transitions, and critique and revisioning of existing epistemologies and pedagogies. It is no surprise that even now, research and pedagogical activities on media take place primarily outside of regular school hours, as an addendum to sanctioned teaching activities, in after-school or alternative programs.

Media and the uses of media as scripted, performative, and personalized text have been at the heart of cutting-edge work in the field of literacy and education more broadly, particularly in the study of inner-city African American and Latino youth. The focus on media in the 1980s and 1990s was simply not the same as it is in 2007, as scholars of media, communications, education, and the social sciences find themselves uniquely linked to each other in the ideation, development, and implementation of different media forms and as teachers and students use these media as modes of self-expression, identity formation and revision, and personal and academic representation.

The work of the authors in the Hill and Vasudevan volume (in press) suggests that media images are at one and the same time narrowly defined and multifaceted, depending on the observer, and that by expanding historically accepted genres in literacy and learning, they invite students to develop and reconfigure literacy practices and behaviors and to create "media text" (Staples, in press). In particular, the focus of the work by newer scholars described earlier on middle and high school students recognizes the significance of adolescence as a particularly complex developmental period of youth, during which students use a range of intellectual abilities, negotiate emerging personal identities, and seek intellectual guidance and support to grasp and grapple with difficult issues.

Youth draw on and revise existing language and linguistic genres to construct their own language(s) and linguistic codes and to make choices about whether and how they enter or remove themselves from the familiar and the strange, irrespective of whether these sit in local or larger spaces. Media, messages of media, and the stories from media are critical to youth's engagement in the acts, events, and processes of learning. Thus, questions about how and why students access different forms of media, how they read media and the academic and personal texts that result, and how students' interactions with different forms of media in settings outside of school are translated into school experiences persist as complex terrains of study and interpretation.

The work on media offers a compelling and well-grounded argument for examining digital production within the context of situated learning, the agentive self, and methodological frameworks that acknowledge the performance of media, the space they create for learners to explore meaning and symbolic images, and the layering of the meaning that results (Denzin, 1997; Gutiérrez, Baquedano-Lopez, & Alvarez, 2001; Hull, 2004; Hull & Katz, 2006; Lave & Wenger1991; Mahiri, 2004; Rogoff, 1990). Readers of this work immediately recognize these frameworks and ways of thinking about the questions, approaches to studying them, and interpretive lenses used to understand them as familiar and appropriate. Research in the arts and education (Eisner, 2002; Greene, 1995), arts and literacy (Bach, 1998), and media and literacy (Duncan-Andrade & Morrell, 2005; Gee, 1992; Morrell, 2002; Staples, 2005) have taken on the intersections of the cultural, social, and cognitive dimensions of learning and the ways in which youth form, inform, and revise traditional genres of thought on literacy while engaging and being engaged by newer forms, created and defined by youth themselves.

This work is complemented by an emerging body of international research discussions often focused on traditional genres (e.g., in Israel, Africa, and Asia) and addressing particularly complex issues of resources (e.g., in India and Australia). For example, Flolu (2000), focusing on music education and visual arts in Ghana, offers an informative commentary on education policy and the absence of a philosophy of arts education (see also Mans, 2000). Research already described in Sweden and England, as well as work in Australia and Asia, focuses on media. United Nations Educational, Scientific, and Cultural Organization (UNESCO)–supported symposia in Australia, Hong Kong, and New Delhi reinforce the increasing attention and significance attached to this often-overlooked area of education (UNESCO, 2005).

ARTS AND EDUCATION: CLOSING CONSIDERATIONS AND POSSIBILITIES

This chapter used a social–cultural–contextual framework to examine issues in the study of the arts and education. It sought to address questions about the role that research on the arts has played and can play to uncover the real and potential contributions of the arts to and in education. A fundamental premise of the chapter is that the present is a particularly important moment to build on past work and to build a future, coherent body of research that complicates and improves the ways in which we create educational theory, conduct educational research, enhance practice, and deepen our understanding of learning and the arts. Perhaps more than any other area of study in education, the arts successfully merge the old and new, traditional and avant-garde, local and global, mainstream and cutting-edge. However, like other areas of inquiry, whether and how the arts are integrated into curricula may be tied to issues of power, cultural practices, and personal and political dispositions.

The arguments for the arts are situated within several different discourses, for example, those that focus on the arts for the sake of the arts (i.e., children's lives are expanded through exposure to the arts) and those that seek to give it credibility within the standards and high-stakes testing arenas. These foci are not always or necessarily polar opposites, however; that is, those who appear to sit in one camp may well sit, depending on the circumstances, in another. One might argue, then, that the problem is not in the polemics but in the circumstances and demands set forth through policies that create the polemics in the first place. On the other hand, a considerable amount of the discourse on the arts and education is located in polemics, not unlike the points–counterpoints between qualitative and quantitative research or between the sciences and the humanities. This type of divide in the arts is augmented and further made problematic when the arts are constructed as oppositional to science.

The different sections of this review were designed to address the major themes that run through conceptualizations and discussions of innovative classroom practices. Not surprisingly, most of the writing, particularly writing about work in the United States, laments cutbacks in government and policy support for programs. Articles written about efforts abroad, including the UNESCO and Australia Council for the Arts Compendium project and symposia held in Asia, often demonstrate several similarities to the United States in the type and nature of problems regarding funding. More active discussions, such as Spain's controversy about whether art education should be more oriented toward the fine arts or toward craft, highlight the question of what counts as the arts. However, recent efforts suggest that some shifts are occurring and need to be sustained at federal and state levels of government.

What is consistent through the materials reviewed for the chapter is their discussion of the potential for the arts to be used more integratively in curricula and made an active part of the preparation of teachers. Other works argue that the problem lies in our failure to deconstruct the multiple dimensions of the arts, particularly as new genres emerge. The critical questions, then, in considering what counts as knowledge and how it is generated are centered, in part, on questions of how to study, hence preserve, historically valued genres such as visual arts and music performance while creating the necessary space for more contemporary and future-sensitive approaches.

The question of what counts as art and the arts is also addressed through the focus on new technologies and genres, some of which have made dramatic leaps within a short time, for example, in digital teaching, multimedia, and technology. None of us could have imagined the ways in which new genres might have expanded the arts: multimodality, diverse musical and literary genres that are attempting to uncover both process and product, and new twists on old genres such as storytelling that provide us with opportunities to understand the learner and build better learning environments. Moreover, these new trends in the arts and the research that is being conducted expand the reach of who is studied, with what facility and results, and with what emergence of new knowledge.

The focus on the arts and education suggests several lines of inquiry, many of which are discussed in documents such as *The Arts and Education* (Arts Education Partnership, 2004). Not unlike that document, the present chapter points to a need to examine critically multiple methodological approaches that draw on a range of disciplines—from the humanities, using historical and literary genres, to the social sciences, using empirical (quantitative and qualitative or ethnographic) methods. In other words, much of what we need to know about the arts and its place in education and schooling will only be understood by considering the diversity of approaches available and the diversity of the contexts and people who will be engaged in the arts. Changes in technology and in "who" constitutes schools, the communities of artists, and art forms require that we revisit, possibly revise, our conceptualizations of art and, by extension, our views of education.

Existing work on the arts and education would be enhanced by an expansion and deepening of conceptual and theoretical analyses, particularly, work that demonstrates the historical and interdisciplinary nature of inquiry in the arts. Within this work, more targeted analyses are needed on the role of the arts in promoting social justice and democracy. The issues have reemerged as scholars from different disciplines demonstrate the ways in which the arts have become increasingly a site for intellectual and social activism (see Eisner, 2000; Levine, 2007).

Given the relatively narrow focus of research on the arts and education, our temptation is to provide a long list of options. In fact, the list of possibilities is long but not equally accessible in the short term. There are some areas in which there has already been important work in the past decade and that concurrently need to be broadened. Hence, there were difficult decisions to be made about the content of a review such as this. Issues in one of these areas—the role of the arts in learning and teaching among children living in poverty and placed at risk for school failure—are embedded in all the sections of the chapter, particularly in discussions of programs designed for students at risk. These areas suggest a need for (re)newed examination of the role of the arts and student persistence and resilience. A second core of important work not discussed as a separate area of study is the range of international studies and commentaries, including a recently edited volume by Bresler (2007). There are several other impressive bodies of work on multimodality that are emerging in Europe (Rostvall & West, 2006a, 2006b), studies of the arts and education in Asia (UNESCO, 2005), and work that questions the disjuncture between teachers' knowledge of students' cultures and students' native artistry (Belver, Ullan, & Acaso, 2005).

In addition, research that examines the meaning of arts learning and how such learning is experienced by diverse learners would contribute to new lines of inquiry that have attempted to take up these issues in teaching, teacher education, teacher inquiry, and classroom practice. Such work would extend questions posed on cognition and the arts, with some researchers (e.g., Schwartz, Bransford & Sears, 2005) noting that traditional studies of transfer often limit themselves to direct application of theories that use tests of "sequestered problem solving."

Last, research that examines the relationship that exists between culture and the arts would lend an especially critical dimension to the broad questions of schooling, the particular issues of classroom practice and student engagement, and the role of social contexts (such as families and communities) in shaping, nurturing, and supporting students' engagement. In areas such as literacy, we know that such social contexts and the cultural experiences within them contribute in ways that we have yet to understand fully in students' learning. The arts—neither the panacea to ameliorate all that troubles us in education nor the beacon of all possibility—offer us a lens through which to examine long-standing questions, provocative ways to (re)consider creativity, opportunity to reimagine engagement, and a renewed sense of possibility that can lead us to the formation of new epistemologies.

NOTE

[1]In much of the earlier work, authors use a range of descriptors to refer to what is described here as the arts and education and the arts in education.

ACKNOWLEDGMENTS

The author thanks Penn graduate students Sue Bickerstaff, Cleo Jacobs, Shannon Kane, and Jie Park for their research assistance.

REFERENCES

Alim, H. S. (2002). Street conscious coupla variation in the hip hop nation. *American Speech*, *77*(3), 288–301.

Alim, H. S., & Baugh, J. (2007). *Talkin Black talk: Language, education, and social change*. New York: Teachers College Press.

Arts Education Partnership. (2004). *The arts and education: New opportunities for research*. Washington, DC: Author.

Bach, H. (1998). *A visual narrative concerning curriculum, girls and photography etc.* Edmonton, Canada: QUAL Institute Press.

Ballengee-Morris, C., & Stuhr, P. L. (2001). Multicultural art and visual cultural education in a changing world. *Art Education*, *54*(4), 6–13.

Begoray, D. (2001). Through a class darkly: Visual literacy in the classroom. *Canadian Journal of Education*, *26*(2), 201–217.

Belver, M., Ullan, A., & Acaso, M. (2005). Integrating art education models: Contemporary controversies in Spain. *Journal of Art & Design Education*, *24*(1), 93–99.

Boykin, A. W., & Bailey, C. T. (2000). *Experimental research on the role of cultural factors in school-relevant cognitive functioning: Synthesis of findings on cultural contexts, cultural orientations, and individual differences* (Center for Research on the Education of Students Placed At Risk [CRESPAR] Technical Report No. 42). Washington, DC, and Baltimore, MD: Howard University and Johns Hopkins University.

Bradley, K., & Szegda, M. (2006). The dance of learning. In B. Spodek and O. N. Saracho (Eds.), *Handbook of research on the education of young children* (pp. 243–250). Mahwah, NJ: Lawrence Erlbaum.

Bransford, J. D., & Schwartz, D. L. (1999). Rethinking transfer: A simple proposal with multiple implications. *Review of Research in Education*, *24*, 61–100.

Bresler, L. (1998). "Child art," "fine art," and "art for children": The shaping of school practice and implications for change. *Arts Education Policy Review*, *100*(1), 3–11.

Bresler, L. (2001). Agenda for arts education research: Emerging issues and directions. In M. McCarthy (Ed.), *Enlightened advocacy: Implications for research for arts education policy and practice* (pp. 43–71). College Park, MD: University of Maryland.

Bresler, L. (Ed.). (2007). *International handbook of research in arts education*. Dordrecht, Netherlands: Springer.

Bresler, L., & Ardichivili, A. (Eds.). (2002). *International research in education: Experience, theory and practice*. New York: Peter Lang.

Bresler, L., DeStefano, L., Feldman, R., & Garg, S. (2000). Artists-in-residence in public schools: Issues in curriculum, integration, impact. *Visual Art Research*, *26*(1), 13–29.

Brooks, W. (2007). The literary voices of urban readers: Multi-factor influences on textual inter-pretations. In R. P. Solomon & D. Sekayi (Eds.), *Urban teacher education and teaching: Innovative practices for diversity and social justice* (pp. 195–206). Mahwah, NJ: Lawrence Erlbaum.

Broudy, H. S. (1977). Types of knowledge and purposes of education. In R. C. Anderson, R. J. Spiro, & W. E. Montague (Eds.), *Schooling and the acquisition of knowledge* (pp. 1-17). Hillsdale, NJ: Lawrence Erlbaum.

Burkhart, A. (2006). Object lessons: Thinking about material culture. *Art Education, 59*(2), 33–39.

Burton, J., Horowitz, R., & Abeles, H. (1999). Learning in and through the arts: Curriculum implications. In E. B. Fiske (Ed.), *Champions of change: The impact of the arts on learning* (pp. 35–46). Washington, DC: Arts Education Partnership.

Burton, L. (2007). Childhood adultification in economically disadvantaged families: A conceptual model. *Family Relations, 56*(4), 329–345.

Cadwell, L. (2003). *Bringing learning to life: The Reggio approach to early childhood education.* New York: Teachers College Press.

Carey, J. (2005). Exploring future media. In J. Flood, S. B. Heath, & D. Lapp (Eds.), *Handbook of research on teaching literacy through the communicative and visual arts* (pp. 62–67). Mahwah, NJ: Lawrence Erlbaum.

Catterall, J. S. (2002). The arts and the transfer of learning. In R. J. Deasy (Ed.), *Critical links: Learning in the arts and student academic and social development* (pp. 151–157). Washington, DC: Arts Education Partnership.

Catterall, J. S., & Waldorf, L. (2000). Chicago arts partnerships in education: Summary evaluation. In E. B. Fiske (Ed.), *Champions of change: The impact of the arts on learning* (pp. 47–62). Washington, DC: Arts Education Partnership.

Cauce, A. M., Stewart, A., Rodriguez, M. D., Cochran, B., & Ginzler, J. (2003). Overcoming the odds? Adolescent development in the context of urban poverty. In S. S. Luthar (Ed.), *Resilience and vulnerability: Adaptation in the context of childhood adversities* (pp. 343–363). New York: Cambridge University Press.

Chessin, D., & Chessin, L. (2006). Every feather tells a story. *Science and Children, 44*(1), 48–51.

Clemens, S. G. (1999). Editing: Permission to start wrong. *Early Childhood Research and Practice, 1*(1). Retrieved June 18, 2007, from http://ecrp.uiuc.edu/v1n1/clemens.html

Cochran-Smith, M. (1995). Uncertain allies: Understanding the boundaries of race and teaching. *Harvard Educational Review, 65*(4), 541–570.

Costa, A., & Kallick, B. (2000). *Assessing and reporting on habits of mind.* Alexandria, VA: Association for Supervision and Curriculum Development.

Association for Supervision and Curriculum Development.

Dartnall, T. (Ed.). (2002). *Creativity, cognition, and knowledge: An interaction.* Westport, CT: Praeger.

Deasy, R. J. (Ed.). (2002). *Critical links: Learning in the arts and student academic and social development.* Washington, DC: Arts Education Partnership.

Denzin, N. (1997). Performance texts. In W. Tierney & Y. Lincoln (Eds.), *Representation and the text: Re-framing the narrative voice* (pp. 179–217). Albany: State University of New York Press.

Detterman, D. & Sternberg, R. (Eds). (1993). *Transfer on trial: Intelligence, cognition and instruction.* Norwood, NJ: Ablex.

Dewey, J. (1934). *Art as experience.* New York: Minton Balch.

Duncan-Andrade, J., & Morrell, E. (2005). Popular culture and critical media pedagogy in secondary literacy classrooms. *International Journal of Learning, 12,* 1–11.

Dyson, A. H. (2003). *The brothers and sisters learn to write: Popular literacies in childhood and school cultures.* New York: Teachers College Press.

Efland, A. D. (1990). *History of art education: Intellectual and social currents in teaching the visual arts.* New York: Teachers College Press.

Eisner, E. (1982). *Cognition and curriculum: A basis for deciding what to teach.* New York: Longman.

Eisner, E. (1994). Revisionism in art education: Some comments on the preceding articles. *Studies in Art Education, 35*(3), 188–191.

Eisner, E. (1997). The state of art education today and some potential remedies: A report to the National Endowment for the Arts. *Art Education, 50*(1), 61–72.

Eisner, E. (1999). Getting down to basics. *Arts Education Journal of Aesthetic Education, 33*(4), 145–159.

Eisner, E. (2002). *The arts and the creation of mind.* New Haven, CT: Yale University Press.

Eisner, E., & Powell, K. (2002). Art in science? *Curriculum Inquiry, 32*(2), 131–159.

Eisner, E. W. (2000). Art education policy? *Arts Education Policy Review, 101*(3), 4–6.

Ennis, R. (1962). A concept of critical thinking. *Harvard Educational Review, 32*(1), 81–111.

Ennis, R. (1994, April). *Assessing critical thinking dispositions: Theoretical considerations.* Paper presented at the meeting of the American Educational Research Association, New Orleans, LA.

Facione, P., Facione, N., & Giancarlo, G. (2000). The disposition toward critical thinking: Its character, measurement, and relationship to critical thinking skill. *Informal Logic, 20*(1), 61–84.

Facione, P., Sanchez, C., & Facione, N. (1994). *Are college students disposed to think?* Paper presented at the sixth international Conference on Thinking, Boston.

Fantuzzo, J. F., Gadsden, V. L., & McDermott, P. (2007). *Evidence-based program for the integration of curricula: Interim report to the National Institute for Child Health and Human Development.* Washington, DC: U.S. Department of Health and Human Services.

Fisher, M. (2004). "The song is unfinished": The new literate and literacy and their institutions. *Written Communication, 21*(3), 290–309.

Fisher, M. (2006). Earning "dual degrees": Black bookstores as alternative knowledge spaces. *Anthropology and Education Quarterly, 37*(1), 83–99.

Fiske, E. B. (Ed.). (1999). *Champions of change: The impact of the arts on learning.* Washington, DC: The Arts Education Partnership and the President's Committee on the Arts and the Humanities.

Flolu, E. J. (2000). Re-thinking arts education in Ghana. *Art Education Policy Review, 101*(5), 25–29.

Flood, J., Heath, S. B., & Lapp, D. (Eds.). (2005). *Handbook of research on teaching literacy through the communicative and visual arts.* Mahwah, NJ: Lawrence Erlbaum.

Frye, D., & Ziv, M. (2005). Teaching and learning as intentional activities. In C. Tamis-LeMonda & B. D. Homer (Eds.), *The development of social cognition and communication* (pp. 231–258). Hillsdale, NJ: Lawrence Erlbaum.

Gadsden, V. L. (2000). Intergenerational literacy within families. In M. Kamil, R. Tierney, and R. Barr (Eds.), *Handbook of reading research* (pp. 871–887). New York: Longman.

Gadsden, V. L. (2003). Expanding the concept of "family" in family literacy: Integrating a focus on fathers. In A. DeBruin-Parecki & B. Krol-Sinclair (Eds.), *Family literacy: From theory to practice* (pp. 86–125). Newark, DE: International Reading Association.

Gadsden, V. L. (2006). Educational equity in post-disaster New Orleans. In E. L. Birch & S. M. Wachter (Eds.), *Rebuiliding urban places after disaster: Lessons from Hurricane Katrina* (pp. 201–216). Philadelphia: University of Pennsylvania Press.

Gadsden, V. L., Frye, D., & Wasik, B. A. (2005, June). *Evidence-based program for the integration of curricula: A partnership between research and practice.* Paper presented at the National Head Start Research Conference, Washington, DC.

Gardner, H. (1989). Zero-based arts education: An introduction to ARTS PROPEL. *Studies in Art Education, 30*(2), 71–83.

Garmezy, N. (1993). Children in poverty: Resilience despite risk. *Psychiatry, 56*(1), 127–136.

Gee, J. (1992). *The social mind: Language, ideology, and social practice.* New York: Bergin & Garvey.

Gee, J., & Green, J. (1998). Discourse analysis, learning, and social practice: A methodological study. *Review of Research in Education, 23,* 119–169.

Glassman, M., & Whaley, K. (2000). Dynamic aims: The use of long-term projects in early childhood classrooms in light of Dewey's educational philosophy. *Early Childhood Research and Practice, 2*(1). Retrieved April 3, 2006, from http://ecrp.uiuc.edu/v2n1/glassman.html

Green, J., & Dixon, C. (2003). Language, culture and knowledge in classrooms: An ethnographic approach to identity potentials, knowledge and language in a bilingual fifth grade. *Encontro International Linguagem, Cultura 3 Cognição, Belo Horizonte, 42*(6), 60–76.

Greene, M. (1994). Carpe diem: The arts and school restructuring. *Teachers College Record, 95*(4), 494–507.

Greene, M. (1995). *Releasing the imagination: Essays on education, the arts, and social change.* San Francisco: Jossey-Bass.

Greene, M. (1997). Metaphors and multiples: Representation, the arts and history. *Phi Delta Kappan, 78*(5), 387–394.

Greene, M. (2000). Imagining futures: The public school and possibility. *Journal of Curriculum Studies, 32*(2), 267–280.

Greene, M. (2001). *Variations on a blue guitar: The Lincoln Center lectures on aesthetic education.* New York: Teachers College.

Greeno, J. G. (1998). Situativity of knowing, learning, and research. *American Psychologist, 3*(1), 5–26.

Gutiérrez, K., Baquedano-López, P., & Alvarez, H. (2001). Literacy as hybridity: Moving beyond bilingualism in urban classrooms. In M. de la Luz Reyes & J. Halcón (Eds.), *The best of our children: Critical perspectives on literacy for Latino students* (pp. 122–141). New York: Teachers College Press.

Haney, W., Russell, M., & Bebell, D. (2004). Drawing on education: Using drawings to document school and support change. *Harvard Educational Review, 74*(3), 241–272.

Heath, S. B. (2001). Three's not a crowd: Plans, roles, and focus in the arts. *Educational Researcher, 30*(7), 10–17.

Heath, S. B., & Roach, A. (1999). Imaginative actuality: Learning in the arts during the non-school hours. In E. B. Fiske (Ed.), *Champions of change: The impact of the arts on learning* (pp. 19–34). Washington, DC: The Arts Education Partnership and the President's Committee on the Arts and the Humanities.

Hill, M. L., & Vasudevan, L. (Eds.). (in press). *Media, learning, and sites of possibility.* New York: Peter Lang.

Hull, G. A., (2004). Youth culture and digital media: New literacies for new times. *Research in the Teaching of English, 38*(2), 229–233.

Hull, G. A., & Katz, M. (2006). Crafting an agentive self: Case studies of digital storytelling. *Research in the Teaching of English, 41*(1), 43–81.

Hull, G. A., & Nelson, M. E. (2005). Locating the semiotic power of multimodality. *Written Communication, 22*(2), 224–261.

Jocson, K. M. (in press). Situating the personal in digital media production. In M. Hill & L. Vasudevan (Eds.), *Media, learning, and sites of possibility.* New York: Peter Lang.

Jordan, W. J., & Plank, S. B. (1998). *Sources of talent loss among high achieving poor students* (Report No. 23). Baltimore: MD: Johns Hopkins University, Center for Research on the Education of Students Placed at Risk.

Kalin, N., & Kind, S. (2006). Invitations to understanding: Explorations in the teaching of arts to children. *Arts Education, 59*(3), 36–41.

Kant, I. (2001). *The basic writings of Kant.* New York: Random House.

Katz, L. G. (1990). Impressions of Reggio Emilia preschools. *Young Children, 45*(6), 11–12.

Kenner, C., & Kress, G. (2003). The multisemiotic resources of biliterate children. *Journal of Early Childhood Literacy, 3*(2), 179–202.

Klein, P. (1998). The concept of knowledge. In E. Craig (Ed.), *Encyclopedia of philosophy* (pp. 266–276). London: Routledge.

Kress, G. (2003). *Literacy in the new media age.* London: Routledge.

Ladson-Billings, G. (1994). *The dreamkeepers: Successful teachers of African American children.* San Francisco: Jossey-Bass.

Ladson-Billings, G. (2006). From the achievement gap to the education debt: Understanding achievement in U.S. schools. *Educational Researcher, 35*(7), 3–12.

Larson, R. W., & Walker, K. C. (2006). Learning about the "real world" in an urban arts youth program. *Journal of Adolescent Research, 21*(3), 244–268.

Lave, J., & Wenger, E. (1991). *Situated learning: Legitimate peripheral participation.* New York: Cambridge University Press.

Lee, W. T. (2007). *Culture, literacy, and learning: Taking bloom in the midst of the whirlwind.* New York: Teachers College Press.

Levine, C. (2007). *Provoking democracy: Why we need the arts.* Oxford, UK: Basil Blackwell.

Lewis, D. (1997). Finkish dispositions. *Philosophical Quarterly, 47,* 143–158

Madhere, S., & MacIver, D. (1996). *The talent development middle school: Essential components* (Center for Research on the Education of Students Placed at Risk [CRESPAR] Technical Report No. 3). Washington, DC, and Baltimore, MD: Howard University and Johns Hopkins University.

Mahiri, J. (Ed.) (2004). *What they don't learn in school: Literacy in the lives of urban youth.* New York: Peter Lang.

Mans, M. E. (2000). The African context. *Arts Education Policy Review, 101*(5), 9–10.

Maturana, H., & Varela, F. (1987). *The tree of knowledge: The biological roots of human understanding.* Boston: Shambhala.

McGillicuddy-De Lisi, A. V., Daly, M., & Neal, A. (2006). Children's distributive justice judgments: Aversive racism in Euro-American children? *Child Development, 77*(4), 1063–1080.

McPartland, J. M., Legters, N., Jordan, W., & McDill, E. L. (1996). *The Talent Development High School: Early evidence of impact on school climate, attendance, and student promotion.* Baltimore, MD: Johns Hopkins University, Center for Research on the Education of Students Placed at Risk.

Meacham, S. (2003, April). *Hip hop literacies: Concepts and strategies for pedagogy and practice for the hip hop generation.* Paper presented at the annual meeting of the American Educational Research Association, Chicago.

Mellor, D. H. (1974). In defense of dispositions. *Philosophical Review, 83,* 157–181.

Mercado, C., & Santamaria, L. J. (2005). A new vision for Latino/a education: A comparative perspective on research agendas. In P. Pedraza & M. Rivera (Eds.), *Latino education: An agenda for community action research* (pp. 11–43). Mahwah, NJ: Lawrence Erlbaum.

Messaris, P., & Moriarty, S. (2005). Visual literacy theory. In K. Smith, S. Moriarty, G. Barbatsis, & K. Kenney (Eds.), *Handbook of visual communication: Theory, methods, and media* (pp. 481–502). Mahwah, NJ: Lawrence Erlbaum.

Molnar, G. (1999). Are dispositions reducible? *Philosophical Review, 49,* 157–181.

Morrell, E. (2002). Toward a critical pedagogy of popular culture: Literacy development among urban youth. *Journal of Adolescent and Adult Literacy, 46*(1), 72–77.

New, R. S. (1993). *Reggio Emilia: Some lessons for U.S. educators* (Report No. EDO-PS-93-3). Urbana, IL: ERIC Clearinghouse on Elementary and Early Childhood Education.

Pedraza, P., & Rivera, M. (Eds.). (2005). *Latino education: An agenda for community action research.* Mahwah, NJ: Lawrence Erlbaum.

Pellegrino, J. W., Chudowsky, N., & Glaser, R. (Eds.). (2001). *Knowing what students know: The science and design of educational assessment.* Washington, DC: National Academies Press.

Perkins, D., Tishman, S., Ritchhart, R., Donis, K. & Andrade, A. (2000). Intelligence in the wild: A dispositional view of intellectual traits. *Educational Psychology Review, 12*(3), 269–293.

Perkins. D. N., & Tishman, S. (2001). Dispositional aspects of intelligence. In J. M. Collis & S. Messick (Eds.), *Intelligence and personality: Bridging the gap in theory and measurement* (pp. 233–257). Mahwah, NJ: Lawrence Erlbaum.

Rand, Y., Tannenbaum, A., & Feuerstein, R. (1979). Effects of instrumental enrichment on the psychoeducational development of low-functioning adolescents. *Journal of Educational Psychology, 71*(6), 751–763.

Rauscher, F. H. (2003). Can music instruction affect children's cognitive development? *Eric Digest.* Retrieved June 18, 2007, from http://www.uwosh.edu/psychology/rauscher/ ERIC03.pdf

Rauscher, F. H., Shaw, G. L., Levine, L. J., Wright, E. L., Dennis, W. R., & Newcomb, R. (1997). Music training causes long-term enhancement of preschool children's spatial-temporal reasoning abilities. *Neurological Research, 19*(1), 1–8.

Rex, J. (1996). Multiculturalism in Europe. In J. Hutchinson & A. Smith (Eds.), *Ethnicity* (pp. 241–245). New York: Oxford University Press.

Rogoff, B. (1990). *Apprenticeship in thinking: Cognitive development in social context.* New York: Oxford.

Rostvall, A., & West, T. (2006a). Multimodality and designs for learning. In J. Allwood, B. Dorriots, & S. Nicholson (Eds.), *Papers from the second Nordic conference on multimodal communication* (Gothenburg Papers in Theoretical Linguistics 92). Gothenburg, Sweden: Göteborg University, Department of Linguistics.

Rostvall, A., & West, T. (2006b). Theoretical and methodological perspectives on designing video studies of interaction. *International Journal of Qualitative Methods, 4*(4), 1–19.

Ruppert, S., & Nelson, A. (2006). *From anecdote to evidence: Assessing the status and condition of arts education at the state level* [AEP research and policy brief]. Washington, DC: Arts Education Partnership.

Rutter, M. (1996). Stress research: Accomplishments and tasks ahead. In J. Haggerty, L. R. Sherrod, N. Garmezy, & M. Rutter (Eds.), *Stress, risk, and resilience in children and adolescents: Processes, mechanisms, and interventions* (pp. 354–85). Cambridge, UK: Cambridge University Press.

Ryle, G. (1949). *The concept of mind.* London: Hutchinson.

Salomon, G. (1994, April). *To be or not to be (mindful)?* Paper presented at the meeting of the American Educational Research Association, New Orleans, LA.

Schirrmacher, R. (2002). *Art and creative development for young children.* Albany, NY: Delmar Thomson Learning.

Schwartz, D. L., Bransford, J. D., & Sears, D. (2005). Efficiency and innovation in transfer. In J. Mestre (Ed.), *Transfer of learning from a modern multidisciplinary perspective* (pp. 1–51). Greenwich, CT: Information Age.

Sleeter, C. E. (2001). *Culture, difference, and power.* New York: Teachers College Press.

Smith, W. (1872). *Art education: Scholastic and industrial.* Boston: James Osgood.

Spencer, M. B. (2006). Phenomenology and ecological systems theory: Development of diverse groups. In W. Damon & R. Lerner (Eds.), *Handbook of child psychology: Theoretical models of human development* (pp. 829–893). New York: John Wiley.

Staples, J. (2005). *Reading the world and the word after school: African American urban adolescents' reading experiences and literacy practices in relationship to media texts.* Unpublished doctoral dissertation, University of Pennsylvania, Philadelphia.

Staples, J. (in press). What's possible: An African American urban adolescent boy's reading engagement through media text. In M. Hill & L. Vasudevan (Eds.), *Media, learning and sites of possibility.* New York: Peter Lang.

Stovall, D. (2006). We can relate: Hip-hop culture, critical pedagogy, and the secondary classroom. *Urban Education, 41*(6), 585–602.

Strasser, J., & Seplocha, H. (2007). Using picture books to support young children's literacy. *Childhood Education, 83*(4), 219–224.

Thompson, C. M. (2006). Repositioning the visual arts in early childhood education: A decade of reconsideration. In B. Spodek & O. N. Saracho (Eds.), *Handbook of research on the education of young children* (pp. 223–242). Mahwah, NJ: Lawrence Erlbaum.

Thornton, C. (2002). Creativity and runaway learning. In T. Dartnall (Ed.), *Creativity, cognition, and knowledge* (pp. 239–249). Westport, CT: Praeger.

Tishman, S., & Andrade, A. (1995). *Thinking dispositions: A review of current theories, practices, and issues* (ACCTION Report No. 1). Washington, DC. ACCTION.

Tishman, S., Perkins, D., & Jay, E. (1995). The thinking classroom: *Teaching and learning in a culture of thinking.* Needham, MA: Allyn & Bacon.

United Nations Educational, Scientific, and Cultural Organization. (2005). *Educating for creativity: Bringing the arts and culture into Asian education.* Report of the Asian Regional Symposia on Arts Education. Bangkok, Thailand: Author.

Vasudevan, L. (2006). Making known differently: Engaging visual modalities as spaces to author new selves. *E-Learning, 3*(2), 207–216.

Welch, G. F. (2006). The musical development and education of young children. In B. Spodek & O. N. Saracho (Eds.), *Handbook of research on the education of young children* (pp. 251–267). Mahwah, NJ: Lawrence Erlbaum.

Wertsch, J. V. (1998). *Mind as action.* New York: Oxford University Press.

Winner, E., & Hetland, L. (2000). The arts in education: Evaluating the evidence for a causal link. *Journal of Aesthetic Education, 34*(3), 3–10.

Wissman, K. K. (2005). *"Can't let it all go unsaid": Self-definition, sisterhood, and social change in the literacy and artistic practices of young women of color.* Unpublished doctoral dissertation, University of Pennsylvania, Philadelphia.

Wolf, D. P. (2000). Why the arts matter in education or just what do children learn when they create an opera. In E. Fiske (Ed.), *Champions of change: The impact of the arts on learning* (pp. 91–98). Washington, DC: Arts Education Partnership and the President's Committee on the Arts and the Humanities.

Wolf, S. A. (2006). "The mermaid's purse": Looking closely at young children's art and poetry. *Language Arts, 84*(1), 10–20.

Wright, R., Lindsay, J., Ellenbogen, S., & Offord, D. R. (2006). Effect of a structured arts program on the psychosocial functioning of youth from low-income communities: Findings from a Canadian longitudinal study. *Journal of Early Adolescence, 26*(2), 186–205.

Zuberi, T. (2001). *Thicker than blood: How racial statistics lie.* Minneapolis: University of Minnesota Press.

Chapter 3

English Education Research and Classroom Practice: New Directions for New Times

MELANIE SPERLING

University of California, Riverside

ANNE DiPARDO

University of Iowa

In exploring the role of research in the secondary school subject traditionally known as "English," we address a host of issues crowded with problems and potentials. Surely the perennially debated contours of the field have never been more in question, as new technologies and transforming patterns of civic, workplace, and global communication challenge us to enlarge our notions of what is truly basic in concert with the myriad opportunities, dangers, and complexities of today's world (Luke, 2004a, 2004b). As those who teach the secondary subject and who provide teachers' professional preparation, English educators are positioned to serve as critical mediators of these new challenges. This is admittedly no easy undertaking, as academics' ongoing efforts to build ever-richer conceptions of literacy remain markedly at odds with the determined emphasis on basic skills both reflected in and reified by the No Child Left Behind initiative in the United States (U.S. Department of Education [USDOE], 2007). English educators therefore face the formidable task of negotiating between the complex vision of contemporary research and the modernist take on literate competency embedded in recent education policies (Yagelski, 2006), with their concomitant conception of research as "market commodity *qua* objective product testing and market research" (Luke, 2004a, p. 1427).

As U.S. states and districts respond to federal pressure to adopt practices based on "scientific" studies (USDOE, 2007), English educators are endeavoring to foster appreciation of the broader intellectual traditions that have shaped understandings of the high school subject through the years—including not only the social sciences but also literary studies, philosophy, and the arts (National Council of Teachers of English [NCTE], 2007; see also the American Educational Research Association [AERA] Task

Review of Research in Education
February 2008, Vol. 32, pp. 62–108
DOI: 10.3102/0091732X07309336
© 2008 AERA. http://rre.aera.net

Force on Standards for Reporting in Humanities Research, 2007; guidelines forthcoming 2008). In light of this intellectual diversity, even tougher challenges lie in articulating just what it means for scholarly perspectives to influence teachers' work in useful and satisfying ways and to foster such influence in English education pre- and in-service preparation programs. In the United States, new urgency and challenge is added to the work of English teacher educators by the nation's changing demographics and persistent socioeconomic divide; as the nation's schools see a growing minority population, ethnic disparities persist in terms of school achievement, drop-out rates, and eventual income (National Center for Education Statistics, 2007).[1]

Although the influence of English education research to date is difficult to ascertain with certainty, its growth and promise are surely not. As this diverse and growing body of work continues to provide substantive insights, questions, and generative new frameworks for contemplating the daily work of classrooms, the time is opportune for a reappraisal of the history, present status, and potential of research in English education in the United States—its place over time in a contested field, its efforts to address questions of relevance to practitioners, and its emergent reimagining as scholars and teachers build better understandings of one another's worlds and work. Perhaps the traditional tendency to speak of a research–practice chasm is but another instance of the binary oppositions that have plagued educational argumentation at least since Dewey's day (1938/1963), a discursive artifact that—given the educational urgencies of a changing world and ill-advised federal interventions—neither English teachers nor researchers can yet afford.

Toward this end, we begin with a look back at the emergence of English education in the social and political context of the United States as a nation, situating the development of the research–practice divide narrative in debates concerning the nature and purpose of English as secondary-school subject in changing times. We turn next to researchers' efforts to provide generative implications for classroom practice as they have widened the scope of their inquiries to situate individual learners in an expanding array of contexts—and ultimately challenged not only the field's traditional focus on language as the prime mode of representation but also its early preoccupation with national identity. As notions of "context" are destabilized by the globalized, digitalized environments of a new century, the time is right for rethinking as well traditional conceptions of the separation of research and practice. Beyond considering the robust implications of research to date, we look to recent efforts to bring the work of research and teaching together in ways that not only offer profound integration but also begin to dissolve altogether the distinction between the work of English educators in the secondary classroom and the academy. Finally, we close by calling on the field to develop more generative theoretic frameworks to enhance our understandings of how research can and does inform practice and to explore how varied research traditions might more explicitly inform one another in moving us toward richer understandings of literacy teaching and learning.

HISTORIC CONTEXTS OF ENGLISH EDUCATION RESEARCH
English Education for the American People(s)

Controversy surrounding the nature and purpose of the U.S. school subject known as English can be traced to its inception a century ago, the questions tenaciously familiar across the decades: Does it serve to transmit a stable body of content and skills or to foster a more dynamic, shape-shifting process of meaning making? Should it reify a cultural mainstream or promote appreciation of diverse points of view and ways with words? Is it more appropriately seen as a higher education gatekeeper or as preparation for life? Narratives of the field have often posited an opposition between what Applebee (1974) called "tradition and reform," as American educators have engaged in curricular debates inexorably embedded in larger questions concerning the role of the subject in a changing nation (see VanSledright, this volume). Our overview of the emergence and development of English education research is therefore also about values and vision, the ends as well as the means of English as high school subject, and the often contentious role of the academy generally and research particularly in informing its direction, scope, and purpose. Even as echoes of the competing concerns that gave birth to English as school subject and English education as profession are clearly discernible in debates between neotraditionalists and neoprogressives in our own time, the challenge of addressing disparities in wealth and opportunity has never seemed greater (see Shannon, 2001). Just as literacy instruction designed to build a sense of unified national identity is no longer sufficient to the challenges of today's globalized, culturally fluid world, so too is the narrative of research–practice divide rendered particularly problematic by the personal, political, and vocational contexts that today's adolescents will both encounter and shape.

The origins of English as secondary-school subject are commonly traced to the Committee of Ten (Applebee, 1974; Hook, 1979), a group of university professors chaired by Harvard's Charles W. Eliot that sought to stipulate subject-area preparation for higher education. In their published report (Committee of Ten of the National Education Association [NEA], 1894), the group described a high school course in English that would meet for 5 hours weekly for 4 years, emphasizing literary masterpieces and judicious training in correct expression. In a companion set of developments, the National Conference on Uniform Entrance Requirements (Hill, 1898) developed rosters of works to be universally read across the high school years (hereafter, the Uniform Lists), reflecting an Arnoldian commitment to fostering cultural unity and countering new-world "intellectual mediocrity" (Arnold, 1875/1971, p. 13) through study of canonical works. In much the same spirit as the cultural literacy movement in our own time (Core Knowledge Foundation, 2007; Hirsch, 1987, 1996), such efforts reflected professorial preoccupation with specifying what every educated American needs to know, promoting an enduringly powerful conception of English as a culturally cohesive body of content to be internalized and passed on to posterity.

In the inaugural issue of NCTE's *English Journal*, Hosic (1912) observed that the Uniform Lists had placed English education in "an educational storm center" (p. 95).

Fred Newton Scott was among many decrying the belief that high schools served only to prepare students for college, attacking the Uniform Lists as higher education "feudalism" (Scott, 1901, p. 365) and "required reverence" (Scott, 1909, p. 14). Attention to diversity was much in the air in the early years of the new century, as unprecedented numbers of adolescents stayed in school through adolescence, most with no plans to attend college. Caught between mandates informed by elite traditionalists and the needs of the students before them, English educators grew restive, activist, and rhetorically extravagant. Cast as the "menace of academic pedantry," the Uniform Lists were seen as products of the "inbred conservatism of the scholar," deemed heedless of the "polyglot immigrant population" thronging the nation's schools (Chubb, 1912, pp. 34, 36). Responses to diversity were as sharply divided then as now, the forebearers of today's English-only and standardization movements aligned against those who would embrace the diversity of the nation's new citizens and the attendant implications for schools.

Rising interest in education for everyday life was apparent in such responsive documents as the NEA Commission on the Reorganization of Secondary Education's (1918) *Cardinal Principles*, a landmark Progressive Era formulation of democratic goals intended to guide school reform, with an emphasis on preparing diverse young people for work, citizenship, raising families, and leading happy, healthy, and ethical lives (see Wraga, 2001). These sentiments found further expression in "Reorganization of English in Secondary Schools" (Hosic, 1917), the official statement of a subcommittee composed of representatives of the NEA's Commission on the Reorganization of Secondary Education and the newly constituted NCTE. Commonly known as the Hosic Report—after its primary author, James Fleming Hosic—the document argued that as most graduates were going not into college but, rather, into "life," high school English should emphasize "basic personal and social needs" (p. 26). Preparation in reading, writing, speaking, and thinking were said to serve three fundamental purposes: (a) cultural ("to open to the pupil new and higher forms of pleasure"), (b) vocational ("to fit the student for the highest success in his chosen calling"), and (c) social and ethical ("to present to the student noble ideals, aid in the formation of his character, and make him more efficient and actively interested in his relations with and service to others in the community and in the Nation") (Hosic, 1917, p. 32). These triadic goals would remain influential in the United States for decades to come, even as new avenues of inquiry provided fresh vistas onto the old debates between canonical traditionalists and literacy-for-life progressives—and the nation's burgeoning cultural, linguistic, and socioeconomic diversity continued to raise a host of issues at once educational, social, and political. (That the most visible players in these debates were European American men is generally cast as a given in histories of the field; for an account of the role of women in the history of NCTE, see Gerlach & Monseau, 1991.)

Born of what many saw as university professors' undue control of secondary curricula, in its early days, NCTE was primarily focused on serving a membership of high school teachers. Concerned about inattention to research and to the early grades, a small group of NCTE members went on to found the National Conference on Research in English (NCRE) in 1932. Although much of NCRE's initial work focused on the elementary level, through its various partnerships with NCTE, publications, and annual meetings, it brought new attention to the relevance of research across the grade levels. In 1959, for instance, NCRE member Guy Bond posed a series of enduringly key questions concerning the relationship between research and practice, challenging the organization to consider ways that research might be "interpreted and reported for wider use," reflected in "instructional materials," and taken up in pre- and in-service teacher education with an emphasis on "critical evaluations of methods used and validity of findings" as well as searching discussion of "their implications for instructional change" (Petty, 1983, p. 43). Though small and selective, NCRE encompassed a range of perspectives, female as well as male leaders, and the promising beginnings of efforts to complement the research efforts of NCTE, the International Reading Association (IRA), and AERA by "synthesizing, interpreting, and implementing the findings of the best research" (Petty, 1983, p. 78). As research efforts gathered momentum in the '50s and '60s, NCRE renewed its commitment to hosting meetings in collaboration with NCTE as well the IRA, enjoying something of a new "heyday" (Petty, 1983, p. 36).

The nature of English education and the potential of research were revisited and debated throughout the1960s, as the crises of the time—Sputnik, the Vietnam war, the struggle for civil rights, enduring disparities in wealth and opportunity—imparted fresh urgency to the underlying questions of what constitutes foundational literacy in a changing and troubled national landscape. Providing empirically informed perspectives on the progressives' notion of individually appropriate preparation for life, conversations of the day also registered occasional echoes of the traditionalist focus on English as a stable body of content. Two meetings during this time make visible the issues being debated in the areas of research and practice. Of the multiple professional gatherings that focused on the challenge of developing a more cohesive and systematic program of research on English education, the 1962 Project English meeting at the Carnegie Institute of Technology was regarded as especially noteworthy (Henry, 1966). Attended by the premiere U.S. English educators of the era, the group charted needed research across the grade levels, calling for linguistic studies, rigorous measurement, and computer modeling of psychological processes (Steinberg, 1963). Cutting-edge work that would prove enduringly influential appeared during these years, including landmark studies of students' oral and written language (e.g., Hunt's [1965] research on the maturation of students' written syntax, employing T-unit analyses, and Loban's [1976] longitudinal studies of student readers and writers [which we take up later]).

Echoes of English education's beginnings as well as a vigorous vision of its future were everywhere apparent at the 1996 Anglo-American Seminar on the Teaching and Learning of English at Dartmouth, funded by the Carnegie Corporation and cosponsored by NCTE and the Modern Language Association (MLA) in the United States as well as the National Association of Teachers of English (NATE) in the United

Kingdom. As the landmark gathering sought to formulate a shared conception of English as school subject and preferred instructional strategies, participants' discussions came to be richly informed by growing British interest in developmental psychology, the relationship between language and learning and engagement and equity (Dixon, 1967/1975; Harris, 1991; Muller, 1967).

And yet the perspectives at Dartmouth were far from consistent (Harris, 1991; E. G. Lewis, 1970; Marckwardt, 1970), the contrasts especially evident in Americans' mixed response to British participants' call for a "Copernican shift from a view of English as something one *learns about* to a sense of it as something one *does*" (Harris, 1991, p. 631), not a "package to be handed over" (Dixon, 1967/1975, p. 81). Dixon (1967/1975) reported that "After the initial shock of hearing this from British lips, there was some U.S. sympathy with this view" (p. 72)—even as other Americans called for a renewed focus on literary scholarship and masterworks modeled after university curricula (Harris, 1991), reflecting the canonical sensibilities of the Committee of Ten as well as Sputnik-era preoccupation with instructional rigor and consistency (see Commission on English, 1965; NCTE, 1961).

Harris (1991) later pointed out that a number of U.K. and U.S. Dartmouth participants who would come to be well known as champions of learner-centered, developmental perspectives (Britton and Dixon among the British and Moffett among the Americans, for instance) presented themselves primarily as teachers, despite their significant scholarly credentials. "In thus rooting their work firmly in the schoolroom but not in the graduate seminar," argued Harris (1991), they in effect ceded the high ground to the scholars . . . [and] ended up reinscribing the split between teaching and research" (p. 641).

It is perhaps too simplistic, however, to ascribe what have been called the "empty echoes of Dartmouth" (Hamilton-Wieler, 1988) to the at once practical and scholarly sensibilities of the event's participants. If English remained as Dixon (1967/1975) described it in the opening line of *Growth Through English*, "a quicksilver among metals—mobile, living and elusive" (p. 1), the new emphasis on teachers' roles in fostering individual development brought an array of important grassroots movements even as federal funding on both sides of the Atlantic dissipated in the ensuing years. As Squire and Britton argued in their foreword to a reissue of Dixon's classic account some years after Dartmouth, the new focus on "learning rather than teaching" (p. xv) was felt in individual teachers' reflections on their work, in an array of grassroots efforts as well as in national professional development efforts in the United States (perhaps most notably, those sponsored by MLA, NCTE, and IRA). Similarly, the growth model animated research endeavors for decades to come, influencing the advent of sociolinguistic and ethnographic research in the '70s and '80s as well as the formation of the National Writing Project (NWP), with its long-term commitment to fostering teachers' consumption as well as production of research. The shaping role of language in student learning would become a major focus of teachers and scholars alike, even as U.S. education policy reflected commitment to standardization and a view of English as a stable body of content and skills.

The Growth of English Education Research

In addition to the intellectual ferment of Project English and the Dartmouth conference among U.S. English educators, the 1960s also saw a wave of new initiatives by professional organizations intended to promote, disseminate, and reward research. For example, NCTE introduced its empirical journal in 1967 (*Research in the Teaching of English*), gave its first Research Foundation grants, established research awards, partnered with ERIC to produce a database of relevant studies (Hook, 1979; NCTE, 2007), and published a landmark review of research on writing (Braddock, Lloyd-Jones, & Schoer, 1963).

Although the organization's Research Foundation may have been more likely in those days "to approve proposals that promised a rather quick classroom pay-off" (Hook, 1979, p. 213), many in NCTE's leadership were strongly committed to building a conceptually rigorous empirical base to guide the work of teachers across the grade levels (Hook, 1979). The inaugural issue of *Research in the Teaching of English* in 1967 reflected the scale of the undertaking, offering two articles providing rudimentary introductions to methodological approaches (Budd, 1967; Gunderson, 1967) and a scattering of essentially atheoretic reports profiling poor writers (Potter, 1967), students' writing frequencies (Hunting, 1967), and the effects of writing teachers' correction techniques (Stiff, 1967). In a companion set of developments, the IRA published the first issue of *Reading Research Quarterly* in 1965, which would evolve from an initial early-literacy emphasis to encompass studies across the grade levels.

Efforts to connect literacy research to classroom practice were manifest in AERA publications during these years as well, perhaps most notably in the first edition of its *Handbook of Research on Teaching* (which included a chapter reviewing separate bodies of work on teaching composition and literature; Meckel, 1963; see review in Spalding, 1963). A chapter in the second edition appearing a decade later found the burgeoning field promising yet flawed, its effects on classroom practice limited by a lack of consensus concerning the objectives of the English curriculum, uneven methodological quality, and absence of coordination across investigations (Blount, 1973). In calling for studies conducted by teachers, Blount anticipated the teacher-research movement of subsequent decades (see Cochran-Smith & Donnell, 2006; Zeichner & Nofke, 2001) while also implicitly recalling Progressive Era interest in Deweyan-oriented lab schools in which teachers both enacted and encouraged a spirit of inquiry (see Putney & Green, in press).

As the influence of research on teaching across the fields of study was increasingly subject to critique (see Clifford, 1973), English education's continuing identity crisis imparted discipline-specific intensity to larger debates regarding the efficacy of research expenditures. Even amid new support for pursuing and publishing English education research, one vocal member of NCTE complained,

There is no applied research unless there is theory to render it practical. . . . Research, to be important, must be in the main stream of the general ideas of a discipline . . . [but] there seemed to be little philosophical effort to determine the river bed or large contexts in which English operates. (Henry, 1966, p. 234)

Freshly honed versions of the familiar questions—English as a situated set of purposeful activities or the transmission of a body of content—would continue to shape debates concerning the role of research in years to come.

Contested Terrains and New Directions

Two decades later, as intensifying concern about standardized test scores provoked calls for a renewed emphasis on a basic-skills approach to instruction, interest in the relevance of research to classroom practice was once again on the rise. Some looked to a growing body of English education research in formulating responses to the back-to-basics movement (see Squire, 1982); in another landmark development, Hillocks (1984) published a much-cited meta-analysis of experimental studies of composition and argued their potential to enhance practice. Although terming experimental work "fool's gold" (Grindstaff, 1987, p. 47) and charging that research to date had been more concerned with the academic reward structure than offering insights of value to teachers, a NCTE report on English education research (Peters & the Conference on English Education [CEE] Commission on Research in Teacher Effectiveness, 1987) did strike a note of tentative optimism in looking to future studies to convey more effectively the nuanced complexities of actual classrooms (Grindstaff, 1987). Others remained more skeptical. The ever-vocal Henry (1984) fumed that English education researchers were "pumping out, shall we say, piles of research" as yet bereft of a rigorous conception of the field and its empirical domain; similarly, Purves (1984) despaired that the NCTE of the '80s had become a "vast network without an intellectual center," plagued by a "general disdain [of] theory and research," "anti-intellectualism," and a tendency to treat teachers as crafts persons rather than professionals (pp. 694–695).

But the field's gathering sense of purpose was much in evidence soon thereafter, as the MLA and NCTE cosponsored the English Coalition Conference—a gathering comprised primarily of teachers and teacher educators that would once again contemplate current challenges, new directions, and as it turned out, the role of research. Although participant Booth (1987) argued that the resultant publications (Elbow, 1990; Lloyd-Jones & Lunsford, 1989) offered little that was strikingly new, the timing of the event—the same year as the release of E. D. Hirsch's influential *Cultural Literacy* (1987) amid Reagan-era interest in conservative educational reform—imparted new exigency to the challenge of articulating a larger vision of the nature and purpose of English education (increasingly conceptualized as K–12 language arts). As conference attendees began their deliberations, Hirsch's book was rendering the old Hosic-era contentions new again, firing fresh volleys at Deweyan progressivism and the spirit of the *Cardinal Principles*, eschewing celebration of active, experiential learning environments in favor of a fact-based curriculum emphasizing study of canonical literary works that gestured back to the Committee of Ten.

In his personal account of the 3-week conference, Elbow (1990) described a series of events that situate the recurrent debate concerning the nature of the field and its relationship to research in the political atmosphere of the times. Chester Finn, then

Assistant Secretary of Education for Educational Research and Improvement, had given a talk critiquing education reforms across recent decades and arguing the promise of Hirsch's book, which was then followed by a visit from the *Cultural Literacy* author himself. Decidedly unsettled, participants would be reinspired some days later by none other than a leading researcher, Shirley Brice Heath, who eloquently described the work of the English classroom as focusing on language—the uses of language toward a variety of purposes and toward a variety of ends, the value of reflection on one's own and others' language use, and the importance of ensuring that students find both personal satisfaction and adequate challenge in their studies. Heath's presentation helped participants articulate their own felt sense that the ever-changing work of teaching and learning is infinitely more complex and satisfying than reading lists and instructional prescriptions would have it. It became an episode, Elbow recalled, "of Chester Finn and E. D. Hirsch laying siege to us and Shirley Brice Heath riding in on a white horse to the rescue" (p. 16). Heath had spoken to the group as decision-making professionals in need not of reductive prescription but generative big ideas that recalled the vision and vitality of Dartmouth.

The secondary group's official statement—published in the report of the conference, titled *Democracy Through Language* (Lloyd-Jones & Lunsford, 1989)—also reflected the post-Dartmouth influence of developmentalist and social-constructivist notions as well as the sociolinguistic, anthropological, and developmental perspectives informing the work of language scholars such as Heath: "Learning is the process of actively constructing meaning from experiences"; "Others—parents, teachers, and peers—help learners construct meanings"; and "Learners at different ages and stages of development may well learn in different ways" (Lloyd-Jones & Lunsford, 1989, p. 17). Although appendices of shared empirical and theoretic reading were included at the end of the report, the influences of these texts on the group's various recommendations for practice were left largely unspecified; and although many of these recommendations seem reasonable enough—"use language effectively to create knowledge, meaning and community" (p. 19) and so on—a casual reader could readily surmise that they emerged from participants' personal values and beliefs alone. For this and no doubt multiple reasons besides, the English Coalition Conference would exert little lasting influence on policy, practice, or research in the ensuing years.

Old Questions and New Urgencies

"The past is never dead," Faulkner (1951/1975) famously observed; "it's not even past" (p. 80). And so it is that as English educators continue to review, debate, and expand their own conceptions of the field, reform initiatives premised on a traditional view of English as a body of stable content knowledge and discrete skills have once again assumed precedence.

In light of recent calls for "evidence-based practice" enacted by "highly qualified teachers" possessing "subject-matter knowledge" (USDOE, 2007), the field faces an escalating need to respond to federal policies that are shaping the work of English teachers and researchers alike. Although representatives of the profession endeavor to argue that research appropriately informs rather than dictates classroom practice and that teachers must be seen as makers as well as receivers of professional knowledge (Cochran-Smith & Lytle, 1999; DiPardo et al., 2006), English education yet awaits more systematic efforts to trace the full variety of ways in which research can and does come to inform classroom practice. Notwithstanding efforts across the disciplines to weave stronger connections between research and teaching (e.g., Donovan, Wigdor, & Snow, 2003) and to foster appreciation of traditions of teacher inquiry (Cochran-Smith & Donnell, 2006; Putney & Green, in press; Zeichner & Nofke, 2001), the ubiquity and complexity of English as school subject lends both added significance and difficulty to such undertakings. As scholars trace broadening conceptions of 21st century literacy, research paradigms proliferate, and policymakers continue to make literacy a key focus, the relationship between English education research and classroom practice is more complex than ever in its contours, potential, and challenges.

Current conversations concerning the scope of English education and the role of research are also marked by an intensified focus on serving all students. Although the field took shape at the turn of the past century amid unprecedented ethnic, linguistic, and socioeconomic diversity in the nation's schools, increasing school enrollments and a fast-growing minority population (NCES, 2007) are imparting a new sense of urgency. Research documenting a persistent literacy achievement gap between minority and poor students and their more affluent Euro-American counterparts is weighing on both policymakers and researchers, stimulating empirical attention to issues of equity and attracting more diverse scholars to the field (see Meacham, 2000–2001). English education is infused with not only a renewed commitment to serving an increasingly diverse student population but also an ever-richer array of researchers, questions, epistemologies, and tools.

As federal insistence on evidence-based practice is provoking a fresh wave of interest in the research–practice relationship, English education is confronted with perils as well as possibilities. Facing the imposition of purportedly research-driven back-to-basics curricula, the field is newly motivated to offer its own formulations of not only what counts as secondary English but also what counts as research and how to characterize the nature of its implications in today's diverse, digitalized, globalized environment (CEE, 2005). As English educators counter demands at once political, empirical, and conceptual—contemplating powerful reforms on one hand and the expansive literacy demands of new times on the other (Hall, 1989/1996; Luke, 1998, 2004a, 2004b)—rethinking the familiar trope of English education research and practice as worlds apart is both necessary and overdue.

Long critiqued for their early tendency to conduct studies devoid of the messy dynamics of real students—their learning pushed, pulled, and shaped by classroom contexts and wider world alike (e.g., Grindstaff, 1987)—English education researchers have responded to proliferating challenges, pushing the horizons of their investigations ever wider in contemplating the many sets of activities, influences, and ways of seeing that compose literacy learning as doing. We turn now to address these investigations.

THEORY AND RESEARCH: TOWARD KNOWING
WHAT TO KNOW

The movement of secondary English across time serves both as backdrop to and voice in dialogue with the field's research history, which has also provided views on what counts as secondary English, what students in secondary English can or should learn, and how teachers can or should contribute toward this learning. Research has been fueled by both popular and academic concerns for the reading and writing skills of an increasing diversity of students, as these bespeak society's changing notions of a fully realized citizenry as well as scholars' perspectives on what secondary English can accomplish for students. Furthermore, it has increasingly reflected the belief that if it is to make headway in helping to shape students as educated readers and writers, research must explore the nuances of classroom complexities to fully understand what it means to read and write in school contexts.

Research has relatedly been influenced by evolving theories about language and literacy from a number of humanist and social science disciplines that have lent increasingly social and cultural perspectives to the cognitive perspectives that were dominant in research the '70s and '80s. These theoretical lenses have helped researchers to develop more sharply tuned antennae for the ways secondary English—that is, reading, writing, and language in the guise of this secondary school subject—reflect and maintain broader social, cultural, and historical processes. Mirroring at least some of the field's historic movement, the research push has thus been toward a broader and richer understanding of the role of context in students' literacy and learning. Emerging in part in response to calls for more practice-sensitive research, these understandings have also complicated and extended notions of what it means for research to hold implications for practice.

We thus review research that has helped shape secondary English, keeping in mind the broadening sense of context—its role and its meaning in students' development as readers and writers—that this work has yielded. With researchers from a number of orientations often complementing and interanimating one another's work, the research lenses have variously narrowed and widened as researchers have focused on (a) students' minds and ways with literacy; (b) the local classroom dynamics of literacy teaching and learning; (c) the ways English teachers, students, and classrooms are situated socially, culturally, and historically; and (d) the challenges and opportunities of a globalized, digitalized, and multimodal world. Although these are not the only ways that researchers have focused and do not encompass every type of research that has been conducted, these foci draw attention to researchers' expanding conceptions of context and the attendant implications for classrooms, constructed in part as responses to the challenges of diverse populations, new technologies, and varied literacies.

Conceptually, these ways of focusing inevitably share fuzzy and permeable boundaries. Studies that have focused, for example, on individual students' minds and ways with literacy have not necessarily ignored broader social, cultural, and/or historical influences. But researchers have tended to foreground or background these factors to varying degrees, and it is what is foregrounded that our four-part succession is intended to capture. Furthermore, any single focus has not been limited to research conducted in particular decades or influenced by particular theories, so each part of the four-part succession also encompasses research across decades and theories. In exploring research within these varied research foci, then, we sometimes traverse back and forth between decades and theories as we consider implications of this work in informing and shaping the field. We do not provide a comprehensive review or history of English education research or theory but, rather, offer key works through the years from influential theoretical perspectives, as well as more current instantiations of research in these traditions, that have contributed to rich and nuanced conceptions of secondary English in a diverse and changing world.

How Do We Understand Students' Minds and Ways With Literacy?

A focus on the minds and literacy habits of students has been strongly evident across the years, even before the midcentury cognitive revolution that would set research on individuals' thinking on a course of exponential expansion in the '70s and beyond. Concerned about the ways the range of secondary students read, write, and interpret literature, this work has rested on the assumption that such insights can lead to knowing both how to teach varied students and what to teach. Although the influence on students' literacy of their wider social and cultural experiences was often acknowledged in this work, its primary gaze was on individual students' more immediate understandings of particular literacy tasks.

Early research focusing on individual students attempted, from a range of theoretical perspectives, to describe their experiences with various aspects of secondary English curricula. The aim was usually to help shape these experiences to curricular goals. In the area of secondary literature, for example, much research centered on how students responded to and understood literary texts. This work was influenced in part by the humanistic literary tradition of New Criticism (Brooks, 1947; Ransom, 1941), which sought to discover the meanings believed to be encoded in texts through close readings and emphases on forms, language, and literary technique (a literary approach that had significantly entered into secondary classroom literature instruction by the '50s and '60; Grossman, 2001), and in part by then-newly-recognized reader-response theories (Rosenblatt, 1938), which, in prescient anticipation of more cognitively based studies of readers and reading that were to occur decades later, suggested that meaning lies within both the reader and the text and must be actively constructed by the reader interacting with text during the reading process (see Marshall, 2000). Although reader-response theory is more often associated with Deweyan progressivism, both approaches responded to the growing diversity of American schools and universities, endeavoring to render literary appreciation available beyond the confines of elite preparatory schools.

Attempting to foster such appreciation, I. A. Richards (1929), arguably one of English education's first teacher-researchers, studied his Cambridge students' readings, examining what they reported to think and feel about the poetry they read. This was also one of the first studies to provide empirical evidence that students' "personal situations" were factors in reading (cited in Beach, 1993, p. 16). Drawing on this work as well as on reader-response theory (Rosenblatt, 1938), investigations in the 1960s into secondary students' responses to literature developed category systems to capture reported differences across reading experiences, sometimes sorting these into hierarchies in an effort to understand what influenced different students' readings (Marshall, 2000). Inspired by a humanistic sense of literary appreciation as well as by more social scientific urges to systematically quantify such appreciation, Squire's (1964) study of 9th- and 10th-graders' responses to short stories was a groundbreaker in this tradition, attempting to capture what students "think, feel, or react to at any moment" (p. 1) as they paused to answer questions at various points in the texts. Yet although he found that students responded to these stories in "unique and selective ways" (frontispiece)—influenced by personal experience, gender, and reading ability, for example—Squire notably valued responses that were in line with New Critical ways of "extracting" meaning from text. Emphasis on such close reading would extend into the coming decades; even as late as the '90s, Blau (1994) could say that the teaching of literature at the high school level often reflected such text-centered values.

Early research in other areas of English and language arts, shaped at least in part by researchers' recognition of diverse students' language needs and practices, examined students' literacy practices developmentally to discover those that appeared to serve students as they grew over time. Much of this work also took inspiration from both humanistic "appreciative" approaches to language as well as quantitative approaches to language phenomena emerging in disciplines such as linguistics and developmental psychology. Basing his work on the premise that just as in biological characteristics, so in language children must surely grow in predictable ways over time, Loban (e.g., 1976) followed one group of more than 200 students for 13 years (what he called a cross-section of students—boys and girls from different racial, ethnic, and socioeconomic status [SES] backgrounds) to identify (through interviews and examinations of their reading, writing, and speaking) stages of language and literacy development and significant changes in language features across time. However, the study tended to conflate SES with race and ethnicity, thereby viewing as one and the same the language characteristics of African American Vernacular English (AAVE) and those associated with working-class speakers. One of the key findings was that students' oral syntax varied significantly by SES, the high-SES students employing what Loban determined to be more complex language as measured by how much it explicitly embedded syntactic structures; this syntax was equated with complexity of thought. The study promoted drills to instill in low-SES students what he called new habits, essentially those of the middle class.

Sociolinguistic studies being conducted at about the same time by linguists and scholars of color, which were to strongly influence English education research in subsequent years were showing such language characterizations to be theoretically naïve and ethnocentric. Labov's (1972) sociolinguistic studies of AAVE, for example, described in fine-grained detail the systematic, complex, and communicatively purposeful patternings of AAVE language features, including syntax and grammar, thereby challenging notions fed by popular opinion as well as academic shortsightedness that AAVE was inferior to mainstream standard dialects or reflected inferior thinking. Other linguistic studies of AAVE, such as Mitchell-Kernan's (1973) and Smitherman's (1977), added to this characterization by systematically tracing the contribution to meaning—making of AAVE artistry and style. Indeed, two decades later, African American discourse in students' writing samples on the National Assessment of Educational Progress (NAEP) writing exam were to correlate with high writing scores (Smitherman, 1994, reported in Meacham, 2000–2001). In light of such work, Loban's (1976) best contributions were less in his language characterizations than in his suggestion of the inevitability of variation in students' language and literacy based on what later researchers would examine as social and cultural influences and his arguing the need English education to speak to this variability. (A strong element of his research, too, was his commitment to studying the same students across a 13-year time period, a phenomenon that has never been duplicated in English education.)

Associated primarily with early cognitive studies, another research direction that proved influential to English education explored students' strategies and procedures during writing and reading. An illustrative early exploration of secondary students' writing, and perhaps the most familiar among professional English teacher groups (e.g., NCTE and NWP) was Emig's (1971) case studies of 12th graders, which showed not only that their composing was complex and nonlinear but also that it was highly influenced by the environments for which they composed. Emig followed eight 12th graders as they composed for school-assigned writing tasks and as they wrote for their own purposes; on the basis of interviews and students' taped accounts of these processes as well as examinations of their writing, Emig found that students followed different strategies depending on what they were writing and for what purposes. What she called school-sponsored writing proved to be especially stultifying to students' thinking and creativity, a key culprit being teachers' adherence to the school-ubiquitous five-paragraph essay across writing tasks and purposes. Emig's findings flagged issues of context as influencing students' writing strategies, thereby challenging notions that what students produced in the context of school was a mirror of their writing abilities and processes writ large.

Increasingly reaching audiences within both NCTE and AERA, research on the writing process was to take a more focused cognitive turn in a spate of studies that shined light on the constructivist premise that readers and writers construct meaning by "organizing, selecting, and connecting information" (Nystrand, Greene, & Wiemelt, 1993, p. 282) as part of complex literacy processes (the premise, as earlier indicated, of reader-response studies as well). Flower and Hayes's (1981; Hayes & Flower, 1980) studies with college students became familiar and enduring and were to help shape perceptions about teaching writing at all grade levels. Flower and Hayes's approaches, although drawing on cognitive theories, were also influenced both by rhetoric (which suggested that writers make choices and decisions about their rhetorical purpose and audience and in doing so deal with varied constraints on the shape and direction of their work) and by the problem-solving research of Newell and Simon (e.g., 1972) in psychology (which suggested that writing constitutes such a problem-solving process). By studying college freshmen thinking out loud as they composed essays to researcher-determined writing prompts, Flower and Hayes traced students' composing ideas and strategies moment by moment, thereby developing a model of this process. The model described how—given immediate contextual constraints such as their "task environment," that is, topic, audience, rhetorical exigencies, and evolving text—writers set rhetorical goals, plan ideas and text strategies, translate plans into text, and evaluate what they have thought about and written. The research suggested the need to understand the ways these processes might vary among skilled and unskilled writers and across writing tasks, and how pedagogy might foster the processes that skilled writers were seen to employ.

In their review of the research stemming from this work, Sperling and Freedman (2001) note that although these studies were able to describe expert and novice writing processes, they did not fully unpack either immediate or broader contextual influences on these processes and thus did not examine the contextual bearings on moving from unskilled to skilled levels (also see reviews of this work in Scardamalia & Bereiter, 1986). Yet these studies offered to practice an opportunity to think about individual students in the act of composing and complemented pedagogies (emerging especially in the United Kingdom) that approached the teaching of writing by focusing on writers' processes. Indeed, cognitively based research in writing was to continue through the decades into present time (see, for example, Olson & Land's [2007] study of cognitive-strategies approaches to teaching and learning writing).

Both at the time writing process research was getting a toehold in the writing research community as well as in later years, other researchers were taking stock of the application of process approaches in classrooms. Applebee (1986), for example, noted from his observational research that the notion of a writing process was sometimes narrowly construed in practice, becoming a rigid set of procedures rather than a way of thinking about what it means to write. The causes for this traditional approach to an essentially new pedagogy, Applebee maintained, were such practical realities of secondary schooling as the workload, time constraints, and challenge of student diversity. More than 15 years later, Scherff and Piazza (2005), conducting large-scale survey research of secondary school writing practices in Alabama, found that the constraints of other realities—specifically, state writing assessments and the rigidity of "pre-determined standards" (p. 271)—stacked the deck in favor of traditional practices based on drilling correct form over supporting students' reading and writing processes. Such accounts flag broader contextual constraints that shape day-to-day pedagogy; despite such challenges, writing process approaches (however well or fully they may have been enacted) became widespread in secondary English classrooms across the United States.

Cognitive perspectives also penetrated the area of reading, where a rich corpus of work was focusing on the individual reader engaging in comprehension processes. Bringing to bear a cognitive framework for thinking about comprehension and memory, scholars described an array of strategies by which readers construct and retain meaning from text, for example, drawing on text cues and prior knowledge to comprehend text both literally and inferentially. Perhaps the most familiar reading comprehension models came from Anderson (e.g., 1994), Kintsch (e.g., 1998), and Meyer (e.g., 1975), much of this work developed at the federally funded Center for the Study of Reading that was established in 1976 to focus on cognitive approaches.

In Anderson's (1994) schema-theoretic model, the text was seen as a catalyst to a process in which readers' cognitive schemata provide ideational scaffolding, facilitate allocation of attention, and enable inferential elaboration across knowledge of text, language, and everyday and disciplinary experience; Kintsch (1998) described a process in which readers process words and sentences linearly, integrating new information into working memory with old and building representations of meaning (see Hamm & Pearson, 2002). Although this cognitive research did not always account for the environment in which reading occurred (as was the case with cognitive accounts of writing), cognitive studies of reading did move the field forward by enlightening both researchers and practitioners on the role of metacognition and knowledge of text structures in reading and writing processes. Moreover, they identified the crucial role of background knowledge and experiences in how readers understand written texts (see reviews in Barr, 2001; Calfee & Drum, 1986; Hamm & Pearson, 2002). Barr (2001), in fact, characterized this research as fairly consistent on this point, showing in her review of these studies that such knowledge is "trainable" (p. 396) in classroom experiences, with students' comprehension improved when teachers provide them with relevant background knowledge to their reading. On the basis of this early work, researchers would increasingly come to understand how cultural differences in background knowledge can lead readers to different interpretations of the same works (in subsequent sections, we provide research perspectives that have furthered these understandings). Such understandings of the cognitive dimensions of reading would inform efforts to enhance secondary reading teaching through to the present time (see, for example, Schoenbach, Greenleaf, Cziko, & Hurwitz, 1999).

The work discussed above focused on individual students and sought to understand the dimensions of reading and writing "inside students' heads." Researchers were to expand on this work in myriad ways by speaking more fully to the role of context in these reading and writing processes (see Bloome, 1987; Tierney & Pearson, 1983).

Helping to set the conceptual stage for such work were Scribner and Cole's (1981) studies of literacy among the Vai of Liberia. Clearly situated as cognitivists (in anthropology and psychology) in the late 1970s, Scribner and Cole assumed a critical stance on their early findings, looking beyond the individual as the unit of analysis to explore the contexts in which individuals functioned. They combined cognitively based experimental studies of text-based logic and thinking processes with ethnographic studies of the nature and uses of literacy in Vai society to study the connection between literacy and thinking, studying reading and writing as it occurred in varied home, school, and religious settings as tribe members enacted literacy in particular contexts.

Scribner and Cole (1981) were able to compare members' memory, logic, and analytic processes as these were associated with different literacy situations. Their studies identified different forms of literacy with different cognitive skills, helping scholars to understand that the functions and purposes of writing and reading in different social contexts, including the context of school, might influence not only the nature of writing and reading but also the thinking processes associated with them.

Anticipating the burgeoning interest in sociocognitive and sociocultural as well as varied linguistic perspectives on thought and language (see Ball, 2002; Vasquez, 2006), which highlighted the importance of meaning-making contexts (a topic we take up in the next section), Scribner and Cole's (1981) work represented a widening of the research focus beyond the individual reader or writer toward the workings and functions of contexts in which reading and writing take place. This focus, stemming from varied complementary research traditions, was to include especially the social and linguistic dimensions of context that shape what counts as writing and reading in secondary school English (see Bloome, 1987; Green & Wallat, 1981; Rex, Green, Dixon, & the Santa Barbara Classroom Discourse Group, 1998).

How Do We Understand the Local Classroom Dynamics of Literacy Teaching and Learning?

Research focusing on local classroom contexts of literacy took hold in the late 1970s and 1980s, finding inspiration from multiple theoretical sources. These included ethnomethodological and sociolinguistic approaches that explored how language is constructed and used in varied social situations and among varied social groups, work that was applied in classrooms (e.g., Cazden, 2001; Green, 1983; Mehan, 1979; see review in Ball, 2002), and sociocognitive and sociocultural perspectives (e.g., Vygotsky, 1978, and later, Bakhtin, 1981) that were influencing English education researchers to better understand the role of language in learning and the role of others in students' literacy learning and development.

Much of the linguistic work explored classrooms as sites with their own discourse norms, roles, and conventions, with discourse shaping and displaying teachers and students' rights and responsibilities in varied literacy learning contexts. Key to English educators' understanding of classroom discourse were Mehan's (1979) studies of classroom lesson conventions, which described the deeply entrenched discourse patterns through which teachers dominate the discourse with their known-answer questions and evaluations of students' minimal responses—the IRE structure, in which teacher initiates, student responds, and teacher evaluates—reflecting not only teacher and student role differentials but also shaping and displaying traditionalist transmission approaches to teaching. (For a recent revisiting of Mehan and IRE sequences, see Macbeth, 2003).

In English education, this work was complemented by Vygotskian perspectives on learning, which focused on teacher–student verbal interactions as foundational to the literacy learning process. Such discourse patterns as the entrenched IRE would seem to stultify students' own participation in the learning process if learning was, as Vygotsky (1978) suggested, an interactive process that "presupposes a specific social nature and a process by which children grow into the intellectual life of those around them"

(p. 88). To explain the process of learning and development, Vygotsky used the metaphor of "buds" or "flowers" (p. 86) that, with assistance, will fruit into independent accomplishments. These buds or flowers, Vygotsky claimed, need to be nourished through classroom interactions, for through such interactions, teachers and students construct not only new knowledge and skills but also "the ideas, language, values, and dispositions" (Vasquez, 2006, p. 36) that reflect classroom culture.

English education researchers had, in the perspectives coming from both linguistic frameworks and from Vygotskyan psychology, then, complementary lenses for exploring what goes on in classroom literacy learning when students interact with peers and teachers in reading, writing, and literary study. This research rested in part on the assumption that analyzing instructional discourse could make classroom dynamics visible and available to scrutiny and critique, thereby revealing avenues for change (see Lee & Smagorinsky, 2000).

A number of studies of classroom dynamics attempted to understand the effects of different social organizations of classrooms on students' learning, from whole-class discussions, in which teachers were seen usually to dominate, to smaller groups or dyads. Questions centered on how patterns of language use in these contexts affect what counts as knowledge and what occurs as learning, how these patterns affect the equality or inequality of students' learning opportunities, and what communicative competencies these patterns presume or foster (see Cazden, 2001, p. 3). Much of the research took the form of either qualitative case studies or ethnography and often drew on sociolinguistic methods influenced by linguistic anthropology (e.g., Cook-Gumperz, 2006; Gumperz, 1982) to explore the relationship between discourse patterns and what and how students learned literacy. Perspectives from linguistic anthropology allowed researchers to examine, for example, tacit language cues that contextualize meaning, such as teacher and student use of intonation patterns, prosody, and nonverbal cues, exploring how and whether participants from different language or cultural backgrounds picked up on or ignored such cues and what was gained or lost as a result.

Together with linguistic perspectives on broader teacher–student interaction structures (e.g., Sinclair & Coulthard's [1975] research on what they called IRF—initiation, response, and feedback), this work led to two general observations. The first was that teachers and students who followed the same tacit discourse cues were seen to engage in smoother and sometimes more productive learning interactions, whether these were whole-class discussions or smaller configurations (e.g., Cazden, 2001; Michaels & Cazden, 1986). And the second was that it was particularly difficult for even excellent teachers to move beyond IRE recitation structures in class discussions (Athanases, 1993, 1998).

These notions formed the premise for research examining teacher–student discourse in different areas of secondary English, including writing and literary study. Much research examining teaching–learning discourse was in the area of writing, where modes of teacher response beyond traditional markings on student papers were being explored, for example, using teacher–student writing conferences and peer response groups (see Hillocks, 2006; Sperling & Freedman, 2001). Closely examining the discourse of peer response groups (see review in DiPardo & Freedman, 1988) or teacher–student writing conferences (see reviews in Prior, 1998; Sperling, 1998), researchers often found that in these configurations, traditional teacher-dominated classroom patterns could give way to more conversational and collaborative interactions in which students, with one another or with their teacher, might discover and together solve writing issues and problems as they built on one another's talk to negotiate writing information and strategies.

Yet many case studies were showing, too, that these varied configurations could not guarantee such collaborative approaches to learning. Conversations were often seen to be marked by miscommunication and missed opportunities for learning or to more resemble teacher monologues than dialogues, especially when teachers pressed to get across their own agendas for students' work (Sperling, 1998). When such studies of classroom discourse were grounded in larger classroom ethnographies, researchers were able also to show that the ways different discourse configurations worked depended greatly on the ethos of the greater classroom context (Athanases & Heath, 1995). "Response-rich" classrooms, for example, were seen often to nurture more dialogic exchanges for students to reflect on and interpret their own writing strategies (Sperling & Freedman, 2001).

Despite at least some research showing the possibilities of reorganizing classroom interaction configurations, such as using small groups or teacher–student dyads, however, when word about these varied configurations was beginning to infiltrate professional conversations (for example, at meetings of NCTE and NWP), even very capable teachers reported difficulties making them work and thus only occasionally used them (Freedman, 1987). Indeed, a good 10 years after this research was being reported, Nystrand (1997) found that dialogic classrooms of the kind that incorporated more collaborative configurations were, at least across the United States, still rare. Despite some notable exceptions, the entrenched patterns, enacting wonted social relationships between teachers and students and traditional notions of teaching and learning, did not easily disappear.

The studies reported above were focused case studies and ethnographies. Large-scale studies of local classroom dynamics have been scant but have tended to provide compatible findings; these include national data on English teaching practices, such as the data gathered by the NAEP studies (e.g., Applebee, Langer, Mullis, Latham, & Gentile, 1994) that reflected teachers' reports of the kinds of configurations they used in their English classes. These data have tended to show that peer groups and teacher–student dyads in secondary English, if they have existed at all, have more consistently characterized suburban middle-class schools than others. (See also Gamoran & Carbonaro, 2002.)

In an exemplary large-scale study, Nystrand (1997) and colleagues brought sociocognitive and sociocultural theoretic perspectives to a range of classrooms reflecting a range of teaching epistemologies. The study reflected the rise of Bakhtin in English education research, with his theories on language and learning not only compatible with Vygotsky's but also extending and enriching Vygotsky's perspectives. Gee (2000–2001), discussing both Vygotsky and Bakhtin, for example, asserted,

Vygotsky shows how people's individual minds are formed out of, and always continue to reflect, social interactions in which they engaged as they acquired their "native" language or later academic languages in school. Bakhtin stresses how anything anyone thinks or says is, in reality, composed of bits and pieces of language that have been voiced elsewhere, in other conversations or texts. . . . For Bakhtin, what one means is always a product of both the meanings words have "picked up" as they circulate in history and society and one's own individual "take" or "slant" on these words (at a given time and place). (pp. 114–115)

Drawing on this theoretical lens, Nystrand (1997) framed his study, which focused on classroom dynamics in the teaching and learning of literature, with Bakhtin's (e.g., 1981) conception of the relationship of discourse to thought: Because discourse is "dialogic," which is to say, "structured by tension, even conflict" between conversants, "one voice 'refracts' another . . . [and] it is precisely this tension—this relationship between self and other . . . that . . . lies at the heart of understanding as a dynamic, sociocognitive event" (Nystrand, 1997, p. 8). Nystrand (1997) examined more than 100 eighth- and ninth-grade English and language arts classrooms in urban, suburban, and rural communities across the United States, drawing not only on survey data but also on interviews and discourse analyses of spoken and written interactions observed in those classrooms. His study supported what the numerous case studies had been suggesting, that students can learn English and language arts most meaningfully in dialogic classrooms; moreover, it provided evidence that forms of discourse might be related to concept development (Wertsch, 1991, as cited in Nystrand, 1997).

This research supported the efficacy, then, of what Nystrand (1997) framed as genuine dialogue across communicative contexts, from class discussions marked by teachers' open-ended questions and uptake of students' ideas into discussion to written dialogue-journals about literary readings. Nystrand's study offered ways to see both the state of literature instruction from a national perspective and the potential of fresh theoretic conceptions to push against traditional patterns of classroom discourse. (For similar arguments, see Bakhtinian studies in Ball & Freedman, 2004; and Vygotskian studies in Lee & Smagorinsky, 2000.)

Concern about classroom dynamics, as reflected in the studies above, was centrally connected to concern about diverse learners (see Green, 1983). As Cazden (2001) suggested, if education is to serve diverse students, one must carefully pay attention to who speaks and who receives thoughtful responses. Progenitors for this work were studies in ethnography of communication and sociolinguistics (e.g., Hymes, 1977) that addressed the extent to which students' diverse home and community discourses in literacy match those of mainstream classrooms (Cook-Gumperz, 1986, 2006; Gilmore & Glatthorn, 1982; Treuba, Guthrie, & Au, 1981). These studies showed that mismatch of discourses could lead to missed opportunities for learning and to teachers' misconstruals of students' abilities. This issue was paramount in Heath's (1983) 10-year ethnography, grounded in cultural anthropology, which explored language and literacy in the homes and communities of working-class African Americans and Whites in the Carolina Piedmont. Heath described in this study how discourse dynamics of reading and writing in different facets of community life differed both between these communities and as she set them against White middle-class schools.

Cazden (2001) and colleagues, too, centered their studies in these home–school mismatch concerns and showed both how the classroom discourse dynamics that she and colleagues explored in different classrooms tended to echo those found in middle-class White homes and communities and how African American and other students of color had difficulty entering into these classroom discourses. Cazden drew on diverse theories, analytic strategies, and kinds of empirical research to show the complexity of classroom discourse and difficulty in shaping it to diverse students' discourse and learning needs, especially when teachers were being encouraged to rely less on IRE structures and to add the kinds of nontraditional discussions that serve to foster students' thinking and learning. This work also, importantly, showed how teachers' and students' language and cultural backgrounds could strongly influence what is viewed as appropriate or useful classroom talk.

The notion of cultural appropriateness, and how classroom dynamics shape and maintain what is seen to be appropriate, has sat at the center of a number of studies in secondary English, including the study of literature (Underwood, Yoo, & Pearson, 2006). Studies of secondary literature teaching that have explored classrooms in which reader-response theories focus instruction have found that the ways students discuss their literary responses are heavily influenced by the predominant White middle-class conventions of schooling, including ways of talking and of writing (Marshall, 2000).

In her review of reading research, Barr (2001) has suggested that although the "conceptual center" (p. 401) of reading research has for some time been on students' response to literature, in practice, organizing instruction so all students have a chance to respond is not easy and is a problem exacerbated by the reality that classroom dynamics privilege certain ways of responding over others. Grossman (2001) has suggested that the IRE script strongly structures students' responses to literature, with teachers' questions designed not to tap students' own responses so much as to shape their skills at text-centered "close readings" and students getting few opportunities to construct interpretations of their own. This work supports Nystrand's (1997) findings of teacher-dominated literature discussions, directing discussions to develop particular kinds of literary interpretations over others.

Focus on discussion format has yielded a variety of insights. Alvermann and colleagues (1996) found that middle school and high school students were aware of the norms and responsibilities contributing to productive discussions, including all students' contributing to talk (reported in Grossman, 2001). Altering discussion format so that students discuss literature in small groups has been found to encourage more student talk, although as with writing discussions, these have also been found to mirror larger classroom discourse or to exacerbate status differences between students (Grossman, 2001). Echoing the field's past, this body of research has shown that even practices that many would deem progressive (for example, reader-response literature pedagogy) have often been shaped by conservative and deeply rooted cultural forces as instantiated through traditional classroom discourse patterns—and have been not-so-paradoxical reminders that new wine can be readily stored in traditional bottles.

These studies used a variety of complementary theoretical perspectives and research approaches to allow the research community to understand the discursive underpinnings of day-to-day classroom dynamics. Classroom dynamics have tended to follow traditional IRE scripts and have tended often to shape traditional approaches to reading and writing; yet when altered, they have resulted in dialogic discourse, allowing students to construct and negotiate meanings and interpretations as they read and write (see, e.g., Alvermann et al., 1996). These studies have also shown how immediate social and cultural contexts shape ways with words and thinking, sharing intellectual affinity with studies that have been widening their focus to consider the broader social, cultural, and political contexts of English teaching and learning.

How Do We Understand How English Teachers, Students, and Classrooms Are Situated Socially, Culturally, and Historically?

As studies of classroom dynamics showed, context reflects socially, culturally, and historically embedded beliefs and values that shape the nature and consequences of literacy practices and learning. As secondary English has attempted to be responsive to diversity and change, researchers have opened up theoretical orientations and research approaches to better capture context's shaping power. Fine-tuned examinations of context have sat side by side with more macro-level analyses, allowing researchers to encompass in their thinking about English teachers, students, and classrooms requisite issues of identity, membership, and power. Research has drawn on psychological and sociocultural theories as well as newer outgrowths of these that allow complex contextual understandings. Activity theory has been particularly prominent, viewing behavior in terms of the contexts in which behavior occurs, and accounting for how the motives of varying settings shape the goals of these settings and determine which activities and behaviors will be maximized or minimized to accomplish these goals (see Beach, Green, Kamil, & Shanahan, 2005; Wertsch, 1985). Different types of studies have sat side by side, complementing one another and helping to create a larger portrait of secondary English as contextually situated. Case studies and ethnographies have proliferated, with multiple data sources and modes of analyzing data adding to understandings of the beliefs, values, urges, and constraints related to secondary English teachers, students, and classrooms (see Marshall, 2000; Sperling & Freedman, 2001).

Such work sits amid research on the status of the field in which the old tensions between conservative and progressive views continue to show up—for example, in a secondary English literary canon that has changed only at glacial speed (see, e.g., Applebee, 1993), persistently reflecting a predominantly White and male sensibility (e.g., Agosto, Hughes-Hassell, & Gilmore-Clough, 2003; Stallworth, Gibbons, &

Fauber, 2006). Yet contrary to what might be taken as these studies' implications of intractable curricular conservatism, a growing body of work has shown that the picture is not that simple.

A number of studies endeavoring to penetrate the contextual nuances of secondary English have centered on teachers, probing their beliefs and self-identities to better understand what drives instructional decisions and why. In their research reviews related to English education, Barr (2001), focusing on reading, and Grossman (2001), focusing on literature, have shown the close relationship between teachers' practices and their beliefs about literacy and learning. Grossman shows how teachers literary orientations—these being primarily either text centered or reader centered—determine how teachers teach literature to their students, a finding supported by qualitative case studies based on interview and observation as well as large-scale survey studies (e.g., Applebee, 1993; Purves, 1981). Studies of teachers in the United States have consistently found few teachers to have other orientations to literature, such as critical orientations as fostered in Australia (e.g., Musspratt, Luke, & Freebody, 1997)—for example, critical feminist or Marxist orientations—that would lend social, cultural, historical, and political perspective to texts and ways readers read (Appleman, 2000). Likewise, critical genre approaches to both reading and writing—centering on the ways conventions of genre are related to cultural norms and values—have had more influence in Canada and Australia than in the United States (see review by Cope & Kalantzis, 1993).

Many studies probing teachers' beliefs have taken a psychological approach (as exemplified by Shulman, 1987), relating what teachers know about secondary English content, pedagogy, students, and learning to what occurs in classrooms. The premise of these studies has been that how one teaches English grows from different understandings of the nature of writing, literature, and learning to write and read.

Hillocks (1999), following in this tradition, investigated how secondary and community college teachers made sense of English by exploring their beliefs about English as well as their beliefs about students' capacities to learn. By interviewing them and observing them teach, Hillocks found teachers' epistemologies about literary reading to be a major influence on what they chose to teach and how. These teachers reflected a range of literary epistemologies, but the dominant epistemology among the group was "current traditional rhetoric" (Berlin, 1982), encompassing New Critical approaches to literature and teaching with the assumption that "reality must be [and can be] apprehended directly through the senses" (Hillocks, 1999, p. 111). Hillocks (1999) tried to change these teachers' practices through intensive seminar readings of contemporary literacy research; what he found, however, was stability in their practices, not the hoped-for change. Hamel (2003), in case studies of teachers conducted from the perspective of reading development as well as literary study, found that teachers' own experienced ways of reading literature qua literature prevented them from considering how students' basic reading skills and knowledge were related to their literary readings. Such studies demonstrate the need to unpack teachers' epistemologies, and although researchers such as Hillocks have worked with teachers toward developing new ways of seeing their teaching and their students' learning, this line of work has also suggested the need to work with teachers in multiple ways over time to do so.

Other studies of secondary English teachers have demonstrated that teachers' identities as decision makers in the classroom can be fluid and are ultimately subject not only to their underlying epistemologies about what constitutes reading and writing, and knowledge and learning, at given moments but also to their own positioning in relation to students and the culture of classrooms and schools. Research has underscored the ways varying and sometimes competing conceptions about reading and writing, knowledge and learning, can live side by side as teachers navigate such often-contradictory influences on their teaching and thinking as high-stakes assessments of their students' reading and writing, school-level evaluations of their teaching, English department policies and practices, district and state policies, their own ways of reading and writing, and their own professional development experiences (e.g., Franzak, in press; Johnson, Smagorinsky, Thompson, & Fry, 2003; Marshall, Smagorinsky, & Smith, 1995; Sperling, 2004).

Studies that have looked at a range of influences on teachers' thinking and practices have been able to offer highly nuanced teacher portraits. Drawing on activity theory, Johnson et al. (2003), for example, provided a longitudinal look at one case-study teacher's persistence in teaching the five-paragraph essay to eighth graders, exploring competing influences on her beliefs and the logic of her ultimate decisions. The researchers followed her from preservice years to first years of teaching, tracing through multiple data sources the evolution of this persistence. Enacting one kind of researcher–practitioner connection—in this case the teacher was at the end of the study part of the research team—the study raised questions about what influences might compel different teachers to identify with certain norms and standards versus others, underscoring in this way broad-based social, cultural, and political dimensions of teacher identity.

Studies of teachers have been complemented by numerous studies of students. Drawing on a range of theories of literacy, teaching, and learning, these too have offered varied and nuanced portraits of students as contextually situated, many of these destabilizing conventional categories or labels (as applied to student ability, for example, or to SES and race). Some of this work has explored influences on students' reading and writing by tracing their interactions with texts, peers, and teachers in classroom settings. In the area of secondary literature, a number of such studies have explored students enacting their membership in what Fish (1980) called "interpretive communities," that is, the sociocultural contexts in which students read—which as Marshall (2000) pointed out is quite different from focusing on individual students' psychology. Marshall's review shows how cultural norms and values situate students' conceptions of what constitutes different genres of literature, their beliefs in the power of literature to affect their views on issues, and their choices for what to read. As indicated in the previous section on studies of the dynamics of literary response, Marshall's (2000) review also shows that students' responses to literature, including how they talk and write about literature, are influenced by the norms, values, and preoccupations of their cultural context.

Much of the research focusing on context has been ethnographic, with researchers immersing themselves in the communities in which students live and learn. Finders (1997), for example, followed both working- and middle-class girls engaging in school literacy practice (including those sanctioned and not sanctioned by teachers) as well as out-of-school literacy practices, making connections between the norms and expectations of gender, social class, and age in shaping these girls' literacies across in-school and out-of-school contexts. She showed that what and how they read and wrote served to display and construct their classed and gendered identities, including their social and school relationships.

Fairbanks and Ariail (2006), in an ethnography including case studies of three adolescent girls, drew on theories of positioning and identity to explore the social, cultural, and political meanings underlying the kinds of social and cultural resources that each girl brought to literacy and schooling and the consequences of these resources to their literacy learning. Dressman, Wilder, and Connor (2005) used multiple methodological approaches, gathering ethnographic as well as quantitative data, to trace the personal and academic histories of eight adolescents' struggles with literacy, finding the sources of their struggles to be varied and tangled and causing the researchers to assert that any one theoretical account of such struggles is inadequate to explain them.

Another area that has drawn on varied theories of literacy and learning is the study of students in nontraditional activities inside and outside school contexts, with scholars exploring how context connects to what students' texts are and how they are produced and considering implications for building and extending theoretic conceptions of literacy engagement, performance, and learning. Within this area of study, DiPardo and Schnack (2004) studied intergenerational writing in an eighth-grade English project, Fisher (2003) studied spoken-word poetry performances in community settings, and Mahiri (2005) and colleagues studied literacies in different urban settings. Still other researchers of literacy practices explored students' meaning making by raising awareness of language. For example, Lee (1993) explored connections between students' literary understanding and their knowledge of the African American discourse practice of "signifying" (a study we take up later); Fecho and Meacham (2007) explored connections between literacy and hip-hop; and Morrell (2004a) studied apprenticing urban youth as critical researchers of literacy practices.

Responding to students' diverse social and cultural worlds, the above studies showed students inquiring into and theorizing about meaning making and school experience as they connected their lived-in and familiar worlds to developing knowledge and skills in language and literacy. Such explorations have taken reading and writing beyond traditional English classroom definitions, not necessarily to promote in classrooms the literacy activities of nontraditional contexts—although some research (e.g., DiPardo & Schnack, 2004; Fecho & Meacham, 2007; Lee, 1993) did just that—but to understand the literacy skills and knowledge that students bring to bear in these contexts and to what ends. These studies weigh the place and function of such knowledge and skills in the

English class and suggest by contrast how secondary English can constrain students' skills and knowledge in narrow construals of what counts as literacy in a socially, culturally, and linguistically diverse and changing world.

Many of these studies viewed teachers, students, and classrooms through a critical lens, exposing the ways historic privileging profoundly affects what counts as knowledge and learning. A growing body of work has taken critical lenses explicitly to studying teachers, students, and classrooms. Drawing on Gee's (1992) notion that discourse is in effect an "identity kit" (p. 21) that reflects and shapes social roles, Hartman's (2006) case study of working-class White girls in their high school English course revealed the mismatch between the classed and gendered discourses of the girls and those of their school and the effects of this mismatch in constraining how the girls participated and made meaning as readers of literature and students in secondary English.

In another study, Moje and Lewis (2007) drew on activity theory and critical discourse analysis (e.g., Fairclough, 1992)—the analysis of discourse to unpack language's shaping of privilege and identity—to examine the ways writing and speaking of an eighth-grade English language arts class constructed classroom identities, social and power relationships, and literacy knowledge. They found that students' learning was constrained by their unwillingness to speak against prevailing cultural models and discourses.

Taking a critical lens to students' writing, a number of scholars have exposed the racialization of schooling by studying students' narratives of self (e.g., Quoroz, 2001; Schultz, Buck, & Niesz, 2005), that is, students' written stories exploring their identities and educational experiences. Such narratives have been shown to expose schooling's silencing of different racial groups and normalizing other negative experiences in the fabric of everyday school structure and experience.

Many of the studies reviewed in this section have highlighted not only the reciprocal relationship between literacy learning and the cultural and social practices of classrooms and communities (see Gutierrez & Stone, 2000) but have also shed light on the ways these practices are located in relation to the practices granted privilege in the broader culture. Much of this work suggests that different ways with literacy and discourse maintain gender, race, and class differentials rooted in the broader culture (see also, in this regard, Prendergast's [2003] critique of Heath's [1983] study) but that there are ways to address this problem by exposing it to students and studying it.

How to work against historically rooted constraints remains a serious question, continuing to inform research conducted by university-based and schools-based researchers alike (e.g, Fecho, Allen, Mazaros, & Inyega, 2006; Greene & Abt-Perkins, 2003; Ladson-Billings, 1994). Such studies highlight the suppression of race–class–gender issues in classrooms as well as the challenging task of exploring these silences in both classroom research and practice. These studies have contributed to a growing view of the complexity facing teachers and students as researchers have attempted to understand the consequential nature of life in secondary English as it sits within broader school and nonschool contexts. The studies also make apparent the need for researchers to examine secondary English and its contextual groundings over time, employing varied methods and drawing on varied theoretical lenses that continue to help shift the angle of vision from students and teachers as individuals to students, teachers, texts, and contexts interanimating one another across changing social, cultural, and political landscapes.

How Do We Understand and Address the Literacy Challenges and Opportunities of a Globalized, Digitalized, Multimodal World?

Recent studies tracing adolescents' participation in digital multimedia have both drawn on and challenged conceptions of the shaping power of context, presenting a socially and economically diffuse world in which the challenge of ensuring satisfying personal, civic, and vocational futures has taken on new complexities (Kress, Jewitt, & Tsatsarelis, 2000). Providing glimpses of the fluid, globally distributed spaces that compose the milieu of digital literacies, this work suggests the potential of new and emerging tools (e.g., instant messaging, online journaling, wikis, chat spaces, and so on) to extend communication across space, time, and culture (Lam, 2004; Leander & McKim, 2003; Leander & Sheehy, 2004; Rowsell & Pahl, 2007; Stein, 2007). This potential carries important consequences not only for young people's language and literacy learning but also for the emergence of affiliations and identities that "cut across national, ethnic, and linguistic lines" (Lam, 2006a). Furthermore, as researchers explore adolescents' uses of these new tools in particular contexts, the field is continuing to weigh the implications of a semiotic "design" conception of literacy (New London Group, 1996) and the concomitant notion that digital multimedia provide "not just a new way to make meaning, but a different kind of meaning" (Hull & Nelson, 2005, p. 225).

A number of studies have highlighted the potential of digital literacies in fostering motivation, creativity, and connection (e.g., Guzzetti & Gamboa, 2005; Hull & Nelson, 2005; Knobel & Lankshear, 2007; C. Lewis & Fabos, 2005). Recent examinations of culturally and linguistically diverse students' online practices are challenging English education teachers and researchers to rethink traditional conceptions of personhood, offering contextualized glimpses of digital contact zones and hybridized identities. In her studies of bilingual chat and anime spaces, for example, Lam (2004, 2006b) has provided portraits of adolescents inventing transnational ways with words and presentations of self as they forge connections with fellow participants half a world away; similarly concerned with issues of power, diversity, and identity, Stein (2004, 2007) has examined South African youths' engagement in multimodality in postapartheid classrooms emphasizing criticality.

What is at stake in terms of teaching and learning involves more than promoting facility with new technological tools—for as social-cultural literacy researchers have long maintained, it is the nature and purpose of their use rather than tools alone that shape their consequences (Greenleaf, 1994). Studies of new technologies are therefore often informed by how they are taken up by young people in the context of "globalization"—that is, the "movement of capital, labor, media, technologies, images, ideas, and symbolic mediums such as language across geographical and social spaces" (Lam, 2006a, p. 215)—with its accompanying demands for creativity, collaboration, and innovation (Kalantzis, Cope, & the Learning by Design Project Group, 2005). Such work offers opportunities to think beyond the commercial hype surrounding new technologies, inviting teachers and researchers alike to reflect on young people's engagement with these multimodal venues and to consider what their participation suggests by way of expanded perspectives on the nature of context, identity, culture, and text.

Although much of the existing work on youth participation in digital literacies has taken place in out-of-school settings (e.g., Hull & Katz, 2006; Hull & Nelson, 2005; Mahiri, 2004; Morrell, 2004b), researchers have drawn on their findings to argue the need to integrate new media in classrooms in conceptually grounded and reflective ways (see Hull & Schultz, 2002; Stein, 2007). A recurrent theme in this work has been the need to foster criticality concerning the texts (and authors) that students encounter in their online travels. In a study of classroom uses of the Internet, for instance, Fabos (2004) observed students inundated with commercial content that sometimes found its way into their "research" projects.

Frequently, studies of students' online literacies conclude with arguments for fostering active reflection as part of students' digital sensibilities particularly (e.g., Lam, 2006b; Stein, 2004) and perusals of new media generally (Alvermann & Hagood, 2000). The stakes are especially high for less advantaged youth, who are likely to enjoy diminished access to digital literacies in their out-of-school lives; for instance, in his comparison of well-funded laptop programs in schools in more and less affluent communities, Warschauer (2006) found programs in wealthier areas to be consistently more effective in promoting student participation and learning. Where online tools are appropriated to a traditional teacher-centered ethic—an ethic arguably more likely to prevail in schools serving less advantaged youth—their potential to foster meaningful engagement has been seen as compromised (Knobel & Lankshear, 2006).

In addition to extending conceptions of context, community, and classroom, digital literacies are also challenging the English educators' traditional focus on the primacy of language. Even as "literacy" is becoming a too-expansive metaphor for understandings and representations of all kinds (Kress, 2000), researchers are increasingly arguing that semiotic expansion is inevitable and, indeed, already taking place in the world beyond schools. Drawing on the early work of the New London Group (1996) as well as subsequent efforts to extend and enact these ideas (e.g., Kalantzis et al., 2005), a new wave of English education research is beginning to suggest ways that the school subject might be reimagined with an eye to fostering critical and creative approaches to multimodal understanding and design (Beach, 2006).

English educators are increasingly noting the power of the transformation taking place all around us—not just in terms of textual tools but also in literacy practices and their personal, economic, and political repercussions—although efforts to study multimodal texts and practices and to chart implications for classroom practice remain in their infancy (Hull & Nelson, 2005).

Efforts to understand and address the challenges and opportunities of these new technological, social, and global contexts are meanwhile beset with questions as old as the field of English education. Although theorists are beginning to build conceptual frameworks (Kress, 2003) that can usefully guide research into multimodal teaching and learning (Jewitt & Kress, 2003; Kress et al., 2005), the larger issues are all too familiar, albeit infused with higher stakes than ever: What should English as school subject ultimately accomplish? What kinds of people, citizens, and workers should it help create? How does one reconcile contemporary calls for a more creative, innovative, collaborative, globally minded workforce with the traditional view of English as stable skill set and knowledge of a Western canon? As English education researchers endeavor to address an expanding array of activities, texts, and settings, drawing on the field's diverse scholarly traditions is in many ways an easier task than crossing the bridge to practice, with its concomitant uncertainties concerning what English will or should be in the fluid, dynamic, globalized contexts of another new century (Lam, 2006a; Sefton-Green, 2006).

A Closing and an Opening: Toward Expanding Directions

As this brief overview of major trends has suggested, "English education research" has become a multiplicity of complementary perspectives, approaches, lenses, and tools. And although the field's growing variety is in some ways indicative of the differing epistemologies and agendas continually in play whenever the purpose, contours, and ends of "English" have been taken up, it is tempting to cast the varied developments in the field during the past quarter-century in modernist terms of inexorable progress with a definable end. Reflective of its own social and cultural context, English education research has offered increasingly nuanced and generative perspectives on reading and writing both responding to changing times and helping meaningfully to shape them and our vision of them. In these contexts, we find promise and possibility for continued shaping and reshaping of research–practice integrations.

Yet much remains to be learned concerning the nature of the research–practice connection in English education. Although the understandings teachers take away from their immediate readings of research have been studied at some length (e.g., Bartels, 2003; Gitlin, Barlow, Burbank, Kauchak, & Stevens, 1999; Kennedy, 1997, 1999; Zeuli, 1994), given the social-cultural, critical, and semiotic turns in literacy studies in recent years, the field is well positioned to explore the understandings teachers are constructing in light of the myriad influences that inform their long-term planning and moment-by-moment practices. Too often, policymakers have clung to the naïve belief that a given study can provide transportable "how-tos"—as if knowledge were stable and transmittable through prescriptive training. In the case of English education, the uncertainty concerning what research has to offer is multiplied exponentially—not only because of historic debate concerning what the field is or should be and attendant notions concerning the role of research and researchers, but now also because of this array of lenses and vantage points. In developing this review of empirical trends commonly regarded as rich with implications for practice, we were abidingly aware that relatively little is known concerning the extent to which these implications have actually been realized, let alone what that process of realization has entailed.

The amount of theorizing and research that awaits in this regard is formidable and surely beyond the scope of this chapter. As we draw this chapter to a close, however, we offer a few glimpses of new realizations, instances where research and teaching have intertwined, showing us expanding views of both research and practice, as each better understands the world of the other.

BEYOND BRIDGING: EXEMPLARS OF INTEGRATION

Further countering the research–practice great-divide narrative, a number of English education's professional leaders—both university-based scholars and classroom teachers—have engaged in work that has challenged with particular emphasis the tendency to cast research and practice as worlds apart. We offer these brief portraits not as taxonomy or comprehensive guide to such efforts but, rather, generative instances of long-term collaborations that exemplify more than the well-worn metaphor of the research–practice "bridge" affords, offering knowledge both for and of practice.

Researchers as Teachers

The tradition of university-based researchers working in K–12 classrooms to build, enact, and refine theories of learning dates back to Brown's (1992) pioneering "design experiments." Although a number of literacy educators have written about the challenging experience of reentering classroom teaching (e.g., Cazden, 1992; Dudley-Marling, 1997; Mahiri, 2004), such accounts at the secondary level are relatively rare. Given the many constraints on high school English teachers' work—the paperload, accountability pressures, and a widening achievement gap among students ill served by the system along the way—the passage from ivory tower to the untidy bustle of compulsory schooling can be overwhelming (Scherff & Kaplan, 2006).

Working with real adolescents in real schools demands a commitment of time and energy that can undermine scholarly productivity—or, alternatively, as in the work of the researcher-teacher we briefly sketch here, function at once as matrix and catalyst. Building on her prior work exploring culturally responsive approaches to language arts pedagogy for African American students, Northwestern University's Carol Lee (2001, 2007a) developed the multiyear Cultural Modeling Project, in which she participated not only as theorist and researcher but also as public-school teacher and colleague. Designed to help speakers of AAVE understand the relevance of their everyday linguistic practices and cognitive resources to literary study, the Cultural Modeling Project fostered intellectual communities engaged in rigorous exploration of complex issues. In her own daily classroom teaching, Lee drew on microethnographic (Green & Dixon, 1994) and neo-Vygotskian notions of situated learning to draw students into increasingly participatory stances in challenging class discussions (Lave & Wenger, 1991). As Lee modeled analytic strategies demanding close attention to texts, she emphasized connections between literary interpretation and students' everyday worlds. By explicitly naming the proficiencies represented in such AAVE practices as signifying and rapping, Lee rendered these language-play strategies available tools in approaching literary texts. She gradually stepped back as students stepped in, engaging in dynamic discussions of literary characters, language, and connections to their own worlds.

Lee (2001) is quick to point out that the process was far from smooth or easy. As her students left the school's "rowdy, noisy" halls and entered Lee's classroom, they brought along well-reified beliefs that little would be expected of them beyond factual recall and obedience. Ensuring that even the most reluctant students participate takes "a great deal of energy" (p. 118), Lee allowed, acknowledging that students "actively resisted" her efforts from Day 1 (p. 133). Even their richest moments could seem overwhelming to a less culturally attuned teacher, as a rising decibel level and overlapping talk signaled their growing engagement.

Staying the course with these young people involved more than adherence to a set of abstract beliefs. Rather, Lee (2001) saw these young people

as she saw her own biological children, for whom failure is simply not an option. She had to appreciate the humanity of these young people, their innate talents, and their infinite ability to learn, grow, and develop. They could not garner enough resistant behavior to deter her determination that they would learn and master intellectually difficult problem solving. (p. 133)

Lee's research, theory building, and teaching offer not just new cognitive strategies but a vibrant look into a challenging urban classroom. Lee brought mind, hand, and heart to this work, melding the work of theory building and implementation— at the levels of her own classroom as well as those of the school colleagues with whom she closely collaborated—into a seamless whole.

Teachers as Researchers

Nowhere have traditional conceptions of "teachers" and "researchers" been more vigorously challenged than in English education, where the teacher-research movement has found advocacy and support from AERA and the Teacher Research Special Interest Group, NCTE (see Stock, 2005), and NWP (2007). Although this work is too ample and wide-ranging to allow full treatment, we offer three brief snapshots that illustrate the potential of teacher research to inform English classroom practice— three boundary-blurring instantiations of what Cochran-Smith and Lytle (1999) have called "inquiry as stance" (p. 18).

In *Teacher Research for Better Schools* (Mohr et al., 2004), a K–12 network of Virginia teachers explored the implications of their investigations across multiple school sites. Led by veteran teachers who functioned as colleagues as well as coaches, these teacher-researchers found their appetite for "useful theory" (p. 9) whetted as they pursued their own local inquiries; that is, as they became creators as well as consumers of research, they found that their own research informed their understandings of published research and vice versa. At one participating high school, teachers collaborated with school administrators to use their findings to enhance student achievement and effectively implement a new ninth-grade block schedule; at another, teacher-researchers participated in program assessment, professional development, and school planning. It is regrettable that funding for such work has diminished in the years since, as *Teacher Research for Better Schools* so compellingly demonstrates the potential of practitioner inquiry to enrich the evidence base guiding local decisions concerning curricula, programming, and teacher development.

The Brookline Teacher Researcher Seminar (BTRS) is perhaps best known through the publications of its elementary members, though this long-running Boston-area group encompassed high school instructors as well. Guided in the initial years by work with local sociolinguists such as Sarah Michaels and Courtney Cazden, BTRS's regular gatherings came to include visits from a diverse and distinguished roster of scholars, including Shirley Brice Heath, James Gee, Lisa Delpit, Vivian Paley, Sylvia Ashton-Warner, and Douglas Barnes (BTRS, 2004). As high school teacher Roxanne Pappenheimer (2004) exemplifies, BTRS research often focused on dilemmas, mysteries, and unresolved problems. When a student teacher engaged Pappenheimer's special-education English class in a discussion of M. E. Kerr's (1987) young-adult novel *Night Kites*, she was uneasily aware that the book's attention to homophobia would likely elicit highly charged responses. The classroom conversations that Pappenheimer went on to record and analyze took often unexpected turns, including imaginative dramatizations and searching attention to the many questions of values, ethics, and roles that the book raises. Pappenheimer found these events both heartening and provocative, turning back to her own teaching and inquiry, wondering, "How can we best use the power that imagination obviously holds to further our students' learning?" (p. 104).

Finally, in his award-winning book *Is This English? Race, Language, and Culture in the Classroom*, Bob Fecho (2004) takes us into the world of urban Philadelphia's Simon Gratz High School. Fecho provides a series of provocative scenarios that raise theoretically and pedagogically generative questions concerning issues of power, equity, achievement, and what it means to work together as members of a multicultural classroom community of relevance not only to preservice teachers but also to teacher educators, veteran teachers, and literacy researchers. Now a university professor, Fecho continues to serve as an influential advocate and conceptual guide to teachers seeking new lenses through which to examine the complexities of their own classrooms and practices (Fecho, 2003). More recently coauthoring with public-school colleagues (Aaron et al., 2006) and writing, as well, for audiences of researchers (Fecho & Botzakis, 2007) and policymakers (Schultz & Fecho, 2005), Fecho exemplifies a growing cohort of English educators whose work transcends the very categories of teacher and researcher.

Teachers and Researchers Together

The field has seen many instances of university-based researchers listing teachers as research-report coauthors (e.g., DiPardo & Schnack, 2004; Smagorinsky & Coppock, 1995; Smith & Connolly, 2005), reflecting a growing recognition that long-term observation in accomplished practitioners' classroom tends to promote a mutual intellectual influence. Given the differing pressures and priorities of their respective work, however, far less often do professors and teachers collaborate closely in sustained and systematic data analysis. Even given the relative convenience of electronic communication, finding time and energy to sift through data and take up issues of interpretation is hardly easy. And even where they firmly believe that their perspectives can contribute more together than they could alone, formulating that shared vision means living in one another's worlds to an extent that time and circumstance rarely permit.

Exceptions, then, are well worth noting, and we focus here on one: the work of Sarah Warshauer Freedman of the University of California, Berkeley, and Berkeley High School teacher Verda Delp, authors of a *Research in the Teaching of English* article honored with the Alan C. Purves Award for its implications for classroom practice (Freedman & Delp, 2007; Freedman, Delp, & Crawford, 2005). Delp and Freedman had known one another for many years before first collaborating as university- and schools-based researchers in the M-Class Project (Freedman, Simons, Kalnin, Casareno, & the M-Class Teams, 1999). As they undertook a joint study of Delp's untracked eighth-grade English class, Freedman became a regular presence in Delp's school, even as Delp deepened her own understandings of theory and research by pursuing a doctorate; that is, while retaining primary membership in their respective places of employment, each gained insights into the norms, rituals, and priorities of the other's world and work. In weekly research meetings, they pored over data, challenged one another's understandings, and hammered out collaborative interpretations.

Their article, "Teaching English in Untracked Classrooms" (Freedman, Delp, & Crawford, 2005), offers a vivid illustration of a veteran teacher negotiating the Bakhtinian heteroglossia of her diverse classroom as well as an effort to extend social-cultural theory. Having since completed a doctoral dissertation that further explored the nature of talk, interaction, and learning in her classroom (Delp, 2005), Delp continues to teach at Berkeley High School as well as in the University of California, Berkeley, Multicultural Urban Secondary English teacher-education program (MUSE); Freedman, meanwhile, remains a regular presence Delp's classroom, as the two extend their efforts to chart the nature of student learning in what they call the "grand dialogic zones" (Freedman & Delp, 2007) of diverse whole-class settings. Their collaboration serves as a further instantiation of Bakhtinian heteroglossia— that is, more than pooling their existing wisdom, as Freedman and Delp move between these sites of teaching and learning, they are challenging, extending, and enriching one another's approaches to teaching and research alike.

Preparing New Teachers to Understand and Use Research

Although professional-development efforts that explore research–practice connections are many (e.g., the National Writing Project Institutes, the various National Endowment for the Humanities–sponsored Literature Institutes for Teachers, NCTE's Co-Learn; see also Appleman, 2000; Olson & Land, 2007), comparable work with preservice teachers is somewhat harder to find, although promising new efforts, such as the University of Arizona College of Education's (2007) Research

Initiative on Preparing Teachers for Mexican American Students, are endeavoring to fill this void. With the multiple and well-documented demands on neophyte teachers' intellectual and emotional energies, helping them also to incorporate research has required profound belief in the power of research to help realize teaching's fullest potentials.

George Hillocks's work with preservice teachers at the University of Chicago has been notable in this regard. Guided by decades of his own research on the teaching of writing, Hillocks has worked through the years with his master's of arts in teaching (MAT) students to prepare them to teach and conduct research in a diversity of secondary schools. He has brought to this work an abiding concern for young African American and Hispanic students' acquisition and development of literacy skills and knowledge in the contexts of public schools and has carefully developed empirical evidence that certain approaches to teaching writing have measurable effects on these. His recent work has addressed the teaching of narrative (Hillocks, 2007)—for the power of its generativity, its ability to bring into perspective the experiences that are part of students' developing lives, and the complex problem solving that it entails—which Hillocks and his MAT students aimed to make visible to middle and secondary school students.

The research–practice connection in this endeavor was multilayered. Working together in workshop fashion, Hillocks (2007) and his MAT students prepared, tried out, and then refined the daily lessons and strategies for teaching that would foster young students' narrative writing knowledge and skills. They went into classrooms to teach and observe one another teaching, went back to the university with samples of students' writing to read them critically and analytically and to reflect on their teaching following research precepts, and revised their teaching strategies accordingly in a process that covered the weeks it took to teach narrative—and in which the MAT students learned how to encourage rich and thoughtful writing, guide revision, and track student progress. In part, this was a case of a research explicitly informing and guiding MAT students' classroom experiences and reflections.

But another research layer added even more dimension to the experience. With his MAT students, Hillocks (2007) designed an experiment to assess the effects of their teaching on students' work. They set up a study with treatment groups (the classrooms in which they had taught) and control groups and administered pre- and posttest evaluations of students' writing across these classrooms, quantitatively measuring gains. (They found gains, indeed, in treatment compared with control groups and substantial gains for African American and Hispanic students.) This work offers a theoretical model for teaching in which new teachers come to understand the conceptual, technical, and pedagogical principles behind their work and to develop ways to probe and test them out in theoretically and methodologically systematic ways (see Lee, 2007b).

REWRITING THE NARRATIVE

We have attempted in this chapter to craft a narrative of the emergence, development, and present status of English education in the United States, exploring its early preoccupation with national identity, its long-ambivalent relationship with university-based scholarship, the cumulative contributions of research to date, and emerging efforts to bring research and practice into unprecedented interaction. Theorists have pointed out that the narratives we craft are born of a desire to find generative meaning in what would otherwise stand as disparate chronologies (e.g., Sarbin, 1986). Disparity aplenty remains in the necessarily incomplete story we have told here concerning the nature and purpose of English as school subject and on the role of research from multiple and related disciplines in its advancement.

As the field endeavors to respond to reductionist conceptions of the appropriate priorities of high school English, this panoply of scholarly perspectives is at once promising and problematic. On one hand, given its focus on fostering young people's meaning-making capacities—and the globalized, digitalized, politically charged contexts in which literacy activities are currently situated—the questions before English educators demand inquiry and debate informed by diverse perspectives, methods, and insights. Although its scholarly variety holds benefits both realized and potential, the field's diverse range is also further complicating the always-complicated relationship between research and practice. Even as so-called scientifically based approaches to research have been widely condemned by English educators as lacking sensitivity to the range of literacy demands and opportunities before today's high school students, the field has only begun to take up the challenge of enacting and describing the array of ways that research *can* inform classroom practice. Just as the term *literacy* has shifted to the plural, so too is the "research–practice relationship" more appropriately cast as a diverse range of intellectual stances, enacted strategies, and nuanced patterns of effect. Absent redoubled and carefully sustained efforts to chart the contours of these relationships, the task is ceded to those who would posit a singular, transmission-oriented view of things, in which university-based scientists generate best practices to be enacted by teacher-technicians.

As the field nears its 100th anniversary, the challenge of preparing young people for the literacy demands of their personal, vocational, and civic futures is more pressing, complex, and contested than ever. Although nation building may have sat at the core of English education historically, as unfolding years and the broadening contexts of our research have pushed us to rethink the nature of nationhood in a globalizing world, new questions emerge concerning the implications for English as a secondary subject. As English educators address these challenges in the midst of policy initiatives informed by reductionist assumptions concerning the nature of literacy teaching and learning, rewriting the narrative of research–practice estrangement will afford new ways of seeing the connections between research and practice that, as this chapter has suggested, are "always already" there. What we need at this moment in our history is a way to theorize the relationship between English education research and practice in ways that honor and account for the field's conceptual diversity and expanding contours.

The questions driving the challenges before English education research and researchers are still those that scholars have asked for generations: "What is the scope of English education and what is the role of research in shaping English education practice?" Yet the social, cultural, and political conditions that give these questions meaning have changed dramatically across the generations, and the challenges ahead that revolve around these questions are conceptually, empirically, and politically intertwined in new ways.

These questions are firmly grounded in a sense that students and teachers are contextually situated, shaped by multiple social and cultural influences and identifying as well with multiple ways of using language and of enacting literacy. One challenge for research, then, is to foster reading and writing that speak to these influences and to the varied worlds in which students make and take meaning. This sense of students' and English education goals casts anew the old Dartmouth focus on growth and equity: How can we better understand student literacy growth as fostering multiple, diverse, or hybridized identities? Put another way, what will count as literacy growth, and what will count as equitable growth across literacies as the range of student readers and writers expands in varied directions?

Another challenge is for researchers and teachers to develop understanding of the other: How can researchers better understand and conceptualize the complexities of practice? How do teachers develop as both consumers and facilitators of research as well as investigators or collaborators in research projects? We will need widespread initiatives for working with emerging teachers and researchers in these directions—fostering the kind of work conducted by academics and classroom teachers that advances knowledge and theory and that yields theoretically grounded and productive practice.

As researchers press forward with the varied research foci that have evolved through the decades, empirical challenges emerge. Research that focuses on individual students—future instantiations of which will likely emphasize emerging technologies for tracking thinking and learning—can give one kind of perspective on what is involved when students learn and develop as writers and readers over time and in changing material conditions. Research on the local dynamics of teaching and learning, which yield understandings about how reading and writing are constructed in real time, can give another perspective as researchers focus on diverse students and teachers with varied and expanding curricula. And as secondary English gets shaped by shifting political winds, technological tides, and other contextual forces, studies emphasizing these broader contexts can continue to add new social, cultural, and political perspectives to literacy and learning as these play out for different students and teachers in different school settings. Given change as the one true constant, we would argue that only such diverse methods and perspectives can help us read the moment at hand and give us insight about those to come.

In this complex empirical context, researchers face key questions: How can one type of research be critically in dialogue with others? How can "research in dialogue" be presented to inform policy or to be shared with others? What new genres of research presentation await? We need to know more about the ways teachers and researchers together can make sense of findings from different traditions as traditions evolve and sometimes merge.

Politically, challenges revolve around funding research from such multiple pathways, with varied researchers and teachers as key players, to include not only large-scale "scientifically based" projects but also critical social and cultural investigations in local settings. Projects across traditions complement and enrich one another, give one another meaning and perspective, and mutually shape their value to practice.

In sum, as the research story that we have told suggests, our field's most promising vision for research is not somehow to unify its theoretical and empirical scope, and not to settle the issues of English education in recipe-fashion or to shut questions down. Rather, the promise of research is to provide multiple ways of seeing, critiquing, and generating questions—about teachers, students, reading, and writing—in the context of English and language arts as a school subject shaping membership on a world stage. We end with the thought that we need to construe English education's story in new ways—to embrace, in a world of fluid boundaries, the field's complexities, which research, in its generativity, has helped to account for and thus to make salient.

NOTE

[1]According to the National Center for Education Statistics (2007), racial and ethnic minorities composed 42% of the K–12 public school population in 2005, up from 22% in 1972 (p. 26). A gap in reading proficiency between European American students and both Black and Hispanic students has meanwhile persisted; in 2005, on a 0-to-500 scale, Blacks scored 29 points lower than Whites, and Hispanics scored 26 points lower than Whites (p. 39), a gap that showed little sign of narrowing into middle school and beyond. Though drop-out rates for Black and Hispanic students declined slightly since 1972, Whites continued to drop out at significantly lower rates (p. 54). Not surprising, Black and Hispanic youth were more likely than their White counterparts to be neither enrolled in school nor working in 2006 (11% of Hispanic and 11% of Black youth as compared to 6% of Asian and 6% of White youth; p. 46).

REFERENCES

Aaron, J., Bouchereau Bauer, E., Commeyras, M., Dowling Cox, S., Daniell, B., Elrick, E., et al. (2006). *No deposit, no return: Enriching literacy teaching and learning through critical inquiry pedagogy*. Newark, DE: International Reading Association.
Agosto, D. E., Hughes-Hassell, S., & Gilmore-Clough, C. (2003). The all-White world of middle-school genre fiction: Surveying the field for multicultural protagonists. *Children's Literature in Education, 34*, 257–275.
Alvermann, D. E., & Hagood, M. (2000). Critical media literacy: Research, theory, and practice in "New Times." *Journal of Educational Research, 93*, 193–205.
Alvermann, D. E., Young, J. P., Weaver, D., Hinchman, K. A., Moore, D. W., Phelps, S. F., et al. (1996). Middle and high school students' perceptions of how they experience text-based discussions: A multicase study. *Reading Research Quarterly, 31*, 244–267.
American Educational Research Association. (2007). AERA task forces working for the Association and education research. *Educational Researcher, 36*, 165–166.
Anderson, R. C. (1994). Role of the reader's schema in comprehension, learning, and memory. In R. B. Ruddell, M. R. Ruddell, H. & Singer. (Eds.), *Theoretical models and processes of reading* (4th ed., pp. 469–482). Newark, DE: International Reading Association.
Applebee, A. N. (1974). *Tradition and reform in the teaching of English: A history*. Urbana, IL: National Council of Teachers of English.

Applebee, A. N. (1986). Problems in process approaches: Toward a reconceptualization of process instruction. In A. Petrosky & D. Bartholomae (Eds.), *The teaching of writing: 85th yearbook of the National Society for the Study of Education* (Part II, pp. 95–113). Chicago: University of Chicago Press.

Applebee, A. N. (1993). *Literature in the secondary school: Studies of curriculum and instruction in the United States.* Urbana, IL: National Council of Teachers of English.

Applebee, A. N., Langer, J. A., Mullis, I. V. S., Latham, A. S., & Gentile, C. A. (1994). *NAEP 1992 writing report card* (Report No. 23-W01). Washington, DC: U.S. Department of Education, Office of Educational Research and Improvement.

Appleman, D. (2000). *Critical encounters in high school English: Teaching literary theory to adolescents.* New York: Teachers College Press.

Arnold, M. (1971). *Culture and anarchy.* New York: Bobbs-Merrill. (Original work published 1875)

Athanases, S. (1993). Discourse about literacy and diversity: A study of two urban tenth-grade classes. *Dissertation Abstracts International, 54* (05). (UMI No. 9326420)

Athanases, S. (1998). Diverse learners, diverse texts: Exploring identity and difference through literary encounters. *Journal of Literacy Research, 30,* 273–296.

Athanases, S., & Heath, S. B. (1995). Ethnography in the study of the teaching and learning of English. *Research in the Teaching of English, 29,* 263–287.

Bakhtin, M. (1981). *The dialogic imagination.* Austin: University of Texas Press.

Ball, A. (2002). Three decades of research on classroom life: Illuminating the classroom communicative lives of America's at-risk students. *Review of Research in Education, 26,* 71–111.

Ball, A., & Freedman. (Eds.). (2004). *Bakhtinian perspectives on language, literacy, and learning.* Cambridge, UK: Cambridge University Press.

Barr, R. (2001). Research on the teaching of reading. In V. Richardson (Ed.), *Handbook of research on teaching* (4th ed., pp. 390–415). Washington, DC: American Educational Research Association.

Bartels, N. (2003). How teachers and researchers read academic articles. *Teaching and Teacher Education, 19,* 737–753.

Beach, R. (1993). *A teacher's introduction to reader-response theories.* Urbana, IL: National Council of Teachers of English.

Beach, R. (2006). *Teachingmedialiteracy.com: A Web-linked guide to resources and activities.* New York: Teachers College Press.

Beach, R., Green, J., Kamil, M., & Shanahan, T. (Eds.). (2005). *Multidisciplinary perspectives on literacy research.* Cresskill, NJ: Hampton.

Berlin, J. A. (1982). *Writing instruction in nineteenth-century American colleges.* Carbondale: Southern Illinois University Press.

Blau, S. (1994). Transactions between theory and practice in the teaching of literature. In J. Flood & J. A. Langer (Eds.), *Literature instruction: Practice and policy* (pp. 19–52). New York: Scholastic.

Bloome, D. (1987). *Literacy and schooling.* Norwood, NJ: Ablex.

Blount, N. S. (1973). Research on teaching literature, language and composition. In R. M. W. Travers (Ed.), *Second handbook of research on teaching* (pp. 1072–1097). Chicago: Rand McNally for American Educational Research Association.

Booth, W. (1987). Foreword. In R. Lloyd-Jones & A. Lunsford (Eds.), *The English Coalition Conference: Democracy through language* (pp. vii–xii). Urbana, IL, and New York: National Council for Teachers of English and Modern Language Association.

Braddock, R., Lloyd-Jones, R., & Schoer, L. (1963). *Research in written composition.* Urbana, IL: National Council for Teachers of English.

Brookline Teacher Researcher Seminar. (2004). *Regarding children's words: Teacher research on language and literacy.* New York: Teachers College Press.

Brooks, C. (1947). *The well-wrought urn: Studies in the structure of poetry.* New York: Harcourt Brace.

Brown, A. (1992). Design experiments: Theoretical and methodological challenges in creating complex interventions in classroom settings. *Journal of the Learning Sciences, 2,* 141–178.

Budd, W. C. (1967). Research designs of potential value in investigating problems in English. *Research in the Teaching of English, 1,* 1–9.

Calfee, R., & Drum, P. (1986). Research on teaching reading. In M. Wittrock (Ed.), *Handbook of research on teaching* (3rd ed., pp. 804–849). New York: Macmillan.

Cazden, C. B. (1992). *Whole language plus: Essays on literacy in the United States and New Zealand.* New York: Teachers College Press.

Cazden, C. B. (2001). *Classroom discourse: The language of teaching and learning* (2nd ed.). Portsmouth, NH: Heinemann.

Chubb, P. (1912). The menace of pedantry in the teaching of English. *School Review, 20,* 34–45.

Clifford, G. J. (1973). A history of the impact of research on teaching. In R. M. W. Travers (Ed.), *Second handbook of research on teaching* (pp. 1–46). Chicago: Rand McNally for American Educational Research Association.

Cochran-Smith, M., & Donnell, K. (2006). Practitioner inquiry: Blurring the boundaries of research and practice. In G. Camilli, P. Elmore, & J. Green (Eds.). *Complementary methods for research in education* (2nd ed.). Washington, DC: American Educational Research Association.

Cochran-Smith, M., & Lytle, S. L. (1999). The teacher research movement: A decade later. *Educational Researcher, 28*(7), 15–25.

Commission on English. (1965). *Freedom and discipline in English: Report of the Commission on English.* New York: College Entrance Examination Board.

Committee of Ten of the National Education Association. (1894). *Report of the Committee of Ten on secondary school studies.* New York: American Book Company.

Conference on English Education. (2005). *The relationship between research and teaching.* Retrieved July 17, 2007, from http://www.ncte.org/groups/cee/positions/122897.htm

Cook-Gumperz, J. (Ed.). (1986). *The social construction of literacy.* Cambridge, UK: Cambridge University Press.

Cook-Gumperz, J. (Ed.). (2006). *The social construction of literacy.* Cambridge, UK: Cambridge University Press.

Cope, B., & Kalantzis, M. (Eds.). (1993). *The power of literacy: A genre approach to teaching writing.* London: Falmer.

Core Knowledge Foundation. (2007). *About core knowledge.* Retrieved April 16, 2007, from http://www.coreknowledge.org/CK/index.htm

Delp, V. (2005). *Meaning-making journeys in the untracked English classroom: Students thinking and writing interpretively about literature and themselves.* Unpublished doctoral dissertation, University of California, Berkeley.

Dewey, J. (1963). *Experience and education.* New York: Simon & Schuster. (Original work published 1938)

DiPardo, A., & Freedman, S. W. (1988). Peer response groups in the writing classroom: Theoretic foundations and new directions. *Review of Educational Research, 59,* 119–149.

DiPardo, A., & Schnack, P. (2004). Expanding the web of meaning: Thought and emotion in an intergenerational reading and writing program. *Reading Research Quarterly, 39,* 14–37.

DiPardo, A., Whitney, A., Fleischer, C., Johnson, T., Mayher, J., McCracken, N., et al. (2006). Understanding the relationship between research and teaching. *English Education, 38,* 295–311.

Dixon, J. (1975). *Growth through English set in the perspective of the seventies.* Oxford, UK: NATE/Oxford. (Original work published 1967)

Donovan, M. S., Wigdor, A. K., & Snow, C. E. (Eds.). (2003). *Strategic education research partnership*. Washington, DC: National Research Council.

Dressman, M., Wilder, P., & Connor, J. J. (2005). Theories of failure and failure of theories: A cognitive/sociocultural/macrostructural study of eight struggling students. *Research in the Teaching of English, 40*, 8–61.

Dudley-Marling, C. (1997). *Living with uncertainty: The messy reality of classroom practice*. Portsmouth, NH: Heinemann.

Elbow, P. (1990). *What is English?* New York and Urbana, IL: Modern Language Association and National Council of Teachers of English.

Emig, J. (1971). *The composing processes of twelfth graders*. Urbana, IL: National Council of Teachers of English.

Fabos, B. (2004). *Wrong turn on the information superhighway: Education and the commercialization of the Internet*. New York: Teachers College Press.

Fairbanks, C., & Ariail, M. (2006). The role of social and cultural resources in literacy and schooling: Three contrasting cases. *Research in the Teaching of English, 40*, 310–354.

Fairclough, N. (1992). *Critical language awareness*. London: Longman.

Faulkner, W. (1975). *Requiem for a nun*. New York: Vintage. (Original work published 1951)

Fecho, B. (2003). Yeki bood/Yeki na bood: Writing and publishing as a teacher researcher. *Research in the Teaching of English, 37*, 281–294.

Fecho, B. (2004). *Is this English? Race, language, and culture in the classroom*. New York: Teachers College Press.

Fecho, B., Allen, J. B., Mazaros, C., & Inyega, H. (2006). Teacher research in writing classrooms. In P. Smagorinsky, *Research on composition: Multiple perspectives on two decades of change* (pp. 108–140). New York: Teachers College Press.

Fecho, B., & Botzakis, S. (2007). Feasts of becoming: Imagining a literacy classroom based on dialogic beliefs. *Journal of Adolescent and Adult Literacy, 50*, 548–558.

Fecho, B., & Meacham, S. (2007). Learning to play and playing to learn: Research sites as transactional spaces. In Lewis, C., Enciso, P., & Moje, E. B. (Eds.), *Reframing sociocultural research on literacy: Identity, agency, and power* (pp. 163–187). Mahwah, NJ: Lawrence Erlbaum.

Finders, M. (1997). *Just girls: Hidden literacies and life in junior high*. New York: Teachers College Press.

Fish, S. (1980). *Is there a text in this class? The authority of interpretive communities*. Cambridge, MA: Harvard University Press.

Fisher, M. T. (2003). Open mics and open minds: Spoken word poetry in African diaspora participatory literacy communities. *Harvard Educational Review, 73*, 362–389.

Flower, L. S., & Hayes, J. R. (1981). A cognitive process theory of writing. *College Composition and Communication, 32*, 365–387.

Franzak, J. (in press). On the margins in a high-performing high school: Policy and the struggling reader. *Research in the Teaching of English*.

Freedman, S. W. (with Greenleaf, C., & Sperling, M.) (1987). *Response to student writing* (Research Report No. 23). Urbana, IL: National Council of Teachers of English.

Freedman, S. W., & Delp, V. (2007). Conceptualizing a whole-class learning space: A grand dialogic zone. *Research in the Teaching of English, 41*, 259–268.

Freedman, S. W., Delp, V., & Crawford, S. M. (2005). Teaching English in untracked classrooms. *Research in the Teaching of English, 40*, 62–126.

Freedman, S. W., Simons, E. R., Kalnin, J. S., Casareno, A., & the M-Class Teams (1999). *Inside city schools: Investigating literacy in multicultural classrooms*. New York: Teachers College Press.

Gamoran, A., & Carbonaro, W. J. (2002). High school English: A national portrait. *High School Journal, 86*(2), 1–13.

Gee, J. P. (1992). *The social mind: Language, ideology, and social practice.* New York: Bergin and Garvey.

Gee, J. P. (2000–2001). Identity as an analytic lens for research in education. *Review of Research in Education, 25,* 99–125.

Gerlach, J. M., & Monseau, V. R. (Eds.). (1991). *Missing chapters: Ten pioneering women in NCTE and English education.* Urbana, IL: National Council of Teachers of English.

Gilmore, P., & Glatthorn, A. (Eds.). (1982). *Children in and out of school: Ethnography and education.* Washington, DC: Center for Applied Linguistics.

Gitlin, A., Barlow, L., Burbank, M., Kauchak, D., & Stevens, T. (1999). Pre-service teachers' thinking on research: Implications for inquiry oriented teacher education. *Teaching and Teacher Education, 15,* 753–769.

Green, J. (1983). Research on teaching as a linguistic process: A state of the art. *Review of Research in Education, 10,* 151–252.

Green, J. L., & Dixon, C. N. (1994). Talking knowledge into being: Discursive and social practices in classrooms. *Linguistics and Education, 5,* 231–239.

Green, J. L., & Wallat, C. (Eds.). (1981). *Ethnography and language in educational settings.* Norwood, NJ: Ablex.

Greene, S., & Abt-Perkins, D. (2003). *Making race visible: Literacy research for cultural understanding.* New York: Teachers College Press.

Greenleaf, C. (1994). Technological indeterminacy: The role of classroom writing practices and pedagogy in shaping student use of the computer. *Written Communication, 11,* 85–130.

Grindstaff, F. L. (1987). The context variable of the organic field model. In W. H. Peters (Ed.), *Effective English teaching: Concept, research, and practice* (pp. 45–92). Urbana, IL: National Council of Teachers of English.

Grossman, P. L. (2001). Research on the teaching of literature: Finding a place. In V. Richardson (Ed.), *Handbook of research on teaching* (4th ed., pp. 416–432). Washington, DC: American Educational Research Association.

Gumperz, J. (1982). *Discourse strategies.* Cambridge, UK: Cambridge University Press.

Gunderson, D. V. (1967). Flaws in research design. *Research in the Teaching of English, 1,* 10–16.

Gutierrez, K. D., & Stone, L. D. (2000). Synchronic and diachronic dimensions of social practice: An emerging methodology for cultural-historical perspectives on literacy learning. In C. D. Lee & P. Smagorinsky (Eds.), *Vygotskian perspectives on literacy research: Constructing meaning through collaborative inquiry* (pp. 150–164). Cambridge, UK: Cambridge University Press.

Guzzetti, B., & Gamboa, M. (2005). Online journaling: The informal writings of two adolescent girls. *Research in the Teaching of English, 40,* 168–206.

Hall, S. (1996). The meaning of New Times. In D. Morley & K.-H. Chen (Eds.), *Stuart Hall: Critical dialogues in cultural studies* (pp.223–237). New York: Routledge. (Original work published 1989)

Hamel, F. (2003). Teacher understanding of student understanding: Revising the gap between teachers' conceptions and students' ways with literature. *Research in the Teaching of English, 38,* 49–84.

Hamilton-Wieler, S. (1988). Empty echoes of Dartmouth: Dissonance between the rhetoric and the reality. *Writing Instructor, 8,* 29–41.

Hamm, D., & Pearson, P. D. (2002). Reading-comprehension processes. In B. J. Guzzetti (Ed.), *Literacy in America: An encyclopedia of history, theory, and practice* (pp. 508–515). Santa Barbara, CA: ABC-CLIO.

Harris, J. (1991) After Dartmouth. *College English, 53,* 631–646.

Hartman, P. (2006). "Loud on the inside": Working-class girls, gender, and literacy. *Research in the Teaching of English, 41,* 82–117.

Hayes, J. R., & Flower, L. S. (1980). Identifying the organization of writing processes. In L. W. Gregg & E. R. Steinberg (Eds.), *Cognitive processes in writing* (pp. 31–50). Hillsdale, NJ: Lawrence Erlbaum.

Heath, S. B. (1983). *Ways with words: Language, life, and work in communities and classrooms.* Cambridge, UK: Cambridge University Press.

Henry, G. (1966). English teaching encounters science. *College English, 28,* 220, 229–235.

Henry, G. (1984). The council: How shall it survive? *College English, 46,* 668–678.

Hill, F. (1898). Conference on uniform entrance requirements in English. *School Review, 6,* 745–746.

Hillocks, G. (1984). What works in composition: A meta-analysis of experimental treatment studies. *American Journal of Education, 93,* 133–170.

Hillocks, G. (1999). *Ways of thinking: Ways of teaching.* New York: Teachers College Press.

Hillocks, G. (2006). Middle and high school composition. In P. Smagorinsky, *Research on composition: Multiple perspectives on two decades of change* (pp. 48–77). New York: Teachers College Press.

Hillocks, G. (2007). *Narrative writing: Learning a new model for teaching.* Portsmouth, NH: Heinemann.

Hirsch, E. D. (1987). *Cultural literacy: What every American needs to know.* Boston: Houghton Mifflin.

Hirsch, E. D. (1996). *The schools we need and why we don't have them.* New York: Doubleday.

Hook, J. N. (1979). *A long way together: A personal view of NCTE's first sixty-seven years.* Urbana, IL: National Council of Teachers of English.

Hosic, J. F. (Compiler). (1912). The influence of the uniform entrance requirements in English. *English Journal, 1,* 95–121.

Hosic, J. F. (Compiler). (1917). *Reorganization of English in secondary schools: A report by the national joint committee on English representing the Commission on the Reorganization of Secondary Education of the National Education Association and the National Council of Teachers of English* (Bureau of Education Bulletin No. 2). Washington, DC: Government Printing Office.

Hull, G. A., & Katz, M-L. (2006). Crafting an agentive self: Case studies of digital storytelling. *Research in the Teaching of English, 41,* 43-81.

Hull, G. A., & Nelson, M. E. (2005). Locating the semiotic power of multimodality. *Written Communication, 22,* 224–261.

Hull, G. A., & Schultz, K. (2002). *School's out! Bridging out-of-school literacies with classroom practice.* New York: Teachers College Press.

Hunt, K. (1965). *Grammatical structures written at three grade levels.* Urbana, IL: National Council of Teachers of English.

Hunting, R. (1967). Recent studies of writing frequency. *Research in the Teaching of English, 1,* 29–40.

Hymes, D. (1977). *Foundations of sociolinguistics: An ethnographic approach.* London: Tavistock.

Jewitt, C., & Kress, G. (Eds.). (2003). *Multimodal literacy.* New York: Peter Lang.

Johnson, T. S., Smagorinsky, P., Thompson, L., & Fry, P. G. (2003). Learning to teach the five-paragraph theme. *Research in the Teaching of English, 38,* 136–176.

Kalantzis, M., Cope, B., & the Learning by Design Project Group. (2005). *Learning by design.* Melbourne, Australia, and Altona, Australia: Victorian Schools Innovation Commission and Common Ground.

Kennedy, M. M. (1997). The connection between research and practice. *Educational Researcher, 26*(7), 4–12.

Kennedy, M. M. (1999). A test of some common contentions about educational research. *American Educational Research Journal, 36,* 511–541.

Kerr, M. E. (1987). *Night kites.* New York: HarperTeen.

Kintsch, W. (1998). *Comprehension: A paradigm for cognition.* Cambridge, UK: Cambridge University Press.

Knobel, M., & Lankshear, C. (2006). Weblog worlds and constructions of effective and powerful writing: Cross with care, and only where signs permit. In K. Pahl & J. Rowsell (Eds.), *Travel notes from the new literacy studies: Instances of practice* (pp. 72–92). Clevedon, UK: Multilingual Matters.

Knobel, M., & Lankshear, C. (Eds.). (2007). *A new literacies sampler.* New York: Peter Lang.

Kress, G. (2000). "You've just got to learn how to see": Curriculum subjects, young people and schooled engagement with the world. *Linguistics and Education, 11,* 401–415.

Kress, G. (2003). *Literacy in the new media age.* NY: Routledge.

Kress, G., Jewitt, C., Bourne, J., Franks, A., Hardcastle, J., Jones, K., et al. (2005). *English in urban classrooms: A multimodal perspective on teaching and learning.* London: Routledge/Falmer.

Kress, G., Jewitt, C., & Tsatsarelis, C. (2000). Knowledge, identity, pedagogy: Pedagogic discourse and the representational environments of education in late modernity. *Linguistics and Education, 11,* 7–30.

Labov, W. (1972). *Language in the inner city: Studies in Black English vernacular.* Philadelphia: University of Pennsylvania Press.

Ladson-Billings, G. (1994). *The dreamkeepers: Successful teachers of African American children.* San Francisco: Jossey-Bass.

Lam, W. S. E. (2004). Second language socialization in a bilingual chat room: Global and local considerations. *Language Learning and Technology, 8*(2), 44–65.

Lam, W. S. E. (2006a). Culture and learning in the context of globalization: Research directions. *Review of Research in Education, 30,* 213–237.

Lam, W. S. E. (2006b). Re-envisioning language, literacy, and the immigrant subject in new mediascapes. *Pedagogies: An International Journal, 1,* 171–195.

Lave, J., & Wenger, E. (1991). *Situated learning: Legitimate peripheral participation.* Cambridge, UK: Cambridge University.

Leander, K., & McKim, K. K. (2003). Tracing the everyday "sitings" of adolescents on the Internet: A strategic adaptation of ethnography across online and offline spaces. *Education, Communication & Information, 3,* 211–240.

Leander, K. & Sheehy, M. (Eds.). (2004). *Spatializing literacy research and practice.* New York: Peter Lang.

Lee, C. D. (1993). *Signifying as a scaffold for literary interpretation: The pedagogical implications of an African American discourse genre* (NCTE Research Report No. 26). Urbana, IL: National Council of Teachers of English.

Lee, C. D. (2001). Is October Brown Chinese? A cultural modeling activity system for underachieving students. *American Educational Research Journal, 38,* 97–142.

Lee, C. D. (2007a). *Culture, literacy, and learning: Taking bloom in the midst of the whirlwind.* New York: Teachers College Press.

Lee, C. D. (2007b). Foreword. In G. Hillocks, *Narrative writing: Learning a new model for teaching* (pp. vii-xi). Portsmouth, NH: Heinemann.

Lee, C. D., & Smagorinsky, P. (Eds.). (2000). *Vygotskian perspectives on literacy research: Constructing meaning through collaborative inquiry.* Cambridge, UK: Cambridge University Press.

Lewis, C., & Fabos, B. (2005). Instant messaging, literacies, and social identities. *Reading Research Quarterly, 40,* 470–501.

Lewis, E. G. (1970). Postscript to Dartmouth—Or poles apart. In L. Joseph & E. Steinberg (Eds.), *English education today* (pp.616–629). New York: Noble and Noble.

Lloyd-Jones, R., & Lunsford, A. (Eds.). (1989). *The English coalition conference: Democracy through language.* Urbana, IL, and New York: National Council of Teachers of English and Modern Language Association.

Loban, W. (1976). *Language development: Kindergarten through grade twelve* (Research Report No. 18). Urbana, IL: National Council of Teachers of English.

Luke, A. (1998). Getting over method: Literacy teaching as work in "New Times." *Language Arts, 73,* 305-313.

Luke, A. (2004a). Teaching after the market: From commodity to cosmopolitan. *Teachers College Record, 106,* 1422-1433.

Luke, A. (2004b). The trouble with English. *Research in the Teaching of English, 39,* 85–95.

Macbeth, D. (2003). Hugh Mehan's *Learning Lessons* reconsidered: On the differences between the naturalistic and critical analysis of classroom discourse. *American Educational Research Journal, 40,* 239–280.

Mahiri, J. (2004). Researching teaching practices: "Talking the talk" versus "walking the walk." *Research in the Teaching of English, 38,* 467–471.

Mahiri, J. (Ed.). (2005). *What they don't learn in school: Literacy in the lives of urban youth.* New York: Peter Lang.

Marckwardt, A. H. (1970). The Dartmouth seminar. In L. Joseph & E. Steinberg (Eds.), *English education today* (pp. 630–636). New York: Noble and Noble.

Marshall, J. D. (2000). Research on response to literature. In M. Kamil, P. Mosenthal, P. D. Pearson, & R. Barr (Eds.). *Handbook of reading research* (Vol. III, pp. 381–402). Mahwah, NJ: Ablex.

Marshall, J. D., Smagorinsky, P., & Smith, M. W. (1995). *The language of interpretation: Patterns of discourse in discussions of literature* (NCTE Research Report No. 27). Urbana, IL: National Council of Teachers of English.

Meacham, S. J. (2000–2001). Literacy at the crossroads: Movement, connection, and communication within the research literature on literacy and cultural diversity. *Review of Research in Education, 25,* 181–208.

Meckel, H. (1963). Research on teaching composition and literature. In N. L. Gage (Ed.), *Handbook of research on teaching* (pp. 966–1006). Chicago: Rand McNally for American Educational Research Association.

Mehan, H. (1979). *Learning lessons.* Cambridge, MA: Harvard University Press.

Meyer, B. J. F. (1975). *The organization of prose and its effects on memory.* Amsterdam: North Holland.

Michaels, S., & Cazden, C. (1986). Teacher-child collaboration as oral preparation for literacy. In B. B. Schieffelin (Ed.), *The acquisition of literacy: Ethnographic perspectives* (pp. 132–154). Norwood, NJ: Ablex.

Mitchell-Kernan, C. (1973). Signifying. In A. Dundes (Ed.), *Mother wit from the laughing barrel: Readings in the interpretation of Afro-American folklore* (pp. 310–328). Englewood Cliffs, NJ: Prentice Hall.

Mohr, M., Rogers, C., Sanford, B., Nocerino, M., MacLean, M., & Clawson, S. (2004). *Teacher research for better schools.* New York: Teachers College Press.

Moje, E., & Lewis, C. (2007). Examining opportunities to learn literacy: The role of critical sociocultural literacy research. In C. Lewis, P. Enciso, & E. B. Moje (Eds.), *Reframing sociocultural research on literacy: Identity, agency, and power* (pp. 15–48). Mahwah, NJ: Lawrence Erlbaum.

Morrell, E. (2004a). *Becoming critical researchers: Literacy and empowerment for urban youth.* New York: Peter Lang.

Morrell, E. (2004b). *Linking literacy and popular culture: Finding connections for lifelong learning.* Norwood, MA: Christopher-Gordon.

Muller, H. J. (1967). *The uses of English.* New York: Holt, Rinehart, and Winston.

Musspratt, S., Luke, A., & Freebody, P. (Eds.). (1997). *Constructing critical literacies: Teaching and learning textual practice.* Cresskill, NJ: Hampton.

National Center for Education Statistics. (2007). *The condition of education: Participation in education.* Retrieved August 23, 2007, from http://nces.ed.gov/programs/coe/2007/section1/indicator05.asp

National Council of Teachers of English. (1961). *The national interest and the teaching of English: A report on the status of the profession.* Urbana, IL: Author.

National Council of Teachers of English. (2007). *Squire Office for Policy Research in English Language Arts.* Retrieved July 19, 2007, from http://www.ncte.org/edpolicy

National Education Association Commission on the Reorganization of Secondary Education. (1918). *Cardinal principles of secondary education.* Washington, DC: National Education Association.

National Writing Project. (2007). *Teacher research/inquiry.* Retrieved August 1, 2007, from http://www.nwp.org/cs/public/print/resource_topic/teacher_research_inquiry

New London Group. (1996). A pedagogy of multiliteracies: Designing social futures. *Harvard Educational Review, 66,* 60–92.

Newell, A., & Simon, H. A. (1972). *Human problem solving.* Englewood Cliffs, NJ: Prentice Hall.

Nystrand, M. (1997). *Opening dialogue: Understanding the dynamics of language and learning in the English classroom.* New York: Teachers College Press.

Nystrand, M., Greene, S., & Wiemelt, J. (1993). Where did composition studies come from? An intellectual history. *Written Communication, 10,* 267–333.

Olson, C. B., & Land, R. (2007). A cognitive strategies approach to reading and writing instruction for English language learners in secondary school. *Research in the Teaching of English, 41,* 269–303.

Pappenheimer, R. (2004). What's real about imagination? In Brookline Teacher Researcher Seminar (Ed.), *Regarding children's words* (pp. 85–105). New York: Teachers College Press.

Peters, W. H., & the Conference on English Education Commission on Research in Teacher Effectiveness. (1987). *Effective English teaching: Concept, research, and practice.* Urbana, IL: National Council of Teachers of English.

Petty, W. T. (1983). *A history of the National Conference on Research in English.* Urbana, IL: National Council of Teachers of English for National Conference on Research in English.

Potter, R. (1967). Sentence structure and prose quality: An exploratory study. *Research in the Teaching of English, 1,* 17–28.

Prendergast, C. (2003). *Literacy and racial justice: The politics of learning after* Brown vs. Board of Education. Carbondale: Southern Illinois University Press.

Prior, P. (1998). Contextualizing instructors' responses to writing in the college classroom. In N. Nelson & R. Calfee (Eds.), *The reading-writing connection: Yearbook of the National Society for the Study of Education* (pp. 153–177). Chicago: University of Chicago Press.

Purves, A. (1981). *Reading and literature: American achievement in international perspective.* Urbana, IL: National Council of Teachers of English.

Purves, A. (1984). NCTE: The house of intellect or Spencer gifts. *College English, 46,* 693–696.

Putney, L., & Green, J. (in press). The roots and routes of teacher-based action research and curriculum inquiry: An historical perspective. In B. McGaw, P. L. Peterson, & E. Baker (Eds.), *International encyclopedia of education* (3rd ed.). Amsterdam: Elsevier.

Quoroz, P. A. (2001). The silencing of Latino student "voice": Puerto Rican and Mexican narratives in eighth grade and high school. *Anthropology and Education Quarterly, 32,* 326–349.

Ransom, J. C. (1941). *The new criticism.* Norfolk, CT: New Directions.

Rex, L., Green, J., Dixon, C., & the Santa Barbara Classroom Discourse Group. (1998). What counts when context counts: The uncommon "common" language of literacy research. *Journal of Literacy Research, 30,* 405–433.

Richards, I. A. (1929). *Practical criticism: A study of literary judgment.* New York: Harcourt, Brace and World.

Rosenblatt, L. M. (1938). *Literature as exploration.* New York: Modern Language Association.

Rowsell, J., & Pahl, K. (2007). Sedimented identities in texts: Instances of practice. *Reading Research Quarterly, 42,* 388–404.

Sarbin, T. R. (1986). The narrative as a root metaphor for psychology. In T. R. Sarbin (Ed.), *Narrative psychology* (pp. 3–21). New York: Praeger.

Scardamalia, M., & Bereiter, C. (1986). Research on written composition. In M. Wittrock (Ed.), *Handbook of research on teaching* (3rd ed., pp. 778–803). New York: Macmillan.

Scherff, L., & Kaplan, J. (2006). Reality check: A teacher educator returns home. *Studying Teacher Education, 2*, 155–167.

Scherff, L., & Piazza, C. (2005). The more things change, the more they stay the same: A survey of high school students' writing experiences. *Research in the Teaching of English, 39*, 271–310.

Schoenbach, R., Greenleaf, C., Cziko, C., & Hurwitz, L. (1999). *Reading for understanding*. San Francisco: Jossey-Bass.

Schultz, K., Buck, P., & Niesz, T. (2005). Authoring "race": Writing truth and fiction after school. *Urban Review: Issues and Ideas in Public Education, 37*, 469–489.

Schultz, K., & Fecho, B. (2005). Literacies in adolescence: An analysis of policies from the United States and Queensland, Australia. In N. Bascia, A. Cumming, A. Datnow, K. Leithwood, & D. Livington (Eds.), *International handbook for educational policy* (pp. 677–694). Amsterdam, Netherlands: Kluwer Academic.

Scott, F. N. (1901). College entrance requirements in English. *School Review, 9*, 365–378.

Scott, F. N. (1909). What the West wants in preparatory English. *School Review, 17*, 10–20.

Scribner, S., & Cole, M. (1981). *The psychology of literacy*. Cambridge, MA: Harvard University Press.

Sefton-Green, J. (2006). Youth, technology, and media cultures. *Review of Research in Education, 30*, 279–306.

Shannon, P. (2001). Turn, turn, turn: Language education, politics, and freedom at the turn of three centuries. In P. Shannon (Ed.), *Becoming political, too: New readings and writings on the politics of literacy education* (pp. 10–30). Portsmouth, NH: Heinemann.

Shulman, L. (1987). Knowledge and teaching: Foundations of the new reform. *Harvard Educational Review, 57*, 1–22.

Sinclair, J. M., & Coulthard, R. M. (1975). *Towards an analysis of discourse: The English used by teachers and pupils*. London: Oxford University Press.

Smagorinsky, P., & Coppock, J. (1995). The reader, the text, the context: An exploration of a choreographed response to literature. *Journal of Reading Behavior, 27*, 271–298.

Smith, M. W., & Connolly, B. (2005). The effects interpretive authority on classroom discussions of poetry: Lessons from one teacher. *Communication Education, 54*, 271–288.

Smitherman, G. (1977). *Talkin and testifyin: The language of Black America*. Detroit, MI: Wayne State University Press.

Smitherman, G. (1994). The blacker the berry the sweeter the juice: African American student writers. In A. H. Dyson & C. Genishi (Eds.), *The need for story: Cultural diversity in classroom and community*. Urbana, IL: National Council of Teachers of English.

Spalding, W. B. (1963). Review of *Handbook of Research on Teaching. Journal of Teacher Education, 14*, 346–350.

Sperling, M. (1998). Teachers as readers of student writing. In N. Nelson & R. Calfee (Eds.), *The reading-writing connection: Yearbook of the National Society for the Study of Education* (pp. 131–152). Chicago: University of Chicago Press.

Sperling, M. (2004). Is contradiction contrary? In A. Ball & S. W. Freedman (Eds.), *Bakhtinian perspectives on language, literacy, and learning* (pp. 232–251). Cambridge, UK: Cambridge University Press.

Sperling, M., & Freedman, S. W. (2001). Research on writing. In V. Richardson (Ed.), *Handbook of research on teaching* (4th ed., pp. 370–389). Washington, DC: American Educational Research Association.

Squire, J. (1964). *The responses of adolescents while reading four short stories* (Research Report No. 2). Champaign, IL: National Council of Teachers of English.

Squire, J. (1982). The collision of the basics movement with current research in writing and language. In G. Hillocks (Ed.), *The English curriculum under fire: What are the real basics?* (pp. 29–37). Urbana, IL: National Council of Teachers of English.

Squire, J., & Britton, J. (1975). Foreword. In J. Dixon, *Growth through English set in the perspective of the seventies* (pp. vii–xviii). London: NATE/Oxford.

Stallworth, B. J., Gibbons, L., & Fauber, L. (2006). It's not on the list: An exploration of teachers' perspectives on using multicultural literature. *Journal of Adolescent and Adult Literacy, 49,* 478–489.

Stein, P. (2004). Representation, rights, and resources: Multimodal pedagogies in the language and literacy classroom. In B. Norton & K. Toohey (Eds.), *Critical pedagogies and language learning* (pp. 95–115). Cambridge, UK: Cambridge University Press.

Stein, P. (2007). *Multimodal pedagogies in diverse classrooms: Representation, rights and resources.* New York: Routledge.

Steinberg, E. R. (1963). *Needed research in the teaching of English.* Proceedings of Project English research conference, Carnegie Institute of Technology, Pittsburgh, PA. (ERIC Document Reproduction Service No. ED020154)

Stiff, R. (1967). The effect upon student composition of particular correction techniques. *Research in the Teaching of English, 1,* 54–75.

Stock, P. L. (2005). 2004 NCTE presidential address: Practicing the scholarship of teaching. What we do with the knowledge we make. *College English, 68,* 107–121.

Tierney, R. J., & Pearson, P. D. (1983). Toward a composing model of reading. *Language Arts, 60,* 568–580.

Treuba, H. T., Guthrie, G. P., & Au, K. H. P. (Eds.). (1981). *Culture and the bilingual classroom: Studies in classroom ethnography.* Rowley, MA: Newbury House.

U.S. Department of Education. (2007). *U.S. Department of Education: Promoting educational excellence for all Americans.* Washington, DC: Author. Retrieved April 22, 2007, from http://www.ed.gov/index.jhtml

Underwood, T., Yoo, M., & Pearson, P. D. (2006). *Understanding reading comprehension in secondary schools through the lens of the Four Resources Model.* Retrieved August 7, 2007, from http://seedsofscience.org/PDFs/UnderstandingReadingComp.pdf

University of Arizona College of Education. (2007). *Research initiative on preparing teachers for Mexican American students.* Tucson, AZ: Author. Retrieved August 6, 2007, from http://coe.arizona.edu/pages/dep_tte/researchinitiative.php

Vasquez, O. A. (2006). Cross-national explorations of sociocultural research on learning. *Review of Research in Education, 30,* 33–64.

Vygotsky, L. S. (1978). *Mind in society.* Cambridge, MA: Harvard University Press.

Warschauer, M. (2006). *Laptops and literacy: Learning in the wireless classroom.* New York: Teachers College Press.

Wertsch, J. (1985). *Vygotsky and the social formation of mind.* Cambridge, MA: Harvard University Press.

Wertsch, J. (1991). *Voices of the mind: A sociocultural approach to mediated action.* Cambridge, MA: Harvard University Press.

Wraga, W. (2001). A progressive legacy squandered: The "Cardinal Principles" report reconsidered. *History of Education Quarterly, 41,* 494–519.

Yagelski, R. (2006). English education. In B. McComiskey (Ed.), *English studies: An introduction to the discipline(s)* (pp. 275–319). Urbana, IL: National Council of Teachers of English.

Zeichner, K., & Nofke, S. (2001). Practitioner research. In V. Richardson (Org.), *Handbook of research on teaching* (pp. 298–330). Washington, DC: American Educational Research Association.

Zeuli, J. (1994). How do teachers understand research when they read it? *Teaching and Teacher Education, 10,* 39–55.

Chapter 4

Narratives of Nation-State, Historical Knowledge, and School History Education

BRUCE VANSLEDRIGHT
University of Maryland, College Park

In spring of 2006, the Florida state legislature, in a virtually unprecedented step, chose to make how U.S. history is taught a matter of public policy. The Florida omnibus bill contained the sentence,

American history shall be viewed as factual, not as constructed, shall be viewed as knowable, teachable, and testable, and shall be defined as the creation of a new nation based largely on the universal principles stated in the Declaration of Independence. (Florida House of Representatives, 2006, p. 44.)

Apparently, protecting the hallowed ground of the nation-building story of American history from threatening forces prompted state policymakers to legislate its protection. Such a move provoked yet another in a decades-old raft of reactions, accusations, and criticisms from across the political spectrum.[1]

Why all the fuss, a reasonable observer might ask, and to what end? This, of course, is itself a historical question. And of course, an answer would beg a response that includes a multitude of causes. In this review, I attempt to address the question in a series of broad but also specific strokes. I begin by suggesting that in the United States, for example, late 20th century immigration patterns have been perceived by some who consider themselves American natives because they were born in the country (even though their ancestors are of European stock) as threatening to soften the glue that preserves their vision of the right and true American culture. In 2006, the U.S. Census Bureau estimated that there were approximately 34.3 million foreign-born persons (largely from Mexico) living in a country of 300 million people, or about 11.4% of the U.S. population. Contrast that with 1967, when there were 200 million people in the United States, of whom only 4.8% (9.7 million) were foreign born (largely from Italy). Recently, the idea about erecting a giant wall along the U.S.-Mexico border—ostensibly

Review of Research in Education
February 2008, Vol. 32, pp. 109–146
DOI: 10.3102/0091732X07311065
© 2008 AERA. http://rre.aera.net

to stop the flow of *indocumentados* into Arizona, Texas, New Mexico, and California—was bandied about. In 1998, California citizens voted to require public school teachers to use only English in their classes. Other states pursued similar policies (e.g., Arizona in 2000 and Massachusetts in 2002). Such efforts have long been part of the cultural landscape in the United States. American "nativists" challenged immigration policies in the late 19th century and again after the First World War.

To explore the role changes in immigration patterns may play in how public school history education is shaped, understood, taught, and with what consequences in the United States—the larger focus of this review—I examine selective recent historical scholarship in that vein. After briefly attending to this scholarship as a means of providing some historical context, I move to analyzing what often passes for U.S. history education in American grade-school classrooms—a narrative of national development and progress. I rely on textbook research literature and that which comes from classroom studies of how U.S. history is taught. In this effort, I ask, what exactly does an Americanizing narrative or (hi)story contain? How does *a* story become *the* story; that is, how is that story authorized? How is it then promulgated? I summarize how scholarship attends to these questions by drawing on selected work related to history education as heritage and collective memory, noting that history—in the sense that it is practiced in the discipline—is rarely taught at all in public grade schools.

Then, using additional research on teaching and learning U.S. history, I turn to considering a series of consequences that stem from asking children and young adults to accept a collectively memorialized nation-building story as their own, as a part of their cultural identity. In particular, I labor to show that the U.S. nation-building story that sits at the center of how most children are taught and learn in history classes in American public schools is largely a prescriptive and conserving one that often molds and shapes in particular ways. I finish up by exploring alternative conceptions of history education, ones that might result if educators pursued different visions of what such an education might accomplish.

IMMIGRATION HISTORY AND NATION BUILDING

It is not difficult to surmise a role for history education in the current iteration of the ebbing and flowing immigration drama. The U.S. nation-building story at the center of what often passes for history education has long been considered pivotal in "Americanizing" the "unwashed," "the outsiders," and the otherwise naïve (read children in general). Countries all over the planet use them to shape the identities of their citizens.[2] Historian Gary Gerstle (1997a), a scholar who has studied immigration patterns and histories in the United States, has argued that some coercion is typically involved in such a process. The public school in the United States can serve as a powerful force in attempting to detach outsiders and the naïve from their culturally "unacceptable" and "alien" customs and teaching them appropriate "American ways" to think and behave. Repetition of the American nation-building story in U.S. history classes in grade school functions as one potentially productive vehicle.

To become an American then requires that one know and be able to repeat this story, what the late Arthur Schlesinger Jr. (after Gunnar Myrdal) once termed the "American Creed" (Schlesinger, 1991). But customs and traditions are seldom elided or displaced with others without struggle. And those who advocate for the importance of thoroughly "Americanizing" the hordes believe that the struggle is more than worth fighting, as recent efforts at national immigration "reform" and legislative events in Florida have attested. In some measure, cultural disputes more broadly and the dustups over the history curriculum more specifically represent a range of battles along this horizon of struggle. Policymakers and average American citizens themselves often disagree about the amount of coercion that should be used in "Americanizing" the masses. They also quarrel over what the term *American*, and therefore *Americanizing*, might mean.

Building and maintaining a nation state has long been a precarious undertaking in the United States (and, of course, in other countries as well[3]). As a nation of immigrants—some voluntary, others forced—it has been difficult to construct and maintain a sense of national community. Disparate peoples, and their different customs that give shape to and have shaped the nation's past, present opportunities for conflict at almost every turn. Holding together such difference under the banner of "one nation" gave rise to the American Civil War in the 19th century. It brought on Jim Crow laws in the South and de facto segregation in the North in the wake of that Civil War. It forced indigenous American Indians onto reservations. It spawned the Red Scare and its attendant repressive policies of "100% Americanism" following World War I. It produced reactionary immigration quotas in the 1920s, and such quotas and other measures are being considered again in the early 21st century. Following September 11, 2001, it birthed an anti-Islamic backlash that targeted American citizens of Middle Eastern descent as potential enemies of state. It also brought on a new desire for a form of 21st-century 100% Americanism, perhaps epitomized best by Chevrolet-produced pickup trucks with an American flag and *God Bless America* emblazoned across the rear window. Although the United States as nation-state was founded on such ideals as justice before the law; one person, one vote; and a panoply of rights for individual citizens and propertied interests, those ideals sometimes have been abdicated to serve the interests of maintaining the nation-state itself.

Immigration historian Gerstle (1997b) argues that despite a nod to liberty and pursuits of happiness, "Our history suggests that building a national community depends on repression and exclusion" (p. 576) and manifests such coercions in both civic and ethnoracial spheres.[4] In a debate with historian David Hollinger (1997) on the possibility of what Hollinger calls a postethnic America, in which citizens would be free to pursue any identity they desired without repercussion, he accepts Hollinger's argument that a common culture is shaped by both liberal political principles and anthropological phenomena such as shared customs, music, and language. However, Gerstle (1997b) observes,

American nationalism has also derived its power from its ability to exclude and denigrate others. Within our borders, Indians, blacks, Tories, Irish Catholics, Asians, southern and eastern Europeans, Communists, anarchists, homosexuals, and even monopolists and "plutocrats" have served as "others" against whom "we" have defined our Americanness. (p. 577)

He then notes that, despite some success at expanding the reach of democratic principles, throughout much of the 20th century, the United States has either been at war or on the brink of it about 80% of the time and ponders how such wars or threats of war serve "to stoke the engines of American nationalism" (p. 576), as proponents and caretakers further the nation-building and maintenance project. He even wonders if the United States could "build a cohesive national community without a war or a common internal enemy" (p. 576). With an uncanny prescience, Gerstle predicts the need for new prospects in the early 21st century that could be served up as enemies against whom "we" would define ourselves. These prospects, of course, turned out to be the Taliban, Saddam Hussein, insurgent Iraqis, and more recently, immigrant Latinos and Latinas.

The historiographical myths of the great American melting pot and Americanization-as-emancipation promulgated by Hector St. John de Crevecoeur (1782/1912) and his followers gave way to the new immigration scholarship of Robert Park and colleagues (Park & Miller, 1921) in the 1930s and Oscar Handlin (1951/1973) in the 1950s. The latter moved away from the Crevecoeurian emancipation motif by noting how culturally disruptive and potentially coercive being an immigrant to America was. After about 1980, some historians of the Park and Handlin schools of thought returned again to the idea that, although often difficult and intrusive to ethnoracial identity formation as immigration could be, Americanization allowed room for newcomers to exercise agency and forge an identity of their desire.[5] In some respects, Hollinger's (1995) work in his book *Postethnic America* imagines a country in which the Crevecoeurian notion held greater currency. Thus, Hollinger shares some space with the historians who are attracted to maintaining such notions.

However, for other historians of Americanization processes, the 1960s ushered in a radical shift in the historiographical scholarship regarding the workings of immigration, ethnicity, and identity development.[6] The post-1960 historians began to look more deeply at the consequences of being an immigrant in America, at the culturally and intellectually coercive effects immigrants endured and to what end. These historians probed more deeply into how immigrants and American ethnics considered on the margins of mainstream culture (e.g., African Americans, Japanese Americans) encountered and dealt with the ruptures, uprootedness, and difficulties they experienced.[7] They concluded in various ways that Americanization, rather than being emancipatory, was likely to be experienced as more coercive than even benign: ethnoracial inventiveness battling to override powerful normative and legal constraint, and individual agency fighting to overcome unyielding institutional and structural impediment. Gerstle (1997a) describes the effect as being a result of "the complex and contradictory nature of the Americanizing process" (p. 547), one that beckons those who seek to possess the American creed with the promise of liberty and its pursuit while often erecting barriers that can fence off the place in which it can occur in ways that render its achievement onerous at best, impossible at worst. And such contradictory forces can arise under a variety of conditions.

Similar conditions, no doubt, exist in many nations around the globe.[8] Presently, the struggles around them have become particularly visceral in the United States, something a number of Americanist historians (and others) have been working to describe.

GRADE SCHOOL HISTORY EDUCATION

If we accept this treatment of the immigration–Americanization scholarship, one that demonstrates greater sensitivity to complexity in identity formation and presents more balance between the upbeat Crevecoeurian account and the dour Handlinian version, then it would be fair to ask how the historiography has reshaped the American story that attendees at U.S. schools are asked to learn. Has the narrative line or history (one might say *high*-story) of national development been influenced by this recent historical scholarship? Does the narrative arc reflect this more balanced emancipation– coercion dialectic?

These are difficult questions to answer with any precision, for it would be impossible to know for certain what the narrative sweep is in the hundreds of thousands of U.S. history classes taught across the country in any given year or whether all students encounter a narrative at all. Nonetheless, we can infer the story from several different sources. The U.S. history textbook that remains ubiquitous in these courses offers up opportunities to assess the nature of the narrative of nation building and state development. Research on what students are taught in such courses, both of the case variety and large sample, also presents occasions to examine the story students have opportunities to learn.

U.S. History Textbooks

If schooling in general and a history education in particular are designed in good measure to socialize cultural outsiders and the naïve to the American creed, then perhaps the single most important repository of the nation-building narrative that provides symbolic shape and substance to that creed is the U.S. history textbook. The nature of the narrative it contains shifts and is modified as a function of change with time and, to a degree, who does the textbook authoring. However, work in the field of U.S. history-textbook analysis has demonstrated that despite occasional adjustments, the principal narrative arc of progressive and continuous national development has remained largely impervious to serious amendments.[9]

These books are not stories of various tribes and their fortunes or troubles. Nor are they compilations of eyewitness accounts that chronicle intriguing or lurid events that readers might find engaging. To be sure, the books may contain some of these elements. But in the end, they are typically submerged under the weight of narrating the growth of the nation-state. The arc is predominantly concerned with military, economic, and political processes from British colonization along the Atlantic coast to war for independence with Britain; from early government formation through challenges to the fragility of that government to industrialization; and onto the world wars and the Cold War of the 20th century and victories over Communism and the triumphs of globalized capitalism from the late part of that century and into the next. The story is primarily populated with champions of politics (presidents especially), business (entrepreneurs and CEOs and their technological advancements), and military campaigns (generals). The cast is decidedly Eurocentric, with preferences leaning toward an anchoring in the accomplishments of Anglo-Saxon men.

The primordial theme is Manifest Destiny, that powerful 19th-century idea that the Judeo-Christian God mandated the immigrant Anglo-Saxon "race" to create the

United States, connect it from one coast to the other, advocate for its democratic and capitalist values, and sow liberty and the freedoms carried by assertions of natural rights to all those who would claim its birthright. It is a story that repeatedly forefronts the ideals of America's Founding Fathers. It makes plain that the citizens of the United States grow ever closer to achieving those ideals. Attaining freedom for all is pivotal. The tone is one of gloriousness. Blemishes and heretofore unachieved ideals are glossed in service of that tone. Internecine and racial conflicts and coercive forms of nationalist enforcement are noted but typically in the context of how the United States, by the way it settles these disputes, moves ever closer toward achieving its founding ideals.

In an analysis of the treatment of immigration history in grade-school U.S. history textbooks, Stuart Foster (2006) noted that despite critics' contentions that after about 1970 too much attention was paid to the fortunes and travails of ethnic groups, most of these textbooks continued to traffic in traditional nation-building themes in which freedom is the most powerful motif. The themes were described typically in Anglocentric and conservative terms. Foster maintained that in the last four decades especially, textbook writing practices could be characterized by three phenomena: (a) a focus on the nation-state as the carrier of meaning in which the goal was not to examine or reexamine the American past but to celebrate the nation's achievements, (b) an effort to underplay a long American history of conflict and controversy with special care taken to avoid stirring the caldron of ethnoracial antagonisms, and (c) a marked tendency to deal with issues and historical agents that may be perceived as controversial—with regard to success in realizing national ideals—through a strategy of mentioning previously invisible ethnoracial characters and the organizations they headed. The latter approach hinges on providing such representations largely in service of their contributions to the achievement of mainstream goals in the spirit of Manifest Destiny, achieving freedom, and national political, economic, and military triumphalism.[10]

The United Farm Workers Union, led by Cesar Chavez, and the civil rights movement, led by Dr. King and Malcolm X, in the 20th century, as just two examples, are incorporated into the narrative arc as historical agents and organizations that helped solve ethnoracial and labor conflicts. Such incorporations allow textbook authors to claim favorable treatment toward ethnoracial groups while leaving the larger Anglocentric nationalistic arc undisturbed. Celebratory progress in achieving a "we-ness" trumps a past of ethnoracial conflict and violence. It is a history of success, seldom if at all struggle or failure. A sense of *unum* is wrung from a disconcerting national *pluribus*.

By absorbing animosity, conflict, and struggle into a story of progress in achieving American ideals, textbook authors, and the publishing industry that underwrites their work, co-opt difference and make it part of the American creed. It is a largely symbolic act, one that gains its potency by controlling the definition of terms[11] and demarcating boundaries of Americanness in ways set within prevailing Anglocentric traditions of Manifest Destiny and national progress, often circumscribed by the widening of the franchise and the freedoms so doing provides.

Sociologist Michael Olneck (1989), after historian John Higham (1955/2002), has illustrated, for example, how immigrant contributions are frequently characterized as offerings to America and thus are symbolically uprooted from the ethnoracial contexts in which they originated and are subsequently made distinctly American. In this sense, they can be historically embedded in a textbook narrative of progress, one that demonstrates repeated successes in overcoming the divisiveness and battles that occur over the span of liberty, those that arise when immigrants' customs and behaviors clash with how native-born Americans would otherwise define them. Olneck observes, "It is precisely on this account that the construct of contributions, to the extent that it shapes [Americans'] thinking about the tolerable limits of diversity and pluralism, is exceptionally significant" (p. 419) in the symbolic process of defining Americanism by those who would attempt control of those definitions.

History textbooks, then, play a vital role in the definitional process. Coercion—in the form of co-optation—to Anglocentric tradition, ideals, and values is subtle here, so subtle that it appears disguised in a narrative of expanding liberty, eager inclusion of immigrants' and ethnoracial groups' "offerings," and the disappearance of conflict and division. The books aim to celebrate and proscribe the terms in which the celebration is cast, not to investigate and carefully report on the American past on the basis of available evidence. Because they are the textbooks' principal authors, such results can implicate Americanist historians in a celebratory national-development and nationalistic effort, as historian Donna Gabaccia (1997) has noted.[12]

Another feature of U.S. history textbooks described at length in the analysis literature outlines how authors offer up the narrative in largely omniscient voices.[13] The narrative is presented as though there were no alternative or counternarratives possible. Rhetorical hedges, interpretive dissension, evidence trails, and concerns about conflicting archival sources so common to historical scholarship are typically shorn from the books. This omniscient voice appears to be the voice from everywhere but nowhere simultaneously. It is as though the spirit of Manifest Destiny—the granting of the birthright to settle and control North America by an omniscient God to the Anglo-Saxon visitors of the 17th and 18th centuries—reappears even in the prose and tonal qualities of the symbolic presentation of the narrative.

The narrative voice traffics in freedom, progress, and celebration of national development. The voice that carries the arc appears etched in a timeless quality as though it were awarded by the divine to the authorial chosen. Its power, again, is derived from the authority to symbolically define terms and configure landscapes. That authority has its roots in national beginnings, in the mythologies (symbolically transferred as truths into the books) of nation building and the trials and tribulations faced by those Anglo forefathers who battled many demons and enemies to wrest a distinctive nation-state from the wildernesses of North America. Once conveyed and represented narratively by those with great investments and interests in maintaining the privileges such struggle and success imbue, each generation is effectively charged with a vital legacy to continue the effort to which so much energy was given and for which so much blood was shed.

It may take a few generations before the narrative becomes officialized. Yet myths are reified into truths, oppositional accounts are symbolically co-opted, and omniscient voice constructions come to dominate presentation. At least in the United

States, conflict, controversy, and counternarratives almost always compete for limited space against the prevailing one.[14] However, to the extent that the official narrative is compelling, sounds authoritative, is often repeated, its heroes and seismic turning points routinely celebrated, and is supported by and reified in important social and political institutions (e.g., school), its officialized status remains difficult to challenge. Caretakers find ways to embrace opposition by submerging potentially subversive elements into symbolic "cultural offerings." The officialized narrative, then, becomes a pivotal conduit through which the nation-states' collective memory passes. The authors and publishers of U.S. history textbooks, and the school personnel who authorize and use them, have been engaged fully in this ongoing practice for at least 100 years.[15]

As historians Max Paul Friedman and Padraic Kenney (2005) argue, there are certainly disputes over the visions of history such tomes should present.[16] It is the nature of democratic nation-states to argue over the memories of the past they wish to cherish and repeat to successive generations. However, arguments are rarely between the kinds of evidence-based, archive-driven histories produced by the professional historians and those celebratory myths and legends offered up and maintained by cultural leaders, politicians, and policymakers.[17] Although professional historians aspire to be faithful to the past by being as objective as possible, they rarely if ever achieve this goal, largely because they are cognizant of the fact that as authors, they are implicated in and products of the sociocultural milieu in which their histories are produced.[18]

Yet when these same historians become authors of grade-school history textbooks, a shift occurs. The omniscient authorial tone of these texts conveys a sense that objectivity has been achieved, that the story line narrated is precisely what happened and is therefore ultimately true and beyond dispute. This is precisely the point: "In . . . national contests for power . . . , history becomes a weapon in the struggle for symbolic capital, wielded to acquire legitimacy for one's own side while delegitimizing the opposition," Friedman and Kenney (2005, p. 2) point out. They add that all actors in this drama of creating collective memories "recognize that the past is a rich source of stories, images, metaphors, and 'lessons' that have compelling power over the imagination and can move people to action" (p. 2). History textbooks assist in performing this symbolic function, one that, in the case of the United States, has been turned to the practice of committing to memory and celebrating the Crevecoeurian, progressive, freedoms-based arc described in the textbook-analysis literature.[19]

To those who have explored U.S. history textbooks even casually, none of this would seem surprising. It might be argued as peculiar, though, that in a pluralistic democracy such as the United States, formed out of the cauldron of waves of immigrants and periodically mired in ethnoracial conflict, there would not be more potent and visible long-term competition to reconceptualize U.S. textbook accounts.[20] I would argue that it is just these features—periods of prodigious immigration brought on by changes in commerce and attendant shifts in social stratification globally, a long history of ethnoracial divisiveness, the appearance of more *pluribus* than *unum*—that place significant pressure on textbook authors, publishers, and the marketplace to carefully reiterate a nation-building story characterized by motifs of unification and shared national heritage. Fear that purchase on the American creed might dissolve and disunification would follow remains palpable in U.S. society, as the popularity of books such as Arthur Schlesinger's (1991) *The Disuniting of America* testifies. The palpability of that fear is further illustrated by the battle over the release of standards for U.S. history in 1994. The standards' authors arguably attempted to place more emphasis on recent work in the discipline, the type of more balanced scholarship that Gerstle, for example, describes. This effort was immediately met by a vociferous preemptive attack that suggested in thinly veiled ways that the standards' authors work was un-American at best and anti-American at worst.

The dustup eventually resulted in the U.S. Senate's voting overwhelmingly to reject the standards because they were said to reflect a history of the United States that no good American would recognize.[21] Cultural leaders appear to prefer instead a form of nostalgia. "Nostalgia, with its wistful memories," Michael Kammen (1991) once noted, "is essentially history without guilt" (p. 688). Memories of a heroic, celebratory, freedom-imbued American heritage—historical guilt's apparent antidote—"is something that suffuses us with pride rather than shame. . . . History and memory are not merely fractured. They are frequently at odds" (p. 688). That fractured and divisive relationship was on display in the U.S. Senate the day of the vote on the history standards.

Not all democracies approach history textbooks or history education from a decidedly collective-memory perspective. For example, in England, there is greater emphasis placed on understanding the textbook as only one of many different textual sources to be used to teach the subject in school. Considering the textbook as one account among many appears more consistent with practices in the discipline of history, in which evidence gleaned from multiple sources becomes the site of investigations into the past with the goal of building whatever interpretations such evidence can withstand on close scrutiny. The discipline-centric approach in England appears to be the exception rather than the rule among democratic nation-states.[22]

Teaching U.S. History in School

For their part, teachers of U.S. history typically follow the narrative register framed by the textbooks. Periodic surveys of what students encounter textually in U.S. courses indicate that the textbook plays a predominant role in their history education. In 2002, the U.S. Department of Education reported that 84% of high school students surveyed said they read history textbooks at least once a week, and just more than half that many reported reading them for the most part daily.[23]

In a broad-ranging survey of 158 high school history teachers in the United States, researchers asked them, among other things, what their purposes were for teaching history, what they thought their students should learn, and what their goals were for using source materials in class. Regarding overall purposes, the most frequent response was that they wanted to assist their students in understanding common historical knowledge. Although not saying so directly, that purpose would be directly linked to the textbook, which represented the principal common knowledge source. A key response to the question about what students should learn referred to their efforts at helping the students achieve a degree of mastery of committing the story of America to memory. Again, the broadest account of that story in U.S. history classrooms is the textbook. Nontextbook source materials were primarily used for looking up additional ideas concerning key individuals and events that had been represented in the textbook account.[24]

Such surveys support the image of the U.S. history teacher engaged in a common, long-standing practice of using and covering the vast textbook, occasionally supporting it with additional print materials and visual imagery (films, documentaries), and reinforcing the ideas the textbook conveys with classroom lectures. Larry Cuban (1991) has studied and written extensively about this common practice and noted its resilience in the face of repeated efforts to modify it. He suggests that the resilience of this practice is connected to the cultural assets it provides those who succeed in assisting their students in acquiring a degree of learned mastery of the story of America.

Case studies of U.S. history teachers also bear out this pattern.[25] Teachers feel driven to and are rewarded for covering the textbook, reinforcing its narrative arc in classroom activities, and eventually testing the capacity of their students to recall elements of the story line, when things occurred, and who the central characters were as ostensible measures of their facility with that story line.[26] To follow a much different tack would be at least to appear as veering off the path of transmitting the collective memory to the young and the cultural outsiders and, as a result, to have failed in the important mission of properly socializing them to the story that binds Americans together. At worst, one could be labeled as a "disunifier," especially if multiple story lines were introduced and it was not made clear, at least eventually, that the account represented in the textbook was the best one to commit to memory.[27] Teachers also face growing pressure from accountability forces outside the immediate province of their classrooms and schools (through tests and surveillance) to faithfully present the account officialized in the textbook and underpinned by state-level curriculum and learning standards.[28]

A few history teachers in the United States report studies in which their teaching practices have defied the norm.[29] They approach history more in the tradition of common practice in England, where a reliance on the activities that occur within the discipline of history is more prevalent. These history teachers—operating in part outside or at the margins of the school community and its sanctioned practices—approach history education with a much different vision in mind. History as story or narrative is understood as an outcome of disciplined investigation into the relics and sources and archival materials surviving from the past. These *residua* provide evidence for what can or cannot be said about that past. Because relics and sources seldom speak in unified ways and suffer from breaks and ruptures that require investigative imagination to fill, and because historical investigators cannot fully shed their various present temporal bearings, histories end up being multiple, partial, unstable, and prone to revision.

To learn to understand history this way requires particular epistemological commitments and complex cognitive and analytic capacities. History teachers who teach their students with these ideas in mind find the celebratory account encapsulated between the covers of the typical history textbook problematic. They teach it, much as they do in England, as one of many sources and without any special elevated authority. However, the literature suggests that such teachers are exceptionally rare in grade-school classrooms, frequently associate actively in different communities (colleges and universities), hold more powerful affiliations to them than to the grade-school cultures in which they teach, and therefore are perceived to be cultural outsiders who may be partially (or fully) immune to faithfully teaching the sanctioned form of collective memory. They are remarkable primarily because of their rarity.

And Histories Away From School

Textbooks, teachers, and schooling can be important influences in socializing and shaping the identities of U.S. students to the American creed and its collective memories. However, students have opportunities to learn powerful lessons in that vein from a plethora of sources outside of school and history courses.[30] Mass culture in America is littered with references to the narrative register of freedom triumphant, predictable progress, and democratic and capitalistic norms and values. Political holidays appear regularly on the calendar. Heroes are celebrated, with the American "pioneer" and the "patriot" being the most primal.[31] Leaders extol the virtues of "we, the people" and the oneness of the American spirit. Interest groups such as Daughters of the American Revolution and think tanks such as the American Heritage Institute clamor for news, influence, and public attention. Presidents on national television exhort citizens to overcome their woes and fears and take advantage of American freedom by going shopping. The American creed and its manifold mass-cultural accoutrement are omnipresent, reinforcing and reinforced by the story line repeated in school.

AMERICANIZATION AS SOCIALIZATION BY NECESSITY

To be sure, public school personnel in a nation-state have an obligation to society to assist in the process of socializing their charges to its dominant ways of thinking, understanding, and behaving. The young in general and the young of newcomers and outsiders in particular if, for example, they are to acclimate successfully to a culture where rule by law with enforcement by elected legal authorities is central to social norms, must learn how it operates, what rights and responsibilities individuals possess with regard to the law, and how its evolution has been shaped by history. For some who have had no experience or history with rule-by-law governance, the liberties afforded by natural rights, and democratic practices, public schooling may be perhaps the most effective way of socializing behavior and instilling understandings that can lead to responsible social participation. It is hard to imagine that this process would occur without some degree of ideological and intellectual coercion, especially for those whose experience and customs run counter to this way of public life.

What passes for history education in public schools can and does perform a vital role in this ideological and intellectual shaping. However, the process of so doing is not willy-nilly; it represents choices by those who regard nationalism and, in this case, its attendant Americanization forces to be the most important. It reflects decisions about the role schooling should play in the Americanization and nation-building dynamics. Typically, it endorses tradition and continuity and stares more often at the rear-view mirror instead of through the front windshield.[32] There is nothing inherent to schooling that unnecessarily ordains its role to be such a force.

However, mass public schooling in the United States began, was rationalized, and expanded during periods of significant population growth that was as much a result of immigration by outsiders as it was fertility by those native born.[33] As historians have shown, these sorts of immigration patterns can threaten social cohesion and national development or at least be perceived that way. Liberal progressive national-ists such as Theodore Roosevelt and Woodrow Wilson saw public schooling (and in that they were historians themselves, history education, particularly) as a powerful vehicle for strengthening *unum* in the face of the potential destabilizing effects of a growing *pluribus*. We revisit such landscapes today, as I noted at the outset. In fact, because the United States is a nation of immigrants and because of its volatile ethno-racial past, a threat to *unum* has more or less been constant at least since the incep-tion of mass public schooling. Given these historical contingencies, decisions to use public schools and history education as prime vehicles for nationalistic purposes seem understandable. But they are not inevitable or immutable.

A question then is begged: Is what passes for an official history education in the United States that I described in the foregoing really an education in history? Work by Michael Kammen (1989) and David Lowenthal (1998), for example, is instructive here.[34]

Both Kammen and Lowenthal distinguish between history and what they call her-itage, or in the former's lexicon, the "heritage phenomenon." Kammen (1989) has argued that despite a powerful nostalgic yearning in the United States, Americans (both young and old) are largely ignorant and indifferent to important events of the national past, noting that "the variety of topics affected by this amnesia . . . is alarm-ingly broad" (p. 139). He then wonders if the escapist nostalgia afflicting so many Americans, coupled with their ignorance of the past, suggests that we have "perpe-trated upon ourselves a self-deception?" Answering his own questions, he observes, "I believe that we have, in fact, and that highly selective, sentimental, sanitized versions of American history have produced a severely simplified vision of how we came to the society we are now" (p. 139). That "simplified vision" is what he calls heritage.[35] By his lights, heritage serves often as an inaccurate synonym for history, clusters selective social memories into a broader collective memory that substitutes for history, and is "up-beat and affirmative in an unqualified way about the American past" (p. 151).[36]

History, although encompassing the "heritage phenomenon," is a more careful examination of the past. It investigates, wrestles with, and interprets that past in an uncomfortable, ongoing struggle to wrest some meaning from it, all on its own terms as much as is possible. Little of it is stable: Meanings and understandings shift as new evi-dence comes to light, changes in historical investigators' research lenses affect what is considered significant and therefore what stories emerge,[37] and each new generation of investigators are wont to rework the ideas and stories of their predecessors with or without new evidence or reconceptualizations of significance. Kammen (1989) notes that heritage, in spite of its powerful nostalgic appeal, "really isn't an alternative to history, or a surrogate for it, but [only] a prologue and a preparation for the pasts (wars and all) that produced the present (warts and all)" (pp. 153–154). An American *history*, then, reveals the blemishes, leaves rough edges intact, and eschews cosmetics. American *heritage* selects out and papers over those elements of the past not conducive to a story line of celebratory successes and, at present, nation-building ones. Two sides to the same coin of pastness: One tarnished, stained, heavy from the weight of its journey, and tricky to read; the other shiny, bright, easily legible, but possessing little substance.

David Lowenthal (1998) generally makes many of these same arguments and distinctions. Whereas Kammen's is a chapter-length treatment, Lowenthal explores what he calls the "heritage crusade" across the span of a book.[38] He offers a plethora of examples, from collective, celebratory memorializing of Columbus and the Jamestown settlers to the heroics of World War II and Korean War veterans, from "history" theme parks to the work of the Smithsonian Institution.

For Lowenthal (1998), the primary distinction between heritage and history is in their different purposes. History strives to tell the truth about the past, even though "that truth is a chameleon and its chroniclers fallible beings" (p. 119). Heritage, by contrast, primarily uses the past for celebratory purposes, cherry-picking it along the way. History, as the result of work by historical investigators, is an account of the past made testable within and through the practices of the disciplinary guild. Heritage is more a "declaration of faith in that past." They are also different in their primary modes of persuasion, Lowenthal asserts: "History seeks to convince by truth and succumbs to falsehood. Heritage exaggerates and omits, candidly invents and frankly forgets. . . . Heritage is immune to critical appraisal because it is not erudition but catechism" (p. 121). Lowenthal concludes, "*Heritage diverges from history not in being biased but in its attitude toward bias.* Neither enterprise is value-free. But while historians aim to reduce bias, heritage sanctions and strengthens it" (p. 122, original emphasis).

If Kammen's and Lowenthal's assessments are accurate, then it seems reasonable to conclude that what goes on in American classrooms is largely an exercise in heritage consumption and collective memorialization, not history. Based on this primary purpose, then, courses in American history might be more aptly be called American Heritage I and II, or Collective U.S. Memory A and B, or even more broadly and simply, The U.S. Collective-Memory Project.

If coursework in school American history is fundamentally an exercise in collective memorialization, that helps to explain why the warts-and-all effort by historians to rewrite the history of American immigration and identity development of the past 50 years remains largely absent from current school history textbooks. It also helps us understand why textbooks and teaching have largely been impervious to periodic measures to invoke change in their century-old practices. Americans appear to prefer nostalgia and dislike history's tendency to unearth cause for guilt and shame. Accepting for the moment these understandings, the question I turn to now is, What consequences does this history-education-as-collective-memory have for the students who are its recipients in school? From a potentially long list, I examine six areas that appear to me to matter most.[39] I selectively draw and summarize from empirical research on history education that spans about 20 years here in the United States but goes back farther in Great Britain.[40] This research has explored both teaching and learning. I focus here on the learning research but refer to studies on the way in which learners are taught when it is relevant.

CONSEQUENCES OF HISTORY EDUCATION AS COLLECTIVE MEMORY

It would be tempting to conclude that tracing out consequences reveals their intentionality. My treatment of the following six areas of consequence, however, is more an exercise in inferential correlation. Whereas there might be some indication that the consequences turned up by the research on history education are the ones intended, there are also equal, if not more plausible, reasons to believe that a number of the consequences are unintended; but to tell the difference is an uncertain enterprise at best. What we do know is that the evidence for a cluster of learning consequences in history education coexists with a collective-memory approach in American history classrooms, if we accept the premise that such classrooms traffic more in collective memory than history. It is reasonable to believe that the intentions of those who authorize and sanction what turn out to be collective-memory courses make no distinctions between them and history courses, that the role of such courses is to rightly instill in students knowledge of and appreciation for the nation-building narrative, and that those individuals are convinced that these courses are important to creating good American citizens who feel proud of their pledge of allegiance. Few would argue with these ideas. However, even the best intentions can be foiled occasionally by unanticipated results.

Such situations create interesting policy–practice paradoxes. Part of my purpose is to explore such consequences for students as a means of raising questions about what history-education-as-collective-memory appears to accomplish and to what end, salutary, objectionable, or indifferent. This further allows me to consider alternatives to it that might ameliorate some of its more problematic and/or unintended outcomes. As such, research evidence and issues of educational policy and practice engage each other in conversation.

A "Freedom-Quest Narrative" as Cultural Tool

There is evidence to suggest that students who are engaged by the collective-memory approach in school (and have it reinforced for them away from school) retain and can recount the general contours of a nation-building narrative, the centerpiece repeated most often in history textbooks. In one study, a group of 24 American college undergraduates were asked to write an essay response to the question, What is the origin of the United States? Twenty-three of them crafted essays that bore uncanny similarities. Persecuted Anglos fled Europe and their oppressive overlords and traveled to the New World in search of freedom. The birth of the United States, the 23 reasoned, was the culmination of a struggle to overthrow European-imposed tyrannies and establish a new nation founded on individual liberty and unfettered pursuits of happiness. Following this birth, a period of two centuries ensued in which the people further distanced themselves from the Old World, hunting limitless progress as they expanded and settled the vast expanse that was western North America. With copious amounts of hard work and the goal of individual liberty beckoning them from every horizon, patriots and pioneers threw off their Old World trappings and were born anew. The nation they built stood for liberty, democracy, and the right to live and produce all their minds and hearts could desire, unobstructed by a government that tampered with their yearnings, coddling them instead. The result was a nation populated by freedom seekers, who created the best and most powerful experiment in nation building the world had yet to see.[41]

Struck by the similarities in these freedom-quest narratives, psychologist James Wertsch (1998) argued that such narratives are powerful because they can be encapsulated into succinct story lines, contain thematic elements that are seductive and thus memorable, and can be repeated easily because they are linked to self-identification with core features of the story line and what it represents symbolically. Wertsch referred to these story lines as schematic narrative templates. They function as powerful cultural tools in that they enable their carriers to claim allegiances to particular nation-states and their representative institutions in a world in which such allegiances are important to success in identity development. The schematic-narrative-template-as-cultural-tool contrasts with specific narratives that people encounter, sometimes create, and certainly sample. The latter tend to be transitory, serve local and sometimes brief purposes, and are retained only if their elements can be blended with or subsumed by the broader, more powerful narrative template. Wertsch has also studied the presence of these templates in Russia with special attention to their changing character associated with the collapse of the Soviet Union. He alludes to their ubiquity among diverse nation-states.[42]

The story of freedom and progress that animates the U.S. history textbooks and is oft repeated in history classrooms is, without much doubt, a schematic narrative template, functioning as a powerful cultural tool complete with identity markers. To know it, believe it to be true, and be able to repeat it with conviction function as declarations of a speaker's Americanness. Without it, one remains a cultural outsider. Learning the narrative in school can begin early.

Elements of the template appeared among 9- to 11-year-old upper elementary students in one study in Kentucky (Barton, 1996). As with the college students, the younger ones saw national progress as generally linear and rational, moving steadily forward as Americans became progressively smarter and developed crucial new inventions. The students also tended to imagine history through a lens of much reduced scope in ways that were reminiscent of the reductionist and telescopic narratives the college students produced. Already by upper elementary school, students apparently were developing several of the precursory ingredients of the freedom-quest schematic narrative template echoed by textbooks.

Some key patriots and pioneers that populate that template are also retained in memory. However, the list is relatively short and fairly uniform. In a study of more than 1,000 entering college students across a 10-year period in Buffalo, New York, a historian invited them on the first day of his survey history course to list without reflection 10 names they could remember after they saw the prompt "American history from its beginning through the Civil War."[43] The results revealed rather remarkable consistency. Presidents particularly and similar national leaders and generals topped the lists. Fourteen of the same names appeared consistently across samples of students during the 10-year span of data collection. President responses (e.g., Washington, Jefferson, Lincoln, Jackson) were so common that the historian conducting the research, Michael Frisch, asked students to produce a similar list without naming any presidents. These second lists turned up consistent mentions of the same set of celebrated American patriots and pioneers noted by John Bodnar. Betsy Ross, Paul Revere, Harriet Tubman, and Lewis and Clark were top recollections. Presidents, generals, patriots, and pioneers are all part of the supporting cast of characters that give a degree of substance to the freedom-quest narrative template.

The results of the study prompted its author to remark that "they are evidence that cultural imagery seems to be reproduced in our young people with startling consistency and regularity" (Frisch, 1989, p. 1150). By way of a conclusion, he observed, "The consistency and extraordinary uniformity in the images offered up by these students indicates that [cultural leaders] and their followers have little cause for concern: the structure of myth and heroes, martyrs and mothers, is firmly in place" (p. 1154). However solid the list, Frisch's data suggest that it remains short and homogeneous.

At their best, U.S. collective-memory courses, in which this freedom-quest narrative is so pivotal, succeeds well at binding it as a tool to the historical consciousness of the students who encounter it. At the very least, the courses successfully reinforce the narrative template that is imbued upon the consciousness of the larger mass culture. If the goal of the effort is to provide children and adolescents with a thematically linear, simple, and upbeat story line of national development (with an abbreviated list of American heroes, martyrs, and mothers mixed in), then research evidence indicates that the consequences remain salutary. Yet asking for a more intricate story replete with plot complexities, indeterminacies, and an occasional wart or two appears to request too much.

Command of Details and Events

A curious national pastime in the United States involves periodically testing a sample of young people on what they can recall about the specifics of the American past. This pastime is coupled with hand wringing and teeth gnashing, as the results repeatedly demonstrate that these youngsters have a thin grasp of a broader array of details.[44] A much-quoted line from one such secondary analysis of students' limited capacity to recall what some think are crucial elements of the national narrative arc complains that a shocking number of 17-year-olds could not even remember correctly in which half century the American Civil War was fought (Ravitch & Finn, 1988). Perhaps one of the earliest teeth-gnashing episodes came from two researchers who, after giving a recall test to 1,500 precollegiate students, grumbled in 1917, "Surely a grade of 33 in 100 on the simplest and most obvious facts of American history is not a record in which any high school can take pride" (Bell & McCollum, 1917, p. 257).

In 1923, the study was replicated with a smaller sample of students (Eikenberry, 1923). The results were similar. In the 1940s, another survey was commissioned by *The New York Times*. Almost 7,000 students were involved. The grumbling and complaining continued as the data were shown to repeat earlier patterns (Nevins, 1942). Surveys were conducted among adults in 1975 and among college freshmen in 1976; the same results emerged (Kammen, 1991, p. 664). More recently, the pace at which the pattern is unearthed has intensified. Since the late 1980s, the National Assessment of Education Progress (NAEP) U.S. history test is given about every 4 or 5 years. Following each administration, a spokesperson from the National Assessment Governing Board (a policy body regulating NAEP tests) or someone from the National Center for Educational Statistics (an agency that oversees the test administrations and reports out trends) appears in a public forum to reiterate what previous tests results had made clear decades previously.

American students appear able to recount a general narrative arc, but they have difficulty populating that arc with supporting specifics and casts of characters at least some think are essential to know. However, given the ways in which the collective-memory effort appears to function with so much stress placed on a 400-year story line of endless freedom horizons and boundless progress, details and specifics all piled atop one another, gave at least one student cause to say, "I just don't remember—the ideas are all jumbled in my head" (VanSledright, 1995). Collective-memory courses, although effective at transmitting a coherent (although simplistic) narrative, come up short at giving that narrative much historical substance. For reasons that remain to be investigated more fully, possessing a detailed understanding of the American past and the complexities of its change with time that provide additional flesh to the nation-building story line appear less crucial to acquiring an American creed, one bestowed upon those who can produce the contours of a succinct freedom-quest narrative template on demand. It is as if students are saying, "Understanding the details and exigencies of the past? Who needs all that? I don't." And they could be right if Michael Kammen (1989) is correct in his observation that even many otherwise well-adjusted and productive American adults possess significant levels of historical amnesia.

Death of the Subject in School

As some have observed, there is a curious irony in the presence of profound wistfulness about the past residing alongside concentrations of serious historical amnesia.[45] Seeking the past in theme parks, in "retro" clothing, in genealogical traces, in roots music and sampling practices, and in acts of historical preservation has grown markedly in popularity recently. Collective memorialization is on the rise. Yet grade-school students report finding the courses that deal directly with the American past dull and uninspiring. They tell researchers that history is their least liked school subject and that they would avoid it if they could (e.g., Schug, Todd, & Beery, 1984). Put bluntly, they report that the subject is presented to them in lifeless fashion, a fait accompli that is stripped of the dynamic, investigative, revisionist lifeblood that animates those who plumb its depths in search of hidden treasure and answers to ancient mysteries only rummaging about in the *residua* of the past can address. Although students appear to learn (or have reinforced) the contours of a freedom-quest narrative and its heroes and martyrs by putting in their seat time, little else seems to make an impression, except how much they wish the courses could be over more quickly.

This ironic circumstance may be more a result of the way such courses are organized, taught, and tested than a consequence of students' disliking the subject per se. The research studies turn up a familiar pattern. Teachers battle the clock in a losing race to deal with all the chapters (and thus the chronology) in the weighty textbook. The offerings to the American creed by disparate groups of immigrants to America are legion. Mentioning them becomes an important strategic maneuver in textbook production, as we have seen. The books grow in size and length almost exponentially with each generation and new struggle over whose offerings will be included. The authoritative, omniscient voice of the textbook author(s) lends credibility and importance to such mentions. If each mention or offering to the narrative arc appears as credible as any other, all must be treated with some sense of equality, and the list continues to grow as more of those who perceive themselves to be "outsiders" rattle cages, signaling for their inclusion. Teachers, without much sanctioned authority to pick and choose (selection is typically a job for curriculum policymakers and school boards at some remove from daily classroom life), must attend to it all while blending the details into the larger master narrative of freedom and progress. Students appear to be overwhelmed, twitch in their seats, sleep, or fidget with the latest electronica under their desks. Occasionally, they threaten overt dissension.

In response, history teachers are pushed to teach defensively. They make textbook reading and writing assignments, give quizzes and tests, and attempt to bring compliance with threats of poor grades and more homework that typically means more textbook reading. Teachers and students sometimes reach a truce by engaging in collective bargaining over the degree of reading, writing, and serious attention to test taking that will be exchanged in return for nominal behavioral and cognitive compliance. The unwritten contract has students appearing to be learning the historical details mentioned in the textbook in trade for the promise of reductions in teacher-assigned schoolwork (McNeil, 1988). Those who have taught the subject in school know that this arrangement gets played out in some collective-memory classroom and in some manner almost every day.

Couple this practice with a regime in which a state or educational jurisdiction engages in surveillance of teaching efforts through accountability schemes and standardized-testing measures, and the resolve of many history teachers to teach defensively only increases. The pressure to cover the textbook's details feverishly increases because teachers (and students) never quite know which of those details will appear on the year-end assessment. And the assessments typically measure only recall of specific events and items dealt with in the textbooks. They do so most frequently in a multiple-choice format, items that are easy to administer and score and thus remain relatively inexpensive. Rarely are students given opportunities on such standardized assessments to craft essays in which they analyze certain events, make a claim about their significance (for national development or otherwise), and mount an argument that supports that claim with evidence.[46] The tests turn on asking students to recall those particularities they encountered, and with some luck acquired, in their collective-memory courses.

With accountability stakes ratcheted up sufficiently, teachers, for good or ill, tend to match their teaching practices to the ways assessments measure results. The study of the patriotic deeds and somewhat lesser mentions in the textbook that provide the underpinning to the freedom-quest narrative template are thrust to the center of classroom practice. Yet assumptions by educational policymakers appear to suggest that emerging from school having committed the official, general narrative to memory is insufficient. Students need to be able to recall a broader panoply of celebrated nation-building events and their supporting casts; exactly how many remains unclear. The apparent worry among policymakers is that a failure to recount enough specific detail undergirding the narrative means one does not really know that narrative and so, therefore, has not acquired the American creed. If too many students depart school with such deficiencies, some reason, the nation state is threatened.[47] This concern may well have driven the actions of those Florida legislators in the spring of 2006.

In this regard, the moves to ensure collective remembering appear to get derailed. As stakes rise and accountability provisions tighten, students try to bargain them back down in the classroom or subtly resist by neglecting, for example, their assigned reading (McNeil, 1988). This result may give teachers the impression that they need to intensify their efforts at narrating the textbook story to ensure that their charges get it. However, it can also redouble students' desire to sleep, fidget, and otherwise disengage. As Michael Frisch (1989) has noted, "Alienated students cannot be bullied in attention or retention; that [type of] authoritarian cultural intimidation is likely to be met with further and more rapid retreat" (p. 1154).

The periodic surveys of young peoples' grasp of the narrative's supporting details, as we have seen, reveal no significant increase in mastery of those details and have not revealed one across a century of efforts to improve it. Recently in the state of Virginia, results on the standardized collective-memory exams were so poor initially, the state's policymakers were forced to modify the tests and raise the cutoff points that signaled a passing grade. NAEP history results in the past 20 years, likewise, show little significant score increase among 17-year-olds, despite rapid expansion in efforts to hold students to higher standards during that same period. This situation provoked several observers to note that efforts to press teachers to teach more details and teach them more fervently were akin to insisting that a patient suffering from life-threatening bronchial pneumonia repeatedly take over-the-counter antihistamines in the hope that doing so would provide a cure (Kelly, Meuwissen, & VanSledright, 2007). That proponents of collective-memory courses would embrace such a questionable antidote may seem surprising. On the other hand, if you succumb to a robust concern that the layers of veneer holding together the freedom-quest narrative, and by extension the nation-state, are delaminating, then more of the same dispensed with greater vigor may seem like an effective strategy.

Resistance to the Official Narrative

Some students respond to collective memorializations with suspicion, cynicism, and sometimes outright cognitive resistance. Here, again, history-education-as-collective-memory appears to nurture results that are unintended. One such study that revealed these kinds of outcomes took place in the Detroit area in the 1990s.

Researchers compared differences between American adolescents of European and African descent on a task in which they had to sort into a top-10 list both names and events drawn from the U.S. past by rank order of their perceived importance. The European American students, not unlike the collegians in the Buffalo study, ranked as most important key names and events marking traditional elements of the freedom-quest, nation-building narrative arc and the presidents, patriots, and pioneers often associated with it. For the European American students, George Washington and John Kennedy were most often at the top of their lists, and the Civil War (because it saved the union of states) and the Declaration of Independence and Constitution periods were most pivotal. The civil rights movement, the Civil War (because it signaled an end to slavery), and slavery and emancipation ranked at the top of the African American students' lists, as well as did Martin Luther King and Malcolm X. A close third to the latter was Harriet Tubman. Neither Tubman nor Malcolm X was ranked by any of the European American students.

In an effort to understand more about the differences observed, the researchers asked students to explain what influenced their decisions. For the European American students, the textbook and teachers' lectures served as most influential in structuring their selections, suggesting the power that the narrative register those sources contained held in mediating ideas about historical significance. The African American students, by contrast, talked about the influence of parents and relatives especially and lumped teachers, television, and film together as secondary influences. In interviews with a subsample of students, several African American students registered suspicion about the "whitewashing" agenda textbook and school curricula were perceived to promote. They claimed that the books and lectures tended to ignore or marginalize contributions of African Americans and otherwise sanitize or omit the long history of racial oppression, struggle, and violence necessary to overcome it. In short, several found the narrative arc transmitted in the classroom to be part of an age-old conspiracy to keep African Americans in a type of perpetual bondage. Turning away from it and toward localized, specific narratives conveyed by family and community members became an exercise in cultural survival.[48]

Knowing the narrative and some of its romanticized heroes and their patriotic national sacrifices and accomplishments does not necessarily result in the appropriation of or self-identification with that narrative. Instead, in this case, the collective-memory approach appears to promote and reinforce among some Americans conspiracy theories and counternarratives that, with enough repeating, serve to nurture a cynical view of it and the larger school system that serves as its officializing and sanctioning agent. If the collective-memory proponents cannot find means for co-opting competing specific and local narratives through offerings, or by broadening the approach's appeal through genuine inclusion, it risks saliency among some groups and ironically may actually increase resistance and alienation.[49] Rather than enhance *unum*, one consequence is that memorialization can exacerbate the fractiousness of *pluribus* the more it insists on a program that can be taken by the excluded to be riddled with partisan political aims. As David Lowenthal (1998) notes, it is the excesses of collective memorialization, its often irrational exuberance and desire to secure allegiance to *particular* remembrances of nation, that can imperil its success.

Limited Opportunities to Achieve High-Status Cognitive Capabilities

"Everyday" conceptions of history are widespread. They reflect the idea that it is composed of predetermined ideas and facts that form a finished story—indeed, that there is a single story of the past.[50] Laypeople seldom appreciate the idea that historical narratives are constructed from evidence that has been questioned, pieced together, and interpreted.[51] Consistent with this conception is the belief that one does not interact with or question evidence or offer counterevidence that challenges the story of the past.[52] Many people also tend to view the past through presentist lenses in which they regard evidence from the past through the lenses of their own lives' contexts. Such conceptions of history, ones reinforced every day in history classrooms in which the teaching of nation-building narratives predominate, tend to retard the development of key cognitive capabilities that make history possible in the first place.

Classrooms in which collective memory is the preoccupation turn on the "everyday" view of history, with heavy reliance on learning to repeat a simplified national narrative. This leaves little room for making sense of multiple historical sources, considering and working from evidence, asking questions, developing one's own interpretation, or writing interpretive arguments. As such, it is difficult to learn to reason in these classrooms. Indeed, many focus most on memorization (Page, 1991; Ravitch & Finn, 1988). That focus implicates particular classroom strategies. It is rare for time to be spent reasoning about the past, writing extended answers to historical questions, or reading primary and secondary sources (Lapp, Grigg, & Tay-Lim, 2002).

In describing this pattern, one extensive study noted that the "preponderance of classroom activity involv[ed] listening, reading textbooks, completing workbooks and worksheets, and taking quizzes" (Goodlad, 1984, p. 213). In another study, of different tracks of classes, a classroom researcher found that both high- and low-track history classes treated history as memorization, but lower tracks spent more time completing worksheets and higher tracks focused more on recitation of textbook narratives (Page, 1991).

Facing unrelenting growth in the number of events and details that need adding to the narrative to keep it reasonably current and the pressures this then exerts on teachers, continuing to embrace a collective-memory approach to history education results in learners' encountering serious opportunity costs. Historian Tom Holt (1990) describes these costs for one student, Debbie. For her, history was about collecting and ordering other people's facts. Her own curiosity, interpretations, questions, and historical consciousness and cognition were largely irrelevant when it came to her experience with school history. Historical reasoning, the sort that begets deeper historical understandings, was traded off for a steady stream of requirements that invited Debbie to do little more than commit the nation-building story to memory.

Other studies have turned up similar opportunity-cost compromises. In one, a history education researcher carefully documented a U.S. history teacher's practices (Monte-Sano, 2006). The teacher lectured daily, gave multiple-choice and identification questions to answer as homework, assigned reading from the textbook only, and required that students write summaries of what they had been studying every 2 weeks. As the semester progressed, students improved little in their ability to write historical arguments or reason with evidence, despite doing a considerable amount of writing in response to the summary assignments.

What students instead learned involved mining the textbook for information that they needed to define terms, people, and events for their writing assignments. During class, they sat and listened to the teacher talk at them about historical topics, or, disinterested, they turned to work on homework for other classes. When asked to write essays, the students took to reporting out what they understood to be the factual details found in their textbook. Little evidence emerged that the students could reason about historical topics in writing or convey an underlying understanding of the topics about which they wrote. Opportunities to reason thoughtfully and thereby understand history more profoundly were nonexistent. Analyzing the American story, reading for comprehension, writing analytical and interpretive papers, and reasoning with evidence were sacrificed in the name of memorizing the textbook story. Acquiring the American creed by reading about its persona on the pages of the textbook overshadowed learning to think deeply and reason effectively about that creed.

In information-laden, pluralistic democracies, capabilities for thinking through, assessing, and evaluating (in speech and/or in writing) the plethora of political, product, and media claims that appear in startling numbers every day may well be understood as necessities.[53] These cognitive capabilities are considered high-status forms of knowledge that can be (perhaps need to be) matched to the growing intellectual demands life in the 21st century makes on citizens of such democracies. If studying history in school can teach those capabilities, then it remains paradoxical that opportunities to engage them are frequently jettisoned in favor of the Americanizing function that pressing for a nationalistic collective-memory program entails. Coming to understand the story of national development may be necessary; however, it is hardly educationally sufficient, proponents of this position argue.

Becoming Good Consumers

Lest this treatment of consequences suggest an overabundance of unintended, ironic, or paradoxical results, I end this examination by noting another feature of the collective-memory approach at which it succeeds, perhaps more coincidentally than anything else. Returning to the heritage (collective memory)–history distinction discussed in the foregoing, it is important to note that the latter concerns itself with the study of the past. It is investigative in nature, accepts no claims without evidentiary support, and subjects the results of investigations to community practices of criticism and peer review. Those who engage in these practices can be said to be producing histories or evidence-based historical accounts that attempt to explain what a complex, unstable past means to us here today. The pivotal metaphor register is participation in a production process. Investigators do consume to acquire ideas and evidence for making claims. But consumption—of the *residua* of the past, for example—is almost always pressed into the service of the more salient goal of producing histories.

In the world of school's collective-memory courses, the metaphorical relationship takes an inverted form. The message of schooling can be construed to involve privileging consumption at the expense of production in the sense just noted. Participants are required to consume a product that has been produced by others.[54] To the extent that any production is required, it involves the reproduction of that which has already been consumed, a largely symbolic process that creates nothing new or marketable other than through its exchange value. That value is managed by the adults who require, judge, and sanction the reproduction, not the reproducer herself. In many ways, this schooling arrangement can mirror life in the wider consumer-driven, market economy.

Whether intended or not, history-education-as-collective-memory, with its valorization of capitalism and free-market practices, dovetails nicely with the consumer culture that has come to dominate the global marketplace. The collective-memory approach appears to do double duty in this regard, teaching allegiance to and identity with a nation-state while also giving its recipients practice in becoming efficient consumers of the products made available in a marketplace supported by that nation-state. Such a relationship may be merely coincidental. However, the powerful message of consumption reverberating off the billboards, media conduits, subway tunnels, and satellite dishes of popular culture are echoed each day in a process in which students are told to crack the covers of their history textbooks, consume its pages, and then pause to have it reinforced by the voice emanating from behind the lectern or on the audiovisual screen behind it. Here is yet another location—this one predominantly symbolic rather than material—in which the messages of mass culture and schooling meet each other in a mutually sustaining, perhaps even symbiotic, socioeconomic dance.

ALTERNATIVE CONCEPTUALIZATIONS

At the risk of belaboring the point, the principal target of history-education-as-collective-memory in U.S. schools involves socializing "outsiders" and the naïve and enhancing allegiance to the nation-state and what that nation-state embodies as framed by its myths, legends, values, and norms. The freedom-quest narrative template is the conduit. It requires that the narrative be consumed, be committed to memory, and then be reproduced as a sign of membership. Student consumers are asked to wrap themselves in its mantle, don the American creed, and thereby assume Americanness.

If there is resistance, it is met by coercion, sometimes forceful but most often subtle. In trade for success at this process, budding student citizens can legitimately speak in terms of "we" Americans and about "our" America.

Transcendental Narrative as Collective Memory

Allegiance to nation-state and the story it seeks to tell about itself, however, need not be the ultimate target. A centerpiece of a community's specific narrative can also play the role. Simone Schweber (2006), for example, has explored how a transcendental entity—in this case, the Judeo-Christian God—can as easily suffice. Studying how the Holocaust is taught in history courses in a Protestant, evangelical Christian school in the United States, she has noted that it is the narrative template of God the Father and the world He has wrought and controls that deserves ultimate allegiance and reverence. The nation-state exists only at that God's command and is subservient to it. All actions, behaviors, and agency are the will of the Lord God of this narrative register. Although that God manages all historical events, even those that otherwise appear manifestly evil, such as the Holocaust, it is our weakness as humans that prevents us from fully understanding the divine and goodly providence in even those occurrences. The story of the nation-state and God's will may possibly cohere in a larger transcendental meta-narrative, but evangelical Christians would never fully trust the nation-state, particularly if it lays claim to secular order. It is to God's bidding that they must incline.

The point here is that specific localized narratives with significant reach, power, and enough adherents can serve well as organizing frameworks and therefore function as (high) stories in school. Allegiance to the nation-state need not be the central objective; the U.S. history textbook need not function as the symbolic carrier of the narrative. The Bible, for example, with its Judeo-Christian themes, tropes, and characters, could supplant the secular freedom-quest narrative of the textbook. In several respects, this is precisely what appeared to be happening in the evangelical Christian school studied. Therefore, one alternative conception to nationalistic collective memorializing would be to encourage adherence to a transcendental narrative template around which all other specific templates could turn, the freedom-quest narrative, for example. U.S. history, or world history for that matter, would be constructed, read, and consumed through the narrative prism of what God's will was for the human race rather than through the secular light refractions cast by national political, military, and economic leaders popular in the historical consciousness of Frisch's college students.[55]

Schweber (2006) cautions, however, that the type of fundamentalist master narrative template pursued in the context of the evangelical school history courses she studied presents its own set of consequences, some perilously close to morally dangerous. She submits that adherence to such a narrative reifies God's plan for the world and subsequently results in breeding hubris among those who claim to be children of that plan, who possess certain knowledge of it, and who claim that knowledge as a means of telling others how they should live. Simultaneously, it creates a form of complacency, in which human agency is elided as sinful creatures lie prostrate before the

Divine's plan for their lives. If God is in charge, then believers cannot intervene in events lest they risk disrupting God's will for the world. Most of the students Schweber studied, she observes, "seemed caught in this theological pitfall, being unwilling as they were to even consider saving Jews when asked to imagine living during the Holocaust" (Schweber, 2006, p. 410). Excesses of a different sort plague such transcendental-narrative conceptions.

History as Vernacular Narrative

A second alternative could be construed as one in which all local, vernacular narratives supplant the nationalistic one. Here, each tribe or ethnoracial group tells its own (high) story in school. Allegiance is to the specific narrative told within those circles. Each in different ways replaces the story of national development or, if it so chooses, writes that story as one of contribution to or claim over that development. History textbooks proliferate, becoming regional, ethnoracial, or state based.[56] Such a conception privileges local interests and narratives and could be understood as a more thorough democratization of history than the current nationalistic-memory effort in school permits.

Although perhaps attractive to those who would welcome a more complete multiculturalization of school history, there is something antithetical about pursuing it to the degree such a conceptualization encourages. In the United States, by Constitutional provision, public education is the responsibility of the 50 individual states. To permit, as an example, each of a state's local tribes or ethnoracial groups to assume control of the focus of narrative register, write its curriculum to suit it, and publish its own textbook version could be interpreted as an abdication of responsibility and control by a state over its mission to educate the public. States as large and ethnically diverse as California and Texas, for example, would encounter great difficulty retaining more centralized control while simultaneously granting disparate local groups the right to craft their own narratives and teach them. If such an approach could actually be realized, there is some reason to fear, as critics of multiculturalism in schools and in history education have pointed out, that sociocultural cohesiveness would be jeopardized, sectarian and ethnic disagreement would increase, and internal strife and warfare might be an eventual result. The United States' 19th-century Civil War, history suggests, was fought, in part, because of profound regional, sociocultural, and economic differences (with competing vernacular high stories or specific narrative templates) that fundamentally threatened the glue holding together the nation-state.

As with the former conceptualizations of collective memory—the current nation-state and the transcendental-narrative approaches—the vernacular-narrative version traffics in related excesses and portends worrisome consequences. Those who can exert control over collective memories and point them in particular directions (e.g., the Florida legislature and the Florida State Department of Education that must comply with the law) see clearly the benefits such power and control can reap. Therein lies the ground spring of excess. To the extent that excesses of a memory approach go unchecked by countervailing forces, they only grow in magnitude. In a collective as diverse as the United States, for example, sanitized remembrances, celebratory glee, selective rituals, omissions, co-optation by offering, and coercion all can be ingredients in reinforcing otherwise desirable aims of promoting "Americanization" and fostering cross-ethnic cohesion.

Yet those practices necessarily walk a fine line that leaves them open to sociocultural and political manipulation with unintended consequences. Should either the transcendental narrative register or the vernacular-memories templates replace the current nationalist collective-memory version, we would likely witness one set of excesses supplanted by others. And it is difficult to gauge with any certainty whether any one set is preferable. Such is the often treacherous and troublesome landscape on which collective-memory efforts of the sort I have been describing appear to operate. At once, they seem necessary and unavoidable but riddled with serious deficiencies and cause for concern.

Another way of conceptualizing alternatives to the current nation-state collective-memory approach is to ask, as the foregoing discussion alludes, whether the nation-state is a powerful enough object for allegiance in a 21st-century world. If postcolonial and postmodern globalizations of commerce and their attendant population migrations and blurring of boundaries only increases, what is the fate of the nation-state in such a reformulated world? Multinational corporations with powerful commitments to and interests in globalized commerce and no particular national identifications have proliferated in recent years. They expatriate their workers to satisfy rising labor demands and the opening of new markets in various world regions. The purchase a national identity may hold over these corporate migrants weakens with each move. Corporate loyalty could well displace nation-state allegiance in a foreseeable future.

Moreover, as time is compressed by instantaneous communication, travel distances shortened by air travel, and the world brought home each day to personal living spaces by Internet and satellite television, how long will nation-states be able to sustain their roles as central carriers and protectors of meaning and loyalty? Do they need, as Gary Gerstle wonders about the United States, periodic wars with rival nation-states to reignite flagging patriotism and rekindle ebbing loyalties to the nation's institutions and memory? Do schools and the collective-memory programs they favor as symbolic carriers of nationalism need to redouble their efforts? Perhaps the boredom adolescents in American public schools report about their U.S. history courses and the poor results they consistently turn in on tests that measure their command of the national narrative signal a palatable increase in the perceived irrelevance of those exercises in nation-state memorialization.

A World History

Given new directions in the 21st century, it is possible to conceptualize an alternative to the nationalistic collective-memory approaches by using world history courses as their replacement in public schools. The U.S. history course as it is presently curricularized, sanctioned, and taught would disappear. History would be engaged from a world perspective. Nation-state origins and their ongoing historical developments would be placed into a larger temporal sweep. Growth of late-20th-century nations could be taught as historical evolutions, as outgrowths of changes in transportation, the economics of surplus, the politics and forces of colonization, and resistance to them, for example. Comparisons and contrasts could be investigated, analyzed, and criticized. If done effectively, no nation, nation-building process, or nationalistic undertaking would be immune from an examination of its strengths and weaknesses, much the way dynasties, city-states, and feudal empires are often considered. In this sense, nationalistic collective memorializations would take on a different cast, understood through the lenses of comparative analysis.[57] Excesses would be exposed and consequences could be more candidly considered. Under this guise, nationalism and nation building become objects of historical study rather than ends in themselves.

Yet lurking beneath the façade of reasoned, dispassionate analysis and comparison might be the urge to turn world history into a course in Western civilization, at least among Western democracies such as the United States. Here, collective memory could slide in through the back door. The accomplishments of the West are taught and understood as more important than those of other nations around the globe. The world's preeminent recent colonizers, for instance, were able to colonize because of their ethnoracial superiority. Trafficking in tropes of White, Western, capitalist supremacy could reappear only thinly disguised.

The United States could be understood as the quintessential embodiment of such superiority. Excesses thought to be checked and abandoned would quickly resurface in other costumes without a careful analysis, temporalization, and a historicized critique of nationalism. If replacing the nationalist collective-memory effort with a world history course seems only likely to provide a remedy to the excesses and unintended consequences of nationalistic energies, what sort of alternative conceptualization might offer the best hope of providing checks and balances for the consequential excesses of collective-memory projects?

Discipline-Based History

One candidate involves mirroring school historical study on what transpires in the community of practice called disciplinary history. This is the practice embodied principally by the activities of academic historians. It also has been popular among those in the field of history education research as an advocated pedagogical method for checking the excesses and arresting the unintended consequences of collective memorializing and its oversimplified and authoritative narrative arcs.

The argument for adopting this conceptualization of history education involves putting into play an investigative, critical approach to the past common to the disciplinary community. History, as I have alluded, is considered a product of careful analysis of the remnants of the past. Those remnants are understood as forms of evidence for answering questions investigators pose about what had occurred in that past. The accounts (stories) that can be generated are multiple (perhaps infinite), necessitating critical mechanisms for judging their quality. Investigators read and critique others' accounts and challenge questions posed, how evidence gets appropriated

to address those questions, and the relationship of the accounts (stories) to those produced by earlier investigators.[58] Revisions follow as new accounts (stories) of the past
are generated.[59]

In its rational, idealized form, the processes of careful systematic analysis and peer
critique produce historical accounts generally freed of the celebratory, simplified, artificially stabilized narratives that make up collective-memory high stories. In
Lowenthal's (1998) and Kammen's (1989) vocabulary, history displaces heritage, critical questioning overrides commemoration, and production replaces passive consumption. Metaphorically speaking, *participation in* a process of generating and critiquing
the past serves to provide the basis for the *acquisition of* historical knowledge and
understanding. Reliance on simple acquisition of a central narrative account via a
process of repeated exercise in memorization drops out. "While the single authoritative
interpretation of the past, conveyed as what really happens, is consistent with an
authoritarian political culture," observes Peter Seixas (2000), "the epistemology that
underlies [the disciplinary] approach is suited to the education of critical citizens in a
liberal democracy." He then adds, "It should help [students] to develop the ability and
the disposition to arrive independently at reasonable, informed opinions" (pp. 24–25),
thus reducing the grip identity politics and myopic, intolerant ethnocentric commitments have on their lives and sense making about the past. Such is its promise. And
there is some emerging research evidence that this promise is indeed realizable in
schools, that students can learn to think in this way while simultaneously coming to
understand and master the narrative of U.S. nation building.[60]

However, that promise can be attenuated by several factors. Historical investigators cannot escape the sociocultural positionalities that frame how they come to pose
questions, address them, craft historical accounts, and offer critique. Their intellectual and social milieu shapes how they understand the past's *residua*, and as such,
how the way in which their own nationalistic commitments prefigure the telling of
stories (e.g., Gabaccia, 1997; Trouillet, 1995). In other words, investigators cannot
escape completely from the influences of nationalistic collective memorializing precisely because, for them as for others, the narrative register of those efforts serve as a
powerful culture tool that gives meaning to experience. Nationalistic sympathies can
simply creep back in camouflage.

Other factors also press against the realization of this conceptualization. The disciplinary approach, if engaged fully, possesses the capacity to weaken nationalistic ties,
it is possible to argue. Consequently, protectors and defenders of such loyalties might
resist efforts to trample on those ties, especially because access to power is tied up, in
part, in maintaining them. And these defenders can appeal to the protected ground
on which nation-state narratives are thought to stand. Purveyors of the disciplinary
approach can be accused of un-Americanism and antipatriotism, or at least allusions
to these unacceptable attitudes can be broached, much as we saw in the battles over
the adoption of the standards for U.S. history in the 1990s. Discrediting proponents
of a threatening approach using such vocabularies pays quick dividends in the struggle to protect cherished nationalist memories. Yet another claim is that weakening

devotion to the nation-state produces a corrosive cultural relativism that can undermine the need citizens have to understand the origin of their identity, for which the nation-state often can offer more than any other current source.

Despite these attenuating factors, advocates continue to stress the importance the discipline-based conceptualization holds for tempering and/or excising some of the excesses and unintended consequences of a nationalistic collective-memory approach, broadening and deepening students' understanding of the subject, and helping students learn to more effectively deal with the mixed messages and counternarratives so common to globalized and time-compressed cultural life in the 21st century.[61] They argue that although this approach is flawed and unlikely to fully realize its ideals, it possesses greater promise as an antidote to the exaggerations and misuses of the past of collective memory than any other approach to history education.[62] In Great Britain, where approaching history from a disciplinary perspective has held some currency since the 1970s, adherents maintain that generally speaking, most of the fears critics advance have not been realized in school children there.[63]

CODA

In an effort to come to some reasonable terms with the firm hold a triumphal national narrative has over the way history education—or heritage education, if you will—is practiced in the United States, I have labored to show that it serves a powerful sociocultural purpose. It attempts to provide the ingredients necessary to secure allegiance to the nation-state, a set of loyalties important to gluing together the disparate ethnicities, interests, and commitments a society made from immigrants—past and present—and the naïve requires. Yet in its exuberance, it traffics in problematic unintended consequences and promotes excesses by omission and commission.[64]

Defenders of liberal, democratic nationalism, of which perhaps the late Richard Rorty is one of the more notable, argue that at present, such practices are the best we have.[65] Democratic politics and an open, liberal society allow interests and commitments a space in which to battle each other for allegiances and loyalties. Recent struggles about whose history will be taught are arguably an object lesson in the vitality of a democratic, liberal nation-state and the people who claim fealty to it to reimagine itself and themselves, to choose and rechoose who it and they wish to become. Nonetheless, the quiet coerciveness, excesses, and distortive consequences of our schooling arrangements remain and are borne out in history classrooms every day across the United States (and in other liberal national-states as well), as the research literature makes clear.

By my lights, the challenge for those interested in thinking about what a history education might look like in such liberal, democratic nations is to extend the conversation in ways that allow us to productively imagine how history—rather than shiny, happy heritage celebrations or progressive, tidy collective memories—can be taught while also attending to the need for a generally affirmative narrative arc that provides enough sociocultural cement to ignite loyalties to its best democratic elements. That one day national narratives become virtually or completely unnecessary is possible. But for the near-term conversation, I am of the mind that we must first address the excessiveness and problematic consequences that are the outcomes of the current collective-memory education. None of the alternatives I have considered are panaceas; none will fully arrest the outcomes that trouble those who survey the landscape of history education. However, systems of checks and balances have their own time-honored place in liberal, democratic nations. I read those who would infuse what currently passes for history education in such nation-states with a dose or two of the critical practices found in the discipline of history to be engaged in a conversation about how to make good on just such a democratic tradition. Inattention or resistance to this conversation in amelioration likely will result in little more than a continuation of subtle intellectual and sociocultural coercion, unworthy of being called a history *education* in any liberal, democratic sense, despite stated claims to the contrary.

ACKNOWLEDGMENTS

Jane Bolgatz, Michael Singh, and the volume editors provided thoughtful comments and assistance to me at various points. Sam Wineburg was instrumental in pointing me toward work—others and prepress versions of his own—that served to underpin some of my readings of the research literature. Chauncey Monte-Sano kindly offered erudite criticisms and contributions to certain portions of the review. To all I owe a debt of gratitude. I should note, however, that the positions I stake out and possible errors I have overlooked remain entirely of my own making. Thanks are also in order to the University of California, Berkeley's Graduate School of Education (and especially to P. David Pearson and Dan Perlstein, my sponsors) for the support offered me during the initial research and writing phases of this review while I was on sabbatical leave there in the fall of 2006.

NOTES

[1]See, as examples, Dolinski (2006) and Norton (2006).

[2]As I finished work on this review, *The Washington Post* published an article dealing with two new manuals, one for reshaping history education, that appeared in Russia. The author of the article, Peter Finn (2007), stated in the opening line, "With two new manuals for high school history and social studies, written by Kremlin political consultants, Russian authorities are attempting to imbue classroom debate with a nationalist outlook" (pp. A1, A16).

[3]For treatments of other nations' efforts, see, for example, Foster and Crawford (2006), Friedman and Kenney (2005), Hein and Selden (2000), and Seixas (2004).

[4]The summary of immigration and Americanization historiography that follows does not do full justice to its complexity. Its brevity is a function of space limitations. For a more detailed treatment, see, for example, Gerstle (1997a). For the sake of consistency, throughout the remainder of the review, I use Gerstle's term *ethnoracial* to refer to the many ethnic and racial groups and identities that form the fabric of American culture.

[5]For example, see Lawrence H. Fuchs (1990) and Werner Sollors (1989).

[6]See Gerstle (1997a) on this point, pages 534–536 especially.

[7]See works by Lizbeth Cohen (1990), Herbert Gutman (1976), David R. Roediger (1991), and Rudolph J. Vecoli (1979).

[8]For specific accounts of how history is used as a device to shape and socialize in democracies beyond the United States, see Friedman and Kenney (2005) and Hein and Selden (2000).

[9]See especially reviews by Michael V. Belok (1981), Frances FitzGerald (1980), Stuart Foster (2006), Jesus Garcia (1986), Gilbert T. Sewall (1987), and Leah H. Washburn (1997).

[10]For more on the ways in which these matters are treated in grade-school U.S. history textbooks, see FitzGerald (1980), Michael Olneck (1989), Christine E. Sleeter and Carl A. Grant (1991), and Jonathan Zimmerman (2002).

[11]On the power to name historical facts and thus control definitions, see Michel-Rolph Trouillot (1995, pp. 114–115).

[12]On this point, see also Friedman and Kenney (2005, pp 1–6).

[13]For a detailed review on this feature of textbooks, see Richard Paxton (1999). See also Isabel Beck, Margaret McKeown, and Jo Worthy (1995).

[14]For more on these competing versions and their roles, see work by historian John Bodnar (1992).

[15]On how certain interests attempt to control the marketplace of ideas and nation-state myths through textbook story lines, see, for example, Michael Apple and Linda Christian-Smith (1989) and Gary B. Nash, Charlotte Crabtree, and Ross E. Dunn (2000).

[16]See Friedman and Kenney's (2005) "Introduction: History in Politics."

[17]On the role the professional disciplinary guild plays in such arguments, see also Trouillot's (1995) chapter 1.

[18]For more on this point, see Gabaccia (1997), Friedman and Kenney (2005), Novick (1988), and Schlesinger (2007).

[19]For a detailed account of how textbooks (and history teachers and schooling) participate and reinforce a particular collective memory concerning Quebec history, see Jocelyn Letourneau and Sabrina Moisan (2004). With respect to Japan and its Ministry of Education's tight grip on the story textbooks tell, see, for example, Keith Crawford (2006).

[20]Most democracies do use history textbooks as a means of controlling and maintaining particular collective memories. These memories shift somewhat depending on changing national agendas, the degree of national control over the textbook industry and school curricula, who the policymakers are, and which interests they represent. But as with U.S. history textbooks, narrative registers remain relatively stable unless powerful events bring severe crisis to nationalism projects. Most democracies in the world engage in collective memorializing that is more mythical than evidence based. For more on comparative treatments, see, again, Foster and Crawford (2006), Friedman and Kenney (2005), Hein and Selden (2000), and Letourneau and Moisan (2004).

[21]See, for example, Lynne Cheney (1994); Nash, Crabtree, and Dunn (2000), especially chapters 1 and 2; and Zimmerman (2002), "Epilogue."

[22]On this comparative point, see especially Jason Nicholls (2006). For more on international comparisons between democratic states, see the different chapter authors in Friedman and Kenney (2005).

[23]See the report by Michael Lapp, Wendy Grigg, and Brenda Tay-Lim (2002).

[24]See the article by David Hicks, Peter Doolittle, and John Lee (2004).

[25]There are clearly exceptions among history teachers to this basic pattern, as I note in what follows. However, a number of studies have turned up that pattern repeatedly. See, for example, John Goodlad (1984), Karen Wiley and Jeanne Race (1977), and Larry Cuban's (1993) wider study of teaching.

[26]See, for example, the two cases in S. G. Grant (2003), the case of David in Cynthia Hartzler-Miller (2001), the case of new teacher Angela in Stephanie van Hover and Elizabeth Yeager (2003), and the case of Ed Barnes in Suzanne Wilson and Sam Wineburg (1993).

[27]On the grip of the common collective-memory approach on history education and historical consciousness generally, see Peter Seixas (2000). See also Bodnar (1992), Lowenthal (1998), and Kammen (1991). Also of note is Linda Levstik's (2000) account of how students' fascination with the seamier sides of American history were ushered off the educational stage

to give the history teachers she studied more time to focus on the positive, celebratory aspects embedded in the freedom-quest narrative.

[28]For an account of such pressure in the state of Virginia, see Stephanie van Hover and Walter Heineke (2005).

[29]At the high school level, see Bob Bain (2000). In the upper elementary school grades, see Bruce VanSledright (2002) and Suzanne Wilson (1990).

[30]For empirical studies on these influences, see Keith Barton (2001), Terrie Epstein (2000), Bruce VanSledright (1997), Sam Wineburg and colleagues (Wineburg, Mosborg, Porat, & Duncan, 2007), and a review by James F. Voss (1998).

[31]These terms are from Bodnar (1992).

[32]Although to see into the mirror, one must look toward the front windshield. And so nationalism projects lean in the direction of deploying what can be seen in the reflection (the past) for particular present and forward-going enterprises.

[33]For more on the development of American public schools and the curriculum, see, for example, Lawrence Cremin (1964), Herbert Kliebard (1985), and David Tyack (1974).

[34]In a similar vein, see pages 1–6 in Friedman and Kenney (2005) and especially Eric Hobsbawm's (1997) distinction between partisan histories and the sort of subjective partisanship that can creep into professional historical writing.

[35]All these preceding quotes are taken from Kammen (1989, p. 139).

[36]See Kammen (1989, pp. 145–151). The quote is from page 151. Kammen's (1991) later work in *Mystic Chords of Memory* (especially chapter 19) is also instructive.

[37]Gerstle's (1997a) treatment of changes in immigration history in America is a case in point.

[38]Kammen (1991) explores the heritage phenomenon more deeply in *Mystic Chords of Memory*. I rely here on his chapter-length treatment for its more direct application to school history.

[39]For a different treatment, see Keith Barton and Linda Levstik (2004), especially chapter 9.

[40]There are studies of history teaching and learning, and their results, that predate the period from which I draw. However, these studies tend to be rather spasmodic and scattered. By contrast, work begun in the late 1980s in North America tends to be more systematic and more common, causing some to refer to it as a cottage industry. For a sample of studies conducted before the period I draw from, see a review by Sam Wineburg (1996). For a detailed review of the growing cottage industry in history education research (both national and international) from 1996 to 2006, see Bruce VanSledright and Margarita Limon (2006).

[41]See James V. Wertsch and Kevin O'Connor (1991). Anecdotally, I conducted a close approximation of Wertsch and O'Connor's (1991) study, using the same prompt with a group of 27 undergraduate prospective elementary teachers in 2002. Twenty-four of the 27 wrote responses that virtually mirrored those written by students in the earlier study.

[42]See James V. Wertsch (1998) and especially his chapter "Specific Narratives and Schematic Narrative Templates" (Wertsch, 2005) and Wertsch and O'Connor (1991).

[43]See Michael Frisch (1989). Frisch does not give readers a breakdown of the ethnoracial composition of the students from whom he collected data. Presumably, they were predominantly White and of European lineage. If so, as I will show, this may matter in important ways.

[44]For a more detailed review of this body of research, see Wineburg (1996). The hand wringing is, of course, ironic if we consider that the collective-memory approach is fairly adept at leaving its mark on the recollections of the average high school graduate, at least the ones sampled by Michael Frisch. See also Kammen (1991), chapter 19, on this point.

[45]Good treatments on this point come from historians. See Kammen (1989), Lowenthal (1998), Bodnar (1992), and Rosenzweig and Thelen (2000).

[46]The state of New York uses document-based questions on its standardized tests in history (as does the Advanced Placement program) that can encourage this sort of essay writing. See S. G. Grant (2003). But most other educational jurisdictions follow the practice of Virginia

and rely exclusively on multiple-choice items that sample recall of details ostensibly attended to in class and in the textbook. See van Hover and Heinecke (2005).

[47]To date, the U.S. Department of Education has spent approximately $500 million on its Teaching American History grant program designed, as Senator Robert Byrd of West Virginia—the program's sponsor—had argued, to improve the purchase the nation's youth had on the "traditional" story of that nation and thus help to undermine the threat.

[48]See Epstein (2000). For more detail on this point, see also Signithia Fordham (1996) and Peter Murrell (2001).

[49]Genuine inclusion can be seen as risky because some fear it might dilute the potency of the officialized narrative arc and therefore only alienate those who are its staunchest defenders while also implying that those defenders be willing to relinquish hold on previously unshared socio-cultural assets.

[50]On the everyday conception of history, see Carl Becker (1935). On its presence among school-age students, see Peter Lee (2004). See Seixas (2000) regarding the single-story conception of the past.

[51]For descriptions of these differences in conceptions, see Tom Holt (1990) and Roy Rosenzweig (2000).

[52]On this point about the unquestioned "sacredness" of understandings about certain aspects of the American past, work by Edward Linenthal and Thomas Engelhardt (1996) is deeply instructive.

[53]For evidence-backed arguments about why such capabilities are necessities in the 21st century, see, for example, Barton and Levstik (2004), VanSledright (2002), and Wineburg et al. (2007).

[54]For more on what this looks like, see the "exhibition stance" described by Barton and Levstik (2004).

[55]On this point, secular and religious narratives are seldom as distinct and separated as I imply in stories of the American past. Manifest Destiny, for example, that ancient theme of national development, is thoroughly infused with potent Protestant religious tropes and iconography. But currently, if U.S. history textbooks are any guide, it is within the province of the secular care-takers of the narrative of nation-state and its development to choose the nature of those tropes and icons. Organized religious groups can only lobby these caretakers for inclusion and are cir-cumscribed by the state's provision preventing overlap of nation-state and organized religious functions and iconographies in places such as public schools. Nonetheless, the divine–secular boundaries often can be more opaque than transparent.

[56]By state based, I mean in this case a story derived, say, by the development of a state of the union, such as California or Oklahoma or Vermont.

[57]For an example of this idea and how it might be taught, see Thomas Bender (2006).

[58]For a more systematic and erudite overview of the rudiments of disciplinary approach applied to school history, see Peter Lee (2004).

[59]Gerstle's (1997a) treatment of immigration history in America and his efforts to offer what he argues is a more balanced account of the interplay of emancipation and coercion in Americanization processes is a case study of how this process can unfold.

[60]See the classroom-based studies by, for example, Bain (2000), VanSledright (2002), and Wilson (1990).

[61]The following studies, for example, and their authors represent these aspects of disciplined-based history education advocacy: Bain (2000), Seixas (2000), VanSledright (2002), and Wineburg et al. (2007).

[62]Seixas (2000) argues that another approach that he terms "the postmodern" may actually possess even greater promise. Although I find his argument compelling, in the interest of space, I do not consider it here.

[63]A good example here is a chapter-length treatment by Peter Lee (1995).

[64]Of course, I am far from the first to make such a case. Yet as I note in the following para-graph, it is seldom too late to intensify and broaden the conversations we have about these

matters and to what end we pursue them. Such conversations are perhaps at the heart of the best liberal, democratic systems many of us live by permit.

[65]See, for example, chapters 4 and 9 in Rorty's (1989) *Contingency, Irony, and Solidarity* and his *Achieving Our Country: Leftist Thought in Twentieth Century America* (1998).

REFERENCES

Apple, M., & Christian-Smith, L. (1989). The politics of the textbook. In S. de Castell, A. Luke, & C. Luke (Eds.), *Language, authority, and criticism: Readings on the school textbook* (pp. 155–169). London: Routledge.

Bain, B. (2000). Into the breach: Using research and theory to shape history instruction. In P. Stearns, P. Seixas, & S. Wineburg (Eds.), *Knowing, teaching, and learning history: National and international perspectives* (pp. 331–352). New York: New York University Press.

Barton, K. (1996). Narrative simplifications in elementary students' historical thinking. In J. Brophy (Ed.), *Advances in research on teaching: Vol. 6. Teaching and learning history* (pp. 51–84). Greenwich, CT: Elsevier Science.

Barton, K. (2001). "You'd be wanting to know about the past": Social contexts of children's understanding in Northern Ireland and the USA. *Comparative Education, 37*, 89–106.

Barton, K., & Levstik, L. (2004). *Teaching history for the common good.* Mahwah, NJ: Lawrence Erlbaum.

Beck, I., McKeown, M., & Worthy, J. (1995). Giving text a voice can improve understanding. *Reading Research Quarterly, 30*, 252–276.

Becker, C. (1935). *Everyman his own historian.* New York: Quadrangle Paperbacks.

Bell J. C., & McCollum, D. (1917). A study of the attainments of pupils in United States history. *Journal of Educational Psychology, 8*, 257–274.

Belok, M. V. (1981). Schoolbooks, pedagogy books, and the political socialization of young Americans. *Educational Studies, 12*, 35–48.

Bender, T. (2006). *A nation among nations: America's place in world history.* New York: Hill and Wang.

Bodnar, J. (1992). *Remaking America: Public memory, commemoration, and patriotism in the twentieth century.* Princeton, NJ: Princeton University Press.

Cheney, L. V. (1994, October 20). The end of history. *The Wall Street Journal,* pp. A26(W), A22(E).

Cohen, L. (1990). *Making a new deal: Industrial workers in Chicago, 1919–1939.* New York: Cambridge University Press.

Crawford, K. A. (2006). Culture wars: Japanese history textbooks and the construction of official memory. In S. J. Foster & K. A. Crawford (Eds.), *What shall we tell the children? International perspectives on school history textbooks* (pp. 49–68). Greenwich, CT: Information Age.

Cremin, L. A. (1964). *The transformation of the school.* New York: Knopf.

Crevecoeur, H. S. J. de. (1912). *Letters from an American farmer.* New York: E. P. Dutton. (Original work published 1782)

Cuban, L. (1991). History of teaching in social studies. In J. Shaver (Ed.), *Handbook of research on social studies teaching and learning* (pp. 197–209). New York: Macmillan Reference.

Cuban, L. (1993). *How teachers taught: Constancy and change in American classrooms.* New York: Teachers College Press.

Dolinski, C. (2006, May 18). Whose facts? *Tampa Tribune.* Available from http://www.tbo.com/life/education/MGBE0HSHCNE.html

Eikenberry D. H. (1923). Permanence of high school learning. *Journal of Educational Psychology 14*, 463–481.

Epstein, T. (2000). Adolescents' perspectives on racial diversity in U.S. history: Case studies from an urban classroom. *American Educational Research Journal, 37*, 185–214.

Finn, P. (2007, July 20). New manuals push a Putin's-eye view in Russian schools. *The Washington Post*, pp. A1, A16.

FitzGerald, F. (1980). *America revised: History schoolbooks in the twentieth century.* Boston: Knopf.

Florida House of Representatives HB 7087 (2006).

Fordham, S. (1996). *Blacked out: Dilemmas of race, identity, and success at Capital High.* Chicago: University of Chicago Press.

Foster, S. (2006). Whose history? Portrayal of immigrant groups in U.S. history textbooks, 1800–Present. In S. J. Foster & K. A. Crawford (Eds.), *What shall we tell the children? International perspectives on school history textbooks* (pp. 155–178). Greenwich, CT: Information Age.

Foster, S. J., & Crawford, K. A. (Eds.). (2006). *What shall we tell the children? International perspectives on school history textbooks.* Greenwich, CT: Information Age.

Friedman, M. P., & Kenney, P. (2005). Introduction: History in politics. In M. P. Friedman & P. Kenney (Eds.), *Partisan histories: The past in contemporary global politics* (pp. 1-13). New York: Palgrave Macmillan.

Frisch, M. (1989). American history and the structures of collective memory: A modest exercise in empirical iconography. *Journal of American History, 75*, 1130–1155.

Fuchs, L. H. (1990). *The American kaleidoscope: Race, ethnicity, and civic culture.* Hanover, NH: Wesleyan University Press.

Gabaccia, D. R. (1997). Liberty, coercion, and the making of immigrant historians. *Journal of American History, 84*, 570–575.

Garcia, J. (1986). The White ethnic experience in selected secondary U.S. history textbooks. *Social Studies, 76*, 117–180.

Gerstle, G. (1997a). Liberty, coercion, and the making of Americans. *Journal of American History, 84*, 524–558.

Gerstle, G. (1997b). The power of nations. *Journal of American History, 84*, 576–580.

Goodlad, J. (1984). *A place called school: Prospects for the future.* New York: McGraw-Hill.

Grant, S. G. (2003). *History lessons: Teaching, learning, and testing in U.S. high school history classrooms.* Mahwah, NJ: Lawrence Erlbaum.

Gutman, H. (1976). *Work, culture, and society in industrializing America: Essays in American working-class and social history.* New York: Knopf.

Handlin, O. (1973). *The uprooted: The epic story of great migrations that made the American people.* Boston: Little, Brown. (Original work published 1951)

Hartzler-Miller, C. (2001). Making sense of "best practice" in teaching history. *Theory and Research in Social Education, 29*, 672–695.

Hein, L., & Selden, M. (Eds.). (2000). *Censoring history: Citizenship and memory in Japan, Germany, and the United States.* Armonk, NY: M. E. Sharpe.

Hicks, D., Doolittle, P., & Lee, J. (2004). Social studies teachers' use of classroom-based and Web-based historical primary sources. *Theory and Research in Social Education, 32*, 213–247.

Higham, J. (2002). *Strangers in the land: Patterns of American nativism, 1860–1925.* New Brunswick, NJ: Rutgers University Press. (Original work published 1955)

Hobsbawm, E. J. (1997). *On history.* London: New Press.

Hollinger, D. A. (1995). *Postethnic America: Beyond multiculturalism.* New York: HarperCollins.

Hollinger, D. A. (1997). National solidarity at the end of the twentieth century: Reflections on the United States and liberal nationalism. *Journal of American History, 84*, 559–569.

Holt, T. (1990). *Thinking historically: Narrative, imagination, and understanding. New York*: College Board.

Kammen, M. (1989). History is our heritage: The past in contemporary American culture. In P. Gagnon (Ed.), *Historical literacy: The case for history in American education* (pp. 138–156). Boston: Houghton Mifflin.

Kammen, M. (1991). *Mystic chords of memory: The transformation of tradition in American culture.* New York: Knopf.

Kelly, T., Meuwissen, K., & VanSledright, B. (2007). What of history? Historical knowledge within a system of standards and accountability. *International Journal of Social Education, 21,* 115-145.

Kliebard, H. M. (1985). What happened to American schooling in the first part of the twentieth century? In E. Eisner (Ed.), *Learning and teaching the ways of knowing: Eighty-fourth yearbook of the national society for the study of education* (Part II, pp. 1–22). Chicago: University of Chicago Press.

Lapp, M., Grigg, W., & Tay-Lim, B. (2002). *The nation's report card: U.S. history 2001.* Jessup, MD: United States Department of Education.

Lee, P. (1995). History and the national curriculum in England. In A. Dickinson, P. Gordon, P. Lee, & J. Slater (Eds.), *International yearbook of history education, Vol. 1* (pp. 73–123). London: Woburn.

Lee, P. (2004). Putting principles into practice: Understanding history. In S. Donovan & J. Bransford (Eds.), *How students learn: History in the classroom* (pp. 31–78). Washington, DC: National Academies Press.

Letourneau, J., & Moisan, S. (2004). Young people's assimilation of a collective historical memory: A case study of Quebeckers of French-Canadian heritage. In P. Seixas (Ed.), *Theorizing historical consciousness* (pp. 109–128). Toronto, ON: University of Toronto Press.

Levstik, L. (2000). Articulating the silences: Teachers' and adolescents' conceptions of historical significance. In P. Stearns, P. Seixas, & S. Wineburg (Eds.), *Knowing, teaching, and learning history: National and international perspectives* (pp. 284–305). New York: New York University Press.

Linenthal, E. T., & Engelhardt, T. (1996). *History wars: The Enola Gay and other battles for the American past.* New York: Henry Holt.

Lowenthal, D. (1998). *The heritage crusade and the spoils of history.* Cambridge, UK: Cambridge University Press.

McNeil, L. M. (1988). *Contradictions of control: School structure and school knowledge.* New York: Routledge.

Monte-Sano, C. (2006). *Learning to use evidence in historical writing.* Unpublished doctoral dissertation, Stanford University, Palo Alto, CA.

Murrell, P. C. (2001). *The community teacher: A new framework for effective urban teaching.* New York: Teachers College Press.

Nash, G. B., Crabtree, C., & Dunn, R. E. (2000). *History on trial: Culture wars and the teaching of the past.* New York: Vintage.

Nevins, A. (1942, May 4). American history for Americans. *The New York Times Magazine,* pp. 6, 28–29.

Nicholls, J. (2006). Beyond the national and the transnational: Perspectives on WWII in U.S.A., Italian, Swedish, Japanese, and English school history textbooks. In S. J. Foster & K. A. Crawford (Eds.), *What shall we tell the children? International perspectives on school history textbooks* (pp. 89–112). Greenwich, CT: Information Age.

Norton, M. (2006, May 2). History under construction in Florida. *The New York Times.* Available from http://weblogs.elearning.ubc.ca/ross/archives/028613.html

Novick, P. (1988). *That noble dream: The "objectivity question" and the American historical profession.* Cambridge, UK: Cambridge University Press.

Olneck, M. R. (1989). Americanization and the education of immigrants, 1900–1925: An analysis of symbolic action. *American Journal of Education, 92,* 398–423.

Page, R. N. (1991). *Lower track classrooms.* New York: Teachers College Press.

Park, R., & Miller, H. A. (1921). *Old world traits transplanted.* New York: Harper and Brothers.

Paxton, R. J. (1999). A deafening silence: History textbooks and the students who read them. *Review of Educational Research, 69,* 315–339.

Ravitch, D., & Finn, C., Jr. (1988). *What do our 17-year-olds know? A report on the first national assessment of history and literature.* New York: HarperCollins.

Roediger, D. R. (1991). *The wages of Whiteness: Race and the making of the American working class.* London: Verso.

Rorty, R. (1989). *Contingency, irony, and solidarity.* Cambridge, UK: Cambridge University Press.

Rorty, R. (1998). *Achieving our country: Leftist thought in twentieth century America.* Cambridge, MA: Harvard University Press.

Rosenzweig, R. (2000). How Americans use and think about the past: Implications from a national survey for the teaching of history. In P. Stearns, P. Seixas, & S. Wineburg (Eds.), *Knowing, teaching, and learning history: National and international perspectives* (pp. 262–283). New York: New York University Press.

Rosenzweig, R., & Thelen, D. (2000). *The presence of the past: Popular uses of history in American life.* New York: Columbia University Press.

Schlesinger, A., Jr. (2007). Reflections on the national history center and the purposes of history. *Perspectives, 45,* 16–17.

Schlesinger, A. M., Jr. (1991). *The disuniting of America: Reflections on a multicultural society.* New York: Whittle Communications.

Schug, M., Todd, R., & Beery, R. (1984). Why kids don't like social studies. *Social Education, 48,* 382–387.

Schweber, S. (2006). Fundamentally 9/11: The fashioning of collective memory in a Christian school. *American Journal of Education, 112,* 392–417.

Seixas, P. (2000). Schweigen! Die kinder! or, Does postmodern history have a place in the schools? In P. Stearns, P. Seixas, & S. Wineburg (Eds.), *Knowing, teaching, and learning history: National and international perspectives* (pp. 15–37). New York: New York University Press.

Seixas, P. (Ed.). (2004). *Theorizing historical consciousness.* Toronto, ON: University of Toronto Press.

Sewall, G. T. (1987). *American history textbooks: An assessment of quality.* New York: Educational Excellence Network.

Sleeter, C. E., & Grant, C. A. (1991). Race, class, gender, and disability in current textbooks. In M. Apple & L. K. Christian-Smith (Eds.), *The politics of the textbook* (pp. 78–110). New York: Routledge.

Sollors, W. (Ed.). (1989). *The invention of ethnicity.* New York: Oxford University Press.

Trouillot, M.-R. (1995). *Silencing the past: Power and the production of history.* Boston: Ingram.

Tyack, D. (1974). *The one best system.* Cambridge, MA: Harvard University Press.

van Hover, S. D., & Heineke, W. F. (2005). The impact of accountability reform on the "wise practice" of secondary history teachers: The Virginia experience. In E. A. Yeager & O. L. Davis Jr. (Eds.), *Wise social studies teaching in an age of high-stakes testing: Essays on classroom practices and possibilities* (pp. 89–116). Greenwich, CT: Information Age.

van Hover, S. D., & Yeager, E. A. (2003). Making students better people? A case study of a beginning history teacher. *International Social Studies Forum, 3,* 219–232.

VanSledright, B. (1997). And Santayana lives on: Students' views on the purposes for studying American history. *Journal of Curriculum Studies, 29,* 529–557.

VanSledright, B. (2002). *In search of America's past: Learning to read history in elementary school.* New York: Teachers College Press.

VanSledright, B., & Limon, M. (2006). Learning and teaching social studies: A review of cognitive research in history and geography. In P. Alexander & P. Winne (Eds.), *The handbook of educational psychology* (2nd ed., pp. 545–570). Mahwah, NJ: Lawrence Erlbaum.

VanSledright, B. A. (1995). "I don't remember—the ideas are all jumbled in my head": Eighth graders' reconstructions of colonial American history. *Journal of Curriculum and Supervision, 10,* 317–345.

Vecoli, R. J. (1979). The resurgence of American immigration history. *American Studies International, 17,* 46–66.

Voss, J. F. (1998). Issues in the learning of history. *Issues in education: Contributions from educational psychology, 4*, 163–209.

Washburn, L. H. (1997). Accounts of slavery: An analysis of United States history textbooks from 1900–1992. *Theory and Research in Social Education, 25*, 470–491.

Wertsch, J. V. (1998). *Mind as action.* New York: Oxford University Press.

Wertsch, J. V. (2005). Specific narratives and schematic narrative templates. In P. Seixas (Ed.), *Theorizing historical consciousness* (pp. 49–62). Toronto, ON: University of Toronto Press.

Wertsch, J. V., & O'Connor, K. (1991). Multi-voicedness in historical representation: American college students' accounts of the origin of the US. *Journal of Narrative and Life History, 4*, 295–310.

Wiley, K., & Race, J. (1977). *The status of pre-college science, mathematics, and social science education: 1955–1975* (Vol. III). Washington, DC: National Science Foundation.

Wilson, S. (1990). *Mastodons, maps, and Michigan: Exploring uncharted territory while teaching elementary school social studies* (Elementary Subjects Center Report No. 24). East Lansing, MI: Center for the Learning and Teaching of Elementary Subjects.

Wilson, S., & Wineburg, S. (1993). Wrinkles in time and place: Using performance assessments to understand the knowledge of history teachers. *American Educational Research Journal, 30*, 729–769.

Wineburg, S. (1996). The psychology of teaching and learning history. In R. Calfee & D. Berliner (Eds.), *Handbook of educational psychology* (pp. 423–437). New York: Macmillan Reference.

Wineburg, S., Mosborg, S., Porat, D., & Duncan, A. (2007). Common belief and the cultural curriculum: An intergenerational study of historical consciousness. *American Educational Research Journal, 44*, 40–76.

Zimmerman, J. (2002). *Whose America? Culture wars in the public schools.* Cambridge, MA: Harvard University Press.

Chapter 5

Language Moves: The Place of "Foreign" Languages in Classroom Teaching and Learning

DIANE LARSEN-FREEMAN
DONALD FREEMAN
University of Michigan

Language as subject matter is highly protean; it has been defined in various ways in schools, usually as a reflection of predominant images of teaching and learning. Language is also *in, of,* and *for* the world. It exists and flourishes *in* the lives and circumstances of its users, created *of* their worlds; it is thus a way of both being in and knowing about the immediate and more distant world. This quality of making present what is not actually there means that language exists *for* purposes beyond itself. This complicated ecology masks a dynamism in language that is difficult to capture, let alone work with within normal disciplinary boundaries and within the organized activities of schools. It also leads to definitional challenges.

In this review, we focus on the relationship between disciplines, knowledge, and pedagogy in foreign language instruction, as we have been invited to do. However, we acknowledge that the designation *foreign* is, of course, relative to the speaker and mutable in the situation. For instance, Spanish has a heterogeneous identity in the United States: It could be considered as a "foreign" language to those with little or no knowledge of it, or as a "second" language to those who use it in addition to their first language, or as a "native" language to those for whom it is a home or heritage language. To cope with these ambiguities, colleagues within the field of language teaching often prefer the term *modern languages* or *world languages*, although these terms have associated problems as well. To facilitate recognition, we will use the term *foreign language* for this review, but to problematize it, hereafter we will use "foreign" with quotation marks.

We need to acknowledge at the outset a second, and related, decision in framing this review, which is to how to address English. Other chapters in this volume (Sperling, this volume) address the teaching and learning of English through language arts and through the issues of access to the curriculum faced by students who are not fluent in English

Review of Research in Education
February 2008, Vol. 32, pp. 147–186
DOI: 10.3102/0091732X07309426
© 2008 AERA. http://rre.aera.net

(Duran, this volume). We have chosen instead to treat English differently and in two main ways: as the geopolitical linguistic influence that it has become and for the professional influence it exerts on the teaching of "foreign" languages as a specific school subject. In terms of the former, we need to be explicit that this chapter does not present a global sociopolitical analysis of the role of English; however, we will consider how the globalization of English has influenced conceptions of "foreign" language teaching. In the latter area, we recognize that there will be readers who will likely be dissatisfied with our drawing connections between the teaching of English and other "foreign" languages, preferring perhaps to maintain what they may see as the analytical integrity of the latter. We would simply argue that to avoid discussions of how English as what we will call a "subject-language" is (re)shaping "foreign" language instruction would be to turn a blind eye to one of the critical language moves that is now happening in education.

In fact, the complexity of positioning this review goes well beyond these immediate questions of terminology, which in a sense are emblematic of ambiguities about the place of language in the larger landscape of educational research and theorizing. As indicated by some of the other chapters in this volume, there are several lines of thinking and development in language education, "foreign" language education being one of them. Each of these lineages draws on its own foundational models and operational definitions and makes its own presuppositions on this basis. Our remit in this chapter is to examine the subfield of "foreign" language teaching and learning. We therefore acknowledge from the outset that the models and definitions we draw from, and the presuppositions we may make, will be reflective of that lineage. To trace the interrelations—and potential disagreements and discontinuities—between the various different subfields in language education would be another task. All we can reasonably do, then, in this review is to acknowledge the positioning we adopt, not claiming it as exclusive but as reflective of the domain of the study of classroom "foreign" language teaching and learning.

In addressing this review to "foreign" language teaching, we are writing about what we will call subject-languages, be they either languages other than English (LOTE) or English as a "foreign" language depending on the national and school context. A subject-language is a language that has been designated as subject matter within a school curriculum and thus has certain teaching practices and learning expectations associated with it. We intend to use the examination of subject-languages to probe some of the changing assumptions about knowledge and pedagogy in "foreign" language teaching and learning. The word *moves* in our title is intended to capture the dynamism of those changes. Examining the ways in which language moves in "foreign" language teaching and learning shows, we will argue, how the complex relationships between parent disciplines, school knowledge, and pedagogy in "foreign" language instruction are shifting. Furthermore, because these shifts occur in and through language, they may presage wider moves in disciplinary knowledge.

OVERVIEW OF CHAPTER

The argument in this review is organized around the core elements of these moves in classroom practice: the content (in this case subject-languages), how they are learned, and how they are taught. Casting these elements in terms of "foreign" language instruction, we begin by asking three questions: (a) How has "foreign" language been defined as a school subject and how have those definitions changed in the last century? (b) What does it mean to have learned, and thus to know, a language as a school subject? and (c) How is knowledge in language teaching being reconstituted these days? It is clear these three areas overlap and respond to one another; however, they can serve as a useful heuristic in structuring consideration of "foreign" language as a school subject.

As our responses to these questions will reveal, there has been a rapid succession of redefinitions of "foreign" language in the past hundred years that seems to have been propelled by intense pressures that are external to the professional language teaching community itself. Fueled by geopolitical, economic, and strategic forces, current definitions of language have become far more utilitarian than in the past so that subject-languages are often defined by their uses or "specific purposes," that is, language for economic advancement, for technological purposes, or for political or security purposes. This utilitarian view is further reflected in the rhetorical references to language as an instrument of war (cf. the recent emphasis on the "critical languages" such as Arabic, Chinese, or Pashto) or as a political weapon as in the recent immigration debate in the United States, France, or Russia,[1] for example.

When language is defined in more utilitarian terms, we will show that what it means to come to know a language also shifts from knowledge of an autonomous system of linguistic competence to a means of communication. Indeed, we will argue that the move from language as a structure-based mental system to language as a functional tool for communicative purposes has had a major impact on "foreign" language instruction. The notion of "plurilingualism" has recently accompanied this shift, whereby languages are seen not to exist as hermetically sealed and distinct intact systems in the minds of language users but rather more generally to grow from experience, which makes knowledge of language dynamic, situated, sometimes partial, and shaped through time by use.

To explore a dynamic view of language, we next turn to chaos and complexity theories (hereafter, C/CTs[2]) to frame our observations. Although we can only briefly outline the tenets in this chapter, we feel that C/CTs, which probe the complexity, dynamism, and nonlinearity of systems, provide a useful way of characterizing the protean quality of "foreign" language and how it has moved as a school subject.

Later in this review, we argue that there is a certain tension between the global and the local. The impetus that seems to drive the utilitarian redefinitions of language has stemmed in large measure from moves toward globalization and the concomitant development of so-called knowledge economies and the "technocratic discourse" they have spawned (Luke, Luke, & Graham, 2007); in contrast, the intense localness of the various practices of subject-language teaching has defined language knowledge in increasing local and contextual terms.

This move to localness has fueled the decomposition of a unified view of classroom practices, which is our next point. We see evidence that the field of "foreign" language teaching is becoming fractured in a decomposition that is animated by second-language acquisition (SLA) research, the changing roles for language teachers, the blurring of professional identities, and the globalization of English; in essence, there is no grand theory or primary discipline to anchor it. Although we argue that this is true of "foreign" language teaching, we believe it is also the case of other subjects as we enter into a period of "postdisciplinarity," a time in which the overarching definitions of knowledge in many disciplines are decomposing and are being overtaken by local practices. Because language provides the discursive basis through which disciplines are defined and articulated, as well as the interactive medium through which they are realized, we conclude our review by reasoning that this postdisciplinarity is perhaps most immediately evident in subject-language teaching and learning but that it may eventually affect other fields.

OVERVIEW OF "FOREIGN" LANGUAGE AS A SCHOOL SUBJECT DURING THE 20TH CENTURY

Language as a subject, arguably more than any other content area, is constantly being redefined. It is the tool that everyone uses in learning and teaching but one that they find hard to define in its own right. This may be because language teaching,[3] unlike mathematics or history, has not had a consistent disciplinary home in which to anchor its content or theories of learning, teaching, and knowing, or mastery.[4] Certainly, linguistics offers an importance disciplinary base, but linguistic descriptions of subject languages, as helpful as they may be, are not the sole or even the defining content of what is taught in the "foreign" language classroom. There is also the thriving field of applied linguistics, which is largely interdisciplinary in its orientation. Although applied linguistics has had an impact on the teaching and learning of "foreign" languages, applied linguistics also does not dictate the content of "foreign" language instruction. Neither do the disciplines of anthropology or psychology, although they too have influenced "foreign" language teaching.

At the beginning the 20th century, "foreign" language teaching was generally seen as a means of support for the study of literatures and the fine arts. Growing out of traditions associated with grammar schools and the teaching of Latin, the focus was on languages as grammatical systems that could be taught and learned primarily through translation of literary texts (Kelly, 1969; Titone, 1968). The rather loose set of practices that enacted this pedagogical view became known (largely in retrospect) as "grammar-translation" teaching. Its teacher-fronted pedagogy, which entailed explanations of grammatical systems and new lexicon or vocabulary while students copied notes and read and translated texts in the new language, flowed quite readily from the general style of teaching in other subject areas in U.S. schools (Tyack & Cuban, 1995). Thus, in the prevailing thinking, learning a language as a subject in school depended on memorizing equivalences between one language system (the language of instruction) and the other (the subject-language) such that teaching the new or target language could be built on the first or mother tongue.

In this period, language learning in classrooms bore little or no connection to language learning or language use in the world outside of school. One could argue that in a very real sense, the focus on explaining grammar and on translating new vocabulary helped the teacher to circumscribe and package a classroom subject matter out of language; such packaging focused on literacy, which was a broadly accepted aim of schooling (Tyack, 1974). Thus, language as a school subject was distanced from language as it was learned and spoken on the street, a gulf that the language-teaching profession has sought to bridge ever since. There was little to challenge or problematize this view. Although the multilingualism of communities around the world was well documented in anthropology and ethnography, it was largely invisible in schools. Classroom pedagogies were founded on the concepts of language equivalence, which gave rise to the rather pernicious concept of "nativeness," which was understood as knowing the language from birth and learning it through the social processes of growing up in a particular language community. Anchored in determinations of social position and power, this concept of nativeness became a persistent feature of subject-language instruction through the 20th century.

Beginning in the 1940s, the conceptualizing of language, how it was learned and therefore how it might be taught, changed rather dramatically. Although the direct method and the reading method[5] had challenged the supremacy of grammar translation, the dramatic changes were primarily driven externally, which began with the need during World War II for people to learn foreign languages rapidly for military purposes. Later, beginning in 1957, the Sputnik revolution furthered the geopolitical dimension[6] in language teaching in the United States, as having citizens who could speak Russian and other "foreign" languages was defined more explicitly as a key element of U.S. national security policy under the auspices of the National Defense Education Act (Ninkovich, 1981).

Faced with the need to train speakers of languages deemed strategic by the government, views of language as subject matter and how it might be learned altered radically. In an approach called the Army Specialized Training Program, or ASTP, which drew heavily on the disciplines of structural linguistics and behavioral psychology, subject-language was portrayed as a set of habits or behaviors that could best be taught through teacher-led drills and rigorous and constant teacher correction coupled with the positive reinforcement of praise. This approach later became known as the audiolingual method (or ALM; Brooks, 1960). "Foreign" language learning then was a matter of forming appropriate linguistic habits in keeping with those of fluent or "native" language speakers. In contrast to the grammar-translation view of language learning that had focused on literacy, primarily through learning to read and, to a lesser extent, to write in the "foreign" language, ALM teaching emphasized the development to automated use or "native-like" mastery of spoken language (Larsen-Freeman, 2000b; Richards & Rodgers, 2000). The corresponding focus on listening as a way to absorb new language input—the audio aspect of the method—drew on images of how children learned their first language and contrasted with the focus on seeing, reasoning, and memory that had undergirded learning language through translating their grammatical and lexical systems.

It could be argued, then, that structural linguistics and behavioral psychology introduced through ALM a "unifying" theory of language, teaching, and learning that clearly framed a definition of language as the content of instruction (i.e., "verbal habits"; cf. Skinner, 1957) and, extending from that basis, how instruction should operate and how learning could be defined and assessed. This view, which integrated the processes of learning and teaching through a definition of language as mental habit, worked in an interesting way against the basic notion of "foreignness" in second or other languages. In contrast to grammar translation, which depended on the "native" and the "foreign" languages as being parallel and therefore commensurate systems, ALM and its antecedent pedagogies focused on the learning process itself. If language learning could be a natural matter of habit formation, then, exposed to the right models, with the proper amount of drill, practice, and correction, anyone could become a fluent speaker of another language. Thus no language was inherently "foreign"; it was simply a "second" or "other" or "additional" language from the point of view of the learner, and with proper instruction, he or she could master it.

Throughout the decades that followed, language teaching would wrestle with this notion of a unifying theory that could bring together, if not integrate, definitions of language as classroom content with understandings of how that content could be learned in classrooms and how instruction should support and manage such learning. In the 1960s, the disciplines of cognitive psychology and generative linguistics became ascendant influences in understanding learning in both first and second languages. As a result, the definition of language underwent another major shift. In major part because of Chomsky's (1959) scathing review of Skinner's (1957) *Verbal Behavior*, language was no longer seen to be a set of verbal habits or behaviors; instead, it was construed as a rule-governed system. Building on this definition, the development of child language acquisition as a field of study (Brown, 1973) introduced constructs such as "creative construction," which helped to reconceive of language learning as a cognitive process, one that entailed an active search for the generative rules underlying the language system. At the same time, the study of first-language (or L1) acquisition raised inevitable questions about how second-language (or L2) learning might be similar or different and, furthermore, how classrooms as instructed settings might differ as language learning environments from the natural social (or noninstructed) settings in which children learned their first languages. Some argued there was little difference. They called for a "natural approach" (Krashen & Terrell, 1983; Terrell, 1977), in which classroom conditions simulated the environment in which children learned their first languages. These, they believed, included a positive affective climate in which learners were exposed to abundant comprehensible input with little or no pressure to produce the language until they themselves determined that they were ready to speak.

Other methodologists stressed differences between L1 and L2 learning. Although taking into account the L1 and building from it, they argued for actively engaging learners with the new language while supporting them affectively (e.g., Curran, 1976; Gattegno, 1972, 1976; Stevick, 1976, 1980). Interestingly, although these pedagogical approaches differed quite starkly from one another in practice,[7] they shared common attributes. Each pedagogy articulated a defined basis in learning theory, which included a view of language and from which flowed a distinct set of

classroom practices. These views of learning addressed the learner as an active participant in learning of the new language; thus, they tended to complement the thinking
about learners and language acquisition that was emerging from studies in first- and
second-language acquisition (Corder, 1967). Due, in part, to this focus on constructivist views of learning and the learner, the "foreign" language teaching approaches of
the 1970s were loosely grouped under the term *humanistic methods* (Stevick, 1990).
The use of this term underscored the contrast in basic assumptions with those of
behaviorism, which portrayed the learner as more or less a habit-forming automaton.

The liveliness of the humanistic pedagogies that competed for teachers' attention
might have been less influential had there not been a vehicle for the attention, which
was provided through the global spread of English. During the period of the 1970s and
1980s, this expansion of English was propelled, in part, by Anglo-American interests in
foreign, economic, and education policy operating under the rubric of cultural diplomacy. It is interesting to trace this expansion through the promulgation of professional
teachers' associations. In the United States, the "foreign" language teaching profession
was supported by two main associations, one focused principally on literature (the Modern Language Association [MLA], founded in 1883) and the other started in 1967 as an
offshoot of the MLA to focus mainly on spoken proficiency or what would later be
called "communicative competence" (the American Council on Teaching Foreign Languages [ACTFL]). Support for teaching English as a second or foreign language
emerged as a new enterprise through two international professional groups, one head-
quartered in England, the International Association of Teaching English as a Foreign
Language (IATEFL), started in 1967, and the other based in the United States, Teachers of English to Speakers of Other Languages (TESOL), which began in 1966.

The geopolitics of this expansion became evident in the split between English and
other languages. Although ACTFL (n.d.) states it "was founded as . . . the only national
organization representing teachers of all languages at all education levels [in the United
States]," both IATEFL and TESOL frame their missions, respectively, as "to link,
develop and support English Language Teaching professionals throughout the world"
(capitalization in the original; IATEFL, n.d.) and "to ensure excellence in English language teaching to speakers of other languages" (TESOL, n.d.). Thus the creation of
these two associations in the late 1960s started to position English language teaching as
a transnational phenomenon and something apart from "foreign" language teaching
communities that were largely defined nationally; we return to this theme later in
this review.

During this period, conceptualizations of language took a decidedly social turn. Prior
to this time, the field was operating under the distinction Chomsky had made between
the capacity to use language, whether first or second, and the actual use of that capacity
in specific situations. Chomsky (1965) referred to the former as "competence" and the
latter as "performance." From the standpoint of linguistics and the theoretical study of
language, Chomsky's choice to focus on competence was justifiable; however, it was
more difficult to conceptualize, let alone apply, to the specifics of using language,
whether in communities or in classrooms. While preserving the notion of competence,

anthropological linguist Dell Hymes extended it to *"communicative* competence" (Hymes, 1972), which included speakers' knowing whether (and to what degree) something is appropriate in relation to the context and whether (and to what degree) it is actually performed. Insofar as this broader concept included knowing how to act on this knowledge in actual language use, it was yet another significant attempt to reinsert the importance of language use as opposed to simply knowledge of the underlying system. As such, it became highly influential in "foreign" language teaching (Savignon, 1972).

By the 1980s, communicative competence was firmly established as a foundational concept in language teaching (Canale & Swain, 1980), which provided to some degree the new unifying theory. In parallel, a view of learning that was based on interaction with others came to prominence in SLA research (Hatch, 1978). Writing about the history of "modern" languages in the European context, Trim (2007) links this move to communicative competence with the practical need for communication for international purposes:

The accelerating internationalisation of life was at its point of take-off, as technical developments in the communications and information industries massively transformed social life in many interconnected aspects. Multinational industries; global financial markets; mass tourism and entertainment; science and medicine were creating a mass demand for practical proficiency in modern languages, particularly for English, which was rapidly establishing itself as the first foreign language in schools and the primary medium of international communication outside the Soviet bloc. (p. 16)

The fertile view of knowing a language offered by communicative competence also helped to reshape thinking about the nature of language itself. Inasmuch as knowing a language meant using it appropriately in particular settings, then language itself might be more usefully understood as a tool or instrument for agency in those settings. Writing in 1976, applied linguist David Wilkins took precisely this view. In contrast to the heavily grammar-based syllabi of the day, Wilkins argued for what he termed "notional-functional syllabi," which sought "to change the balance of priorities by placing emphasis on the meanings expressed or the functions performed through language" (Wilkins, 1976, p. 83). There were many responses to implementing this approach to language, all of which grappled with the challenge of distilling and abstracting those language uses out of the particulars of situations. A major initiative of the Council of Europe, known as *Threshold Languages* (van Ek, 1975), introduced the view into wider circulation as it described

a detailed specification of the minimum language requirements of people who want to prepare themselves, in a general way, to be able to communicate socially on straightforward everyday matters with people from other countries who come their way, and to be able to get around and lead a reasonably normal social life when they visit another country. (van Ek, as cited in Trim, 2007, p. 19)

Other attempts to operationalize "target communicative competence" were less successful. Munby (1978), for example, proposed a model of target competence that included an unwieldy 260 microskills, highlighting the basic problem that even though they tried to be comprehensive, such efforts still foundered in the inherent plasticity and indeterminacy of language. It might be possible, for example, to specify which greetings would be needed in various situations because greeting as a language function uses a finite number of language exponents (i.e., lexical items or words). But for almost any other language function (e.g., apologizing, complaining, complimenting), which is far less formulaic, it is very difficult to specify a small number of possible language realizations because the functional intent can be expressed in many different ways. Not coincidentally, this problem is one reason why it is difficult to program computers to speak or understand natural languages (Davies, 1981).

Nevertheless, communicative competence and its applications have continued to be highly influential in conceptualizing language as the subject matter of classroom pedagogy. Although communicative competence has largely been confined to oral and transactional use of language, thus making it poorly suited for fostering academic work (Byrnes, 2006), its persuasiveness as a unifying theory of "foreign" language instruction has been widespread. Developing during a period of the rapid expansion of language use for political and economic purposes, communicative competence brought a focus on a variety of contexts for that use and thus helped to surface questions of authority and who determines the appropriateness or acceptability of language use in settings. The legacy of the behavioral view of language suggested a singular standard for acceptability because habitual forms do not vary according to situation or speaker. However, as soon as a particular variety of a language is treated as the appropriate or standard one, then other varieties, by implication, become labeled as nonstandard and consequently as less prestigious. The communicative revolution brought about a heightened criticality and raised questions of whose judgment would designate standards of language appropriateness or acceptability. These challenges extended well beyond definitions of subject-languages to broaden notions of purpose and identity in language learning. In the 1990s, critical theorists argued that to understand language, use one had to account for relations of power in the practices and interactions in which learners sought to participate (e.g., Norton, 1995), whereas others, drawing on critical theories applied to literature, questioned the construct of individual identity itself and how learning a foreign language could affirm (Brown Mitchell & Ellingson Vidal, 2001) or even transform one's identity (J. N. Davis, 1997). Thus, these debates began to outline the formal issues involved in defining the outcomes of instructed "foreign" language learning: what it means to know an (other) language.

THE NATURE OF KNOWING (AN)OTHER LANGUAGE(S)

Knowing a language is something that we all do as part of being human, yet it is very difficult to define the nature of the capacity that allows us to do so. In terms of "foreign" language teaching, the question is more than simply a philosophical one; it becomes critical to all those involved in the enterprise, whether directly as teachers and students or indirectly as curriculum developers, policymakers, test designers, parents, and the broader community. In this section, we revisit the operational history of "foreign" language teaching we have just outlined but this time through the lens of how knowing (an)other language(s) has been defined at various points in that history. We see this move as critical both to the construction of subject-language in school and to how it has influenced the decomposition of "foreign" language classroom practices at the threshold of what we think is a time of postdisciplinarity. However it is defined— as mastery, proficiency, competency, or so on—this concept of outcome, what it means to know (an)other language(s), anchors the classroom teaching–learning enterprise and shapes in both explicit and implicit ways how the work of language teaching is understood and carried out.

Since the early 20th century, when Saussure (1916/1959) proposed a distinction between *langue* (the abstract linguistic system) and *parole* ("speaking"), wherein the latter was the audible (and visible) instantiation of this abstraction, linguists have worked with the tension between the use of language in particular situations and the abstracted totality that connects these specifics as exemplars within one coherent system. It is interesting to try and define what it means to know a language within this paradigm: On one hand, it means knowing the abstracted system, the language in its entirety, but such a system exists only as a theoretical construct. On the other, it means knowing a wide variety of individual uses that depend on the communicative intent, the situation, the relationship of the interlocutors, and many other factors.

The definitional challenge becomes further complicated when one examines what it means to know a "foreign" language or one beyond one's first or mother tongue. In a real sense, to "know" one's first or mother tongue is a tautological undertaking, somewhat like knowing the proverbial water in which fish swim. Using this de facto tautology, which is often referred to as "native-speaking proficiency," as the standard for what it means to know (an)other language(s) and to define the goal of learning subject-language(s) through instruction has only compounded the difficulty. Throughout the first half of the 20th century, when "foreign" languages were primarily taught through grammar translation, knowing a second language was implicitly defined as being able to read and write it as one would one's first or mother tongue. This assumption skirted the basic question, however, because it simply defined the capacity a priori in terms of what the student could already do as a user of his or her first language. With the advent of audiolingual teaching, under the influence of behaviorism as discussed earlier, knowing a second language was understood as acting in routine or habitual ways similar to what a "native" user or speaker of that language would do. Thus, the definition was largely a circumstantial one in which linguistic performance was measured against the construct of "native-like" proficiency. So again, as with grammar-translation teaching, the notion of knowing, or mastering, a new language was understood as a sort of static abstraction in terms of the competence of a fluent language user.

There were several issues with such a definition. At the core, the definition of knowing a language was entirely a priori, framed in terms of those language users who were already socially positioned, often by birth or nationality, class, and race, as fluent users or speakers of the standard variety. This positioning was captured in the construct of the "native speaker," which was essentially more geopolitical than linguistic, in effect balkanizing the world into communities of language competence anchored by history and geographical boundaries. Thus, when a language was identified "native" by and to one group of users, it became ipso facto "foreign" to others. In spite of a growing awareness of the complexity of emerging language systems, such as pidgins, creoles, and other language hybridities, identities were based in linguistic terms on the dominant language version, which in many places was the language transplanted through the socioeconomic process of colonization. So the very term *foreign language* was rooted in a conception of knowing and using a language that was based on geography rather than psychology. In the face of a world that is a collection of multilingual communities, the apparent simplicity of the "native" versus "nonnative" or "foreign" dichotomy overlooked the complexity of language use in favor of the pragmatic necessity to define language as the subject matter of language curricula.[8]

Hymes' (1972) redefinition of competence challenged this illusion of simplicity, however. By conceptualizing communication as knowledge of appropriate use in interaction rather than simply knowledge of linguistic rules, and by basing measures of competence on what interlocutors could (or could not) do in specific situations, Hymes and his followers relativized the notion of knowing language. In this sense, a child of 5 could be seen as "communicatively competent" in forms of play as an adult might be in forms of argument.[9] This concept of ability as circumscribed by context likewise helped to shift operational notions of language learning, particularly in defining goals of "foreign" language learning.

Throughout the 1970s and 1980s, the metric of a static, geographically defined, native speaker was increasingly blurred by circumstance. Propelled by a confluence of factors, including the diversification of teaching methodologies, the global expansion of English, the developing dialects of English or "World Englishes" by "outer circle" countries (such as Nigerian or Indian Englishes; Kachru, 1986), and the rapid acceleration of language contacts both actual (through travel and various forms of social relocation) and increasingly virtually (by the Internet and Web), it has become more and more problematic to define succinctly what it means to learn or to know (an)other language(s). Language curricula and classroom pedagogies have moved to emphasize learners' ability to use language effectively in multifarious sets of circumstances. Capturing this widening gyre of communicative language use has called for a different concept of proficiency, not one that was understood as mastering the language system in its entirety but rather one that envisions competence as a dynamic and expanding proposition driven by need and tailored to situation.

It was in this context that the idea of proficiency scales began to take root in the U.S. "foreign" language teaching community. Once again, the government had an impact on language teaching—this time in launching the Proficiency Movement (Omaggio, 1983). The Proficiency Movement got its initial impetus from the oral proficiency interview (OPI) scales defined by the U.S. government's Interagency Language Roundtable (scales that became popularly known as the "Foreign Service Institute" or FSI ratings). The OPI provided a model of knowing a new language that acknowledged five ascending levels of development, which were extended from speaking to the other commonly defined language skills—listening, reading, and writing. Interestingly, the end point continued to be anchored in the concept of "native speaker," as Level 5 of the FSI scales is defined as the ability to "function as an educated native speaker."

This developmental view of language learning offered an instrumental solution to the problem of how to limit language for curricular purposes. Whereas previous versions of language curricula essentially organized language by topic and within topic by the complexity of grammatical structure and lexical demands, the communicative language-teaching "revolution," which began in the 1980s, brought with it a boundless view of language use, which necessitated a reconceptualization of language as curricular content. The overarching notion of learning or mastering the entire language that had been at the core of achieving "native-like" proficiency within the framework of audiolingual teaching needed to be rethought. Because the "entirety" of the new language is an abstract concept that has no reality in teaching or learning terms, it made operational sense to replace this vast and ungainly notion with definitions of language use in various contexts. In this way, attention shifted away from the language as an abstract system to language use and skills to achieve particular purposes. This change was evident in the U.S. national curriculum projects of the 1990s, which were managed by professional teachers' associations (e.g., the ACTFL standards in 1996, *Standards for Foreign Language Learning: Preparing for the 21st Century*, and in 1999, *Standards for Foreign Language Learning in the 21st Century*).

As definitions of language curricula focused on use, "foreign" language teaching saw the increase of "language for specific purposes" as another means to limit the pedagogical focus; thus, specific curricula were defined as language for banking, or health care provision, or academic purposes (e.g., the program at the University of Rhode Island for a bachelor of science in German and engineering ; Grandin, 1989, as cited in Byrnes, 2005). Generally, however, such instruction for specific purposes focused on language learners at the intermediate or advanced levels, in other words, those students who had already developed a foundational control of the basic linguistic structures and vocabulary of the new language. Thus, arguably, this view of curriculum was less radical than it might have appeared, because in essence it simply substituted specific contexts of language use (e.g., law, engineering, academic study) for the study of literature and the fine arts that had been the goal and domain of advanced language study.

The preceding critique notwithstanding, the focus on escalating developmental definitions of language competence that informed and reshaped curriculum and instruction throughout the 1990s did help to define a different concept of participation in language. Rather than seeing language as a linguistic competence to be acquired, learning a language was seen as learning to participate in particular communities of practice (Lave & Wenger, 1991; Rogoff, 1995; Sfard, 1998). In this sense, then, analyzing what it means to know (an)other language(s) for curricular purposes became enumerating the various forms it might take in contexts of use, what Widdowson (2003) called its "culturally informed ways of thinking and communicating" (pp. 68–69). Similarly, the extensive work done on genre analysis (Bhatia, 1993; Swales, 1990) seeks to identify the particular conventions for language use in certain domains of professional and occupational activity. This approach differs from teaching language for specific purposes in that "it seeks not simply to reveal what linguistic forms are *manifested* but how they *realize,* make real, the conceptual and rhetorical structures, modes, thought and action, which are established as conventional for certain discourse communities" (Widdowson, 2003, p. 69). This argument notwithstanding, the view of language use raises complex questions about its relation to what has conventionally been termed "culture" for the "foreign" language teaching community.

Closely aligned with this way of thinking about language use is systemic-functional linguistics (Halliday, 1973, 1994). Halliday and other proponents of this approach view language as a code that is functionally motivated, one that has meaning potential that is realized when it comes in contact with actual use. This approach is becoming increasingly influential in the development of "foreign" language curricula (Byrnes, 2007; Colombi, 2007) and as a tool in reforming general instruction in English-medium education to create better access for English learners (Schleppegrell, 2004). In the systemic-functional view, what is encoded in the language is not the grammatical system in the restricted Chomskyan sense but a complex system of lexico-grammatical relations that derive from the communicative functioning of language. Thus, the user's purpose or intent is centrally important in defining what it means to know and use (an)other language(s) appropriately and effectively.

The work on corpus linguistics (e.g., O'Keeffe, McCarthy, & Carter, 2007) is somewhat allied with this general view of the centrality of language use. Such research, which has been made feasible with the advent and use of computer technology, allows for the investigation of regularities in textual patterning found in existing bodies (or corpora) of language data. The main aim of such corpus analyses has been to inform the preparation of curricula and teaching materials (see Tao, 2005, for an example in Mandarin Chinese). However, although both systemic-functional linguistics and corpus linguistic analyses have helped to redefine language as tool of use, neither approach speaks directly to the core dilemma of defining what it means to know—and thus to be able to successfully use— (an)other language(s).

This challenge of conceptualizing language as a tool for social and economic participation has also been taken up at the level of educational policy with the development of the Council of Europe's (2001) *Common European Framework of Reference,* or *CEFR.* Like the FSI scales of the 1980s and the ACTFL standards of the 1990s, the *CEFR* has framed language competence in terms of skills in ascending contexts of use. Referring to it as "frame of reference," developers of the *CEFR* cast it as a descriptive framework that supports the comparative mapping of competences in various languages. In this way, they seek to distinguish it from a set of standards, which has been the approach in the United States. Although this may be more of a political than a conceptual distinction, it does shift the focus from the abstracted assessment of competence squarely to the level of individual use and instrumentality with the new language. The fact that the descriptors in the *CEFR* are written as "can do" statements from the user's point of view, and that the document suggests that users compare what they can do with what they want to be able to do in the new language, encourages users to locate their competence as they perceive it and to relate it to their own needs in the language.

At the heart of this view of language as a tool for participation is the *CEFR*'s concept of plurilingualism, which

emphasizes the fact that . . . an individual's experience of language and its cultural contexts expands from the language of the home to that of the society at large and then to languages of other peoples (whether learnt at school or college, or by direct experience). (Council of Europe, 2001, p. 4)

In this view, all language use is partial (or plural), and measures of this partiality depend on what the user intends. Because intentions can grow and change over time with life experience, plurilingual competence articulates a different perspective on language learning and what it means to know (an)other language(s), one that is dynamic, situated, and use driven (Ellis & Larsen-Freeman, 2006). This view contrasts in important ways with the concept of multilingualism, which has undergirded "foreign" language instruction from the concept of communicative competence to the FSI scales and the ACTFL curriculum standards. Multilingualism holds the image of a learner or user seeking to be equally capable in all languages and in all domains of activity. A plurilingual individual, in contrast, "does not keep these languages and cultures in strictly separate mental compartments, but rather builds up a communicative competence to which all knowledge and experience of language contribute and in which all languages interrelate and interact" (Council of Europe, 2001, p. 4).

From this view, it follows that users and knowers of (an)other language(s) are seen as "successful multi-competent speakers, not failed native speakers" (V. Cook, 1999, p. 204). It follows, then, that bilinguals should not be assessed as two monolinguals in one. If comparisons need to be made, they should be made appropriately. For example, Kasper (1997) warns against the comparative fallacy, in which the performance of the second-language learner is compared with that of native speakers and is therefore seen to be deficient. She asks the important question, "Who should learners be compared with? The solution to the comparative fallacy does not renounce on comparison but selects more appropriate baselines" (p. 310). "For instance," Kasper maintains, "when you study the phonological development and ultimate attainment of Anglo-Canadians learning French, do not choose as a baseline monolingual speakers of Canadian French; choose highly competent French-English bilinguals" (p. 310) instead.

This shift in perspective from multi- to plurilingualism may appear to be a small one; however, it has widespread implications for how the processes of learning, teaching, and indeed, knowing (an)other language(s) are conceived and operationalized. Instead of projecting learning outcomes as a final state, the *CEFR* and related documents argue for an emergent or process view in which use and the user's perceptions guide judgments of these outcomes. Instead of focusing on mastery of a system, it emphasized language use. We thus come full circle to seeing "foreign" languages as dynamic creatures of use in the world rather than as frozen by the artificially stasis of subject-languages in schools.

RECONSTITUTING KNOWLEDGE IN LANGUAGE TEACHING: CHAOS AND COMPLEXITY THEORIES (C/CT)

In the two previous sections of this review, we have traced the changing views of "foreign" languages as school subjects, first through how they have been taught and then retracing that history in how they have been defined as having been learned. We contend that each of these moves carries a different view of knowledge; these changes thus foreshadow what we call postdisciplinarity. To bridge this argument between the history of "foreign" language teaching and how learning outcomes have been defined, on one hand, and shifts in the broader plate tectonics of disciplinary knowledge in schools, on the other, we find it helpful to seek out a broader conceptual frame to help make sense of these dynamics. We suggest that C/CTs offer a fruitful way of conceiving of these moves that point toward what we have termed postdisciplinarity. C/CTs are ecological theories (Kramsch, 2002) that attempt to account for the behavior of complex, dynamic, nonlinear, self-organizing, and adaptive systems, of which language or a unified "languaculture" (Agar, 1994), with its protean quality, is surely one (Larsen-Freeman, 1997).

If, as we have argued, language more than any other subject matter defies disciplinary positioning, it may be because language itself is a normative fiction (Klein, 1998). From a C/CT perspective, language is seen as not an entity but instead as a space in which an infinite number of possible trajectories may be realized. None of these trajectories comes into being until language is used in a specific context (e.g., the classroom). Context, in this sense, does not mean just the physical space; it includes the intentional or intersubjective space between users (Firth & Wagner, 1997). Thus in this dynamic view, there is no such thing as a uniform, homogeneous, static entity that can be called "Spanish," "Urdu," or "Japanese"; rather, a particular language comes into a sort of evanescent existence as users muster it according to their ends and intentions. Language users "soft-assemble" their language resources in the moment to deal with the communicative exigencies at hand; by so doing, they not only adapt their resources to those of their interlocutor, but also the communicative partners together transform the language system they are using (Larsen-Freeman & Cameron, in press).

Therefore, because language itself is changing all the time at the local level, no centralized authority can actually control or govern the structure or lexicon of a particular language, which emerges from local interactions (Tomasello, 2003) and whose forms are constantly undergoing modification and adaptation through use (Bybee, 2006). There is stability in a language, of course, for without it, communication and learning would be impossible (Givón, 1999). It is the stability that linguists have tried to capture with their research on the language system; however, there is no enduring or innate architecture to language, and even the most carefully documented rules are not inviolable, offering language users a great deal of choice in how they use language forms to express themselves (Larsen-Freeman, 2002). The imposition of certain conventions through the written language and social norms that prescribe and proscribe certain forms may give the appearance of a static system, but although there is a system, there is no stasis. Instead, language is clearly a dynamic system, one that is continuously changing and one whose learning does not involve mere reproduction of the "foreign" language but rather entails a morphogenetic process, or the creation of new forms (Larsen-Freeman, 1997). C/CTs thus offer us a way forward from the persistent struggle between the view of language as a system and the view of language use. Language as a dynamic system is, at one and the same time, both system and its use.

However, the traditional contrast between the fixed, yet artificial, nature of subject-languages and the fluid and self-defining experiences of that content as it is used in the wider world foregrounds a very basic tension. In schools, language is a means to an end as well as an end in itself. Thus students need a level of knowledge and skill in the language that is the medium of instruction to access and learn content in the school environment, even as they may also be studying other languages as "foreign" languages. The fact that language is treated simultaneously in two ways—as a medium of instruction and as a subject—tends to blur, if not confuse, issues of educational access and achievement.[10] So for some students, language learning in school is focused on reaching a level of academic and social proficiency in the language of schooling so that they can have access to the rest of the curriculum, whereas for other students, often in the same school building, learning language is a companion undertaking to learning math, science, or social studies as subjects. That these two experiences of language learning are rarely linked, and certainly not reconciled within a common frame, offers continuing evidence of a schizophrenia that surrounds languages in school (Freeman, 2004).

One could argue, from the perspective of C/CTs, that such disjunctions are inevitable if language is truly a situated dynamic system. It is not only its vastness that makes it resistant to the standard activities of teaching, such as defining curricular units; the problem lies in attempts to corral it, atomize it, and fix its units to make them learnable as subject matter. Control, fragmentation, and stasis run contrary to a complex, dynamic system in which everything is changing, everything is connected to everything else, and the slightest change in one part of a system can have profound effects for another part. Instead of attempting to acquire its parts, students need to experience its use. Understanding blends meaning with context. When students get to experience language as a resource for making meaning in context, the pedagogical boundaries between subject-languages and language use in the world are blurred.

This blurring of boundaries lies at the heart of the postdisciplinary challenge to knowledge more generally. The fuzziness challenges two long-standing assumptions in mainstream linguistics: that all languages can be described and theorized in essentially the same way and that the concept of the native speaker can define both a language and language knowledge (G. Cook, 2005). These concepts have been the building blocks of professional knowledge and practices in language teaching; furthermore, we would contend that because almost all teaching is in language, they undergird teaching and learning in schools more broadly. To further compound the issue, when it is framed as content, the dynamic nature of language as a "system" is artificially frozen, and so, too, sometimes are the practices of the people who use it in teaching, contributing to "the inert knowledge" problem (Whitehead, 1929), whereby language learners know the rules but cannot apply them in communication (Larsen-Freeman, 2003).

As with any subject area, classroom teaching is primarily and most directly shaped by social forces and expectations of schooling; however, language as subject matter (subject-language) brings a complexity to that relationship for several reasons. Unlike other school subjects, languages can be readily learned outside of classrooms, and furthermore, the proficiency that can come with learning a language in the world is often seen as the standard of mastery for the subject in the classroom. Thus, language classrooms have attempted to approximate both the results that people can achieve in the world and to mirror the ways in which to do so. Debates about the efficacy of classroom methodologies generally focus on the degree to which these approaches are (or claim to be) able to achieve the types of learning that learners seem to be capable of without formal instruction.

This tension is exemplified, as we have said in previous sections, in the status quo ante of classroom language teaching in the 20th century, which lay in the undifferentiated, or perhaps unexamined, practice of teaching through translation as a vehicle for literary and cultural studies. In a real sense, this approach to pedagogy strived to make language like other school subjects: It was teacher dominated, was syllabus and text based, and embodied the prevailing literacy practices—primarily decoding and analyzing texts—of the time. In contrast to this prevailing view, the audiolingual revolution of the 1950s and 1960s brought a theoretical basis that integrated a view of language (as behavior) and learning (as habit formation), both of which directly supported a particular view of instruction (as drill accompanied by vigilant correction). This integration of views of language and learning to support practices in teaching created a theoretical framing that brought language as "subject-language" into the classroom.

Thus, we suggest the audiolingual revolution reframed the disciplinary basis, in the broadest sense, for "foreign" language as subject matter and for its teaching. That basis was shifted from literary and cultural studies to psychology, primarily, and the standards of "native-like" fluency across any and all situations of use. Rather quickly, however, this recast basis for subject-language and teaching began to unravel, as seen in the new construct of communicative competence and relative proficiencies. We contend that this unraveling shows both the inadequacy of the grand disciplinary narrative in anchoring subject-language teaching and, more fundamentally, indicates how language influences classrooms.

To grasp and make sense of these moves, a theoretical stance that is more supple, and one that honors the complexity, is needed; this we find in C/CTs. Viewed from this perspective, these language moves can reveal the seeds of postdisciplinarity. Classical theories, based in traditional modernist rationality established in the first half of the 17th century, reject complexity in a number of ways (Cilliers, 2007). One way pertinent to our discussion is the enactment of "the principle of disjunction," which consists of isolating and separating disciplines one from another (Morin, 2007), just as in the "foreign" language field, linguists artificially separated the language system from its use. One of the ways the limitations of disjunction are already manifest is in the proliferation of "hyphenated" areas of study, for example, psychobiology, which implicitly tear down the walls that the principle of disjunction has built. From a C/CT perspective, we need to realize the limitations of disjunction and to look for what connections can be made.

In the following section, we unpack four themes in the unraveling of "foreign" language as a school subject, themes that suggest how subject-language has moved toward a postdisciplinary view. The first theme examines how a unified view of classroom practice in "foreign" language teaching has decomposed; the second traces how, in the face of this decomposition, research knowledge has come to supply what we call microtheoretical justifications for these teaching practices in which space, third, teachers have increasingly been cast as (or allowed to be) arbiters of their own practices, and thus, fourth, to be seen as knowledge-generators.

THE UNRAVELING OF SUBJECT-LANGUAGE: THE DECOMPOSITION OF A UNIFIED VIEW OF CLASSROOM PRACTICES IN "FOREIGN" LANGUAGE TEACHING

In the diversification of pedagogical approaches in "foreign" language teaching that flourished into the 1970s and 1980s, the integrated theoretical position represented by behaviorism and audiolingualism began to decompose, although the three broad categories of language, learning, and classroom practices remained foundational. The proficiency movement cleaved a further division between methods and classroom practices, as it became accepted that many methods could be used to attain proficiency or meet standards (Brown Mitchell, & Ellingson Vidal, 2001). In fact, some argue that "method" is no longer a viable pedagogical construct for precisely this reason, and they therefore refer to the field of language teaching as being in a "post-method condition" (Kumaravadivelu, 1994). In place of methods, Kumaravadivelu offers "macrostrategies" derived from theories related to language learning and teaching. Somewhat ironically in our view, his analysis seems to replace one form of standardization (methods) with another (postmethod strategies) and thus ultimately reinforces a unified view, whether imposed as a modern standard or resisted in a "postmethod" condition.

The experience and documentation of teachers' day-to-day classroom practices seem to point in a different direction, however. Although characterized as resistance to reform and change (see Evans, 1996, for a good discussion) or as stasis within the educational system, there is abundant evidence that teachers' classroom practices are highly individual and durable. When viewed from the perspective of the decentralization or emergence inherent in any complex, dynamic, nonlinear system, attempts to impose a standard or uniform way of acting are likely to fail, at least from the standpoint of achieving or maintaining uniformity. Such systems do not change simply on the basis of interventions of power instituted from the top down. In the foreign-language teaching field, as in many other areas of intentional educational reform, top-down attempts to introduce pedagogical innovations by uncritically transposing those forged in one context to another, no matter how well researched and well intentioned, rarely succeed.

We offer two examples. After the government of Singapore instituted a shift in language pedagogy from a more teacher-centered approach to one of cooperative learning and group work, teachers either did not use group work at all or did so for reasons such as "student enjoyment or pleasure." They thus did not make the reform-intended connection to the pedagogic value of cooperative learning and the importance of interaction in fostering the SLA process (Silver, 2007). In the second case, the introduction of task-based language teaching into Dutch-medium primary schools in Brussels was done with abundant support, including classroom "coaching" for the pedagogic innovation. Despite teachers' sense that their structurally based approaches to language teaching were not meeting the needs of the new, rapidly growing immigrant population in Belgium, "very few of teachers appeared to be inclined to radically change their subjective beliefs or behavior in the classroom" (Van den Branden, 2007).

In both cases, the prevailing analysis would argue that teachers were purposefully countering the reform by not carrying it out as intended. Such an analysis would suggest, however, perhaps a greater coherence and top-down power to affect change than we generally see exists in subject-language teaching or, indeed, in teaching generally. An alternative view suggests that neither teaching behavior nor the thinking that supports it will ever transfer as replicas of what the reformers intend (Freeman, 1994, 2006). In a complex dynamic system, in which all elements are interconnected, non-linearity and adaptation is the norm. Thus what may appear as static and unchanged, in this instance, teachers' classroom practices, may be part of a wide and less predictably shaped web of thinking and reasoning from which vantage point the stability and continuity makes sense. Subject-languages in schools are, we would say, the most illustrative of this fact, because the very definitions and understandings of the subject-matter are determined by conditions in the world. These tenuous relationships, and the wider chaotic and complex web that connects them, are in what we are calling a postdisciplinary frame. The singularity of a disciplinary anchor, be it psychology or literature, no longer obtains so that uniform rationales and theoretical bases of language teaching are unraveling.

This decomposition of the theoretical bases for classroom practice is traceable in three broad areas: in what we will call the "microtheoretical" uses of SLA research constructs to shape classroom teaching; in the notion of teachers as creators and arbiters of their practices through the mental work of thinking and decision making; and in the knowledge generation by teachers from their classroom practices. In a sense, each of these three areas is talismanic of the fluidity that seems to characterize the complexification and localization of complex systems and a postdisciplinary frame. We explore each in turn as we further subdivide them into the five themes that follow.

Microtheoretical Uses of Second Language Acquisition Research

Some would argue that learning theory, and specifically, SLA research and theorizing, should fill in the gaps left by the decomposition of a unified methodological view. After all, if that unified view included, as it did in the 1950s and the 1960s, both a theory of learning and practices of teaching based on it, and if the practices themselves were decentralizing, then could not a new learning theory, or set of theories, reassert the explanatory power that had been lost? What happened, however, was in a way the opposite. In a sense, the genesis of the subfield of SLA in the 1970s further fueled this diversification of pedagogical practices and the complexification of teachers' roles. Examining three examples of SLA research that have contributed to language teaching practices—the notions of "interlanguage," interactional tasks, and content-based instruction—is instructive in showing how research supported the diversification of teaching practices.

The construct of interlanguage recast thinking about student errors from the bad-habits view based in behaviorism (Larsen-Freeman & Long, 1991). Corder (1967), whom we mentioned earlier, argued that language learners' errors were not a reflex of the native language (L1) but rather were reflective of the learners' underlying second language (L2) competence. This perception was later extended in the claim that learners were actively involved in constructing a system out of the linguistic input to which they had been exposed, a linguistic system called an interlanguage (Selinker, 1972). Interlanguage supports a view of language learning as a developmental process through which learners evolve ever-closer approximations to the new or target language. As with other languages, these approximations are seen to each have internal logic and consistency, and learners' developmental stages can be mapped onto an "interlanguage continuum." This view of learning then suggested that teacher correction of student errors in language, rather than trying to obliterate "bad habits" as it had in audiolingual teaching, should focus on understanding how the student was making sense of the target language system as she or he was expressing and comprehending ideas or meanings. Students' errors were seen as inevitable by-products of the influence of their native language and of their active engagement with figuring out how the new system worked. Thus, the teacher's role could shift from exclusively enforcing the standards of the new language to encouraging its exploration, a role with far less specification of exactly what was expected, leaving a standard definition of "good" teaching far more elusive.

In the areas of curriculum and activity in classroom teaching, the concept of tasks had a similar effect on reorganizing activity in classroom teaching. Because tasks permitted learners to negotiate for meaning rather than explicitly practice linguistic forms, SLA researchers saw in tasks the kind of learning that was consistent with the findings from SLA research (e.g., Long & Crookes, 1993). When student performance on tasks could be accompanied by a judicious "focus on form" (Long, 1991), it was thought that the basic ingredient for successful SLA, that is, meaningful or communicative interaction among speakers, was provided. So in a way, tasks offered to language curricula what interlanguage did to language learning: an inherently decentralizing view of the core work in the classroom. Both microtheoretical concepts recast the learner as an independent and generative actor within a larger, more chaotic, and thus less plannable activity of language teaching.

In an interesting way, this attention to task as an organizing factor in classroom teaching furthered the undoing of the unifying thinking about communicative language teaching. Writing of the Bangalore/Madras Communicational Teaching Project in

India, the founder, Prabhu (1980) observed, "Communicative teaching in most Western thinking has been training *for* communication . . . whereas the Bangalore Project is teaching *through* communication; and therefore the very notion of communication is different" (p. 164). Teaching through communication called for students to be engaged in tasks whereby they are encouraged "to arrive at an outcome from given information through some process of thought" (Prahbu, 1987, p. 24), such as solving some problem by piecing together certain clues or by conducting a survey of student preferences. Thus, the central tenet of language curricula was anchored not in situations or dialogues but in the execution of the task, which generated language almost as a by-product. This view likewise recasts the role of the teacher. Because the task is the scaffold and even the source of the new language, the teacher's role became one of facilitator and guide rather than as language model, again, a role that was much more open to interpretation than the roles that had been prescribed by earlier methods.

A similar logic underlies two initiatives in using content as a vehicle for language instruction. Although their proponents argue for certain differences (principally about which domain drives the integration, the language structures and lexicon or the content), "content-based language instruction," as it is called in the United States (Snow & Brinton, 1997), or "content learning in language" (CLIL), as it is referred to in Europe (Marsh & Langé, 2000), each blends the learning of traditional disciplinary content, such as history or science, with the learning of a new language. These pedagogies see teaching curriculum subjects through a language other than the school's medium of instruction as achieving dual ends of curriculum knowledge and linguistic mastery. Unlike the original immersion designs, such as the French immersion programs in Canada, in content-based or CLIL classrooms, explicit attention is given to the "foreign" language (usually students are not beginners in the language), so that language learning objectives are formulated alongside the objectives for the learning of the traditional disciplinary content (Schleppegrell, 2004). Many of these proposals for practice do not call for exclusivity. For example, focusing on form can take place in any communicative approach. Then, too, it has also been suggested that curricular proposals that marry a content-based approach with genre-based notions of task can prove effective in teaching languages at an advanced level (Byrnes, 2005; see also, Wesche & Skehan, 2002).

Although each of these proposals, which we have termed microtheoretical, might make a great deal of sense by itself, they illustrate our earlier point about how the diversification of teaching practices places increased demands on teachers. At the same time, there has been an increasing recognition that the decision to adopt and adapt such practices needed to be more socially situated (Larsen-Freeman, 2007). Challenging the SLA field to adopt a more socially contextualized view of language learning, Firth and Wagner (1997) urged SLA researchers to reconsider unquestioningly accepted and well-established concepts such as nonnative speaker, learner, and interlanguage. As they put it in their 1998 response to commentators, "We are unable to accept the premises of 'interlanguage'—namely, that language learning is a transitional process that has a distinct and visible end" (Firth & Wagner, 1998, p. 91). Furthermore, these authors contended that since its founding by Corder, second-language acquisition had been concerned with individual acquisition and its relation to language-specific cognitive systems—the acquisition of L2 competence in the Chomskyan sense. "As such, it is flawed," they wrote, "and obviates insight into the nature of language, most centrally the language use of second of foreign language (S/FL) speakers" (Firth & Wagner, 1997, p. 285). This call to consider language learning as centrally concerned with language use, thus being a much more context-bound proposition, has been key to other theories as well (Zuengler & Miller, 2006). For instance, speaking to the situatedness of learning from a sociocultural theory perspective, Hall (2000) writes of language teaching that "effecting change in our classrooms will not result from imposing solutions outside but from nurturing effectual practices that are indigenous to our particular contexts" (p. 295).

It has further become apparent that individual differences between language learners could no longer be overlooked or attributed to "noise" or random variation in the data (Larsen-Freeman, 2006). Whereas many first- and second-language acquisition researchers conceived of language learning as a universal process, it has become clear that there are significant differences between learners with regard to all kinds of motivational, attitudinal, and aptitude factors and so on and that these factors can make a commensurately large difference in instructional outcomes. Learners vary between themselves and follow their own paths in learning another language. In fact, from a C/CT perspective, the learner and the environment cannot be separated. Although it is possible, of course, to separate context and person for the purpose of analysis, such separation requires the untenable assumption that the two are independent (van Geert & Steenbeck, in press). Indeed, "it is no longer sufficient to talk about individual differences in SLA against a backdrop of a universal learner. . . . Variation becomes the primary given; categorization becomes an artificial construct of institutionalization and scientific inquiry" (Kramsch, 2002, p. 4) such that it may not be possible "to tell the dancer from the dance," to paraphrase Yeats, as Kramsch does.

These examples from SLA research are several among many that contributed to shaping classroom practices in "foreign" language teaching throughout the past two decades. In a sense, they represent both the theoretical diversity and the attempted explanatory power that research knowledge invoked in relation to classroom practices. They also demonstrate its limitations. For it is clear that universal solutions that are transposed acritically, often accompanied by calls for increased standardization, and that ignore indigenous conditions, the diversity of learners, and the agency of teachers are immanent in a modernism that no longer applies, if it ever did. Recognizing the inconclusive cycle of pedagogical fashion in teaching methods, Widdowson (2004) observes that what is needed is a "shift to localization," in which pedagogic practices are designed in relation to local contexts, needs, and objectives (Larsen-Freeman, 2000a). Such a shift answers the objections of some critical theorists (e.g., Pennycook, 2001) to the attempts to "export" language-teaching methods from developed to developing countries with the assumption that one size fits all. Treating localization of practices as a fundamental "change in attitude," Widdowson adds that "local contexts of actual practice are to be seen not as constraints to be overcome but conditions to be satisfied" (p. 369). In a sense, the microtheoretical frames from SLA research that have

shaped classroom practice exemplify language *for* the world in that the example constructs proposed in interlanguage and its continuum, in tasks as sites of negotiated
meaning, and in the various intertwining of content and language each link subject-
language to purposes of use in the wider world.

Teachers as Arbiters of Their Practice

Coinciding, and in a sense supporting, this diversification view of "foreign" language instruction was the development of a new research base in teacher learning in
language teaching during the 1990s (Freeman, 2002). Influenced by related work in
general education throughout the 1980s (e.g., Calderhead, 1987; Clark & Peterson,
1986), as well as antecedents in "foreign" language teacher education (see Schultz,
2000), the rationale was grounded in the then relatively novel assertion that teachers
engage in mental activity as they teach, and thus they might have what Walberg (1971)
had termed "mental lives." The concepts of teacher thinking or cognition also shaped
research and thinking in second-language teacher education, particularly through the
influential notion that these mental lives could be a central aspect of teaching and thus
of how individuals learned to teach (Kennedy, 1991) through what Lortie (1975) had
termed "the apprenticeship of observation." These constructs of mental activity, as
applied to teachers and their professional learning, as contrasted with beliefs[11] about
language learning itself,[12] found their way into the field of language teaching through
seminal studies of teacher decision making (Woods, 1996) and research on teacher
learning in language teaching (Freeman & Richards, 1996). And they were instru-
mentally embedded in many language teacher preparation and professional development programs through the increasingly widespread emphasis on reflective teaching
(e.g., Richards & Lockhart, 1994; Wallace, 1991). Thus language became a dual vehicle in a sense: as subject-language, it was the content of practice, yet as professional discourse, it became the medium of analysis of that practice (Freeman, 1996).

As teachers have been recognized as decision makers in practice, so too has the
activity of teaching been resituated, primarily through the influence of sociocultural
theory (e.g., Engeström, 1999; Lantolf, 2000). The view that the activity of teaching is itself socially constructed, emerges and develops with time, and is contextualized not just physically but also socially and temporarily (Freeman & Johnson, 1998)
has furthered this orientation toward decentralizing methodologies and localizing
classroom practices. In contradistinction to this localized conceptualization of teachers' work, policy environments of the 1990s in many countries, usually operating
from a neoliberal view, sought to regulate the "quality" of instruction through licen-
sure requirements and other provisions to ensure the "fidelity" to designated teaching approaches. Ironically, therefore, just as teachers were being recast through
research and theorizing as agents of their practices, many governmental entities were
increasingly trying to standardize their work, a push we have argued is doomed to
failure, given the nature of subject-languages and of language teaching as a social
activity.

This push to localize practice through the diversification of theoretical constructs
found companion support in a simultaneous move toward methodology as eclecticism

in teaching. "Principled eclecticism" vested in the teacher the capability to make decisions or "informed choices" (Stevick, 1982) about what to teach and how to teach it. The impetus of this view suggested that even when the curriculum and syllabus defined quite precisely the subject-language to be taught, the teacher was still left—or could carve out—space to define how to teach that content to that particular class of students. This sense of "freedom" could be quite illusory, however, were it not for the companion forces of decomposition that surrounded it, namely, the views of teachers as knowledge generators and the globalization of content, which we discuss in the next sections.

Teacher-Research: Knowledge Generation in and Through Classroom Practice

Arguably, the logical trajectory of the localization of teaching practices, which was supported in the ways we have noted above, was the emphasis on teachers as generators of knowledge of their practice—literally using language *of* their work to describe and interrogate their worlds. The teacher-research movement of the 1990s, broadly conceived,[13] was persuasive in repositioning the language teacher in several ways. The idea of generating knowledge in and through classroom practices seemed inherently attractive to a field and profession whose content was often more easily acquired in the world outside the classroom.[14] Beyond that, capturing and channeling the agency of the teacher seemed like an attractive way to improve instruction, though it was implicitly a strategy of localization. Often major reforms in "foreign" language teaching turned on this idea of local knowledge generation to improve teaching, for example, the LOTE Project in Australia and "exploratory teaching," which has been applied in Brazil and other countries (Gieve & Miller, 2006). In exploratory teaching, general guiding principles, such as "involve everybody"—students, teacher, and community—are given to teachers, but their implications need to be worked out for local practice (Allwright, 2003).

Some might challenge our analysis to this point, observing the application of dissected research knowledge (which we have termed microtheoretical frames); the recasting of teachers as thinkers, decision makers, researchers, and theorizers of their own work; and the recognition of classroom practitioners as knowledge generators are all documented developments in general education as well and as such are not limited or unique to foreign- or second-language teaching as a field. We would accept this observation but reply that there are two key factors that shape the atypicality of "foreign" language teaching in these areas and point this decomposition of practice in the direction of a broader postdisciplinarity. Both factors stem from the very nature of language. When it becomes a subject-language in classrooms and schools, as we have discussed, language refracts (as all content does) through the person of the teacher, and likewise, like any content, it reflects the wider world. But in the case of subject-language, these two refractions are caught in the dynamic of language as a complex, dynamic system and the teacher as user (and exemplar) of that language in the classroom (what we have called language *in* the world).

The Person of the Teacher

It is the person of the language teacher that truly instantiates the issue of language being *in* the world. Insofar as subject matter helps to frame a teacher's professional identity as well as the practices that enact that identity, language plays a rather ambiguous role, particularly in view of its dual role as subject matter and as means of instruction. As long as knowing a language was understood in multilingual terms as being as proficient in all areas of endeavor in a second language as one might be in the first, then the teacher's identity was defined in terms of linguistic proficiency according to a standard of "nativeness." However, as the notions of pluralism and eclecticism have taken hold in classroom methodology, combined with the global transformation of English, professional identities have become increasingly blurred.

If all users shape and reshape language, then each native speaker creates and uses a different individual dialect, or ideolect, shaped by that particular individual and his or her social experience. It follows then that language versions have no inherent natural privilege and that there is no such thing as "native speaker" proficiency, as we have said; rather, socioeconomic-political forces, usually operating through geography and social class, bestow such judgments. However, this makes them no less real, and native-speaker proficiency is often advertised as the preferred qualification for language teachers, even though such judgments are misguided and counterproductive. For example, those who have mastered the language that they are teaching as a "foreign" language are often in a much better position to identify the learning challenges for other learners than a native speaker who has come to the language as a birthright.

The Globalization of/in English

That language is simultaneously *in* and *for* the wider world beyond the classroom captures how content refracts the wider domains from which it is drawn and that it is assumed to represent. In the case of subject-languages, as we have commented in previous sections, the geopolitical influences that have shaped language teaching, particularly, English[15] in the past 25 years, have propelled its transnational expansion. These factors have included the increasingly networked character of knowledge development, particularly in the natural sciences, economic forces of globalization, and especially the expansion of free trade, mass migration in certain regions, the rise of the Internet, and the foreign policy objectives of major English-speaking countries (e.g., United States, United Kingdom, Canada, and Australia).

The rise of English is further blurring pedagogical boundaries between the classroom and the world. Estimating the number of language users is a highly dynamic undertaking, especially in the case of English. For example, a decade ago, Crystal (1997) estimated there were around 427 million native English speakers, with English speakers falling far behind Mandarin Chinese speakers at around 726 million. He and others have pointed out, however, that the number of second- and foreign-language speakers of English, which is conservatively estimated to be approximately 750 million, dramatically augments those figures.[16]

Thus, even conservative estimates put English in the historically unprecedented position (except for perhaps Latin) of having more second- or foreign-language than first-language or "native" speakers, and these speakers often use English, and therefore transform it, in multimodal contexts that are far outside the purview of classrooms. English is like Latin in another respect. Just as Latin was incomprehensible to the masses of vernacular speakers, the English of the academy, international finance, and law is as opaque for most native speakers of English as it is to its nonnative speakers. What could be called "technocratic English" is principally a literate language, composed of registers that are acquired only through the institutionalized learning and use of writing, not through birth into an English-speaking community (Luke et al., 2007).

As it has moved in most national contexts from a "foreign" language to a global basic skill, English is more and more a tool that is being (re)shaped, actually and virtually, by a global group of users. Although some argue that the emergence of English as a global lingual franca is threatening the existence of other languages (Skutnabb-Kangas, 2000; Skutnabb-Kangas & Phillipson, 1995), there are reasonable arguments about whether the expansion is fueled, intentionally or not, by an Anglophone push for economic and political hegemony, as some argue, or is a by-product of various forces, which include economic globalization, technology, and geopolitical alignments, among others. Although there may not be a concerted bid for supremacy, it is certainly the case that English instruction is increasingly called for in educational policies around the world, although instructional quality varies considerably. To achieve a more equitable distribution of resources within the world, therefore, the real obstacle may be the unequal access to quality instruction in technocratic discourse and technical registers within a given language, even though the language may not always be English (A. Luke, personal communication, June 28, 2007). Indeed, recent evidence (see Graddol, 2006) suggests that it is German and Spanish for economic purposes that are on the ascendancy of use in Europe, presumably because of the same pressures and opportunities that have promoted the learning and teaching of English. Thus, "issues of language rights are now compounded by another level of complexity: the shifting and ambiguous positions and relations of the state, the nation, the multinational corporation and their real and virtual borders" (Luke et al., 2007, p. 2), such that the matter of "whose language" will dominate may as much be a question of a particular discourse as one of a particular lingua franca per se.

It is also the case that the need for lingua franca transnational languages (of which there are many in the world; McGroarty, 2006) has been because of reasons other than the economic and political forces of colonialism. For example, the use of Mandarin in many parts of Southeast Asia is the result of the Chinese diaspora, and Arabic is likewise a language both of diaspora and transnational secular and religious identity. It is clear, as G. Cook (2005) observes, that there is no longer—if there ever was—a "strong correlation between a place, a people, a culture, and a language. For English, these distinctions and this correlation have broken down" (p. 291).

Scholars who study English as a lingua franca (Jenkins, 2000; Seidlhofer, 2001) have for similar reasons suggested that "native-speaker" English should be considered a dialectal variety distinct from "international" English, which implies that speakers of English from birth will need to become bilingual in their own language to converse with other speakers of global English. As Byrnes (2007) notes,

In a globalized environment in which the sovereign nation state, including its construction through national languages, is being reshaped, many of the assumptions that have undergirded mostly beginning and intermediate level language instruction are in any case being questioned severely, thereby at the very least attenuating their validity (e.g., single and/or fixed norms, canonical texts, separation of nativeness and foreignness, structurally rather than functionally oriented notions of language and language learning). (pp. 10–11)

It is interesting to position the above perspective alongside the view of critical discourse analysts who argue that because different languages condition the ways in which people see the world, it is a linguistic right that people be able to conduct their lives and educate their children in their "own" language (Fairclough, 1995). Learning any other language, they contend, should not lead to abandoning one's first language. If, however, the dynamic of language as a complex system is actually redefining "ownership" through constantly expanding use, the situation may be changing. Although the concerns are well founded if taken from the standpoint of languages that are stable and thus invasive systems, the C/CT analytic frame suggests another view.

When we entertain a view of language that is less mechanistic and more organic, as a complex adaptive system, we recognize that every use of language changes the language resources of the learner-user, and these changed resources are then potentially available for the next speech event (Larsen-Freeman & Cameron, in press). "The act of playing the game has a way of changing the rules," as Gleick (1987, p. 24) put it in describing naturally occurring complex adaptive systems. From a C/CT point of view, the mutually constitutive processes of using and learning a language are not just reproducing a shared system; instead, they are creative processes, blending and blurring, not of conforming to uniformity (Larsen-Freeman, 2003). As such, using and learning a language is not simply proceduralizing declarative knowledge by developing automaticity with the rules of a steady-state grammar (DeKeyser, 1998). Instead, language users change the linguistic context itself. As the noted biologist Lewontin (2000) put it, "Organisms do not find already existent ecological niches to which they adapt, but are in constant process of defining and remaking their environments. Thus organism and environment are both causes and effects in a co-evolutionary process" (pp. 125–126).[17]

This coevolution, or what Larsen-Freeman and Cameron (in press) have called "coadaptation," creates these hybridities. This eddying form of development, although it differs from the linear images of modernist teleologies, has always been the case, as Luke and Luke (2000) note:

Hybridity, then is not an invention of postmodernism, globalization, and postcolonial theory. Rather it is a social and culture formation born out of complex and intersecting histories that often predate direct contact with the industrial and imperial west. (pp. 283–284)

They illustrate this point writing about Thai youth responding to, appropriating, and shaping Western cultural norms and practices, particularly in music, that are available to them through economic and social globalization:

Certainly, an emergent middle-class youth culture [in Thailand] is reconstructing itself around images and texts that are Thai appropriations of Western rock and popular culture. Yet, such a position risks flattening out, one dimensionalizing, the complex processes of globalization. These processes are not simply uncritical reproductions of western cultures. Rather, their formation flows out of (1) a hybridization and reappropriation of western cultures; and (2) long-standing incorporations and appropriations of other Asian regional cultures. . . .

None of these are carbon copies of the Western music industry. Indeed, there is evidence that Thai popular music . . . has taken on a substantial life of its own, not only shaping youth culture but providing a space for innovative forms of social comment and cultural expression. (Luke & Luke, 2000, p. 283)

In this section, we have argued that the decomposition of classroom practices from the unifying theory of behaviorist psychology and audiolingualism, which had itself supplanted literature and cultural studies as the disciplinary anchor for subject-language teaching in many settings, was shaped itself by the nature of language. We have pointed to several factors that obtain in this analysis, principally, that from a schooling perspective, subject-language teaching has no disciplinary home per se, largely because it cannot. We have also pointed out that language is a dynamic system, which changes through use. Because it is always changing, its users always innovating, hybridity is the norm, not the exception. In addition, from a use perspective, the globalizing of English, and to some extent other languages such as Mandarin, is further eroding the boundaries between the classroom and the world. From human experience, school learners know language, what it does and can do, so very often, the versions that they are asked to study in classrooms are pale versions of that experience.

This gap has driven "foreign" language teaching pedagogy for the past 50 years, even as the very construct of "foreignness" is increasingly irrelevant. But if a language is not "foreign," if it is not part of the other, then why take time in school to study and to try to learn it? This fundamental tension, we would contend, positions "foreign" language teaching as a postdisciplinary enterprise. We have suggested that we find C/CTs a very valuable frame through which to understand these language moves. When viewed as an inherently stable and standardized system, as they often are in many education reform efforts, classrooms and teachers can seem irrational in the status quo and resistant to the new. From a C/CT perspective, however, the decomposition, diversification, and localization of teaching practices simply echo the reality of language as a complex dynamic system that we vainly try to capture and segment as a subject matter. In closing, then, we turn to a more elaborate discussion for how subject-languages move school subjects in this direction of postdisciplinarity.

THE LANGUAGE "MOVE" TOWARD POSTDISCIPLINARITY

To briefly recapitulate, in this chapter, we have made the argument that language in school is responding to two contrapuntal forces—from the world and from the way that language has traditionally been treated in curricula—and furthermore, we have said that these forces are moving language toward a different relationship to disciplinary knowledge. In the world, the broad sweep of globalization—the accelerating access to and dissemination of information, the simultaneous broadening and consolidation in certain hands of economic activity, the fluidity of migration (whether for economic or political purposes)—is recasting the place of language. As for the curricula, we have seen that there are ever-changing definitions of language as a school subject (what we have termed subject-languages) and of how subject-languages are taught and judged to have been learned.

We began this chapter with the argument that "foreign" language is atypical among classroom subject matters in several ways. In comparison to other disciplines that can be said to be "content full," in which the discipline anchors not only the content but the ways of thinking or habits of mind that underlie it, there is no agreed-on content to be taught and learned in "foreign" language classes. The result is that how learning and knowing (an)other language(s) is defined in school is often at odds with the context of use in the world. In essence, the trajectory of curricula and formal assessments in "foreign" language teaching since the 1950s has sought increasingly to fashion classrooms and teaching to parallel the ways in which languages are seen to be used in the world. As we have said previously, when in the 1950s and 1960s, knowing (an)other language(s) was defined as being able to respond automatically depending on situation, language teaching was organized to create language as patterned habits in students. During the 1980s and 1990s, when knowing (an)other language(s) came to be seen as learners' interactively achieving their ends, language teaching focused on communicative competence, language for specific purposes, tasks, negotiation of meaning, and content.

To capture these moves of language as it appears in school curricula, we have suggested the term *subject-languages*. These are languages that are designated as subject matter within the school curriculum but are not the medium of instruction in those settings (e.g., French or Chinese in an Anglophone U.S. school or English or Korean in a Japanese secondary school). As subject matter, they have certain teaching practices and learning expectations associated with them. In conventional terms, they are often referred to as "foreign" or "world" languages, but this notion of subject-language, which is in essence a shorthand for language-as-subject-matter, catalyzes central questions about the interrelation between language and disciplinary knowledge. Clearly, the description of language, and its study in schools, has been widely influenced by several disciplines (especially psychology, linguistics, anthropology, philosophy, applied linguistics, and even the natural sciences), but the content of language has not been informed by those disciplines. In comparison, for example, to the ways in which the discipline of history informs the teaching of social studies or the field of mathematics shapes the teaching of math as a school subject, the content of subject-languages is not defined by a specific discipline. Furthermore, if a central goal of disciplinary content areas is to help students develop habits of mind (see Sizer, 1986) and come to think within the knowledge structures of the discipline (e.g., Hill, Rowan, &

Ball, 2005), then subject-languages are at a bit of a loss. Thinking within a particular language as a school subject means coming to use the language as one who is identified as a member of that language community.

The fact that language has no direct disciplinary progenitor makes it problematic as a content area in school. In this sense, subject-languages are hybrid phenomena: Like any subject matter, they are creatures of schools, but unlike other subjects, their referential frame beyond school is not disciplinary. Instead, language can be seen variously as constitutive of individual and social identities, thus as utilitarian in social, political, and economic terms and as historical in the deitic sense.

To examine these features of the relationship between subject-languages and their referential frame, we see the notion of postdisciplinarity as a promising direction. We propose *post-* rather than *inter*disciplinary, because in our view, the idea of subject-languages necessitates working backward from the "problem space" that they create, or inhabit, in schools and schooling. In doing so, we want to extend the argument made by the Australian linguist, M. A. K. Halliday, when he challenged the idea of inter- or multidisciplinary thinking. Halliday (2001) put forward the term *transdisciplinary*:

> I say "transdisciplinary" rather than "inter" or "multidisciplinary" because the latter terms seem to me to imply that one still retains the disciplines as the locus of intellectual activity, while building bridges between them, or assembling them into a collection; whereas the real alternative is to supercede them, creating new forms of activity which are thematic rather than disciplinary in their orientation. (p. 176)

We agree with Halliday's analysis that what is needed is "creating new forms of activity which are thematic rather than disciplinary in their orientation," but we suggest that in terms of subject-language, there is a more fundamental problem. The increasing pace of knowledge creation and exchange not only is diversifying what is known, expanding knowledge in a traditional sense, but more critically, it is accelerating how things are known.

To concretize this argument in a particular example, consider the contrast between the *Encyclopedia Britannica* and Wikipedia as two compendia of what is known on subject entries. The former is selectively authored, print based, and centrally published, and thus it is structured and fixed. The *Encyclopedia Britannica* is updated periodically, and it is accessible through ownership of the volumes themselves. Wikipedia, in contrast, is publicly authored, electronic and Web based; it is thus highly malleable and is constantly updated and updatable. The whole design depends on a new gateway, accessibility through the Web, that blurs the boundaries between authors and readers to the point that both become in effect users. Counterposing these two as knowledge sources raises some fundamental questions: For example, What constitutes authorship and the source of information? Is the standard of accuracy and knowledge commensurate in the two forms? Is that the aim, or do the two diverge in fundamental ways about what knowledge is and who can create it?

Regardless of how one assesses these new fora of knowledge—their warrants for knowledge and standards of accuracy—it is clear that the media themselves create platforms for levels of participation in processes of authoring, editing, and publishing that are extremely different. This distinction points to a further issue in relation to the notion of transdisciplinarity: how knowledge is (deemed to be) created. The dynamic of knowledge creation seems increasingly to be split between the canonical and the local, wherein the former (like the *Encyclopedia Britannica*) expresses a unified and stable view of knowledge or a grand narrative, whereas the latter (like Wikipedia) introduces dynamic, multiple, and sometimes parallel readings. These readings are not simply interpretations; they have become more and more–alternative versions. Clearly, various fields have worked from multiple readings of knowledge previously, if we consider, for example, the parallel, and sometimes conflicting, explanations offered by allopathic, osteopathic, and homeopathic forms of medical diagnosis. The principal difference, however, is that these multiple readings were anchored in a set of shared definitions of the phenomena (human physiology, in these cases) and even sometimes etiologies of disease and malfunction; they differed in strategies for addressing (diagnosing, treating, and curing) the problems. In the case of postdisciplinarity, the tension between global or universal and local expertise; the acceleration of creating and access to new knowledge, however it is defined; and breadth of reach of human contact through technology, where there is no single authoritative source for what is known, seem to combine to unravel a common basis for knowing. And language, we would argue, is at the heart of that unraveling.

To this mix is added the expanding place of English globally. The irony or tension is that although English is now dominant as the lingua franca, it is less and less a language that is "owned" by one geographical or social community. Thus, the singular metrics that have in the past been invoked around "foreignness," "nativeness," "fluency," and "proficiency" are being problematized by and unraveling through the use of English as a tool for social, economic, and political access and participation. Simply put, as more and more students are learning English around the world, they are being taught by teachers who fulfill their role as "English" teachers based on circumstance rather than on proficiency (to whatever level), education, or professional training. As English becomes the subject-language in these settings, it is very much localized—interpreted, presented, practiced, assessed all within local circumstances. By itself, this fact might simply suggest a lack of equal educational quality for students in these situations, were it not that the standards of use, both formal and informal, are themselves changing radically, as well.

In that the vast majority of English users use English as a second or additional language, coupled with the fact that they are—and will increasingly—use English with others for whom it is also a second or additional language, it is inescapable that the language will rapidly diversify and evolve into new polyglottal forms that will ultimately appear "foreign" and even incomprehensible to those who use English as their first or mother tongue (Graddol, 2006). In this sense, students learning English as a "foreign" language in a Thai secondary school are participating in the creation and definition of what "English" becomes in the world. As those who speak it at home, and from birth, become a smaller numerical minority, the language itself moves. Of course, at present, there is no denying that although the language is less owned by one geographical location, there is still an ideological ownership that has not changed—and that those who buy into this ideological ownership and defer to native-speaker models sustain the current differences in power relationships among the World Englishes.

We still maintain, however, that the content of English is being reconstituted by the venues in which it is being taught, learned, and used, much like the common children's game of "telephone" or "Chinese whispers," in which each participant in the circle repeats in a whisper what she or he has heard from the person on the left to the person sitting on the right. This dynamism and fluidity is largely possible, we would suggest, because English, like other languages, does not have a clear link to a disciplinary frame. Thus, as a subject-language in school, English particularly, and other languages as well, is caught, or perhaps creates, a tension between the inherent stability sought through the exercise of curriculum, methodologies, and teaching practices and the turbulence of how these languages function in the world. This turbulence creates a fungibility of opportunity and of use with languages. Learners, as students of subject-languages in schools, have access to English, and other languages, through technology and through human interaction; they are exposed to, and often realize directly, the fungible opportunities for language use. And as they participate in these opportunities, they are changing in a dynamic and nonlinear sense what constitutes the systems of these languages themselves.

In this way, we have argued that the various practices of language teaching and learning, and the language knowledge from which they operate, are increasingly locally defined and contextually determined. This dynamic is creating a tension between the artificial stasis of language as a school subject and the use of that language in the world, eroding a sense of constancy in language, which is now not only more broadly accessible to learners but also more transiently defined. In this sense, "foreign" language teaching can be seen as leading, or at least signaling, a path of change that will ultimately influence other disciplines as they are invoked and enter into educational practice. All school knowledge, and the disciplines that undergird it, are practically speaking *in* language. Texts are read or written, problems are explained or solved, arguments are made, lab experiments are set up and run . . . all *in* language. So as language moves, so too may other aspects of classroom content.

This analysis suggests two principle harbingers of the influence of change on other disciplines as knowledge bases for teaching and learning in schools. The technological features of knowledge creation and dissemination that blur the boundary between authorship or generation and use or consumption (viz. the Wikipedia example) are contributing to anarchistic definitions for knowledge, a process that must ultimately influence the disciplines. These same features are propelling technocratic English, and perhaps other languages, globally, even as they are decentralizing it. Then, because knowledge dissemination is *in* language, and primarily in English at this point in history, the medium is likely to reshape the message such that knowledge dissemination decomposes even as it becomes more accessible. Lest this seem like an assertion that the tail will wag the dog, we would point out that language in our analysis is metaphorically the bone and muscle structure of the tail; it is how—not what—the dog wags.

This returns us, in closing, to the notion of postdisciplinarity. We differ from Halliday's (2001) suggestion of transdisciplinarity in that we do not see the issue so much as "creating new forms of activity which are thematic rather than disciplinary in their orientation" (p. 176), in his words, but rather as acknowledging that the structure and categories of disciplinary knowledge themselves are now in play. Terming this complex dynamic as postdisciplinarity, we refer to this present period in which the overarching definitions of knowledge in many disciplines are decomposing and are being overtaken by local practices. Although the grand narratives of the disciplines will continue to exist, their persuasiveness is being eroded primarily by language itself. Thus, because language provides the discursive bases through which disciplines are defined and articulated, as well as the interactive medium through which they are realized, it is reasonable—and, indeed, perhaps even to be expected—that this postdisciplinarity is more immediately evident in language teaching and learning than in other fields. This is, we contend, not a unique circumstance. For as language moves, so do—and will eventually—other school subjects. As its ownership and authorship decomposes, through and in language, so perhaps will the warrants in other disciplines that are based on predictable notions of stability and singularity. And as its uses change, it seems almost inevitable that the knowledge forms and disciplines that must depend on language will themselves ultimately be transformed.

NOTES

[1]In April 2007, Russian immigration chiefs proposed compulsory language tests for foreigners wanting to work in Russia, the latest in a series of measures to tighten up on immigration (message posted to lgpolicy-list@ccat.sas.upenn.edu, May 4, 2007).

[2]Chaos theory and complexity theory have developed from the source disciplines of mathematics and biology, respectively (Larsen-Freeman & Cameron, in press). However, they have much in common, so we have chosen to combine them as does the American Educational Research Association Special Interest Group as "chaos and complexity theories."

[3]From this point forward in this review, when we refer to *language teaching*, we mean the teaching of "foreign" language as a school subject, or what we have called "subject-language." Thus the complete phrase would be *subject-language teaching*; however, that is a bit cumbersome, so we have shortened it.

[4]There are foreign language departments at universities, but these have been by and large concerned with literature, the teaching of language being provided by service courses, with no disciplinary status.

[5]For descriptions of both, see Rivers (1972).

[6]"Foreign" languages had been a dimension of U.S. national security for some time. The founding of the Office of Strategic Services, the predecessor to the Central Intelligence Agency, included linguists. Interestingly, several key academic leaders of the 1950s and 1960s in the "less commonly taught" languages (e.g., Donald Keene in Japanese; Burton Watson in Mandarin Chinese) came from this background. Most recently, the U.S. president announced (January 5, 2006) the National Security Language Initiative, which invests millions of dollars in an attempt to expand the number of Americans mastering "critical need" languages (such as

Arabic, Chinese, Russian, Hindi, Farsi, and others) and to start teaching them at a younger age (kindergarten). The United States is not alone in targeting younger learners. The government in the United Kingdom recently announced that from 2010, the learning of a modern foreign language will be compulsory for children from the age of 7 to 14 (*Education Guardian*, March 12, 2007).

[7]Probably the most dramatic contrast could be seen between the Silent Way (Gattegno, 1976), which literally used teacher silence as a key teaching practice, and Suggestopedia (Lozanov, 1978), in which the teacher gave dramatic readings of long stretches of dialogue accompanied by classical music.

[8]Such dichotomies also obscure the fact that the status of these designations may not be constant. For example, there have been many documented cases where heritage speakers of particular languages in the United States, that is, the children of immigrants who speak a language other than English at home, could be said to have "lost" their native language.

[9]Methodologist Caleb Gattegno captured this apparent contradiction in language development when he would ask teachers in training seminars, "When did you become 'fluent' in your native language?"

[10]It bears noting, for example, that until the passage of the U.S. federal legislation known as No Child Left Behind, there was no requirement that state or school authorities define what was meant, in operational terms, by proficiency in English as the language of instruction (see Freeman & Riley, 2005).

[11]The study of beliefs, particularly in language teaching, has a complex history because there are no standard definitions for the concept either as descriptive notion or as research tool (see Bernat & Gvozdenko, 2005**).**

[12]This work had been in some ways foreshadowed by research on beliefs in foreign-language teaching about communicative fluency (De Garcia, Reynolds, & Savignon, 1976) as well as by Kern's (1995) work on beliefs about language learning, the major distinction being that the teacher cognition research summaries of the late 1980s addressed the place of thinking generally in teachers' work, of which beliefs about learning, content, or instruction were a possible subset.

[13]There are many progenitors of this movement. One can trace its roots to the work of Stenhouse (1975) in Britain, Kemmis and McTaggart (1988) in Australia, and Cochran-Smith and Lytle (1993) in the United States, among many others. It found its way into "foreign" languages primarily through individual emphases on action research (e.g., Nunan & Lamb, 1996), teacher research (e.g., Freeman, 1998), or collective projects on classroom teaching (e.g., the Languages Other Than English [LOTE] Project in South Australia; Burton, 1997).

[14]Field learning of languages has always seemed a sort of "gold standard," such that self-taught learners—those who acquire language and who become proficient by whatever measure—are often regarded as more successful than those who "learn" that same language in instructed settings. In fact, language teaching is, we think, the only educational field in which there has been a terminological difference drawn in the processes between field-based *acquisition* and classroom or instructed *learning*.

[15]Some see that in the future, English will be replaced by Chinese for the same globalization reasons. According to a prediction by the Chinese National Office for Teaching Chinese as a Foreign Language, by the year 2010, 100 million non-Chinese will be studying Chinese.

[16]More recently, Graddol (2006) quotes estimates that put English and Mandarin on a par when second-language users are included. He further quotes M. Davis (2004), who estimates that the percentage of the global economy (GDP) accounted by English (28.2%) and Mandarin (22.8%) by 2010 will be roughly comparable.

[17]This is reminiscent of an earlier statement by Gee and Green (1998) to the effect that "language simultaneously reflects and constructs the situation in which it is used" (p. 134).

ACKNOWLEDGMENTS

We would like to thank the editors of this volume, Judith Green, Greg Kelly, and Allan Luke, for their feedback during the preparation of this chapter. In addition, Jin Sook Lee, Audra Skukauskaite, Heidi Byrnes, and Karen E. Johnson offered us helpful comments, for which we are grateful.

REFERENCES

Agar, M. (1994). *Language shock. Understanding the culture of conversation.* New York: Quill.

Allwright, R. L. (2003). Exploratory practice: Rethinking practitioner research in language teaching. *Language Teaching Research, 7,* 113–141.

American Council on Teaching Foreign Languages. (1996). *Standards for foreign language learning: Preparing for the 21st century.* Yonkers, NY: ACTFL.

American Council on Teaching Foreign Languages. (1999). *Standards for foreign language learning: Preparing for the 21st century.* Yonkers, NY: ACTFL.

American Council on the Teaching of Foreign Languages. (n.d.). *About ACTFL.* Retrieved April 19, 2007, from http://www.actfl.org/i4a/pages/index.cfm?pageid=3274

Andalo, D. (2007, March 12). *All primary children to teach foreign languages by 2010.* Retrieved from http://education.guardian.co.uk/schools/story/0,,2032012,00.html

Bernat, E., & Gvozdenko, I. (2005). Beliefs about language learning: Current knowledge, pedagogical implications, and new research directions. *TESL-EJ, 9*(1), 1–21.

Bhatia, V. J. (1993). *Analysing genre: Language use in professional settings.* London: Longman.

Brooks, N. (1960). *Language and language learning.* New York: Harcourt, Brace and World.

Brown, R. (1973). *A first language.* Cambridge, MA: Harvard University Press.

Brown Mitchell, C., & Ellingson Vidal, K. (2001). Weighing the ways of the flow: Twentieth century language instruction. *Modern Language Journal, 85*(1), 26–38.

Burton, J. (1997). Sustaining language teachers as researchers of their own practice. *Canadian Modern Language Review, 54*(1), 84–109.

Bybee, J. (2006). From usage to grammar: The mind's response to repetition. *Language, 82*(4), 711–733.

Byrnes, H. (2005). Content-based foreign language instruction. In C. Sanz (Ed.), *Minds and context in adult second language acquisition* (pp. 282–302). Washington, DC: Georgetown University Press.

Byrnes, H. (2006). Locating the advanced learner in theory, research, and educational practice. In H. Byrnes, H. Weger-Guntharp, & K. Sprang (Eds.), *Educating for advanced foreign language capacities: Constructs, curriculum, instruction, assessment* (pp. 1–14). Washington, DC: Georgetown University Press.

Byrnes, H. (Ed.). (2007). *Advanced language learning. The contribution of Halliday and Vygotsky.* London: Continuum.

Calderhead, J. (1987). *Exploring teachers' thinking.* London: Cassell.

Canale, M., & Swain, M. (1980). Theoretical bases of communicative approaches to second language teaching and testing. *Applied Linguistics, 1*(1), 1–47.

Chomsky, N. (1959). Review of *Verbal Behavior* by B. F. Skinner. *Language, 35*(1), 26–58.

Chomsky, N. (1965). *Aspects of the theory of syntax.* Cambridge, MA: MIT Press.

Cilliers, P. (2007). *Knowing complex systems: The limits of understanding.* Unpublished manuscript.

Clark, C. M., & Peterson, P. L. (1986). Teachers' thought processes. In M. C. Wittrock (Ed.), *Handbook of research on teaching* (3rd ed., pp. 255–296). New York: Macmillan.

Cochran-Smith, M., & Lytle, S. (Eds.). (1993). *Inside-outside: Teacher research and knowledge.* New York: Teachers College Press.

Colombi, M. C. (2007, July). *Spanish as an academic language in the U.S.: A functional approach to the language of the humanities.* Paper presented at the International Systemic Functional Congress, Odense, Denmark.

Cook, G. (2005). Calm seas or troubled waters? Transitions, definitions and disagreements in applied linguistics. *International Journal of Applied Linguistics, 15*(3), 282–301.

Cook, V. (1999). Going beyond the native speaker in language teaching. *TESOL Quarterly, 33*(2), 185–209.

Corder, S. P. (1967). The significance of learners' errors. *International Review of Applied Linguistics, 5,* 161–170.

Council of Europe. (2001). *Common European framework of reference for languages: Learning, teaching, assessment.* Cambridge, UK: Cambridge University Press.

Crystal, D. (1997). *English as a global language.* Cambridge, UK: Cambridge University Press.

Curran, C. (1976). *Counseling-learning in second language.* East Dubuque, IL: Counseling-Learning Publications.

Davies, A. (1981). Review of *Communicative Syllabus Design* by John Munby. *TESOL Quarterly, 15*(3), 332–336.

Davis, J. N. (1997). Educational reform and the Babel (babble) of culture: Prospects for the standards for foreign language learning. *Modern Language Journal, 81*(1), 151–163.

Davis, M. (2004). *GDP by language* (Unicode Technical Note 131). Retrieved May 23, 2007, from http://www.unicode.org/notes/tn13/tn13–1/html

De Garcia, R., Reynolds, S., & Savignon, S. (1976). Foreign-language attitude survey. *Canadian Modern Language Review, 32,* 302–304.

DeKeyser, R. (1998). Beyond focus on form: Cognitive perspectives on learning and practicing second language grammar. In C. Doughty & J. Williams (Eds.), *Focus on form in classroom in second language acquisition* (pp. 42–63). New York: Cambridge University Press.

Ellis, N., & Larsen-Freeman, D. (2006). Language emergence: Implications for applied linguistics. Introduction to the special issue. *Applied Linguistics, 27*(4), 558–589.

Engeström, Y. (1999). Expansive visibilization of work: An activity-theoretical perspective. *Computer Supported Cooperative Work, 8,* 63–93.

Evans, R. (1996). *The human side of school change.* San Francisco: Jossey-Bass.

Fairclough, N. (1995). *Critical discourse analysis: The critical study of language.* London: Longman.

Firth, A., & Wagner, J. (1997). On discourse, communication, and (some) fundamental concepts in SLA research. *Modern Language Journal, 81*(3), 285–300.

Firth, A., & Wagner, J. (1998). SLA property: No trespassing! *Modern Language Journal, 82*(1), 91–94.

Freeman, D. (1994). Knowing into doing: Teacher education and the problem of transfer. In D. C. S. Li., D. Mahoney, & J. C. Richards (Eds.), *Exploring second language teacher development* (pp. 1–21.) Hong Kong: City Polytechnic of Hong Kong.

Freeman, D. (1996). "To take them at their word": Language data in the study of teachers' knowledge. *Harvard Educational Review, 66*(4), 732–761.

Freeman, D. (1998). *Doing teacher-research: From inquiry to understanding.* Boston: Heinle/Thomson.

Freeman, D. (2002). The hidden side of the work: Teacher knowledge and learning to teach. *Language Teaching, 35*(1), 1–13.

Freeman, D. (2004). Teaching in the context of English-language learners: What do we need to know? In M. Sadowski (Ed.), *Teaching immigrant and second language students* (pp. 7–20). Cambridge, MA: Harvard University Press.

Freeman, D. (2006). Teaching and learning in the "age of reform": The problem of the verb. In S. Gieve & I. Miller (Eds.), *Understanding the language classroom* (pp. 239–262). Basingstoke, UK: Palgrave Macmillan.

Freeman, D., & Johnson, K. D. (1998). Re-conceptualizing the knowledge-base of language teacher education. *TESOL Quarterly, 32*(3), 397–417.

Freeman, D., & Richards, J. C. (Eds.). (1996). *Teacher learning in language teaching*. New York: Cambridge University Press.

Freeman, D., & Riley, K. (2005). When the law goes local: One state's experience with NCLB in practice. *Modern Language Journal, 89*(2), 264–268.

Gattegno, C. (1972). *Teaching foreign languages in schools: The silent way* (2nd ed.). New York: Educational Solutions.

Gattegno, C. (1976). *The common sense of teaching foreign languages*. New York: Educational Solutions.

Gee, J. P., & Green, J. L. (1998). Discourse analysis, learning, and social practice: A methodological study. *Review of Research in Education, 23*, 119–169.

Gieve, S., & Miller, I. (Eds.). (2006). *Understanding the language classroom*. Basingstoke, UK: Palgrave Macmillan.

Givón, T. (1999). Generativity and variation. The notion "rule of grammar" revisited. In B. MacWhinney (Ed.), *The emergence of language* (pp. 81–114). Mahwah, NJ: Lawrence Erlbaum.

Gleick, J. (1987). *Chaos: Making a new science*. New York: Penguin.

Graddol, D. (2006). *English next*. London: British Council.

Grandin, J. (1989). German and engineering: An overdue alliance. *Die Unterrichts-praxis, 22*, 146–152.

Hall, J. (2000). Classroom interactions and additional language learning: Implications for teaching and learning. In J. K. Hall & L. S. Verplaetse (Eds.), *Second and foreign language learning through classroom interaction* (pp. 287–298). Mahwah, NJ: Lawrence Erlbaum.

Halliday, M. A. K. (1973). *Explorations in the functions of language*. London: Edward Arnold.

Halliday, M. A. K. (1994). *An introduction to functional grammar* (2nd ed.). London: Edward Arnold.

Halliday, M. A. K. (2001). New ways of meaning: The challenges to applied linguistics. In A. Fill & P. Mühlhäusler (Eds.), *The ecolinguistics reader: Language ecology and environment* (pp. 175–202). New York: Continuum.

Hatch, E. (1978). Discourse analysis, speech acts and second language acquisition. In W. Ritchie (Ed.), *Second language acquisition research* (pp. 137–155). New York: Academic Press.

Hill, H. C., Rowan, B., & Ball, D. L. (2005). Effects of teachers' mathematical knowledge for teaching on student achievement. *American Educational Research Journal, 42*(2), 371–406.

Hymes, D. (1972). On communicative competence. In J. Pride & J. Holmes (Eds.), *Sociolinguistics: Selected reading* (pp. 269–293). Harmondsworth, UK: Penguin.

International Association of Teachers of English as a Foreign Language. (n.d.). *Welcome to IATEFL*. Retrieved April 19, 2007, from http://www.iatefl.org/content/about/index.php

Jenkins, J. (2000). *The phonology of English as an international language*. Oxford, UK: Oxford University Press.

Kachru, B. (1986). The power and politics of English. *World Englishes, 5*(2/3), 121–140.

Kasper, G. (1997). "A" stands for acquisition: A response to Firth and Wagner. *Modern Language Journal, 81*(3), 307–312.

Kelly, L. (1969). *25 centuries of language teaching*. Rowley, MA: Newbury House.

Kemmis, S., & McTaggart, R. (1988). *The action research reader*. Melbourne Australia: Deakin University Press.

Kennedy, M. (1991). *An agenda for research on teacher learning*. East Lansing: Michigan State University, National Center for Research on Teacher Learning.

Kern, R. G. (1995). Students' and teachers' beliefs about language learning. *Foreign Language Annals, 28*(1), 71–92.

Klein, W. (1998). The contribution of second language acquisition research. *Language Learning, 48*(4), 527–490.

Kramsch, C. (2002). Introduction. In C. Kramsch (Ed.), *Language acquisition and language socialization* (pp. 1–30). London: Continuum.

Krashen, S., & Terrell, T. (1983). *The natural approach.* New York: Pergamon.

Kumaravadivelu, B. (1994). The postmethod condition: Emerging strategies for second/foreign language teaching. *TESOL Quarterly, 28*(1), 27–48.

Lantolf, J. (Ed.). (2000). *Sociocultural theory and second language learning.* Oxford, UK: Oxford University Press.

Larsen-Freeman, D. (1997). Chaos/complexity science and second language acquisition. *Applied Linguistics, 18*(2), 141–165.

Larsen-Freeman, D. (2000a). On the appropriateness of language teaching methods in language and development. In J. Shaw, D. Lubelske, & M. Noullet (Eds.), *Partnership and Interaction: Proceedings of the fourth international Conference on Language and Development* (pp. 65–71). Bangkok, Thailand: Asian Institute of Technology.

Larsen-Freeman, D. (2000b). *Techniques and principles in language teaching* (2nd ed.). Oxford, UK: Oxford University Press.

Larsen-Freeman, D. (2002). The grammar of choice. In E. Hinkel & S. Fotos (Eds.), *New perspectives on grammar teaching in second language classrooms* (pp. 103–118). Mahwah, NJ: Lawrence Erlbaum.

Larsen-Freeman, D. (2003). *Teaching language: From grammar to grammaring.* Boston: Thomson/Heinle.

Larsen-Freeman, D. (2006). The emergence of complexity, fluency, and accuracy in the oral and written production of five Chinese learners of English. *Applied Linguistics, 27*(4), 590–619.

Larsen-Freeman, D. (2007). Reflecting on the cognitive-social debate in second language acquisition. *Modern Language Journal, 91*(5), 771–785.

Larsen-Freeman, D., & Cameron, L. (in press). *Complex systems and applied linguistics.* Oxford, UK: Oxford University Press.

Larsen-Freeman, D., & Long, M. (1991). *An introduction to second language acquisition research.* London: Longman.

Lave, J., & Wenger, E. (1991). *Situated learning: Legitimate peripheral participation.* New York: Cambridge University Press.

Lewontin, R. (2000). *The triple helix: Gene, organism, and environment.* Cambridge, MA: Harvard University Press.

Long, M. H. (1991). Focus on form: A design feature in language teaching methodology. In K. de Bot, R. Ginsberg, & C. Kramsch (Eds.), *Foreign language research in cross-cultural perspective* (pp. 39–52). Amsterdam and Philadelphia: John Benjamins.

Long, M. H., & Crookes, G. (1993). Units of analysis in syllabus design: The case for task. In G. Crookes & S. M. Gass (Eds.), *Tasks in pedagogical context: Integrating theory and practice* (pp. 9–54). Clevedon, UK: Multilingual Matters.

Lortie, D. (1975). *Schoolteacher: A sociological study.* Chicago: University of Chicago Press.

Lozanov, G. (1978). *Outlines of suggestology and suggestopedy.* London: Gordon and Breach.

Luke, A., & Luke, C. (2000). A situated perspective on cultural globalization. In N. Burbules & C. Torres (Eds.), *Globalization and education: Critical perspectives* (pp. 275–297). New York: Routledge.

Luke, A., Luke, C., & Graham, P. (2007). Globalisation, corporatism, and critical language education. *International Multilingual Research Journal, 1*(1), 1–13.

Marsh, D., & Langé, G. (2000). *Using languages to learn and learning to use languages.* Jyväskylä, Finland, and Milan: TIE-CLIL.

McGroarty, M. (Ed.). (2006). *Annual review of applied linguistics: Vol. 26. Lingua franca languages.* Cambridge, UK: Cambridge University Press.

Morin, E. (2007). Restricted complexity, general complexity. In C. Gershenson, D. Aerts, & B. Emonds (Eds.), *Worldviews, science and us: Philosophy and complexity* (pp. 5–29). Singapore: World Scientific.

Munby, J. (1978). *Communicative syllabus design.* Cambridge, UK: Cambridge University Press.

Ninkovich, F. (1981). *The diplomacy of ideas: U.S. foreign policy and cultural relations, 1938–1950.* New York: Cambridge University Press.

Norton, B. (1995). Social identity, investment and language learning. *TESOL Quarterly, 29*(1), 9–31.

Nunan, D., & Lamb, C. (1996). *The self-directed teacher.* New York: Cambridge University Press.

O'Keeffe, A., McCarthy, M., & Carter, R. (2007). *From corpus to classroom: Language use and language teaching.* Cambridge, UK: Cambridge University Press.

Omaggio, A. (1983). Methodology in transition: The new focus on proficiency. *Modern Language Journal, 67*(3), 330–341.

Pennycook, A. (2001). *Critical applied linguistics: A critical introduction.* Mahwah, NJ: Lawrence Erlbaum.

Prabhu, N. S. (1980). *Theoretical background to the Bangalore project. New approaches to teaching English.* Bangalore, South India: Regional Institute of English.

Prabhu, N. S. (1987). *Second language pedagogy.* Oxford, UK: Oxford University Press.

Richards, J. C., & Lockhart, C. (1994). *Reflective teaching in second language classrooms.* New York: Cambridge University Press.

Richards, J. C., & Rodgers, T. (2000). *Approaches and methods in language teaching* (2nd ed.). Cambridge, UK: Cambridge University Press.

Rivers, W. (1972). *Teaching foreign language skills.* Chicago: University of Chicago Press.

Rogoff, B. (1995). Observing sociocultural activity on three planes: Participatory appropriation, guided participation, and apprenticeship. In J. Wertsch, P. del Rio, & A. Alvarez (Eds.), *Sociocultural studies of mind* (pp. 139–164). Cambridge, UK: Cambridge University Press.

Saussure, F. de. (1959). *Course in general linguistics* (W. Baskin, Trans.). New York: Philosophical Library. (Original work published 1916)

Savignon, S. (1972). *Communicative competence: An experiment in foreign language teaching.* Philadelphia: Center for Curriculum Development.

Schleppegrell, M. (2004). *The language of schooling: A functional linguistics perspective.* Mahwah, NJ: Lawrence Erlbaum.

Schultz, R. (2000). Foreign language teacher development: MLJ perspectives, 1916–1999. *Modern Language Journal, 84*(4), 495–522.

Seidlhofer, B. (2001). Closing a conceptual gap: The case for a description of English as a lingua franca. *International Journal of Applied Linguistics, 11*(2), 133–158.

Selinker, L. (1972). Interlanguage. *International Review of Applied Linguistics, 10,* 209–231.

Sfard, A. (1998). On two metaphors for learning and the dangers of choosing just one. *Educational Researcher, 27*(2), 4–13.

Silver, R. E. (2007, March). *Language awareness and teacher expertise: Moving from collaborative learning to collaborative language learning.* Paper presented at the meeting of Teachers of English to Speakers of Other Languages, Seattle.

Sizer, H. (1986). *Horace's compromise: The dilemma of the American high school.* Boston: Houghton-Mifflin.

Skinner, B. F. (1957). *Verbal behavior.* New York: Appleton-Century-Crofts.

Skutnabb-Kangas, T. (2000). *Linguistic genocide on education—Or worldwide diversity and human rights?* Mahwah, NJ: Lawrence Erlbaum.

Skutnabb-Kangas, T., & Phillipson, R. (Eds.). (1995). *Linguistic human rights: Overcoming linguistic discrimination.* Berlin: Mouton de Gruyter.

Snow, M. A., & Brinton, D. M. (Eds.). (1997). *The content-based classroom: Perspectives on integrating language and content.* New York: Addison-Wesley Longman.

Stenhouse, L. (1975). *An introduction to curriculum research and development.* London: Heinemann.

Stevick, E. (1976). *Memory, meaning and method.* Rowley, MA: Newbury House.

Stevick, E. (1980). *Teaching languages: A way and ways.* Rowley, MA: Newbury House.

Stevick, E. (1982). *Teaching and learning languages.* Cambridge, UK: Cambridge University Press.

Stevick, E. (1990). *Humanism in language teaching.* New York: Oxford University Press.

Swales, J. (1990). *Genre analysis.* Cambridge, UK: Cambridge University Press.

Tao, H. (2005). The gap between natural speech and spoken Chinese teaching material: Discourse perspectives on Chinese pedagogy. *Journal of the Chinese Language Teachers Association, 40*(2), 1–24.

Teachers of English to Speakers of Other Languages. (n.d.). *Bylaws.* Available from http://www.tesol.org

Terrell, T. (1977). A natural approach to second language acquisition and learning. *Modern Language Journal, 61*(3), 325–337.

Titone, R. (1968). *Teaching foreign languages: An historical sketch.* Washington, DC: Georgetown University Press.

Tomasello, M. (2003). *Constructing a language.* Cambridge, MA: Harvard University Press.

Trim, J. (2007). *Modern languages in the Council of Europe, 1954–1997.* Strasbourg, France: Council of Europe.

Tyack, D. (1974). *The one best system: A history of American urban education.* Cambridge, MA: Harvard University Press.

Tyack, D., & Cuban, L. (1995). *Tinkering toward utopia: A century of public school reform.* Cambridge, MA: Harvard University Press.

Van den Branden, K. (2007, March). *Towards a school-based, practice-oriented coaching: Bridging the gap between second.* Paper presented at the meeting of Teachers of English to Speakers of Other Languages, Seattle, WA.

van Ek, J. (1975). *The threshold level.* Strasbourg, France: Council of Europe.

van Geert, P., & Steenbeek, H. (in press). A complexity and dynamic systems approach todevelopment assessment, modeling and research. In A. Battro, K. Fischer, A. Battro, & P. Léna (Eds.), *Mind, brain, and education.* Cambridge, UK: Cambridge University Press.

Walberg, H. (1971). Decision and perception: New contructs in research on teaching offects. *Cambridge Journal of Education, 7*(1), 12- 20

Wallace, M. (1991). *Training foreign language teachers: A reflective approach.* Cambridge, UK: Cambridge University Press.

Wesche, M., & Skehan, P. (2002). Communicative, task-based, and content-based instruction. In R. Kaplan (Ed.), *The Oxford handbook of applied linguistics* (pp. 207–228). Oxford, UK: Oxford University Press.

Whitehead, A. N. (1929). *The aims of education.* New York: Macmillan.

Widdowson, H. G. (2003). *Defining issues in English language teaching.* Oxford, UK: Oxford University Press.

Widdowson, H. G. (2004). A perspective on recent trends. In A. P. R. Howatt with H. G. Widdowson, *A history of English language teaching* (2nd ed., pp. 353–372). Oxford, UK: Oxford University Press.

Wilkins, D. (1976). *Notional syllabuses.* Oxford, UK: Oxford University Press.

Woods, D. (1996). *Teacher cognition and language teaching.* New York: Cambridge University Press.

Zuengler, J., & Miller, E. (2006). Cognitive and sociocultural perspectives: Two parallel SLA worlds? *TESOL Quarterly, 40*(1), 35–58.

Chapter 6

Culture and Mathematics in School: Boundaries Between "Cultural" and "Domain" Knowledge in the Mathematics Classroom and Beyond

NA'ILAH SUAD NASIR
Stanford University

VICTORIA HAND
University of Colorado at Boulder

EDD V. TAYLOR
Northwestern University

This chapter is about culture and mathematics teaching and learning. Our goal is to offer a thoughtful treatment of the role of culture in the teaching and learning of mathematics and to synthesize literature that is relevant to this concern from multiple subdisciplines in education, including math education, educational anthropology, sociology, sociolinguistics, and critical theory. As we do so, we will consider boundaries between what is commonly thought of as "cultural" knowledge (that is, knowledge derived from settings outside of school, typically in students' homes and communities) and "domain" knowledge (that is, knowledge valued in the practices prescribed by mathematicians and math educators). Of course, in reality, all knowledge is cultural. All knowledge is related to our experience in the social and cultural worlds that we inhabit, and all knowledge comes to us as it passes through social and cultural systems and institutions through the socializing of norms, values, conventions, and practices. Some have even argued that the dichotomy between "everyday" and "school" mathematics is false (Moschkovich, 2007).

It is also true that knowledge is not neutral with respect to power—some types of knowledge are more aligned with communities of practice that hold more power, whereas other types of knowledge are more aligned with communities of practice that have less power. When viewed through this lens, any discussion of boundaries between mathematical knowledge and cultural knowledge must respect that these issues of power are implicated in our definitions, issues of concern, and the very

Review of Research in Education
February 2008, Vol. 32, pp. 187–240
DOI: 10.3102/0091732X07308962
© 2008 AERA. http://rre.aera.net

conversation in which we are engaged through our scholarship. Furthermore, knowledge is fundamentally tied to the kinds of people we (and others) view ourselves to be and the trajectory we (and others) view ourselves to be on. In other words, issues of identity are critical to understanding both the development of mathematical knowledge for individuals and communities but also to considering how we draw lines between cultural and domain knowledge.

We would like to begin with a story about the experience of cultural and domain mathematics for one group of African American students in California. For us, this story illustrates important themes in understanding the cultural nature of mathematics learning and tensions to consider in elucidating boundaries between domain and cultural knowledge in mathematics. As a part of a study on thinking and learning across contexts (Nasir, 1996, 2000) middle and high school basketball players were asked to solve average and percentage problems two ways: In one set of tasks, the problems were framed by the practices of basketball, and in the other, problems were given in the format of a typical school math worksheet. Two examples of problems in both formats are presented in Table 1.

Players' responses to these two sets of problems were striking. Overall, players were better able to solve the problems in the context of basketball, and they used quite different strategies across the two contexts. On basketball problems, players tended to use invented strategies, such as a strategy for computing the average that involved adding and subtracting between the numbers until they were all the same or a strategy for calculating percentages that involved assuming each shot was worth 10% (so that the problem above would be 70% because the players made seven shots). On school math problems, players used algorithms, often misremembered, to manipulate numbers. How do we think about which of these kinds of responses are more mathematically sound? Through one lens, the use of algorithms is a powerful and concise way to solve math problems involving average and percentage and speaks to one's ability to leverage the collective wisdom in the field for a reliable and tidy solution. However, players often misapplied the algorithms and may not have understood the mathematics behind the operations that they performed. Through another lens, the invented strategies (in some cases) show understanding of fundamental mathematical principles. The average strategy presented above is founded on an intuitive understanding of the principle of an average (a number that represents a group of numbers). However, other strategies, although useful for some problems, could lead to mathematically incoherent solutions on other problems. For instance, the percentage strategy cited above is a mathematically inflexible solution path for generalization across different problem contexts. Furthermore, the point can also be made that the very problems students are solving across these contexts are different in nature. On the basketball problems, students were reasoning about discrete quantities—quantities that had shape and form in the real world. The school problems asked students not to reason about quantities directly but to work with symbolic representations of quantities. We argue, though, the differences in students' solutions were not solely because of the presence or absence of symbolic representations;

TABLE 1   School and Basketball Format Problems

Problem Type	Basketball Format	School Format
Calculating a percentage	"Say you are at the free-throw line. You take 11 shots and you make seven of them. What's your percentage from the line?"	$7/11 =$ _____ %
Calculating the average of a series of numbers	"In the first game of the season, you score 15 points. In the second game you score 20 points. In the third game you score 10 points. What is your average score for those three games?"	Students were shown a list of the numbers with a blank box in which to write the average of (15, 20, 10). Instructions were written as "Calculate the average for these sets of numbers and write the solution in the box."

rather, they reflect differences in students' sense of themselves and their abilities in these settings.

Basketball players' patterns of solutions and strategies illustrate what is often a discontinuity between students' everyday cultural knowledge about math and the type of mathematics instruction and classroom activities many students are exposed to in school. The observed response patterns also point to one way that culture can become salient (even if it is not recognized as so) in the math classroom. That is, the basketball players possessed knowledge about average and percentage that was inaccessible in the math classroom and that their teachers likely did not know that they had.

Thus far, our analysis of players' solution patterns across problems has been primarily cognitive. However, the findings also speak to the sociocultural aspects of the boundaries between domain and cultural knowledge in math. When players were asked to solve the basketball problems first, they did better on all of the problems. When they were asked to solve the school problems first, they scored lower on all of the problems. This order effect has implications for considering what these two problem sets may have indexed beyond mathematical knowledge. It may be that players who solved the school problems first experienced relative failure and incompetence, which rendered them unable to call up complex reasoning strategies when they solved the basketball problems. When players got the basketball problems first, they took up positions as knowledgeable experts and were emotionally equipped to take on both sets of problems. Interestingly, getting the school problems first left the boundaries between cultural and domain knowledge intact, whereas getting the basketball problems first may have begun to blur these boundaries. Students' sense of themselves as mathematical thinkers and capable learners are at play here. This sense of themselves is rooted in students' histories of participation in mathematics in basketball and in school mathematics.

This analysis raises questions about what counts as mathematical knowledge and productive mathematical activity. It also points to the importance of discerning how the features of different social contexts, in interaction with the proclivities and dispositions of students, mediate what is learned. This dual lens is critical in that learning occurs at the intersection of individual learners (their preferences, sensibilities, and histories of participation in math classrooms) and social contexts with sets of norms and conventions for engagement, availability of supports, and assumptions about learners.

In this chapter, we consider relations between cultural and domain knowledge in mathematics, exploring multiple ways that culture has been viewed by scholars as having relevance to math teaching and learning. Underlying our discussion in this chapter is a concern for the experiences of teaching and learning for nondominant and other marginalized students in American schools, particularly, students who belong to ethnic and social groups currently "underperforming" in mathematics. We draw from Perry, Steele, and Hilliard (2003) in our concern for three kinds of "gaps" in mathematics education: the racial "achievement gap," the gap between potential and achievement for students of color, and the "service gap" widely documented in studies of schools and classrooms across communities. We are all familiar with the racial achievement gap in mathematics and more generally (Haycock, 2001; Secada, 1992; Tate, 1997). White and Asian students continue to outperform African American and Latino students on national tests of mathematics, even when social class is controlled for.[1] This long-standing gap in math achievement is a major national concern and points to the continuing inequities in access to opportunities to learn rich mathematics on multiple levels (Oakes, Joseph, & Muir, 2003). Perry et al. (2003) argue that although this achievement gap by race is important, there are other important "gaps" in education that receive much less attention. First, they argue, there is a gap between "current levels of performance of African [American] students and levels of excellence" (p. 138). In other words, they argue that we know that excellence (not simply adequacy) is in full reach of the masses of African American (and by extension other minority) students, yet many students are not supported to reach this potential for excellence.

Second, they argue that there is quality-of-service gap. They write,

Nothing is more peculiar than the continuing seeming inability of our leading educators to acknowledge these well-documented savage inequalities and to use them as a basis for explaining the academic, social, and cultural achievements of students. (p. 140)

In pointing out these other two gaps, these authors challenge the mainstream conversation about students of color and about culture and learning, but they also make the argument that reducing all of these gaps is about good teaching.

In this chapter, we take all of these gaps seriously in our discussion of cultural and domain knowledge in mathematics. We consider both theoretical treatments about the relation between culture, race, and math learning, and we also review important contributions with respect to what kinds of practices (both teaching practices and professional development practices) support the reduction of the gaps described above. We also address these issues from a policy perspective, considering the production and reproduction of inequity with respect to math reforms in the past decade.

More specifically, in the second section, we offer our assumptions about knowledge (or knowing) as an inherently cultural activity. In the third section, we briefly explore relations between "everyday" informal math knowledge and school math as a way to enter the conversation about the cultural nature of mathematics. In the fourth section, we attend to the ways in which the field has conceptualized how issues of culture matter in mathematics classes, highlighting three lenses that researchers have used to understand culture and math learning: (a) the way that language mediates knowledge, (b) features of math classrooms as contexts that support or constrain different forms of knowledge, and (c) the way that racialized identities and expectations play out in mathematics classes. In the fifth section, we examine how these issues of culture have taken shape in conversations and research about reforms in mathematics education. In the sixth section, we explore distinct programs and approaches that offer tools and ideas for blurring the line between domain and cultural knowledge in mathematics and briefly reflect on the implications of these issues of culture and math learning for teacher professional development. We conclude by returning to the discussion we began in this introduction—What are the multiple ways that the responses of the basketball players can be interpreted? What might they suggest about cultural and domain knowledge and the empowerment of all students to think and reason mathematically?

KNOWLEDGE AS CULTURAL ACTIVITY

The view of knowledge we take in this chapter is motivated by our experience both as researchers who study students' acts of cognition and cognizing across a variety of informal and formal contexts for learning and as individuals who are concerned about a system of education that continually tells youth from nondominant groups that they are poor learners. As described above, we have observed some of these youth demonstrating rich mathematical problem-solving strategies in nonschool contexts in a form markedly different from what we typically consider school knowledge. We have also found that these out-of-school environments hold quite different opportunities for youth in terms of authentic problem solving, ongoing feedback, and meaningful relationships (Nasir & Hand, in press). These experiences have led us to reject the notion of knowledge as context independent and thus transportable. Instead, we examine the various forms and functions of knowledge as it is situated in activity. We join with a growing number of educational researchers in the field who conceptualize knowing as both as an in-the-head phenomenon and as constituted in and by cultural practices (Cole & Engeström, 1993; K. D. Gutiérrez, 2002; Kirshner & Whitson, 1997; Moll, 2000; Rogoff, 1990; Rogoff & Lave, 1984).

Central to this view of knowledge is Vygotsky's (1962, 1978b) premise that mental functioning is part and parcel of, even follows, our activity in the social world.

Vygotsky and those who have followed in his stead argue that knowledge is necessarily mediated by tools and signs that we construct and adapt as we coordinate activities with each other to solve problems and achieve our goals (Wertsch, 1991, 1998). We develop goals by assessing what we have the potential to do within a particular context and by negotiating the tools, relationships, and roles that help us carry out our plans in interaction with others (Leontiev, 1978). The past 20 years of research has led us to understand that what one comes to know is necessarily *situated* within socially organized systems of activity (J. S. Brown, Collins, & Duguid, 1989; Cobb & Bowers, 1999; Gibson, 1986; Goodwin, 1981; Greeno & Middle School Math Through Applications Program, 1998; Lave & Wenger, 1991; Rogoff, 1994), *embodied* as individuals project and manage themselves and their goals within these systems (Barsalou, 1999; Varela, Thompson, & Rosch, 1991), and *distributed* through the coordination of informational, material, and interpersonal aspects of these systems over time (Cole & Engeström, 1993; Hutchins, 1995, 1997; Moll, Tapia, & Whitmore, 1993; Pea, 1993). Knowledge in activity, then, or knowing, emphasizes the inextricable links between person and context over interactional history (Cole, 1996; Cole & Scribner, 1974).

Research that takes knowing and coming to know as inseparable focuses on the relation of the individual to the role, position, and patterns of activity that are made available to them as they participate in the practices of various communities (A. L. Brown & Campione, 1994; Lave, 1993; Lave & Wenger, 1991). Researchers have found that students who take their role as learners to be purposeful, integral, and active to the collective enterprise may be more engaged in knowledge-building activities than individuals who simply do what is necessary to succeed (or not to get caught failing) on an immediate task (Engle & Conant, 2002; Nasir, 2002). For example, in the case of the basketball players, participation in the social context of basketball playing required that each individual actively play a role in the execution of a play—their moves being inextricably linked to the moves of others and publicly available for feedback from other players, the coach, and even the fans. Players described how these moves could be broken down into component parts and how they were related both to their overall performance and the success of the team. In the case of a mathematics classroom, however, the players differed in the nature and level of engagement. Some players viewed their role as integral to the mathematics learning of the class by answering the teacher's questions or providing help to their peers. However, other players did not take (nor were they required to take) an active role in the class and instead sat quietly in the background. Lave and Wenger's (1991) model of legitimate peripheral participation explicates how learners may become well practiced at, barely adopt, and even reject the roles and practices of the various communities they encounter. In the mathematics classroom, there was significant opportunity for students to disengage from practices that supported developing mathematical understanding, whereas in the basketball context, high levels of engagement were required by the team.

This perspective challenges the notion, then, that individuals will embrace the opportunities for knowledge development in a learning community in the same way.

Instead, it acknowledges the importance of recognizing the process of *negotiation* that learners undertake as they reconcile new ways of learning and being with the practices and positions they enacted in prior experiences. This process of negotiation forms the contours and texture of their trajectory of participation and necessarily entails issues of power and status. For example, Danny Martin (2006a) poignantly describes the fortitude of adult African American mathematics students who had to reconcile experiences of racism and marginalization around mathematics in grade school with their decision to pursue mathematics in community college many years later. It is also the case that newcomers can challenge their local situations by introducing ways of participating and perceiving into a community of practice that serve to act back on local structures and processes and produce cultural change. We see this occur, for example, in research on professional development and school change where the grassroots initiatives of a small group of teachers can reverberate throughout their district (Dutro, Fisk, Koch, Roop, & Wixson, 2002).

The turn in the field of mathematics education research toward a conceptualization of knowledge as socially situated represents a major shift in thinking about the nature and role of culture in learning. Although there are numerous ways that theorists have conceptualized and operationalized culture (Bishop, 1988; Geertz, 1973; Gonzalez, 1999; Kroeber & Kluckhohn, 1952; Wax, 1993), we draw on a *cultural practice* perspective of culture, with roots in Vygotskian theory of learning, culture, and development (Vygotsky, 1978a). This perspective highlights the culturally organized practices and activities that make up the daily lives of individuals in societies (Lave, 1988; Saxe, 1999; Wertsch, 1998). Such practices are seen as local sites of cultural processes, calling for attention to social interaction, mediation of cognitive processes by tools and artifacts, and multiple interacting levels of context (Cole, 1996; Nasir & Hand, 2006). The metaphor of culture as a "blanket" that surrounds individual cognition in this case is replaced by one as the "fabric" of knowing, where culture and activity are inseparable at the level of individual, group, and societal development. This means that the cultural practices that we engage in as we move across everyday, school, and professional contexts both shape and constitute our learning.

Viewing culture solely in terms of the variations and similarities among practices and orientations misses the role of power in determining which forms of knowledge are considered competent and productive in different contexts. A number of researchers have drawn on Bourdieu's (1977) notion of *cultural capital* to illustrate how a cultural practice, such as school math, is historically and socially reified through broader social structures and processes that privilege certain groups of individuals over time (Cobb & Hodge, 2002; Mehan, Hubbard, & Villanueva, 1994). That some cultural practices are viewed as taken for granted, normative, or independent of their cultural underpinnings is partly a result of the longer time scales of some processes and events (Lemke, 2000; Saxe & Esmonde, 2005) and the tendency of social practices to coalesce into broader, more encompassing constellations. We see this in the way that calculus is presented in today's textbooks, which on the face of it appears static and incontestable. However, the adoption of a Lagrangian perspective of calculus as a set of rigorous algebraic processes versus MacLaurin's perspective of it as geometries and velocities is a decision embedded in a set of conversations that date back to Euler and Newton (Grabiner, 1997). Thus, in addition to locating knowing and doing mathematics within sociocultural activity, and recognizing the differences in how this activity is organized within communities and interpreted by individuals, it is critical to consider how communities (and thus representations and forms of mathematics) come to be privileged over one another.

We perceive the boundaries between cultural and domain knowing and coming to know as being taken up in the research on mathematics education in three ways: (a) mathematics knowing as a cultural activity (the structures and discourse of everyday vs. school math), (b) mathematics learning as a cultural enterprise (the structures and discourse of the classroom vs. students' home and local community), and (c) the system of mathematics education as a cultural system (access to and positioning in the field of mathematics). (See Figure 1.)

This tripartite model of the role of culture in mathematics learning and teaching illustrates how the boundaries between mathematical and cultural knowing are being confronted and examined by researchers at different levels of social activity. These include the cultural entailments of what it means to know mathematics (e.g., basketball vs. classroom mathematical knowing), the cultural entailments of what it means to be and become a mathematics learner within a particular community, and the cultural entailments of what stories get told and decisions made about how, when, and why mathematics is (and is not) learned (e.g., No Child Left Behind [NCLB] vs. the "service gap"). However, though we treat them as analytically distinct for the purposes of this chapter, we recognize that these levels of activity necessarily constitute each other and are reflexively related. In this chapter, we shift our gaze between these levels to capture the myriad ways that researchers perceive the relations between culture and mathematical knowledge.

MATHEMATICAL KNOWLEDGE AND CULTURAL PRACTICE

These three levels allude to a conceptualization of math knowledge as inherently tied to cultural practices. This point has been highlighted in studies that examine the mathematical thinking and problem solving that students take part in outside of school. This body of research has highlighted both the complexity of mathematical thinking in everyday practices (even for unschooled people) and the ways that such knowledge transfers or fails to transfer into classrooms. As such, it speaks to issues of mathematics knowing as a cultural activity, or the first level of our model.

Researchers have studied a wide range of out-of-school mathematics practices, including shopping in grocery stores (Lave, Murtaugh, & de la Rocha, 1984), loading dairy cases (Scribner, 1983/1997, 1984), carpet laying (Masingila, 1994), money exchange (Brenner, 1998a; Guberman, 1996; Taylor, 2004), selling candy (Saxe, 1988, 1999) and other goods on the street (Carraher, Carraher, & Schliemann, 1985; Nunes, Schlieman, & Carraher, 1993), playing basketball (Nasir, 1996, 2000, 2002), dieting and measuring food portions (de la Rocha, 1985), farming in Brazil (de Abreu,

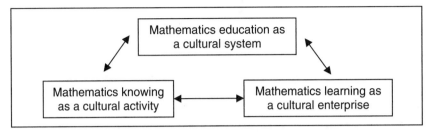

FIGURE 1   Analytic Framework of the Boundaries Between Cultural and Mathematics Knowing

1995), and math at work (Hall, 2000; Hall & Stevens, 1995; Hoyles, Noss, & Pozzi, 2001). There is also a body of research in ethnomathematics (Ascher, 1994; D'Ambrosio, 1985; Powell & Frankenstein, 1997) that highlights the various indigenous systems and practices of mathematics to problematize Eurocentric assumptions about valid mathematics and the power issues at play in deciding whose mathematics to legitimize. We do not undertake a review of research on ethnomathematics here, as our focus is on relations between domain and cultural knowledge for students in the United States. However, we begin with seminal cross-cultural research conducted in other countries that greatly informed this line of research.

One of the earliest studies in this area was a part of a broader effort to understand why Kpelle students in Liberia were underachieving in their Western-style mathematics classes. Cole, Gay, Glick, and Sharpe (1971) set out to better understand the kind of mathematics that the Kpelle encountered in their everyday lives (Cole et al., 1971; Gay & Cole, 1967. They documented extensive measurement practices (the Kpelle were rice farmers), including counting, classification, and the use of geometric knowledge for building houses. They designed studies that showed that the Kpelle did not use school-type approaches to solving these everyday mathematical situations but rather relied on visual and perceptual cues and specific cultural artifacts to estimate mathematical quantities. Similarly, Scribner (1983/1997), in a study of dairy case workers reported that although the workers were highly efficient in their solutions of on-the-job math problems, they solved such problems without the use of calculations, instead using routine visual displays. Lave et al. (1984) also explored everyday mathematics, examining the kinds of mathematical problems people solve as they go about their grocery shopping and also documented the difference between the nature of individuals' solutions to routine problems and approaches taught in school.

Similar findings have been reported for street vendors in Brazil (Carraher et al., 1985; Saxe, 1991, 1999) and African American high school basketball players (Nasir, 1996, 2000). Such studies have also found that when asked the same questions in an everyday and a school format, individuals tended to score higher on tasks more closely linked to their everyday practices, though schooled people do sometimes bring their school knowledge to bear to solve out-of-school problems. This line of research has illustrated that it is quite common for there to be strong boundaries in the minds of individuals (and in the practices themselves) between the kinds of local, practice-linked mathematical knowledge that people construct outside of school and school-linked mathematics. The extended example that opened this chapter is a part of this body of research. The players' response patterns are representative of similar patterns across other practices and clearly illustrate the boundaries between school math and out-of-school math for many youth.

Not only are there differences between school and out-of-school math knowledge, there is also wide variation within practices outside of school. In a study of the purchasing practices of elementary school African American students in an urban neighborhood, Taylor (2007) highlights important ways that the practice of purchasing outside of school is structured and scaffolded by others such that there is wide range of mathematical thinking that students engage in, depending on the difficulty of the problem that they are solving, the supports available to them, and potential time constraints for solving the problem. Furthermore, other research has explored the variation in solution strategies between school and out-of-school contexts and has highlighted the way in which solutions to math problems outside of school can draw on common sense, estimation, and cultural artifacts. For example, in one study, researchers documented that a woman faced with the problem of measuring three fourths of two thirds of a cup of cottage cheese simply filled a 1-cup measuring cup two thirds of the way full, dumped it onto an cutting board, and carved out one fourth of it, then put the remaining cottage cheese on a plate (Lave, 1988). This woman and others used nonconventional strategies rather than school-taught algorithms for solving mathematical problems in situ.

In addition to documenting the practice-linked nature of individuals' mathematical understandings and a widespread lack of usefulness of school-taught procedures in solving everyday mathematical problems, research has also highlighted the ways that math problems are solved in practices outside of school. Specifically, learners in everyday settings are often supported in various ways by social others as they attempt to solve authentic math problems in their everyday lives (Brenner, 1998a; Lave & Wenger, 1991; Nasir, 2000; Saxe, 1991, 1999). This support in the process of carrying out authentic tasks (formally termed an apprenticeship model of teaching) has been used as the basis for reforms in teaching practices in classrooms (J. S. Brown et al., 1989).

Another important finding from this work was that students who participated in the mathematics practices of their communities and who also attended school did not view both of these practices as having the same value or worth. Although students often used practices from their everyday or home math, they clearly felt that such practices were inferior and that the school math was of higher status or was more highly valorized by students (de Abreu, 1995; de Abreu & Kline, 2006). This issue of the way in which people make sense of the mathematical practices that they engage in and what those practices mean for who they are and how they fit into society brings to the fore issues of identity (Beach, 1995; Martin, 2000; Sfard & Cole, 2003). One way that these studies have been interpreted is that mathematics instruction should seek to better contextualize and make relevant to the real world its content (National Council for Teachers of Mathematics [NCTM], 2000). Sfard and Cole (2003) argue that these conclusions are a misreading of the findings from everyday math studies. Instead, they propose that these studies point to the importance of supporting the mathematical literacy of all students and that in the process, students' identities as math learners must be nurtured as well.

This body of research has supported a notion of math as inherently cultural activity, in part by pointing to how math knowing and learning looks different across different practices. In some ways, however, at the first level of our model, this set of studies has reified and made salient the boundary between cultural and domain knowledge. Yet at the second level, the studies also show how the teaching and learning practices in settings outside of school are constructed in ways that support novices in the development of cultural knowledge. Furthermore, these studies point to the constrained nature of school knowledge and problematize the privileging of school math knowledge. This body of research also provides an important lens through which to understand and study school mathematics classrooms, which are sometimes viewed as being acultural. Research on mathematical practices outside of school highlights the inherently cultural nature of mathematical activity and offers some insight into the types of cultural processes that are embedded in mathematical practices. Next, we consider three aspects of culture and math classrooms that have been prevalent in the research literature.

CULTURE IN THE MATH CLASS

Considerations of the ways in which issues of culture show up in the math classroom are central to each of the three analytic planes. The math classroom is the local site through which the cultural system of math education is enacted, where particular types of math knowing are privileged over others, and where the cultural enterprise of math learning plays out in interactional space. In this section, we review research that has focused on the cultural nature of teaching and learning in math classrooms, highlighting three ways that research has considered culture in math classroom: (a) the way that language mediates knowledge, (b) features of math classrooms as contexts that support or constrain different forms of knowledge, and (c) the way that racialized identities and expectations play out in mathematics classes.

Knowledge in Language

One important way that research has considered math learning as cultural activity is through an examination of the role of language in mathematics learning. How language in mathematics classrooms mediates meaning making and instructional practice (Cobb, Wood, & Yackel, 1993; Forman, 1996; Lemke, 1990; Lerman, 2001; Van Oers, 2001), as well as differential access for second-language learners (Brenner, 1994; R. Gutiérrez, 2002a; Khisty, 1995; Moschkovich, 1999, 2002; Warren, Rosebery, & Conant, 1994), has been the focus of considerable research during the past 15 years. Within these discussions, language has been conceptualized in myriad ways, relating to the nature of mathematical talk in the classroom, the discourse practices entailed in the learning of mathematics, and the challenges and opportunities of linguistically and culturally diverse mathematics classrooms.

First, and foremost, we follow theorists like Bakhtin (1981, 1986) and Vygotsky (1962), who considered language to be both a window into the meanings people make of themselves and their activities and the substance of these formulations. Language is a primary symbolic means through which we come to participate in and understand the world. In a sense, then, language constitutes and is constituted by knowledge. The understandings we develop as we enter into dialogue with social others (on the interpersonal plane) gradually become internalized (on the intrapersonal plane) and form the social and cultural fibers of our knowledge base (Vygotsky, 1962). It is this conception of language, as the primary source of our interaction with and reflection on the world (or how we know), that problematizes the ancillary position it is often relegated to with respect to knowledge (or what we know).

There is much to be said about the role of language in cognition and learning. Here, we will focus on aspects of it that are implicated in our analysis of the social and cultural aspects of knowing and doing mathematics. It is important to acknowledge that although language reveals and exposes certain meanings and interpretations, it necessarily obscures others. Like knowledge, it is never neutral. As our primary form of communication, however, language also allows us to achieve *intersubjectivity* (Lerman, 1996; Rommetveit, 1987; Schegloff, 1992), or the development of a shared understanding of the perspectives we bring to our activity together (Clark, 1996; Greeno, 2006b). These two characteristics of language—that it both hides and reveals meaning—are critically important to understanding the cultural processes of teaching and learning. As Erickson (2004) and many others have noted, the intricate linguistic acts involved in the coordination of meaning leave open the possibility for much misunderstanding and confusion.

The symbolic and abstract nature of the language of mathematics complicates the processes of communication even more (Durkin & Shire, 1991; Pimm, 1987). This complexity lies not only with mathematical syntax and register (or the terms, notations, and specific uses of them; Nemirovsky, DiMattia, Ribeiro, & Lara-Meloy, 2005) but also with the very structure of the practice of mathematics, which represents a distinct semiotic system (Lemke, 2002; O'Halloran, 2000, 2003). As an aspect of this semiotic system, language cannot be separated from other communicative practices such as gesture, alignment, and gaze, which function together to produce a discourse, or "the social activity of making meanings with language and other symbolic systems in some particular kind of situation or setting" (Lemke, 1995, p. 6). By positioning language as one of many components of a discourse, we limit the possibility of reducing complex interactions of mathematical activity to patterns in linguistic moves. We also understand why visual cues, artifacts, and social interaction play such a critical role in learning in everyday cultural practices.

Early work on discourse in the mathematics classroom tended to focus on how participants coordinated their activities through various discursive acts and how these emerged into patterns that came to characterize a particular type of classroom community. Researchers found that it was typically confined to a number of configurations. Historically prominent among these is the initiation–response–evaluation structure (Heath & McLaughlin, 1994), or IRE (Cazden, 1988; Mehan, 1979), which represents a closed system of meaning making in which the teacher poses a question, students attempt to respond to it, and this response is evaluated. This structure tends to constrain students' everyday mathematical register (Lemke, 1990), their mathematical conjectures (Wood, 1992), and the participation of lower socioeconomic groups of students (Heath, 1983). Despite this, the IRE structure continues to be pervasive in many "traditional" mathematics classrooms and limits the opportunities for classroom participants to engage in discourse that allows them to think together (Spillane & Zeuli, 1999).

Central to this analysis was the recognition that this coordination took place on multiple levels that comprised, for example, talking about mathematics and talking about talking about mathematics (Cobb et al., 1993). In other words, attention was paid not only to how particular mathematical meanings and conventions became regular features of the classroom conversation (both in whole-class discussions and small-group work) but also whether tacit assumptions about what it means to do mathematics were made explicit to students. In contrast to classrooms that used IRE structures, studies of discourse practices such as revoicing (O'Conner & Michaels, 1993), redirecting, probing, and such illustrated how expert teachers explicitly positioned students' mathematical utterances as meaningful with respect to the broader mathematics community, while at the same time clarifying what counts as a mathematical contribution (Ball & Bass, 2000; Boaler & Greeno, 2000; Cobb et al., 1993; Lampert, 2001; Rittenhouse, 1989).

Another line of research on classroom discourse also began to look more broadly at the relation between language, social practices, and power in shaping classroom life. Drawing on theorists in symbolic interactionism and sociolinguistics, such as Bernstein, Bahktin, and Goffman, researchers attempted to examine the multiple voices and historical artifacts within the mathematics classroom that stemmed from local communities and broader communities of practice (Forman & Ansell, 2001; Lerman, 2001; Van Oers, 2001). These accounts drew from cultural psychology and other anthropological traditions to consider the reflexive relations between the nature of mathematical conversations taking place in mathematics classrooms and the various positions from which different participants in the conversation are speaking. These studies found that teachers and students shifted between different discourse practices, depending on the goals of their activities, their cultural positions, and their alignment with different communities. For example, communicating social norms and exposing hidden characteristics of mathematical talk was marked by direct, explicit, and authoritative discursive moves (generally on the part of the teacher) to reshape conversation and, ultimately, the classroom culture. On the other hand, interaction regarding students' mathematical sense making was characterized by open-ended conversations and shared authority structures to foster students in making conjectures and taking risks (Cobb et al., 1993; Forman & Ansell, 2001). Whereas the latter focuses on negotiating meanings of mathematical ideas and procedures, the former helps students to understand why it makes sense to do this work within this community (Van Oers, 2001).

These findings led researchers to question the strong ties between mathematics classrooms and the mathematics community, suggesting that the two fundamentally differ in purpose and character (Moschkovich, 2000, 2002). In contrast to the mathematics community, a great deal of what goes on in a mathematics classroom is that students from different backgrounds are determining for themselves, in relation to the classroom community, what it looks like for someone like them to learn and do mathematics. However, as Van Oers (2001) argues, drawing on Bahktin, the *speech genre* of the mathematics community still predominates school mathematics and as such has significant sway over the look and feel of legitimate (and illegitimate) mathematical activity. We see this in the case of the basketball studies, where players described being able to express themselves through the practice of basketball while they either did or did not fit with the culture of the mathematics classroom (Nasir & Hand, in press). Lerman (2001) reiterates the importance of accounting for alignment and power in analyzing language in the mathematics classroom, arguing that (a) classroom discourse practices necessarily shape what is viewed as legitimate mathematical participation and (b) the official language of the classroom can position certain groups with power and privilege.

With respect to the first point, Wells and Arunz (2006) argue that the IRE structure limits classroom mathematical learning, as it assumes perfect intersubjectivity on behalf of the participants. They propose that classrooms need to be organized to foster dialogic inquiry, where the participants actively work to understand the speaker's perspective and attend to the speaker's focus of attention (Wells & Arunz, 2006). This perspective considers classroom learning to depend not only on the processes of acculturation—or learning the tools, meanings, and values of the mathematical community—but also on transformation, where the consideration of alternative explanations leads to new understandings. New reform mathematics practices support teachers in eliciting and building on students' ideas, thus opening up the possibility for dialogic learning experiences.

Even as mathematics researchers and reformers push for new and expanded discourse structures in mathematics, however, these initiatives do not necessarily conceptualize discourse as being embedded within critical social and cultural contexts, and indexing both local and broader discourses (Gee, 1990; Lemke, 1995; Lerman, 2001)—what our third level would push us to consider. The study of what Gee calls "Big D" discourse maintains the positionality of language within hierarchical power structures. It makes visible the various layers of meaning and relations that are indexed by and constituted in discursive acts. The discourse of school mathematics, then, can be traced to the activities and historical practices of particular communities that won decisive power struggles. In their work on hybrid discourse practices, *Third Space*, Kris Gutierrez and her colleagues argue that classrooms should be organized to circumvent or disrupt the societal power structures that leak into classrooms and constrain access to nondominant groups of students (K. D. Gutiérrez, Baquedano-López, Alvarez, & Chiu, 1999; K. D. Gutiérrez, Baquedano-López, & Tejada, 2000; K. D. Gutiérrez, Rymes, & Larson, 1995). One way to do this in classroom interaction is to position students' discourse practices as authorized ways of participating productively in the classroom. The hybrid discourse practices that result represent an expansive learning activity (Engeström, 2001), where participants reach new understandings by working toward common ground.

This is particularly important in classrooms with students from diverse linguistic and cultural backgrounds. As Moschkovich (2002) argues, students' mathematical sense making is grounded in their everyday discourse practices, which originates in the home and local communities. When the classroom linguistic structures are restricted to English, or teachers do not attend to the gestures, representations, and everyday descriptions that second-language learners draw on to create and communicate meaning, they inadvertently miss the multiple, rich resources that students bring to the classroom. The research of Rosebery, Warren, Conant, and others working with Haitian students in Chèche Konnen Center at TERC reinforces why it is critical to afford the development of the hybrid interactional spaces in the classroom. They have found that to create truly dialogic communities requires that teachers actively work to draw out and on students' resources for meaning through extended turns of talk and by puzzling out words and meanings that they can use to leverage students' disciplinary understandings (Rosebery, Warren, & Conant, 1992; Warren, Ballenger, Ogonowski, Rosebery, & Hudicourt-Barnes, 2001).

These perspectives illustrate the social and interdependent nature of the language, conventions, tools, values, and meanings of school mathematics. As a discourse practice, mathematics learning encompasses cultural ways of participating in mathematical activity that privilege (though not explicitly) particular ways of knowing and being in the mathematics classroom. Thus, developing mathematical and cultural intersubjectivity among students and teachers in ethnically, racially, and linguistically diverse classrooms depends not only on making an attempt to understand the meaning of a person's discursive act but also on creating space to renegotiate issues of power and status involved in this process.

Features of Mathematics Classrooms

A second way that researchers have studied the relation between culture and math learning is by examining how opportunities to learn mathematics are structured in different ways within mathematics classrooms. For example, researchers concerned with design principles for mathematics classrooms explore how the norms and practices of mathematics classroom organize (and are organized by) different forms of agency (Chazan, 2000; Chazan & Ball, 1999; Engle, 2006), authority (Lampert, 1990), and accountability (Cobb, Gravemeijer, Yackel, McClain, & Whitenack, 1997) for students with respect to mathematical knowledge and the classroom community (Boaler, 2003; Cobb, Gresalfi, & Hodge, in press; Engle & Conant, 2002;

Greeno, 2006a; Kazemi & Stipek, 2001; Yackel & Cobb, 1996). However, the bulk of this work considers how these features support and constrain different forms of knowing and being for students in a general sense, instead of examining how they may be differentially available to particular groups of students. One of the reasons for this is that we have yet to develop an overarching analytic framework that captures how opportunities tied to classroom structures are shaped by processes that take place at multiple levels and time scales of classroom and social interaction.

One of the most careful and thorough studies of the teaching and learning of mathematics that addresses classroom structures at multiple levels of classroom interaction is Magdalene Lampert's (1990, 2001) practitioner-based research in her fifth-grade mathematics classroom. Lampert videotaped her classroom on a regular basis and kept detailed records of her practice, including her preclass preparation, on-the-fly decision making, and postclass reflections. In her analysis of these data, she examined how her students came to do mathematics over time by "zooming in" on particular classroom exchanges and "zooming out" on the patterns of activity that began to emerge over time. Through this process, she illustrates how classroom moments add up to the practices of a particular classroom community (in her case, modeled after the practices of mathematicians).

Yackel and Cobb's (1996) notion of sociomathematical norms helps us to further analyze how the practices of mathematicians became instantiated in Lampert's classroom. For example, part of what it meant to be a student in Lampert's classroom was to try out different mathematical ideas and to respectfully critique the ideas of other students, often in public. Through the processes of eliciting students' mathematical ideas and modeling appropriate questions to ask about these ideas, the students in Lampert's class became more practiced at constructing and responding to mathematical arguments in a form that mirrored the conversations of mathematicians. Thus, a sociomathematical norm emerged concerning "how one engages in a mathematical argument." Classroom exchanges in which this norm was violated were noticed by other participants and often repaired. This type of analysis contributes to our understanding of how the ritual ways of interacting around mathematical ideas, tools, and participants in a classroom evolve into a particular classroom culture (Franke, Kazemi, & Battey, 2007).

A line of research that has investigated the different types of cultures we find in mathematics classrooms has identified a number of key features of reform mathematics classrooms that foster students' productive, domain-based inquiry. These features include giving students the opportunity to problematize the subject matter in a way that is meaningful to them, distributing authority to them to develop and evaluate their mathematical methods, supporting students in exercising agency over the development of their mathematical understanding, and holding students' accountable to each other's mathematical thinking and questioning (Boaler, 1997, 2003; Boaler & Greeno, 2000; Chazan, 2000; Chazan & Ball, 1999; Cobb, Gresalfi, & Hodge, in press; Engle & Conant, 2002; Greeno, 2006a; Hiebert et al., 1997; Lampert, 1990, 2001; Yackel & Cobb, 1996). At the same time, researchers have also posed an important challenge to this research by questioning how what counts as an argument, method, or even mathematical activity is related to the forms of participation that students bring from home, local, and broader communities and discourses (Cobb & Hodge, 2002; Diversity in Mathematics Education [DiME], 2007; Moschkovich, 2002).

In the past 10 years, Jo Boaler and her colleagues have found that on the whole, reform-driven mathematics classrooms are more successful at narrowing the achievement gap than classrooms that focus on rote memorization and recall of procedures (Boaler, 1997, 2003, 2006a; Boaler & Staples, in press). She argues that in mathematics classrooms that use reform versus traditional mathematics curricula, students are more likely to be engaged in active problem posing and problem solving with the teacher and each other, where they are supported in thinking across ideas, methods, and formulas to build stronger and deeper connections to fundamental mathematical ideas. In her latest study of Railside High School, Boaler illustrates that the use of Complex Instruction (Cohen & Lotan, 1997), a multiple-ability treatment designed to rearrange status, in conjunction with reform mathematical practices can create multidimensional mathematics classrooms that broaden what it means to be "smart" in a mathematics classroom (Boaler, 2006b, 2006c). In Railside detracked math classrooms, students worked in groups on groupworthy mathematical tasks, which were structured by broader classrooms processes promoting explicit mathematical sense making and group accountability. Importantly, this study found that in the course of 5 years, students from diverse racial and ethnic backgrounds not only pursued higher-level mathematics courses throughout high school but also were more interested in the mathematics they were doing (Boaler & Staples, in press).

This research points to the growing recognition that it is crucial to locate issues of equity in mathematics education with curriculum and classroom structures rather than with individuals or groups of students. Multidimensional classrooms also challenge us to look beyond the a priori distinctions between mathematical and social activity we often make to how different forms of participation are framed and positioned around productive mathematical activity (D'Amato, 1996; Hand, 2003).

However, none of these accounts explicitly attend to how students negotiate the cultural practices they develop in communities outside of the classroom with those they encounter in the mathematics classroom. K. D. Gutiérrez and Rogoff (2003) have suggested that one way researchers might begin to explore these relations is by documenting students' repertoires of practice, which "characterize the commonalities of experience of people who share cultural background, without 'locating' the commonalities within individuals" (p. 21).

These studies on classroom mathematical structures illustrate how classrooms function as and in social cultural space to afford and constrain certain ways of doing mathematics and becoming a mathematics learner. This research has been increasingly concerned with the role of identity and how students come to see themselves as mathematics thinkers and doers.

Racial Identities and Access

In a third category of research on culture in the mathematics classroom, scholars are exploring the ways in which students' racial identities and racialized opportunities and expectations have implications for their achievement in mathematics.

Ladson-Billings (1997) and others (Nasir & Cobb, 2006; Oakes et al., 2003; Secada, 1992; Silver, Smith, & Nelson, 1995; Tate, 1994, 1995) have pointed out the persistent achievement gaps in mathematics achievement by race. Although Ladson-Billings lays inferior instruction at the feet of these differences in achievement (citing Oakes, 1990, who shows that teachers of African American and other minority students are least likely to be prepared to teach mathematics),[2] she also suggests that one potential source of this disparity is the "nerdy" or "geeky" image of White males in horn-rimmed glasses that are conjured up in the public mind at the thought of high levels of mathematics achievement. In this section, we synthesize the emerging body of research on identities at the intersections of race and math learning as well as differential access (by race or ethnicity) to a wide range of schooling and mathematics learning resources.

In recent years, math education researchers have begun to explore not only the nature of students' experiences in math classrooms but also the extent to which students feel a sense of connection to math, or their mathematics identities. Boaler and colleagues (Boaler, 2002; Boaler & Greeno, 2000) have studied mathematical identities and math achievement for middle and high school students. Boaler's findings show that not all capable students in math have high mathematical identities and that the style of teaching had much to do with the types of mathematical identities students developed and their desires to continue to pursue mathematics (Boaler, 2002; Boaler & Greeno, 2000). Gresalfi and Cobb (2006) use the term *dispositions* to capture both the discipline of math as it is realized in particular classrooms and the extent to which students come to identify with the discipline. They recognize interest and connection as critical aspects of engaging in the practices of mathematics and draw on their own and others' work (Engle & Conant, 2002; Greeno & Hull, 2002; Greeno, Sommerfeld, & Wiebe, 2000) to focus on the way that students are positioned in interactions in math classes.

Martin (2000, 2006b) explores the way in which sociohistorical context and community norms come to influence students' mathematical identities through socialization processes. Martin argues that African American community members often identify their own limited mathematics achievement as being related to the constriction of opportunities to learn math because of racism and racial stratification. Students in mathematics classrooms must negotiate these historically rooted collective narratives about mathematics, which many students do with great success and assertion of individual agency. Martin argues that mathematical identities are constructed in relation to these sociohistorical forces as well as through local interactions and practices in schools and families. Furthermore, students are not mere pawns in their reactions to multiple conflicting narratives about math learning, race, and achievement—rather, they make agentic decisions that reflect their own ideas and goals.

Cobb and Hodge (2002) also employ the construct of mathematical identities to examine relations between culture and math learning. They theorize that power is an important factor in understanding identity and learning processes in mathematics. A number of researchers have conceptualized power relations within mathematics systems and classrooms in terms of classroom opposition (D'Amato, 1996; Diamondstone,

2002; Fordham & Ogbu, 1986; Hand, 2005; Stinson, 2006). In particular, Hand's (2005) research documented how opposition became a form of competent participation that grew among a highly diverse group of students in a low-track reform mathematics classroom. This opposition was related to the lack of opportunities for students to engage in mathematics, a discourse of tracking that positioned them as the "slow" and "dumb" students, and the teacher's resistance to a high-status discourse practice in the students' peer community that contained aspects of their mathematical sense making.

The studies cited thus far have primarily taken a qualitative approach to the study of race, culture, identity, and math learning. An important consideration is the extent to which these findings and issues define the experience of students on a broader scale. Although there is relatively little research on the relation between race or ethnicity, identity, and math learning or achievement, there is a large body of research on racial or ethnic identity and schooling outcomes more broadly. Research on the relation between racial or ethnic identities and academic achievement for African American and Latino students shows mixed findings (Burrow, Tubman, & Montgomery, 2006). Some studies find that students with stronger racial or ethnic identities achieve better (or have stronger academic identities; Sellers, Chavous, & Cooke, 1998; Supple, Ghazarian, Frabutt, Plunkett, & Sands, 2006; Thomas, Townsend, & Belgrave, 2003; Zarate, Bhimji, & Reese, 2005), whereas others report that students with stronger ethnic or racial identities perform worse (or have lower academic identities; Fordham & Ogbu, 1986; Steele & Aronson, 1995). Others argue that the effect of racial or ethnic identity on academic achievement is mediated by self-esteem (Lockett & Harrell, 2003).

One recent study has looked explicitly at the relationships between math identities, racial identities, and math achievement (Nasir, Atukpawu, O'Connor, & Davis, 2007). African American, Asian American, Latino, and White high school students were surveyed with respect to their mathematical identities, racial identities, academic identities, and math grades. Findings showed that although there were few variations in levels of students' racial or ethnic, mathematical, and academic identities by racial or ethnic group, African American students were less likely to connect their math grades to their sense of academic or mathematical identities than students from other groups and that particular versions of racial or ethnic identities were more supportive of achievement in mathematics than others.

Students' taking on or resisting identities as math learners do not occur in a vacuum. Although we will not do an extensive review here, we do want to acknowledge at least two other ways that culture comes to the fore in math classrooms. First, culture comes to play when teachers hold lower expectations for achievement and learning for students from particular racial or cultural communities (Ferguson, 2003). Studies on teacher expectations and race have highlighted the ways that differential treatment and expectations by teachers can greatly affect students' access to learning opportunities (Beady & Hansell, 1981). Second, issues of access can also constrict students' learning opportunities as well as opportunities to develop mathematical identities. More specifically, nondominant students, particularly, African American and Latino students and poor students, consistently have less access to a wide range of resources for learning mathematics, including qualified teachers, advanced courses, safe and functional schools, textbooks and materials, and a curriculum that reflects their experiences and communities (Apple, 1995; Darling-Hammond, 1997; King, 2005; Oakes et al., 2003).

Studies on racialized identities and expectations and their role in the teaching and learning of minority students in U.S. schools represents an important line of research. This work views the math classroom as both a space where students develop a sense of themselves as doers and learners of math and also where broader issues of power and access play out in fundamental ways.

Overall, research on the multiple ways that culture intersects with math learning highlights the myriad of ways that knowledge is inextricably linked to culture, language, identity, and power; situated in practice; distributed across individuals, tools, and forms of social activity; and structured by the features of social contexts that organize what constitutes knowing, how knowing is demonstrated, and how knowing is related to doing and being. In multiple ways, then, mathematics classrooms are inherently cultural spaces where different forms of knowing and being are validated. From the perspective of our model, the recognition of mathematics knowing as a cultural activity motivates a closer inspection of school mathematics learning as a particular type of cultural enterprise where these activities take place. This assertion counters the common assumption that mathematics knowledge is clear and precise and can be accessed by all and, thus, that mathematics teaching it is culturally neutral. However, as the research above indicates, what it means to know and understand mathematics, and what counts as productive activity toward knowing and understanding both in our classrooms and in society, is socially and culturally mediated.

This research on culture in the math classroom has spoken to all three levels of our analytic foci (see Figure 1). We have seen how knowing is defined locally (Level 1) and how configurations of activity in classrooms form cultural systems that students learn to navigate (Level 2). This body of work has also highlighted issues of access and power (Level 3), with an eye toward how these issues play out in local interactions in and out of mathematics classrooms.

CULTURE AND MATH REFORM

Given this fundamental intertwining of culture and math learning, we must consider the ways that stakeholders in mathematics education have talked about and attended to issues of culture. In this section, we present a historical and critical examination of the treatment of culture within the context of reform mathematics and the challenges that have been faced in deeply considering culture and mathematical knowledge. We focus squarely on the third level of the model, or the cultural system of mathematics education in the United States. We argue that many of the challenges related to considering culture in mathematics classrooms are related to the historical motivations for mathematics reform and its resulting influence on the ways current mathematical goals and standards address issues related to the teaching of students.

Historical Context of Considering Culture in Math Reform

The complex and situated nature of mathematics classrooms and mathematical thinking is made more complex by considering the relationship between the nature of student engagement and patterns of implementation of reform mathematics. The movement away from teacher-directed, top-down instruction and toward engaging students in meaningful problem-based instruction, as we have outlined in the previous sections, entails a greater consideration of aspects of students lived experiences. Tenets of reform result in increased communication, challenging of teachers and peers, and collaborative group work (NCTM, 2000), thus creating greater space for the influence of students' lived experiences and cultural communication patterns.

Underlying approaches to math reform is the belief that students learn best when they are asked to understand mathematics conceptually, not just apply formulas. This is certainly not a new idea. As early as 1899, the National Education Association (NEA) made calls for math instruction that demonstrated a strong interest in focusing on conceptual rather than procedural ideas. In its annual report, the group stated,

While not wishing to undervalue models which are presented to the pupils ready-made, the committee believes that, as a rule, the pupils gain more by constructing their own models, and that this can de done very easily in a sufficient number of theorems. (NEA, 1899/1970, p. 203)

However, although it is a long-standing idea, math reformers did not begin to reconstruct approaches to teaching math for the masses until much later.

Interestingly, major changes in the need for math reform did not stem from a deep concern for issues of equity between students who are disenfranchised and those from the dominant culture or for a curriculum that was a more natural approach to teaching children. The reform movement grew out of an increasing concern for what seemed impending doom demonstrated by the perceived superiority of Russian scientific and mathematical capabilities as signaled by the launch of Sputnik (Schoenfeld, 2004). Central to this fear about international competition and losing the Cold War was a concern for the perceived need for mathematically and technologically skilled workers in industry and in the military.

These fears were summarized by the documents *A Nation at Risk* (Denning, 1983) and *Everybody Counts* (National Research Council [NRC], 1989), in which the authors call for serious change in the United States' commitment to education and raise concerns about the effects of the prevailing belief that mathematics education was a field of study reserved for the elite. These documents argued that the nation required greater numbers of students to achieve in mathematics education, attributed to the perceived deficiencies in the workforce caused by deficient skill in mathematics and science. It was posited that this workforce deficiency could weaken the nation's position in the world. According to the President's Commission on Excellence in Education,

"America's position in the world may once have been reasonably secure with only a few exceptionally well-trained men and women. It is no longer" (Denning, 1983, p. 470). These documents were influential in bringing to the public not only the gap between U.S. math achievement and that of other countries but also the low number of students of color who were achieving in mathematics. They argued for the importance of an increase in the number of graduates prepared to take on roles in the fields of mathematics and education and that the low number of students of color in these fields contributed to this shortfall. Thus, although reducing the achievement gap was not the motivating goal of math reform, preparing a great number of the nation's citizens to be mathematically skilled was an important aspect of an agenda to maintain the strength of U.S. global power. Indeed, the italicized *all* in the emerging slogan "math for *all*" was pseudonymous for low-income students and students of color. Teaching "all" students resulted in a need to address the needs of students that were previously neglected in math education.

The concern for increasing achievement levels and learning in math and science also opened space for a reexamination of mathematics instruction. One argument suggested,

Industry spends as much on remedial mathematics education for employees as is spent on mathematics education in schools, colleges, and universities. . . . This massive repetition is grossly inefficient, wasting resources that could be used better to improve rather that to repeat mathematics education. (NRC, 1989, p. 13)

Thus the neglect students in low-income and minority communities faced were not being addressed primarily from beliefs about the responsibility of government but rather as a cost-efficient solution for industry.[3]

Despite these initial motivations for addressing issues of equity and the consideration of culture, the impact from this "wake-up call" was twofold. First, it began to change the ways people perceived mathematics, and it also began to address beliefs about who can and should learn mathematics. Both of these goals would begin to shape the ways culture and race were viewed in relation to mathematics teaching and learning.

From Crisis to Standards

Despite the shortcomings, *A Nation at Risk* and the calls from *Everybody Counts* led to a new set of standards for mathematics teaching that more carefully considered culture a significant role in curriculum and instruction in mathematics. Central to NCTM's concerns in the *Principles and Standards for School Mathematics* (NCTM, 2000) is the equity principle, which simply states, "Excellence in mathematics education requires equity—high expectations and strong support for all students" (p. 11). Equity and the idea that math reform should serve all students appear in multiple places in the NCTM standards document as well. Consider the following excerpts:

- "Because students learn by connecting new ides to prior knowledge, teachers must understand what their students already know." (p. 18)

- "Expectations must be raised—mathematics can and must be learned by all students." (p. 13)
- "Teachers need help to understand the strengths and needs of students who come from diverse linguistic and cultural backgrounds, who have specific disabilities, or who possess a special talent and interest in mathematics. . . . They can then design experiences and lessons that respond to, and build on this knowledge." (p. 14)
- "All students should have access to an excellent and equitable mathematics program that provides solid support for their learning and is responsive to their prior knowledge, intellectual strengths, and personal interests." (p. 13)

Creating success for all meant that addressing culture in the math class got operationalized as understanding what individual students already know and raising expectations for a wide range of "diverse" students. However, with this acknowledgement, the document places race and culture with language and disability as challenges to teaching rather than a central consideration in mathematics instruction.

General calls for higher standards and better math instruction for all students does not, however, address the root of inequality, nor does it acknowledge the social realities in schools for many marginalized communities and students (Martin, 2007). Apple (1992) cautions against such calls for high standards and emphasis on technology without considering the existing social and political context that influence how and what students can learn. He states, "Originating motives *do not guarantee at all* how arguments will be used, whose interests they will ultimately serve, and what the patterns of differential benefits will be, giving existing relations of unequal power in society" (p. 438). Indeed, this may only exacerbate the difference in the quality of education received by those who have been traditionally disenfranchised. Apple calls such approaches a "slogan system" that provides challenges to issues of equity. He asks whether it is appropriate to write standards under the assumption that there is equality between communities in their access to technology when communities are, in fact, demonstrably unequal. Tate (1994) goes further to state,

The federal government's position on mathematics standards is akin to the concept of a toll road. In order to benefit from a toll road, the driver must be able to afford the cost of driving on it. Similarly, those school districts that cannot pay the long-term costs of implementing the new mathematics standards will have students who do not benefit. (p. 387)

Others simply argue that the math being taught has such little relationship to mathematics used in industry that the current system does much to add to inequities in education (Noddings, 1994).

Although we have alluded to some of the pedagogical differences between traditional and reform curricula, we should also highlight some fundamental differences in beliefs between supporters of each of these types of curricula in defining what constitutes mathematics and the purpose it should serve for individuals and society. Many of these differences are highlighted in the book *The Saber Tooth Curriculum*

(Benjamin, 1939), a satirical account of a "caveman" society where elders try to determine what children in their prehistoric community should be taught. In the book, New-Fist asks, "What things must we tribesman know how to do in order to live with full bellies, warm backs, and minds free from fear?" (p. 28) Emblematic of this, the New-Fist curriculum was full of important knowledge such as fire scaring and horse clubbing. When these animals no longer roamed their lands, an argument ensued between elders in determining whether to continue to teach these now-obsolete skills because they were fundamental to all learning or to teach new hunting and fishing skills relevant to the present day. This book, written by an education professor under a pseudonym, parodies the arguments of academics and politicians of the time who stood by what he saw as an outdated system of education. These questions continue to mark a sharp contrast in math education today. Is math to be taught as skills that develop "discipline of mind" or an aesthetic understanding of a cultural invention, or rather, should mathematics be a continuously developing tool based on logic and problem solving that can be used effectively in society?

Equity Promises and Challenges of Reform Math

In addition to putting forth a vision of the goals for mathematics teaching, the standards also outlined a set of practices and approaches that constituted "reform" mathematics. A standard traditional problem that asks students to find the mean, for example, by following the procedure of summing amounts and dividing by the number of items summed looks very different than a corresponding reform task where students are asked to collect data from fellow students, compile data, and make arguments about which measure of central tendency is most appropriate for the particular data set.

A major tenet of reform mathematics is problem-based instruction, where students make conjectures and reasoning about particular mathematical ideas. As compared to traditional mathematics with often one solution and where the teacher or textbook serves as the ultimate authority as to right and wrong solutions, reform math asks students to serve as their own authority, to make mathematical arguments. These shifts in both problem-solving process and the distribution of authority may have implications for the participation of low-income and/or minority students.

Researchers have described both affordances and constraints for reform approaches' consequences for equity and the learning of nondominant students. For instance, as mentioned earlier, Boaler's (1997, 2006b) longitudinal research on mathematics education in the United States and the United Kingdom in the past 10 years has identified positive links between the classroom features of reform math and learning outcomes. Building on this work, Horn's (2006) research illustrates how reform mathematics curricula also afford development of a different set of categories with which teachers can begin to challenge deficit perspectives of their students. She found that in contrast to assigning labels such as *fast*, *slow*, or *lazy* to children who struggled under a curriculum that emphasized competition, speed, and the memorization of procedures, teachers who taught from a reform curriculum were concerned with developing ways to elicit their students' mathematical understanding and sought out techniques and strategies from colleagues to help build on the knowledge that they knew their students possessed.

Communication is central to reform mathematics learning. Yet these approaches often privilege a type of communication that is more prevalent in particular communities. Lubienski (2002), for example, found that although students from higher socioeconomic-status families expressed confidence in expressing their ideas during classroom discussions, stating, "I want other people to understand my ideas," lower-income students were more likely to report that they did not participate in classroom discussions for reasons related to confidence, such as "I don't like to be wrong in front of the whole group." Similarly, these students' small-group discussions were qualitatively different from that of the higher-income students; the form of communication by these students allowed for discussions of the work that did not necessarily include the deeper mathematical ideas that the lessons were designed to support.

Norms that privilege particular socioeconomic groups or ethnic groups have also been demonstrated with respect to cultural expectations of peer and teacher interaction. The idea that it is appropriate to argue with peers or with teachers has been a challenge for some students as they engage in reform classroom discourse (Murrell, 1994). How does one address the perceived conflict between respecting elders and the expectation to challenge teachers' explanations and solutions to mathematical problems? How do students balance this expectation with their own cultural norms?

Challenges to Equitable Implementation

In addition to these potential challenges inside of reform math classrooms, there are also substantial challenges to the implementation of reform in schools that serve students from nondominant and poor communities. An examination of National Assessment of Educational Progress data demonstrated that schools with students of color were more likely to adopt more traditional practices, such as multiple-choice assessments, as compared with White students who received greater instruction using reasoning in solutions of novel problems (Strutchens & Silver, 2000).

This unbalanced relationship between ethnicity and class with the implementation of reform appears to be threefold. First, students who attend low-performing schools were most likely to receive a back-to-basics curriculum (Oakes, 1990; Oakes et al., 2003), often to improve state-mandated test scores. Low-performing schools have been consistently associated with a low-income and minority student body. Second, studies suggest that a reform curriculum requires greater pedagogical knowledge and preparation by teachers to ensure optimal learning outcomes. Teachers in these disenfranchised districts more often have less content and pedagogy training to effectively teach using these new curricula (Darling-Hammond & Sykes, 2003). This lack of training greatly decreases the value of reform curricula. Research has found little difference in students' learning of mathematics concepts in classrooms where teachers used a reform curriculum paired with traditional teaching techniques as compared to those where teachers used a traditional curriculum alone. Only in classrooms where teachers used both reform pedagogy and a reform curriculum did students demonstrate more advanced mathematical thinking (Saxe, Taylor, McIntosh, & Gearhart, 2005).

These challenges to the implementation of reform, taken together, create a cycle of underachievement where students in low-performing schools experience back-to-basics instruction and have little exposure to larger conceptual issues highlighted in reform approaches. Because of a lack of success with reform curricula attributed to poor implementation, training, and incompatible beliefs about student behaviors, these schools are likely to change to traditional curricula or never adopt reform curricula initially.

Third, social and sociomathematical norms in many of these schools may be in conflict with the norms and expectations of reform mathematics. Ladson-Billings (1997) states that in many urban communities, the definition of "good school" is one that maintains high levels of order and control. This privileging of order and control are seen both in goals set by urban districts in regard to zero-tolerance policies (Casella, 2003) and in media portrayals of strong-handed principals such as "Crazy Joe" of the movie *Lean on Me* (Twain & Avildsen, 1989). This privileging of order and control may be in conflict with tenets of reform that include the need to question, to argue, and to explore.

A relatively new influence on the way a reform curriculum is implemented and the quality of that instruction in classrooms that serve students of color is the NCLB of 2001. This influence is related to requirements of NCLB with respect to the hiring of teachers, allocation of funds, and particular forms of progress standards used by individual states to measure the adequate yearly progress (AYP) of all students. But the built-in flexibility of the federal policy may result in widely differing effects on student achievement because of the different ways states and districts implement particular portions of the act (Jones, 2006).

As we have noted, much of the challenge of successful implementation and sustained support for reform mathematics implementation may be linked to teachers' discomfort with reform curricula and competency with deep mathematical ideas. Thus in districts with lower-income students, successful implementation may be directly related to the increase in licensed teachers or those holding majors in mathematics. As a focal issue, NCLB called for all teachers to be "highly qualified" in the subject they teach by the end of the 2006–2007 academic year. This call was a reaction to findings that demonstrated wide differences in the mathematical preparation of teachers from various districts and states as well as the generally low numbers of math teachers with mathematics degrees in the United States as compared to other industrialized nations. In the year 2000, whereas 90% of middle and high school math teachers in Minnesota held majors in mathematics, states such as California and Tennessee had dramatically lower rates, 57% and 54%, respectively (Erpenbach, Forte-Fast, & Potts, 2003). Though data are still being collected to determine the extent to which NCLB has made substantial changes, the trend has certainly moved to greater licensing of teachers and greater numbers with mathematics degrees in even the most impoverished communities. Although these changes may not guarantee an increase in the implementation of any particular type of curriculum, it is likely that high-quality teachers are better able to implement the more difficult mathematical tasks presented in a reform curriculum, if indeed this measure represents better mathematical understanding.

Another aspect of NCLB that may also influence this implementation in many low-income and minority communities is the focus on standardized annual testing. Indeed, this requirement brings to the fore chronic academic neglect in some districts, but its effect on curriculum implementation and instruction is dependent on the way that states define progress and, indeed, learning. Because NCLB allows for states to determine an appropriate level of progress and, indeed, sufficient mathematical knowledge, much of the influence on reform implementation will be related to goals and proficiency levels decided on by individual states. Assessments that focus specifically on basic skills, or broader assessments that include more difficult problem-solving tasks but also set the "passing" benchmark at a basic skill level, leave higher-order mathematical problem solving unmeasured or merely as superfluous advanced knowledge. It is these higher-order skills that align more closely with reform mathematics curricula; thus if basic skills are used to determine success, then traditional methods and basic goals may be reinforced, ignoring benefits of reform curricula. What remains to be understood is the way that particular communities have measured success as a function of class, race, and language.

The equitable distribution of opportunities to learn powerful mathematics is clearly one of most pressing issues in the multiple gaps in mathematics education that exist at the intersection of cultural and domain knowledge (Moses & Cobb, 2001; Schoenfeld, 2002). The history of mathematics reform indicates that this issue is bound up in communities with more or less power; political and social systems that perpetuate systemic poverty, injustice, and privilege; and "folk" discourses about differential achievement of various groups of students, which together implicate mathematics learning as a cultural system. The fact that this cultural system has historically reinforced a narrow vision of what it looks like to learn and become good at mathematics suggests that implementing reform mathematical practices with fidelity into more low-income classrooms with predominantly students of color may not be adequate (DiME, 2007; Martin, 2007).

BLURRING THE LINE BETWEEN DOMAIN KNOWLEDGE AND EVERYDAY KNOWLEDGE AS A SOURCE OF EMPOWERMENT

In the prior section, we considered the role of culture in both the history and practices of reform math. We noted that some teachers have demonstrated that reform classrooms can be optimal learning spaces for a wide range of students. Other researchers and educators have developed teaching approaches specifically geared toward teaching and empowering nondominant students, families, and communities. One approach has been to leverage students' everyday social and cultural knowledge to improve domain-related understanding. These approaches seek to make use of the rich sources of knowledge that exist outside of the classroom in the varied activities of cultural life to improve students' participation in classroom activity. In doing so, they attempt to blur the line between domain versus everyday knowing and learning and often work at all three levels of our analytic model. Such approaches also take seriously issues of race, academic identities, and access. Consequentially, students are potentially afforded opportunities to gain increased authority to participate in mathematics in ways that honor and validate their everyday identities and practices.

In this section, we consider several specific programs of research and approaches to teaching that seek to challenge the boundaries between domain understandings and cultural knowledge. These approaches draw on the everyday cultural understandings of students to support domain knowledge in mathematics. In addition to making an explicit link between the everyday and the academic, these programs position their work as challenging existing hegemony in educational spaces, opening up such spaces as sites for inquiry, and repositioning "minority" students with respect to the knowledge they produce in mathematics class. Thus, an important aspect of these projects is to challenge positions of power and privilege that are reinforced in traditional separations of domain and cultural knowledge.

We discuss and offer examples of programs that have attempted this "blurring," including the Funds of Knowledge Algebra Project, social justice approaches to mathematics, and culturally relevant pedagogy. Clearly, because of space constraints, this list is not exhaustive (other important examples of this work include that of Lipka, 1994, 2005; Lipka & Mohatt, 1998; and Brenner, 1998b). Rather, we use these programs as a way to illustrate the themes that are present in this approach. For each, we will briefly describe the research and teaching approach, highlighting the core aspects of the program, and its stated goals. We also explore important themes that cut across these various approaches and consider challenges to these approaches.

Funds of Knowledge

The Funds of Knowledge approach (Civil, 2002; Gonzalez, Andrade, & Carson, 2001; Gonzalez et al., 1993; Gonzalez & Moll, 2002; Moll, Amanti, Neff, & Gonzalez, 1992) takes as a central the idea that cultural communities have strengths and important knowledge bases that currently are not tapped in schools. Their work focuses on Latino and Native American families and communities and documents the wide range of important skills and knowledge bases parents, students, and other community members hold that could be viewed as a resource to teachers and schools. Their work has focused on three different aspects of the relation between parents' and community funds of knowledge and schools. Early phases of the project involved trained ethnographers conducting extended visits to the homes and families of students and documenting the extensive community and family cultural practices that students and parents engaged in as a part of their daily lives. Ethnographers found that parents and youth were involved in a wide range of important and domain-relevant practices, including folk medicine and animal husbandry, construction, sewing, mining, religion, and appliance and automobile repairs. Findings from these studies were shared with teachers, and teachers were asked to consider how understanding families in these new ways might change their teaching practices.

A second aspect of this project involved establishing teacher–researcher working groups, in which teachers were supported in conducting their own ethnographic studies of the home lives of a few of the students in their classrooms. Researchers and teachers met regularly to discuss observations and brainstorm ideas about how to better incorporate the findings from the ethnographic investigations into classroom instruction as well as to debrief the process of the conducting of the research itself. Teachers' involvement with their students' home lives shifted their perceptions of students and their capabilities drastically (in many cases) and offered teachers a better sense of the "whole child" in their classrooms as opposed to just the part of the child that showed up in the life of the classroom.

A third aspect of the project built on the other two and involved incorporating parents and community members directly in classroom instruction as experts. In one example, a parent drew on her skills at making candy and did a lesson with the students on making Mexican candy. This lesson led to a discussion with students on variations in the economies and buying and selling practices in the United States and Mexico.

The Funds of Knowledge approach bridged cultural and domain knowledge by connecting families, communities, and schools. This bridging process involved building multiple kinds of connections, from community practices outside of school to school practices. An important component of the connection between community and school knowledge was content knowledge about mathematics and other domains, such as science and literacy. In other words, students' experiences outside of school—with gardening and construction, for example—were used by classroom teachers to better support students' learning of important mathematical concepts (Civil, 2002).

Another type of bridging that the project supported was a bridging of power. In other words, the project shifted the normal asymmetrical power relations between families, teachers, and schools by repositioning families and students as smart and capable and as having knowledge that is valuable to the whole school community. The project fostered relations between parents and teachers, where the parents took on the role of the expert and teachers took on roles of learners and facilitators. In essence, this project recognizes that typically, certain kinds of knowledge are privileged in schools and that "school" knowledge tends to hold power and position those who have it as powerful, whereas everyday knowledge tends not to hold the same level of status and power. One important aspect of this work, then, is the ways in which power is reconstructed when teachers come into parents' homes as learners and when parents come into classrooms as teachers.

The Algebra Project

The Algebra Project was started by Robert Moses, a well-known civil rights organizer, to support the learning of algebra for African American and other disenfranchised students who may not have access to learning higher-level mathematics (Davis et al., 2006; Moses & Cobb, 2001). Moses views mathematics as an important civil rights issue, because having access to strong algebra instruction in middle school can prepare students to complete higher levels of math in high school and thus to be competitive for college and gain access to important technological fields of study at advanced levels. Underlying this focus are both long-standing racial gaps in mathematical achievement and course-taking patterns and the traditional separation of formal mathematics from the experience of young people.

Algebra Project instruction differs in fundamental ways from textbook approaches to the teaching of algebra. Instead, the curriculum takes a project-based approach, grounding the solution of algebra problems in the real-life experiences of students, then asking them to reflect mathematically on those experiences. Moses and Cobb (2001) write,

> We are using a version of experiential learning; it starts where the children are, experiences that they share. We get them to reflect on these drawing on their common culture, then to form abstract conceptualizations out of their reflection, then to apply the abstract back to their experience. . . . Each step is designed to help students bridge the transition from real-life to mathematical language and operations. (pp. 119–120)

Moses and Cobb (2001) outline five steps to the Algebra Project curriculum process: (a) physical events, where students share a physical real experience in the world; (b) pictorial representation or modeling, where students find a way to represent that experience on paper; (c) intuitive language or "people talk," where students discuss and write about the physical event in their own language; (d) structured language or "feature talk," where students make use of structured language for the purposes of selecting and encoding features of the even that are relevant for further study; and, finally, (e) symbolic representation, where students construct symbols to represent their mathematical ideas. One important physical event occurs as a part of the mathematics-of-trips unit, where students take a physical trip on a bus or subway and then reflect mathematically on various aspects of the trip.

Further dissemination and supporting the developmental trajectories of young people in mathematics are important aspects of the Algebra Project. Dissemination and making the project available to a wide range of youth in communities across the nation come as a product of extensive teacher-training programs and the will on the part of the project to argue for reflective teaching in a standards-based educational climate. Youth are supported beyond their experiences as middle school algebra students through the young people's project (YPP) for late adolescents and young adults, which offers young people a continued connection to other young people pursing the learning of mathematics and also provides mentorship and tutoring for the younger students.

Funds of Knowledge and the Algebra Project illustrate pedagogical approaches that leverage different forms of knowing and build on strengths and funds of knowledge that each student brings to his or her learning to create a richer and more inclusive learning environment. In doing so, they work at all three levels of the model simultaneously, creating spaces where cultural knowledge has an important place in the math classroom, where the cultural system is fundamentally inclusive and encourages participants in the larger mathematical enterprise. However, researchers concerned with issues of power and race may argue that this is not enough. Instead, they contend that schools must provide students with the knowledge and tools to act back on those structures that currently (and historically) serve to disenfranchise them and their communities. It is not simply a matter of giving students greater access to what has been labeled by some as "dominant" mathematics knowledge (R. Gutiérrez, 2002b; Gutstein, 2006), or knowledge that is fixed within the culture of power and perpetuates the existing social hierarchies. As we have argued, knowledge (or a knowledge system) is never neutral and as such is necessarily linked to power in the way that it privileges and marginalizes certain perspectives and narratives. This aspect of knowledge, as a source of power, has traditionally been overlooked in research that examines the relations between knowledge, culture, and differential achievement.

Social Justice Curriculum

A social justice approach to mathematics teaching raises issues about the purposes (political and social as well as cognitive) for which we engage in or ask students to engage in the study of mathematics. Such curricula ask teachers and students to employ mathematics as a tool to critically analyze and act on inequitable situations in their communities. Frankenstein (1983) cites several reasons for taking this approach toward mathematics education. The first is to expose the myth that (mathematics) knowledge is a value- and culture-free product of an objective and rational process of deduction. Exploring the tradeoffs we make in the process of using particular forms of mathematics to capture and represent various social phenomena, for example, positions mathematics as a tool for cultural and political purposes.

A second reason is to challenge what Freire (1970) called "massified" consciousness, where individuals who are oppressed take part in their oppression by believing that they operate independently, out of free choice, instead of within broader social and cultural systems. Citing Apple (1979) and others, Frankenstein (1983) describes how prevailing ideologies and categories that frame what it means to be a mathematics knower (and thus an elite member of the technical ruling class) perpetuate the belief that effort is unrelated to mathematical competence and that failure is an individual consequence. Critical literacies (and in this case, critical mathematical literacy) with special emphasis placed on unpacking language and nurturing conflicting views foster the development of *conscientização*, or "critical consciousness," which can motivate individuals to challenge a system of mathematics that leaves them with less power.

The third reason for a social justice orientation in mathematics education is, to Freire, the most important to realize and, in practice, perhaps the most difficult to achieve—to directly involve students in social activism. According to Freire (1970), it is not enough to simply present students with mathematical problems that authority figures (such as the teacher) view as unjust or unfair. (This serves only to deepen the massified orientation.) To emancipate themselves from the tyranny of their own oppressed thinking, students must be given the opportunity to determine which issues are most relevant to them in their schooling and how mathematics can be used to address these.

The emphasis on action is deliberate. Social justice theorists contend that granting students access to more and higher quality mathematics education only continues to foster their complicit participation in a system that disenfranchises them. At the same time, however, Frankenstein and others have acknowledged the realities of teaching mathematics for social justice in today's mathematics classrooms. We discuss some of these issues in the sections that follow.

Gutstein (2003, 2006) navigated these tensions directly in his work as a middle school mathematics teacher teaching for social justice in an urban Latino school. Drawing on Freire's critical consciousness and problem-posing pedagogy, as well as the notion of positive sociocultural identities in Ladson-Billing's work on culturally relevant pedagogy, Gutstein presents a framework that maps the components of a pedagogy for social justice directly to mathematical goals. The three social justice pedagogical goals include (a) reading the world with mathematics, (b) writing the world with mathematics, and (c) developing positive cultural and social identities (Gutstein, 2006, p. 23). These correspond directly to three mathematical pedagogical goals that include (a) reading the mathematical word, (b) succeeding academically in the traditional sense, and (c) changing one's orientation to mathematics. Following Freire's claim that reading and writing the world are dialectical, Gutstein (2006) emphasizes that the social justice and mathematics goals function interdependently and are mutually reinforcing, which he documented through his students' reflections and mathematics work.

In the course of 2 years, Gutstein observed his students using mathematics to pose and solve mathematics problems that allowed them to critique the material and social conditions of their lives (including his knowledge as their teacher). For example, when exploring the unequal distribution of wealth among nations, students questioned whether one could truly assess which country had more wealth without knowing about how these resources were distributed within each country. In another project, students constructed complex arguments about why racism may or may not play a role in median housing prices across neighborhoods and how they would know for certain. In each case, mathematics was positioned as a tool to make sense of the world at the same time as it was situated within and for particular purposes. The mathematical findings that students discovered also led them to generate new questions about hidden patterns and relationships that they deemed relevant.

After seeing that mathematics was within their reach and had a direct impact on their lives, a majority of Gutstein's students also developed a stronger relationship with mathematics. Not all of them liked mathematics, but most recognized its role and power in shaping their world. This is echoed by one of the students when asked how much her views had changed from being in the class:

A lot. Two years ago I didn't really care at all. I've just noticed that since the past two years, I've been more interested in the world, and the ways things are (in terms of wealth distribution and population). I've been watching the news ever since. (as cited in Gutstein, 2006, p. 63)

Culturally Relevant Pedagogy

Demands to consider the substandard education of students of color as a political imperative is echoed in the work of Gloria Ladson-Billings (1994, 1995) on *culturally relevant pedagogy.* Speaking to the disheartening findings that desegregation appeared to be favoring White students at the expense of African American students, Ladson-Billings provoked the field to take seriously the concerns of educating African American children as a unique population of students. Culturally relevant pedagogy represented a significant move away from superficial and essentialist versions of multicultural education epitomized by celebrations of ethnic foods and holidays toward an awareness of the different ways of communicating and being that African American students brought to the classroom (Ladson-Billings, 1994, 1995; Tate, 1995). Ladson-Billings asserts that teachers who taught the color-blind perspective that all students should be treated the same tend to perceive nondominant students constantly in relation to (and inferior to) their White peers. The pervasiveness of a deficit perspective of African American children also led to a missionary approach to teaching, where teachers entered the profession to "save" underachieving students of color from dropping out of school, instead of holding them to high standards for their academic work.

Examining the work of teachers who are effective at both holding their African American students to high standards and ensuring their place in the classroom community, Ladson-Billings (1994) has developed a set of definitions and indicators for culturally relevant pedagogical practice. This level of detail of teacher practice is situated below three overarching components, including academic achievement, cultural competence, and sociopolitical consciousness. By *academic achievement,* she means the capacity of teachers to effectively articulate and meet multifaceted and individualized goals that correspond to the needs of each student. By *cultural competence,* she means the propensity of teachers to spot, consider, and capitalize on the cultural practices and sensibilities of their students. By *sociopolitical consciousness,* she means the orientation that teachers have on social issues such as racism, social justice, and privilege and the ways they relate content to context. Broadly speaking, these components are less about the teaching of particular subjects and more about the stance that teachers' take toward the relation between school, cultural, and political knowledge. In other words, the aim of culturally relevant pedagogy is to explore the nexus of school, home, community, and society in the context of African American achievement.

Themes in culturally relevant pedagogy pervade much of the research we have described above (Gutstein, Lipman, Hernandez, & de los Reyes, 1997) and theories for teaching diverse learners (Banks et al., 2005; Foster, 1995). Foremost among these is the recognition that there is no single knowledge base that encompasses what teachers need to know to foster culturally responsive and academically rigorous classrooms. Instead, these theories consider knowledge for teaching to be embedded in teacher practice and continually evolving through teachers' reflections on their interactions with their students, their students' communities, peers, and others.

Similar to the Algebra Project and Funds of Knowledge, both social justice approaches and culturally relevant pedagogy integrate all three levels of the model in their approaches to teaching (see Figure 1). These approaches integrate a concern with mastery of knowledge and broadening what counts as knowledge, shifting norms of and discourse about important mathematical problems, and repositioning students to extend greater access and power over their mathematical experiences.

Cross-Cutting Themes and Challenges

Several themes cut across the approaches we have reviewed to blurring the lines between cultural and domain knowledge in mathematics teaching and learning. First, there is an acknowledgement that mathematics teaching and learning are fundamentally cultural activities that to date have privileged certain students and communities rather than others. Second, (and it follows, that) all of these programs challenge traditional assumptions that some students are more able to learn than others (and too often these two categories correspond to racial and social class groups). Last, all of the approaches we have described make the assumption that all learners are capable, given the appropriate support, challenge, and instruction.

These approaches also take as central the task to connect students' experiences in the mathematics classroom to their experiences in everyday life as well as to political and social issues relevant to their lives (but that they may not have considered). Thus math teaching is both about building on what students are familiar with, so as not to alienate them, but it is also about introducing new ideas, concepts, and sensibilities. This involves a complex process of validating students' current identity and sense of themselves while expanding them to include new kinds of social, political, and mathematical activity. In doing so, these models of teaching and learning view math not simply as cognitive activity but also as social and political activity—activities that we do with one another as we seek to improve our world and push for social justice. In this way, the teaching and learning of mathematics becomes a vehicle for shifting current power relations, to use mathematics for the purposes of empowerment at both the individual and community levels.

However, these approaches are not without challenges. We discuss three of these challenges: (a) the difficulty of keeping the math in full view when building on everyday knowledge or when talking about social justice; (b) implications for ethnically heterogeneous classrooms, where students may not share cultural background or community experiences; and (c) the mismatch between these approaches and the teacher workforce and structure of the profession.

The first challenge that has been identified particularly in the work of Funds of Knowledge and teaching math for social justice is the difficulty of keeping the math in view while deeply inquiring into the everyday social world. Activities such as constructing gardens (Civil, 2001) and analyzing world distributions of resources (Gutstein, 2006), for example, are necessarily social and cultural phenomena in which mathematical forms and expressions can be oversimplified (e.g., calculating averages) or extremely complicated (e.g., high-level statistical modeling). It is also the case that students' mathematical moves in these activities may be quite varied and unconventional and thus pose a challenge for teachers to build on productively. In the Funds of Knowledge work, Civil (2001) has found that mathematical dilemmas often arise naturally out of students' everyday activities but that it is important for the teacher to be able to shift students' focus from the concreteness of the everyday situation to abstract principles and procedures in mathematics.

The research on the implementation of social justice tasks in the mathematics classroom has also prompted questions about the difficulty of balancing discussions of complex social issues with the mathematics. For example, Bartell (2006) reports that teachers in her professional development course on social justice in mathematics found it challenging to move flexibly between the mathematics content and conversations about social injustice. Gutstein (2006) also admits that in his class, he had to occasionally forgo opportunities to pursue mathematical investigations to deepen the conversations about social issues. Because students often hold strong perspectives about social injustice and these can trigger emotional responses, it is clearly important for teachers to be able to adeptly and sensitively guide students back to the mathematics at hand. We wonder, then, if teachers are being prepared and have bargained for doing this multifaceted work. Also, can social justice activities stemming from students' social realities sufficiently drive students' development of sophisticated mathematics knowing across an extended period of time? Or should they mainly serve as supplemental materials to the existing mathematics curriculum, used to convince students that learning mathematics is relevant and even critical to improving their lives and the lives of others?

A second challenge is in thinking about how one might apply these approaches in racially or ethnically heterogeneous classrooms. This is an especially salient issue for Funds of Knowledge and the Algebra Project, as to some degree, these approaches assume a degree of coherence within the communities that are being served. How might these approaches be adapted in classrooms where students are from multiple communities? What might it mean to draw on students' experiences in such multicultural classrooms? This may be less of an issue with social justice approaches, but it still leaves more to be negotiated with and between students in classrooms where there is a wide range of race, class, or socioeconomic groups represented. How are teachers to deal with kids from communities that do not share a social justice perspective or see social justice in terms of their own philanthropy? Would such students (not from working-class families) buy into the basic premises of this approach? What additional support might they need to do so? Another critical issue with social justice approaches is that the time spent on social justice issues is potentially time not spent on math. What about the middle-class and upper-class parents who are unwilling to sacrifice time for "basic math" and relegate these approaches as appropriate only for those from nondominant groups? Similarly, in considering heterogeneity and culturally relevant pedagogy, it may be more difficult in heterogeneous classrooms and communities to have a sense of the community that students come from; there may be greater differences in achievement and histories with school among the students as well as variety in issues of identity that may need to be attended to.

A third challenge involves the constraints imposed by the racial and gender makeup of the teaching force in this country and the structure of the profession.

The vast majority of teachers in the United States are White, middle-class women (Howard, 1999; Nieto, 2004). This is potentially a population of teachers for whom the approaches we describe may be particularly difficult, as they likely have the most to learn about their students' communities. Although mathematics teachers are often marginalized within the broader mathematics community, they may not share the same level of marginalization with their nondominant students. Furthermore, teaching is a profession that is largely underpaid and overworked (Darling-Hammond, 1997). Most teachers, given the structure of the school day and demands on their time, have little time to conduct the kind of in-depth investigations of their students and their communities these approaches suggest. Even more important, in the broader context of increased reliance on standardized testing with high stakes for teachers and schools, these approaches that require more of teachers may be unrealistic. Any approach that argues for particular teaching strategies must take into account these very real constraints.

However, despite these challenges, we see great promise in the work of the aforementioned approaches, and we offer these critiques as a way to continue to make progress on ways to support increased equity in math classrooms. It is important to note that these approaches highlight the critical role of teachers in reproducing patterns of inequity. In the next section, we focus on the implications our review may have for the knowledge teachers need to have to best support equity and begin to "blur the lines" between cultural and domain knowledge and work simultaneously at all three levels of our model. Because of space, we do not undertake a full review of the vast literature on teacher professional development that includes a cultural or equity lens (see Sowder, 2007; Wilson & Berne, 1999). Rather, we reflect on the implications for teacher training of the research we have reviewed in this chapter, drawing on some of the relevant work in teacher professional development.

Toward this end, we briefly consider two questions. What knowledge do teachers need to know, and what professional development models might prove productive possibilities for sharing that knowledge with teachers?

Implications for Teacher Knowledge

The work of teachers has grown considerably more complex in the past 10 years (Ball & Cohen, 1999; Cochran-Smith & Lytle, 1999; Cochran-Smith & Zeichner, 2005; Lampert & Ball, 1998; Putnam & Borko, 2000). Standards-based instructional practices require that teachers develop a specialized form of mathematics knowledge for teaching (MKT; Ball, 2005; Hill, Schilling, & Ball, 2004; Hill, Sleep, Lewis, & Ball, 2007) that reflects a particular blend of connected domain understanding with techniques and strategies to facilitate productive classroom interactions. Although the details of MKT are currently being worked out, the domain understanding required for eliciting, evaluating, and building (Carpenter, Fennema & Franke, 1996; Lampert, 1990, 2001; Schifter, 2001) on students' mathematical ideas reflects a facility with and deep understanding of mathematical concepts and procedures across the terrain of K–12 mathematics (Greeno, 1991; Ma, 1999; NCTM, 1991, 2000). Teachers need to have the opportunity to develop mathematics knowing in practice through ongoing reflection in the classroom and with their peers through the use of records of practice, video, and other learning materials (Kazemi & Franke, 2004; Lampert & Ball, 1998).

As Rochelle Gutiérrez (2002b) argues, however, knowledge of dominant mathematics must also be balanced with knowledge of how to enable students to critique the role of mathematics in society and to "contribute toward a positive relationship between mathematics, people, and society in ways that erase inequities on this planet" (p. 172). Delineating a set of teaching practices that encompasses both dominant and critical perspectives on mathematics is complicated by the fact that some classrooms are becoming increasingly diverse while others slip into hypersegregation (Orfield, Frankenberg, & Lee, 2003). Students themselves are also quite complex, as they negotiate hybrid practices, identities, and time scales through new global technologies that transcend traditional racial, social, and linguistic boundaries (Barab, Hay, Barnett, & Squire, 2001; Delpit, 2002; Gergen, 1991; Moje, Ciechanowski, Ellis, Carrillo, & Collazo, 2004). Thus, as we noted, in this chapter we do not presume to be able to comprehensively outline the knowledge teachers need to teach mathematics effectively and fairly. Instead, we juxtapose recent theoretical shifts that blur the boundaries between mathematics and cultural knowledge, with the implications of the various programs we reviewed above to propose ideas about effective mathematics teaching in classrooms with diverse populations of students.

First, the Funds of Knowledge approach would suggest that an important aspect of teacher preparation would support teachers in viewing their students as whole people with rich social and intellectual lives outside of the classroom. Activities for prospective teachers might include spending time with students and families outside of school (Civil, 2002; Foote, 2006) and bringing families into schools to better understand students' interests and skills outside of the classroom and those that exist as funds of knowledge in their communities. Additionally, professional development activities might include a study of modules developed with students' and families' funds of knowledge at the center and might offer models for alternative ways to incorporate family and community members into classroom activities. An important aspect of this work would be to support prospective or current teachers in understanding the value (both for students' learning and for social justice) of shifting the traditional power relations between families and schools and of opening communication channels.

Similarly, the activities of the Algebra Project would also suggest that supporting teachers in understanding the importance of and offering suggestions for how to better get to know the young people they are teaching is a critical focus for teacher preparation. The Algebra Project might also share an orientation for teachers that views math teaching as political activity and sees subverting current patterns of unequal access to higher mathematics as an immediate concern. Moses and Cobb (2001) argue that students need to be taught to "demand to understand" when learning mathematics, arguably placing the teacher in the role of civil rights activist. Central to this approach would be specific training in how to provide opportunities for students to

physically and experientially engage mathematics, to describe mathematical relationships both in their own language and in the formal language of mathematics, and to
represent mathematical ideas symbolically.

Culturally relevant pedagogy has been met with widespread appeal from educators,
yet there is little research to date focusing explicitly on how to organize culturally relevant pedagogy in mathematics classrooms (although this is changing). Culturally relevant pedagogy suggests that teachers' orientation toward students is crucial—that
they should hold themselves accountable for the success of *all* of their students, recognizing the capacity for success of each. In the mathematics classroom, this might
mean the use of instructional strategies such as Complex Instruction (Boaler, 2006c;
Cohen, 1994), where teachers attempt to disrupt traditional status hierarchies by
assigning competence and fostering accountability among students. However, culturally relevant pedagogy also points to the need for a critical approach to race and privilege within mathematics teacher education (DiME, 2007; Grant & Sleeter, 2003).
For White teachers to develop the cultural and intellectual awareness to engage with
their African American students at a deep level, Ladson-Billings (1995) argues that
they need to

- spend a significant amount of time in the African American community,
- receive structured and prolonged experiences with African American students in
  their preservice teaching, and
- learn how to critique our educational system in ways that inspire them to be agents
  of change.

This framework for teacher preparation addresses concerns raised by Sleeter (1997),
who found that multiple, day-long sessions with teachers on topics in multicultural
education did not provide them with sufficient depth to understand the connections
between the cultural and mathematical implications of their teaching. Essential to
teachers' development of culturally relevant pedagogical knowledge, then, is a shift
in their perceptions about what it means to be African American in the mathematics classroom (Martin, 2000) and what is encompassed in their role as mathematics
educators of African American children.

The primary aim of a social justice curriculum is to involve students directly in
using mathematics to question and eventually uproot social injustice. To support
this process, teachers must be trained to allow students to pose questions about local
situations that they feel are unfair and to generate mathematics with their students
to investigate these questions (see also *Rethinking Mathematics*; Gutstein & Peterson,
2005). This may be a chicken-and-egg situation, though, because teachers may find
it difficult to build trust with students who are traditionally marginalized without
first showing them that they are on their side. This also requires that teachers know
how to motivate sophisticated mathematical conversations from social justice activities. And similarly, as Bartell (2005) suggests, teachers must seek out the underlying
causes of unjust situations and processes to prevent reductionist discussions of cause

and effect. These new roles for teachers are not easy. As Aguirre's (2007) reflections on her social justice mathematics methods course suggest, teacher resistance to change at both pedagogical and ideological levels can make it difficult for teacher educators to foster a social justice orientation to mathematics teaching.

The proliferation of equity-oriented mathematics teacher preparation and professional development programs suggests that the field is moving toward a broader understanding of how to prepare teachers for cultural diversity and justice. Enacting changes in teacher education in the ways described above, however, substantially reshapes and enlarges the boundaries of the practice of mathematics teachers. We argue, with others (Franke & Kazemi, 2001; Little, 2002), that teachers cannot do this work alone, in isolated classrooms, without the support of their peers, institutions, and mathematical and cultural *brokers* (Lave & Wenger, 1991). We also draw on Cochran-Smith and Lytle's (1999) distinction between *knowledge for practice* and *knowledge of practice* to argue that knowledge of teaching and teaching practice are not separate acts. A knowledge-of-practice perspective assumes that teachers' knowing emerges from their participation in teacher and other (cultural, ethnic, racial, socioeconomic) communities and is connected to their practice in relation to broader sociopolitical processes and institutions.

CONCLUSION

We reviewed literature relevant to what we consider to be a critical area for mathematics education research—the cultural nature of mathematics teaching and learning and the ways in which we maintain or blur boundaries between cultural knowledge and domain knowledge in mathematics. In doing so, we have explored both research that focuses on relations between cultural and domain knowledge and research that examines issues of race and culture inside of math classrooms. It is interesting to note in our review that often, contributions to our understanding of mathematics teaching and learning have not explicitly attended to issues of race and culture, and contributions to our understanding of the relation between domain and cultural knowledge often do not stem from the study of mathematics classrooms.

The reasons often given for this disjuncture—that our society views mathematics as culture free or that mathematics education researchers are not concerned with issues of race and culture in the learning of mathematics—do not capture the complexity of the situation. Although these explanations may very well be valid, we would also like to offer the following possibilities:

1. Mathematics may be a particularly challenging domain to map students' everyday cultural practices onto, as its very purpose is to abstract and generalize (rather than to reflect on the details of any particular experience). This is different from an argument that math is culture free; rather, culture is less visible from a mathematical lens.

2. Mathematics education researchers have yet to develop and agree on methods that can be used to document cultural practices and processes within mathematics classrooms and systems. That is, we simply have few conceptual and practical

tools to understand issues of culture in mathematics classrooms and even fewer models of how to account for multiple levels of culture, race, and access simultaneously (Nasir & Hand, 2006).

3. Mathematics holds a privileged status in our society as an elite activity for the smartest of citizens. That assumption supports a view of math as out of the reach of the "common" man and thus disconnected from and inaccessible through everyday experiences.

Given these ideological and practical constraints, mathematics education research in general remains underdeveloped with respect to issues of cultural versus mathematical knowledge. However, study of the intersections of cultural and domain knowledge in mathematics may push the field of educational research in productive directions. In our view, this would mean attending to some of the issues that we have outlined in this chapter, including making connections between everyday and mathematical ideas, revisiting what counts as mathematics, who makes the decisions about what counts (and about whose knowledge is privileged), and how these play out in the classroom in terms of the practices, roles, materials, and tools authorized for mathematical activity.

We would like to highlight what we view as critical tensions and issues that could serve as directions for research and practice.

First, many of the scholars whose work we review in this chapter, social justice perspectives in particular, argue that given that all mathematical problems reside in some sort of context—particularly at the lower grades—we need to make the context reflect the realities of students' lives. Furthermore, we cannot impose these contexts on the basis of racial group membership or social class categories; rather, we must build them with students through conversations and shared experiences. This perspective raises a set of questions. Is it important to make the context relevant (e.g., creating social justice tasks), or the structures for classroom participation (e.g., fostering multidimensional classrooms)? How are they different? Is one better for a particular group of students? How is developing social justice within the mathematics classroom (or what Boaler, 2006b, calls "relational equity") related to the development of critical mathematics literacy? Embedded in these concerns are varying assumptions about the purpose of mathematics education—assumptions that we must lay bare and investigate.

Second, another major thrust in the work that we reviewed is intersubjectivity as an important aspect of math learning and "third space" (K. D. Gutierrez et al., 1995) as a potential way to conceptualize the blurring of cultural and domain knowledge in mathematics classrooms. How does a third space (which is related to hybrid discourse structures) develop in mathematics classrooms, and how does it relate to the type of engagement in mathematics available to nondominant students? As classroom participants work toward understanding the meanings of the mathematical context, content, method, or representation produced by others, how are these meanings negotiated? What does it mean to foster dialogical inquiry within a culturally diverse classroom? Will questions about who is making these meanings and what is the social and cultural context of their meaning-making system begin to emerge?

Third, given all of the research that we have reviewed, what can we glean with respect to how to best prepare students (and especially urban students) to productively engage in mathematics classrooms and high-level mathematics? One aspect of this involves thinking about how to incorporate students' voices and experiences into the math classroom. We want to draw a distinction between using everyday cultural knowledge (for instance, the basketball players' knowledge about average and percentage) as a point of entry into a mathematical discussion and using it to limit what students can learn to what they already know. We strongly support the former usage and argue that the math knowledge students accrue in everyday practices should be used as both a conceptual and a social lever to support students' deeper engagement in math and their identities as capable math learners, not as a limit on their ability to engage abstract mathematics.

Finally, our review raises important concerns about what mathematics to cover in schools. What are the constraints and affordances of a "mathematics-for-all" approach? How do we think about this in the context of the current NCLB climate of standards, high-stakes testing, and threats of state takeovers? What are the compromises involved in creating specialized mathematics instruction for groups of students? Would such an approach lead to artificial distinctions and stereotypes?

In our view, the tripartite model that we offered at the beginning of the chapter may offer some traction in thinking about and making progress on these critical issues. Keeping in view the three levels at which math learning and culture intersect may offer us a way to conceptualize the multiple, simultaneous ways that math learning and culture become intertwined in math classrooms. More specifically, the model points to the intertwined nature of concerns with math knowing as a cultural activity, math learning as a cultural enterprise, and math education as a cultural and political activity. With respect to math knowing as a cultural activity, we have highlighted the importance of building on what students know and on understanding how they express what they know. This is deeply connected to viewing math learning as a cultural enterprise and broadening what it means to learn math and be a mathematics learner. This broadening is related to issues of identity—recognizing that students have to negotiate membership across different social contexts (including math) and creating opportunities for them to make the practice their own. Finally, we have argued for the critical nature of understanding mathematics as a cultural system and using mathematics as a tool of empowerment and awareness in issues of social justice (both in the classroom and more broadly through more careful analysis of the outcomes of NCLB).

We would like to return briefly to reflect on the example of the solution strategies of the basketball players with which we opened the chapter. We made sense of this example in the introduction by arguing that it illustrates the distinction the players made between the math of everyday life and the math of school. In some ways, it could be argued that this example, then, reflects the first level of our model—math knowing as cultural activity—as it is concerned with the way the individual student is developing knowledge of mathematics across practices and not challenging the disjuncture between the two.

But the pattern of solutions we encountered also reflects students' experiences of mathematics and mathematics classrooms as places where they are not central participants, where they are not constructors of knowledge, and where "smart" responses mean applying algorithms. These experiences left many of them with the view that Boaler and Greeno's (2000) calculus students articulate: that math does not have to make sense and does not have to be personally meaningful. This corresponds to the second level of the model, that learning in math classrooms is a cultural enterprise with particular norms, values, and appropriate stances and activities.

This example also illustrates the third aspect of the model, that math education itself is a cultural (and indeed political) activity. The basketball players' responses reflect their social and political position in our society—as urban African American young men. They are not afforded access to mathematics teaching or resources at the school level that might allow them to use mathematics to challenge existing hierarchies and injustices and at the same time to create more prosperous futures for themselves and their families.

This last point highlights the ways in which our task, with respect to the preparation of students from nondominant groups and students from impoverished communities, is multipronged. We must prepare urban students to simultaneously challenge existing hierarchies of knowledge and to be competitive in a system that relies on such hierarchies. This involves both relatively long-range and short-term goals. Again, this cannot happen simply through lone teachers acting in isolated classrooms—rather, it must be a part of a collective effort on the part of researchers, educators, and policymakers. It must involve a paradigm shift with respect to the purposes for teaching mathematics and the desired outcomes. When these shifts occur, multiple cultures will be part and parcel of the math classroom, and no longer will the boundary between domain and cultural knowledge be constructed so forcefully by our collective assumptions.

NOTES

[1]Gloria Ladson-Billings (2006) has cast this as a national educational debt to highlight that these are socially and historically located trends, not merely differences in scores between individuals.

[2]We consider culture and approaches to teaching math in the next section.

[3]Similar arguments were successful in passage of Head Start funding.

REFERENCES

Aguirre, J. B. (2007, March). *Examining counter resistance strategies to promote mathematics and equity in teacher preparation and professional development: A Latina mathematics educator's perspective.* Paper presented at the National Conference of Teachers of Mathematics, Atlanta.

Apple, M. (1979). *Ideology and curriculum.* London: Routledge & Kegan Paul.

Apple, M. (1992). Thinking more critically about the challenges before us: A response to Romberg. *Journal for Research in Mathematics Education. 23,* 438-440.

Apple, M. (1995). Taking power seriously: New directions in equity in mathematics education and beyond. In W. Secada, E. Fennema, & L. B. Adajian (Eds.), *New directions for equity in mathematics education* (pp. 329–348). New York: Cambridge University Press.

Ascher, M. (1994). *Ethnomathematics: A multicultural view of mathematical ideas.* London: Taylor and Francis/CRC.

Bakhtin, M. M. (1981). *The dialogic imagination: Four essays by M. M. Bakhtin.* Austin: University of Texas Press.

Bakhtin, M. M. (1986). *Speech genres and other late essays* (V. W. McGee, Trans.). Austin: University of Texas Press.

Ball, D. (2005, May). *What mathematical knowledge, skills, and habits do teachers need in order to teach effectively?* Paper presented at Mathematical Knowledge for Teaching (K–8): Why, What and How? Berkeley, CA.

Ball, D., & Bass, H. (2000). Making believe: The collective construction of public mathematical knowledge in the elementary classroom. In D. Phillips (Ed.), *Yearbook of the national society for the study of education: Constructivism in education* (pp. 193–224). Chicago: University of Chicago Press.

Ball, D. L., & Cohen, D. K. (1999). Developing practice, developing practitioners: Toward a practice-based theory of professional education. In L. Darling-Hammond & G. Sykes (Eds.), *Teaching as the learning profession: Handbook of policy and practice* (pp. 3–32). San Francisco: Jossey-Bass.

Banks, J. A., Cochran-Smith, M., Moll, L., Richert, A., Zeichner, K., LePage, P., et al. (2005). Teaching diverse learners. In L. Darling-Hammond & J. D. Bransford (Eds.), *Preparing teachers for a changing world* (pp. 232–275). San Francisco: Jossey-Bass.

Barab, S., Hay, K., Barnett, M., & Squire, K. (2001). Constructing virtual worlds: Tracing the historical development of learner practices. *Cognition and Instruction, 19*(1), 47–94.

Barsalou, L. W. (1999). Perceptual symbol systems. *Behavior and Brain Sciences, 22,* 577–600.

Bartell, T. G. (2006, November). *Striving for equity in mathematics education: Learning to teach mathematics for social justice.* Paper presented at the 28th annual meeting of the North American chapter of the International Group for the Psychology of Mathematics Education, Merida, Yucatan, Mexico.

Beach, K. (1995). Activity as a mediator of sociocultural change and individual development: The case of school-work transition in Nepal. *Mind, Culture, and Activity, 2*(4), 285–302.

Beady, C., & Hansell, S. (1981). Teacher race and expectations for student achievement. *American Educational Research Journal, 18*(2), 191–206.

Benjamin, H. R. W. (1939). *The saber tooth curriculum.* New York: McGraw-Hill.

Bishop, A. (1988). *Mathematics enculturation: A cultural perspective on mathematics education.* Dordrecht, Netherlands: Kluwer.

Boaler, J. (1997). *Experiencing school mathematics: Teaching styles, sex, and setting.* Philadelphia: Open University Press.

Boaler, J. (2002). The development of disciplinary relationships: Knowledge, practice, and identity in mathematics classrooms. *For the Learning of Mathematics, 22*(1), 42–47.

Boaler, J. (2003). Learning from teaching: Exploring the relationship between reform curriculum and equity. *Journal for Research in Mathematics Education, 33*(4), 239–258.

Boaler, J. (2006a). How a detracked mathematics approach promoted respect, responsibility, and high achievement. *Theory Into Practice, 45*(1), 40–46.

Boaler, J. (2006b). Promoting respectful learning. *Educational Leadership, 63*(5), 74–78.

Boaler, J. (2006c). Urban success: A multidimensional mathematics approach with equitable outcomes. *Phi Delta Kappan, 87*(5), 364–369.

Boaler, J., & Greeno, J. G. (2000). Identity, agency, and knowing in mathematics worlds. In J. Boaler (Ed.), *Multiple perspectives on mathematics teaching and learning* (pp. 171–200). Westport, CT: Ablex.

Boaler, J., & Staples, M. (in press). Creating mathematical futures through an equitable teaching approach: The case of Railside School. *Teachers College Record.*

Bourdieu, P. (1977). *Outline of a theory of practice.* Cambridge, UK: Cambridge University Press.

Brenner, M. E. (1994). A communication framework for mathematics: Exemplary instruction for culturally and linguistically diverse students. In B. McLeod (Ed.), *Language and learning: Educating linguistically diverse students* (pp. 233–268). Albany: State University of New York Press.

Brenner, M. E. (1998a). Adding cognition to the formula for culturally relevant instruction in mathematics. *Anthropology and Education Quarterly, 29*(2), 214–244.

Brenner, M. E. (1998b). Meaning and money. *Educational Studies in Mathematics, 36*(2), 123–155.

Brown, A. L., & Campione, J. C. (1994). Guided discovery in a community of learners. In K. McGilly (Ed.), *Classroom lessons: Integrating cognitive theory and classroom practice* (pp. 229–272). Cambridge, MA: MIT Press.

Brown, J. S., Collins, A., & Duguid, P. (1989). Situated cognition and the culture of learning. *Educational Researcher, 18*(1), 32–42.

Burrow, A., Tubman, J., & Montgomery, M. (2006). Racial identity: Toward an integrated developmental psychological perspective. *Identity, 6*(4), 317–339.

Carpenter, T. P., Fennema, E., & Franke, M. L. (1996). Cognitively guided instruction: A knowledge base for reform in primary mathematics instruction. *Elementary School Journal, 97*(1), 3–20.

Carraher, T. N., Carraher, D. W., & Schliemann, A. D. (1985). Mathematics in the streets and in the schools. *British Journal of Developmental Psychology, 3,* 21–29.

Casella, R. (2003). Zero tolerance policy in schools: Rationale, consequences, and alternatives. *Teachers College Record, 105*(5), 872–892.

Cazden, C. B. (1988). *Classroom discourse: The language of teaching and learning.* Portsmouth, NH: Heinemann.

Chazan, D. (2000). *Beyond formulas in mathematics and teaching: Dynamics of the high school algebra classroom.* New York: Teachers College Press.

Chazan, D., & Ball, D. (1999). Beyond being told not to tell. *For the Learning of Mathematics, 19*(2), 2–10.

Civil, M. (2001). Mathematics instruction developed from a garden theme. *Teaching Children Mathematics, 7*(7), 400–405.

Civil, M. (2002). Culture and mathematics: A community approach. *Journal of Intercultural Studies, 23*(2), 133–148.

Clark, H. H. (1996). *Using language.* Cambridge, UK: Cambridge University Press.

Cobb, P., & Bowers, J. (1999). Cognitive and situated learning perspectives in theory and practice. *Educational Researcher, 28*(2), 4–15.

Cobb, P., Gravemeijer, K., Yackel, E., McClain, K., & Whitenack, J. W. (1997). Mathematizing and symbolizing: The emergence of chains of signification in one first-grade classroom. In D. Kirschner & J. Whitson (Eds.), *Situated cognition: Social, semiotic and psychological perspectives* (pp. 151–233). Mahwah, NJ: Lawrence Erlbaum.

Cobb, P., Gresalfi, M., & Hodge, L. L. (in press). An interpretive scheme for analyzing the identities that students develop in mathematics classrooms. *Journal for Research in Mathematics Education.*

Cobb, P., & Hodge, L. L. (2002). A relational perspective on issues of cultural diversity and equity as they play out in the mathematics classroom. *Mathematical Thinking and Learning, 4*(2/3), 249–284.

Cobb, P., Wood, T., & Yackel, E. (1993). Discourse, mathematical thinking, and classroom practice. In E. Forman, N. Minick, & C. A. Stone (Eds.), *Contexts for learning: Sociocultural dynamics in children's development* (pp. 91–119). New York: Oxford University Press.

Cochran-Smith, M., & Lytle, S. L. (1999). Relationships of knowledge and practice: Teacher learning in communities. In A. Iran-Nejad & P. D. Pearson (Eds.), *Review of research in education* (Vol. 24, pp. 249–305). Washington, DC: American Educational Research Association.

Cochran-Smith, M., & Zeichner, K. (2005). *Studying teacher education: The report of the AERA panel on research and teacher education.* Mahwah, NJ: Lawrence Erlbaum.

Cohen, E. G. (1994). *Designing groupwork: Strategies for the heterogeneous classroom.* New York: Teachers College Press.

Cohen, E. G., & Lotan, R. A. (1997). *Working for equity in heterogeneous classrooms.* New York: Teachers College Press.

Cole, M. (1996). *Cultural psychology: A once and future discipline.* Cambridge, MA: Belknap.

Cole, M., & Engeström, Y. (1993). A cultural-historical approach to distributed cognition. In G. Salomon (Ed.), *Distributed cognitions: Psychological and educational considerations* (pp. 1–46). New York: Cambridge University Press.

Cole, M., Gay, J., Glick, J. A., & Sharp, D. W. (1971). *The cultural context of learning and thinking.* New York: Basic Books.

Cole, M., & Scribner, S. (1974). *Culture and thought.* New York: John Wiley.

D'Amato, J. (1996). Resistance and compliance in minority classrooms. In E. Jacob & C. Jordan (Eds.), *Minority education: Anthropological perspectives* (pp. 181–208). Norwood, NJ: Ablex.

D'Ambrosio, U. (1985). Ethnomathematics and its place in the history and pedagogy of mathematics. *For the Learning of Mathematics, 5*(1), 44–48.

Darling-Hammond, L. (1997). *The right to learn.* San Francisco: Jossey-Bass.

Darling-Hammond, L., & Sykes, G. (2003). Wanted: A national teacher supply policy for education: The right way to meet the "highly qualified teacher" challenge. *Education Policy Analysis Archives, 11*(33). Retrieved April 10, 2006, from http://epaa.asu.edu/epaa/v11n33/

Davis, F., West, M., Greeno, J., Gresalfi, M., & Martin, T. (with Moses, R.) et al. (2006). Transactions of mathematical knowledge in the Algebra Project. In N. Nasir & P. Cobb (Eds.), *Improving access to mathematics: Diversity and equity in the classroom* (pp. 69–88). New York: Teachers College Press.

de Abreu, G. (1995). Understanding how children experience the relationship between home and school mathematics. *Mind, Culture, and Activity, 2*(2), 119–142.

de Abreu, G., & Kline, T. (2006). Social valorization of mathematical practices: The implications for learners in multi-cultural schools. In N. S. Nasir & P. Cobb (Eds.). *Improving access to mathematics* (pp. 118–131). New York: Teachers College.

de la Rocha, O. (1985). The reorganization of Arithmetic Practice in the kitchen. *Anthropology and Education Quarterly, 16*(3), 193–198.

Delpit, L., & Dowdy, J. K. (Eds.).(2002). *The skin that we speak.* New York: New Press.

Denning, P. J. (1983). A nation at risk: The imperative for educational reform. *Communications of the ACM, 26*(7), 467–478.

Diamondstone, J. (2002). Keeping resistance in view in an activity theory analysis. *Mind, Culture, and Activity, 9*(1), 2–21.

Diversity in Mathematics Education. (2007). Culture, race, power, and mathematics education. In F. Lester (Ed.), *Handbook of research on mathematics teaching and learning* (2nd ed., pp. 405–434). Reston, VA: National Council for Teachers of Mathematics.

Durkin, K., & Shire, B. (1991). *Language in mathematics education: Research and practice.* Buckingham, UK: Open University Press.

Dutro, E., Fisk, M. C., Koch, R., Roop, L. J., & Wixson, K. (2002). When state policies meet local district contexts: Standards-based professional development as a means to individual agency and collective ownership. *Teachers College Record, 104*(4), 787–811.

Engeström, Y. (2001). Expansive learning at work: Toward an activity theoretical reconceptualization. *Journal of Education and Work, 14*(1), 133–156.

Engle, R. A. (2006). Framing interactions to foster generative learning: A situative explanation of transfer in a community of learners classroom. *Journal of the Learning Sciences,* 15(4), 451–498.

Engle, R. A., & Conant, F. R. (2002). Guiding principles for fostering productive disciplinary engagement: Explaining an emergent argument in a community of learners classroom. *Cognition and Instruction, 20*(4), 399–483.

Erickson, F. (2004). *Talk and social theory.* Cambridge, UK: Polity.

Erpenbach, W. J., Forte-Fast, E., & Potts, A. (2003). *Statewide educational accountability under NCLB: Central issues arising from an examination of state accountability workbooks and U.S. Department of Education Reviews under the No Child Left Behind Act of 2001.* Washington, DC: Council of Chief State School Officers.

Ferguson, R. (2003). Teachers' perceptions and expectations and the Black-White test score gap. *Urban Education, 38*(4), 460–507.

Foote, M. (2006). *Supporting teachers in situating children's mathematical thinking within their lived experience.* Unpublished doctoral dissertation, University of Wisconsin, Madison.

Fordham, S., & Ogbu, J. (1986). Black students' school success: Coping with the burden of "acting White." *Urban Review, 18,* 176–206.

Forman, E. (1996). Learning mathematics as participation in classroom practice: Implications of sociocultural theory for educational reform. In L. P. Steffe, P. Nesher, P. Cobb, G. Goldin, & B. Greer (Eds.), *Theories of mathematics learning* (pp. 115–130). Mahwah, NJ: Lawrence Erlbaum.

Forman, E., & Ansell, E. (2001). The multiple voices of a mathematics classroom community. *Educational Studies in Mathematics, 46*(1/3), 115–142.

Foster, M. (1995). African American teachers and culturally relevant pedagogy. In J. A. Banks & C. Banks (Eds.), *Handbook of research on multicultural education* (pp. 570–581). San Francisco: Jossey-Bass.

Franke, M. L., & Kazemi, E. (2001). Teaching as learning within a community of practice: Characterizing generative growth. In T. Wood, B. Nelson, & J. Warfield (Eds.), *Beyond classical pedagogy in elementary mathematics: The nature of facilitative change* (pp. 47–74). Mahwah, NJ: Lawrence Erlbaum.

Franke, M. L., Kazemi, E., & Battey, D. (2007). Mathematics teaching and classroom practice. In F. Lester (Ed.), *Second handbook of research on mathematics teaching and learning* (pp. 225–256). Reston, VA: National Council of Teachers of Mathematics.

Frankenstein, M. (1983). Critical mathematics education: An application of Paulo Freire's epistemology. *Journal of Education, 165*(4), 315–339.

Freire, P. (1970). *Pedagogy of the oppressed* (M. B. Ramos, Trans.). New York: Herder and Herder.

Gay, J., & Cole, M. (1967). *The new mathematics and an old culture.* New York: Holt, Rinehart, and Winston.

Gee, J. P. (1990). *Social linguistics and literacies: Ideology in discourse* (1st ed.). New York: Falmer.

Geertz, C. (1973). *The interpretation of culture.* New York: Basic Books.

Gergen, K. J. (1991). *The saturated self: Dilemmas of identity in contemporary life.* New York: Basic Books.

Gibson, J. J. (1986). The ecological approach to visual perception. Hillsdale, NJ: Lawrence Erlbaum.

Gonzalez, N. (1999). What will we do when culture does not exist anymore? *Anthropology and Education Quarterly, 30*(4), 431–435.

Gonzalez, N., Andrade, R., & Carson, C. (2001). Creating links between home and school mathematics practices. In E. McIntyre, A. Rosebery, & N. Gonzalez (Eds.), *Classroom diversity: Connecting curriculum to students' lives* (pp. 100–114). Portsmouth, NH: Heinemann.

Gonzalez, N., & Moll, L. (2002). Cruzando el Peunte: Building bridges to funds of knowledge. *Educational Policy, 16*(4), 623–641.

Gonzalez, N., Moll, L., Floyd-Tenery, M., Rivera, A., Rendon, P., Gonzales, R., et al. (1993). *Teacher research on funds of knowledge: Learning from households* (Educational Policy Report No. 6). Santa Cruz, CA: National Center for Research on Cultural Diversity and Second Language Learning.

Goodwin, C. (1981). *Conversational organization: Interaction between speakers and hearers.* New York: Academic Press.

Grabiner, J. (1997). The calculus as algebra, the calculus as geometry: LaGrange, MacLaurin, and their legacy. In R. Calinger (Ed.), *Vita mathematica: Historical research and integration with teaching* (pp. 131–143). Washington, DC: Cambridge University Press.

Grant, C. A., & Sleeter, C. E. (2003). *Turning on learning: Five approaches for multicultural teaching plans for race, class, gender, and disability* (3rd ed.). New York: John Wiley.

Greeno, J. G. (1991). Number sense as situated knowing in a conceptual domain. *Journal for Research in Mathematics Education, 22*(3), 170–218.

Greeno, J. G. (2006a). Authoritative, accountable positioning and connected, general knowing: Progressive themes in understanding transfer. *Journal of the Learning Sciences, 15*(4), 537–547.

Greeno, J. G. (2006b, July). *Learning as perspective taking: Conceptual alignment in the classroom.* Paper presented at the International Conference on the Learning Sciences, Bloomington, IN.

Greeno, J. G., & Hull, G. (2002). *Identity and agency in non-school and school worlds.* Manuscript submitted for publication.

Greeno, J. G., & Middle School Math Through Applications Program. (1998). The situativity of knowing, learning, and research. *American Psychologist, 53*(1), 5–26.

Greeno, J., Sommerfeld, M., & Wiebe, M. (2000). Practices of questioning and explaining in learning to model. In L. R. Gleitman & A. K. Joshi (Eds.), *Proceedings of the 22nd annual conference of the Cognitive Science Society* (pp. 669–674). Mahwah, NJ: Lawrence Erlbaum.

Gresalfi, M., & Cobb, P. (2006). Cultivating students' discipline-specific dispositions as a critical goal for pedagogy and equity. *Pedagogies: An International Journal, 1*(1), 49–57.

Guberman, S. R. (1996). The development of everyday mathematics in Brazilian children with little formal schooling. *Child Development, 67*(4), 1609–1623.

Gutiérrez, K. D. (2002). Studying cultural practices in urban learning communities. *Human Development, 45*, 312–321.

Gutiérrez, K. D., Baquedano-López, P., Alvarez, H. H., & Chiu, M. M. (1999). Building a culture of collaboration through hybrid language practices. *Theory Into Practice, 38*(2), 87–93.

Gutiérrez, K. D., Baquedano-López, P., & Tejada, C. (2000). Rethinking diversity: Hybridity and hybrid language practices in the third space. *Mind, Culture, and Activity, 6*(4), 286–303.

Gutiérrez, K. D., & Rogoff, B. (2003). Cultural ways of learning: Individual traits or repertoires of practice. *Educational Researcher, 32*(5), 19–25.

Gutiérrez, K. D., Rymes, B., & Larson, J. (1995). Script, counterscript, and underlife in the classroom: James Brown versus "Brown v. Board of Education." *Harvard Educational Review, 65*(3), 445–471.

Gutiérrez, R. (2002a). Beyond essentialism: The complexity of language in teaching mathematics to Latina/o students. *American Educational Research Journal, 39*(4), 1047–1088.

Gutiérrez, R. (2002b). Enabling the practice of mathematics teachers in context: Toward a new equity research agenda. *Mathematical Thinking and Learning, 4*(2/3), 145–187.

Gutstein, E. (2003). Teaching and learning mathematics for social justice in an urban, Latino school. *Journal for Research in Mathematics Education, 34*(1), 37–73.

Gutstein, E. (2006). *Reading and writing the world with mathematics: Toward a pedagogy for social justice.* London: Taylor and Francis.

Gutstein, E., Lipman, P., Hernandez, P., & de los Reyes, R. (1997). Culturally relevant mathematics teaching in a Mexican American context. *Journal for Research in Mathematics Education, 28*(6), 709–737.

Gutstein, E., & Peterson, B. (Eds.). (2005). *Rethinking mathematics: Teaching social justice by the numbers.* Milwaukee, WI: Rethinking Schools.

Hall, R. (2000). Following mathematical practice in design-oriented work. In C. Hoyles, C. Morgan, & G. Woodhouse (Eds.), Rethinking the mathematics curriculum (pp. 29–47). London: Routledge.

Hall, R., & Stevens, R. (1995). Making space: A comparison of mathematical work in school and professional design practices. In S. L. Star (Ed.), *The cultures of computing* (pp. 118–145). Cambridge, MA: Blackwell.

Hand, V. (2003). *Reframing participation: Meaningful mathematical activity in diverse classrooms.* Unpublished doctoral dissertation, Stanford University, Stanford, CA.

Hand, V. (2005, April). *Race, culture, and the construction of opposition in mathematics classrooms.* Paper presented at the meeting of the American Educational Research Association, Montreal, Canada.

Haycock, K. (2001). Helping all students achieve: Closing the achievement gap. *Educational Leadership, 58*(6), 6–11.

Heath, S. B. (1983). *Ways with words: Language, life and work in communities and classrooms.* Cambridge, UK: Cambridge University Press.

Heath, S. B., & McLaughlin, M. W. (1994). Learning for anything everyday. *Journal of Curriculum Studies, 26*(5), 471–489.

Hiebert, J., Carpenter, T. P., Fennema, B., Fuson, K. C., Wearn, D., & Murray, H. (1997). *Making sense: Teaching and learning mathematics with understanding.* Portsmouth, NH: Heinemann.

Hill, H. C., Schilling, S. G., & Ball, D. L. (2004). Developing measures of teachers' mathematics knowledge for teaching. *Elementary School Journal, 105*(1), 12–30.

Hill, H. C., Sleep, L., Lewis, J., & Ball, D. (2007). Assessing teachers' mathematics knowledge: What knowledge matters and what evidence counts? In F. Lester (Ed.), *Second handbook of research on mathematics teaching and learning* (pp. 111–156). Reston, VA: National Council of Teachers of Mathematics.

Horn, I. (2006). Lessons learned from detracked mathematics departments. *Theory Into Practice, 45*(1), 72–81.

Howard, G. (1999). *We can't teach what we don't know: White teachers, multiracial schools.* New York: Teachers College Press.

Hoyles, C., Noss, R., & Pozzi, S. (2001). Proportional reasoning in nursing practice. *Journal for Research in Mathematics Education, 32*(1), 4–27.

Hutchins, E. (1995). *Cognition in the wild.* Cambridge, MA: MIT Press.

Hutchins, E. (1997). Mediation and automatization. In M. Cole, Y. Engeström, & O. Vasquez (Eds.), *Mind, culture, and activity: Seminal papers from the Laboratory of Comparative Human Cognition* (pp. 338–353). Cambridge, UK: Cambridge University Press.

Jones, V. (2006). *Response to national policy: Perspective of government and business.* Paper presented at the conference titled "Raising the Floor: Progress and Setbacks in the Struggle for Quality Mathematics Education for All," Mathematical Sciences Research Institute, Berkeley, CA.

Kazemi, E., & Franke, M. (2004). Teacher learning in mathematics: Using student work to promote collective inquiry. *Journal of Mathematics Teacher Education, 7*(3), 203–235.

Kazemi, E., & Stipek, D. (2001). Promoting conceptual understanding in four upper-elementary mathematics classrooms. *Elementary School Journal, 102,* 59–89.

Khisty, L. L. (1995). Making inequality: Issues of language and meanings in mathematics teaching with Hispanic students. In W. G. Secada, E. Fennema, & L. B. Adajian (Eds.),

New directions for equity in mathematics education (pp. 279–297). New York: Cambridge University Press.

King, J. (Ed.) (2005). *Black education: A transformative research and action agenda for the new century.* Washington, D.C. : American Educational Research Association/Lawrence Erlbaum.

Kirshner, D., & Whitson, J. (1997). *Situated cognition: Social, semiotic, and psychological perspectives.* Mahwah, NJ: Lawrence Erlbaum.

Kroeber, A. L., & Kluckhohn, C. (1952). *Culture: A critical review of concepts and definitions.* New York: Random House.

Ladson-Billings, G. (1994). *The dreamkeepers: Successful teachers of African American children.* San Francisco: Jossey-Bass.

Ladson-Billings, G. (1995). But that's just good teaching! The case for culturally relevant pedagogy. *Theory Into Practice, 34*(3), 159–165.

Ladson-Billings, G. (1997). It doesn't add up: African American students' mathematics achievement. *Journal for Research in Mathematics Education, 28*(6), 697–708.

Ladson-Billings, G. (2006). From the achievement gap to the educational debt: Understanding achievement in U.S. schools. *Educational Researcher, 35*(7), 3–12.

Lampert, M. (1990). When the problem is not the question and the solution is not the answer: Mathematical knowing and teaching. *American Educational Research Journal, 27*(1), 29–63.

Lampert, M. (2001). *Teaching problems and the problems of teaching.* New Haven, CT: Yale University Press.

Lampert, M., & Ball, D. L. (1998). *Teaching, multimedia, and mathematics: Investigations of real practice.* New York. Teachers College Press.

Lave, J. (1988). *Cognition in practice: Mind, mathematics and culture in everyday life.* Cambridge, UK: Cambridge University Press.

Lave, J. (1993). Situating learning in communities of practice. In L. Resnick, J. Levine, & S. D. Teasley, (Eds.), *Perspectives on socially shared cognition* (pp. 63–85). Washington DC: American Psychological Association.

Lave, J., Murtaugh, M., & de la Rocha, O. (1984). The dialectic of grocery shopping. In B. Rogoff & J. Lave (Eds.), *Everyday cognition: Its development in social context* (pp. 67–94). Cambridge, MA: Harvard University Press.

Lave, J., & Wenger, E. (1991). Situated learning and legitimate peripheral participation. Cambridge, UK: Cambridge University Press.

Lemke, J. L. (1990). *Talking science.* Norwood, NJ: Ablex.

Lemke, J. L. (1995). *Textual Politics: Discourse and social dynamics.* London: Taylor and Francis.

Lemke, J. L. (2000). Across the scales of time: Artifacts, activities, and meanings in ecosocial systems. *Mind, Culture, and Activity, 7*(4), 273–290.

Lemke, J. L. (2002). Mathematics in the middle: Measure, picture, gesture, sign, and word. In M. Anderson, A. Sáenz-Ludlow, S. Zellweger, & V. Cifarelli (Eds.), *Educational perspectives on mathematics as semiosis: From thinking to interpreting to knowing* (pp. 215–234). Ottawa, ON: Legas.

Leontiev, A. N. (1978). *Activity, consciousness, and personality.* Englewood Cliffs, NJ: Prentice Hall.

Lerman, S. (1996). Intersubjectivity in mathematics learning: A challenge to the radical constructivist paradigm. *Journal for Research in Mathematics Education, 27*(2), 133–150.

Lerman, S. (2001). Cultural, discursive psychology: A sociocultural approach to studying the teaching and learning of mathematics. *Educational Studies in Mathematics, 46*(1/2), 87–113.

Lipka, J. (1994). Changing the culture of schooling: Navajo and Yup'ik cases. *Anthropology and Education Quarterly, 25*, 266–284.

Lipka, J. (2005). Math in a cultural context: Two case studies of a successful culturally based math project. *Anthropology and Education Quarterly, 36*(4), 367–385.

Lipka, J., & Mohatt, G. V. (1998). *Transforming the culture of schools: Yup'ik Eskimo examples. Sociocultural, political, and historical studies in education.* Mahwah, NJ: Lawrence Erlbaum.

Little, J. W. (2002). Locating learning in teachers' communities of practice: Opening up problems of analysis in records of everyday work. *Teaching and Teacher Education, 18*(8), 917–946.

Lockett, C., & Harrell, J. (2003). Racial identity, self-esteem, and academic achievement: Too much interpretation, too little supporting data. *Journal of Black Psychology, 29*(3), 325–336.

Lubienski, S. (2002). Research, reform, and equity in US mathematics education. *Mathematical Thinking and Learning, 4*(2/3), 103–125.

Ma, L. (1999). *Knowing and teaching elementary mathematics.* Mahwah, NJ: Lawrence Erlbaum.

Martin, D. (2000). *Mathematics success and failure among African-American youth.* Mahwah, NJ: Lawrence Erlbaum.

Martin, D. (2006a). Mathematics learning and participation as racialized forms of experience: African American parents speak on the struggle for mathematics literacy. *Mathematical Thinking and Learning, 8*, 197–229.

Martin, D. (2006b). Mathematics learning and participation in African American context: The co-construction of identity in two intersecting realms of experience. In N. Nasir & P. Cobb (Eds.), *Diversity, equity, and access to mathematical ideas* (pp. 146–158). New York: Teachers College Press.

Martin, D. (2007). *Researching race in mathematics education.* Manuscript submitted for publication.

Masingila, J. (1994). Mathematics practice in carpet-laying. *Anthropology and Education Quarterly, 25*(4), 429–462.

Mehan, H. (1979). *Learning lessons: Social organization in the classroom.* Cambridge, MA: Harvard University Press.

Mehan, H., Hubbard, L., & Villanueva, I. (1994). Forming academic identities: Accommodation without assimilation among involuntary minorities. *Anthropology and Education Quarterly, 25*(2), 91–117.

Moje, E., Ciechanowski, K., Ellis, L., Carrillo, R., & Collazo, T. (2004). Working toward third space in content area literacy: An examination of everyday funds of knowledge and discourse. *Reading Research Quarterly, 39*(1), 38–70.

Moll, L. C. (2000). Inspired by Vygotsky: Ethnographic experiments in education. In C. D. Lee & P. Smagorisky (Eds.), *Vygotskian perspectives on literacy research* (pp. 256–268). New York: Cambridge University Press.

Moll, L. C., Amanti, C., Neff, D., & Gonzalez, N. (1992). Funds of knowledge for teaching: A qualitative approach to connect homes and classrooms. *Theory Into Practice, 31*(1), 132–141.

Moll, L., Tapia, J., & Whitmore, K. (1993). Living knowledge: The social distribution of cultural resources for thinking. In G. Salomon (Ed.), *Distributed cognitions: Psychological and educational considerations* (pp. 139–163). New York: Cambridge University Press.

Moschkovich, J. N. (1999). Supporting the participation of English language learners in mathematical discussions. *For the Learning of Mathematics, 19*, 11–19.

Moschkovich, J. N. (2000). Learning mathematics in two languages: Moving from obstacles to resources. In W. Secada (Ed.), *Changing the faces of mathematics: Vol. 1. Perspectives on multiculturalism and gender equity* (pp. 85–93). Reston, VA: National Council of Teachers of Mathematics.

Moschkovich, J. N. (2002). A situated and sociocultural perspective on bilingual mathematics learners. *Mathematical Thinking and Learning, 4*(2/3), 189–212.

Moschkovich, J. N. (2007). Examining mathematical discourse practices. *For the Learning of Mathematics, 27*(1), 24–30.

Moses, B., & Cobb, C. (2001). *Radical equations: Math literacy and civil rights.* Boston, MA: Beacon.

Murrell, P. (1994). In search of responsive teaching for African American males: An investigation of students' experiences of middle school mathematics curriculum. *Journal of Negro Education, 63*(4), 556–569.

Nasir, N. (1996). *Statistics in practice: African American youth in the play of basketball.* Unpublished master's thesis, University of California, Los Angeles.

Nasir, N. S. (2000). Points ain't everything: Emergent goals and average and percent understanding in the play of basketball among African American students. *Anthropology and Education Quarterly, 31*, 283–305.

Nasir, N. S. (2002). Identity, goals, and learning: Mathematics in cultural practice. *Mathematical Thinking and Learning, 4*(2/3), 213–248.

Nasir, N. S., Atukpawu, G., O'Connor, K., & Davis, M. (2007). *How racial identity meanings matter for racial identity, academic identity, mathematical identity, and math achievement among urban high school students.* Manuscript submitted for publication.

Nasir, N. S., & Cobb, P. (Eds.). (2006). *Improving access to mathematics: Diversity and equity in the classroom.* New York: Teachers College.

Nasir, N. S., & Hand, V. (2006). Exploring sociocultural perspectives on race, culture, and learning. *Review of Educational Research, 76*(4), 449–475.

Nasir, N. S, & Hand, V. (in press). From the court to the classroom: Opportunities for engagement, learning, and identity in basketball and classroom mathematics. *Journal of the Learning Sciences.*

National Council of Teachers of Mathematics. (1991). *Professional standards for teaching mathematics.* Reston, VA: Author.

National Council for Teachers of Mathematics. (2000). *Principles and standards for school mathematics.* Reston, VA: Author.

National Education Association. (1970). Report of committee on college education requirements. Washington, DC: National Academy Press. (Original work published 1899).

National Research Council. (1989). *Everybody counts.* Washington, DC: National Academy Press.

Nemirovsky, R., DiMattia, C., Ribeiro, B., & Lara-Meloy, T. (2005). Talking about teaching episodes. *Journal of Mathematics Teacher Education, 8*(5), 363–392.

Nieto, S. (2004). *Affirming diversity.* Boston: Pearson.

Noddings, N. (1994). Does everybody count? *Journal of Mathematical Behavior, 13*, 89–104.

Nunes, T., Schliemann, A., & Carraher, D. (1993). *Street mathematics and school mathematics.* Cambridge, UK: Cambridge University Press.

Oakes, J. (1990). *Multiplying inequalities: The effects of race, social class, and tracking on opportunities to learn mathematics and science.* Santa Monica, CA: RAND.

Oakes, J., Joseph, R. & Muir, K. (2003). Access and achievement in mathematics and science: Inequalities that endure and change. In J. A. Banks & C.A. Banks (Eds.), *Handbook of research on multicultural education* (2nd ed., pp. 69–90). San Francisco: Jossey-Bass.

O'Connor, M. C., & Michaels, S. S. (1993). Aligning academic task and participation status through revoicing: Analysis of a classroom discourse strategy. *Anthropology and Education Quarterly, 24*(4), 318–335.

O'Halloran, K. (2000). Classroom discourse in mathematics: A multisemiotic analysis. *Linguistics and Education, 10*(3), 359–388.

O'Halloran, K. (2003). Educational implications of mathematics as a multisemiotic discourse. In M. Anderson, A. Sáenz-Ludlow, S. Zellweger, & V. Cifarelli (Eds.), *Educational perspectives on mathematics as semiosis: From thinking to interpreting to knowing* (pp. 185–214). Ottawa, ON: Legas.

Orfield, G., Frankenberg, E. D., & Lee, C. (2003). The resurgence of school segregation. *Educational Leadership, 60*(4), 16–20.

Pea, R. (1993). Practices of distributed intelligence and designs for education. In G. Salomon (Ed.), *Distributed cognitions: Psychological and educational considerations* (pp. 47–87). New York: Cambridge University Press.

Perry, T., Steele, C. M., & Hilliard, A., III. (2003). *Young, gifted, and Black: Promoting high achievement among African American students.* Boston: Beacon.

Pimm, D. (1987). *Speaking mathematically: Communication in mathematics classrooms.* London: Routledge.

Powell, A., & Frankenstein, M. (1997). *Ethnomathematics: Challenging Eurocentrism in mathematics education.* New York: State University of New York Press.

Putnam, R., & Borko, H. (2000). What do new views of knowledge and thinking have to say about research on teacher learning? *Educational Researcher, 29*(1), 4–15.

Rittenhouse, P. S. (1989). The teacher's role in the mathematical conversation: Stepping in and stepping out. In M. Lampert & M. L. Blunk (Eds.), *Talking mathematics in school: Studies of teaching and learning* (pp. 163–189). Cambridge, UK: Cambridge University Press.

Rogoff, B. (1990). *Apprenticeship in thinking: Cognitive development in social context.* Oxford, UK: Oxford University Press.

Rogoff, B. (1994). Developing understanding of the idea of communities of learners. *Mind, Culture, and Activity, 1,* 209–229.

Rogoff, B., & Lave, J. (Eds.). (1984). *Everyday cognition: Its development in social context.* Cambridge, MA: Harvard University Press.

Rommetveit, R. (1987). Meaning, context, and control. *Inquiry, 30,* 77–99.

Rosebery, A. S., Warren, B., & Conant, F. R. (1992). Appropriating scientific discourse: Findings from language minority classrooms. *Journal of the Learning Sciences, 2,* 61–94.

Saxe, G. B. (1988). The mathematics of child street vendors. *Child Development, 59*(5), 1415–1425.

Saxe, G. B. (1991). *Culture and cognitive development.* Mahwah, NJ: Lawrence Erlbaum.

Saxe, G. B. (1999). Cognition, development, and cultural practices. *New Directions for Child and Adolescent Development, 83,* 19–35.

Saxe, G. B., & Esmonde, I. (2005). Studying cognition in flux: A historical treatment of Fu in the shifting structures of Oksapmin mathematics. *Mind, Culture, and Activity, 12*(3/4), 171–225.

Saxe, G. B., Taylor, E. V., McIntosh, C., & Gearhart, M. (2005). Representing fractions with standard notation: A developmental analysis. *Journal for Research in Mathematics Education, 36,* 137–157.

Schegloff, E. (1992). Repair after next turn: The last structurally provided defense of intersubjectivity in conversation. *American Journal of Sociology, 97,* 1295–1345.

Schifter, D. (2001). Learning to see the invisible: What skills and knowledge are needed in order to engage with students' mathematical ideas? In T. Wood, B. Scott Nelson, & J. Warfield (Eds.), *Beyond classical pedagogy: Teaching elementary mathematics* (pp. 109–134). Mahwah, NJ: Lawrence Erlbaum.

Schoenfeld, A. H. (2002). Making mathematics work for all children: Issues of standards, testing, and equity. *Educational Researcher, 31*(1), 13–25.

Schoenfeld, A. H. (2004). The math wars. *Educational Policy, 18*(1), 253–286.

Scribner, S. (1984). Studying working intelligence. In B. Rogoff & J. Lave (Eds.), *Everyday cognition: Its development in social context* (pp. 9–40). Cambridge, MA: Harvard University Press.

Scribner, S. (1997). Mind in action: A functional approach to thinking. In M. Cole, Y. Engeström, & O. Vasquez (Eds.), *Mind, culture, and activity: Seminal papers from the Laboratory of Comparative Human Cognition* (pp. 354–368). Cambridge, MA: Cambridge University Press. (Original work published 1983)

Secada, W. G. E. (1992). The reform of school mathematics in the United States. *International Journal of Educational Research, 17*(5), 399–516.

Sellers, R., Chavous, T., Cooke, D. (1998). Racial ideology and racial centrality as predictors of African American college students' academic performance. *Journal of Black Psychology, 24,* 8–27.

Sfard, A., & Cole, M. (2003). *Literate mathematical discourse: What is it and why should we care?* Retrieved February 18, 2007, from http://lchc.ucsd.edu/vegas.htm

Silver, E., Smith, M., & Nelson, B. (1995). The Quasar project: Equity concerns meet mathematics reform in the middle school. In W. G. Secada, E. Fennema, & L. Byrd (Eds.). *New directions for equity in mathematics education* (pp. 9–56). Cambridge, UK: Cambridge University Press.

Sleeter, C. E. (1997). Mathematics, multicultural education, and professional development. *Journal for Research in Mathematics Education, 28*(6), 680–696.

Sowder, J. (2007). The mathematics education and development of teachers. In F. Lester (Ed.), *Second handbook of research on mathematics teaching and learning* (pp. 157–224). Reston, VA: National Council of Teachers of Mathematics.

Spillane, J. P., & Zeuli, J. S. (1999). Reform and teaching: Exploring patterns of practice in the context of national and state mathematics reforms. *Educational Evaluation and Policy Analysis, 21*, 1–27.

Steele, C., & Aronson, J. (1995). Stereotype threat and the intellectual test performance of African Americans. *Journal of Personality and Social Psychology, 69*(5), 797–811.

Stinson, D. W. (2006). African American male adolescents, schooling (and mathematics): Deficiency, rejection, and achievement. *Review of Educational Research, 76*(4), 477–506.

Strutchens, M. E., & Silver, E. A. (2000). NAEP findings regarding race/ethnicity: The students, their performance, and their classrooms. In E. A. Silver & P. A. Kenney (Eds.), *Results from the seventh mathematics assessment of the National Assessment of Educational Progress* (pp. 45–72). Reston, VA: National Council of Teachers of Mathematics.

Supple, A., Ghazarian, S., Frabutt, J., Plunkett, S., & Sands, T. (2006). Contextual influences on Latino adolescent ethnic identity and academic outcomes. *Child Development, 77*(5), 1427–1433.

Tate, W. F. (1994). Mathematics standards and urban education: Is this the road to recovery? *Educational Forum, 58*, 380–390.

Tate, W. F. (1995). Returning to the root: A culturally relevant approach to mathematics pedagogy. *Theory Into Practice, 34*(3), 166–173.

Tate, W. F. (1997). Race-ethnicity, SES, gender, and language proficiency trends in mathematics achievement: An update. *Journal for Research in Mathematics Education, 28*(6), 652–679.

Taylor, E. V. (2004, April). *Engagement in currency exchange as support for multi-unit understanding in African-American children.* Paper presented at the meeting of the American Educational Research Association, San Diego, CA.

Taylor, E. V. (2007). *Purchasing practice of low-income students: The relationship to mathematical development.* Manuscript submitted for publication.

Thomas, D., Townsend, T., & Belgrave, F. (2003). The influence of cultural and racial identification on the psychosocial adjustment of inner-city African American children in school. *American Journal of Community Psychology, 32* (3/4), 217–228.

Twain, N. (Producer), & Avildsen, J. G. (Director). (1989). *Lean on me* [Motion picture]. United States: Warner Bros.

Van Oers, B. (2001). Educational forms of initiation in mathematical culture. *Educational Studies in Mathematics, 46*(1/3), 59–85.

Varela, F., Thompson, E., & Rosch, E. (1991). *The embodied mind: Cognitive science and human experience.* Cambridge, MA: MIT Press.

Vygotsky, L. S. (1962). *Thought and language.* Cambridge, MA: MIT Press.

Vygotsky, L. S. (1978a). Interaction between learning and development. In M. Cole, V. John-Steiner, S. Scribner, & E. Souberman (Eds.), *Mind in society: The development of higher psychological processes* (pp. 79–91). Cambridge, MA: Harvard University Press.

Vygotsky, L. S. (1978b). *Mind in society: The development of higher psychological processes.* Cambridge, MA: Harvard University Press.

Warren, B., Ballenger, C., Ogonowski, M., Rosebery, A. S., & Hudicourt-Barnes, J. (2001). Rethinking diversity in learning science: The logic of everyday sense-making. *Journal of Research in Science Teaching, 38*(5), 529–553.

Warren, B., Rosebery, A. S., & Conant, F. R. (1994). Discourse and social practice: Learning science in bilingual classrooms. In D. Spener (Ed.), *Adult literacy in the United States.* Washington, DC: Center for Applied Linguistics and Delta Systems.

Wax, M. L. (1993). How culture misdirects multiculturalism. *Anthropology & Education Quarterly, 24*(2), 99–115.

Wells, G., & Arunz, R. M. (2006). Dialogue in the classroom. *Journal of the Learning Sciences, 15*(3), 379–428.

Wertsch, J. V. (1991). A sociocultural approach to socially shared cognition. In L. B. Resnick, J. M. Levin, & S. Teasley, D. (Eds.), *Perspectives on socially shared cognition* (1st ed., pp. 85–100). Washington, DC: American Psychological Association.

Wertsch, J. V. (1998). *Mind as action.* New York: Oxford University Press.

Wilson, S. M., & Berne, J. (1999). Teacher learning and the acquisition of professional knowledge: An examination of research on contemporary professional development. In A. Iran-Nejad & P. D. Pearson (Eds.), *Review of research in education* (Vol. 24, pp. 173–209). Washington, DC: American Educational Research Association.

Wood, D. (1992). Teaching talk: How modes of teacher talk affect pupil participation. In K. Norman (Ed.), *Thinking voices* (pp. 203–214). London: Hodder and Stoughton.

Yackel, E., & Cobb, P. (1996). Sociomathematical norms, argumentation, and autonomy in mathematics. *Journal for Research in Mathematics Education, 27*(4), 458–477.

Zarate, M., Bhimji, F., & Reese, L. (2005). Ethnic identity and academic achievement among Latino/a adolescents. *Journal of Latinos and Education, 4*(2) 95–114.

Chapter 7

Multimodality and Literacy in School Classrooms

CAREY JEWITT

Institute of Education, University of London

The characteristics of contemporary societies are increasingly theorized as global, fluid (Bauman, 1998), and networked (Castells, 2001). These conditions underpin the emerging knowledge economy as it is shaped by the societal and technological forces of late capitalism. These shifts and developments have significantly affected the communicational landscape of the 21st century. A key aspect of this is the reconfiguration of the representational and communicational resources of image, action, sound, and so on in new multimodal ensembles. The terrain of communication is changing in profound ways and extends to schools and ubiquitous elements of everyday life, even if these changes are occurring to different degrees and at uneven rates (A. Luke & Carrington, 2002). It is against this backdrop that this critical review explores school multimodality and literacy and asks what these changes mean for being literate in this new landscape of the 21st century. The two key arguments here are that it is not possible to think about literacy solely as a linguistic accomplishment and that the time for the habitual conjunction of language, print literacy, and learning is over. As Kress (2003) writes,

It is no longer possible to think about literacy in isolation from a vast array of social, technological and economic factors. Two distinct yet related factors deserve to be particularly highlighted. These are, on the one hand, the broad move from the now centuries long dominance of writing to the new dominance of the image and, on the other hand, the move from the dominance of the medium of the book to the dominance of the medium of the screen. These two together are producing a revolution in the uses and effects of literacy and of associated means for representing and communicating at every level and in every domain. (p. 1)

My claim here is that how knowledge is represented, as well as the mode and media chosen, is a crucial aspect of knowledge construction, making the form of representation integral to meaning and learning more generally. That is, the ways in which something is represented shape both *what* is to be learned, that is, the curriculum content, and *how* it is to be learned. It follows, then, that to better understand learning and teaching in the multimodal environment of the contemporary classroom, it is essential to explore the

Review of Research in Education
February 2008, Vol. 32, pp. 241–267
DOI: 10.3102/0091732X07310586
© 2008 AERA. http://rre.aera.net

ways in which representations in all modes feature in the classroom. The focus here, then, is on multimodality on the representations and the learning potentials of teaching materials and the ways in which teachers and students activate these through their interaction in the classroom.

This review, organized in three parts, does not provide an exhaustive overview of multimodal literacies in and beyond classrooms. Instead, it sets out to highlight key definitions in an expanded approach to new literacies, then to link these to emergent studies of schooling and classroom practice. The first part outlines the new conditions for literacy and the ways in which this is conceptualized in the current research literature. In particular, it introduces three perspectives: New Literacies Studies, multiliteracies, and multimodality. Contemporary conceptualizations of literacy in the school classroom are explored in the second part of the chapter. This discussion is organized around themes that are central to multimodality and multiliteracies. These include multimodal perspectives on pedagogy, design, decisions about connecting with the literacy worlds of students, and the ways in which representations shape curriculum knowledge and learning. Each of these themes is discussed in turn, drawing on a range of examples of multimodal research. The third and final part of the chapter discusses future directions for multiple literacies, curriculum policy, and schooling.

My focus here is primarily on the school classroom as a site of literacy and learning. Discussion of out-of-school literacies, in particular, how technologies are remaking the boundaries between sites such as home and school, is an intensive focus of current work (Lam, 2006; Lankshear, Peters, & Knobel, 2002; Leander, 2001, 2007; Marsh, 2003; Pahl, 1999; Sefton-Green, 2006). This work demonstrates how learning traverses institutional boundaries, seeping across and at times collapsing the boundaries between in-school and out-of-school literacies (Leander, 2001). Indeed, the trajectories of students, teachers, and knowledge across and between these spaces are not only physical, but they are also social, emotional, and cognitive (Nespor, 1994). Sefton-Green's (2006) *Review of Research in Education* review of how current media debates frame children's interactions with media as pedagogic argues that interest in children's media culture opens wider notions of learning beyond education and school systems. In that same volume, Lam (2006) examines how learning and teaching take place in new digital landscapes and other translocal contexts as a way of understanding the opportunities and challenges of the contemporary era. Both pieces argue that the contemporary conditions of communication and digital technologies create the movement of images and ideas across geographical and social spaces in ways that affect how young people learn and interact.

I begin by focusing on the new conditions of literacy and how these have affected contemporary conceptualizations of literacy and learning. Key terms and ideas associated with multiliteracies and multimodality are introduced and outlined to provide a theoretical backdrop and context to the discussion of multiple literacies.

NEW CONDITIONS AND CONCEPTUALIZATIONS FOR LITERACY

The concept of multiple literacies has emerged in response to the theorizations of the new conditions of contemporary society. This can be broadly characterized by a number of factors, including the accelerated transnational flows of people as well as information, ideology, and materials in contexts in which knowledge is highly situated, rapidly changing, and more diverse than ever before (Appadurai, 1990; Kalantzis, Cope, & Harvey, 2003). Alongside this, the representational and communicational environment is also changing in highly significant ways that can be described as a shift from print as the primary medium of dissemination toward digital media (Boulter, 1999; Kress, 2003). Against this backdrop, writing as the dominant mode is increasingly brought into new textual relationships with, or even exchanged for, visual and multimodal forms of representation (Bachmair, 2006). In consequence, new relationships between production and dissemination are made possible across a range of media and technologies, remaking the conditions and functions of authorship and audience (Adkins, 2005; Lury, 1993). In scientific endeavor, new digitalized workplaces, and new culture industries, disciplinary boundaries and expertise are increasingly blurred, reformulated, or collapsed in ways that open up new configurations and types of texts.

The potential impact of new social and material conditions on communication and education is profound. They allow for new possibilities and constraints for representation and communication. They also place emergent demands on the communicative repertoires of people to participate in the global economy as well as on the construction of knowledge and the performativity of self in face-to-face, local, and virtual contexts (Bauman, 1998; Beck, 1992; Butler, 1990; Leander & Wells Rowe, 2006). Hence, multimodal representation and globalization are close companions, providing new foundations for processes of remixing and remaking genres and modal resources in ways that produce new forms of global and commercial processes. These in turn are constantly personalized, appropriated, and remade in local workplaces, communities, and institutions.

These multimodal processes and their global scale and impact on local situated literacies are exemplified by a recent ethnographic study on the ascendancy of the Nike Swoosh as a global cultural icon. Bick and Chiper (2007) examined how the Nike Swoosh performs in the cultural contexts of two cities in Romania and Haiti, cities and countries that sit on the fringes of global capitalism. The Nike global trademark has been appropriated, transformed, and remade locally in Romania and Haiti in ways that express people's identities across numerous places—from logos on jackets and trucks to inscriptions on tombstones. This process of remaking happens across different scales and sites. Pahl's (2003) U.K. ethnographic study of three 5- to 7-year-old boys examines how meanings are constructed in multimodal texts made in the home. She demonstrates how young children consume and appropriate Pokemon and Yugio characters across television, film, and game cards, making and remaking features in their own cards and activities. Buckingham and Sefton-Green's (2004) study of Pokemon shows how theories of learning and multimodal meaning making can be applied to the relationship between media and user.

These studies suggest that the conditions for available resources and designs are dynamic, with distributed tools for transforming and (re)distributing these resources and designs in development and transition (Leander, 2007). Taken together, this work highlights the changing requirements of communication, literacy, and knowledge economy of the 21st century. The implications for the educational system differ significantly from those of the nation-bound industrial economies of the recent past, with the industrial–print nexus continuing to dominate literacy policy and practice in schools (Gee, 2004; Gee, Hull, & Lankshear, 1996; A. Luke & Woods, in press). Against this changing communicational landscape, which can be typified by diversity and plurality, the dominant view of literacy as a universal, autonomous, and monolithic entity is at best dated and in need of reconsideration.

Literacy to Literacies

Literacy is increasingly pluralized and multiplied in educational discourses. It is, however, important to note that literacy studies has a long history of attending to the visual character of some scripts and symbol systems. Furthermore, the fields of New Literacies Studies (hereafter, NLS), multiliteracies, and multimodality each build on a range of traditions, disciplines, and histories. These include critical literacy and discourse studies (Fairclough, 1992; Foucault, 1980; Lankshear & McLaren, 1993; A. Luke, 1996; Street, 1995), genre studies based on systemic functional linguistics (Cope & Kalantzis, 1993; Freedman & Medway, 1994a, 1994b), gender studies (Cranny-Francis, 1993), and critical cultural studies (Hall, 1997).

Nonetheless, within this broader picture, NLS has been central in the theorization of the complexity of literacies as historically, socially, and culturally situated practice (Barton, Hamilton, & Ivanic, 2000; Street, 1998). Key to this attempt to rethink literacy is the analytical focus of NLS on literacy events and literacy practices with texts in people's everyday lives and the bid to document emergent literacies across different local contexts. This marks a shift in focus from the idea of literacy as an autonomous neutral set of skills or competencies that people acquire through schooling and can deploy universally to a view of literacies as local and situated. This shift underlines the variable ideological character of school literacy practices, that is, how the official institutional construction of literacy may or may not dovetail with emergent practices in homes and communities. Furthermore, this perspective enables an analysis of how the social practices of literacy in schools realize social structures through the formation of specific power relations, forms of knowledge, and identities (A. Luke & Carrington, 2002).

Within NLS, there is increasing recognition of the complex interaction between local and global literacies (Brant & Clinton, 2006). For example, Marsh's (2003, 2005) ethnographic studies on new technologies and the literacy practices of nursery school children (ages 2.5 to 4 years) describe how global discourses of Disney mediate children's everyday literacy practices. Marsh mapped children's mediascapes and patterns in media use through interviews, literacy diaries during a month period, questionnaires, and home observation with 62 families. She concludes that global media has a fundamental role in very young children's identity formation and construction of themselves as literate. This and other studies highlight the need to be sensitive to how children's literacy practices traverse physical and virtual spaces (Alvermann, Hagood, & Williams, 2001; Leander, 2007; Pahl, 1999). The empirical description of children's and adolescents' new mediascapes is essential to understanding how they negotiate social identity in relation to the economies and cultures of late modernity.

Multiliteracies

The term *multiliteracies* was introduced to educational researchers by the New London Group (1996). In this key position paper, a team of leading literacy educators called for literacy pedagogy to respond to the changing social conditions of global capitalism, in particular, the new demands it places on the workforce. The multiliteracies model highlights two interconnected changes in the communicational landscape that impinge on what it means to be literate. These are the increasing significance of cultural and linguistic diversity in a global economy and the complexity of texts with respect to nonlinguistic, multimodal forms of representation and communication, particularly, but not limited to, those affiliated with new technologies. Multiliteracies has evolved into an international pedagogic agenda for the redesign of the educational and social landscape. To this end, multiliteracies sets out to stretch literacy beyond the constraints of official standard forms of written and spoken language to connect with the culturally and linguistically diverse landscapes and the multimodal texts that are mobilized and circulate across these landscapes. Therefore, multiliteracies can be seen simultaneously as a response to the remaking of the boundaries of literacy through current conditions of globalization and as a political and social theory for the redesign of the curriculum agenda. It is an educational agenda that calls for the redrawing of the boundaries and relationships between the textual environments toward the ideological purposes of the design of new egalitarian and cosmopolitan social futures (A. Luke & Carrington, 2002).

Although sharing many of the assumptions of NLS, multiliteracies has at its center the idea of a social and culturally responsive curriculum. It is informed by political pedagogies of literacy, including Paulo Freire and Donaldo Macedo's (1987) construction of literacy as "reading the word and reading the world," Australian approaches to the teaching of writing as genre (Cope & Kalantzis, 1993), and critical literacy and pedagogy models. The transformative agenda of multiple literacies sets out to redesign the social futures of young people across boundaries of difference. With this explicit agenda for social change, the pedagogic aim of multiliteracies is to attend to the multiple and multimodal texts and wide range of literacy practices that students are engaged with. It therefore questions the traditional monologic relationship between teacher and student, setting out to make the classroom walls more porous and to take the students' experiences, interests, and existing technological and discourse resources as a starting point. From this perspective, the social and political goal of multiliteracies is to situate teachers and students as active participants in social change, the active designers of social futures (Cope & Kalantzis, 2000). Overall, multiliteracies pedagogy can be described as developing models of effective critical engagement with student values, identity, power, and design. I return to illustrations of this agenda later in this chapter.

Yet even in its plural form, this and other emergent approaches to literacy continue to be strongly focused on competencies and written lettered representation (Kress,

1997; Marsh, 2005). In what follows, I turn to focus on literacies that move beyond the cognitive and analytic processes of written and spoken language.

Multimodality

Multimodality (Kress, Jewitt, Ogborn, & Tsatsarelis, 2001; Kress & van Leeuwen, 2001), like multiliteracies, has emerged in response to the changing social and semiotic landscape. Key to multimodal perspectives on literacy is the basic assumption that meanings are made (as well as distributed, interpreted, and remade) through many representational and communicational resources, of which language is but one (Kress & van Leeuwen, 2001). This and other aspects of multimodal theory are outlined by Kress and van Leeuwen's (2001) *Multimodal Discourse.* Multimodality attends to meaning as it is made through the situated configurations across image, gesture, gaze, body posture, sound, writing, music, speech, and so on. From a multimodal perspective, image, action, and so forth are referred to as *modes*, as organized sets of semiotic resources for meaning making.

To some extent, multimodality can be described as an eclectic approach, although it is primarily informed by linguistic theories, in particular, the work of Halliday's (1978) social semiotic theory of communication and developments of that theory (Hodge & Kress, 1988). Multimodality has developed in different ways in the decade since its inception around 1996. Although a linguistic model was seen as wholly adequate for some to investigate all modes, others set out to expand and reevaluate this realm of reference, drawing on other approaches (e.g., film theory, musicology, game theory). Multimodality thus extends past the traditional psychological and linguistic foundations of print literacy to draw from anthropological, sociological, and discourse theory (specifically, the work of Barthes, 1993; Bateson, 1977; Foucault, 1991; Goffman, 1979; and Malinowski, 2006; among others). In addition, the influence of cognitive and sociocultural research on multimodality is also present, particularly, Arnheim's (1969) models of visual communication and perception.

From decades of classroom language research, much is known about the semiotic resources of language; however, considerably less is understood about the semiotic potentials of gesture, sound, image, movement, and other forms of representation. A number of detailed studies on specific modes have helped begin to describe these semiotic resources, their material affordances, organizing principles, and cultural referents. Alongside Kress and van Leeuwen's (1996) work on images, other key works that contribute to an evolving "inventory" of semiotic modal resources include van Leeuwen's (1999) work on the materiality of the resources of sound (e.g., pitch, volume, breathing, rhythm, and so on). Martinec's (2000) work focuses on movement and gesture. With a focus on writing as a multisemiotic resource, Kenner's (2004) ethnographic case studies show how young bilingual learners (Spanish, Chinese, and Arabic) use directionality, spatiality, and graphic marks to realize meaning and express identities.

From this work, we know that people draw on their available modal resources to make meaning in specific contexts. Furthermore, the resources come to display regularities through everyday patterns of use. The more a set of resources has been used in the social life of a particular community, the more fully and finely articulated its regularities and patterns become. Consequently, any given mode is contingent on fluid and dynamic resources of meaning, rather than static skill replication and use. These modes are constantly transformed by their users in response to the communicative needs of communities, institutions, and societies: New modes are created, and existing modes are transformed. Flewitt's (2006) multimodal study of preschool classroom interaction demonstrates the strong link between the communicative demands of a context and the modes in use. Flewitt's research draws on data from ethnographic video case studies of young children communicating at home and in a preschool play-group. By focusing on all modes of communication (talk, gesture, movement, gaze, and so on), she is able to scrutinize young children's multifunctional uses of different modalities in meaning making. Flewitt's "analysis of children's uses of different semiotic modes as intentional, socially organized activity in the construction of meaning" argues against "pathologizing the absence of talk" (p. 47). This work, then, offers a different account of classroom language by locating the analysis of classroom talk in the broader context of children's total multimodal resources.

The concept of *modal affordance* refers to what it is possible to express and represent easily. How a mode has been used, what it has been repeatedly used to mean and do, and the social conventions that inform its use in context shape its affordance. Where a mode "comes from" in its history of cultural work becomes its provenance, shaping available designs and uses (Kress, 2003). Furthermore, the affordance of a mode is material, physical, and environmental. For instance, an image in the form of graphic marks on a two-dimensional surface offers different potentials for the expression and representation of meaning than the affordances of speech in the form of sounds. Physical, material, and social affordances affiliated with each mode generate a specific logic and provide different communicational and representational potentials. For instance, the sounds of speech occur in time, and this temporal context and location shape what can subsequently be done with (speech) sounds. This makes the logic of sequence in time unavoidable for speech: One sound has to be uttered after another, one word after another, one syntactic and textual element after another. This sequence therefore constitutes an affordance, producing the possibility and constraint for putting things first or last or somewhere else in a sequence. It can be said, therefore, that the mode of speech is governed by a temporal logic. By contrast, the affordances of (still) images can be understood as being governed by the logic of space and simultaneity. In sum, multimodality approaches affordance as a complex concept connected to the material *and* the cultural, social, historical use of a mode.

Alongside the assumption that all modes in a communicative event or text contribute to meaning, models of multimodality assert that all modes are partial. That is, all modes, including the linguistic modes of writing and speech, contribute to the construction of meaning in different ways. Therefore, no one mode stands alone in the process of making meaning; rather, each plays a discrete role in the whole. This has significant implications in terms of epistemology and research methodology: Multimodal understandings of literacy require the investigation of the full multimodal ensemble used in any communicative event. The imperative, then, is to incorporate the nonlinguistic representation into understandings of literacy in the contemporary classroom. It also has implications for contemporary theorizations of literacy pedagogy, curriculum, and learning in the school classroom.

MULTIPLE LITERACIES IN THE SCHOOL

The question of how theories of literacy are understood and used by educational policymakers and educators directly affects classroom teaching and learning. In the processes of "doing" literacy, students learn "what counts as literacy" (Unsworth, 2001). The classroom construction of literacy occurs through the legitimation and valuing of different kinds of texts and interactions.

Multiple literacies challenges the current organization of traditional schooling. It gives rise to questions of the relevance of dominant models of literacy as it is currently taught in the majority of schools around the world in relation to the communicative and technological requirements of contemporary, digitalized society. Generally speaking, school literacy is criticized where it continues to focus on restrictive print- and language-based notions of literacy (Gee, 2004; Lam, 2006; Leander, 2007; Sefton-Green, 2006). In this context, what is positioned as *new* literacy practices in the school may be *new to school* but are often already well established among many young people (Lankshear & Knobel, 2003). Increasingly, the communicational landscapes occupied by young people originate outside of the school. This has entailed changes in family life, the traditional access point for children's texts, enabling new ways for children to be the producers and disseminators of information (Carrington, 2005).

Five key themes that draw on multiple and multimodal literacies are discussed in the next section of the chapter: pedagogy, design, the new literacy worlds of students, shapes of knowledge, and shapes of learning. Given emergent local foci of multimodal practices, research in this area is small scale, ethnographic, and case based—with limited analysis on the impact on teaching and learning. Much of this work is descriptive and offers detailed inventories of the resources used by students and teachers, how these are designed into multimodal ensembles, and the implications for the construction of school knowledge, pedagogic relations, and learner positions.

Pedagogy

The theoretical frameworks of multiple literacies have been taken up, adapted, and extended to explore literacy development in a variety of contexts. This has led to the articulation of multiliteracies theory into pedagogic models and practices. Five factors are identified as key to these pedagogic models (Cope & Kalantzis, 2000; New London Group, 1996). Although the following pedagogic sequences are not necessarily linear, the model begins with immersion in an acquisition-rich environment. The starting point is that of the students and a focus on *situated practice* based on the learners' experiences. Situated practice involves the immersion in students' experience and the designs available to them in their life worlds. *Overt instruction* is the key pedagogic strategy through which students are taught metalanguages of design, that is, the systematic and explicit teaching of an analytical vocabulary for understanding the design processes and decisions entailed in systems and structures of meaning. *Critical framing* is key to this pedagogical model, explicitly connecting meanings to their social contexts and purposes to interpret and interrogate the social and cultural context of designs. *Transformed practice* is the fourth pedagogic factor, which relates to the ways in which students recreate and recontextualize meaning across contexts (Cope & Kalantzis, 2000). This model has evolved and been developed by others; for example, Unsworth (2001) offers a pedagogic learning development cycle model that combines systemic functional grammar with the four stages of multiliteracies pedagogy. The model is designed to make the multimodal design of texts explicit to children as one way to explore the construction of stories in both conventional print and digital formations (Unsworth, 2001; Unsworth, Thomas, Simpson, & Asha, 2005). Some examples of research on multimodality and multiliteracies and learning are discussed below to show multiple literacies in action.

Significant pedagogic work is realized through a range of modes. Ethnographic studies of multimodal practices of science and English classrooms in the United Kingdom show that this holds true even in a curriculum context such as English where talk and writing dominate the classroom (Kress et al., 2005). The Multimodal Production of School English project (Kress et al., 2005) involved detailed video recording and observation of 9 English teachers in three inner London schools, interviews with teachers and students, and the collation of texts made and used in the classroom. The project shows the complex ways in which image, gesture, gaze, interaction with objects, body posture, writing, and speech interact in the classroom production of school subject knowledge. The School English project highlighted how students and teachers coproduce notions of ability, resistance, and identity in the classroom through their nonverbal interaction. The way in which classroom displays, space, furniture, and artifacts were designed to realize versions of English as a school subject was also documented. This research showed that the work of interpreting school English is beyond language and requires the ability to make sense of a range of modes and the relationships between them. It also highlighted the complex multimodal identity work that students are engaged with in the classroom.

A considerable body of work has been undertaken in schools within the diverse cultural and linguistic context of South Africa. Both examples demonstrate how multimodality and multiliteracies can be operationalized as pedagogic practice.

The Arndale Alphabet (Janks & Comber, 2006), *A is for Arndale, A is for Atteridgeville*, was set up as a shared, cross-continent primary school project that situated literacy in the students' experiences and concerns of their neighborhoods (one in South Africa and one in Australia). The project recruited learners and teachers from Grades 3 to 6. Data involved videotapes, teacher and student interviews, and students' work with alphabet books. Working with a class of students in each school, an alphabet book was made that drew on the students' experiences and use of available designs. The students were given overt instruction through the analysis of the representational meanings in other alphabet books, analysis of how image and word were organized, and identification of patterned meanings. The students undertook deconstructive and reconstructive critical analysis and text design. The students engaged in critical interpretations of the social and cultural contexts of designs of meanings. The project moved beyond literacy as recount to literacy as explanation across differences, involving the students in the work of imagining the other class in another context as the audience for their book. Such pedagogic projects that involve the development of students' literacy resources and a range of modes of representation in conscious ways have been developed to provide students with tools for critical analysis and the redesign of meaning. By establishing a transnational pedagogic context, Janks and Comber (2006) document the impact of new, multimodal pedagogic spaces and practices on social and cultural identities.

In the Olifantsvlei fresh stories project, Stein (2003) undertook a literacy project for 6 months with Grades 1 and 2 teachers and students at a Johannesburg primary school that serves children of unemployed and migrant families living in informal settlements. She worked with multimodal literacy practices and pedagogy through a systematic use of different semiotic modes to develop forms of learning beyond language. The project explored the relations between creativity, multimodal pedagogy, representation, and learning. Student case studies involved observation and interviews, students' use of 2-D drawings, writing, 3-D figures, spoken dialogues, multimodal play, and performance to create narratives of identity and culture. The focus was on the representation of doll and child figures and their symbolic meanings. Stein describes the children's transformation and recontextualization of culturally and historically situated practices of these representations. Stein argues that multimodal pedagogy enables the assertion of student identity, cultural practices, and community to enter the school context in ways that are significant for literacy and teaching.

Significant research has been conducted on the technologization of school literacies and pedagogy (e.g., Alvermann et al., 2001; Cope & Kalantis, 2000; Lankshear & Knobel, 2003; Leander, 2007; Marsh, 2005; Unsworth et al., 2005). It explores and theorizes the nature of image and text relations in literacy narratives, relationships between book- and computer-based versions of texts, and the role of online communities of various kinds in the critique as well as the interpretation and generation of new forms of multimodal and digital narratives and literacies. This work often describes new forms of literacy in an attempt to remap the territory of new literacies and the kinds of practices that help move across it, such as blogging and culture jamming (Lankshear & Knobel, 2003; Sefton-Green & Sinker, 2000). Knobel and Lankshear (2006; Lankshear & Knobel, 2003), for example, discuss the potential of new forms of literacy for learning, including blogging and the use of wikis. Their detailed case describes the out-of-school technoliteracies of young people and the extent to which it is possible or desirable to import these out-of-school cultural practices into the classroom for school literacies such as extensive writing. They identify the difficulties in bringing out-of-school cultural practices into the classroom, including the compulsory character of schooling, the individualization of student identities, the lack of authentic purposeful activities, and how interests and technoliteracies are socially constituted and regulated through adult control in classroom spaces. They conclude that different conditions and new virtual and institutional spaces will be required to enable their effective use (Knobel & Lankshear, 2006; Owen, Grant, Sayers, & Facer, 2006).

Although it is the case that multimodal research and multiliteracies are often strongly associated with the introduction of new technologies, this perspective is relevant for the analysis of traditional classroom technologies. These approaches have been used to examine the ways in which teachers orchestrate a range of modal resources, gesture, gaze, position, posture, action with books and boards, and talk in the classroom. In addition, multimodal research has examined the ways in which language policy, student identities, official curriculum, examination, and school knowledge are mediated through multimodal communication in the classroom (Bourne & Jewitt, 2003; Kenner & Kress, 2003; Kress et al., 2001, 2005). Comparative multimodal analysis has examined how these patterns vary across systems and cultural contexts (Bhattacharya et al., 2007). Working across three cities (Delhi, Johannesburg, and London), Bhattacharya and colleagues (in press) undertook in-depth case studies focused on English lessons (with students ages 14 to 15 years), interviewing teachers and students. The multimodal analysis examined and compared how texts were pedagogically activated, circulated, and drawn into practices and processes to be remade and transformed by students. The project identified ways in which language policy, modal conventions and practices, teacher identities, and subject histories were realized through the textual cycle of the classrooms. Here, the multimodal approach engages with the entire classroom event as a kind of text in motion in which multimodal texts are caught up and actualized in the stream of practice. Work within this framework tends to be analytical research that identifies the conditions and processes of learning, the ways in which students draw on practices, the social categories and practices that inform pedagogy, and so on, rather than presenting a theory of pedagogy itself.

In light of a general move toward explicitness and transparency in educational approaches to literacy, pedagogic models drawing on multimodality and multiple literacies are often accompanied by overt instruction and critical framing. These aim to introduce technical metalanguages for different modes. This has led to efforts to augment the technical language of linguistics (e.g., genre, grammar, and discourse) to describe and explain the semiotic contribution of each mode to multimodal texts (Unsworth, 2001). Substantial theoretical descriptions of the dynamics of interaction between image and language have been offered, for example, by the early work of Kress and van Leeuwen (1996) and Lemke's (1998) work on science textbooks. Recent work by Kress and Bezemer (2007) examines contemporary curriculum materials and investigates the learning gains and losses of different multimodal ensembles. This work draws on a corpus of learning resources for secondary school in science, mathematics, and English from the 1930s, the 1980s, and the first decade of the 21st century as well as digitally represented and online learning resources from the year 2000 onward. It sets out to provide a social semiotic account of the changes to the design of these learning resources (textbooks and websites, etc.) and of their epistemological and social-pedagogic significance. Through investigation of the relationship between image, writing, action, and layout, they show that image and layout are increasingly meshed in the construction of content. Research on the multimodal resources of digital screen-based texts also supports this finding: that in complex multimodal texts, the boundaries between modes blur and mesh in new configurations. These affect the construction of knowledge and identities (Jewitt, 2006; Leander, 2007; Pelletier, 2005, 2006).

This potential remaking of modes in new contexts raises fundamental questions about how best to articulate their relationships (Kress et al., 2001, 2005; Kress & van Leeuwen, 2001; Unsworth, 2006). It also places a crucial reservation on the teaching of a technical metalanguage of multimodal meaning: the risk of a static grammar of modes that cannot account for the power of context and the transformative character of systems of making meaning. In addition, this has the unintended potential to produce another form of "Big 'L' Literacy" (Gee, 1990), a normative resource to regulate meaning and uphold and reproduce dominant cultural practices across all modes. There is the potential, then, for the overt teaching of metalanguages to reproduce the links between available designs (e.g., genres) and their cultural and ideological relations and functions. As parts of the social system of communication, all modes work to realize culture and power. Image is as ideological and as power laden as word. This raises important issues about how image, word, and design of other modes are understood as available resources for meaning making in the classroom.

Design

Traditional pedagogic models for print literacy are based on the acquisition and mastery of sets of established practices, conventions, and rules. The multiple literacies model holds that limited models of skill and competence are incomplete. Models of critique encourage students to be aware of principles of dominant notions of literacy, to question these and the ideologies they represent, and to explore the production of innovation and change. In contrast to traditional competence-based pedagogic models, the New London Group (1996) and Kress (2000) identify the notion of design as an active and dynamic process central to communication in contemporary society. Design refers to how people make use of the resources that are available at a given moment in a specific communicational environment to realize their interests as sign makers. In this way, design has been used to theorize the relationships between modes, pedagogy, and context and to understand the changed dispositions toward information and knowledge. It foregrounds the importance of multimodal resources, the sign maker's social purpose and intentions, context, and audience (Kress, 2000, 2003). Furthermore, the New London Group (1996) draws on design to understand the multimodal organization of social relations through the design of communicative resources, including linguistic meaning, visual meaning, audio meaning, and gestural and spatial meaning. Although design incorporates some of the aims inherent in models of competence and critique, it provides a more flexible and dynamic analytical frame that responds to the interests of the sign maker and the demands of the context.

As a research tool and way of thinking about literacy as process, design is useful in analyzing how materials in the classroom (e.g., textbooks and the materials displayed on interactive whiteboards [IWB], media images) include image and writing and other modes, in configurations that distribute meanings across the boundaries of modes and multimodal connections. This is but one part of pedagogic design, which can be conceptualized as a semiotic chain of meanings across different contexts. From this perspective, design can be used to refer both to teachers' pedagogic designs of learning processes and students' designed constructions of meaning. This includes student engagement, interaction, and remaking of the available designs. For instance, a printed textbook, website, or other teaching material is designed, accessed by the school or teacher, downloaded, and printed or perhaps scanned and made digital to be displayed on a screen or IWB. These materials may then be manipulated by students, annotated by the teacher, and saved and stored. Later, the remade text may be accessed, reappraised, and reworked on an Internet revision site. The emphasis is on the activities and processes of interpretation students engage with, framing how students make sense of ("read") multimodal signs in the classroom as itself a process of redesign. Moss's (2003) ethnographic research focuses on U.K. students working with junior-age nonfiction texts as objects of design. Moss's research draws on a large data set built up from a series of interlinked ethnographic research projects consisting of observations, field notes, interviews, and conversations about reading between boys perusing nonfiction together in informal contexts within the school classroom. Her research shows how the layout structure of factual books affects the ways in which it is read by young boys, specifically, how they sequence the page, create reading paths, negotiate their roles and identities in the classroom, and identify opportunities for performing being a reader. In so doing, Moss's study begins to describe and theorize the broader set of practices of remaking, "mashing," and "remixing" in the digital, multimodal mediascape.

Efforts to retheorize the design of school pedagogy have drawn on notions of design. Kress and Selander (in press) have developed a model, learning design sequences, which is based on the need to move away from designed information and teaching sequences involving prefabricated learning resources, formalized work, and strict timetables, which, they argue, place the teacher as the conduit of knowledge. They argue instead for the need to shift toward learning design sequences that encompass the multiplicity of learning. Their model attempts to map critical incidents across learning as sign making, moments of transformation, representation, and presentation. This work, although at an early stage, sets out a model of pedagogy based on the theorization of the redesign (transformation) of knowledge.

Literacy Worlds of Students

Recent ethnographic studies suggest that conventional print literacy pedagogy proceeds independently of the everyday multimodal social and communicative worlds of many urban children (e.g., Marsh, 2006). It is axiomatic in NLS that schools construct and shape students' literacy in particular ways for specific social purposes. It follows that the extent to which school literacies across the curriculum engage, incorporate, or colonize students' out-of-school literacy practices is a matter of power; it is about what is allowed to count, to whom, and for what purpose. The physical and social boundaries of schools and the curriculum vary in their porosity. Although there are clearly many similarities across schools, it is nonetheless true that in general, primary schools are differentially permeable than secondary schools, London schools are differentially positioned in relation to community practice than those in Delhi or Johannesburg, and subject English is differentially permeable than school science. Furthermore, different texts and experiences are allowed into these different schools and legitimated and mobilized for pedagogic purposes in distinct ways. An example of this is shown in the research on the multimodal production of school English introduced earlier. That study demonstrated how teachers' multimodal design of the classroom environment conveyed what was to be done and learned in it and the place of students' life worlds of "English" (Jewitt & Jones, 2005; Kress et al., 2005). Across the nine teacher case studies, the design of the room connected with the life worlds of students and teachers in different ways. For instance, one case study teacher covered her wall with posters of films and music stars brought in by the students, another displayed carefully framed elements drawn from curriculum and examination documents, and yet another displayed posters of poetry and art exhibitions. These different versions of English (and Englishness) placed students in different relationships to the curriculum content of English and in turn attempted to connect or disconnect English in specific ways to the experiences of those students in ways that are significant for the construction of literacy.

It is the often the case that connecting with students' literacy experiences and knowledge translates into teachers' permitting authorized fragments of students' lives into the classroom. Multiliteracies, as the earlier discussion of pedagogy illustrates, calls for a reexamination of the relationship between school and out-of-school communicative environments. Stein and Mamabolo (2005) undertook detailed ethnographic research in Johannesburg on the connections between home and school and literacy practices across these sites. Drawing on three case studies, they show in detail how families draw on their own resources to negotiate home–school relationships in distinct and different ways. Their findings suggest that this is a key part of the construction of literate identities of students and how they build and negotiate their educational and literacy pathways through school and community life. Marsh's (2006) studies investigate young children's (ages 2.5 to 4 years) mediascapes to identify the complex multimodal communicative practices that they are engaged with in the home. Her focus is on understanding the functions that these digital media expressions have in maintaining the social relations of the family, accessing knowledge, self-expression, and the development of literacy skills. She documents how migrant students reappropriate and use media designs in creative play, family life, and home–school transitions. These studies suggest the possibilities for curriculum that connects with students' out-of-school multimodal repertoires. The questions of where to draw these boundaries, when, and who gets the power to draw are central to the development of new pedagogic approaches to traditional and emergent literacies.

Current pedagogies built on multiple literacies encourage teachers to build classroom work on students' knowledge, experiences, and interests. This involves integrating students' knowledge of narrative characterization and structure developed from visual modes (films, videos, picture books) into the planning and creation of narratives, either print based (e.g., Millard, 2005; Newfield, Andrew, Stein, & Maungedzo, 2005) or multimedia multimodal narratives (e.g., Burn and Parker, 2003; Marsh, 2006; Pahl,

2003). Multiple literacies projects build stories based on and arising from young people's lives and experiences and cultural forms of representation to engage with and gain access to student agency, cultural memory, and home and school learning within local contexts. Newfield and colleagues (2005) undertook a multimodal pedagogy intervention and research project in a Soweto secondary school to develop the students' literacy practices. The starting point for this project was the literacy worlds of the students, infused with many different languages, cultures, music, and performance not usually heard or seen in the classroom. These provided the focus for poetry writing, featuring the design and production of an anthology. The use of performance and visual arts opened up the voices of the students identified as reluctant writers.

Gee's (2003) work on video games and learning connects multimodality, multiliteracies, and the out-of-school literacy worlds of children and young people. He sees game playing as a new space for learning and what it means to be a learner in the 21st century. His theorization of games and learning is based on his own experiences of game play (including observing his son's game playing). Through this account, he identifies 36 learning principles present in game designs that he suggests could be useful for rethinking more formal education. Sefton-Green (2006) questions the generalizability of such an approach. He asks if games are a kind of literacy, whether it is a kind of literacy that can "do anything other than support the playing of more games" (p. 291)

Across different contexts, the concern of multiple literacies is with the promotion of a pluralized notion of literacy and forms of representation and communication to help students negotiate a broader range of text types and modes of persuasion (Morgan & Ramanathan, 2005). This makes it increasingly important for schools to attend to the literacy practices of students and diverse ways of making meaning, in particular, the multilingual, the multimodal, and the digital. In short, there is a need for further investigation of literacy practices as an intertextual web of contexts and media rather than isolated sets of skills and competences. Because of the simultaneity of different modes in everyday community and educational contexts, the decontextualized study of particular practices, assuming their universality and transfer, has clear limitations.

A multimodal approach to literacy focuses on the representations of students across different sites of learning and raises questions for how curriculum knowledge is organized, classified, represented, and communicated. It asks how different representations and modes of communication shape knowledge as well as locate and connect knowledge to the world. It queries what and how teachers and students can do with school knowledge. The focus of the following section is on how these shapes of knowledge affect the interpretative and meaning-making demands made on students.

Shapes of Curriculum Knowledge

As noted at the onset of this review, one of the characteristics of the contemporary communicational landscape is a shifting and remaking of disciplinary boundaries. In the U.K. classroom, for instance, this is realized in a general move to build connections across discourses of specialized knowledges and everyday knowledges, an emphasis on context-based learning, and the introduction of new cross-curricular projects. This redefining of the boundaries and frames of school knowledge raises interesting challenges for literacies as they are shaped by disciplinary practices and histories. One aspect of this is the reframing and blurring of the boundaries between texts, media, and contexts—which in turn produces new and unsettled genres (Kress, 2003; Moss, 2003). Increasingly, for example, the concept and shape of the book is remade as it is being fully linked to websites and online resources. Leander (2007) has described how textbooks are organized by structures in which the visual dominates. He goes on to examine learning resources that introduce new relationships between image and action and bodies through the use of avatars. Such representations make new demands on students in relation to both how knowledge is represented and communicated and how those representations circulate and are mobilized across time and space (Nespor, 1994). In this technological context, the challenge is for the curriculum to engage with epistemologies that reflect radically different knowledge structures and learning processes (Lankshear & Knobel, 2003).

Image and other nonlinguistic modes take on specific roles in the construction of school knowledge. Kress et al. (2001) undertook an ethnographic study of London school science classrooms. This involved observation and video recording of nine science classes across a half-term topic unit, interviews with students and teachers, and analysis of the texts used and made during the lessons. A key finding of the research was that different modes of representation led to radically different constructions of the scientific and natural world. For example, representation of a cell in the science classroom as an image or through writing, in color or black and white, or as 3-D model or an animated sequence on a CD-ROM or website makes available and foregrounds different aspects of the concept of cell. Each of these representational forms makes different demands on the learner. There was also evidence that different modes have differential potential effects for learning, the shaping of learner identities, and how learners create pathways through texts. The choice of mode, then, is central to the epistemological shaping of knowledge and ideological design. What can be done and thought with image or writing or through action differs in ways that are significant for learning. In this regard, the long-standing focus on language as the principal, if not sole, medium of instruction can at best offer a very partial view of the work of communicating in the classroom.

Furthermore to this, the technology of production, dissemination, and communication that is chosen is also key to the shaping of curriculum knowledge. These curriculum and pedagogic choices and configuration of modes systematically favor specific patterns of interaction and artifact production. Therefore, the teacher's and students' interaction with the materiality of modes (an inextricable meshing of the physical materiality of a mode and its social and cultural histories) and the facilities of technologies shape the production of school knowledge.

There is, then, an increasing interest in investigating the role that different semiotic modes or sign systems have in classroom communication. Multimodal research has shown, for example, that images feature in significant ways across the curriculum, as sound, animation, and multimodal configurations are increasingly understood as key to how people learn in the science classroom (Kress et al., 2001; Lemke, 1998; Marquez,

Izquierdo, & Espinet, 2005; Prain & Waldrip, 2006; Scott & Jewitt, 2003). Even in the subject English classroom, where common sense would have it that language is the dominant communicative means, the meanings of language, speech, and writing are embedded in a multimodal ensemble. There, significant, often contradictory, meanings are realized visually or through gesture, proximics, image, and so forth (Kress et al., 2005).

Across both print and digital media, the relationship between image and writing in educational materials (e.g., textbooks, websites, etc.) appears to be in historical transition (Jewitt, 2006; Kress & Bezemer, 2007). This change relates both to quantity and, perhaps more importantly, to the quality and function of images in a text (Jewitt, 2002). Images are no longer illustrative of writing on the page or screen; rather, a phenomenon may now be introduced and established visually. On-screen resources frequently place image, action, sound, and other modes (including the body) in new intertextual relationships that redefine and foreground space and time (Leander, 2007). The relationship between modes in learning materials raises important questions for learning, all of which require a better understanding of the gains and losses realized through the representation of curriculum concepts in one mode as compared with another (Kress & Bezemer, 2007).

Although these issues are not exclusive to the use of new technologies, the multimodal facilities of digital technologies enable image, sound, and movement to enter the classroom in new and significant ways. These new multimodal configurations can affect pedagogic design, text production, and interpretative practices. The visual character of writing comes to the fore on screen to function as objects of literacy in fundamentally different ways than it does on the page (Boulter & Grusin, 1998; Jewitt, 2002, 2005). Jewitt's (2002) case study on the transformation from printed novel to novel as CD-ROM showed how the visual character of writing on screen combined with the dominance of image alongside action serves to restructure texts and fragment and break up forms of writing. A study of the use of IWBs in London secondary schools (Moss et al., 2007) suggests that this kind of modularization can be seen across the curriculum as information breaks up across the screen. However, similar findings have emerged on the organization of time in nontechnologized classrooms. This breaking up of information into bite-size chunks occurs regardless of media and mode as a pedagogic response to the management of information and attention (Jewitt, Moss, & Cardini, 2007). Another potential resource of digital technologies is the mode of hypertext, which embeds writing and image (and other modes) into web-like patterns and layers of information and genres that make meaning making a process of navigation and choice and create new resources (and demands) on meaning making (Jewitt, 2002; Lemke, 2002; C. Luke, 2003; Zammit, 2007).

Multimodal approaches to shapes of knowledge raise serious issues about teachers' access to materials (e.g., websites, CD-ROMs, games and simulations, textbooks and worksheets) and technologies and how these are used in the classroom. Freitas and Castanheira (2006) studied the use of textbook images in 1st-year high school biology classrooms (36 students ages 17 to 30 years old) in Brazil. In these classrooms, only 20% of students were able to afford to purchase the textbook adopted for the class; the effect is that the graphic representations are available only to the teacher. Their research shows that it is essential to better understand how teachers' display and use of the textbook representations, their classroom talk, and gesture all interact in the construction of scientific knowledge. Drawing on video recordings of classroom interaction, interviews with the teacher and students, field notes on classroom interaction, and copies of notebooks, textbooks, and tests, they found that teachers' coordinated use of semiotic modes to supplement each other in the construction of biology concepts was relied on by students to infer conventionalized meanings. At the same time, however, they found that the contradiction between the frames of reference in teachers' gesture and talk and the visual image in the textbook led to breakdowns in students' understandings of the concepts taught.

The issue of breakdowns and multimodal interpretation across resources is equally salient for students working independently with a CD-ROM or watching a teacher model a process on the whiteboard or visualizer. The point is that learners, whatever their age, may engage with some modes and not others or privilege (trust) one mode over another. For example, case study observation of 11- and 12-year-old students using an animation of particles in a science lesson found that students interpreted the visual information independently from the written information provided on the CD-ROM screen (Jewitt, 2006). This appeared to be because of the CD-ROM's emphasis on empirical reality, observation, and visual evidence supported by the classroom practices within school science. Many students missed important cues about the observed sequence. This finding serves to emphasize the need to examine literacies through the "tension between the meaning potential of the text, the meaning potential of the context in which it will be read and the resources that the reader brings to that exercise" (Moss, 2003, p. 85). When using learning resources that demand the interpretation of movement, image, and color, students are engaged in a complex process of sense making. Multimodal analysis thus offers a way to broaden the lens of educational research and investigate the role of image and other nonlinguistic modes as well as to better understand the role of language as one multimodal resource.

The examples here highlight the importance of understanding how knowledge is shaped through the teacher's choice of one mode over another and the consequent constraints and possibilities those choices introduce. In this way, the representation of curriculum knowledge can be viewed as a process of pedagogic multimodal design, of the matching of target knowledges with particular modal affordances. In this process, meanings are made and remade (designed) when representations are enlivened in the classroom and again when students engage with them for the purposes of making their own meanings in lesson practices.

Learning

Seeing the communicational landscape of the classroom through a multimodal lens has significant implications for conceptions and processes of learning. Thinking about learning as a process of design and choice of representation gives a renewed focus on the role of the learner. Design, diversity, and multiplicity emphasize the meaning-making practices and interpretative work of students. From this perspective, the multimodal texts and artifacts that students make can be viewed as one kind of sign of learning, a material trace of semiosis. These texts can be understood as material instantiations of students' interests, their perception of audience, and their use of modal resources mediated by overlapping social contexts. The interpretative work of students is reshaped through their engagement with a range of modes, image, animation, hypertext, and layered multimodal texts. In such a view, students need to learn how to recognize what is salient in a complex multimodal text, how to read across the modal elements in a textbook or IWB, how to move from the representation of a phenomenon in an animation to a static image or written paragraph, and how to navigate through the multiple paths of a text. These complex tasks—as against traditional taxonomies of print skills—are central to multimodal learning and development. Learning increasingly involves students in working across different sites of expression, negotiating and creating new flexible spaces for planning, thinking, hypothesizing, testing, designing, and realizing ideas (Jewitt, 2006).

New skills for reading, finding information, authenticating information, and manipulating, linking, and recontextualizing information are demanded in this multimodal symbol-saturated environment (Beavis, 2006; Kress, 2003; Leander, 2007; A. Luke, 1996). Along with the choice of what mode to read, the structure of many digital texts opens up options about where to start reading a text—what reading path to take. This is a question that is intrinsically linked to how the relationship between modes and layout (itself an emergent mode) mediates the practices of reading and writing. The multimodal design of texts in the contemporary digital landscape often offers students different points of entry into a text and alternative possible paths through a text, highlighting the potential for readers to *remake* a text via their reading of it. The reader is involved in the task of finding and creating reading paths through the multimodal, multidirectional texts on the screen—an openness and fluidity of structure that seeps onto the page of printed books (Kress, 2003; Moss, 2001). Writing, image, and other modes combine to convey multiple meanings and encourage the reader to reject a single interpretation and to hold possible multiple readings of a text (Coles & Hall, 2001). In addition, new technologies make different kinds of cultural forms available, such as computer games and websites.

Flexible, interactive, and relatively fluid hypertexts offer the ability to redefine reader, author, and text relations (as the reader constructs the text in reading it). The ability to work fluently across many modes and "historically discrete domains" is required by new technologies (Sefton-Green & Reiss, 1999, p. 2). These facilities combine to increasingly align reading with the production and consumption of images alongside writing. The conceptual shift demanded by hypertext is, C. Luke (2003) suggests, from one of "collection to connection" (p. 400), a move that underlies the production of complex hybrid semiotic systems and new repertoires and demands for literacy. In this rich semiotic environment, a digital novel can be a multimodal configuration of music and songs, voices, sketches, maps and photographs, video clips, and written prose. Complex multimodal texts set the conditions for students to remake genres, to read texts variously as a musical, a short film, a comic book, or any other genre (Jewitt, 2002).

In addition to changing the work of interpretation, new technologies offer the possibility of new spaces for publication and dissemination. This has the potential to build new relationships between readers and writers in a manner that challenges and breaks down some of the traditional distinctions between reader and writer. Online fan-fiction forums, for example, enable children to move between various identity categories, such as writer, reviewer, or editor of other fans' stories; writing mentor involved in coaching other writers, adding paragraphs and offering suggestions; a summary writer, writing summaries for stories posted on the site; illustrator, making graphic art for others' stories; a critic, rating and commenting on posted stories; or a collaborative writer, working as a member of a team. These open up new spaces for identity play and for reflecting on audience and process, which are important for thinking of literacy. The ways in which people use language and make sense is inextricably linked to the beliefs and values of particular communities and the sense of self. A change in discourse practices, Gee (2003, 2004) says, potentially marks a change of identity. Accordingly, as many of the studies reviewed here show, multimodal learning involves the ongoing design and redesign of identities across the social and cultural practices of meaning making.

Learning often involves adopting a specialist language, an epistemological shift leaving one world of experiences for another. This can be expressed as both a loss and a gain of new possibilities and new identities. Any design of learning needs to make clear both the gains and how these are to be offset against what is to be lost (Gee, 2003; Kress, 2003; Kress & Bezemer, 2007). In the context of contemporary theories of education and communication, learning is increasingly discussed in terms of the creation of particular dispositions and orientations to the world rather than people who are in command of a body of knowledge. Accordingly, success at multimodal learning can be coupled with the ability to be autonomous and self-directed designers of learning experiences (Gee, 2004), to possess problem-solving skills with multiple strategies for tackling a task, and to have a flexible solutions orientation to knowledge (Cope & Kalantzis, 2000). The increasing recognition of literacy as a social practice that evolves around the situated interests of people suggests the need to "acknowledge the ways in which we position children within these social practices and landscapes" (Carrington, 2005, p. 121).

The five interconnected themes introduced and discussed above—pedagogy, design, the literacy worlds of students, shapes of knowledge, and multimodal models of learning—feature prominently in the emergent literature on multimodality.

FUTURE DIRECTIONS

This review combined the perspectives of models of multiliteracies and multimodality to examine the character of literacy in the communicational landscape of the 21st century. In doing so, it has highlighted some of the new possibilities and constraints for representation and communication that this landscape may generate in the school classroom. Central to these are the new demands placed on the literacy practices and communicational repertoires of students in terms of their capacities to participate in the global knowledge economy, education, and everyday life. These practices potentially transform how reading, writing, meaning making, and literacy more generally are understood. The studies here have stressed the multimodal character of literacy in the contemporary era and the need to uncouple the traditional conjunction of language and learning. Much of the work reviewed here has been of necessity small scale and case-based, tabling new theories and developing new research methods for observing pedagogy and curriculum across modalities that are still in formation. They raise significant questions for curriculum and pedagogy, and they point to the limitations of research methods that have heretofore focused on language and print as principal learning media. Although some educational systems now officially recognize the importance of multiliteracies and multimodality (e.g., state curricula in Australia, South Africa, and Canada), the implications of this work for teacher education and curriculum policy are still emerging.

Research within multiliteracies and multimodal design provides pedagogic models, principles, and strategies for the classroom. Teachers and policymakers can reflect on, adopt, and adapt these toward developing situated pedagogic approaches that connect with contemporary multimodal literacy practices. Two key aims of these models are, on one hand, to better understand and connect with students' literacy worlds and mediascapes and, on the other, to build on these to develop students' explicit understanding of a broad range of multimodal systems and their design. Both these strategies require educational policy, curriculum, and teachers to place students as active participants at the center of the classroom (at least to some extent). Pedagogy can be seen as a process of design.

Pedagogic understanding of students' mediascapes demands the adoption of strategies for engaging with the literacy worlds of students and their interests and desires. The theoretical and pedagogic focus of multimodality and multiliteracies can support teachers in engaging with the resources that students bring into the classroom. This includes understanding students as sign makers, the texts they make as designs of meaning, and the meaning-making processes that they are engaged in. These can give insights into the kinds of resources that students have access to (as well as those that they do not). Rethinking the role of the learner in literacy in this way raises the question of how to design the relationship between literacy spaces in school and out of school. These are regulated by curriculum and educational policy in different ways: with an increasing acknowledgment in early childhood literacy curriculum of the centrality of students' background knowledge and home practice but little explicit acknowledgment of their multimodal resources.

Furthermore, these connections and disconnections are re-mediated by teachers and schools in different local contexts for different purposes. Teachers, curriculum designers, and policymakers can begin to take the porosity of the classroom or school boundaries (physical, emotional, and technological) as a pedagogic resource to be designed in different ways, depending on their purpose. What is it that it is useful to connect or disconnect with? Why and to what ends? These basic curriculum questions return us to the key finding of this review: that the classroom is one node in the complex intertextual web of the communicational landscape of young people *even when it appears isolated and autonomous.* Indeed, the classroom may increasingly involve, as it does currently in relation to some online spaces, the remaking of the connections and boundaries of different spaces of learning and literacy. A key issue then becomes what kinds of artifacts, modes, and literacy are legitimated in different spaces, and what is enabled to flow and move across these spaces? This is particularly important in the contemporary digital era (at least in some global contexts) where the modal dominance of writing- and print-based medium of school stands in stark contrast to the multimodal spaces of leisure (e.g., games, film, online spaces) out of school.

Multimodality and multiliteracies can help to support the pedagogic task of developing students' explicit understandings of a broad range of multimodal systems and the design of these. The need is to move away from a monocultural and monomodal view of literacy. One way in which teachers, curriculum, and policy can respond to this task is to broaden the diversity of signs and cultural meanings that circulate in the classroom. Multimodal texts may be used by teachers in the classroom as the basis for critical engagement, redesign, or the explicit teaching of how modes construct meaning in specific genres. Teachers may design explicit teaching on a range of modal resources, concentrating, for example, on the main semiotic resources of image. As in the case of language, this will produce norms and grammarlike rules that may later need to be critiqued if the pedagogic focus on diversity and plurality is to be realized. In the New London Group (1996) model, and in much of the U.K., South African, and U.S. work discussed here, multimodality has been linked to an agenda for social justice, equity, and access for all learners but can unintentionally negate the reality that all modes realize ideology and power relations. As a multimodal and global context dominated by corporate and mass media communications, the ideological functions of modes and how these are associated with power and elite forms of literacy are central problematics.

A multimodal approach to shapes of knowledge helps to highlight the particular affordances and resistances of learning resources. This brings to the fore the questions of what curriculum resources can be designed to do (and not do) and what teachers and students actually do with multimodal texts in the classroom. These are important design decisions that affect the selection and shaping of knowledge. For instance, the ways in which teachers design and use pedagogic materials shape how students can remake a text through its possibilities and resistances or how they can navigate the designed relationship of image and writing and identify possible reading paths. These are everyday design decisions that students and teachers make constantly in the classroom. At another level, they are decisions that curriculum developers and policymakers are also engaged in, including through the possibilities for interaction and identity formation that are designed into a curriculum, the interpretative demands that these make on students, and the criteria and activities for assessing this. Multimodal research offers ways of making the design of these decisions explicit and sheds light on breakdowns in understanding and the variety of readings of a text by a class of students. How teachers and students use gaze, body posture, and the distribution of space and resources produces silent discourses in the classroom that affect literacy.

Multimodality offers teachers the potential to reflect on their pedagogic use of the resources of their body, to critique and redesign these aspects of their practice.

A multimodal perspective highlights the complex pedagogic work of designing curriculum knowledge across modes in the classroom. Teachers as well as curriculum designers and policymakers may employ multimodal tools (such as modal resource or modal affordance) to reflect on how image, action, and other modes feature in the classroom. Multimodality offers new ways to think about learning via a focus on meaning making as a process of design. It approaches communication as a process in which students (as they are socially situated and constrained) make meanings by selecting from, adapting, and remaking the range of representational and communicational resources (including physical, cognitive, and social resources) available to them in the classroom. Through understanding how people select modal resources, multimodality emphasizes the dynamic character of meaning making toward an idea of change and design. In this way, meanings, as well as meaning making resources, are constantly reconfigured and newly remade through the social work of the sign maker. Rethinking literacy beyond language can support teachers, curriculum, and educational policy in the work of connecting the school, children, young people, and the demands of the contemporary communicational landscape.

REFERENCES

Adkins, L. (2005). The new economy, property and personhood. *Theory Culture Society, 22*(1), 111–130.

Alvermann, D. E., Hagood, M. C., & Williams, K. B. (2001). Images, language, and sound: Making meaning with popular culture texts. *Reading Online.* Retrieved October 12, 2007, from http://www.readingonline.org/newliteracies/action/alvermann/index.html

Appadurai, A. (1990). Disjuncture and difference in the global cultural economy. *Theory, Culture and Society, 7,* 295–310.

Arnheim, R. (1969). *Visual thinking.* Berkeley and Los Angeles: University of California Press.

Bachmair, B. (2006). Media socialisation and the culturally dominant mode of representation. *Medien Padagogik.* Retrieved November 14, 2007, from http://www.medienpaed.com/2006/bachmair0606.pdf

Barthes, R. (1993). *Mythologies.* London: Vintage.

Barton, D., Hamilton, M., & Ivanic, R. (2000). *Situated literacies.* London: Routledge.

Bateson, G. (1977). *Step to ecology of mind.* London: Ballantine.

Bhattacharya, R., Gupta, S., Jewitt, C., Newfield, D., Reid, Y., & Stein, P. (2007). The policy-practice nexus in English classrooms in Delhi, Johannesburg, and London: Teachers and the textual cycle. *TESOL Quarterly 41,* 465–487.

Bauman, Z. (1998). *Globalization: The human consequences.* Oxford, UK: Polity.

Beavis, C. (2006). English at a time of change: Where do we go with text? *English in Australia, 41*(2), 61–68.

Beck, U. (1992). *Risk society: Towards a new modernity.* London: Sage.

Bick, P., & Chiper, S. (2007). Swoosh identity: Recontextualizations in Haiti and Romania. *Visual Communication, 6*(1), 5–18.

Boulter, J. D. (1999). *Writing space: The computer, hypertext, and the history of writing.* Hillsdale, NJ: Lawrence Erlbaum.

Boulter, J. D., & Grusin, R. (1998). *Remediation: Understanding new media.* Cambridge, MA: MIT Press.

Bourne, J., & Jewitt, C. (2003). Orchestrating debate: A multimodal approach to the study of the teaching of higher-order literacy skills. *Reading (UKRA), 37*(2), 64–72.

Brant, D., & Clinton, K. (2006). Afterword. In K. Pahl & J. Rowsell (Eds.), *Travel notes from the New Literacy Studies: Instances of practice* (pp. 254–258). Clevedon, UK: Multilingual Matters.

Buckingham, D., & Sefton-Green, J. (2004). Structure, agency and culture in children's media culture. In J. Tobin (Ed.), *Pikachu's global adventure: The rise and fall of Pokemon* (pp. 379–399). Durham, NC: Duke University Press.

Burn, A., & Parker, D. (2003). Tiger's big plan: Multimodality and moving image. In C. Jewitt & G. Kress (Eds.), *Multimodal literacy* (pp. 56–72). New York: Peter Lang.

Butler, J. (1990). *Gender trouble: Feminism and the subversion of identity.* London: Routledge.

Carrington, V. (2005). Txting: The end of civilization again. *Cambridge Journal of Education, 35*(2), 161–175.

Castells, M. (2001). *The Internet galaxy.* Oxford, UK: Oxford University Press.

Coles, M., & Hall, C. (2001). Breaking the line: New literacies, postmodernism and the teaching of printed texts. *UKRA, 35*(3), 111–114.

Cope, B., & Kalantzis, M. (Eds.). (1993). *The powers of literacy: A genre approach to teaching writing.* Pittsburgh, PA: University of Pittsburgh Press.

Cope, B., & Kalantzis, M. (Eds.). (2000). *Multiliteracies.* London: Routledge.

Cranny-Francis, A. (1993). Gender and genre: Feminist subversion of genre fiction and its implications for critical literacy. In B. Cope & M. Kalantzis (Eds.), *The powers of literacy: A genre approach to teaching writing* (pp. 90–115). Pittsburgh, PA: University of Pittsburgh Press.

Fairclough, N. (1992). *Discourse and social change.* Cambridge, UK: Polity.

Flewitt, R. (2006). Using video to investigate preschool classroom interaction: Education research assumptions and methodological practices. *Visual Communication, 5*(1), 25–51.

Foucault, M. (1980). *Power/Knowledge.* New York: Pantheon.

Foucault, M. (1991). *Discipline and punish: The birth of the prison.* London: Penguin.

Freedman, A., & Medway, P. (Eds.). (1994a). *Genre and the new rhetoric.* London: Taylor and Francis.

Freedman, A., & Medway, P. (Eds.). (1994b). *Learning and teaching genre.* Portsmouth, NH: Boynton/Cook.

Freire, P., & Macedo, D. (1987). *Literacy: Reading the word and the world.* Greenwood, CT: Praeger.

Freitas, C., & Castanheira, M. (2006, January). *Talked images: Examining the contextualized nature of image use.* Paper presented at Thematic School on Ethnography in Education, Federal University of Minas Gerais, Brazil.

Gee, J. P. (1990). *Social linguistics and literacies: Ideology in discourses.* New York: Falmer.

Gee, J. P. (2003). *What video games have to teach us about learning and literacy.* New York: Palgrave/Macmillan.

Gee, J. P. (2004). *Situated language and learning: A critique of traditional schooling.* London: Routledge.

Gee J. P., Hull, G., & Lankshear, C. (1996). *The new work order: Behind the language of the new capitalism.* Sydney, Australia: Allen and Unwin.

Goffman, E. (1979). *Gender advertisements.* London: Macmillan.

Hall, S. (1997). *Representation: Cultural representations and signifying practices.* London: Sage.

Halliday, M. (1978). *Language as a social semiotic.* London: Edward Arnold.

Hodge, R., & Kress, G. (1988). *Social semiotics.* Cambridge, UK: Polity.

Janks, H., & Comber, B. (2006). Critical literacy across continents. In K. Pahl & J. Rowsell (Eds.), *Travel notes from the New Literacy Studies: Instances of practice* (pp. 95–117). Clevedon, UK: Multilingual Matters.

Jewitt, C. (2002). The move from page to screen: The multimodal reshaping of school English. *Journal of Visual Communication, 1*(2), 171–196.

Jewitt, C. (2005). Multimodal "reading" and "writing" on screen. *Discourse: Studies in the Cultural Politics of Education, 26*(3), 315–332.

Jewitt, C. (2006). *Technology, literacy and learning: A multimodal approach.* London: Routledge.

Jewitt, C., & Jones, K. (2005). Managing time and space in the new English classroom. In M. Lawn & I. Grosvenor (Eds.), *Material cultures of schooling* (pp. 192–218). Oxford, UK: Symposium.

Jewitt, C., Moss, G., & Cardini, A. (2007). Pace, interactivity and multimodality in teacher design of texts for interactive white boards in the secondary school classroom. *Learning, Media and Technology, 32*, 303–317.

Kalantzis, M., Cope, B., & Harvey, A. (2003). Assessing multiliteracies and the new basics. *Assessment in Education: Principles, Policy and Practice, 10*(1), 15–26.

Kenner, C. (2004). Becoming biliterate: Young children learning different writing systems. Stoke-on-Trent, UK: Trentham.

Kenner, C., & Kress, G. (2003). The multisemiotic resources of biliterate children. *Journal of Early Childhood Literacy, 3*(2), 179–202.

Knobel, M., & Lankshear, C. (2006). Weblog worlds and construction of effective and powerful writing: Cross with care, and only where signs permit. In K. Pahl & J. Rowsell (Eds.), *Travel notes from the New Literacy Studies: Instances of practice* (pp. 72–92). Clevedon, UK: Multilingual Matters.

Kress, G. (1997). *Before writing: Rethinking the paths to literacy.* London: Routledge.

Kress, G. (2000). Multimodality. In B. Cope & M. Kalantzis (Eds.), *Multiliteracies* (pp. 182–202). London: Routledge.

Kress, G. (2003). *Literacy in the new media age.* London: Routledge.

Kress, G., & Bezemer, J. (2007, June). *Gains and losses.* Paper presented at the 14th International Conference of Learning, Witwatersrand University, Johannesburg, South Africa.

Kress, G., Jewitt, C., Bourne, J., Franks, A., Hardcastle, J., Jones, K., et al. (2005). *English in Urban classrooms: A multimodal perspective on teaching and learning.* London: RoutledgeFalmer.

Kress, G., Jewitt, C., Ogborn, J., & Tsatsarelis, C. (2001). *Multimodal teaching and learning: The rhetorics of the science classroom.* London: Continuum.

Kress, G., & Selander, S. (in press). Designs for learning—Individual and institutional formations of meaning. In Säljö, R. (Ed.), *Information and communication technologies and the transformation of learning practices.* Pergamon: Oxford, UK.

Kress, G., & van Leeuwen, T. (1996). *Reading images: The grammar of visual design.* London: Routledge.

Kress, G., & van Leeuwen, T. (2001). *Multimodal discourse: The modes and media of contemporary communication.* London: Arnold.

Lam, W. (2006). Culture and learning in the context of globalization: Research directions. *Review of Research in Education, 30*, 213–237.

Lankshear, C., & Knobel, M. (2003). *New literacies: Changing knowledge and classroom learning.* Buckingham, UK: Open University Press.

Lankshear, C., & McLaren, P. L. (Eds.) (1993). *Critical literacy: Politics, praxis, and the postmodern.* New York: State University of New York Press.

Lankshear, C., Peters, M., & Knobel, M. (2002). Information, knowledge and learning: Some issues facing epistemology and education in a digital age. In M. Lea & K. Nicolls (Eds.), *Distributed learning* (pp. 16–37). London: RoutledgeFalmer.

Leander, K. (2001). Producing and hybridizing space-time contexts in pedagogical discourse. *Journal of Literacy Research, 33*(4), 637–679.

Leander, K. (2007, June). Youth Internet practices and pleasure: Media effects missed by the discourses of "reading" and "design." Keynote delivered at ESRC Seminar Series: Final Conference, Institute of Education, London.

Leander, K., & Wells Rowe, D. (2006). Mapping literacy spaces in motion: A rhizomatic analysis of a classroom literacy performance. *Reading Research Quarterly, 41*(4), 428–460.

Lemke, J. (1998). Multiplying meaning: Visual and verbal semiotics in scientific text. In J. R. Martin & R. Veel (Eds.), *Reading science* (pp. 87–113). London: Routledge.

Lemke, J. (2002). Travels in hypermodality. *Visual Communication, 1*(3), 299–325.

Luke, A. (1996). Text and discourse in education: An introduction to critical discourse analysis. *Review of Research in Education, 21,* 3–48.

Luke, A., & Carrington, V. (2002). Globalisation, literacy curriculum practice. In R. Fisher, M. Lewis, & G. Brooks (Eds.), *Raising standards in literacy* (pp. 231–250). London: Routledge.

Luke, A., & Woods, A. (in press). Policy and adolescent literacy. In L. Christensen, R. Boomer, & P. Smagorinsky (Eds.), *Handbook of adolescent literacy.* New York: Guilford.

Luke, C. (2003). Pedagogy, connectivity, multimodality, and interdisciplinarity. *Reading Research Quarterly, 38*(3), 397–403.

Lury, C. (1993). *Cultural rights: Technology, legality and personality.* New York: Routledge.

Malinowski, B. (2006). *Crime and custom in savage society.* London: Read.

Marquez, C., Izquierdo, M., & Espinet, M. (2005). *Multimodal science teachers' discourse in modelling the water cycle.* Available from Wiley InterScience: http://www.interscience .wiley.com

Marsh, J. (2003). One-way traffic? Connections between literacy practices at home and in the nursery. *British Educational Research Journal, 29*(3), 369–382.

Marsh, J. (Ed.). (2005). *Popular culture, new media and digital literacy in early childhood.* London: Routledge/Falmer.

Marsh, J. (2006). Global, local/public, private: Young children's engagement in digital literacy practices in the home. In K. Pahl & J. Rowsell (Eds.), *Travel notes from the New Literacy Studies: Instances of practice* (pp. 19–38). Clevedon, UK: Multilingual Matters.

Martinec, R. (2000). Construction of identity in Michael Jackson's "Jam." *Social Semiotics, 10*(3), 313–329.

Millard, E. (2005). To enter the castle of fear: Engendering children's story writing from home to school at KS2. *Gender and Education, 17*(1), 57–63.

Morgan, B., & Ramanathan, V. (2005). Critical literacies and language education: Global and local perspectives. *Annual Review of Applied Linguistics, 25,* 151–169.

Moss, G. (2001). To work or play? Junior age non-fiction as objects of design. *Reading, Literacy and Language, 35*(3), 106–110.

Moss, G. (2003). Putting the text back into practice: Junior age non-fiction as objects of design. In C. Jewitt & G. Kress (Eds.), *Multimodal literacy* (pp. 73–87). New York: Peter Lang.

Moss, G., Jewitt, C., Levacic, R., Armstrong, V., Cardini, A., & Castle, F. (2007). *The interactive whiteboards, pedagogy and pupil performance evaluation* (Research Report 816). London: Department for Education and Skills.

Nespor, J. (1994). *Knowledge in motion: Space, time and curriculum in undergraduate physics and management.* London: Routledge.

New London Group. (1996). A pedagogy of multiliteracies: Designing social futures. *Harvard Educational Review, 66,* 60–92.

Newfield, D., Andrew, D., Stein, P., & Maungedzo, R. (2003). No number can describe how good it was: Assessment issues in the multimodal classroom. *Assessment in Education: Principles, Policy and Practice, 10*(1), 61–81.

Owen, M., Grant, L., Sayers, S., & Facer, K. (2006). *Social software and learning.* Bristol, UK: Future Lab.

Pahl, K. (1999). *Transformations: Children's meaning making in nursery education.* Stoke-on-Trent, UK: Trentham.

Pahl, K. (2003). Children's text-making at home: Transforming meaning across modes. In C. Jewitt & G. Kress (Eds.), *Multimodal literacy* (pp. 139–154). New York: Peter Lang.

Pelletier, C. (2005). The uses of literacy in studying computer games: Comparing students' oral and visual representations of games. *English Teaching: Practice and Critique, 4*(1), 40–59.

Pelletier, C. (2006). Reconfiguring interactivity, agency and pleasure in the education and computer games debate: Using Žižek's concept of interpassivity to analyse educational play. *E-learning, 2*(4), 317–326.

Prain, V., & Waldrip, B. (2006). An exploratory study of teachers' and students' use of multimodal representations of concepts in primary science. *International Journal of Science Education, 28*(15), 1843–1866.

Scott, P., & Jewitt, C. (2003). Talk, action, and visual communication in the teaching and learning science. *School Science Review, 84*(308), 117–124.

Sefton-Green, J. (2006). Youth, technology, and media culture. *Review of Research in Education, 30*, 279–306.

Sefton-Green, J., & Reiss, V. (1999). Multimedia literacies. In J. Sefton-Green (Ed.), *Young people, creativity, and new technology: The challenge of digital art* (pp. 1–11). London: Routledge.

Sefton-Green, J., & Sinker, R. (Ed.). (2000). *Evaluating creativity: Making and learning by young people.* London: Routledge.

Stein, P. (2003). The Olifantsvlei fresh stories project: Multimodality, creativity and fixing in the semiotic chain. In C. Jewitt & G. Kress (Eds.), *Multimodal literacy* (pp. 123–138). New York: Peter Lang.

Stein, P., & Mamabolo, T. (2005). Pedagogy is not enough: Early literacy practices in a South African school. In B. Street (Ed.), *Literacies across educational contexts: Mediating, learning and teaching* (pp. 25–42). Philadelphia: Caslon.

Street, B. (1995). *Social literacies: Critical approaches to literacy in development, ethnography and education.* London: Longman.

Street, B. (1998). New literacies in theory and practice: What are the implications for language in education? *Linguistics and Education, 10*(1), 1–24.

Unsworth, L. (2001). *Teaching multiliteracies across the curriculum: Changing contexts of text and image in classroom practice.* Buckingham, UK: Open University Press.

Unsworth, L. (2006). *E-literature for children: Enhancing digital literacy learning.* London and New York: Routledge/Falmer.

Unsworth, L., Thomas, A., Simpson, A., & Asha, J. (2005). *Children's literature and computer-based teaching.* Maidenhead, UK: Open University Press.

van Leeuwen, T. (1999). *Speech, music, sound.* London: Macmillan.

Zammit, K. (2007). *The construction of student pathways during information-seeking sessions using hypermedia programs: A social semiotic perspective.* Unpublished dissertation, University of Western Sydney, Australia.

Chapter 8

Science Education in Three-Part Harmony: Balancing Conceptual, Epistemic, and Social Learning Goals

RICHARD DUSCHL

Rutgers, the State University of New Jersey, New Brunswick

Two major reform efforts in K–12 science education have taken place during the past 50 years. The first was the 1950–1970 curriculum reform efforts motivated by the launching of Sputnik and sponsored by the newly formed National Science Foundation (NSF) in the United States and by the Nuffield Foundation in the United Kingdom. The signature goal for these reformed programs was to produce courses of study that would get students to "think like scientists," thus placing them in a "pipeline" for science careers (Rudolph, 2002).

The second U.S. and U.K. reform effort in science education began in the 1980s and continues to this day as part of the national standards movement. Referred to as the "Science for All" movement in the United States and the "Public Understanding of Science" in the United Kingdom, here the education goal was and is to develop a scientifically literate populace that can participate in both the economic and democratic agendas of our increasingly global market–focused science, technology, engineering, and mathematics (STEM) societies. In addition to the economic and democratic imperatives as a purpose for science education, more recent voices of science education reform (Driver, Leach, Millar, & Scott, 1996; Millar, 1996; Millar & Hunt, 2002; Osborne, Duschl, & Fairbrother, 2002) have advocated that the proper perspective for science education in schools ought to be the cultural imperative. The cultural imperative perspective sees STEM disciplines, knowledge, and practices as woven into the very fabric of our nations and societies. What the cultural imperative provides that the democratic and economic imperatives do not is recognition of important social and epistemic dimensions that are embedded in the growth, evaluation, representation, and communication of STEM knowledge and practices. New perspectives and understandings in the learning sciences about learning and learning environments, and in science studies about knowing and inquiring, highlight the importance of science

Review of Research in Education
February 2008, Vol. 32, pp. 268–291
DOI: 10.3102/0091732X07309371
© 2008 AERA. http://rre.aera.net

education teaching and learning harmonizing conceptual, epistemological, and social learning goals.

Traditionally, science curriculum has focused on what one needs *to know* to do science. Schwab (1962) called this the "rhetoric of conclusions" approach to science education, and he advocated that science education be an "enquiry into enquiry." Thirty years later, Duschl (1990) commented on the problem of "final form science" instruction, a signal that little progress had been made toward shifting the focus of science education from what we know to how we know and why we believe. The new perspective of science education focuses on what students need *to do* to learn science. The notion of *to do* in science education has traditionally been associated with the manipulation of objects and materials to engage learners with phenomena to teach what we know. This is embodied in disconnected, modularized, hands-on and textbook approaches that have been a hallmark of elementary and secondary science curricula since the 1960s reform efforts. The dominant format in curriculum materials and pedagogical practices is to reveal, demonstrate, and reinforce via typically short investigations and lessons either (a) "what we know" as identified in textbooks or by the authority of the teacher or (b) the general processes of science without any meaningful connections to relevant contexts or the development of conceptual knowledge. What has been missing is a sense of *to do* that embodies the dialogic knowledge-building processes that are at the core of science, namely, obtaining and using principles and evidence to develop explanations and predictions that represent our best-reasoned beliefs about the natural world. In other words, missing from the pedagogical conversation is how we know what we know and why we believe it.

Two recent National Research Council (NRC) reports—*Rising Above the Gathering Storm* (*RAGS*; NRC, 2007a) and *Taking Science to School: Learning and Teaching Science in grades K–8.* (*TSTS*; NRC, 2007b)—serve as evidence, though, that competing perspectives and agendas in science education persist. The *RAGS* report is a response to STEM workforce issues, for example, shortages in attracting and retaining students and teachers in science programs and careers. The *TSTS* report reflects new research understandings about how children learn science and how to design and implement effective science learning environments. The *RAGS* report emphasizes the economic imperative of keeping the United States competitive in STEM global markets. The *RAGS* focus is on the "pipeline," the emergence of new interdisciplinary sciences, the integration of sciences and technologies, and the need for more Advanced Placement courses at the high school level.

The *TSTS* report puts emphasis on the cultural imperative and harmonizing learning goals by advocating the development of four strands of scientific proficiency for all students. Students who understand science

1. know, use, and interpret scientific explanations of the natural world;
2. generate and evaluate scientific evidence and explanations;
3. understand the nature and development of scientific knowledge; and
4. participate productively in scientific practices and discourse.

The four strands of scientific proficiency reflect an important change in focus for science education, one that embraces a shift from teaching about *what* to teaching about *how* and *why*. But as one of the *TSTS* research recommendations indicates, more research knowledge exists for how children perform in Strands 1 and 2 than exists for children's performance in Strands 3 and 4.

The focus of this chapter is to examine research and development efforts on the critical role epistemic understanding and scientific reasoning play in the development of understanding science. The first section of the chapter presents an overview of salient developments in two new scholarly domains—learning sciences and science studies—that inform the framing of research on epistemic reasoning and learning goals in science education. The second section examines specific programs of research that seek to develop classrooms as epistemic communities. The third and final section moves to a discussion of the design of science curriculum, instruction, and assessment models. Issues are raised about what constitutes the appropriate "grain size" of ideas, evidence, information, and explanations for K–12 science education that seeks to harmonize across conceptual, epistemic, and social learning goals.

SHIFTING THE AGENDA IN SCIENCE EDUCATION

The agenda for science education has broadened in ways that demand a rethinking of approaches to curriculum, instruction, and assessment. We live in a time when there is rapid growth of scientific knowledge, scientific tools and technologies, and scientific theories. Like the first science education reformers in the 1950s and 1960s, we are today faced with the challenge of making important decisions about what and how to teach. But unlike the 1960s reform effort, we now have a deeper understanding of how and under what conditions learning occurs. We also have a richer understanding of the dynamics occurring in the growth of or advancements in scientific knowledge. Essentially, we have learned about learning through advancements in two scholarly domains that can help us in our thinking about how to reform K–12 science education:

1. Learning sciences: A group of disciplines focusing on learning and the design of learning environments that draw from cognitive, developmental, and social psychology; anthropology; linguistics; philosophy of mind; artificial intelligence; and educational research.
2. Science studies: A group of disciplines focusing on knowing and inquiring that draw from history, philosophy, anthropology, and sociology of science as well as cognitive psychology, computer science, science education, and artificial intelligence.

It is well beyond the scope of this chapter to provide a thorough review of developments in these two domains. An overview follows below. For comprehensive reviews of developments in the learning sciences, interested readers are directed to recent NRC (1999, 2001, 2007b) reports and to *The Cambridge Handbook of the Learning Sciences* (Sawyer, 2006). For overviews and commentary on the emergence of science studies, refer to Godfrey-Smith (2003), Longino (2002), Kitcher (1993, 1998), Koertge (1998), and Zammito (2004).

Learning Sciences

What the learning sciences literature tells us is that the structure of knowledge and the processes of knowing and learning are much more nuanced than initially described by associative and behavioral learning theories. That is, context and content matter. Thus, there is a general move away from an emphasis on domain-general reasoning and skill development to domain-specific reasoning and practices development. The richer understanding of learning and reasoning domain-specific contexts provide has significant implications for the design of pedagogical models and learning environments.

In a review article titled "The Psychology of Learning: A Short History," Bruner (2004) concludes, "It was the cognitive revolution that brought down [associative and behavioral] learning theory" and "it was the study of language and particularly of language acquisition that precipitated learning theory's decline" (p. 19). The cognitive, social, and cultural dynamics of learning are mutually supportive of one another and intertwined such that "you cannot strip learning of its content, nor study it in a 'neutral' context. It is always situated, always related to some ongoing enterprise" (Bruner, 2004, p. 20). In this sense, psychologists claim that learning has a historical dynamic because learning is shaped by experiences, by the sequencing of those experiences, and by the guiding hand of thoughtful mediation directed toward learning goals (Lehrer & Schauble, 2006b; Rogoff, 1990).

One domain in particular from the learning sciences has helped us understand cognitive development; it is research on infants' and children's learning (NRC, 2007b). This new field of scholarly work reveals how infants and young children are capable of abstract reasoning in core knowledge domains of science and mathematics (e.g., change, form, and function; physical attributes and properties of objects; systems and interactions; number sense; causal inference; distinguishing animate from inanimate). Researchers are learning that young children are capable of complex reasoning, for example, theory building. These and other forms of scientific reasoning are possible when children are provided with multiple opportunities that sustain their engagement with select scientific practices over time such as predicting, observing, testing, measuring, counting, recording, collaborating, and communicating (Carey, 2004; Gelman & Brenneman, 2004; Gopnik et al., 2004; Hapgood, Magnusson, & Palincsar, 2004; Metz, 2004; Spelke, 2000).

Schauble (2007) reminds us, though, that although we certainly want to answer the question, "Where does reasoning and learning come from?" we must also ask, "Where is reasoning going?" and "What conditions support productive change?"

Answers to the first question help us better understand the foundation on which further development can build. Answers to the second provide a sense of developmental trajectory, or more likely, trajectories. What characteristic changes are coming up? What pathways of change are usually observed? And answers to the third question focus on how those changes can get supported in a productive way. (p. 51)

The study of infants and child development is but one important element of the learning sciences. Sawyer (2006), in the preface of *The Cambridge Handbook of the Learning Sciences*, states that the "goal of the learning sciences is to better understand the cognitive and social processes that result in the most effective learning" (p. xi). The emergence of the learning sciences community in the past three decades has shifted the educational and developmental research agenda to the redesign of classrooms and other out-of-school learning environments. The stakeholders in the design of classrooms and learning environments are teachers, parents, administrators, policymakers, and professionals. The learning science constructs for such redesign include (a) transition from novice to expert performance, (b) using prior knowledge, (c) scaffolding, (d) externalization and articulation, (e) reflection, and (f) building from concrete to abstract knowledge.

The learning sciences emerged from the earlier constructivist theories of learning and from the pioneering research in the cognitive sciences. Our deeper understanding of how children's thinking is fundamentally different from that of adults, coupled with richer understandings of expertise, representation, reflection, problem solving, and thinking, provided a foundation for a major tenet of the learning sciences: "Students learn deeper knowledge when they engage in activities that are similar to the everyday activities of professionals who work in a discipline" (Sawyer, 2006, p. 4). Subsequent research on informal learning reveals the importance of participation structures and the development of practices in culturally valued activities (Cole, 1996). Focusing on scaffolding, apprenticeship, legitimate peripheral participation, and guided participation, informal learning researchers provided "broader units of analysis . . . : these views move beyond the study of individuals alone to consider how learning occurs within enduring social groups such as families and communities" (Bransford et al., 2006, p. 24).

One element of the learning sciences and an important dynamic of relevance here is the development of expertise within and among knowledge workers, for example, scientists, engineers, mathematicians, medical doctors, and so on. Cognitive, historical, sociological, and anthropological studies of knowledge workers revealed the importance of practices that are central to the professional activities in these knowledge growth communities. With respect to the scientific disciplines and, in particular, the study of epistemic cultures, cognitive models of science (cf. Giere, 1988; Goldman, 1986; Kitcher, 1993; Thagard, 1992) coupled with sociocultural models of science (cf. Knorr-Cetina, 1999; T. Kuhn, 1962/1996; Longino, 1990, 2002) have established the important role that models, mechanisms, and peers have in the advancement and refinement of scientific knowledge and the methods regarding the growth of scientific knowledge. Science takes place in complex settings of cognitive, epistemic, and social practices.

The implication for science learning is that more and more contemporary science is being done at the boundaries of disciplines. Thus, there is a connectedness in the practices of science that are not typically found in school classroom environments. An examination of school curriculum, for example, reveals disconnected and isolated units of instruction the norm in K–8 science education (NRC, 2007b). An examination of the growth of scientific knowledge as provided by science studies scholars can provide some helpful insights on how to proceed with the redesign agenda.

Science Studies

In very broad brushstrokes, 20th-century developments in science studies can be divided into three periods. In the first, logical positivism, with its emphasis on mathematical logic and the hypothetico-deductive method, was dominant. Some of the major figures in the movement were Rudolf Carnap, Carl G. Hempel, Ernest Nagel, and Hans Reichenbach. Logical positivism views of science held to several assumptions:

1. There is an epistemologically significant distinction between observation language and theoretical language, and this distinction can be made in terms of syntax or grammar.
2. Some form of inductive logic would be found that will provide a formal criterion for theory evaluation.
3. There is an important dichotomy between contexts of discovery and contexts of justification.

In the 1950s and '60s, various writers questioned these and other fundamental assumptions of logical positivism and argued for the relevance of historical and psychological factors in understanding science. Thomas S. Kuhn is the best known of the figures in this movement, but there were numerous others, including Paul Feyerabend, Norwood Russell Hanson, Mary Hesse, and Stephen Toulmin.

T. Kuhn (1962/1996) introduced the conception of paradigm shifts in the original version of *The Structure of Scientific Revolutions* and then revised it in the postscript to the 1970 second edition, introducing the concept of a disciplinary matrix. One important aspect of Kuhn's work was the distinction between revolutionary and normal science. Revolutionary science involves significant conceptual changes, whereas normal science consists of "puzzle solving," of making nature fit into the boxes specified by the disciplinary matrix.

In this view of science, theories still played a central role, but they shared the stage with other elements of science, including a social dimension. Although Kuhn saw the scientific communities as essential elements in the cognitive functioning of science, his early work did not present a detailed analysis. The most recent movements in philosophy of science can be seen as filling in some of the gaps left by Kuhn's demolition of the basic tenets of logical positivism. This movement

1. emphasizes the role of models and data construction in the scientific practices of theory development,
2. sees the scientific community as an essential part of the scientific process, and
3. sees the cognitive scientific processes as a distributed system that includes instruments, forms of representation, and agreed upon systems for communication and argument.

Science is seen as having important social phenomena with unique norms for participation in a community of peers. Perhaps the most important element Kuhn and others added to our understanding of the nature of science is the recognition that most of the theory change that occurs in science is not final theory acceptance but improvement and refinement of a theory. Ninety-nine percent of what occurs in science is neither the context of discovery nor the context of justification, as the logical positivists proposed, but the context of theory development, of conceptual modification. The dialogical processes of theory development and of dealing with anomalous data occupy a great deal of scientists' time and energy. The logical positivist's context of justification is a formal final point—the end of a journey; moreover, it is a destination few theories ever achieve, and so overemphasis on it entirely misses the importance of the journey. Importantly, the journey involved in the growth of scientific knowledge reveals the ways in which scientists respond to new data, to new theories that interpret data, or to both. Some people describe this feature of the scientific process by saying that scientific claims are tentative; I prefer to say that science and scientists are responsive, thus avoiding the connotation that tentative claims are unsupported by evidence or scientific reasoning.

One of the important findings from the science studies literature is that not only does scientific knowledge change with time, but so, too, do the methods of inquiry and the criteria for the evaluation of knowledge change. The accretion growth model of scientific knowledge is no longer tenable. Nor is a model of the growth of knowledge that appeals to changes in theory commitments alone, for example, a conceptual change model. Changes in research programs that drive the growth of scientific knowledge also can be because of changes in methodological commitments or goal commitments (Duschl, 1990). Science studies examining contemporary science practices recognize that both the conceptual frameworks and the methodological practices of science have changed with time. Changes in methodology are a consequence of new tools, new technologies, and new explanatory models and theories that, in turn, have shaped and will continue to shape scientific knowledge and scientific practices.

As science has progressed as a way of knowing, yet another dichotomy has emerged, and it is one that is critically important for a contemporary consideration of the design of K–12 curriculum, instruction, and assessment. That dichotomy is the blurring of boundaries between science and technology and between different branches of the sciences themselves, yet another outcome of learning how to learn that challenges our beliefs about what counts as data, evidence, and explanations. Ackerman (1985) refers to such developments as the shifts in the "data texts" of science and warns that the conversations among contemporary scientists about measurement, observations, data, evidence, models, and explanations is of a kind that is quite foreign from the conversations found in the general population. Consequently, understanding discipline-based epistemic frameworks, as opposed to or in addition to learning-based epistemic frameworks, is critically important for situating school science learning, knowing, and inquiry (Hammer & Elby, 2003; Kelly & Duschl, 2002).

Pickering (1995) referred to this conflation when describing experiments in high-energy physics as the "mangle of practice." Zammito (2004) writes,

Pickering's (1990) "practical realism" or interpretation of "science as practice" offers a robust appreciation for the *complexity* of science, its "rich plurality of elements of knowledge and practice," which he has come to call the "the mangle of practice." Indeed, as Ian Hacking (1988) has noted, it is the "richness, complexity and variety of scientific life" which has occasioned the widespread new emphasis on science as practice. As against the "statics of knowledge," the frame of existing theoretical ideas, Pickering (1990) situates the essence of scientific life in the "dynamics of practice," that is, "a complex process of reciprocal and interdependent tunings and refigurings of material procedures, interpretations and theories." (pp. 225–226)

For Pickering, scientific inquiry during its planning and implementation stages is a patchy and fragmented set of processes mobilized around resources. Planning is the contingent and creative designation of goals. Implementation for Pickering (1989) has

three elements: a "material procedure" which involves setting up, running and monitoring an apparatus; an "instrumental model," which conceives how the apparatus should function; and a "phenomenal model," which "endows experimental findings within meaning and significance . . . a conceptual understanding of whatever aspect of the phenomenal world is under investigation. The "hard work" of science comes in trying to make all these work together. (Zammito, 2004, pp. 226–227)

The role of modeling practices in science and of model-based reasoning has led Lehrer and Schauble (2006a), among others, to investigate ways to design classroom learning environments that promote students' modeling and model-based reasoning. This research focus has, in turn, contributed to new views about the image of science we present to students in school science. The *TSTS* report (NRC, 2007b) interprets these science studies perspectives by stating that science involves the following important epistemic and social practices:

1. Building theories and models
2. Constructing arguments
3. Using specialized ways of talking, writing, and representing phenomena

Science Education

The "pipeline" curriculum agenda is a pushdown curriculum driven by scientists' perspectives of what one needs to know to do science. This orientation was criticized right from the inception of early NSF curricula (Duschl, 1990; Easley, 1959; Rudolph, 2005). The science-for-scientists approach initially ignored research on teaching and learning in the conceptualization and design of science curricula. What ensued, then, was a content–process (CP) curriculum orientation in school science that typically separated one, content learning, from the other, process learning. A competing curriculum orientation is the discovery–inquiry (DI) approach to teaching science introduced during the NSF curriculum reform movement of the 1950s and 1960s, characterized by Rudolph (2002) as the scientist-in-the-classroom period of U.S. science education.

Although the many initial ideas of Schwab (1958, 1962) to orient science learning to an "enquiry of enquiry" and thereby avoid the "rhetoric of conclusions" conditions found in classrooms still have cachet today, something got lost in the translation to curriculum materials. What got lost in the design of inquiry curriculum materials was the focus on the important roles that guiding conceptions, evidence, and explanations have in framing the syntactic, semantic, and pragmatic structures of scientific inquiry, namely, the epistemic criteria, the conceptual clusters, and the experimental and knowledge-building practices used when doing science (Duschl & Grandy, 2007).

Since the first NSF-funded era of science education reform in the 1960s and 1970s, we see a shift in views about the nature of science from science as experimentation to science as explanation and model building, from science inquiry as an individualistic process to scientific inquiry as an individual and social process, and from science teaching focusing on the management of learners' behaviors and hands-on materials to science teaching focusing on the management of learners' ideas, access to information, and interactions between learners. Some of the shifts have been motivated by new technological development, but new theories about learning, as mentioned above, have contributed, too.

One important change that has significant implications for school science concerns the realm of scientific observations and representations. In the past 100 years, new technologies and new scientific theories have modified the nature of scientific observation from an enterprise dominated by sense perception, aided or unaided, to a theory-driven enterprise (Duschl, Deak, Ellenbogen, & Holton, 1999). We now know that what we see is influenced by what we know and by how we "look." In this sense, scientific theories are inextricably involved in the design and interpretation of experimental methods and scientific instrumentation. The implication is that there are additional important details for the development of learners' scientific literacy, reasoning, and images about the nature of science.

Consider that the developments in scientific theory coupled with concomitant advances in material sciences, engineering, and technologies have given rise to radically new ways of observing nature and engaging with phenomenon. At the beginning of the 20th century, scientists were debating the existence of atoms and genes; by the end of the century, they were manipulating individual atoms and engaging in genetic engineering. These developments are representative of the disciplinary details (conceptual, epistemic, and social) that are altering the nature of scientific inquiry and have greatly complicated our images of what it means to engage in scientific inquiry. Whereas once scientific inquiry was principally the domain of unaided sense perception, today scientific inquiry is guided by highly theoretical beliefs that determine the very existence of observational events (e.g., neutrino capture experiments in the ice fields of Antarctica). Whereas once scientific inquiry was practiced by individuals or small groups with established patrons, today scientific inquiry involves large international communities of university and industrial scientists guided by complimentary or competing beliefs and goals, often fighting for limited governmental grants to enable the research.

Scientific databases such as Geographical Information Systems make it possible to engage in rich scientific inquiry without engaging in hands-on science involving the collection of data. Instead, the data are provided and the inquiry begins with the selection of information for analysis. This is one example of how science education has shifted from management of materials for collecting data to management of information for scrutinizing databases. Such a shift has implications regarding the manner in which interactions with phenomena are designed and included in science lessons for all grade levels and the level of details we elect to include pursue. Information in the guise of data, evidence, models, and explanations represents, in an important sense, the new materials for school classrooms and laboratories.

Historically, scientific inquiry has often been motivated by practical concerns; for example, improvements in astronomy were largely driven and financed by the quest for a better calendar, and thermodynamics was primarily motivated by the desire for more efficient steam engines. But today, scientific inquiry underpins the development of vastly more powerful new technologies and addresses more pressing social problems, for example, finding clean renewable energy sources, feeding an exploding world population through genetically modified food technologies, and stem cell research. In such pragmatic problem-based contexts, new scientific knowledge is as much a consequence of inquiry as the goal of inquiry. New tools, new theories, and new technologies have contributed to advances in science such that the very foundational acts of science, such as observation and measurement, have evolved to the point that direct human interactions are no longer required. As mentioned above, entities such as genes and atoms whose existence and precise nature were debated a mere two generations ago are now being manipulated.

The findings from science studies and from the learning sciences suggest new conceptions for school science and new designs for learning environments in terms of models of curriculum, instruction, and assessment. A new generation of educational researchers is turning attention to design research with a shared goal of sorting out the proper trajectories, developmental pathways, or learning progressions that support the growth of knowledge and the development of reasoning. Within this domain of research, epistemic practices are among the salient topics of inquiry. Thus, there is attention to the design of learning environments as epistemic communities of practice.

EPISTEMIC COMMUNITIES OF PRACTICE

When we synthesize the learning sciences research (NRC, 1999, 2001; Sawyer, 2006), the science studies research (cf. Giere, 1988, 1999; Longino, 2002; Nersessian, 1992), and science education research (cf. Millar, Leach, & Osborne, 2000; Minstrell & van Zee, 2000; NRC, 2007b) we learn the following:

1. The incorporation and assessment of science learning in educational contexts should focus on three integrated domains:
   - the *conceptual* structures and *cognitive* processes used when reasoning scientifically,
   - the *epistemic* frameworks used when developing and evaluating scientific knowledge, and
   - the *social* processes and contexts that shape how knowledge is communicated, represented, argued, and debated.

2. The conditions for science learning and assessment improve through the establishment of
   - learning environments that promote *active productive student learning,*
   - instructional sequences that promote *integrating science learning* across each of the three domains listed above in paragraph 1,
   - activities and tasks that *make students' thinking visible* in each of the three domains, and
   - teacher-designed assessment practices that *monitor learning and provide feedback* on thinking and learning in each of the three domains.

Taken together, the recent developments in the learning sciences and science studies have implications for how we conceptualize the design and delivery of science curriculum materials for purposes of supporting students' learning as well as teachers' assessments for promoting learning. However, existing curricula rarely provide these kinds of experiences and learning opportunities (Duschl & Grandy, 2007; Ford, 2005; Hapgood et al., 2004; NRC, 2007b).

Why is this the case? Well, one partial answer, the psychological component, is because of a lack of research on how children learn and develop scientific knowledge and inquiry practices over time when guided with competent instruction, Schauble's (2007) second and third questions above. A second partial answer, the philosophical component, is the image of science that prevails in science education. What does it mean to be doing science? Is it fundamentally about conducting experiments and testing hypotheses? Is it fundamentally about building theories? Or is it fundamentally about participating in a community of practice that uses and tests models that explain the results of experiments and that inform the structure of theories? A third partial answer, the pedagogical component, concerns the teaching and communication of science. What is most worth knowing? Is it what we know? Or is it how we know and why we believe it even in the face of plausible competing alternatives?

The focus and goals of precollege science education have shifted. In brief, the almost exclusive emphases on conceptual goals of science learning are making room for epistemic and social learning goals. In the rapidly changing world of STEM activities, an understanding of criteria for evaluating knowledge claims, that is, deciding what counts, is as important as an understanding of conceptual frameworks for developing knowledge claims. The relation needs to be a symbiotic one; this is not an either–or situation. Conceptual and epistemic learning should be concurrent in science classrooms, situated within curriculum, instruction, and assessment models that promote the development of each. Moreover, they should reinforce each other, even mutually establish each other. To accomplish a redesign of science learning environments, new perspectives regarding the role of CP and DI approaches to science education are needed.

The history of science education since World War II shows numerous attempts to move instruction away from textbooks and lectures to investigations and experiments (Rudolph, 2002, 2005). Curriculum materials were developed to prepare the next generation of scientists, and lessons were written to help students think like scientists. The CP continuum is the dominant paradigm of science education: "Here is what we know and this is how we go about getting the knowledge," where getting the knowledge is following the testing hypothesis scientific method. The persistence of the CP continuum today seems to have more to do with the adherence to the old view of scientific methods and to the way schools are run and organized and less to do with what we understand about effective learning environments and children's learning (NRC, 2007b).

The rival DI continuum was introduced during the time of the 1950s-to-1960s curriculum and teacher-development interventions. The recent focus on science as inquiry in the United States suggests that the DI approach has not made inroads on the CP science education practices. The NRC's (1996) *National Science Education Standards* and *Inquiry and the National Science Education Standards* (NRC, 2000), along with the edited book *Inquiring Into Inquiry Learning and Teaching in Science* (Minstrell & van Zee, 2000), clearly signal dissatisfaction with school science programs that continue to promote CP orientations.

Many of the extant K–8 science curriculum programs have been found wanting in terms of the lean reasoning demands required of students (cf. Ford, 2005; Hapgood et al., 2004; Metz, 1995; NRC, 2007b). What the research shows is that curricula addressing domain-general reasoning skills and surface-level knowledge dominate over curricula addressing core knowledge and domain-specific reasoning opportunities that meaningfully integrate knowledge. This situation is partially because of a lack of consensus about what is most worth learning, for example, the "big ideas" or core knowledge of early science learning, and because of K–8 teachers' knowledge of science. The reasoning-lean curriculum approaches (a) tend to separate reasoning and learning into discrete lessons, thus blurring and glossing over the salient themes and big ideas of science, thus making American curricula "a mile wide and an inch deep" (Schmidt, McNight, & Raizen, 1997); and (b) in the case of middle school textbooks, tend to present science topics as unrelated items with little or no regard to relations between them (Kesidou & Roseman, 2002).

An alternative to the CP and DI approaches is to consider dialectical discourse frameworks based on an evidence–explanation (E-E) continuum that engage learners in conversations of inquiry. Driven by a consideration of the growth of scientific knowledge and coupled with analyses of the cognitive and social practices of scientists, the E-E focus is on engaging learners in conversations examining "science-in-the-making" practices (Kelly, Chen, & Crawford, 1998). During science-in-the-making episodes, the detailed dialectical exchanges between observations and theory and the accompanying data texts play out. The scientific knowledge we hold is put into practice and tested. Importantly, here is how and when the important dialectical discourses about data representations, data and conceptual models, evidence, explanatory theories, and methods are incorporated into science learning environments. An important issue for school science is deciding at what level of detail and in what sequence.

The E-E continuum (Duschl, 2003) has its roots in perspectives from science studies and connects to cognitive and psychological views of learning. The call for conversations is recognition of the value and importance that representation, communication, and evaluation play in science learning. I use *conversation* in a very broad sense to include, among others ideas, argumentation, debate, modeling, drawing, writing, and other genres of language. Such an expanded repertoire helps us to consider an important domain of research in both formal and informal science learning settings, namely, how to mediate the learning experiences.

The position advanced by Schauble, Leinhardt, and Martin (1997) and Pea (1993), and adopted here, is that such learning mediations should focus on promoting talk, activity structures, signs and symbol systems, or collectively what I will call *conversations*. For science learning, the conversations should mediate the transitions from evidence to explanations, or vice versa, and thereby unfold discovery and inquiry. Adopting an image of science education that is guided by the development, evaluation, and deployment of data texts is grounded in the idea that scientific inquiry and scientific reasoning are both fundamentally decision-making activities mediated by epistemological, cultural, and technological factors. The appeal to adopting the E-E continuum as a framework for designing science education curriculum, instruction, and assessment models is that it helps work out the details of the epistemic discourse processes. The E-E continuum recognizes, whereas the CP and DI approaches do not, how cognitive structures and social practices guide judgments about scientific data texts. It does so by formatting into the instructional sequence select junctures of reasoning, for example, *data texts transformations*. At each of these junctures or transformations, instruction pauses to allow students to make and report judgments. Then students are encouraged to engage in rhetoric–argument, representation–communication and modeling–theorizing practices. The critical transformations or judgments in the E-E continuum include

1. selecting or generating data to become evidence,
2. using evidence to ascertain patterns of evidence and models, and
3. employing the models and patterns to propose explanations.

Another important judgment is, of course, deciding what data to obtain and what observations or measurements are needed (Lehrer & Schauble, 2006a, 2006b; Petrosino, Lehrer, & Schauble, 2003). The development of measurement to launch the E-E continuum is critically important. Such decisions and judgments are critical entities for explicitly teaching students about the nature of science (Duschl, 2000; Kenyon and Reiser, 2004; L. Kuhn & Reiser, 2004). How raw data are selected and analyzed to be evidence, how evidence is selected and analyzed to generate patterns and models, and how the patterns and models are used for scientific explanations are important "transitional" practices in doing science. Each transition involves data texts and making epistemic judgments about "what counts." The complex relationship between evidence and explanation in science warrants an examination of the tools we teach children to use (e.g., Tinkerplots) and of changes or boundary adjustments in three kinds of criteria children employ to relate evidence to explanation: (a) criteria for assigning data to one of four categories: fact, artifact, irrelevant, or anomalous; (b) criteria for identifying patterns or models in selected data; and (c) criteria for theories or explanations created to account for the patterns or models (Duschl, 2000). The preceding discussion sets out some of the challenges and attending scientific inquiry details that face recommendations to redesign science learning environments.

Designing Epistemic Learning Environments

Recall from the introduction of the chapter that there is a need for more research on the third and fourth strands of scientific proficiency, "Understand the nature and development of scientific knowledge" and "Participate productively in scientific practices and discourse." There is, however, some good recent research contributing to our understandings of learning environments that advance in tandem (e.g., harmonize) epistemic, social, and conceptual learning.

Lehrer and Schauble (2006a) report on a 10-year program of research that examines model-based reasoning and instruction in science and mathematics. Critical to the design of these learning environments is engagement in analogical mapping of students' representational systems and emergent models to the natural world. Important instructional supports are coordinated around three forms of collective activity: (a) finding ways to help students understand and appropriate the process of scientific inquiry, (b) emphasizing the development and use of varying forms of representations and inscriptions, and (c) capitalizing on the cyclical nature of modeling (p. 381).

Sandoval (2003) has explored how high school students' epistemological ideas interact with conceptual understandings. Written explanations in the domain of natural selection were used as the dependent measure. Analyses showed that students did seek causal accounts of data and were sensitive to causal coherence, but they failed to support key claims with explicit evidence critical to an explanation. Sandoval posits that although students have productive epistemic resources to bring to inquiry, there is a need to deepen the epistemic discourse on student-generated artifacts. The recommendation is to hold more frequent public classroom discourse focused on students' explanations. "Epistemically, such a discourse would focus on the coherence of groups' claims, and how any particular claim can be judged as warranted" (Sandoval, 2003, p. 46).

Sandoval (2005) argues that having a better understanding of how scientific knowledge is constructed makes one better at doing and learning science. The goal is to engage students in a set of practices that build models from patterns of evidence (e.g., the E-E continuum transformations described above) and that examine how what comes to count as evidence depends on careful observations and building of arguments. Schauble, Glaser, Duschl, Shultz, and Johns (1995) found that students participating in sequenced inquiry lessons with explicit epistemic goals (e.g., evaluating causal explanations for the carrying capacity performance of designed boats) showed improved learning compared to students who simply enacted the investigations. Understanding the purposes of experimentation made a difference. Other reports of research that have found positive learning effects of students' working with and from evidence and seeing argumentation as a key feature of doing science include Kelly and Crawford (1997); Sandoval and Reiser (2004); Toth, Suthers, and Lesgold (2002); and Songer and Linn (1991).

Additional insights for the design of reflective classroom discourse environments comes from research by Rosebery, Warren, and Conant (1992); Smith, Maclin, Houghton, and Hennessey (2000); van Zee and Minstrell (1997); and Herrenkohl and Guerra (1998). Rosebery, Warren, and Conant's study spanned an entire school year, whereas that of Smith, Maclin, Houghton, and Hennessey followed a cohort of students for several years with the same teacher. Both studies used classroom practices that place a heavy emphasis on (a) requiring evidence for claims, (b) evaluating the fit of new ideas to data, (c) justifications for specific claims, and (d) examining methods for generating data. Engle and Conant (2002) refer to such classroom discourse as "productive disciplinary engagement" when it is grounded in the disciplinary norms for both social and cognitive activity.

The research by van Zee and Minstrell (1997) shows the positive gains in learning that come about when the authority for classroom conversation shifts from the teacher to the students. Employing a technique they call the "reflective toss," van Zee and Minstrell found that students become more active in the classroom discourse, with the positive consequence of making student thinking more visible to both the teacher and the students themselves. Herrenkohl and Guerra (1998) examined the effect on student engagement of guidelines for students who constituted the audience; that is, the scaffolding was on listening to others. The intellectual goals for students were predicting and theorizing, summarizing results, and relating predictions, theories, and results. The audience role assignments were designed to correspond with the intellectual roles and required students to check and critique classmates' work. Students were directed to develop a "question chart" that would support them in their intellectual roles, that is, what questions they could ask when it was their job to check summaries of results? Examples of students' questions are What helped you find your results? How did you get that? What were your results? What made that happen? Did your group agree on the results? and Did you like what happened? Following the framework developed by Hatano and Inagaki (1991), Herrenhkohl and Guerra used the audience-role procedures to engage students in (a) asking clarification questions, (b) challenging others' claims, and (c) coordinating bits of knowledge. The focus on listening skills and audience roles helps to foster productive community discourse on students' "thinking in science."

LEARNING PROGRESSIONS:
WHAT GRAIN SIZE KNOWLEDGE CLAIMS?

A critical aspect to the development of domain knowledge and reasoning is the appropriation of language in that domain (Gee, 1996; Lemke, 1990). The implication of focusing on evidence, measurement, models, and other data texts (Ackerman, 1985) is that the language of science is different from normal conventions or conceptions of language. The language of science includes mathematical, stochastic, representational, and epistemological elements as well as domain-specific descriptors and forms of evidence. The challenge for learning sciences research that seeks to understand and promote dialogic processes is one of understanding how to mediate and coordinate language acquisition in these various forms of communicating and representing scientific claims. A tension in science education has been deciding the right balance between domain-general learning goals (e.g., control of variables reasoning) and domain-specific learning goals (e.g., building and revising explanatory models). Another tension is deciding the balance between generalized investigative process skills and situated scientific practices.

The thesis being developed in this chapter is to move science education away from a dominant focus on conceptual learning toward a more balanced focus among things conceptual, epistemic, and social. Such a shift has significant implications for the design of curriculum, instruction, and assessment frameworks. For example, one emerging issue in science education, posed as a recommendation from *TSTS* (NRC, 2007b), is to develop learning progressions that function across grade bands, for example, 2 to 5 or 4 to 8. To address the fragmented curriculum problem, one recommendation from the NRC report is to adopt curriculum sequences that facilitate student learning; one of the *TSTS* report conclusions is to begin researching the design of learning progressions. The conclusion states,

Sustained exploration of a focused set of core ideas in a discipline is a promising direction for organizing science instruction and curriculum across grades K-8. A research and development program is needed to identify and elaborate the progressions of learning and instruction that can support students' understanding of these core ideas. The difficult issue is deciding what to emphasize and what to eliminate. (NRC, 2007b, p. x)

The learning-progression approach to the design of curriculum, instruction, and assessment is grounded in domain-specific or core-knowledge theories of cognitive development and learning as documented in recent NRC reports (NRC, 1999, 2001, 2007b; Smith, Wiser, Anderson, & Krajcik, 2006). The emerging notion is for learning progressions at the K–8 grades to be built on the most generative and core ideas that are central to the discipline of science and that support students' science learning. Additionally, the core ideas should be accessible to students in kindergarten and have the potential for sustained exploration across K–8 (NRC, 2007b).

Learning progressions would be designed to also take up epistemic and social goals of science through the teaching of scientific practices, such as measurement, argumentation, explanation, model building, and debate and decision making. Critically important for the children's development of science learning, as discussed above, are the appropriation of criteria for assessing and evaluating

- the status of knowledge claims,
- the status of investigative methods,
- the tools of measurement, and
- the status of representations and audience for communicating ideas and information.

This list represents a sample of elements in the "mangle of practice" for school science. Recall that the *TSTS*'s third and fourth strands of scientific proficiency, respectively, are "Understand the nature and development of scientific knowledge" and "Participate productively in scientific practices and discourse." In other words, the development of epistemic discourse practices is central to learning within learning progressions. But this raises yet again the important issue regarding details or the grain size of information and ideas we ask children to consider. Clearly judging students' ideas as right or wrong does not provide valuable feedback to learners. Formative assessment strategies that seek to make thinking visible are most effective when the appropriate level of details is designed into tasks such that knowledge deepens, reasoning develops, and learning progresses. Within science education, an important issue is the level of detail needed to develop epistemic reasoning. Consider, for example, the various frameworks used to guide and promote argumentation discourse in classroom learning environments and computer-supported classroom learning.

The adoption and development of argumentation frameworks has gained in importance in the past two decades. Jimenez-Aleixandre and Erduran (2007), in the opening chapter of their edited volume on argumentation research in the science classroom (Erduran and Jimenez-Aleixandre, 2007), propose five potential contributions the introduction of argumentation can have on science learning environments. First is supporting access to cognitive and metacognitive reasoning. Second is supporting the development of communication and critical thinking. Third is supporting the development of scientific literacy and enabling students to engage in the language of science. Fourth is supporting participation in practices of scientific culture and developing epistemic criteria to evaluate knowledge. Fifth is supporting the growth of reasoning employing rational criteria. Employing argumentation practices along any one of these five dimensions requires contexts and levels of detail that make such outcomes of argumentation possible, let alone successful.

When looking across the various available options for argumentation frameworks, one sees that there are issues regarding the grain size of information being sought and used (Duschl & Osborne, 2002; Kelly, 2007; Sampson & Clark, 2006). Toulmin (1958), for example, distinguished between field-dependent and field-independent forms of argumentation, with the latter focusing on the general patterns of arguments involving claims, warrants, backings, rebuttals, qualifiers, and conclusions. Perelman and Olbrechts-Tyteca (1958/1969) maintain that argumentation is fundamentally rhetorical in nature, focusing as it does on persuasion. Walton (1996) advocates that argumentation be seen as a dialectical process guided by informal logic, because considerations for goals, intents, values, and audiences creep into the process. Jimenez-Aleixandre and Erduran (2007), using Darwin's "one long argument" *On the Origin of Species* as a context, describe several aspects of argumentation. Arguments provide evidence for the justification of knowledge. Arguments bring about convergence of lines of reasoning and theoretical frameworks. Arguments seek to convince audiences. Arguments can be seen as debates between two parties or two competing theses. As their edited volume demonstrates, there is a wide variety of frameworks employed in science classrooms. The question asked by Sampson and Clark (2006) in a review of five different frameworks for examining rhetorical argumentation is "How does any framework inform us about the quality of students' argumentation?"

Argumentation, although common among many cultures and communities, when played out in science, has particular *what counts* rules for knowledge building. Such knowledge-building rules represent the epistemic demands (Sampson & Clark, 2006), epistemic resources (Hammer & Elby, 2003), epistemic actions (Pontecorvo & Girardet, 1993), and the practices of epistemic communities (Duschl & Grandy, 2007). Thus, as stated above, when thinking about argumentation discourse in classrooms, there is a need to have tools that can support and scaffold students' participation in argumentation discourse and, importantly, teachers' assessment of the students' argumentation to guide its development.

Sampson and Clark (2006) review five frameworks used for the assessment of argument:

- Toulmin's (1958) argument pattern in science education research (Jimenez-Aleixandre, Rodriguez, & Duschl, 2000; Kelly, Druker, & Chen, 1998; Osborne, Erduran & Simon, 2004),
- Zohar and Nemet's (2002) modification of Toulmin,
- Kelly and Takao's (2002; Takao & Kelly, 2003) framework examining the epistemic status of propositions,
- Sandoval's (2003; Sandoval & Millwood, 2005) framework for examining the conceptual and epistemic quality of arguments, and
- Lawson's (2003) framework for examining the hypothetic-deductive validity of arguments.

The focus of the review was "(a) illustrating the logic and assumptions that have pervaded research in the field, (b) summarizing the constraints and affordances of these different approaches, and (c) making recommendations for new directions" (Sampson & Clark, 2006, p. 655). The analyses were conducted with lenses examining the epistemological criteria used by each of the five frameworks. What Sampson and Clark (2006) report is that the extant frameworks do not get down to a precise level of epistemic criteria:

Unfortunately . . . the majority of the analytical methods that have been developed to assess and characterize the nature of the rhetorical arguments . . . have provided very little information about how the rhetorical arguments generated by students reflect these criteria. (p. 659)

Adoption of argumentation frameworks for use in classrooms does indeed have potential to shape the epistemic and social practices of students. Kelly (2007) makes an important cautionary point, though, about classroom discourse practices. He argues that norms of interaction that permit close examination of evidence while preserving pupils' dignity are not well understood. Pointing to the social nature of science epistemology, Kelly goes on to state that epistemic criteria are the accepted norms for justifying and evaluating knowledge among a given community. Making that community a K–12 classroom opens up a broad range of issues about social engagements and the content of those engagements. Following Longino's (2002) social norms for social knowledge scheme, Kelly offers up some suggestions for making science classrooms places where dialectical discourse interactions like argumentation can occur:

- A need for venues and for public discussion and corrections among members.
- A need for uptake of criticism, tolerance for dissent and changing views, but such levels of disagreement may pose problems if left unresolved.
- A need for public standards that would change with relevant criticism and as the inquiring community changes goals and values.
- A need for intellectual authority; teachers' authority needs to be tempered to support open discussions; students' experiences with shared authority can lead to confidence, responsibility, and understanding of cognitive goals of science.

Changing the nature of classroom discourse practices has implications for teachers as well, naturally. A position taken by Osborne et al. (2004) and Erduran, Simon, and Osborne (2004) is that teacher comfort is a justification for using a generic use-of-rebuttal framework that can define levels of engagement and function across science domains. Although there are merits in this position regarding teachers' comfort with the basics of managing a classroom that promotes scientific argumentation discourse, there remains concerns about the quality of argumentation and reasoning that can emerge if more refined epistemic criteria are not introduced to students.

Shifting the focus of learning from *what* to *how* and *why* requires new forms of knowledge to be brought to the classroom conversations. Consider the proficiency of "Understand the nature and development of scientific knowledge." What is the appropriate level of detail or grain size of information to consider? To begin addressing this important issue, let us revisit the idea that philosophers of science have traditionally drawn a distinction between (a) the context of generation and discovery where new ideas, methods, and questions emerge and (b) the context of justification where ideas, methods, and hypotheses are tested against the prevailing evidence and tested for coherence with prevailing beliefs. Contemporary practices in science education reflect this endpoint perspective on nature and development of science.

What we have learned in the science studies as well as in the learning sciences is that a consideration only for the endpoints of generation and justification is not the proper scientific game nor is it the appropriate game of science education. What research suggests is the proper game for understanding the nature and development of scientific knowledge is engagement with the ongoing pursuit and refinement of methods, evidence, and explanations and the subsequent handing of anomalies that are a critical component of proposing and evaluating scientific models and theories. In other words, dialogical processes characterize science-in-the-making approaches and the epistemic and social dynamics that seek to fill in the details between the initial and important context of generation scientific activities and the concluding and necessary context of justification activities.

The epistemic and social dynamics, though, bring new and important practices to bear for learning environments. Key among them is the need for establishing dialogic or dialectical learning environments that facilitate two important activities. One is making students' thinking visible and doing so within a given conceptually grounded learning context that by design promotes the attainment of scientific reasoning and the motivation to learn. The other is enabling dynamic assessments of learning that provide feedback to learners on the conceptual, epistemic, and social dimensions of engaging in science and science education. The focus needs to be on both inquiry practices and on literacy practices. The inquiry practices address the middle ground between the generation and justification endpoints and include such things as obtaining and using measurements, data, evidence, models, anomalies, and explanations. The literacy practices address the communication and representation activities of science, activities that embrace, among other things, mathematics, reading and writing, argumentation, modeling, measurement, and representation.

Once again, though, we are confronted with the issue of grain size and norms of interaction. What is the appropriate level of detail needed in the middle-ground discourse between generation and justification? What is the appropriate level of detail to assume for students' science learning? Should the level of detail be fixed and static, or should it be dynamic, deepening with students' and teachers' level of expertise and experiences? These are but some of the important research questions that we face regarding the coherent infusion of learning science and science studies into K–12 science education.

REFERENCES

Ackerman, R. J. (1985). *Data, instruments, and theory: A dialectical approach to understanding science*. Princeton, NJ: Princeton University Press.

Bransford, J., Barron, B., Pea, R., Meltzoff, A., Kuhl, P., Bell, P., et al. (2006). Foundations and opportunities for an interdisciplinary science of learning. In R. K. Sawyer (Ed.), *The Cambridge handbook of the learning sciences* (pp. 19–34). New York: Cambridge University Press.

Bruner, J. (2004). The psychology of learning: A short history. *Daedalus*, Winter, 13–20.

Carey, S. (2004). Bootstrapping and the origin of concepts. *Daedalus*, Winter, 59–68.

Cole, M. (1996). *Cultural psychology: A once and future discipline*. Cambridge, MA: Belknap.

Driver, R., Leach, J., Millar, R., & Scott. P. (1996). *Young people's images of science*. Philadelphia: Open University Press.

Duschl R. A. (1990). *Restructuring science education. The importance of theories and their development*. New York: Teachers' College Press.

Duschl, R. A. (2000). Making the nature of science explicit. In R. Millar, J. Leach, & J. Osborne (Eds.), *Improving science education: The contribution of research* (pp. 187–206). Philadelphia: Open University Press.

Duschl, R. A. (2003). Assessment of inquiry. In J. M. Atkin & J. E. Coffey (Eds.), *Everyday assessment in the science classroom* (pp. 41–59). Washington, DC: National Science Teachers Association Press.

Duschl, R. A., Deak, G. O., Ellenbogen, K. M., & Holton, D. L. (1999). Explanations: To have and to hold, or to have and to hone? Developmental and educational perspectives on theory change. *Science & Education*, 8, 525–541.

Duschl, R. A., & Grandy, R. (Eds.). (2007). *Establishing a consensus agenda for K-12 science inquiry*. Rotterdam, Netherlands: Sense.

Duschl, R. A., & Osborne, J. (2002). Supporting and promoting argumentation discourse in science education. *Studies in Science Education, 38,* 39–72.

Easley, J. (1959). The Physical Science Study Committee and educational theory. *Harvard Educational Review, 29*(1), 4–11.

Engle, R., & Conant, F. (2002). Guiding principles for fostering productive disciplinary engagement: Explaining an emergent argument in a community of learners classroom. *Cognition and Instruction, 20,* 399–483.

Erduran, S., & Jimenez-Aleixandre, M. P. (Eds.). (2007). *Argumentation in science education: Perspectives from classroom-based research.* Dordrecht, Netherlands: Springer.

Erduran, S., Simon, S., & Osborne, J. (2004). TAPing into argumentation: Developments in the application of Toulmin's argument pattern for studying science discourse. *Science Education, 88,* 915–933.

Ford, D. (2005). The challenges of observing geologically: Third grades descriptions of rock and mineral properties. *Science Education, 89,* 276–295.

Gee, J. (1996). *Social linguistics and literacies: Ideology in discourses* (2nd ed.). London: Taylor and Francis.

Gelman, R., & Brenneman, K. (2004). Science learning pathways for young children. *Early Childhood Research Quarterly, 19,* 150–158.

Giere, R. (1988). *Explaining science: A cognitive approach.* Chicago: University of Chicago Press.

Giere, R. (1999). *Science without laws.* Chicago: University of Chicago Press.

Godfrey-Smith, P. (2003). *Theory and reality.* Chicago: University of Chicago Press.

Goldman, A. (1986). *Epistemology and cognition.* Cambridge, MA: Harvard University Press.

Gopnick, A., Glymour, C., Sobel, D., Schulz, L., Kushnir, T., & Danks, D. (2004). A theory of causal learning in children: Causal maps and Bayes nets. *Psychological Review, 111*(1), 3–32.

Hammer, D., & Elby, A. (2003). Tapping epistemological resources from learning physics. *Journal of the Learning Sciences, 12,* 53–90.

Hapgood, S., Magnusson, S. J., & Palinscar, A. S. (2004). Teacher, text, and experience: A case of young children's scientific inquiry. *Journal of the Learning Sciences, 13,* 455–505.

Hatano, G., & Inagaki, K. (1991). Sharing cognition through collective comprehension activity. In L. B. Resnick, J. M. Levine, & S. D. Teasley (Eds.), *Perspectives on socially shared cognition* (pp. 331–348). Washington, DC: American Psychological Association.

Herrenkohl, L., & Guerra, M. (1998). Participant structures, scientific discourse, and student engagement in fourth grade. *Cognition and Instruction, 16*(4), 431–473.

Jimenez-Aleixandre, M. P., & Erduran, S. (2007). Argumentation in science education: An overview. In S. Erduran & M. P. Jimenez-Aleixandre (Eds.), *Argumentation in science education: Perspectives from classroom-based research* (pp. 3–27). Dordrecht, Netherlands: Springer.

Jimenez-Aleixandre, M. P., Rodriguez, A. B., & Duschl, R. A. (2000). "Doing the lesson" or "doing science": Argument in high school genetics. *Science Education, 84,* 757–792.

Kelly, G. (2007). Inquiry, activity, and epistemic practice. In R. Duschl & R. Grandy (Eds.), *Establishing a consensus agenda for K-12 science inquiry* (pp. 99–117). Rotterdam, Netherlands: Sense.

Kelly, G. J., Chen, C., & Crawford, T. (1998). Methodological considerations for studying science-in-the-making in educational settings. *Research in Science Education, 28*(1), 23–49.

Kelly, G. J., & Crawford, T. (1997). An ethnographic investigation of the discourse processes of school science. *Science Education, 81*(5), 533–559.

Kelly, G. J., Druker, S., & Chen, C. (1998). Students' reasoning about electricity: Combining performance assessments with argumentation analysis. *International Journal of Science Education, 20*(7), 849–871.

Kelly, G. J., & Duschl, R. (2002, April). *Toward a research agenda for epistemological studies in science education.* Paper presented at the annual meeting of the National Association for Research in Science Teaching, New Orleans, LA.

Kelly, G. J., & Takao, A. (2002). Epistemic levels in argument: An analysis of university oceanography students' use of evidence in writing. *Science Education, 86*(3), 314–342.

Kenyon, L., & Reiser, B. (2004, April). *Students' epistemologies of science and their influence on inquiry practices.* Paper presented at the annual meeting of the National Association for Research in Science Teaching, Dallas, TX.

Kesidou, S., & Roseman, J. (2002). How well do middle school science programs measure up? Findings from Project 2061's curriculum review. *Journal of Research in Science Teaching, 39*(6), 522–549.

Kitcher, P. (1993). *The advancement of science: Science without legend, objectivity without illusions.* New York: Oxford University Press.

Kitcher, P. (1998). A plea for science studies. In N. Koertge (Ed.), *A house built on sand: Exposing postmodernist myths about science* (pp. 32-56). New York: Oxford University Press.

Knorr-Cetina, K. (1999). *Epistemic cultures: How science makes knowledge.* Cambridge, MA: Harvard University Press.

Koertge, N. (Ed). (1998). *A house built on sand: Exposing postmodernist myths about science.* New York: Oxford University Press.

Kuhn, L., & Reiser, B. (2004, April). *Students constructing and defending evidence-based scientific explanations.* Paper presented at the annual meeting of the National Association for Research in Science Teaching, Dallas, TX.

Kuhn, T. (1996). *The structure of scientific revolutions* (4th ed.). Chicago: University of Chicago Press. (Original work published 1962)

Lawson, A. (2003). The nature and development of hypothetico-deductive argumentation with implications for science learning. *International Journal of Science Education, 25*(11), 1378–1408.

Lehrer, R., & Schauble, L. (2006a). Cultivating model-based reasoning in science education. In R. K. Sawyer (Ed.), *The Cambridge handbook of the learning sciences* (pp. 371–388). New York: Cambridge University Press.

Lehrer, R., & Schauble, L. (2006b). Scientific thinking and science literacy. In W. Damon, R. Lehrer, K. A. Renninger, and I. E. Sigel (Eds.), *Handbook of child psychology: Vol. 4. Child psychology in practice* (6th ed., pp. 153–196). Hoboken, NJ: John Wiley.

Lemke, J. (1990). *Talking science: Language, learning, and values.* Norwood, NJ: Ablex.

Longino, H. (1990). *Science as social knowledge.* Princeton, NJ: Princeton University Press.

Longino, H. (2002). *The fate of knowledge.* Princeton, NJ: Princeton University Press.

Metz, K. (1995). Reassessment of developmental constraints on children's science instruction. *Review of Educational Research, 65,* 93–127.

Metz, K. (2004). Children's understanding of scientific inquiry: Their conceptualization of uncertainty in investigations of their own design. *Cognition and Instruction, 22,* 219–290.

Millar, R., & Hunt, A. (with Bowers Isaacson, P., Melamed, A., Scorer, D., & Forester, B.). (2002). Science for public understanding: A different way to teach and learn science. *School Science Review,* 83 (304), 35--42.

Millar, R., & Hunt, A. (2001). Science for public understanding: A different way to teach and learn science. *School Science Review, 83*(304), 35–42.

Millar, R., Leach, J., & Osborne, J. (Eds.). (2000). *Improving science education: The contribution of research.* Philadelphia: Open University Press.

Minstrell, J., & van Zee, E. H. (Eds.). (2000). *Inquiring into inquiry learning and teaching in science.* Washington, DC: American Association for the Advancement of Science.

National Research Council. (1996). *National science education standards.* Washington, DC: National Academy Press.

National Research Council. (1999). *How people learn: Bridging research and practice.* Washington, DC: National Academy Press.

National Research Council. (2000). *Inquiry and the national science education standards: A guide for teaching and learning.* Washington, DC: National Academy Press.

National Research Council. (2001). *Knowing what students know: The science and design of educational assessment.* Washington, DC: National Academy Press.

National Research Council. (2007a). *Rising above the gathering storm : Energizing and employing America for a brighter economic future.* Washington, DC: National Academy Press.

National Research Council. (2007b). *Taking science to school: Learning and teaching science in grades K–8.* Washington, DC: National Academy Press.

Nersessian, N. (1992). Constructing and instructing: The role of abstraction techniques in creating and learning physics. In R. A. Duschl & R. J. Hamilton (Eds.), *Philosophy of science, cognitive psychology, and educational theory and practice* (pp. 48–68). New York: State University of New York Press.

Osborne, J. F., Duschl, R., & Fairbrother, R. (2002). *Breaking the mould: Teaching science for public understanding.* London: Nuffield Foundation.

Osborne, J., Erduran, S., & Simon, S. (2004). Enhancing the quality of argumentation in school science. *Journal of Research in Science Teaching, 41*(10), 994–1020.

Pea, R. (1993). Learning scientific concepts through material and social activities: Conversational analysis meets conceptual change. *Educational Psychologist, 28,* 265–277.

Perelman, C., & Olbrechts-Tyteca, L. (1969). *A new rhetoric: A treatise on argumentation.* South Bend, IN: University of Notre Dame Press. (Original work published 1958)

Petrosino, A., Lehrer, R., & Schauble, L. (2003). Structuring error and experimental variation as distribution in the fourth grade. *Mathematical Thinking and Learning, 5*(2/3), 131–156.

Pickering, A. (1989). Living in the material world: On realism and experimental practice. In D. Gooding, T. Pinch, & S. Schaffer (Eds.), *The uses of experiment: Studies in the natural sciences* (pp. 275–298). Cambridge, UK: Cambridge University Press.

Pickering, A. (1990). Knowledge, practice and mere construction. *Social Studies of Science, 20*(4), 682–729.

Pickering, A. (1995). *The mangle of practice: Time, agency and science.* Chicago: University of Chicago Press.

Pontecorvo, C., & Girardet, H. (1993). Arguing and reasoning in understanding historical topics. *Cognition and Instruction, 11*(3/4), 365–395.

Rogoff, B. (1990). *Apprenticeship in thinking: Cognitive development in a social context.* New York: Oxford University Press.

Rosebery, A. S., Warren, B., & Conant, F. (1992). Appropriating scientific discourse: Findings from language minority classrooms. *Journal of the Learning Sciences, 2*(1), 61–94.

Rudolph, J. (2002). *Scientists in the classroom: The Cold War reconstruction of American science education.* New York: Palgrave Macmillan.

Rudolph, J. (2005). Epistemology for the masses: The origins of the "scientific method" in American schools. *History of Education Quarterly, 45*(3), 341–376.

Sampson, V., & Clark, D. (2006). Assessment of argument in science education: A critical review of the literature. In S. A. Barab, K. E. Hay, & D. T. Hickey (Eds.), *Proceedings of the 7th International Conference of the Learning Sciences* (pp. 655–661). Bloomington, IN: International Society of the Learning Sciences.

Sandoval, W. A. (2003). Conceptual and epistemic aspects of students' scientific explanations. *Journal of the Learning Sciences, 12*(1), 5–51.

Sandoval, W. A. (2005) Understanding students' practical epistemologies and their influence on learning through inquiry. *Science Education, 89*(4), 634–656.

Sandoval, W. A., & Millwood, K. (2005). The quality of students' use of evidence in written scientific explanations. *Cognition and Instruction, 23*(1), 23–55.

Sandoval, W. A., & Reiser, B. J. (2004). Explanation-driven inquiry: Integrating conceptual and epistemic scaffolds for scientific inquiry. *Science Education, 88,* 345–372.

Sawyer, R. K. (Ed.). (2006). *The Cambridge handbook of the learning sciences.* New York: Cambridge University Press.

Schauble, L. (2007). Three questions about development. In R. Duschl & R. Grandy (Eds.), *Establishing a consensus agenda for K-12 science inquiry* (pp. 50–56). Rotterdam, Netherlands: Sense.

Schauble, L., Glaser, R., Duschl, R., Schultz, S., & John, J. (1995). Students' understanding of the objectives and procedures of experimentation in the science classroom. *Journal of the Learning Sciences, 4*(2) 131–166.

Schauble, L., Leinhardt, G., & Martin, L. M. (1997). A framework for organizing a cumulative research agenda in informal learning contexts. *Journal of Museum Education, 22*(2/3), 3–8.

Schmidt, W. H., McKnight, C. C., & Raizen, S. A. (1997). *A splintered vision: An investigation of U S science and mathematics education.* Boston: Kluwer Academic.

Schwab, J. J. (1958). The teaching of science as inquiry. *Bulletin of the Atomic Scientists, 14*, 374–379.

Schwab, J. J. (1962). The teaching of science as enquiry. In J. J. Schwab & P. Brandwein (Eds.), *The teaching of science* (pp. 1–104). Cambridge, MA: Harvard University Press.

Smith, C., Maclin, D., Houghton, C., & Hennessey, M. G. (2000). Sixth-grade students' epistemologies of science: The impact of school science experiences on epistemological development. *Cognition and Instruction, 18*(3), 349–422

Smith, C., Wiser, M., Anderson, C., & Krajcik, J. (2006). Implications of research on children's learning for assessment: Matter and atomic molecular theory. *Measurement: Interdisciplinary Research and Perspectives* (Vol. 4, pp. 11–98). Mahwah, NJ: Lawrence Erlbaum.

Songer, N., & Linn, M. (1991). How do students' views of science influence knowledge integration? *Journal of Research in Science Teaching, 28*(9), 761–784.

Spelke, E. (2000). Core knowledge. *American Psychologist, 55*, 1233–1243.

Takao, A., & Kelly, G. J. (2003). Assessment of evidence in university students' scientific writing. *Science and Education, 12*(4), 341–363.

Thagard, P. (1992). *Conceptual revolutions.* Princeton, NJ: Princeton University Press.

Toth, E., Suthers, D., & Lesgold, A. (2002). "Mapping to know": The effects of representational guidance and reflective assessment on scientific inquiry. *Science Education, 86*(2), 264–286.

Toulmin, S. (1958). *The uses of argument.* Cambridge: Cambridge University Press.

van Zee, E. & Minstrell, J. (1997). Using questioning to guide student thinking. *Journal of the Learning Sciences, 6*, 227–269.

Walton, D. N. (1996). *Argumentation schemes for presumptive reasoning.* Mahwah, NJ: Lawrence Erlbaum.

Zammito, J. H. (2004). *A nice derangement of epistemes: Post-positivism in the study of science from Quine to Latour.* Chicago: University of Chicago Press.

Zohar, A., & Nemet, F. (2002). Fostering students' knowledge and argumentation skills through dilemmas in human genetics. *Journal of Research in Science Teaching, 39*(1), 35–62.

Chapter 9

Assessing English-Language Learners' Achievement

RICHARD P. DURÁN

University of California, Santa Barbara

A ssessment of learners' academic achievement in a second language presents important challenges to the fields of educational research and educational practice.
Although these challenges legitimately concern learners' familiarity with a second
language, the challenges are more complex, particularly in the contexts of large-scale
assessments that are intended to hold schools accountable for what students know and
can do on the basis of their performance on assessments. This chapter presents a syn-
opsis of major trends and issues in this regard involving large-scale assessment of English-language learner students (ELLs) in the United States in core achievement areas.
These students are students from non-English backgrounds who are evaluated by
schools as not knowing sufficient English to benefit fully from instruction in this language and who are eligible for receipt of educational support to acquire greater English
proficiency. Although the precise numbers of these students in the U.S. population
cannot be determined for reasons discussed in this chapter, they have been estimated
to number approximately 4.5 million and to constitute about 8% of all students in the
K–12 grade range; about 80% of these students are from a Spanish-speaking background (Zehler et al., 2003). After a discussion of research trends and issues in the
main body of the chapter, the concluding portions of the chapter suggest development
of an alternative foundation for assessments that provide more valid information about
the learning capabilities and achievement of ELLs. This section also presents an example of how one might pursue enriched assessment of ELLs in the context of classroom
activities concerned with acquisition of an important class of academic English skills.

The focus is on assessment of ELLs in U.S. contexts, but the issues raised are pertinent to ELLs in broader international contexts and to learners assessed in second languages other than English. Attention to U.S. contexts, and in particular, the impact of
the No Child Left Behind (NCLB) Act of 2001 on ELL assessment, highlights how in
one country, the United States, policy-motivated attempts to strengthen assessment of

Review of Research in Education
February 2008, Vol. 32, pp. 292–327
DOI: 10.3102/0091732X07309372
© 2008 AERA. http://rre.aera.net

ELLs is tied to resolving better fundamental questions about who ELL students are, what expectations are held about their schooling achievement, how English language proficiency (ELP) affects or mitigates assessment and schooling performance, and what research base exists to answer these questions and inform new directions for linking assessment and schooling practices furthering the education of these students. Similar questions and their resolution are relevant to other international contexts, particularly in industrialized nations that face a rapid growth in their immigrant populations from non-industrialized portions of the world. Just as in the United States, these nations encounter increasingly multicultural and multilingual growth in their population and a need to improve schooling outcomes for all residents in a country (Suarez-Orozco, 2001).

With this broader set of implications as a backdrop, the chapter overviews findings related to improving assessment of ELLs in the United States at the federal, state, and school levels and the ways in which federal and state policies under the NCLB law have affected concern for inclusion of ELLs in assessments. Accordingly, the focus is on how the policies of a particular law affect assessment practices required by states and their school districts and schools and how this affects the validity of assessments administered to ELLs. Attention to large-scale assessments under NCLB is of high interest from an assessment and learning perspective in that the target of state assessments under NCLB is what students are expected to learn in an entire year of schooling in a subject matter given state standards for this expectation. This is very different from attention to how to assess isolated learning and problem-solving skills better where attention can be focused solely on assessing learning that does not bear any intended relation to other kinds of learning expected of students. In contrast, the former is about capturing a wide range of problem-solving skills and knowledge that are interrelated as components of an intended curriculum at a grade level across an entire year and, beyond that, that are capable of showing evidence of a progression in development of skills and knowledge across grades. As will be appreciated, the ensuing discussion blends concern for interpretation of policies with research and assessment issues. This back-and-forth blending of policy and research issues is deliberate. Consistent with current research on education reform and school accountability and assessment, we need to examine carefully how the theories of action surrounding educational policies are tied to research and assessment problems and issues (Baker & Linn, 2004).

Key issues drawing attention in this discussion include (a) who gets identified and assessed under the status *ELL*; (b) how ELLs are included in assessments, including with assessment accommodations and alternative assessments; (c) the performance of ELLs on assessments and associated evidence of measurement reliability and validity; and (d) the emergence of high-stakes assessments, such as high school exit assessments, and their implications for the assessment of ELL students. In addressing the foregoing questions, attention is also given to whether it is realistic to expect extraordinary congruence in ELL population definitions and assessment practices across states, and between states and the federally based national large-scale assessments. The tension between states' rights to govern assessment of students under their individual education laws and federal concerns is such that there is a question about the trumping of

federal goals for coherent assessment practices at the national level by the idiosyncratic policies of individual states. Although this may seem unsound, at first, on scientific measurement and nationally coherent policy grounds, the upshot is that the
privileging of states to decide how they best include and assess ELL students may
have a validity advantage. Allowing states to assert their rights on how to best identify ELL students may actually hold them more accountable, in the ideal and in the
long run, for being sensitive to the particular characteristics and needs of the students
they define as ELL within their jurisdictions. This is especially the case given the heterogeneity among ELLs in different regions and states in the country and the policies and resources in unique state and school district jurisdictions.

The final sections of the chapter shift attention to the inherent limits of large-scale
assessments as accountability tools for ELLs as a means for directly informing a deep
understanding of students' learning capabilities and performance that can be related to
instructions and other kinds of intervention strategies supporting ELL schooling outcomes. This critique is not intended to imply that existing large-scale assessments of
ELLs are uninformative. The existing results of such assessment clearly show that ELLs
often have serious academic content learning needs. But assessments can be designed
to work better for these students, if we take care to have assessments do a better job of
pinpointing skill needs of students developmentally across time, better connect assessments to learning activities across time and instructional units, and better represent the
social and cultural dimensions of classrooms that are related to opportunities to learn
for ELL students. This final portion of the chapter starts with a concrete example for
how to go about improving assessments for ELLs by redefining how assessments are
conceived as tools for evaluating learning goals in the area of learning of academic
English. This discussion adopts an activity theory perspective. The ensuing discussion
is applicable at large to students, but focus on students whom we label as ELL in this
chapter sharpens the concern for the ways that students' background, talents, and
social practices need to be examined more closely with regard to how these affect the
design and implementation of assessments that might guide instruction given classroom and schooling practices and community experiences.

As will be suggested, (a) students' proficiency in a subject matter cannot be captured adequately by one-dimensional constructs of academic competence, such as
those operationalized by existing large-scale assessments; (b) large-scale assessments
can at best provide "thin" coverage of what students know and can do given students'
background; and (c) current research on the social and cultural nature of learning
contexts and cognitive and interaction studies of students' interaction in learning settings suggest new ways to design assessment tools that are different from traditional
tests and assessments. In closing, the chapter discusses, once again, how opening the
question of what educational achievement goals should be can create opportunities
for revitalizing the field of educational assessment of ELL and other students.

The issues discussed go beyond suggesting that large-scale assessments should not
be expected to perform the function of local teacher-developed classroom assessments intended to guide instruction in a differentiated and formative manner and

that development of the latter represents a solution to making existing assessment approaches more valid for ELLs. Classroom instructional and learning practices, and expectations about students' learning goals, are affected by institutional and cross-institutional values, educational policies, and practices that often work at odds with each other as well as in mutual support. As will be discussed, we need to step back and examine what we value and mean by *learning* altogether and what we expect of students as evidence that they have learned, given their developing skills and knowledge and unique linguistic, social, and cultural history.

ASSESSMENT VALIDITY

Concern for assessment validity is central to the chapter. Assessment validity is the most fundamental question underlying the construction and use of assessments. The fundamental question of validity asks, Does an assessment measure what it is supposed to measure given the purposes of an assessment? The question of assessment validity centers on what inferences may drawn from assessment performances given the objectives, design, and implementation of an assessment; see Messick (1989) for a now-classic discussion of this contemporary view of validity. Assessment validity, according to contemporary accounts, is inherently about arguments used to support inferences—in the case of this chapter, what ELL students know and can do on the basis of how they perform on assessments. These arguments, in principle, must involve both conceptual and empirical warrants. Conceptually, the rationale and documentation for the purpose of an assessment, its design and scoring, and score interpretation should offer an educational explanation of what students know and can do in an achievement area and how these conclusions are linked to empirical evidence and statistical or qualitative data interpretation of test performance and their psychometric consistency or reliability. According to validity theory, there should be a tight connection between what an assessment is expected to measure on conceptual grounds and empirical performance data that could support assessment users' claims about achievement competence targeted by an assessment.

Arguably, the historical development of modern assessment validity theory surrounding achievement and ability testing has not shown adequate sensitivity to ways that the characteristics of individuals and groups interact with the sensibility of target skill and knowledge constructs for assessment and ways that assessments seek to provide evidence for these as constructs as personal, stable attributes of individuals regardless of students' background. Although there is a long history of critiques of assessment design and practice from linguistic and ethnic minority community members citing potential bias in standardized assessments (see Sanchez, 1934, for example), only gradually has this perspective been reflected in specific investigations, as in differential item function (DIF) studies that statistically investigate whether given assessment items are significantly harder or easier for two groups of examinees matched in terms of overall performance on an assessment. Although DIF studies are of value, additional work is also emerging that questions whether the very mathematical-statistical models used to represent skills and knowledge on unidimensional, numeric (interval) scales always makes sense for every population of assessment interest (see Hambleton, Merenda, &

Spielberger, 2005). The usual way to approach these issues from an assessment validity theory perspective is to propose that assessment performance has two components: construct-relevant variance and construct-irrelevant variance. In the assessment of ELLs, the focus of research on validity and reliability of assessments in English has taken this perspective, with emphasis given to the possibility that there might be assessment English-language demands that contribute to construct-irrelevant variance rather than construct-relevant variance on assessments that are not intended to assess English language skills per se.

Only rarely, but with increasing frequency, do we see critiques of assessment that question the foundations for how assessments are developed on the basis of item response theory or its earlier antecedent, classical test theory. Some investigators, such as Abedi (2004), propose that the extent of linguistically based construct-irrelevant variance may vary by first-language background and that this needs to be estimated in interpreting assessment scores. Other investigators, for example, Kopriva (in press) and Solano-Flores (2006), propose that psychometric measurement models need formally to incorporate information on how cultural, demographic, and psychological and personality profiles, as well as linguistic factors, affect ELLs' assessment performance. But arguably, these critiques stop short of questioning how assessments and assessment measurement models come to be based on theories of learning and curriculum and how their form, content, and properties as evidence of achievement reflect societal and institutional forces.

Moss, Girard, and Haniford (2006) show sensitivity to these points in a review of contemporary assessment validity theory, proposing a further transformation of the notion of validity so that the concept more closely examines how the target skills and knowledge of an assessment reflect fundamental assumptions about the nature of learning and performance based on the value systems and practices of institutional and policy stakeholders who advocate for and sponsor assessment systems. They suggest a hermeneutic approach where the inferences about the meaning of assessment performances lead to active, ongoing questioning of whether an assessment is really operating as intended. The bottom line here is that validation of an assessment is a process—one might add, a historical, dialectical process—wherein performance evidence from an assessment is examined over time and where the standards for assessments and assessments themselves are improved or redesigned so that they better meet their goals and usefulness to stakeholders.

The hermeneutic approach described by Moss et al. (2006) also addresses the values of assessment stakeholders and the issues of ethics and power relationships between stakeholders as issues that shape assessments and their consequences as part of this dialectical process. Questions that arise in this regard include Who decides what students are expected to know and do? What consequences are there to evidence that students are not attaining competence in target achievement areas? and Who is held accountable for improving the expected educational performance of students?

Why are the foregoing concerns of importance to this chapter? ELLs from certain backgrounds show low achievement performance on large-scale assessments. They are often students from low-income and immigrant backgrounds with parents who have limited formal education attainment. They are also students who have shown evidence of low schooling achievement and schooling engagement based not just on test scores over time but also based on school record indicators, such as matriculation through required courses, classroom grades, attendance records, drop-out rates, and so on. Large-scale assessments consistently show that ELLs as a whole lag behind other students as a whole in their achievement. The magnitude of achievement lag has been found to be between 0.5 to 2 standard deviations in magnitude on standardized tests and assessments such as the National Assessment of Educational Progress (NAEP) that have been designed in accordance with well-established techniques for designing standardized and criterion-referenced tests common to test developers.

What does this lag in achievement test scores tell us? Is limited competence in English, the language of an assessment, the main factor underlying this gap when an assessment is administered in English? Does it tell us that ELLs know and can do less, given received notions of what an assessment is supposed to measure? Or does it also propel us dialectically to ask more deeply what it is that are we expecting ELLs (and other students) to know and be capable of doing, not just in English but in the wider range of languages and language varieties they may command? Furthermore, will we be served by advancing more comprehensive models for achievement performance and evidence of achievement performance that go beyond the constraints of traditional perspectives underlying the design of existing large-scale assessments? These are among the main questions that motivate this chapter that are tied to a deeper look at validity theory underlying assessments as evidence for what ELLs know and can do, given a federal policy such as NCLB—which putatively frames what ELL students should know and be able to do in achievement areas—and how large-scale assessments at the state level then are expected to serve as conceptually and technically sound instruments to measure students' proficiency in target subject matter areas.

Ultimately, resolution of these issues is itself a historical process tied to the evolution of how assessments will evolve over time to incorporate new research paradigms and findings linking cognitive, sociocultural, and policy-organizational research on assessment to more useful and productive accounts of how assessments themselves might guide assessments as tools to inform educational policy and practice. The aim of the concluding part of this chapter is to suggest some ways that reconstructing how we look at ELLs' (and other students') achievement as "activity" could contribute to such a transformation. If our current approaches to the design and implementation of large-scale assessments are not working well enough for ELLs, what might be a better starting point?

But to create this argument, it is important to get back to why and how we assess ELLs and other students in large-scale assessments currently tied to the policy purposes of assessments and what has been done to address the validity and accuracy or reliability of assessments for ELLs.

LARGE-SCALE ASSESSMENT OF U.S. ELLS WITH A FOCUS ON NCLB

Focus on assessment of ELL students in a U.S. context has several advantages not only because of the range of research and data available to foreground challenges but also because of the historical evolution of U.S. federal educational policy in the form of NCLB. For states to receive federal assistance under NCLB, states, school districts, and schools are responsible for accounting for the rate at which different subgroups of students show test-score evidence of having attained competence in the subject matter areas of English language arts, mathematics, and more recently, science learning across the K–12 grades. NCLB requires that states implement learning standards systems in reading, mathematics, and science that specify what students are expected to know and be able to do across grades and that serve to indicate whether schools are doing an adequate job in instructing students. State assessment test items and assessments in English language arts, mathematics, and soon, science are constructed from test blueprints or specifications intended to measure students' attainment of standards.

Under Title I of NCLB, states are required to establish and implement adequate yearly progress (AYP) goals for students, including students from key ethnic–racial groups, special education students, and students classified as limited English proficient (or ELL). The law at present requires that by 2013–2014, all students and target subgroups in a state attain 100% proficiency in meeting standards in reading and mathematics in Grades 3 to 8, individually, on the basis of reading and math assessments and assessments administered at least once in high school. States are also required to meet state targets for high school graduation for all students. The area of science is held to similar AYP requirements but with fewer assessments required in Grades 3 to 8.

ELL students with more than 1 year of attendance in U.S. schools must be administered state assessments in English in the three NCLB target subject matter areas, though they have the option of deferring this assessment in English for up to 2 additional years in some circumstances. States have the option of administering ELL students their regular English version assessment under standard conditions or with appropriate assessment accommodations to facilitate ELLs' access to assessment content. Also, states may elect to administer ELLs modified (sometimes referred to as *alternate*) assessments that are not intended to be measure exactly the same constructs in the same way as a regular or accommodated assessment but that can be argued on analytic or empirical grounds to yield information about the same target skills and knowledge.

Accommodated assessments are versions of the regular state assessment that have modified administration conditions facilitating ELL students' (and special education students') access to the information presented on an assessment while, allegedly, not altering the meaning of an assessment performance given the specification or blueprints for items on the nonaccommodated assessment. In general (and not just for ELLs), assessment accommodations involve a change in the setting, scheduling, timing, presentation, or response mode for the standard assessment. The range of accommodations administered to ELLs include, for example, linguistic modification of test items to reduce ELP requirements, dictionaries or glossaries explaining selected construct-irrelevant terms found on assessment items, side-by-side English and non-English native language (L1) presentation of assessment items, oral translation of assessment instructions, or even the oral reading of an item as a whole in an L1 language. Other accommodations, such as extended assessment time and assessment in small groups, also are available for both ELL and non-ELL students, depending on the state's accommodation policies.

Modified assessments are unlike accommodated assessments in that they present ELLs with an alternative assessment that is not expected (or found) to measure exactly the same skills or knowledge as the regular assessment. For example, such a modified assessment may consist of easier items than found in a regular state assessment and may not cover exactly the same range of skills as the regular assessment. But there are other possibilities, such as use of an off-the-shelf Spanish-version standardized achievement test in math in place of the regular state assessment in math. In this case, *modified assessment* refers to the fact that the standardized math achievement test is measuring a different (though arguably related) set of skills and knowledge when compared to the regular state assessment.

States are required under NCLB peer review procedures to provide psychometric and other related evidence regarding the reliability and validity of all assessments, including accommodated and modified assessments. States must provide evidence that their accommodated and modified assessments are aligned with grade-level student standards and measure the same standards. In the case of alternative (here, modified) assessments, states must make clear a procedure for how performance on a modified assessment meets the same goals as the regular state assessment.

The foregoing requirements hold for students classified by states as ELL, but Title III also requires that states implement English language development (ELD) standards and annually administered ELP tests based on these standards to evaluate ELL students' progress in attaining English proficiency.[1] States are required to establish annual measurement objectives that establish goals for ELL students' growth in English proficiency based on their ELP assessment scores and also based on ELL students' attainment of fully English-proficient status based on assessment scores. Interestingly, although NCLB Titles I and III hold that all ELL students in a state must attain proficiency in reading, mathematics, and science in target grades by 2013–2014, the same 100% proficiency rate does not apply for attainment of ELP. States have been given the flexibility to set lower target rates for ELLs' attainment of full English proficiency based on ELP test scores by 2013–2014.

A more recent requirement under Title III is that states conceptually align their ELD standards and ELP assessments with subject matter standards in reading, mathematics, and science. States are expected to present evidence to the U.S. Department of Education that the content of ELP assessment items includes coverage of language usage encountered in the three target subject matter areas. To meet this requirement, states are expanding their ELD standards and ELP assessment blueprints so that they include "academic language" and problem-solving tasks pertinent to subject matter learning in the three areas, in addition to basic social and functional English characteristic of early acquisition and learning of a second language. The federal goal for this alignment requirement, putatively, is to help schools attend to the academic language-learning needs of ELL students as they strive to support these students' attainment of proficiency in reading, mathematics, and science.

In addition to state assessments under NCLB, the NAEP is also implemented for the purpose of gauging students' mastery of content standards developed from a national perspective in a variety of subject matter areas, including but not limited to reading, mathematics, and science. The NAEP assesses students' mastery independent from states' standards. Under NCLB, states are expected to corroborate the progress of students on their state assessments in reading and mathematics (and eventually science) in light of NAEP results for their state in these subject matter areas. Although NAEP is a separate assessment from state assessments, and the assessment standards of NAEP are different (almost always more demanding than state standards), there is a federal expectation that growth in states' achievement test scores for the same grades over time will also be reflected in growth on NAEP tests for the same grades over time.

In the past 20 years, the NAEP has developed its own policy and reporting agenda concerned with disparities in the performance of ELLs relative to other groups of students, as the national population of ELLs has increased dramatically among the states and as the agency has pursued testing of Puerto Rican students in Spanish. The NAEP agenda has been deeply influenced by U.S. federal laws mandating inclusion of students regardless of background in federal data reporting. This has led the NAEP to undertake a significant body of research on testing accommodation—ways of altering assessment administration conditions—so as to ensure maximal participation of students. ELLs and students with special education status have been particular targets for NAEP accommodation studies.

The question of comparability of ELLs' scores on state and NAEP tests presents a number of issues that illustrate challenges in better understanding what sense we can make of tests supposedly administered to similar ELLs in similar subject matter areas with arguably related measurement objectives.

Attention is now turned to coverage of what research tells us about four key areas that present challenges for adequate assessment of ELLs in large-scale assessments: (a) Who is assessed under the status ELL? (b) How are ELLs included in large-scale assessments? (c) What evidence do we have about the reliability and validity of ELL assessment outcomes on large-scale assessments? and (d) What special issues are arising in the use of large-scale assessments for high school exit purposes?

Who Gets Identified and Assessed as ELL in Large-Scale Assessments?

One of the most consistent findings in current research on assessment of ELLs is that ELL status is not well defined in large-scale assessments (Abedi, 2004). The National Research Council (Koenig & Bachman, 2004), in a major synthesis report on participation of students with disabilities and ELL students in large-scale state assessments and NAEP, concluded that ELLs are not a true demographic population that can be unambiguously defined by a set of well-defined indicators that are reliably measurable in an all-or-none way. ELLs participating in state large-scale assessments are in effect a policy construction, a category of students established by individual states to satisfy their education laws to deal with a growing group of students from non-English backgrounds who show some evidence of limited familiarity with English, patterns of low school achievement, low assessment scores in English, and propensity to drop out of school and not go on to higher education if they do complete high school. It must be admitted that linguistic and educational researchers themselves do not provide a definitive way to resolve the definition of ELLs. Valdes and Figueroa (1994), for example, present numerous typologies that can be used to characterize bilingual background students with importance to interpreting students' test performance. But what is of essence here is what states do in their own definitions with due consideration for large-scale assessments.

All states rely on a home-language background questionnaire to identify students whose parents or caretakers report whether a language (in addition to or) other than English is spoken at home. A *yes* response to this question leads schools to further screen and assess students for the possibility that they can be classified as limited in their English proficiency and hence eligible for ELD support under state and local programs for this purpose. There is no body of research that has investigated the validity and accuracy of home-language surveys. And there is no research investigating the utility of more "textured" analysis of how one or more languages are used by whom and for different purposes in households and how this might be helpful in identifying the English language competencies and needs of students whose parents or caretakers respond *yes* to presence of a non-English language at home.

In most states a *yes* response to the presence of a non-English language at home triggers administration of an ELP assessment. Performance on this assessment is used to determine whether students can be classified initially as ELL or, alternatively, as English proficient. It is important to note, however, that most states do not classify students as ELL solely on the basis of performance on the ELP assessment. Most states allow local school jurisdictions to use additional criteria to make this decision. In California, for example, local schools are allowed to individually weigh other factors in making this decision. Additional factors that are considered typically include falling below a threshold performance level on a designated English language arts and reading test (this could be the same as the state assessment mandated under NCLB), a teacher's or reading specialist's clinical judgment regarding students' English proficiency, and parents' input regarding their child's readiness for English language instruction. Although states such as California monitor whether school districts and schools use allowable criteria such as that mentioned, a state such as California restricts its feedback to advising schools about how to improve their procedures and to advising schools of their vulnerability to litigation by others in the event they do not improve their assessment practices so as to support ELL students' learning needs.

A related set of relevant factors affecting the definition of ELLs concerns the demographic characteristics and resources of their current communities and schools. It may seem odd logically to consider that the meaning of being an ELL student is tied to the current environment surrounding the community and schooling life of an ELL student. However, it is overly simplistic to maintain a separation between student identity in this regard and the characteristics of the community and schools, because the educational meaning of ELL status is constructed, as has been noted, by local communities and schools. As was mentioned in the foregoing, states give local communities and schools liberty to decide ELL status based on local criteria such as locally set criteria derived from English achievement assessment performance, teacher clinical judgment of students' readiness for English instruction, and parental advice. There appears to be much anecdotal evidence, for example, that local schools and school boards may favor liberally identifying, or alternatively, conservatively bestowing, ELL status on students because of pressures to maintain or obtain financial resources to provide more educational services to more students or, conversely, to avoid showing lack of resources to serve the additional educational needs of an increasing number of ELL students. There is no systematic large-scale research on this sensitive issue.

States' adoption of unique ELD standards and unique ELP assessments further leads to inconsistencies in how ELL students are defined across states. Each state undertakes an educational-political process to create its framework for ELD standards that lead to the adoption of its ELP assessment based on these standards. NCLB requires that states have ELD standards and that ELP assessment be based on these standards to measure English proficiency of students initially classified as ELL. NCLB is explicit in requiring that states create ELD standards and ELP assessments that assess skills in speaking, listening, reading, writing, and language comprehension. NCLB also requires that states design their ELD standards and ELP assessments in line with findings from research on language learning and its developmental progression, national-level efforts to define ELD standards (such as by the Teaching English as a Second Language organization), and findings on best-assessment language proficiency practices for ELL students consistent with testing standards (American Educational Research Association, American Psychological Association, & National Council on Measurement in Education, 1999). However, the U.S. Department of Education, under NCLB, leaves it up to states to specify their ELD standards and ELP assessments in accordance with these general requirements.

Furthermore, states are given license to establish performance standards across assessment areas and composite scores on ELP assessments to determine ELLs' movement across proficiency categories indicating increasing English proficiency and, when students have attained sufficient English proficiency, no longer to classify them as limited English proficient. NCLB does not permit states to do just anything. States are held accountable for providing logical-conceptual evidence and some modicum of basic validity and reliability evidence supporting the claim that ELD standards and ELP assessments are aligned and operating empirically as expected.

Nonetheless, given that there is no consensus in the field of language acquisition research and language proficiency on how to best create ELD standards and ELP assessments, there is very limited consistency and established agreement on who gets classified as ELL or English proficient across states (Abedi & Gandara, 2006; Durán, 2006; Koenig & Bachman, 2004).

A further issue complicating identification of ELLs is that there is great heterogeneity in the background characteristics of students so identified using existing procedures (Abedi, 2004). ELLs can be very different in terms of their non-English language and previous exposure to this language as a medium of instruction, as well as differing in their experience in learning and using English prior to enrollment in U.S. schools. Also, ELLs vary at which age and grade they enter U.S. schools and what curricula they have been exposed to in their country of origin prior to entry into U.S. schools.

These factors have implications for understanding the learning needs and readiness for ELLs to transition to all-English instruction. These learning needs and readiness to transition to all-English instruction will be heterogeneous themselves and, furthermore, will complicate the interpretation of ELLs' scores on large-scale assessments. The same scores may have very different instructional significance for different ELLs classified as being at the ELP level.

Paradoxically, the idiosyncratic definition of ELLs as a student population among states might work against a nationally consistent way of defining this population but eventually aid individual states in developing accountability models for supporting the learning and academic progress of their unique ELL populations. As states and their local school districts grapple with the growth of their ELL populations, their heterogeneity, and local community and school resources, there is the possibility—in the ideal—that they are likely to become more concerned with a more refined way to deal with the specific learning needs of heterogeneous groupings of ELLs. For example, as will be discussed later in this chapter, there is an emerging national pattern that long-term ELL students in middle and high school (students who have been in the United States and classified as ELL for 5 years or longer) have different English-learning needs and schooling engagement and motivational characteristics as compared to more-recent-arrival ELLs who have strong educational records of achievement via schooling outside the United States in their primary language. States, school districts, and schools faced with getting students to pass high school exit examinations as a requirement for a high school diploma are faced with developing different strategies to get these different kinds of ELL students to graduate from high school, and different states have different laws and funding mechanisms that need to address these needs.

How Are ELLs Included in Large-Scale Assessments?

Despite the highly heterogeneous nature of ELLs, the criteria for deciding how ELLs are assessed in large-scale assessments relies entirely on whether they are simply classified as ELL or not. Under NCLB, students from non-English backgrounds who are determined to not be ELL are administered assessments in English in the same manner and format as students from a solely English language background. These English-proficient students from non-English backgrounds are folded into the general assessment reporting population of students at large. As a special case, under NCLB, students who were initially classified as ELL but who subsequently were reclassified as fully English proficient may be counted by states as members of the ELL reporting category for up to 2 years for AYP purposes (Frances, Kieffer, Lesaux, Rivera, & Rivera 2006). The U.S. Department of Education permitted this practice after considering how the immediate removal of former ELL students from AYP calculations would necessarily depress evidence that states were making significant progress in getting ELLs to meet AYP goals.

With this AYP reporting caveat in mind, under NCLB, states must include all ELL students in their mandated assessments in reading, mathematics, and science. States are given the option under NCLB to administer their regular English-version assessments to ELLs, to administer their English-version assessments with accommodations to ELLs, or to administer ELLs modified assessments (for the latter to be acceptable under NCLB, a strong argument is required that the modified assessment provides comparable results to the regular state assessment). In implementing these options, under Title I of NCLB, states are held accountable for providing evidence supporting the conclusion that accommodated and alternate assessments administered to ELLs measure the same range of content standards at an ELL student's grade level as the regular English version assessment. States are also required to document that the scores and proficiency-level assignments earned by ELLs have the same meaning as for non-ELLs.

State policies regarding provisions of accommodations and alternate assessments have increased dramatically since 2001, as states have implemented their state assessments responsive to requirements for student inclusion in state assessments under NCLB (Rivera & Collum, 2006). States have only sporadically conducted research examining the validity and reliability of accommodated and modified assessments for ELL students. Research has found that a school's decision to administer assessment accommodations to ELLs is based overwhelmingly on what state policies specify as a permissible accommodation (that presumably is convenient for local schools to administer) and not on a linguistic rationale intended to reduce English language load faced by ELL examinees on an assessment (Abedi & Gandara, 2006). In other words, ELLs are prone to get assessment accommodations, such as extended time or assessment in small groups, because these create less burden on schools when managing the administration of assessments. More recently, Kopriva, Emick, Hipolito-Delgado, and Cameron (2007) report experimental evidence that selection and administration of accommodations tailored to the specific language background, cultural familiarity of ELLs with U.S. schools, and schooling practice can lead to improved state test scores compared to ELLs administered no accommodations or ELLs administered only some of the recommended accommodations given their background.

What Do We Know About the Performance of ELLs on Assessments?

There is consistent research evidence that ELLs, as a whole, perform at lower levels on unaccommodated large-scale assessments administered in English. NAEP data on ELLs shows that students identified as ELL score lower on reading and math assessments at all grade levels (Mazzeo, Carlson, Voelkl, & Lutkus, 2000). Abedi and colleagues (Abedi, Lord, & Hofstetter, 1998; Abedi, Lord, Kim, & Miyoshi, 2000) report several studies conducted in a variety of settings across the United States using assessments built from released NAEP math and science items that have shown that ELLs tend to perform better on these assessments than on assessments of English reading using released NAEP items. This research has also shown that the reliability of assessment performance is high to very high for ELLs on math and science assessments but only moderate to moderately high on English reading assessments, suggesting that greater demand on English can make ELLs' test performance less stable.

Although states have lagged in conducting extensive research of their own on the validity of assessment accommodations administered to ELLs, there has been a growing body of such research, though it has not produced consistent findings. As the field has emerged, two key questions have come to guide research: (a) Is an assessment accommodation effective? That is, does it raise assessment scores for a target population such as ELLs above levels obtained by such examinees administered an assessment without the accommodation? and (b) Is an assessment accommodation valid in preserving the intended meaning of assessment scores as measures of target knowledge and skill areas? (Abedi, Hofstetter, & Lord, 2004; Sireci & Zenisky, 2006)

In the case of ELLs, the first question concerns whether an assessment accommodation does what it is intended to do—namely, facilitate ELLs' ability to access the information required to understand and to work an assessment item without having limited proficiency in English interfere with problem solving—in those cases where ELP is not a skill deliberately intended for assessment in a target knowledge and skill area. The second question addresses the issue of whether any advantage in assessment scores shown by ELLs administered an accommodated assessment may alter the meaning of the underlying constructs intended for measurement. A common way to investigate this is to check whether non-ELLs administered an accommodated assessment show no dramatic increase in assessment scores compared to performance shown when they are administered a nonaccommodated version of an assessment. If non-ELLs show as dramatic an increase when administered an accommodation compared to non-ELLs not administered the accommodation, this is taken as evidence that the accommodation has altered the constructs targeted for assessment. In the research literature on accommodations, a combined test of the effectiveness and validity of an accommodation for ELLs versus non-ELL students is labeled the "interaction hypotheses," referring to the use of a two-way analysis of variance for determining whether an accommodation is statistically more effective for ELLs but not for non-ELLs (Sireci, Li, & Scarpati, 2003).

Syntheses of research evidence on the effectiveness and validity of accommodations have not found consistent results across accommodation types (Frances et al., 2006; Koenig & Bachman, 2004; Sireci et al., 2003). Studies sometimes show evidence of effectiveness, but not validity, as with linguistic simplification of test items where it has been found to aid native English speakers more than ELLs, and in some cases, linguistic simplification has not shown evidence of effectiveness regardless of group (Abedi, 2006; Frances et al., 2006).

Two accommodation types show the most evidence of effectiveness and validity for ELLs (Frances et al., 2006). These include (a) providing ELLs with customized English dictionaries including definitions of a limited range of terms occurring in assessment math or science items and (b) providing (English or bilingual) glossaries elaborating on the meaning of select math or science terms occurring in assessment items in cases where the linguistic access to the meaning of terms was not an assessment construct target.

Extended time as an accommodation has been found to be associated with increases in assessment performance for ELLs, but this accommodation can be confounded with other factors affecting assessment performance because it is seldom administered without being coupled with another assessment accommodation, such as small-group administration or the linguistically based accommodations mentioned above, therefore making it impossible to isolate performance improvement as because of extended time alone.

Another important form of assessment accommodation that has been investigated provides ELLs with assessment items in their primary language. This can occur in the form of separate English and non-English versions of the same assessment or a dual-language assessment where items are presented in both languages on the same assessment instrument. The development and use of translation equivalent assessments is considered a form of "assessment adaptation" for cross-cultural assessment purposes (Hambleton et al., 2005). Although assessment adaptation is a more general concept referring to a range of ways to make assessments potentially more equivalent across populations, it is helpful in the context of discussing assessment in more than one language because it highlights the importance of a variety of sources of cultural issues in assessment content that interact with ways in which different languages affect the meaning and intelligibility of items represented by language on assessments (Geisinger, 1994; Hambleton, 2005; Stansfield, 2003; van der Linden, 1998).

The creation of assessment items that are considered to be translation equivalents is a complex enterprise (Stansfield, 1996; Vijver & Poortinga, 2005). Although there is no one best procedure, assessment items that are "transadapted" (Stansfield, 1996) undergo a rigorous cycle of development and checking for quality of translation. This can involve translation of an assessment item from a second language (L2) such as English to an L1 such as Chinese or Spanish, followed by back translation from an L1 to an L2, to check whether the same meanings are being communicated in the versions of an assessment item in each language. It is also possible to check whether translation of an item to a third language (L3) from an L1 and L2 version leads to recognizable equivalent items in L3. Professional translators are recommended for these purposes, and their work can lead to substitutions in wording, syntax, and idiomatic usage across languages for an assessment item for the item to be matched better with the linguistic and cultural backgrounds of examinees. Piloting and field-testing with examinees and school staff are also used to check for perception of equivalence of meaning across transadapted items. Although perceptions of quality of translation are important as indicators of the validity of translated versions assessments, they do not establish the degree to which translated assessments are psychometrically equivalent.

The general problem of establishing the psychometric equivalence of assessments in two languages is covered by Wainer (1999) in his aptly titled paper "Comparing the Incomparable." Wainer notes that it is impossible psychometrically to equate assessments in two languages in the strongest sense—scores on two assessments have exactly the same score distributions and measurement scale properties—because there can be a confound between the ability required to solve items in one language versus the other and the ability of two groups of examinees who are assigned to be assessed in one language versus the other. When two translated assessment items differ in difficulty, for example, when the item in L1 is solved by a smaller proportion of L1 examinees than when the item is presented in L2 to L2 examinees, what is responsible for this difference? Is it that the L1 version of the item is harder because the linguistic (and cultural) properties of the item make it harder, or is it because L1 examinees have learned less of the knowledge and skills assessed by the item?

The solution to this problem is to relax the meaning of *equivalent* by adding assumptions. As Wainer (1999) explains, one way to do this is to assume that translated items on an assessment are equivalent in difficulty across languages if their degree of difficulty within each language of assessment remains invariant across languages. That is, if we were to order the difficulty of items in each language, would we find the same difficulty order of items in the other language? If this is so, we have met a necessary, but not sufficient, condition for the equivalence of assessments across two languages. Meeting this condition is not sufficient to ensure the strict equivalence of translated assessment because additional statistical properties would need to be met. The other solution to the problem is to assume that two groups, one taking the L1 assessment and the other the L2 assessment, are of equal ability and to adjust scores statistically for any observed differences across groups.

Sireci, Patsula, and Hambleton (2005) and Sireci (2005) outline strategies of this sort to permit linking and comparison of scores on assessments that are intended to be parallel in two languages. Suffice it to say that although there is no perfect method to ensure that scores on the same intended assessment in two languages are strictly equivalent, psychometricians have worked out a variety of ways to verify that there are systematic and expected ways that scores on two assessments are related once assumptions are made. Example techniques, beyond investigating whether items show highly similar difficulty level in each language across two languages, include looking at whether items show no change in difficulty across L1 and L2 groups given their overall score in each language, whether items are measured with the same degree of reliability precision in each language, whether items cluster together in difficulty in each language on the basis of particular knowledge and skills they are designed to assess, and whether persons who are fluent in two languages perform similarly when presented items in both languages.

Before proceeding to a discussion of the cognitive issues raised by the quandary of establishing equivalence of assessments in two languages, it is helpful to add some comments on dual-language assessments of achievement. Dual-language assessments are translated assessments where an examinee is presented with assessment items in two languages simultaneously, such as in a side-by-side format, where the left portion of an assessment booklet has items presented in one language and the right side of a booklet presents the same item in a second language. No clear evidence has emerged that this accommodation leads to enhanced ELLs' performance compared to ELLs administered regular English versions of items (Sireci et al., 2003), but there is evidence also that ELLs perform no more poorly on such assessments compared to regular English assessments (Mazzeo et al., 2000). Some cognitive interview data exist suggesting that

ELLs administered dual-language assessments pick one language instead of the other and only concentrate on that language during an assessment. It also appears that preference for English on such assessments is connected to the fact that ELL students are receiving their current instruction solely in English.

Now let us turn to the problem of equivalence of items and assessments intended to assess the same skills and knowledge via assessment items found on large-scale assessments from a psychometric perspective attuned to cognitive and background issues. This discussion will serve as a bridge to the final section of this chapter suggesting the value in rethinking what counts as evidence for ELLs' learning achievement in content areas given the putative goals of large-scale assessments under policies such as NCLB.

Martiniello (2007) examined the effects of linguistic complexity on DIF for ELLs on solving math word problems. Following prior research by Abedi et al. (1998) and others, she postulated that ELL fourth graders would find Massachusetts Comprehensive Assessment System math test items with greater English language requirements harder than was the case for non-ELL peer students. Indeed, this turned out to be the case. In addition, however, she examined whether presence of visual images representing mathematical relationships necessary to solve problems mitigated the difficulty of items for ELL students. This turned out to be the case. As part of her research, Martiniello interviewed a small sample of 24 students regarding how they solved problems as they solved them. Her protocol collection method involved probing students about difficulties students encountered with interpreting linguistic terms occurring in problems, the math concepts alluded to, and ways that visual images supported performance. Her findings supported the conclusion that the presence of diagrammatic images related to critical problem information supported ELLs' performance when they encountered difficulties in understanding the English statement of problems.

Although the simple conclusion that presence of visual or other aids common to test accommodations is supported by the foregoing study, there is not always clear evidence that these aids really work as intended—a partial reason why the testing accommodation research has not always found that accommodations work as intended (see Kopriva et al., 2007). There is a growing literature regarding the cognitive functioning of persons in a first and second language that builds on cognitive psychology research that is relevant to this disparity. This chapter does not review this research in detail, but its mention is useful, nonetheless, because it suggests that the performance demands of learning tasks are an important issue that needs to be considered in understanding ELLs' learning. This research cited focuses on ELLs' performance of very specific cognitive learning and performance tasks and on how multiple representations of task information— for example, L1 and L2 representation, computer-aided figural representation, or animation—affects emerging bilinguals' accuracy and efficiency in problem solving. Three not-altogether-consistent examples of such research cited here illustrate how the theoretical notion of *cognitive load* can help explain limitations that ELL or other dual language–immersed students face when asked to perform complex learning and other cognitive tasks. According to cognitive load theory (Sweller, 1988), learning and problem solving are dependent on the capacity of working memory to keep track of information relevant to performing the tasks at hand. That working memory capacity is limited to about seven, plus or minus two, chunks or sets of information at a time is one of the earliest findings of cognitive psychology (Miller, 1956).

Plass, Chun, Mayer, and Leutner (2003), using a cognitive load research paradigm, examined the ability of bilinguals asked to learn new vocabulary terms embedded in reading texts in a second language. They postulated that bilinguals' effectiveness in vocabulary learning in a second language is heavily dependent on the working memory capacity of learners. They tested the hypothesis that extra support for reading via computer-provided visual, written, or orally read annotations regarding word meaning in L1 would facilitate L2 vocabulary learning. Contrary to expectations, their findings indicated that visual annotations reduced vocabulary learning for second-language learners relative to other second-language learners or native-language students receiving no annotations or orally read annotations explaining the meanings of words. They concluded that the addition of supplemental visual support, rather than reducing processing load, actually overloaded the memory capacity of second-language students and that this led to a deterioration in their ability to learn. They suggested that offering students a choice in what multiple representation support they would receive would ameliorate this negative effect. Students would be able to decide on their own what form of either visual or oral support would help or hinder their information processing, taking into account their own sense of what was most effective for them.

The latter hypothesis held up in a study by Durán and Moreno (2004), who found that providing ELL elementary school students with a choice of oral support in either Spanish or English during a visually animated mathematics learning task improved students' performance compared to students not provided the extra language support. Research such as the foregoing continues, but although it is informative on cognitive grounds, and suggests strongly that cognitive and assessment tasks presented to ELL students have to be carefully understood in terms of their linguistic and information processing demands to interpret performance on these tasks, research by and large has yet to broach ways in which social and cultural understandings of context may have a concomitant effect on ELLs' performance on typical school learning tasks and assessment tasks intended to reflect school learning. Here is where attention to ELLs' background can add insights that portend such understanding.

Recall that earlier, the issue of the great heterogeneity in ELLs' background was brought up. Abedi et al. (2004), going beyond concern for the effectiveness and validity of assessment accommodations on ELLs, raise concern for understanding how background differences within ELLs might affect assessment scores. Using postassessment questionnaires to gather background information, they found that student information on time lived in the United States, language spoken at home, and self-ratings of understanding English at school, proficiency in the non-English language, and English-language status predicted NAEP science assessment performance significantly better for students not receiving an English dictionary accommodation than for students receiving the accommodation at the fourth-grade level. Although the results at the eighth-grade level did not attain statistical significance, they were in the same direction. The evidence suggests that the dictionary accommodation reduces the importance of the selected background variables as determinates of student performance on the NAEP science assessment. The findings also suggest that students from different non-English backgrounds may benefit differentially from the availability of the dictionary accommodation. In particular, fourth-grade students from a Korean-language background seemed to benefit significantly better from this accommodation.

Solano-Flores (2006) and Solano-Flores and Nelson-Barber (2001) suggest that student, schooling, and language background variables interact in systematic patterns that affect cognitive performance on NAEP and specially developed standards-based science items in English for ELL students. The key idea is that variation in assessment performance on particular items in English for ELLs is not solely because of student ability factors and an unexplainable noise-error factor but also systematic error of measurement that can be explained by an interaction between these factors and student background factors. Consistent with Lee's (2005) advocacy for greater sensitivity to cultural influence on science assessment performance, they argue that there is an underlying notion of assessment cultural validity that needs to be considered when explaining performance on science items (and items in other content areas) by ELLs. Solano-Flores and Nelson-Barber (2001) and Solano-Flores and Trumbull (2003) report generalizabilty theory statistical studies and cognitive lab studies of ELLs with different language, schooling, and national origin backgrounds on specific NAEP assessment items. The generalizability studies found that some ELL student groups from different language backgrounds show more variability in performing on specific assessment items than others. The cognitive lab studies isolated specific comprehension issues encountered by students from different backgrounds in understanding required information in assessment items. Solano-Flores (2006) points to evidence that ELLs from different background might require different numbers of assessment items for assessment reliability to be high enough to support the validity of assessments. However, Solano-Flores and Nelson-Barber are careful to point out that the underlying question of assessment validity needs to take into account more specifically the cognitive and linguistic backgrounds of examinees and how the interpretation of assessment item information is constructed by examinees.

High School Exit Examinations and ELLs

In 2005–2006, there were 25 states implementing high school exit examinations as requirements for receiving the high school diploma (Center for Education Policy [CEP], 2006). These states comprise 65% of the nation's students and 76% of the nation's ethnic minority students. Although not computed formally, this would comprise between 50% to 80% of all ELLs who are thus required to pass high school exit examinations to receive a high school diploma. Use of high school exit examinations for many states is also tied to meeting NCLB requirements for AYP goals in reading, mathematics, and science, but several states, such as New York with its Regents Examination system, include additional areas of subject matter assessment as part of their high school examination system.

ELLs lag considerably across the country in passing high school exit examinations. The CEP (2006) reports that among 22 states providing breakouts of pass rates for ELLs in 2005 on their first try at passing, between 17% and 60% fewer ELLs passed the reading and English arts high school exit exams compared to students as a whole in their respective state (median = 35%). The corresponding gap in mathematics pass rates was noticeably lower, with the gap within a state ranging from 41% to 4% (median = 20%). These differences are consistent with the hypothesis that ELLs will have more difficulty with assessments that require a greater reliance on English language assessments.

There is a lack of research comparing the background and previous achievement records of ELLs who pass or fail their state's high school examination on their first attempt at passing the examination. There is some reason to believe that those failing to pass are heterogeneous in terms of their prior achievement and history in U.S. schools. Specifically, there is evidence (Callahan, 2005) that a significant number of these students represent "long-term ELLs." These are students who have been classified as ELLs for more than 5 years and failed to be reclassified as English proficient by the time they reach the 10th grade. Callahan (2005), in her research on achievement of ELLs in California high schools, suggests that academic tracking of these students is occurring and that these students show a historical pattern of cumulative low school achievement prior to high school entry. She also cites research by Raudenbush, Rowan, and Cheong (1993) reporting that low academic tracking of students is associated with less demanding language and discourse practices in classrooms as well as less demanding academic content. These possibilities are ones deserving greater research attention, as they suggest that the socialization of students to schooling and the opportunity for ELLs to learn and develop an identity as successful students are critical issues tied to both communication and learning of content.

RECONSTRUCTING ELL STUDENTS' ACHIEVEMENT AS ACTIVITY AND AN EXAMPLE OF IMPROVING ASSESSMENT OF ACQUISITION OF ACADEMIC ENGLISH

Classroom Learning Activity

The notion of cultural validity of assessments in the context of the goals of large-scale state assessments under NCLB and on high school exit examinations to measure what ELL students know and can do based on learning standards is an awesome task, given the cumulative issues that have been cited. Both language and culture are deeply implicated in the validity of assessments, and they are also intertwined with ELL students' educational and experiential histories and opportunity to learn what is expected in classrooms under existing educational policies. What can be done to create assessments that go beyond the limitations of existing large-scale assessments as indicators of what ELL students know and can do? It is important to realize that resolving these issues by refining the design and implementation of existing large-scale assessments will get the field only so far.

Baker (2007), looking toward the future, suggested that we need additional tools to complement existing large-scale state assessments to create assessments and bodies of evidence that reflect students' development and learning accomplishments in a manner more sensitive to public policy and the emerging goals of schools in the new millennium. She advocated that current psychometric methods need to be extended to better map curriculum goals and students' growth in subject matter competence and its application to new learning over time. She suggested that educators explore a wide variety of assessment tools and bodies of evidence of student accomplishments that schools and the public at large will value as important learning outcomes of enduring significance for students. She mentioned, in this regard, that we need to consider tools for the accumulation of evidence of achievement growth sensitive to students' background and unique propensities to learn different skills and knowledge in different ways. Also at issue are students' unique pathways through schooling, given these characteristics. Baker cited the distortions to instruction that occur, given schools' and teachers' accountability to raise scores of students on large-scale assessments under state and federal schooling accountability policies. Although these perspectives are relevant to U.S. students at large, they have special relevance for second-language learner and immigrant students in international contexts, given second-language learners' diversity, language needs, and learning needs, as previously cited.

One way through this thicket is to start by reconceptualizing what we can mean by *classroom achievement* itself. Although there is no one way to resolve this issue, researchers in the tradition of cultural historical activity theory (CHAT; Cole, 1996) provide valuable insights that imply we ought to look more closely at classroom interaction itself as the locus of assessment and learning. From a CHAT perspective, human development and competence emerge through socialization processes that support individuals' acquisition of skills and knowledge that allow persons to develop and exercise identities as members of social groups and participants in social domains and social institutions. Fundamental to CHAT and related sociocultural approaches (see, e.g., Gee, 2007), human social interaction is the primary route for learning to take place. This concern, of course, also includes students' functioning and interaction in classrooms as learning sites.[2,3]

Scribner (1979), in her research on the cultural foundations of cognitive and linguistic skills, called attention to the notion that members of cultures and social groups acquire and develop "genres" for thinking, problem solving, and language use attuned to their everyday living circumstances. Building on Vygotsky (1978) and Leontiev (1981), Cole (1996) and Wertsch (1998) call attention to the fundamental principle that human action is tied to how individuals come to perceive and interpret the situations they construe and how they use these construals to project and guide their purposive action. Situations are interpreted in terms of components involving projections about who, where, when, what (goals), why, and how. These are notions that in contemporary cognitive science undergird social and cognitive action described in terms of scripts (Nelson, 1996) or cultural mental models of situations and action (Holland & Quinn, 1987). What do these ideas suggest about conceptualizing the development of learning agency among ELL students, assessment, and opportunity to learn in the classroom?

ELL students need to acquire identities intimately tied to their agency as learners in the context of classroom cultures and genres for thinking, problem solving, and language use that fit the demands of classroom learning goals. Scarcella (2003) and Bailey (2006) provide elaborate accounts of the range of academic English skills ELL students need to acquire, and Adamson (1993) elaborates how cognitive schema and script theory and Vygotskian theory improve our understanding of how ELLs come to be socialized to participate in classroom learning tasks and to meet communicative competence requirements of these tasks. Consistent with the accounts of Nelson (1996), Holland and Quinn (1987), and Cole (1996), ELL students need to acquire mental and cultural models and scripts for how to act out being competent participants in classroom learning activities, and this includes acquiring competence in using language and language structures to participate in learning activities for communicative purposes.

Taking things a bit further from a Vygotskian perspective, Tharp and Gallimore (1988) assert that bona fide instruction can occur only when students are assisted in performing and progressively internalizing knowledge and skills they have not previously mastered. According to this "strong" definition of instruction, true instructional learning does not occur unless students actually come to know and do things that they previously have not mastered through participation in instructional activity. For learning to occur via instruction, students and teachers or teacher aides must jointly construct understandings of what the goals of learning activity are about and of how to evaluate competence in learning progression. Interaction and communication are central to this process, and this must involve participants' assessment of their intentions and common construals of activity and social and self-regulation of performance to respond to assessment. As effective instructional activity proceeds, students go from not being able to perform tasks and apply knowledge to being able to do so with support from more capable others. This support may be in the form of direct advice on how to perform tasks and apply knowledge, to modeling of competence by more capable others, and to reciprocal interaction where a more capable other extends scaffolding via interaction to guide a learner through next steps of competent performance within their "zone of proximal" development. As student learners acquire competence, they begin to internalize this socially shared understanding of competence so that it may be displayed with less overt support from more capable others, though always, competent performance remains a social act requiring that learners recognize how competent performance is realized through shared social perceptions of action in the classroom and its ongoing range of cultural practices.

The importance of the foregoing resonates with the seminal qualitative research findings of Wong Fillmore (1976), who found that ELL children's social interaction with native English speakers provided the ELL children with exposure to native, fluent exercise of English discourse and speech act forms that the ELL children could then approximate in their interaction with the native English–speaking children. Wong Fillmore's research showed that this strategy, when accompanied by the reciprocal response of competent English speakers, acknowledging the functional intent of ELL students' utterances, helped ELL children acquire increased English competence through repeated refinement of the intended linguistic form.

So as we think about how to develop a stronger foundation for ELL assessment, it would seem very helpful to worry about how our assessment designs and assessment targets might benefit from the foregoing perspective.

Assessing ELL Academic English Competency: An Example

In what follows, an account is given of how ELL student assessment might be reconceptualized toward this end, with an emphasis on acquiring one very important class of academic English skills: being able to recognize questions and knowing how to answer them appropriately. The question-recognition and answering contexts under consideration involve reading and understanding a text and answering a question about what was read. This is but one example of the great range of academic language skills in English that ELL students are required to master, but its consideration has much to offer in that it moves the issue of assessment and its connection to learning in a concrete manner. Rather than addressing how assessments might be improved to inform the learning of academic English in the abstract, the example allows us to be concrete about ways that a specific model for a particular class of functional English usage can be coupled with assessment in a manner tied to the improved use of assessment for the purpose of evaluating students' learning.

Questions, like other linguistic forms, do not exist in everyday reality in isolation. They arise and are used as communicative discourse forms within situations and activities where they assist participants in negotiating meanings and getting practical business done. This is certainly the case in classrooms beginning in the earliest grades, where they form a foundational genre for classroom interaction and learning. Students must develop the ability to recognize their occurrence and how they fit into academic tasks as part of classroom cultural practices. And beyond this, students must acquire the ability to go about answering them competently in written as well as oral form.

Durán and Szymanski (1997) reported a study using formal pre- and postassessment of third-grade ELL students' ability to benefit from question-answering instruction. An important feature of this research, with import for new forms of assessment, is that the study also involved analysis of discourse interaction among students and their teacher during question-answering instruction. The research used a CHAT and Vygotskian perspective to analyze when and how students actually worried collectively about the specific linguistic and semantic properties of questions and how they pursued answering them in writing through their interaction.

From a Vygotskian perspective, the challenge of the research was to start with the research issue: How well can individual students working alone answer written questions about meaning conveyed in text passages prior to start of a specific lesson sequence intended to improve question-answering skills? This was the role of the preassessment. A second question was How well can individual students working alone answer questions following participation in the instructional intervention? Evidence of increased independent performance would be consistent with the inference that students had learned from instruction—though a stronger research design would have required a comparison group with no intervening targeted instruction on question answering to control for the possibility that repeated exposure itself to question-answering demands on the posttest improved performance just because students were already familiar with question-answering demands from the pretest.

However, the most critical component of the Vygotskian and activity theory perspective in the Durán and Szymanski (1997) study was its analysis of how the teacher's instructional interaction with students, and students' interaction with each other and the teacher, made visible students' acquisition and use of the teacher's cultural model or schema for how to answer questions. The analysis of this interaction also revealed evidence of formative assessment. As the students interacted, they evaluated their knowledge of the teacher's model of how to analyze and answer questions, and they regulated their understanding of this model through offering feedback to each other so as to better apply the model. Consistent with a Vygotskian account, the talk or explanation of how to answer questions was first shared as interaction between the "expert" teacher and "novice" students. The teacher explained how to identify different "*wh* question" linguistic markers—*who, what, when, why,* and *how*—and that they occurred at the beginning of a question sentence or clause. (Consider, e.g., "What did Jim buy at the store?") She also modeled and explained that the question always pertained to a semantic subject (e.g., "Jim") explicitly mentioned in the question and that the question marker specified the kind of semantic information requested about the subject (e.g., *what* pertained to an object bought by Jim at the store). She showed students how to keep track of the *wh* question marker and subject by underlining pertinent parts of the written question. She next modeled how students might search a portion of a target text for the answer to the question—again underlining possible relevant sections. She also showed how once the relevant information was found in the story, students could next begin planning and writing their answer. This, prototypically, was modeled by the teacher as first "echoing" the subject (e.g., "Jim") at the start of the written answer, followed by restating information already given in the question with an appropriate change in verb tense (as in "Jim bought") and then finishing the answer-sentence with the new information completing the semantic requirement for an answer (e.g., "a shirt"). The teacher in this process also explained to students the difference between answering a written versus spoken answer to a question. She explained that in face-to-face talk, people typically just give the answer without all the other information made explicit in the written academic form of a question answer (e.g., by just uttering, "A shirt").

The Durán and Szymanski (1997) study found evidence of gains on ELL students' ability to answer the same *wh* question forms from pretest to posttest. They also showed evidence that the students were able to emulate the teacher's way of talking about question answering, and steps in question answering, through their social regulation of problem solving to answer questions in small groups. The interaction analyses revealed that students reminded each other of the steps that the teacher had shown them for answering different types of *wh* question forms and that they assessed how well they were carrying out these steps through their interactions with each other and how they refined their problem solving so as to reflect better the teacher's model and explicit steps for answering questions.

This example of research is suggestive of how one might improve assessments of ELL students by having a clear specification of what competencies students are expected to acquire as a result of specific instructional sequences and experiences. It further illustrates the value and importance of having available a specific framework for instruction that can help analyze how students might practice and improve their learning competence through steps that they undertake in performing a complex learning task. The specificity cited does not imply that there is one best or only way to teach question answering. It does imply, however, that having a clear conception of a target skill domain and how instruction in that domain is designed to occur helps and that evidence from formal pre- and postassessments and assessments rendered in instructional interaction can be interpreted to ground an understanding of important learning.

How does an approach to instruction and assessment such as the preceding link with the goals of educational standards–informed instruction for ELLs? First, it is important to note that such links are possible. Statements of learning standards in English language arts can be connected to instructional practices addressing acquisition of those standards by students. Formal pre- and postassessments tied to standards can be used to evaluate whether students have acquired knowledge and skills. Note, though, that large-scale assessments are not capable of such refined diagnosis. Large-scale assessments used by states in an area such as English language arts are "status" instruments and are administered only once per year and intended only to be gross measures of what students know and can do in a subject matter area. These assessments are not intended sensitively to measure growth in students' learning across time.

In addition, it is also important to understand that statements of learning standards in an area such as English language arts or any other academic area cannot adequately treat how learning is supported and how it might use assessments to guide instruction. The notion of "classroom formative assessment" has been explored in recent years to address this issue (Black & Wiliam, 1998). This notion of assessment addresses how teachers can use day-to-day assessment information to guide instruction. Whereas this work has concerned use of formal classroom assessments for this purpose, others have extended the notion of formative assessment so that it is considered as potentially occurring within learning interaction itself (Torrance & Pryor, 1998), consistent with the analyses described by Durán and Szymanski (1997).

Erickson (2007) refers to this interaction-embedded form of assessment as "proximal formative assessment." Proximal formative assessment centers attention to the ways in which instruction is supported through social interaction. Direct instruction of knowledge and skills will not suffice. Students cannot demonstrate acquisition of new knowledge and skills if they are exposed merely to what they are expected to know and do via a "broadcast" model, where teachers explain and model what needs to be learned without students' having the opportunity to practice use of knowledge and skills with feedback from a teacher or other students regarding the suitability of performance. Instructional contexts are socially constructed, started, maintained, and temporarily terminated by participants through their actions and through their interaction. Assessment is provided via interaction and via ability to understand how to take up the implications of assessment by revisions of subsequent action by learners (see Durán, 1994, for how this take-up is tied to Tharp and Gallimore's [1988] notions of assisted performance). Erickson also raises the issue that we ought not to view learning and assessment supported by interaction as bounded by immediate instructional incidents. He states that the danger is that "'what is learned' by students is treated as an entity that comes to exist after instruction has taken place, and thus, can be measured *as a whole thing of the past*" (p. 190). As an alternative, he proposes that learning be considered as a continuously constructed entity in the ongoing course of classroom life and its activities.

Consistent with Erickson (2007), Durán and Szymanski (1997) and Putney, Green, Dixon, Durán, and Yeager (2000) discuss the notion of consequential progression as a concept capturing how present understandings of a context and activity have a historical reality and the potential to shape and support future interpretations of context and activity. ELL students' learning of new knowledge and skills is not historically isolated and understood by considering just one occasion of instruction that seemed to benefit learning. New learning is based on prior learning, and new learning has further consequences for additional learning. Better understanding how formal assessments and assessments in interaction guide the consequences of prior learning on new learning is complex to consider and lies at the heart of enhancing assessment for ELLs' and other students' school learning. For example, ELL students' acquisition of academic English skills in an area such as question answering is not an isolated learning accomplishment. Such knowledge and skill acquisition is coupled with learning of other academic English skills and becomes part of a repertoire of communication skills that enables learning across domains of social and academic experience. The intent of existing standardized English proficiency tests and state English language arts large-scale assessments is to address evidence of what has been learned, but the design of such assessments is incapable of representing or addressing how learning progresses as a real cultural and social interactional process.

As discussed at the start of this chapter, the most fundamental question about assessment is about what valid inferences may be drawn about competence in a target content domain, given assessment performance information. Large-scale assessments have a severe limitation in this regard. Their results can at best provide a long-distance, coarse, static understanding of what ELLs know and can do, and these inferences are severely affected by ELLs' diverse backgrounds and by the limitations in the design and sensitivity of assessments for this population. That stated, this does not imply that such assessments are not without value, and yes, there are improvements in the ways that such assessments can be supplemented by more targeted formal assessments that reveal cognitive and linguistic growth and by proximal formative assessments that look closely at how interaction in classroom learning activity supports learning from the lived perspectives of ELL students as participants with teachers in creating classroom culture.

CONCLUSION AND FUTURE DIRECTIONS

Looking to the future, beyond refinements of the sort suggested above that make instruction and assessment more tightly linked to ELLs' acquisition of specific important skill types, it is helpful to step back and consider a snapshot critique of large-scale assessment. Students' proficiency in a subject matter can be captured in only a limited manner by one-dimensional constructs of academic competence, such as those operationalized by existing large-scale assessments using item response theory. Although there is research on multidimensional versions of item response theory, there are no versions of such assessments used for accountability purposes by states, and it is not clear how such models would have application to highly complex skill and knowledge domains (though see Mislevy, 1997). The heterogeneity among ELLs, as cited, for example, in the work of Abedi (2004), Martiniello (2007), and Solano-Flores (2006), leads to evidence that assessments administered many ELLs are measuring more than an intended skill and knowledge area. The unaccounted-for error variance in assessment scores is not random error; the research cited indicates that it includes systematic variance in performance that that results from an interaction between the knowledge and skills required to solve particular assessment items and the background and schooling characteristics of ELLs. There is information in these interactions that may have instructional value for students, particularly if instruction can be made culturally and linguistically responsive to the backgrounds of ELL students.

A second limitation of large-scale assessments is that, at best, they can provide only a "thin" coverage of what students know and can do. Such assessments are built to sample discrete skills and knowledge specified in subject matter and corresponding assessment blueprint frameworks. Constructive critics of large-scale assessment, such as Popham (2006), suggest that given the reality that large-scale assessments can present only so many items that cover only so many standards in a subject area, it is wiser to have assessments target fewer assessment standards and to do so in a manner that reflects more systematically how standards might be interrelated. The current call under NCLB for growth models exacerbates this issue, in that state assessment systems lack strong developmental progression models based on cognitive and curriculum design theories for representing how students advance in expertise across years in subject matter domains. These issues are important for understanding ELLs' performance on large-scale assessments within and across years. ELL students enter U.S. schools at varying ages, with varying fluency in English, and with different background and schooling experiences in their primary language. Inferences drawn from large-scale assessment results for ELLs may be invalid because the results do not indicate simple presence as opposed to absence of skills. Existing assessment accommodations for ELLs may not be powerful enough to level the assessment playing field for these students. This is more than an issue of reliability of assessment performance; it can also reflect a mismatch between what ELLs are expected to know and do and systematic variation in their opportunity to learn these skills and knowledge. Not understanding this match and mismatch results in lost information on how schools might better serve these students.

A third limitation of existing large-scale assessments is that they do not reflect current research on the social and cultural nature of learning contexts or cognitive and interaction studies of students' interaction in learning settings that suggest new ways to design evidence of achievement that are different from traditional assessments. This critique is very much in evidence in Baker's (2007) American Educational Research Association presidential address, where she focused centrally on cognitive science research on students' development of subject matter expertise and suggestions on the need for 21st-century students to develop complex skills and knowledge sets attuned to developments in technology applications to daily life, social and institutional demands for increased flexibility and adaptability of employees and leaders, and the increasing importance of communication skills across institutional and global communities. Certainly, here, ELLs' fluency in a non-English language becomes a potential asset for learning and expertise development rather than a deficit to be replaced by English and knowing how to apply skills and knowledge solely in English-speaking contexts.

The real-world and instructional learning environments are much too complex to be represented in depth by assessment items presented in an isolated manner from authentic social and cultural settings for learning, where skills and knowledge are deeply interrelated and integrative in nature. Learning standards themselves suffer the same limitation in that they are embodied in stand-alone statements about skills and knowledge that break down what is to be learned in isolation from the actual processes and sociocultural practices that constitute participation in schools. Sociocultural and activity theory research, evidence-centered design of assessments, and postmodern views of assessment suggest possibilities; see, for example, Moss et al. (2006), Mislevy (1997), and Mislevy and Huang (2006). The focus in these accounts is on the validity of assessments. What do we "really" want evidence of and how do we evaluate and use this evidence? Rhetorically, one might ask, do we really want just to know that students have acquired discrete bits of knowledge and skills, or do we really expect more from students, teachers, and schools? Gee (2007) puts it quite concisely:

> To fairly and truly judge what a person can do, you need to know how the talent (skill, knowledge) you are assessing is situated in—placed within—the lived social practices of the person as well as his or her interpretation of those practices. (p. 364)

You in the foregoing can be seen to refer to all stakeholders concerned with educational outcomes, be they parents, teachers, employers, policymakers, and so on. And importantly, *you* can also refer to students' own inferences about their competencies and their peers' inferences of their distributed competence.

Given these challenges, where might we go in improving assessments of ELL students? Baker (2007) provides some suggestions that would seem quite appropriate. She introduced the notion of *qualification*—a "trusted, certified accomplishment" in school, but also possibly outside of classrooms, by a student that would augment accountability assessment performance as indicators of a broader range of student achievement, beyond learning of specific skills. A qualification would involve choices made by students about preferred achievement areas, goals, and a school-sanctioned crediting system for students regarding these accomplishments. A crediting system would need to certify what would count as significant learning experiences, organization of work and effort, required judgment and certification of expertise by others in an achievement area, and validation of such a system based on inferences of what a qualification means. Instead of a test score, a student's qualification would represent a set of significant accomplishments in a complex achievement area that would include but go beyond subject matter expertise, such as application of knowledge and skills to a public service project, complex artistic performance, or some other complex domain of applied knowledge and skills.

It will be very interesting to consider how Baker's call for a qualification system of assessment could be made relevant to ELL assessment in U.S. schools and elsewhere. The immigrant and transnational experience of ELLs presents these students with many linguistic, cultural, and social challenges that, when overcome, represent the resiliency and adaptability of humans and human intelligence at large. This is a new frontier for ELL assessment. The contemporary notion of setting learning and assessment goals through "backward mapping" seems relevant here (Wiggins & McTighe, 1998). In backward mapping, a curriculum, instruction, and accompanying classroom assessments are designed from the top down, starting with a clarification and detailed statement of educational goals, followed by specification of instructional practices and assessments that could be used to achieve goals. Viewed as a dialectical process, what has become popularly known as backward mapping can be represented from a CHAT perspective as being framed by four questions (Durán, Escobar, & Wakin, 1997):

- What is achievement?
- What activities give rise to achievement?
- What evidence is there of achievement in activities?
- What are the socioeducational consequences of the foregoing?

These four questions are interlocking. They form a conceptual schema not unlike the schema underlying the paradigm of critical pedagogy, which sets forth an unending dialectical cycle of investigating how to conceptualize important educational and social problems, how to devise and implement strategies to solve problems, and how to evaluate the success of problem solving and then go on to better reframe problems and strategies and implementation of strategies (Wink, 2005). Deeply understanding these questions and how to approach answering them from a CHAT perspective commensurate with views on how to establish new understandings of what achievement means for ELL and other students is nontrivial. Durán and Szymanski (1997) postulate that students' moment-to-moment interpretation of learning activity as social and cultural practice and as manifestation of identity and agency are central. The notion of consequential progression applies. How might past and current learning experiences add up to form trajectories for personal development and new forms of learning? What activities and evidence provide insights and data into this historical as well as immediately situated development? How does our thinking about education and its goals get transformed by considering enhanced notions of achievement akin to those described by Baker (2007) and others? Within the boundaries of an academic year, it has been possible to use ethnography to trace students' progression through learning sequences that provide interactional evidence of how young elementary school ELL students form ongoing identities as early learners of social science (Putney et al., 2000) or natural science (Reveles, Kelly, & Durán, 2007). How do we augment such research to track both qualitative and quantitative evidence of students' longer range development of identities that can be meaningful parts of students' lives and can show evidence of Baker's endorsements? These are important next questions.

In closing, it is helpful to return to the work of Moss et al. (2006). Along with Rochex (2006), these investigators remind us of the deep interplay that exists between the expectations of educational policymakers at different levels of government, and even across nations, and assessments administered to students. There is no escaping that national and major jurisdictional levels of educational governance motivate and set the expectations of local educational practitioners, teachers, parents, and students themselves regarding the meaning and implications of assessments for schooling accountability purposes and for student high-stakes purposes such as high school graduation (McDonnel, 2004). The reality is that very few educational stakeholders are able to comprehend the technical characteristics of assessments well, if at all. These stakeholders also, by and large, have only a limited grasp of the meaning and implications of terms such as *English-language learner* and *English proficient*, and the complexity of this limited understanding is also caught in scientific and social science debates of the meaning of such terms, as well as in policy debates.

Much work remains to be done to better ground the field of assessment of ELLs. As part of this process, in closing, it is important to understand that the findings and issues cited in this chapter are of equal relevance to all students. Focus on ELLs helps us understand better how important historical, cultural, and linguistic background differences have to be taken into account in interpreting the results of assessments and the design of new assessment strategies aligned to the characteristics of students. Also at issue is how to locate and treat educational practitioners as full partners in pursuing these matters, and it is good to see at the close of 2007 that in the United States, federally funded efforts are under way to create consortia among states to support teachers' development of formative assessments based on general backward-mapping strategies that require discourse and dialogue among teachers, parents, policymakers, and students regarding what is desired and valued as learning and what evidence can count for learning (Cech, 2007). This will certainly contribute to understanding better how locally developed assessments grounded in authentic learning activity can complement information currently provided by large-scale state achievement assessments, though much work will be required. All of the concerns discussed here also deserve further exploration in different national contexts and comparatively across countries in light of variations in nations' education policies and conception of desired schooling outcomes (see Rochex, 2006).

NOTES

[1]The No Child Left Behind stipulation that states develop English language development (ELD) standards requires states to set explicit expectations of about the basic English (reading, writing, listening, and speaking) skills required of ELLs learning English throughout the K–12 grade

span. Typically, these ELD standards are arranged by specific grades or in clusters of adjacent grades, so that they are appropriate to the English language requirements of curricula encountered by students.

English language proficiency (ELP) tests that are administered to English language learner (ELL) students are built to sample the requirements of ELD standards at a given school grade or grade band appropriate to a student. They should not be confused with tests of English language arts administered annually to all eligible students as part of large-scale assessments. The former are to gauge ELLs' mastery of English as a second language and readiness to receive instruction in English. The latter are to assess students' command of English as found and taught in regular English language arts classes at a target grade level. In reality, ELD and English language arts (ELA) competencies are expected to blend for ELLs. As ELLs become more competent in English, they acquire foundational skills for meeting ELA standards.

[2]As mentioned, the discussion regarding cultural historical activity theory (CHAT) as a useful perspective from which to reconceptualize classroom and schooling achievement is not intended to suggest that there are no other perspectives based on alternative statements of theory, research, and practice that address similar concerns with diverse populations of students. For example, Banks and Banks (2001) provide comprehensive coverage of such topics in their *Handbook of Research on Multicultural Education* from multiple disciplinary perspectives.

Much of this relevant theory, research, and practitioner guidance not described explicitly as under the aegis of CHAT often is described as founded on sociocultural, sociolinguistic, or constructivist approaches to learning, instruction, and classroom communication. Early work of this sort emanated, for example, from the writings and research compilations of investigators such Au (1980); Cazden, John, and Hymes (1972); Cook-Gumperz (1986); Erickson and Mohatt (1982); Erikson and Shultz (1981); Green (1983); Green and Wallat (1981); Heath (1983); and Trueba, Guthrie, and Au (1981). Works such as those mentioned were among the first investigations to address how analysis of discourse and interaction laid bare how perception of interactional context and participation in face-to-face interaction was centrally dependent on the cultural, social, and linguistic resources and background of communicants in schooling and other settings. Investigators such as Saravia-Shore and Arvizu (1992), in their edited volume *Cross-Cultural Literacy*, were among the first to extend concern for ethnographic and sociolinguistic study of classroom communication so that it included examination of how schooling policies, and in particular, resistance to bilingual education policies, affected everyday classroom interaction.

Wells (1999), in his volume *Dialogic Inquiry*, was among the first sociolinguistic and discourse analyst researchers to link Vygotskian theory (and issues tied to CHAT) to classroom research. He was also influential in bringing increased attention to the research of functional linguists such as Halliday and British, European, and Australian researchers on what later came to be known as the "new literacies" research paradigm (see, e.g., Gee, 2004; and Barton, Hamilton, and Ivanic, 2000). The new literacies paradigm has proven quite valuable in suggesting that the functions and linguistic form of spoken and written texts arise from socialization to cultural practices and instrumental goals associated with texts.

It is not possible in the present chapter to survey the extensive literature that followed these earlier works that has put increased attention on how sociolinguistic, ethnographic, and new literacies research has addressed how learning in schooling and other contexts is driven by interactive processes. That stated, readers are referred to volumes by Bloome, Carter, Christian, Otto, and Shuart-Faris (2005) and Schleppegrell and Colombi (2002) for examples of recent research in this area. The latter volume is of particular relevance to this chapter because it address how second-language learners (as well as first-language learners) acquire competence in controlling the linguistic and discourse features of texts tied to language as used in academic settings. Freeman and Freeman (2002) do an excellent job of pursuing these issues from the perspective of teachers and focus on the special challenges of addressing the academic literacy needs of long-term high school ELL students.

It is important to note that all of the research cited above has involved primary use of qualitative research methods and virtually no use of quantitative test data or use of experimental design techniques. One upshot of this is that research of this sort has been excluded from consideration in a recent major synthesis of findings in a chapter on findings of sociocultural research on literacy development of second-language learners by August and Shanahan (2006). This omission is logical on the basis of empiricist criteria used in this volume to define what counts as defensible research findings. The criteria are appropriate only for studies that permit comparison groups and use quantitative methods. However, these criteria for valid findings do not hold for researchers in the traditions of sociocultural, sociolinguistic, ethnographic, and CHAT perspectives. See Erickson (2007) and Moss, Girard, and Haniford (2006) for a further explication of this matter.

[3]Also, comprehensive approaches to reconceptualization of classroom and schooling achievement are becoming more and more prevalent from a CHAT perspective. For example, an excellent resource in this regard are papers and reports published electronically by the Center for Research on Education, Diversity, and Excellence (CREDE) at the Internet site http://crede.berkeley.edu/index.html. The CREDE Web site is particularly powerful in its attention to ways that teacher training, staff development, and instructional practice promote effective instruction, given students' cultural and linguistic backgrounds.

REFERENCES

Abedi, J. (2004). The No Child Left Behind Act and English language learners: Assessment and accountability issues. *Educational Researcher, 33*(1), 4–14.

Abedi, J. (2006, August). *The use of accommodations for English language learners: Latest research and current practice.* Presentation at the LEP Partnership Meeting, Washington, DC.

Abedi, J., & Gandara, P. (2006). Performance of English language learners as a subgroup in large-scale assessment: Interaction of research and policy. *Educational Measurement: Issues and Practices, 25*(4), 36–46.

Abedi, J., Hofstetter, C., & Lord, C. (2004). Assessment accommodations for English language learners: Implications for policy-based empirical research. *Review of Educational Research, 74,* 1–28.

Abedi, J., Lord, C., & Hofstetter, C. (1998). *Impact of selected background variables on students' NAEP math performance.* Los Angeles: University of California, Los Angeles, Center for the Study of Evaluation/National Center for Research on Evaluation, Standards, and Student Testing.

Abedi, J., Lord, C., Kim, C., & Miyoshi, J. (2000). *The effects of accommodations on the assessment of LEP students in NAEP.* Los Angeles: University of California, Los Angeles, National Center for Research on Evaluation, Standards, and Student Testing.

Adamson, H. D. (1993). *Academic competence: Theory and classroom practice. Preparing ESL students for content courses.* New York: Longman.

American Educational Research Association, American Psychological Association, & National Council on Measurement in Education. (1999). *Standards for educational and psychological testing.* Washington, DC : American Psychological Association.

Au, K. H. (1980). Participation structures in a reading lesson with Hawaiian children: Analysis of a culturally appropriate instructional event. *Anthropology and Education Quarterly, 11,* 91–115.

August, D., & Shanahan, T. (Eds.). (2006). *Developing literacy in second-language learners.* Mahwah, NJ: Lawrence Erlbaum.

Bailey, A. (2006). *The language demands of school: Putting academic English to the test.* New Haven, CT: Yale University Press.

Baker, E. (2007, April). *The end(s) of testing.* Presidential address given at the annual meeting of the American Educational Research Association. Retrieved September 1, 2007, from http://www.softconference.com/Media/WMP/270409/s40.htm

Baker, E., & Linn, R. L. (2004). Validity issues for accountability systems. In S. H. Fuhrman & R. F. Elmore (Eds.), *Redesigning accountability systems for education* (pp. 47–72). New York: Teachers College Press.

Banks, J., & Banks, C. (Eds.). (2001). *Handbook of research on multicultural education.* San Francisco: Jossey-Bass.

Barton, D., Hamilton, M., & Ivanic, R. (Eds.). (2000). *Situated literacies: Reading and writing in context.* New York: Routledge.

Black, P., & Wiliam, D. (1998). Assessment and classroom learning. *Assessment in Education,* 5(1), 7–74.

Bloome, D., Carter, S. P., Christian, B. M., Otto, S., & Shuart-Faris, N. (2005). *Discourse analysis and the study of classroom language and literacy events: A microethnographic perspective.* Mahwah, NJ: Lawrence Erlbaum.

Callahan, R. M. (2005). Tracking and high school English learners: Limited opportunity to learn. *American Educational Research Journal, 42,* 305–328.

Cazden, C., John, V. P., & Hymes, D. (Eds.). (1972). *Functions of language in the classroom.* New York: Teachers College Press.

Cech, S. (2007, August 15). 10-state pilot preparing teachers to develop tests. *Education Week,* p. 10.

Center for Education Policy. (2006). *State high school exit exams: A challenging year.* Washington, DC: Author.

Cole, M. (1996). *Cultural psychology.* Cambridge, MA: Harvard University Press.

Cook-Gumperz, J. (Ed.). (1986). *The social construction of literacy.* New York: Cambridge University Press.

Durán, R. P. (1994). Cooperative learning for language minority students. In R. A. DeVillar, C. J. Faltis, & J. Cummins (Eds.), *Cultural diversity in schools: From rhetoric to practice* (pp. 145–159). Albany: State University of New York Press.

Durán, R. P. (2006). *State implementation of NCLB policies and interpretation of the NAEP performance of English language learners.* Palo Alto, CA: American Institutes for Research, NAEP Validity Studies.

Durán, R. P., Escobar, F., & Wakin, M. (1997). Improving classroom instruction for Latino elementary school students: Aiming for college. In M. Yepes-Baraya (Ed.), *1996 ETS invitational conference on Latino education issues* (pp. 39–53). Princeton, NJ: Educational Testing Service.

Durán, R. P., & Moreno, R. (2004). Do multiple representations need explanation? The role of verbal guidance and individual differences in multimedia mathematics learning. *Journal of Educational Psychology, 96*(3), 492–503.

Durán, R. P., & Szymanski, M. (1997). *Assessment of transfer in a bilingual cooperative learning curriculum* (CSE Technical Report 450). Los Angeles: University of California, Los Angeles, National Center for Research on Evaluation, Standards, and Student Testing.

Erickson, F. (2007). Some thoughts on "proximal" formative assessment of student learning. In P. Moss (Ed.), *Evidence in decision making: Yearbook of the National Society for the Study of Education* (Vol. 106, pp. 186–216). Malden, MA: Blackwell.

Erickson, F., & Mohatt, G. (1982). Cultural organization of participation structures in two classrooms of Indian students. In G. Spindler (Ed.), *Doing the ethnography of schooling. Educational anthropology in action* (pp. 132–174). New York: Holt, Rinehart & Winston.

Erickson, F., & Shultz, J. (1981). When is a context? Some issues and methods in the analysis of social competence. In J. Green & C. Wallat (Eds.), *Ethnography and language in educational settings* (pp. 147–160). Norwood, NJ: Ablex.

Frances, D. J., Kieffer, M., Lesaux, N., Rivera, H., & Rivera, M. (2006). *Practical guidelines for the education of English language learners: Research-based recommendations for the use of accommodations in large-scale assessments.* Houston, TX: University of Houston, Center on Instruction, Texas Institute for Measurement, Evaluation, and Statistics.

Freeman, Y., & Freeman, D. (with Mercuri, S.) (2002). *Closing the achievement gap. How to reach limited-formal-schooling and long-term English learners.* Portsmouth, NH: Heinemann.

Gee, J. P. (2004). *Situated language and learning. A critique of traditional schooling.* New York: Routledge.

Gee, J. P. (2007). Reflections on assessment from a sociocultural perspective. In P. Moss (Ed.), *Evidence in decision making: Yearbook of the National Society for the Study of Education* (Vol. 106, pp. 362–375). Malden, MA: Blackwell.

Geisinger, K. F. (1994). Psychometric issues in testing students with disabilities. *Applied Measurement in Education, 7,* 121–140.

Green, J. L. (1983). Research on teaching as a linguistic process: A state of the art. In E. W. Gordon (Ed.), *Review of Research in Education, 10,* 151–252.

Green, J. L., & Wallat, C. (Eds.). (1981). *Ethnography and language in educational settings.* Norwood, NJ: Ablex.

Hambleton, R. K. (2005). Issues, designs, and technical guidelines for adapting tests into multiple languages and cultures. In R. K. Hambleton, P. F. Merenda, & C. D. Spielberger (Eds.), *Adapting educational and psychological tests for cross-cultural assessment* (pp. 3–38). Mahwah, NJ: Lawrence Erlbaum.

Hambleton, R. K., Merenda, P. F., & Spielberger, C. D. (Eds.). (2005). *Adapting educational and psychological tests for cross-cultural assessment.* Mahwah, NJ: Lawrence Erlbaum.

Heath, S. (1983). *Ways with words: Language, life, and work in communities and classrooms.* New York: Cambridge University Press.

Holland, D., & Quinn, N. (Eds.), (1987). *Cultural modes in language and thought.* Cambridge, UK: Cambridge University Press.

Koenig, J., & Bachman, L. (Eds.). (2004). *Keeping score for all: The effects of inclusion and accommodation policies on large-scale educational assessment.* Washington, DC: National Academy Press.

Kopriva, R. (in press). *Improving testing for English language learners.* London: Routledge.

Kopriva, R., Emick, J., Hipolito-Delgado, C., & Cameron, C. (2007). Do proper accommodation assignments make a difference? Examining the impact of improved decision making on scores for English language learners. *Educational Measurement: Issues and Practice, 26*(3), 11–20.

Lee, O. (2005). Science education with English language learners: Synthesis and research agenda. *Review of Educational Research, 75,* 491–530.

Leontiev, A. N. (1981). *Problems of the development of the mind* (M. Kopylova, Trans.). Moscow: Progress.

Martiniello, M. (2007). *Linguistic complexity and differential item functioning (DIF) for English language learners (ELL) in math word problems.* Unpublished doctoral thesis, Harvard University, Cambridge, MA.

Mazzeo, J., Carlson, J. E., Voelkl, K. E., & Lutkus, A. D. (2000). *Increasing the participation of special needs students in NAEP: A report on 1996 NAEP research activities* (NCES 2000–473). Washington, DC: U.S. Department of Education, National Center for Education Statistics.

McDonnel, L. M. (2004). *Politics, persuasion, and educational testing.* Cambridge, MA: Harvard University Press.

Messick, S. (1989). *Validity.* In R. L. Linn (Ed.), *Educational measurement* (3rd ed., pp. 13–103). New York: Macmillan.

Miller, G. J. (1956). The magical number seven, plus or minus two: Some limits on our capacity for processing information. *Psychological Review, 63,* 81–97.

Mislevy, R. (1997). Postmodern test theory. In A. Lesgold, M. Feuer, & A. Black (Eds.), *Transitions in work and learning. Implications for assessment* (pp. 180–199). Washington, DC: National Academy Press.

Mislevy, R. J., & Huang, C. W. (2006). *Measurement models as narrative structures.* Los Angeles: University of California, Los Angeles, National Center for Research on Evaluation, Standards, and Student Testing and Center for the Study of Evaluation.

Moss, P. A., Girard, B. J. , & Haniford, L. C. In J. Green & A. Luke (Eds.), (2006). Validity in educational assessment. *Review of Research in Education, 30,* 109–162.

Nelson, K. (1996). *Language in cognitive development: The emergence of the mediated mind.* Cambridge, UK: Cambridge University Press.

Plass, J. L., Chun, D. M., Mayer, R. E., & Leutner, D. (2003). Cognitive load in reading a foreign language text with multimedia aids and the influence of verbal and spatial abilities. *Computers in Human Behavior, 19,* 221–243.

Popham, J. (2006). *What are some general observations about 21st century skills and assessment?* Presentation given at the annual conference of the Council of Chief State School Officers, San Francisco.

Putney, L., Green, J., Dixon, C., Durán, R., & Yeager, B. (2000). Consequential progressions: Exploring collective-individual development in a bilingual classroom. In C. Lee & P. Smagorinsky (Eds.), *Vygotskian perspectives on literacy research* (pp. 86–126). New York: Cambridge University Press.

Raudenbush, S. W., Rowan, B., & Cheong, Y. F. (1993). Higher order instructional goals in secondary schools: Class, teacher, and school influences. *American Educational Research Journal, 30,* 523–553.

Reveles, J., Kelly, G., & Durán, R. P. (2007). A sociocultural perspective on mediated activity in third grade science. *Cultural Studies of Science Education, 1,* 467–495.

Rivera, C., & Collum, E. (Eds.). (2006). *State assessment policy and practice for English language learners: A national perspective.* Mahwah, NJ: Lawrence Erlbaum.

Rochex, J-Y. (2006). Social, methodological, and theoretical issues regarding assessments: Lessons from a secondary analysis of PISA 2000 literacy tests. *Review of Research in Education, 30,* 163–212.

Sanchez, G. (1934). Bilingualism and mental measures: A word of caution. *Journal of Applied Psychology, 18,* 765–772.

Saravia-Shore, M., & Arvizu, S. (Eds.). (1992). *Cross-cultural literacy: Ethnography of communication in multiethnic classrooms.* New York: Garland.

Scarcella, R. (2003). *Academic English: A conceptual framework.* Santa Barbara: University of California, Santa Barbara, Linguistic Minority Research Institute.

Schleppegrell, M., & Colombi, M. (2002). *Developing advanced literacy in first and second languages: Meaning with power.* Mahwah, NJ: Lawrence Erlbaum.

Scribner, S. (1979). Modes of thinking and ways of speaking: Culture and logic reconsidered. In R. Freedle (Ed.), *New directions in discourse processing* (pp. 223–243). Norwood, NJ: Ablex.

Sireci, S. G. (2005). Unlabeling the disabled: A psychometric perspective on flagging scores from accommodated test administrations. *Educational Researcher, 34*(1), 3–12.

Sireci, S. G., Li, S., & Scarpati, S. (2003). *The effects of test accommodations on test performance: A review of the literature* (Center for Educational Assessment Research Report No. 485). Amherst: University of Massachusetts-Amherst, School of Education.

Sireci, S. G., Patsula, L., & Hambleton, R. K. (2005). Statistical methods for identifying flaws in the test adaption process. In R. K. Hambleton, P. F. Merenda, & C. D. Spielberger (Eds.), *Adapting educational and psychological tests for cross-cultural assessment* (pp. 93–116). Mahwah, NJ: Lawrence Erlbaum.

Sireci, S. G., & Zenisky, A. L. (2006). Innovative item formats in computer-based testing: In pursuit of improved construct representation. In S. M. Downing & T. M. Haladyna (Eds.), *Handbook of test development* (pp. 329–348). Mahwah, NJ: Lawrence Erlbaum.

Solano-Flores, G. (2006). Language, dialect, and register: Sociolinguistics and the estimation of measurement error in the testing of English language learners. *Teachers College Record, 108*(11), 2354–2379.

Solano-Flores, G., & Nelson-Barber, S. (2001). On the cultural validity of science assessments. *Journal of Research in Science Teaching, 38*(5), 553–573.

Solano-Flores, G., & Trumbull, E. (2003). Examining language in context: The need for new research and practice paradigms in the testing of English-language learners. *Educational Researcher, 32*(2), 3–13.

Stansfield, C. W. (1996). Content assessment in the native language. *Practical Assessment, Research and Evaluation, 5*(9). Retrieved June 3, 2007, from http://PAREonline.net/getvn.asp?v =5&n=9

Stansfield, C. W. (2003). Test translation and adaptation in public education in the USA. *Language Testing, 20*(2), 189–207.

Suarez-Orozco, M. (2001). Globalization, immigration, and education: The research agenda. *Harvard Education Review, 71*(3), 345–365.

Sweller, J. (1988). Cognitive load during problem solving: Effects on learning. *Cognitive Science, 12*, 257–285.

Tharp, R., & Gallimore, R. (1988). *Rousing minds to life.* Cambridge, MA: Harvard University Press.

Torrance, H., & Pryor, J. (1998). *Investigating formative assessment.* Philadelphia: Open University Press.

Trueba, H., Guthrie, G., & Au, K. (Eds.). (1981). *Culture and the bilingual classroom: Studies in classroom ethnography.* Rowley, MA: Newbury House.

Valdes, G., & Figueroa, R. (1994). *Bilingualism and testing: A special case of bias.* Norwood, NJ: Ablex.

van der Linden, W. J. (1998). Optimal assembly of psychological and educational tests. *Applied Psychological Measurement, 22*, 195–211.

Vijver, F. J. R., van de, & Poortinga, Y. H. (2005). Conceptual and methodological issues in adapting tests. In R. K. Hambleton, P. F. Merenda, & C. D. Spielberger (Eds.), *Adapting educational and psychological tests for cross-cultural assessment* (pp. 39–64). Mahwah, NJ: Lawrence Erlbaum.

Vygotsky, L. S. (1978). *Mind in society: The development of higher psychological processes* (M. Cole, V. John-Steiner, S. Scribner, & E. Souberman, Eds.). Cambridge, MA: Harvard University Press.

Wainer, H. (1999). Comparing the incomparable: An essay on the importance of big assumptions and scant evidence. *Educational Measurement: Issues and Practice, 18*(4), 10–16.

Wells, G. (1999). *Dialogic inquiry: Towards a sociocultural practice and theory of education.* New York: Cambridge University Press.

Wertsch, J. V. (1998). *Mind as action.* New York: Oxford University Press.

Wiggins, G., & McTighe, J. (1998). *Understanding by design.* Alexandria, VA: Association for Supervision and Curriculum Development.

Wink, J. (2005). *Critical pedagogy: Notes from the real world* (3rd ed.). New York: Allyn & Bacon.

Wong Fillmore, L. (1976). *The second time around: Cognitive and social strategies in second language acquisition.* Unpublished doctoral dissertation, Stanford University, Palo Alto, CA.

Zehler, A. M., Fleischman, H. F., Hopstock, P. J., Stephenson, T. G., Pendzick, M. L., & Sapru, S. (2003). *Descriptive study of services to LEP students and LEP students with disabilities: Volume I. Research report. Final report submitted to U.S. Department of Education, Office of English Language Acquisition.* Arlington, VA: Development Associates.

Chapter 10

Reframing Teacher Professional Learning: An Alternative Policy Approach to Strengthening Valued Outcomes for Diverse Learners

HELEN TIMPERLEY
University of Auckland

ADRIENNE ALTON-LEE
New Zealand Ministry of Education
Iterative Best Evidence Synthesis Programme

This chapter engages in the debate about what counts as professional knowledge from the perspective of improving outcomes for diverse learners. We begin by highlighting the importance of assumptions about appropriate roles for teachers and how those assumptions have shaped the debate about what teachers need to know. Then we consider some myths and evidence about teacher agency that have contributed to a recent international shift in policy attention to the importance of teacher knowledge and, more particularly, how to develop teacher agency and capability.

The main focus of the chapter is on a policy approach to building a multidisciplinary evidence base in education that both identifies the kinds of teacher knowledge that has a positive impact on a range of student outcomes and, at the same time, develops that knowledge through a national collaborative knowledge-building and knowledge-use strategy. The approach described is the New Zealand Iterative Best Evidence Synthesis (BES) Programme, which deliberately and systematically draws on and develops a rich multidisciplinary knowledge base in education. We situate our account of this program within (a) a comparison of a range of international policy approaches to strengthening the evidence base informing what teachers need to know, (b) a vision of the role of teaching as responsive to diverse learners and the evolving challenges of the 21st century, and (c) a touchstone of effectiveness as defined by impacts on a range of valued learner outcomes. We present the findings of a new synthesis of the evidence from 97 empirical studies that identify the development of the kinds of teacher knowledge that have a demonstrated positive impact on outcomes for diverse learners. The

Review of Research in Education
February 2008, Vol. 32, pp. 328–369
DOI: 10.3102/0091732X07308968

findings of the synthesis are exemplified through an in-depth case study of effective professional development designed to support student learning, teacher learning, teacher-educator research, and policy learning.

In conclusion, we highlight the potential of such multidisciplinary collaborative approaches to building the kinds of professional knowledge needed to change outcomes for diverse learners in our schooling system. We also discuss the challenges for both policy and research to engage in such transformational knowledge building.

TEACHER ROLE AND TEACHER KNOWLEDGE

As far back as the writings of Plato, there has been advanced a view of the role of teachers as one of maintaining inequalities in society by educating children of different classes differently. In Plato's "myth of the metals," education is the way by which those who are born "gold" are afforded the greatest honor and power and given very different opportunities to learn than the restricted opportunities for those who are born "brass" or "iron" (Plato, 1968 trans., p. 141). Plato explained that education could be a useful and peaceful alternative to a military regime in maintaining differential status and access to material wealth in society.

Different views about the role of teachers as desirably maintaining or challenging social inequities have persisted across centuries to the current day, leading in turn to very different views about the knowledge needed for teaching. In the *Handbook of Research on Teacher Education*, W. Doyle (1990) explained persisting conflicts about what counts as educational knowledge as arising from fundamentally different views of the proper role of teachers. For example, when the view of teachers is one of "good employee" prepared to maintain the prevailing norms of school practices, then appropriate knowledge for teacher education is essentially experiential and technical, sometimes involving a teacher in implementing prescriptions of practice.

An alternative view advanced by W. Doyle (1990) is one of teachers as "reflective professionals" able to draw on an integrated knowledge base to constantly improve practice through knowledge and inquiry:

The knowledge base for the preparation of reflective professionals includes personal knowledge, the craft knowledge of skilled practitioners, and propositional knowledge from classroom research and the social and behavioural sciences. Within this framework, research and theory do not produce rules or prescriptions for classroom application but rather knowledge and methods of inquiry useful in deliberating about teaching problems and practices. (p. 6)

The debates about what teachers need to know, and the potential of research to inform teacher knowledge and practice, are not new. At a time when teaching was widely considered a craft practice, Winch (1911), a school inspector, joined with professorial colleagues at Cambridge University in explaining the hope for strengthening teaching through using research to inform pedagogy in the newly established *Journal of Experimental Pedagogy*. The vision of the journal was not one just of teachers as recipients of research but of teachers as researchers contributing to professional knowledge building and exchange (Reaney, 1911).

Despite such hopeful beginnings, the relationship between teacher education and research has been vexed by the uncertain and fragmented status of initial teacher education in (and out of) universities. W. Doyle (1990) attributed the low status in the United States in part to tensions between disciplinary and professional knowledge: "Professors in academic departments identify with their disciplines rather than teacher preparation and are frequently antagonistic towards teacher education programs and students" (p. 7). In some jurisdictions, policymakers have turned to other approaches to the development of teacher knowledge, such as school-based apprenticeship models, alternative certification routes, and an open market model for initial teacher education.

TEACHER IMPACT MATTERS

Before directly addressing the evidence about the impact of teaching, it is important to note that there is compelling evidence that poverty, nutrition, health, family processes, and wider social, community, and family influences, such as violence, media, and drug use, affect educational outcomes and children's well-being (Biddulph, Biddulph, & Biddulph, 2003; Mayer, 2002). Although the focus of this review is on our BES focused on teacher knowledge, the Iterative BES Programme has a continuing focus on family and community influences and has provided advice to government about giving priority to matters such as child poverty and early undiagnosed hearing loss. Our consideration of teaching as the *key system influence* complements rather than abnegates evidence about and wider policy implications arising from the impact of families and communities on valued outcomes for children and young people.

Since the outset of our new century, there has been a substantial shift in interest across jurisdictions in the development of teacher knowledge as new evidence about the influence of teaching on student outcomes has become apparent. In the 1960s and '70s, influential reports on the impact of schooling on inequality (Coleman et al., 1966; Jencks et al., 1972) painted a grim picture of schools making relatively little difference to student achievement. Coleman and his colleagues (1966) found that only about 10% of the variance in student achievement could be attributed to schools. However, Coleman's analysis averaged the effect of schools and failed to differentiate the effects of different teachers. Preservice teachers in university courses in the sociology of education in many Western educational jurisdictions encountered the legacy of both this influential research and the neo-Marxist theoretical literature that provided a compelling case that teachers were implicated (albeit unknowingly) in the reproduction of a class society (e.g., Bowles & Gintis, 1976). For some prospective teachers, these arguments became a foundation for a sense of little agency and an "informed" view that their influence could never be significantly equitable or transformational.

The more recent use of multilevel models to estimate the magnitude of variance in students' achievement outcomes that include effects at the class and teacher levels has increasingly highlighted the marked impact teachers can have on differences in achievement. The first *International Handbook of Educational Change* (Cuttance, 1998) signaled a marked shift in thinking about the potential for agency in education partly informed by the evidence emerging from the new multilevel modeling studies capturing both school- and class-level impacts on outcomes:

> Recent research on the impact of schools on student learning leads to the conclusion that 8–19% of the variation in student learning outcomes lies between schools with a further amount of up to 55% of the variation in individual learning outcomes between classrooms within schools. In total, approximately 60% of the variation in the performance of students lies either between schools or between classrooms, with the remaining 40% being due to either variation associated with students themselves or to random influences. (pp. 1158–1159)

Some of the strongest evidence of the effects of quality teaching informing this view is derived from the Australian longitudinal study known as the Victorian Quality Schools Project, where teacher influence on variance has been particularly high in upper secondary subjects (Hill & Rowe, 1996; Rowe & Hill, 1998).

In the United States, Nye, Konstantanopoulos, and Hedges (2004) analyzed the experimental data collected for the Tennessee Class Size Experiment and reported that teacher effects were much larger than school effects, much larger in low-socio-economic-status schools, and "certainly large enough to have policy significance" (p. 253). They found that "the effect of one standard deviation change in teacher effectiveness is larger than, for example, that of reducing class size from 25 to 15" (p. 254) and concluded that intervening to improve teacher quality would be cost-effective compared to class-size reductions. Similarly, from the British research, Muijs and Reynolds (2001) highlighted, "All the evidence that has been generated in the school effectiveness research community shows that classrooms are far more important than schools in determining how children perform at school" (p. vii).

Although different methodological designs, different definitions of what constitutes residual variance, and the different schooling levels, contexts, and outcomes of studies have made this a difficult research literature to come to grips with, there is now good evidence that the impact of teaching and classroom differences on variances in student outcomes are substantial in such countries as the United States, Australia, Sweden, Finland, New Zealand, Canada, Israel, France, and Scotland (Bransford, Darling-Hammond, & LePage, 2005; Scheerens, Vermeulen, & Pelgrum, 1989). The policy importance of this finding has been compellingly articulated.

> The results of this study will document that the most important factor affecting student learning is the teacher. In addition, the results show wide variation in effectiveness among teachers. The immediate and clear implication of this finding is that seemingly more can be done to improve education by improving the effectiveness of teachers than by any other single factor. Effective teachers appear to be effective with students of different achievement levels regardless of the level of heterogeneity in their classrooms (Wright, Horn, & Sanders, 1997, p. 63).

In a range of reviews, Darling-Hammond (2000) made evident the link between the impact of teaching and the influence of teacher education:

> The effect of poor quality teaching on student outcomes is debilitating and cumulative. . . . The effects of quality teaching on educational outcomes are greater than those that arise from students' backgrounds. . . .

A reliance on curriculum standards and statewide assessment strategies without paying due attention to teacher quality appears to be insufficient to gain the improvements in student outcomes sought. . . . The quality of teacher education and teaching appear to be more strongly related to student achievement than class sizes, overall spending levels or teacher salaries. (p. 3)

The importance of this new evidence base has become even more compelling for policymakers given the growing awareness of associated economic, social, and cultural implications. A new Organisation for Economic Co-operation and Development (OECD; 2007) project, Understanding the Social Outcomes of Learning, has been established to develop systematic ways of measuring the impact of education on health and social cohesion. The findings of a wide range of research and development about teaching demonstrate ways of strengthening social cohesion among diverse student populations while also supporting better academic outcomes (Alton-Lee, 2003). Examples include effective uses of structured cooperative groups; reciprocal learning; performing arts; pedagogies that interweave care, respect for cultural identity, and academic challenge; and other approaches that support students to manage conflict productively, optimize peer supports for learning, exercise interpersonal respect, and build learning community (E. Cohen, 1994; Colwell, 1999; Hohepa, Hingaroa Smith, Tuhiwai Smith, & McNaughton, 1992; Palincsar & Brown, 1984).

The case has also been made for a relationship between academic outcomes from schooling and economic growth. Hanushek's (2005) policy brief for the International Academy of Education reports, "One standard deviation on test performance (international mathematics and science tests) was related to one percent difference in annual growth rates of per capita GDP" (p. 4). He concluded, "Governmental investments should focus on school quality because they have such powerful economic impacts. . . . The most likely way to improve student performance is to improve the quality of teachers" (pp. 9, 14).

By 2005, the growing international agreement about the new evidence base informed the landmark OECD (2005b) report, "Teaching Matters." In the influential OECD (2005a) "Indicators Report," the new policy importance of both pedagogy and professional development were highlighted: "At the level of the education system, professional development of teachers is a key policy lever" (p. 20).

EVIDENCE-BASED POLICY AND TEACHER KNOWLEDGE

Ironically, as the importance of teaching and teacher knowledge gained a much stronger profile with policymakers, research on teaching was not appearing to offer a sufficiently helpful knowledge base for practitioners. The editor of the *Handbook of Research on Teaching* (4th ed.), Virginia Richardson (2001), provided a challenging commentary on the state of the field and suggested a need for researchers to move beyond radical methodological swings and attend to the importance of teaching action and questions of practitioners. Recent American Educational Research Association (AERA) meeting themes have been sensitive to heightened media and political concern about public-good interests of expenditure on research. In addition, concerns about the state of knowledge with regard to the effectiveness of both initial teacher education and professional development has been a prominent theme in recent publications by the AERA, the U.S. National Academy of Education, and the National Research Council (Bransford, Brown, & Cocking, 2000; Cochran-Smith & Zeichner, 2005; Darling-Hammond & Bransford, 2005; Hammerness et al., 2005). Although Hanushek (2005), for example, headlined the importance of teacher quality, he rejected in-service teacher education as the key policy lever because "despite some success in general they (professional development programs) have been disappointing" (p. 19), and "existing evidence on in-service programs gives insufficient means for selecting a program that is likely to yield significant gains in teaching performance" (p. 19).

One research approach designed to address this problem of limited impact has been to evaluate interventions for the magnitude and consistency of their influence on outcomes. The Institute of Educational Sciences in the United States designed the What Works Clearinghouse (WWC), funded since 2001 "to provide educators, policymakers, researchers, and the public with a central and trusted source of scientific evidence on what works in education" (Boruch & Herman, in press). The emphasis is on scientific standards for randomized trials and quasiexperimental design of interventions. The reports available to teachers on such topics as beginning reading or mathematics provide evidence about specific packages or commercial programs.

Another approach has been to bring together rigorous reviews of disparate evidence about what works around a theme of importance for teachers, educational leaders, and policymakers. The Evidence for Policy and Practice Information and Co-ordinating Centre (EPPI) began at the University of London in 1993 "with the aim of developing and promoting participatory and user-friendly systematic reviews addressing important questions in policy, practice and research in the public interest" (Gough, 2007; Oakley, Moore, Burford, Fahrenwald, & Woodward, 2005). The EPPI and its linked enterprise, the Centre for Research Evidence in Education (CUREE), increasingly seek to involve practitioners, including teachers, and use their questions in knowledge development. An influential contributor to the English approach to systematic review has been Pawson (2002), whose advocacy of realist synthesis has emphasized the importance of theory development to explain particular findings to inform their use and adaptation in different contexts.

A more sustained approach has been explained by Niemi (2007; personal communication, July 2006), who attributes the world-leading Finnish performance in the first two Programme for International Student Assessment (PISA) surveys to a 40-year policy to enhance equity and quality through the use of research evidence. She cites the decision to raise primary school teacher education to master's level (including the requirement that preservice students understand and engage with research activity), the discontinuation of streaming, and the orientation of the educational research sector to the improvement of education as examples of a tradition of primacy afforded to the use of research evidence in informing teaching and educational policy in Finland.

The most systemic new approach to evidence-based policy focused on teaching is the multidisciplinary, multilevel, and longitudinal approach adopted in Singapore. In 2002,

S\$48 million was set aside to establish the Centre for Research on Pedagogy and Practice (CRPP) in Singapore, "a comprehensive research programme that would provide the evidence for evaluating reforms to date and enable the Singapore Ministry of Education to plan medium and long-term policy interventions" (Luke & Hogan, 2006, p. 176). The goal is "education policy that attempts to steer . . . [from] a multilayered empirical data base on teachers' and students' work, everyday lives and interaction in classrooms" (p. 178). The emerging evidence from this investment in research and development is becoming not only a Singaporean but also a global resource for knowledge about teaching and teacher learning.

THE ITERATIVE BES PROGRAMME

In New Zealand, an alternative approach to those identified in the previous section has been adopted. This approach has involved collaborative knowledge building across policy, research, and practice by identifying and building the evidence around the kinds of influences that have impacts on valued outcomes for diverse learners. Within this program, the series of syntheses on the major influences on student outcomes is being progressively developed (Aitken & Sinnema, in press; Alton-Lee, 2003; Anthony & Walshaw, 2007; Biddulph et al., 2003; Farquhar, 2003; Mitchell & Cubey, 2003; Robinson, Hohepa, & Lloyd, in press; Timperley, Wilson, Barrar, & Fung, in press). The wider program draws on a multidisciplinary evidence base, and the syntheses emerging from it have been funded by government to inform educational policy.

The syntheses selectively filter evidence from research and development linked to valued learner outcomes from international and New Zealand research. These outcomes and what has contributed to them have become the touchstone for reframing knowledge. Many researchers and teachers have engaged in educational research and development with remarkable impacts on these outcomes. With rare exceptions, however, such knowledge has been transitory, likely to be named as the work of researchers rather than teachers, inaccessible to other teachers, siloed in academic subdisciplines, and lost amid a plethora of fads or low priority within academic hierarchies of knowledge and reward systems. The BES iterations bring this valuable resource together while excluding studies without an outcomes link.

The initial BES iterations were published in 2003. The approach informed national guidelines (Alton-Lee, 2004) for subsequent BES development. The guidelines were developed in consultation with three national advisory groups in New Zealand. The approach is rigorously eclectic, gives particular weight to local context, uses effect sizes or other ways of evaluating the comparative magnitude of impact, and involves a realist synthesis approach that foregrounds theoretical coherence. Unlike the work of EPPI or WWC, BES requires the use of vignette and case to exemplify the findings in ways that are useful for practitioner users of the BES, whether teachers, teacher educators, or educational leaders. The integral role of practitioners and other users in the process of BES development is taken up later in this chapter.

FOREGROUNDING A RESPONSIVENESS-
TO-DIVERSITY FRAMEWORK

There are new challenges for education systems in knowledge societies. It is no longer sufficient for education systems to follow Plato's myth and sort learners into those who pass and those who fail. There are moral, economic, social, equity, and practical cases that can be made for this position. Some of the most effective professional development identified in our synthesis results in more than 3 times the expected gain over the same time period for students who do not typically achieve well (English & Bareta, 2006; Parr, Timperley, Reddish, Jesson, & Adams, 2006). Even Plato's "iron" craftsmen would need the capabilities of philosopher kings to negotiate the challenges of technology in many societies in today's world. From a policy perspective, the economic arguments can be most persuasive; however, rapidly changing demographics, and the wider benefits for all of social cohesion, are also compelling for policymakers. Others point out that we should be considering all of these arguments simultaneously. McNulty and Daggett (2007), from the International Center for Leadership in Education, argue that the four megatrends of global, demographic, technological, and cultural issues "facing America today cannot be ignored. The factors described above give credence and forewarning to a quietly approaching perfect storm" (p. 8). Governments across the globe are looking to education systems to rise to the challenge to be more responsive to the diversity of their learners and to meet the higher expectations and future focus required by knowledge societies (Froumin, 2007).

The PISA studies show marked differences among education systems in how well 15-year-old students are able to apply their learning in mathematics, science, and reading literacy (OECD, 2001; 2005a). They also show marked differences in disparities between groups of students within countries. New Zealand, for example, has high mean scores, performing in the second-highest band of countries across the PISA studies. But New Zealand's results show relatively high disparities in achievement, particularly in reading literacy, that are stratified by comparison with most OECD countries. Despite high achievement by many Maori and Pasifika learners, there is a pattern of poor outcomes, particularly for Maori who have been underserved in New Zealand schooling. As in many other Western countries, it is these groups that show rapidly growing demographic profiles, highlighting the urgency for systems to become more responsive to all learners.

Because the context for this work is New Zealand, all BES developments are informed by, and inform, educational practice in both Maori and English-medium education. Maori have a treaty relationship with the Crown that protects Te Reo (Maori language) and *tikanga Maori* (Maori culture) and guarantees Maori the same educational opportunities as non-Maori. However, the published BES iterations provide substantial evidence across some decades of inequitable teaching of Maori learners: fewer teacher–student interactions, less positive feedback, underassessment of capability, mispronounced names, and so on (Benton, 1986; Carkeek, Davies, & Irwin, 1994; Cazden, 1990; Clay, 1985; Millward, Neal, Kofoed, Parr, Kuin Lai, & Robinson, 2001; St. George, 1983; Thomas, 1984). Although Maori-medium education has been only a very recent system provision in New Zealand, and despite resourcing challenges in a language revitalization context, early cohorts of students emerging from continuous Maori-medium education have performed more highly than Maori students in English-medium contexts (Murray, 2006).

For many countries, population projections show increasing diversity by ethnicity and multiple cultural heritages. Over and above cultural heritage, classrooms and other educational groupings of students are always characterized by diversity or heterogeneity to some extent. Diversity is a feature of the varied experiences the students bring to their learning of particular topics and their previous achievement levels in relation to the topic or skill area, whether high, average, low, or gifted. What students bring to the classroom is in turn influenced by their gender, families, and wider affiliations and heritages and the extent to which these become resources for their in-school learning. There are substantial numbers of reports in the research literature that show aspects of learner identity and background to be integral to educational achievement or failure, particularly when there are cultural mismatches between home and school (e.g., Alton-Lee, 2003; Beecher & Arthur, 2001; Dilworth & Brown, 2001; Heath, 1982, 1993; McNaughton, 2002; Moll, 2001; Nuthall, 1999; G. Phillips, McNaughton, & MacDonald, 2004).

Difference is salient in education, albeit in complex and context-specific ways. Our approach is to put difference at the center of our knowledge-building work through a responsiveness-to-diversity framework. Because difference is a characteristic that all learners share, the approach allows for a "universalising discourse of difference" (Britzman, 1995; Town, 1998) as a way of moving forward. This approach moves away from "norm" and "other" distinctions that have constrained mainstream educational thinking to focus on the homogeneous and the "mean" and seeks to strengthen our evidence base about what works for all learners. The approach does not downplay, but rather requires, ongoing and systematic attention to groups of learners who are being disadvantaged or underserved for equity purposes, without stereotyping individual students in ways that fail to reflect the complexity of individual identity.

The daily and complex challenge for teachers is that they need to be working effectively and simultaneously with diverse students. This is where the evidence can be particularly helpful, because it identifies evidence-based strategies and approaches that have enabled teachers to be effective with all students in their classes.

THE LINK TO VALUED LEARNER OUTCOMES AS A TOUCHSTONE

In taking an outcomes-linked approach, the BES attends to a range of desired outcomes, including academic, social, well-being, learning, metacognitive, identity, and other outcomes valued by communities, including those from indigenous communities. The search strategy for each BES actively attends to seeking research for a range of outcomes so that the knowledge generated does not unduly focus on only a narrow band of achievement. The approach recognizes that in a democracy, desired outcomes from an education system are and should be subject to a contested and evolving discourse about what parents and wider communities want for all our learners.

Part of the rationale for the incontrovertible concern with impacts on diverse learners is the compelling evidence across studies that well-intentioned, caring, and experienced teachers and teacher educators can unknowingly teach in ways that have impacts counter to their own goals. Bossert (1979), for example, revealed ways in which teacher management of tasks and interactions with students created negative impacts on peer relationships and social outcomes.

W. Doyle (1983) revealed how well-meaning teacher strategies to make learning safer undermined the intellectual demands of tasks and could heighten rather than lessen the risk of failure. Emerging work at Newcastle in Australia is indicating that when teachers pay attention to cultural relevance, scaffolding, and intellectual quality in task construction, Aboriginal and Torres Strait Islanders can achieve comparably with non-Aboriginal students; but they found also a pattern where well-intentioned Australian teachers attempted cultural relevance without attending also to the intellectual quality of tasks, inadvertently undermining these students' achievement (Amosa, Ladwig, Griffiths, & Gore, 2007; Gore, Ladwig, Griffiths, & Amosa, 2007).

The concern for impact on outcomes is similarly critical for well-intentioned policy settings and initiatives that can also have impacts counter to their goals and do harm—for example, policy initiatives related to drug education that inadvertently exacerbate rather than combat illegal drug use (Biddulph et al., 2003).

An outcomes-linked approach can reveal which widely used educational practices can have little or even negative impacts particularly on those students traditionally underserved in schooling. A report by the New Zealand Education Review Office (2003), for example, showed that the learning styles inventory matching approach is widely used in New Zealand (as a result of a wave of professional development). This approach has been found to be problematic in international reviews of effectiveness (e.g., Irvine & York, 1995) and linked to less effective instructional experiences for Maori and Pasifika than for other learners in junior-class mathematics in New Zealand (Higgins, 2001). In this latter study, Maori and Pasifika learners were classified as kinaesthetic learners and encouraged to work with blocks, whereas other learners focused on metacognitive strategies, for which there is, by contrast, evidence of positive links to higher achievement (e.g., Cardelle-Elawar, 1995; Marzano, Pickering, & Pollock, 2001).

Attending to the link to outcomes is important for another reason. As Nuthall (2004) explained,

> The professional knowledge base that is most needed to improve the quality of teaching and teacher education is knowledge about the ways in which classroom activities, including teaching, affect the changes taking place in the minds of students. . . . At the heart of the problem teachers face in the classroom is knowing what is going on in the minds of the students. . . . This is not all that teachers need to know, but it is at the core of what they need to know and what should be included in teacher education and professional development programs. (p. 295)

This poses a problem for teachers and researchers because what is going on in a child's mind is essentially unobservable, and many of the clues teachers take to be signals of what is occurring in students' minds are unreliable or even misleading. Unless teachers are aware of the links between pedagogy and students' learning processes, teaching can bring about student "learning" that is counter to curriculum goals. For example, in one study, despite the teacher's intentions, students became less concerned, rather than more concerned, about the plight of endangered animals (Alton-Lee, 1983, 1984). Having learned that milk comes from cows, wool from sheep, and so on, the children's patterned schema for learning about animals as being for human use and consumption was inadvertently activated and prevailed. The proactive inhibition caused by the children's learned schema became evident when most of the class wrote they were concerned that if elephants died out, their skins would not be available for clothing.

In another study tracing the link between teacher intentions and student learning, the teacher concerned explained how, despite his best intentions, he unknowingly triggered and exacerbated peer racism in a social studies unit designed to increase tolerance of cultural differences (Alton-Lee, Nuthall, & Patrick, 1993). The teacher used New York City as a learning context. Data gathered using broadcast microphones revealed that the New Zealand teacher's unconscious identification with the European settlers in New York effected (Maori) Ricky's exclusion from the European *we* in the enacted curriculum. Ricky's peer, Joe (European heritage), picked on the exclusion and exploited it as an opportunity to engage in racist abuse and kicking. It was Ricky, however, and not Joe, whom the teacher admonished for causing a disturbance through misbehavior:

> Teacher: Because White people . . .
> Joe (talking to Ricky): Honkies.
> Ricky (talking to Joe): Shut up!
> Teacher: Europeans, we were . . .
> Joe (talking to Ricky): Nigger!
> Teacher: Watch this way please, Ricky!—were often wanting to get things . . .
> Joe (talking to Ricky): Black man! Samoan!
>
> (Alton-Lee, Nuthall, & Patrick, 1993, p. 77)

Joe went on to kick Ricky, but it was Ricky who was again reprimanded and later excluded from class lessons for disruptive behavior. What was evident in the transcripts, however, was that the teacher's inadvertent exclusion of Ricky from the *we* of the classroom community *we, Europeans* was the trigger for verbal and physical abuse that Ricky experienced from, and then directed back at, his classmates. Furthermore, our quantitative analyses showed a negative relationship between long-term learning outcomes and racial abuse for both the givers and the receivers of the abuse (Alton-Lee & Nuthall, 1990). John Patrick, the teacher, explained that these research findings were

heart-rending because I would have liked to have thought that I was tuned in to what was happening in the class . . . I just didn't know . . . Prior to doing this research I would've said "Yes, you know, I'm fully aware of these things. It comes as a real blow to find that in actual fact you're not necessarily doing things that are line with what you believe. I believe that (the outcomes) are extremely positive because they've increased my level of awareness. They've altered my action . . . It's altered the things that I think are important when I'm devising a curriculum . . . It's altered the way I treat other people too. (Alton-Lee et al., 1993, p. 80)

Such findings of social studies inadvertently occasioning or exacerbating racism have also been identified in Seixas' (2001) review. These kinds of findings provided the background for the motivation to identify what kinds of professional learning and development situations are most effective in promoting teacher learning in ways that promote student learning. When undertaking this search, it became apparent that counterproductive outcomes were not restricted to classroom teaching. Some professional development interventions also resulted in lowered student achievement and social outcomes (Timperley et al., in press). The remainder of this chapter, therefore, describes the theoretical and methodological approach together with the results of this BES iteration of professional learning and development (Timperley et al., in press).

THEORETICAL UNDERPINNINGS OF THE SYNTHESIS

The kinds of learning opportunities provided to teachers depend to a large extent on what providers believe the purpose of education to be. If, as proposed by Plato (1968 trans.), it should be a sorting process, then very different professional learning opportunities are likely to be provided than in those situations concerned about social justice for all students. Many professional development approaches appear to be based on the teacher-as-good-employee view in that they have assumed teachers can learn and implement what they need to know in relatively short bursts of delivered knowledge from those with superior expertise. The National Staff Development Council (2001), for example, documented the predominance of single-day workshops for teachers in the United States. Sparks (2004) highlighted in the *Handbook of Research on Raising Student Achievement* how such workshops typically delivered the wisdom of administrators and others' expertise to teachers, not necessarily in ways that interested them.

For far too many teachers in the United States, staff development is a demeaning, mind numbing experience as they passively "sit and get." That staff development is often mandatory in nature . . . and evaluated by "happiness scales." As one observer put it, "I hope I die during an in-service session because the transition between life and death would be so subtle." (p. 247)

Others who have come from an assumption that goals of social equity cannot be met by this kind of approach have advocated for developing greater professionalism among teachers rather than treating them as technicians whose responsibility it is to implement others' prescriptions of practice (Cochrane-Smith & Lytle, 1999). The desired impact on student outcomes as a result of teacher engagement in these kinds of opportunities to learn, however, were usually assumed rather than verified empirically. More recently, questions have been raised about whether promoting this kind of teacher learning really does have the desired impact, with an increasing number of researchers advocating that the links need to be tested rather than assumed. Typical of these calls is one by Camburn (1997), who reminds us, "Our public school system is ultimately in the business of educating students not teachers" (p. 60). Guskey (2000) gave considerable impetus to this focus on students in his five-stage evaluation model, which moved beyond teachers' reactions, self-identified learning, and changes in behavior to judging effectiveness in terms of its impact on student learning outcomes. The empirical evidence about what teachers needed to know and the conditions under which they learned best, however, inevitably lagged behind these researchers' advocacy for taking them into account.

To identify the kinds of teacher knowledge that were associated with improved student outcomes and the conditions under which it was best acquired, the BES on teacher professional learning and development justified all its conclusions in relation to the evidence of the impact on valued outcomes for diverse student learners. Given the relative strength of the theoretical compared to the empirical literature, we developed an approach that drew on these strengths while at the same time tested their premises. In undertaking this task, our first challenge was to understand the process of influence, beginning with the professional learning opportunities for teachers and progressing to outcomes for students. Much has been written about the "black box" between acts of teaching and student outcomes (Black & Wiliam, 1998) because there is no direct relationship between a particular act of teaching and what students learn. How students interpret and use the opportunities to learn particular understandings and skills depends on a number of other influences, such as their prior learning, the conceptual and social resources they bring to the task, and their cultural heritage. Both the theoretical and empirical developments in this field, however, are making progress in unpicking this black box for a range of outcomes (e.g., Aitken & Sinnema, in press; Alton-Lee, 2003; Anthony & Walshaw, 2007; Brophy, 2001; Evertson & Weinstein, 2006; Luke & Hogan, 2006; Rex, Green, & Dixon, 1997).

In the professional learning situation, a second black box is added to the sequence, that between professional learning opportunities and outcomes for teachers and is depicted in Figure 1. How teachers interpret and use the available understandings and skills is also a complex process. Teachers, like their students, have prior learning experiences and bring different conceptual and social resources that are influenced by their cultural heritages to the learning experience. To make a difference to their students' learning, however, we have assumed that the content of what teachers learned needed to result in some changes in their practice, because it is teaching practice that influences the learning opportunities for students.

This very basic conceptual model was then unpacked further by analyzing both the theoretical and empirical literature to identify the aspects of teacher learning and development that were purported to make a difference to outcomes for diverse student learners. Eighty-four separate characteristics were developed into a multidisciplinary theoretical map, identified in Figure 2. The basic premises of this framework

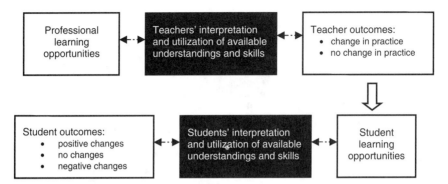

FIGURE 1   The Black Boxes of Teacher and Student Learning

was discussed and shaped by a collaboration between the authors, the national providers of teacher education, the teacher unions, and policy representatives. Our aim was to use this theoretical map to identify from the empirical literature what kinds of teacher knowledge, and the conditions under which it was developed, promoted the learning processes that enabled teachers to change their practice in ways that had a positive impact on student outcomes.

All categories identified in the framework were given equal attention in terms of coding the empirical literature. There were two, however, that discriminated those conditions that were associated with better outcomes for students. These were the content of the professional learning opportunities and the learning processes engaged. For this reason, and those of space, we will elaborate on only these two categories.

Framework Analysis 1: The Content of Professional Learning Opportunities

Given the focus of this chapter on the content of professional knowledge that makes a difference, we have further unpacked this particular part of Figure 2. The first two attributes constituted discipline and curriculum knowledge. There is considerable debate about the relationship between these two kinds of knowledge, with the recognition that curricula are typically structured around discipline knowledge bases but that their content is different. The subject matter of the discipline is transformed into the subject matter of school subjects at particular grade levels to form the curriculum (C. S. Doyle, 1992). In our analysis of the content of the professional learning opportunities, therefore, we distinguished between discipline and curriculum knowledge.

Shulman (1986, 1987) argued for specialized subject matter for teachers comprising pedagogical content knowledge that enabled teachers "to transform the content knowledge he or she possesses into forms that are pedagogically powerful and yet adaptive to the variations in ability and background presented by students" (Shulman, 1987, p. 15). We adopted Shulman's definition and had as our third attribute pedagogical content knowledge. To qualify for this category, however, the professional

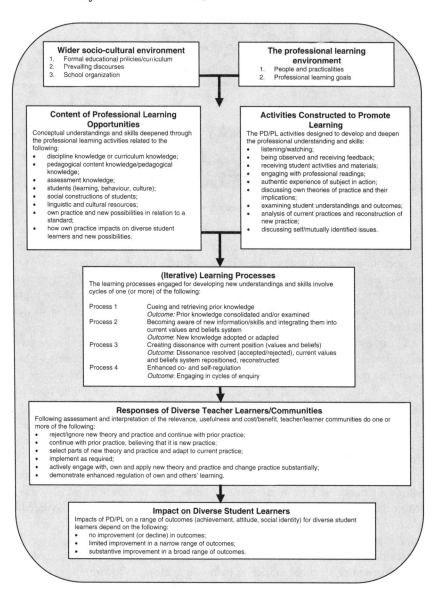

FIGURE 2   Framework for the Analysis of the Effectiveness
of Professional Learning Experiences

Note. PD/PL = professional development/professional learning.

learning opportunities needed to combine a deepening of curriculum content knowledge with particular teaching approaches. Pedagogical content knowledge was distinguished from the fourth category of pedagogical knowledge and practice, which focused on new approaches to teaching alone and did not attempt to deepen curriculum knowledge. This distinction proved to be important for some curriculum areas.

A fifth area of knowledge was that of assessment of student learning. Our reason for its inclusion is that the burgeoning international literature on formative assessment (Black & Wiliam, 1998; Earl & Katz, 2006) convincingly demonstrates that developing teachers' knowledge of how to investigate students' current understandings for the purpose of identifying what needs to be taught next can have a powerful impact on student learning.

The sixth attribute to which we attended focused on improving teachers' knowledge of students in a more generic sense, including their development, their learning, their behavior, and their cultural backgrounds. A related, seventh attribute was teachers' social construction of the students they taught. In this category, we included attributes such as the ways in which teachers' expectations of students affected student learning, because there is a developing acknowledgement of the impact of such expectations on outcomes for students, particularly for those with backgrounds and experiences different from their teachers' (Reyes, Scribner, & Scribner, 1999; Reynolds & Teddlie, 2000).

Linguistic and cultural resources formed the eighth attribute and arose from consulting the literature on education in indigenous communities (Bishop & Glynn, 1998; Smith, 1999). The process of colonization and language loss has led, in many cases, to the need for teachers in these communities to develop this kind of knowledge to connect with and promote the development of particular cultural understandings for their students. Threats to these understandings have been particularly pronounced when Western concepts for which there are no direct indigenous equivalents need to be incorporated into the curriculum for students from indigenous communities (Trinick, 2005).

The next two attributes of the content of the professional learning opportunities had a different orientation in that they focused on developing teachers' understanding of current practice and new possibilities in relation to some external criterion. The ninth attribute examined whether the professional learning opportunities focused on an analysis of current practice and new possibilities in relation to a particular standard of practice, for example, professional standards. The tenth examined how teachers' current practice affected diverse student learners and new possibilities for this relationship and impact. These two attributes were based on the literature related to the place of teachers' current theories of practice in engaging with, overassimilating, or rejecting new theories of practice (Hammerness et al., 2005; Robinson, 1993). The reason for these varying reactions reflects both the differences between teachers as learners and the complexities of teaching itself (Kennedy, 1999). Making sense of change messages is a complex process involving interactions between an individual's existing cognitive structures (knowledge, beliefs, and attitudes), the situation in which they practice, and the providers' messages (Putman & Borko, 2000; Spillane, Reiser, & Reimer, 2002). Decontextualized messages about how to teach in new ways do not take this interplay of influences into account. When analyzing these empirical studies and deciding on whether these attributes formed part of the professional learning opportunities, we noted the extent to which teachers were assisted to understand their personal theories underpinning their current practice and how the new possibilities for practice related to or challenged those theories.

When coding the presence or absence of any of these attributes in the analysis of the empirical studies, we simultaneously considered the depth to which the particular content was addressed. Was the curriculum content unpacked at a deep level of theoretical understanding, or was an approach more consistent with one of "curriculum coverage" adopted? Did teachers understand the curriculum theory underpinning a particular assessment tool, or was the professional learning focused on procedures and categorizing students by test scores? Was the analysis of the impact of current practice on student learning undertaken through testing a range of competing theories, or was it a more superficial analysis?

Framework Analysis 2: Learning Processes

The other categories in Figure 2 (wider social and professional learning contexts and activities in which teachers engaged) were deconstructed in a similar way, but the only other part of the figure that we will unpack further is that relating to learning processes because of the influence they had on student outcomes. The knowledge and skills teachers acquired through participating in the professional learning experience and the learning processes engaged provided the strongest explanations for differential impact on students.

When identifying the learning processes, we accepted Bransford et al.'s (2000) argument that adult learning is fundamentally similar to that of students. In assuming this similarity, we did not intend to discount the obvious differences between adult and student learning situations, such as the richer life experiences on which adults draw, the learning contexts in which they occur, and the greater demand adults place on the relevance of learning to engage. We identified four learning processes to explain particular outcomes. The first process involved cueing and retrieving prior knowledge with the outcome of consolidating it or, alternatively, examining it for its adequacy. It was assumed that cueing prior knowledge on its own was unlikely to result in changed practice, but if it resulted in examination of its adequacy then this could form the basis for change.

The second process involved becoming aware of new information or skills and integrating them into current values and belief systems, with the outcome that new knowledge is adopted or adapted. This process could involve a very superficial level of acquisition of new knowledge or much deeper learning. Most professional development situations described in the empirical literature appeared to be based on the idea that teachers needed to learn "new things" rather than to examine how these new things related to existing knowledge. The problem of overassimilation (Hammerness et al., 2005), where teachers believe they are enacting new practice but represent this practice in only superficial ways, however, is well documented (e.g., Firestone, Schorr, & Monfils, 2004; Spillane, 2000).

The third process involved creating dissonance with current beliefs, attitudes, or knowledge of effective practice. Some authors advocate that such dissonance is a requirement of substantive change, because to realize any proposed reform, teachers will have to unlearn much of what they believe, know, and know how to do (Ball, 1988), but it also runs the risk of rejection of key messages if teachers dismiss new possibilities as impossible in their situation (Coburn, 2001). Resolution of dissonance may, therefore, involve current values, beliefs, and knowledge as reconstructed in ways consistent with the change messages. Alternatively, they may be rejected altogether.

The final process was based on the literature of co- and self-regulation (Butler & Winne, 1995) and examined the extent to which the professional learning opportunities promoted processes of inquiry into the adequacy and improvement of teaching practice. Although there are many theoretical approaches to self-regulation (Zimmerman, 2001), we adopted a position consistent with that of Butler and Winne (1995), in which self-regulated learners are those who "judge performance relative to goals, generate internal feedback about amounts and rates of progress towards goals, and adjust further action based on that feedback" (p. 258). It is, in their view, a deliberate, judgmental, adaptive process. However, we have adapted this original conception of self-regulation to include co-regulation to acknowledge the importance of the social situatedness of learning (Putman & Borko, 2000) and that developing collective responsibility for these self-regulatory processes is more powerful in promoting positive student outcomes than leaving that responsibility to individuals alone (Newmann, 1994). This concept is similar to that of Cochran-Smith and Lytle (1999), who argue for the value of teachers' adopting a deliberate inquiry stance in relation to their own practice where they treat their own work as sites for systematic and intentional inquiry.

MAPPING THE EVIDENCE

All the components of Figure 2 formed a theoretical map against which the empirical studies were analyzed. Each attribute in every category was treated as neutral with regard to its impact on teachers or students until it was tested against the empirical evidence. To do this, a search of the international literature was undertaken using an iterative and "knowledgeable search" (Alton-Lee, 2004) strategy using electronic database searches, hand searches of relevant journals, relevant handbooks, and a network of informants to identify those studies of teacher professional learning and development that reported student outcomes. The application of standard methodological criteria identified 72 individual and groups of related studies of independent interventions with a total of 227 effects (J. Cohen, 1988) that reported quantitative outcomes (46 from the United States, 4 from the United Kingdom, 16 from New Zealand, and 7 from other countries). Effect sizes were not all able to be computed using J. Cohen's (1988) formula, because results were reported in the form of t tests, f values, r coefficients, proportions, and normal curve equivalents, so alternative formulas were used to calculate effect sizes in these cases (Hattie, 1990, 1992; Lipsey & Wilson, 1993; Tallmadge, 1977). Given the substantial difficulties in developing equivalence in effect sizes, they were treated categorically and were not ranked, as is common in a meta-analytical approach. In addition, qualitative studies that met appropriate standards of methodological adequacy were included in the analysis. Some studies providing rich descriptions of the professional learning opportunities but reporting no change in practice by the participating teachers were also used as contrasting examples, because it was assumed that these interventions were unlikely to result in changed outcomes for students.

Our reporting of this list so clinically belies the complexity of the task of locating studies in which the student outcomes could be attributed to teachers' professional learning experiences with some level of confidence. Typically, authors reported details of the professional development with no reference to outcomes, or they reported student outcomes providing only sketchy details of the teachers' learning opportunities. In many cases, we had to refer to groups of linked studies to obtain an accurate picture. It is also probably true that teachers learn a great deal in undocumented after-school meetings and in interaction with their colleagues. This learning is more incremental, with its impact rarely measured.

The reported attributes of the professional development in all studies were then mapped onto the theoretical framework summarized in Figure 2 to identify what kinds of teacher knowledge and the circumstances under which it was acquired were associated with benefits to students.

THE IMPACT OF PROFESSIONAL LEARNING AND DEVELOPMENT ON STUDENT OUTCOMES

From the set of studies analyzed, it appeared that teachers' professional learning opportunities were associated with mostly positive, but at times variable, outcomes for students. A summary of the range and mean effect sizes for all effects are presented in Table 1 (Timperley et al., in press). As can be seen from this table, most categories included some negative effects as well as very positive effects. Academic outcomes had higher means than personal or social outcomes. The high mean effect sizes for literacy were influenced by the inclusion of several studies focused on students with special learning needs whose low starting points resulted in very high effects. In science, the effects were influenced by the large number of studies that used researcher-developed rather than standardized assessments. Not surprising, those studies that used control groups had lower effects than those using within-group comparisons, particularly when objectively scored, standardized instruments were used.

In the remainder of this section, we will briefly describe the situations that were least effective, then report in more detail on those situations that were more effective, with the main focus on what it is teachers need to learn and what learning processes need to be engaged to make a difference to student outcomes.

Characteristics of Professional Learning Opportunities Associated With Limited Impact on Student Outcomes

The circumstances of professional learning and development that appeared to be least effective fell at two extremes, both of which are portrayed as effective by some of

TABLE 1 The Range and Mean Effect Sizes for All Effects

	N	M	SEM	95% CI	Median	SD	Min	Max
Total	227	0.60	0.06	0.24	0.34	0.83	−1.01	5.31
Outcome		$F = 3.30; p = .001; \eta^2 = .13$						
Mathematics	62	0.50	0.12	0.48	0.31	0.94	−1.01	5.10
Reading	44	0.34	0.04	0.16	0.26	0.26	−0.01	1.11
Literacy and language skills	27	1.18	0.24	0.96	0.55	1.27	0.09	5.31
Attitudes toward Subject	21	0.34	0.21	0.84	0.11	0.95	−0.73	4.27
Science	18	0.94	0.19	0.76	0.68	0.80	0.16	2.85
Writing	16	0.88	0.11	0.44	1.06	0.45	0.06	1.34
Self-efficacy	11	0.17	0.06	0.24	0.11	0.21	−0.07	0.68
Other academic skills	10	0.76	0.18	0.72	0.55	0.57	0.22	2.09
Social outcomes	7	0.36	0.11	0.44	0.34	0.29	−0.11	0.86
Cognitive processing	6	0.85	0.18	0.72	0.87	0.44	0.17	1.46
Other personal outcomes	5	0.46	0.10	0.40	0.53	0.23	0.08	0.64
Class of outcome		$F = 3.25; p = .041; \eta^2 = .03$						
Academic	183	0.66	0.06	0.24	0.39	0.85	−1.01	5.31
Personal	37	0.30	0.12	0.48	0.12	0.73	−0.73	4.27
Social	7	0.36	0.11	0.44	0.34	0.29	−0.11	0.86
Grade level grouping (*n*)								
Elementary	172	0.61	0.07	0.28	0.34	0.90	−1.01	5.31
Junior high	23	0.36	0.06	0.24	0.27	0.30	0.05	1.27
Secondary	20	0.60	0.14	0.56	0.45	0.61	0.06	2.85
All	9	0.97	0.32	1.28	0.64	0.95	0.08	2.68
Country (*n*)								
United States	143	0.48	0.07	0.28	0.27	0.80	−1.01	5.10
New Zealand	68	0.87	0.11	0.44	0.53	0.90	−0.14	5.31
Canada	4	0.79	0.44	1.76	0.43	0.88	0.23	2.09
The Netherlands	4	0.48	0.22	0.88	0.36	0.44	0.09	1.12
United Kingdom	4	0.53	0.13	0.52	0.49	0.27	0.29	0.85
Israel	2	0.26	0.01	0.04	0.26	0.01	0.25	0.26
Other country	1	0.31	—	—	0.31	—	0.31	0.31

(continued)

TABLE 1 (continued)

	N	M	SEM	95% CI	Median	SD	Min	Max
Number of participants (*n*)								
<100	20	0.84	0.13	0.52	0.64	0.57	0.21	2.68
100–999	83	0.69	0.11	0.44	0.42	0.96	–0.73	5.10
>1,000	56	0.69	0.13	0.52	0.32	1.00	–0.03	5.31
Type of control				$F = 5.18; p = .02; \eta^2 = .02$				
Control	138	0.50	0.07	0.28	0.31	0.81	–1.01	5.10
Baseline	89	0.75	0.09	0.36	0.45	0.85	0.04	5.31
Type of instrumentation				$F = 18.76; p = .000; \eta^2 = .143$				
Objectively scored	119	0.40	0.05	0.20	0.28	0.51	–0.14	4.27
Researcher	80	0.62	0.10	0.40	0.38	0.92	–1.01	5.10
Verified judgment	28	1.39	0.22	0.88	1.27	1.15	0.16	5.31

Note. CI = confidence interval.

their advocates. The first is that teachers should be considered self-regulating professionals who, if given sufficient time and resources, are able to construct their own learning experiences and develop a more effective reality for their students through their collective expertise. Unfortunately, we found little evidence to support the claim that providing teachers with time and resources is effective in promoting professional learning in ways that have positive outcomes for students. Rather, the evidence pointed to the contrary (Lipman, 1997; Saxe, Gearhart, & Nasir, 2001; Timperley & Parr, 2006). Part of the reason for the failure of these kinds of situations to affect student outcomes arose because they typically did not develop teachers' current knowledge and practice or challenge problematic attitudes. Indeed, in some cases, they served to entrench discriminatory beliefs and practices (e.g., Lipman, 1997).

The alternative extreme occurred when outside experts developed recipes for teaching (typically based on research about what kinds of pedagogies work for improving student outcomes), then presented prescribed practices to teachers with an underpinning rationale and follow-up monitoring to ensure implementation integrity (e.g., Borman et al., 2005). The overall evidence is that these processes can be effective in changing teaching practices and have greater impact on student outcomes than the other extreme of leaving teachers to develop their own solutions, but it is either short-lived (Robbins & Wolfe, 1987; Stallings & Krasavage, 1986) or relatively limited compared to other kinds of professional development (Borman et al., 2005; Datnow, Borman, Stringfield, Overman, & Castellano, 2003). The main reason we propose for this finding is that experienced teachers do not approach professional learning or teaching situations as empty vessels but rather as people who have rich theories about how students learn, how best to teach them, and what constitutes desired content and outcomes. Those who sought to build professional knowledge by prescribing particular teaching behaviors without engaging existing beliefs or understanding the constraints of their practice situation typically failed to take this complexity into account. In some cases, when teachers were closely observed to ensure implementation of particular teaching behaviors, student achievement improved, but once the monitoring was withdrawn, they reverted to previous practice with concomitant losses in student outcomes (Robbins & Wolfe, 1987; Stallings & Krasavage, 1986).

Characteristics of Professional Learning Opportunities Associated With Improved Outcomes for Diverse Learners

Those situations in which the greatest gains were evident in substantive rather than narrow curricula areas were those that sought to deepen teachers' foundation of pedagogical content and assessment knowledge within coherent conceptual frameworks that could then serve as the basis for decisions about practice. Similar patterns were evident in both the elementary and secondary schooling sectors. The synthesis identified that professional learning opportunities that focused on the acquisition of discrete pieces of knowledge independent of a more coherent theory were useful only for the development of discrete skills for students, such as phonemic awareness (Baker & Smith, 1999) or map-reading (Fishman, Marx, Best, & Tal, 2003), and not the more generic understandings, such as reading comprehension or mathematical understandings.

The reason for the integration of pedagogical content and assessment knowledge was that interpreting assessment information allowed teachers to understand in detail what their students knew already and what it was they needed to learn next. This knowledge of how and what to assess was not restricted to test results but included close observation of student learning, examination of student work, and student interviews. For example, in the studies involving cognitively guided instruction (CGI) in mathematics, Fennema, Franke, Carpenter, and Carey (1993) cited a teachers' response to the professional development:

"CGI is really strong and powerful for me because I can get a handle on all my children, from the lowest to the highest . . . I feel that I can know what they are doing and challenge them where they are and help them to feel successful where they are and where they get to." (Fennema et al., 1993, p. 580)

In some instances, more formal assessments played a key part in identifying what students knew and needed to learn. McNaughton, Lai, MacDonald, and Farry (2004), for example, used a reading assessment to assist teachers to understand the strategies used by their upper elementary students from low socioeconomic communities. They found in a cloze test, in which students were required to fill in missing words, the students were not using contextual information from the whole paragraph to identify the correct word to insert into the spaces. They used the meaning of the sentence up to the point of the missing word but not beyond it. Classroom observations of teaching practice identified the teaching strategies that were contributing to the problem. Through a process of negotiating the meaning of both the observations and achievement data with the participating teachers, teaching approaches changed and the students' comprehension improved.

Knowing what students can or cannot do, however, served to shape teaching practice in ways that promoted deep student learning only if teachers had sufficient depth of pedagogical content knowledge on which to base teaching decisions. Otherwise, the learning analysis remained at a superficial level. In the above study by McNaughton et al. (2004), the researchers were able to assist the teachers to develop the necessary knowledge and teaching skills once the problem had been identified. In most of the studies with substantive effect sizes, there was an underlying assumption that students should be taught content at deep conceptual levels rather than more superficial factual-type knowledge. Indeed, in many of the mathematical and science studies, the shift from factual mastery to conceptual inquiry-based knowledge was particularly evident (see, e.g., Adey, 2004; Cardelle-Elawar, 1995; Carpenter, Fennema, Peterson, Chiang, & Loef, 1989; Cobb et al., 1991; Confrey, Castro-Filho, & Wilhelm, 2000; Fennema et al., 1993; Higgins, Irwin, Thomas, Trinick, & Young Loveridge, 2005; Kahle, Meece, & Scantlebury, 2000; McClain & Cobb, 2001; Palincsar, Magnusson, Marano, Ford, & Brown, 1998; Parke & Coble, 1997; Raghavan, Cohen-Regev, & Strobel, 2001; Saxe et al., 2001; Schorr, 2000; University of Hawaii Curriculum Research and Development Group, 2002; Wood & Sellers, 1996).

All studies with high effect sizes also focused on assisting teachers to translate the pedagogical and assessment knowledge into teaching practice, through coaching, workshops, and participation in communities with colleagues. This translation was not left to chance. With one exception (Bishop, Berryman, Powell, & Teddy, 2005), a focus on teaching practices without the accompanying curriculum content knowledge was less successful in achieving substantive student outcomes than those studies that combined both. The relatively low impact of these studies could be an artifact of the intervention approach of many of those studies focusing on teaching practice alone, because they typically involved experts' telling teachers how they should teach, followed by observations to ensure compliance (e.g., Stallings & Krasavage, 1986; Van Der Sijde, 1989). Bishop and colleagues (2005), on the other hand, worked with mainstream secondary school teachers in more collaborative ways to develop interactive and discursive relationships with students from New Zealand's indigenous Maori communities. A combination of 3 days of negotiating the meaning of students' reported reactions to particular teaching approaches, working with indigenous facilitators on how to teach in ways that the students had identified as effective, and follow-up school-based activities served to change teaching practices sufficiently to raise these students' outcomes in mathematics. The school-based activities involved observations and feedback together with participation in teacher meetings that focused on both teaching practices and how these practices were affecting student outcomes.

INTEGRATING NEW KNOWLEDGE AND LEARNING PROCESSES

The acquisition of new pedagogical content and assessment knowledge in the majority of these studies, however, was not the whole picture, and it is here that we bring into consideration the interplay between developing knowledge and the learning processes that appeared to be engaged in most of the interventions. It needs to be stated that in most studies, we have inferred the learning processes from the descriptions provided because they were rarely addressed or described explicitly. In many of the effective interventions, there was a sense of purpose for engagement, typically through identifying a problem to be solved. For example, J. Phillips (2003) describes how the principal of a charter school with high average achievement challenged her teachers to address the learning needs of all their middle school students. She created the catalyst for their engagement by deconstructing students' achievement profiles by subgroups with the teachers. As a result of this process, they could not escape the conclusion that the very low achievement of their local students was masked by the high achievement of students from out of the area. The principal worked with the teachers to review their teaching practices and introduced a more innovative curriculum designed to better meet the needs of all students. The students' achievement improved as a result.

In an earlier review of the professional development literature, Wilson and Berne (1999) noted that the rationale for engagement in professional development experiences is typically not shared between those providing them and the participating teachers. Most professional development providers expected the teachers to change beliefs, practices, or both. Teachers, on the other hand, usually participated with clear ideas of what kinds of knowledge were most helpful and relevant to their ongoing learning but seldom assumed that their views or knowledge of subject matter or student learning needed to change. In many of the effective learning situations included in the current synthesis, this problem did not appear to arise because, as in the study by J. Phillips (2003), a compelling rationale to change became apparent for the participating teachers prior to or in the early stages of engagement. Establishing this kind of rationale to engage involved cueing and retrieving prior knowledge for the purpose of examining its adequacy. Such examination provided the rationale for further engagement.

The second learning process of becoming aware of new information or skills and integrating them into current knowledge systems was more evident in curriculum areas in which teachers were less confident of their knowledge, for example, mathematics, science, and writing in elementary schools rather than reading. In the literacy and numeracy strategies in England and Wales, for example, teachers were more likely to seek new knowledge in numeracy, a curriculum area in which they felt less confident, than in literacy, where they felt more confident of their knowledge and skills (L. Earl, personal communication, October 20, 2006).

Assuming congruence between existing cognitions and new knowledge, even when teachers seek new knowledge, can be a risky assumption that appears to be made by many of those providing professional development for teachers. The problem of dissonance is rarely mentioned. An exception by Coburn (2001) provided a rich description of teachers' reactions to the introduction of literacy reforms in California. Teachers with different theories constructed different understandings of the same messages. In one example, teachers in two groups came to different understandings about what it meant to use assessment to inform instruction. The first group understood reading instruction to be a particular sequence of skills. Using assessment to inform instruction, therefore, meant knowing where in the sequence a child was at and planning and teaching accordingly. A second group working on the same question believed that skills should be taught in response to students' needs rather than in a set sequence. They constructed their understanding of this concept as developing lessons in response to the particular needs of a student, no matter what the sequence.

In more informal settings, these teachers sought like-minded colleagues to negotiate meanings of the reform. These meanings were strongly influenced by existing theories and were far more influential in decisions about which of the reform messages to pursue in classrooms. Many teachers rejected the basic tenets of the reform as impractical and in opposition to what they believed effective reading teaching to be.

One area in which creating dissonance with teachers' current positioning was particularly difficult, yet very important, occurred in relation to teachers' social construction of students, particularly, their expectations of students traditionally underserved by our education systems. An evaluation of the Teacher Expectations and Student Achievement (TESA) program (Kerman, Kimball, & Martin, 1980), purported to be the one most frequently used in the United States, is a case in point. As a result of teachers' participating in the professional development designed to raise their expectations, no improvement in outcomes relating to student achievement, academic self-concept, and attachment to school were evident. The more robust measures actually indicated a negative effect. The rationale provided for these volunteer teachers to participate was a generalized finding that low teacher expectations could disadvantage low-achieving students. Whether the participating teachers did, or did not, disadvantage their students in the ways assumed was never established. In the absence of this analysis, there was no immediate problem to solve. Rather, the teachers were presented with a set of discrete teaching techniques they were expected to implement. Despite the name, teachers' expectations of students were not addressed directly or indirectly, nor was the need to think about their expectations and the impact they may have had on their students addressed.

The more successful projects addressed expectations less directly. One such intervention is described by Timperley and Phillips (2003) for teachers of beginning readers from low-socioeconomic communities. Early in the intervention, teachers were shown and discussed the implications of a video of alternative ways of teaching students from similar backgrounds who demonstrated more rapid progress in learning to read text than their own students. Immediately, cognitive dissonance was created for these teachers, who mostly believed that their students were progressing as fast as they were able. Through a series of other inquiries, they discovered that their own students knew more than they realized because they had not known how to access that information. As they developed their content knowledge in early literacy acquisition, together with the skills of teaching the alterative approach, their students began to make more rapid progress. Through this cyclical process, they began to feel more self-efficacious, and their expectations of themselves and their students increased. Their mean self-ratings of their changed expectations of the progress students could make in their 1st year of schooling was 7.6 on a 10-point scale where 1 represented *no change* and 10 represented *a great deal of change.*

This study demonstrates some of the elements of the fourth of our identified learning processes, which related to developing co- and self-regulation. Of concern is that documentation of these processes was relatively rare yet appeared to be essential to sustaining ongoing improved student outcomes once external providers had withdrawn from directing the professional learning experiences. In the few cases for which student outcomes continued to be reported (Alton-Lee et al., 2000; Carpenter et al., 1989; Datnow et al., 2003; Fennema et al., 1993; Higgins et al., 2005; McNaughton et al., 2004; Robbins & Wolfe, 1987; Stallings & Krasavage, 1986; Timperley, 2005), sustainability appeared to be dependent on teachers' developing a strong theoretical pedagogical content knowledge base that was able to serve as the basis for principled changes to practice together with the skills to inquire into the impact of teaching on student learning. This latter skill became particularly important when students' thinking showed problematic assumptions. Teachers also needed to be working in situations where the organizational conditions provided for collective, evidence-informed inquiry with ongoing opportunities to improve pedagogical content and assessment knowledge. In these studies, continued engagement was motivated by teachers' and leaders' continuing to take responsibility for identified problems with student outcomes together with the belief they had the capability to solve them.

The above analysis led us to develop a model of inquiry (Figure 3) that combines the different elements into a co- and self-regulatory learning cycle, the fourth learning process identified in our initial theoretical framework presented in Figure 2. By co- and self-regulation, we mean that through the inquiry process, teachers collectively and individually identify important issues, become the drivers for acquiring the knowledge they need to solve them, monitor their impact, and adjust practice accordingly (Butler & Winne, 1995). The key claims in the figure are also aligned with the work of Donovan, Bransford, and Pellegrino (1999) in that it integrates their propositions about how people learn. These include their engagement of prior understandings and preconceptions about how the world works, a deep foundation of factual and conceptual knowledge organized in ways that allow its retrieval, and a metacognitive awareness that allows them to take control of their own learning by defining learning goals and monitoring their progress in achieving them.

When developing co- and self-regulatory processes, goals are central, and in this model, teachers' learning goals are grounded in those for their students, as shown in Inquiry A, identifying student learning needs. To make a difference to student outcomes, these goals must also be informed by knowledge of the diversity of students

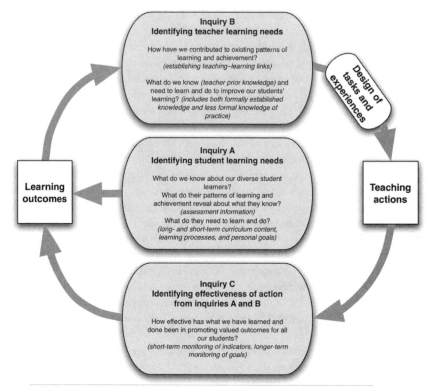

FIGURE 3   Inquiry Cycles for Developing Teacher
Knowledge and Effectiveness

in a given teaching situation, what they already know, and what they need to know. To undertake Inquiry A, teachers need to have sophisticated assessment knowledge together with a variety of assessment tools that can be flexibly applied to meet situational demands. This assessment knowledge can then be used as a basis for planning when answering the question, "What do the students need to learn and do?" In this way, instruction becomes more evidence informed and targeted to student needs.

Inquiry B is focused on identifying teacher learning goals. This inquiry demands much more of teachers than using assessment information to inform planning, because it asks them to reflect on how their particular approaches and teaching emphases have contributed to existing patterns of student learning and achievement. This requires a collective rather than individual analysis, because students are taught by more than one teacher in the course of their education, and the evidence from the synthesis indicates that participation in mutual inquiry is a necessary (but insufficient) condition for promoting professional learning that has an impact on students. Inquiry B begins by focusing teachers on existing teaching—learning links and the outcomes for students.

Having identified these links, it then asks teachers to understand what it is they need to learn and do to promote the students' learning. An essential element of Inquiry B is that teachers see themselves as agents of change for their students and their own learning. Learning cannot be co- or self-regulatory in the absence of this condition, and in most of the studies showing sustained outcomes, these conditions were reported.

Inquiry C involves identifying the effectiveness of action from Inquiries A and B and is central to the co- and self-regulatory processes. Having established student and teacher learning goals and enacted appropriate teaching strategies, it is then important to monitor effectiveness in terms of their impact on students. Inquiry C is essential if the inadvertently negative outcomes for students from well-meaning teaching activities that were described in the introductory sections of this chapter are to be averted. Enacting Inquiry C may involve teachers' creating their own inquiry tools, such as observations and questioning students as well as analyzing achievement information over time.

In situations where this monitoring shows problematic student outcomes, improvement is likely to require adjustment to some other part of the process. This adjustment may include the goals, the plans, or their enactment. Thus the inquiry process cycles back to Inquiry A.

Throughout the process, co-construction of the meaning of the assessment information and the implications for practice of new pedagogical content knowledge is integral to the process. It is not possible to develop co- or self-regulatory learning in the absence of this deep understanding. At the same time, the sophistication of the analyses required during the inquiry cycle is likely to require high levels of expertise in the particular content areas. Part of the challenge is to find out whether existing knowledge is adequate or inadequate. Given that it is difficult for any individual to identify what he or she does not know, it is unlikely that these co- and self-regulatory processes will achieve this without organizational support and external expertise. The evidence from the synthesis indicates this to be the case, because all situations in which substantive outcomes for students were achieved have involved this support. It must be noted, however, that external experts were also involved in ineffective professional development. It is not, therefore, the presence of experts that makes the difference; rather, it is the way they assist in promoting teacher learning. School leaders can be highly influential in the process. In the synthesis on leadership currently in progress, for example, one of the highest effect sizes is associated with leaders promoting and participating in teacher learning and development as a leader, a learner, or both (Robinson et al., in press).

AN ILLUSTRATIVE CASE

This case describes how many of the conditions identified in the analysis above were evident in a project designed to promote professional learning and development. This project was part of a national initiative on the part of the New Zealand Ministry of Education to address its problematic profiles of achievement (English & Bareta, 2006; Parr et al., 2006) as described in the first part of this chapter. The projects' first 2 years of operation involved 91 elementary schools from throughout the country, with half opting for a focus on writing and half focused on reading. The effect sizes for writing were 1.27 on average with a greater effect ($ES = 2.05$) for the lowest 20% of students whose achievement was the primary target of the initiative. For reading, the effect size for the group as a whole was 0.87, but this was depressed as a result of a ceiling effect on the assessment employed. A more accurate reflection of its impact was the effect size of 1.97 for the lowest 20% of students. In this case description, only the writing aspect of the project will be described for reasons of space, although the approach to the professional development was similar for both curricular areas.

The project was focused on outcomes since its inception. The primary requirement of the contract between the Ministry of Education and the providers was evidence of improved student achievement. The other three contract requirements were those believed to promote student achievement. These were evidence of improved teacher content knowledge, evidence of improved transfer of understanding of literacy pedagogy to practice, and evidence of effectively led professional learning communities.

The project providers appointed a team of 25 visiting facilitators and organized training in approaches to professional development involving knowledge building and inquiry. Schools volunteered to be part of the project, but it was highly variable as to whether staff were given any say about their participation. Two researchers worked alongside the project in both a consultancy and formative research capacity. The consultancy part of the role focused on building the knowledge of the project leadership and facilitator team. The research focused on 13 of the 91 schools. In these schools, the researchers analyzed the student achievement data and teachers' responses to a scenario of a classroom lesson designed to assess their pedagogical content knowledge and attitudes toward their responsibility for student learning, undertook classroom and meeting observations, and interviewed school leaders and teachers. Later in the project, they also observed facilitator-led workshops and the feedback facilitators gave to teachers following classroom observations. These events were audiotaped and the transcripts were used to judge progress. These tools and events formed part of the project in all schools, but their analysis in the nonresearch schools was the responsibility of the schools and visiting facilitators.

Consistent with Figure 3, the project began in each school by identifying student learning needs using an assessment tool (Ministry of Education & University of Auckland, 2001) that allowed teachers to analyze students' understanding of both surface and deep features of writing for particular communicative purposes. At the same time, the teachers' writing lessons were observed, and all completed the lesson scenarios. Together, these tools helped to develop an integrated picture of teaching–learning influences. Even in these initial stages, the need for Inquiry B, identifying teacher learning needs, became apparent. Few teachers, for example, were able to score the students' writing assessment accurately, because their theories of writing did not include an understanding of the deeper features of writing for particular communicative purposes. A carefully analyzed situation of three teachers within one school where achievement was particularly low, for example, showed that their writing lessons were dominated by motivating students to write particular content but that the teaching of writing itself was limited to surface features. Not surprising, interviews of students during the lesson by the researcher indicated that they did not know what they were supposed to be learning about writing in the lesson beyond the surface features of punctuation, spelling, neatness, and length. Through the process of negotiating the meaning of these data, the teachers became aware of their own learning needs. They identified these as needing to improve their pedagogical content knowledge through facilitated readings and learning how to mark and level students' writing samples. Inquiry B was directly related to the information that became available through Inquiry A.

Not all schools in the project were so expertly facilitated or so willing initially to identify their own learning needs; however, all who were involved began with analyzing the profiles of student learning and identifying those students achieving least well together with assessing their own levels of pedagogical content knowledge through the analysis of the scenario responses. Initially, few were able to undertake the analysis of the students' writing in the absence of expert assistance. Although it is difficult to provide a normative measure of teachers' pedagogical content knowledge because standardized assessments and comparative data are not available, student progress for a sample of classes in the research schools significantly correlated with this measure of pedagogical content knowledge, $r(15) = .642, p < .01$.

An emphasis of the project was to encourage teachers to plan and execute more deliberate acts of teaching specifically aligned with what students needed to learn. The ability to do this, however, was dependent on deepening knowledge; otherwise, these acts were limited to the more surface features of writing with which they were already familiar. During the 2nd year of the project, when teachers were more familiar with the inquiry processes, each developed professional learning goals with the visiting facilitators based on their analysis of their own learning needs.

The processes of Inquiry C began in informal ways during the 1st year of the project. Teachers were encouraged to interview their students, for example, to find out how well they understood the learning aims of the lessons. A more formal process was undertaken at the end of the year, when the students were reassessed using the same writing assessment tool. Through discussion of moderated writing samples and comparison of beginning- and end-of-year results, the teachers and their leaders were able to analyze the students' patterns of progress and begin a more formal process of Inquiry C. Through this process, they were able to identify the effectiveness of changes in their teaching in response to Inquiries A and B. This reflection led into more a more focused Inquiry A that became possible through more sophisticated pedagogical content and assessment knowledge. Thus, an iterative process was set in train.

As a result of engaging in these inquiry processes with school leaders and teachers, ways in which the project itself needed to become more inquiry oriented became apparent. Policy officials realized that to reach the project goals, more than 1 year that was initially planned was needed, so they adjusted budget priorities to include a 2nd year. Project leaders became aware through school-based observations that in some areas, the national facilitators' pedagogical content knowledge was inadequate to engage in the depth of inquiry needed, so formal opportunities were provided to improve this knowledge. A more unexpected need was revealed through research observations of the facilitators' work in the schools. Although some understood the co-constructed nature of inquiry, many who were more entrenched in a "delivery mode" of professional development did not. Through a series of workshops that included an analysis of transcripts of their interactions in the schools and questionnaires to gauge teachers' reactions to their facilitation efforts, they became more skilled in conducting conversations in which meanings were co-constructed and inquiry focused.

A random sample of 15 schools were visited a year after the facilitators withdrew their support to determine whether student achievement gains were being sustained and the in-school processes that were associated with those gains continued. Preliminary analyses indicate that improved student achievement gains continued in those schools that maintained these inquiry processes and systematically aligned other aspects of the schools' operations with the principles of the project to create cross-curricula coherence in their teaching approaches.

IMPLICATIONS FOR TEACHER EDUCATION RESEARCH AND POLICY

In this chapter, we have provided an overview of the findings from a first-iteration BES of the international literature about professional learning and development that improved valued outcomes for the students of the participating teachers. As illustrated in the above case, the impact on the learning of some of our most underserved students can be accelerated by 2 to 3 years in the period of a year through professional development. The findings of this BES are further reinforced by the outcomes-linked findings emerging from other BES iterations (e.g., Anthony & Walshaw, 2007; Robinson et al., in press). The parallel Educational Leadership BES, for example, has identified the promotion of, or participation in, effective professional development as the single-most influential leadership practice in strengthening student outcomes (Robinson et al., in press). School leaders who involve themselves or others in leadership roles to ensure that the organizational conditions of the school support effective teacher learning can make substantive differences to student outcomes compared with leaders in similar schools who do not give precedence to teacher learning. Professional development for teachers is clearly a powerful policy lever.

Yet these claims appear to contradict the reservations about the potential of professional development to make a systemic difference to student outcomes expressed by the practitioners, policymakers, and researchers we quoted in the introduction to this chapter. The evidence from the synthesis on professional learning and development (Timperley et al., in press) has identified that it is not professional development per se that is the problem; rather, it is the way it is typically undertaken. Provision needs to recognize the complexity of professional practice and bring capable and effective expertise to supporting teachers to better meet the needs of diverse learners in changing times, particularly for our most underserved children. Such expertise needs to engage rather than bypass teachers' theories and provide and exemplify alternative visions and practices. Teachers need to have a problem to solve, to have multiple opportunities to learn relevant pedagogical content and assessment knowledge in ways that integrate theory and practice, and to maintain a constant focus on how teaching affects students. Better outcomes for students are sustained when the organizational conditions support ongoing evidence-informed inquiry into the impact of practice on students. Take any of the ingredients out, and its impact is likely to diminish.

This BES is part of the New Zealand Ministry of Education's Iterative BES Programme, which seeks to do more than identify particular educational conditions that lead to particular outcomes. It has sought also to build capability across the education sector and to create conditions where the relevant knowledge is owned and used by the whole sector, rather than remaining within a project or the property of individual researchers. The approach has been to engage stakeholders, especially those who actually teach, throughout the process, because the evidence can ultimately make a difference only through the actions of practitioners. To achieve this end, the New Zealand Ministry of Education has enacted a collaborative brokerage model to generate all the syntheses (Alton-Lee, 2005) that put into practice the sentiments described by Ginsburg and Gorostiaga (2003):

Our preference is also based on the belief that in the long run dialogue and participation by a wide range of stakeholders produce better and more relevant educational research, policy and practice. . . . Certainly, it may be easier—and, in that sense, more efficient—for researchers, policy makers, and practitioners in education to engage in action (or even in praxis) in isolation of members of the other groups. However, the decisions that are made and the actions that are pursued are likely to be less effective. This is the case not only because the quality of judgements may be lower but also because the activities of one group may detract from or cancel out those of other groups. (p. 10)

The results of this approach have been the development of a partnership with the teacher unions, as described by an advisory officer:

PPTA (Post Primary Teachers Association) regards itself as a partner in the BES programme. As the policy adviser at PPTA specialising in professional issues, I have been closely involved with the Best Evidence Synthesis work ever since 2003.

I believe that the BES programme is absolutely committed to promoting social justice, and for that reason our union, like NZEI [primary teacher union], has committed itself to working alongside this research programme. (Judie Alison, advisory officer for professional issues, personal communication, February 23, 2006)

This partnership has contributed to stakeholder ownership of the new knowledge generated by the synthesis and the inclusion of the Teacher Professional Learning and Development BES in a teacher union industrial claim (PPTA, 2007).

In the remainder of this section, we examine more closely the implications of the teacher professional learning and development BES iteration for research, teacher education, and policy.

Implications for Research and Teacher Education

The outcomes-linked evidence about effective professional learning poses challenges to researchers and teacher education scholars in relation to the approach taken both to knowledge building in this field and to providing professional development. It is timely to reflect on the moral purpose of education in taking research and development forward in the field of professional development and teacher knowledge. If we accept that our schooling systems are ultimately in the business of educating students, not teachers (Camburn, 1997), then we must use outcomes for students as the criteria for effectiveness of our various improvement efforts.

There are now numerous journals dedicated to teacher education. Even a superficial search of studies on the Educational Resources Information Center (ERIC) for the past 40 years yields more than 11,000 studies for professional development and a further 17,000 for in-service teacher education. That this literature is largely self-referential to the perspectives of the adults and not to the benefits for children is apparent in how small the literature is that includes systematic attention to student outcomes. In the interests of both children and their teachers, there needs to be far more attention to the nature and the outcomes for both teachers and students of professional development, and the links between these, in this research field. There are major gaps in the research knowledge about capability development in teacher education.

Although initial teacher education is outside the scope of this synthesis, and therefore, this chapter, this issue of research focus applies as much to the area of initial teacher education as it does to promoting ongoing professional learning. Given the limited attention this research literature has given to the circumstances that have a positive impact on learner outcomes, it would be difficult to undertake a similar synthesis in this area. It is likely, however, that the conditions identified in this synthesis that promote professional learning for those already practicing would apply in a modified form to those learning to teach.

Implications for Educational Policy

The implications for policy were well articulated by Knapp (2003) in a landmark chapter in a previous volume of this journal: "Professional Development as a Policy Pathway." Knapp called for attention to structures and supports, the development of sufficient expertise, more attention to content, and a shift to new norms concerning ongoing professional development. He called for serious reconsideration of investment in professional development as a policy pathway and attention to building and maintaining political support for professional development from outside the education system. The findings of this BES signal also the need for attention from policy to the time needed to allow the multiple opportunities for professionals to learn new knowledge and skills if deep change is to occur.

An immediate challenge for policy is to attend to situations where teacher professional development may be doing harm or wasting investment through undermining rather than optimizing educational opportunities for students. Several published studies were located that showed no or negative impact on student outcomes (e.g., Kerman et al., 1980; Stallings & Krasavage, 1986; Van Der Sijde, 1989). Given publication bias toward success rather than failure, there are no doubt many more such situations.

Perhaps the biggest challenge for policy is scale. Systemic responses are needed from different jurisdictions whether at national, federal, state, or regional levels. These are critical for sustainable rather than siloed and transitory development in education. Coburn's (2003) consideration of the evidence about the effectiveness of school reform suggests the success of policy interventions is likely to be dependent on the extent to which the conditions of depth, breadth, ownership, and sustainability are achieved. Such conditions require the development of systemic infrastructure, capability and expertise in research and development in teacher professional learning, and solutions that are available to all schools.

Policy jurisdictions need to recognize also the value and potential of cyclical research and development for contributing to educational development. The findings of the synthesis illuminate the potential of outcomes-focused research and development as a resource for strengthening teacher knowledge. A recent OECD (2003) review shows expenditure in research and development in education to be very low in many jurisdictions, particularly when education is compared with other engines of social and economic development, such as industry, technology, and health. The value of such research and development should not be underestimated as a contribution to the public good. Given strategic investment and valued outcomes as a touchstone, research and development can be a critical lever for enabling our schools not only to navigate the challenges and opportunities facing our education systems but also in providing the conditions for systemic transformation such challenges offer.

Although the Iterative BES Programme is a strategy to strengthen policy access to trustworthy research, there are challenges in the uptake of research findings by policymakers (Walter, Nutley & Davies, 2005), particularly in democratic systems where more than the research evidence inevitably influences decisions. For policymakers, however, the findings confirm the importance of professional development as possibly one of the highest impact policy levers in education, with potentially transformational effects on both social and academic outcomes from the education system.

As a first-iteration synthesis that illuminates the links between professional development and desired student outcomes, the BES foreshadows the significance of this kind of knowledge building to address the evidential gap identified by Hanushek (2005). Given the promise of addressing that gap, there is a foundation for policymakers to progressively have confidence in making investments in the kinds of professional development that, given the conditions of effective ongoing professional inquiry, evaluation, and development, can make a difference to the success and wellbeing of all of our children, our wider communities, and societies.

ACKNOWLEDGMENTS

Such a substantial work as this happens only with the contribution of others. We wish to acknowledge the assistance of Aaron Wilson, Heather Barrar, and Irene Fung in searching for and analyzing the studies and Dr. Gavin Brown and Junjun Chen for calculating the effect sizes related to student outcomes. Many groups and individuals have participated in the development process, and to name a few would be to exclude others, but special mention needs to made of Dr. Lorna Earl, who acted as a critical friend throughout the process. We also wish to acknowledge the financial and operational support of the New Zealand Ministry of Education.

REFERENCES

Adey, P. (2004). *The professional development of teachers: Practice and theory.* London: Kluwer Academic.

Aitken, G., & Sinnema, C. (in press). *Effective pedagogy in social sciences/Tikanga-a-iwi. Best evidence synthesis iteration.* Wellington, New Zealand: Ministry of Education.

Alton-Lee, A. (1984). *Understanding learning and teaching: An investigation of pupil experience of content in relation to immediate and long-term learning.* Unpublished doctoral dissertation, University of Canterbury, Christchurch, New Zealand.

Alton-Lee, A. (2003). *Quality teaching for diverse students in schooling.* Wellington, New Zealand: Ministry of Education. Available from http://educationcounts.edcentre.govt.nz/goto/BES

Alton-Lee, A. (2004). Guidelines for generating a best evidence synthesis iteration. Wellington, New Zealand: Ministry of Education. Available from http://educationcounts.edcentre/govt.nz/goto/BES

Alton-Lee, A. (2005, September). *Collaborating across policy, research and practice: Knowledge building for sustainable educational development.* Paper presented at the Netherlands Evidence Based Policy Research Conference Linking Evidence to Practice, The Hague, Netherlands. Available from http://educationcounts.edcentre.govt.nz/goto/BES

Alton-Lee, A., & Nuthall, G. (1990). Pupil experiences and pupil learning in the elementary classroom: An illustration of a generative methodology. *Teaching and Teacher Education, 6*(1), 27–45.

Alton-Lee, A., Rietveld, C., Klenner, L., Dalton, N., Diggins, C., & Town, S. (2000). Inclusive practice within the lived cultures of school communities: Research case studies in teaching, learning and inclusion. *International Journal of Inclusive Education, 4*(3), 179–210.

Alton-Lee, A. G. (1983). *Organizing for learning. SET research information for teachers* (No. 2, Item 5). Wellington: New Zealand Council for Educational Research.

Alton-Lee, A. G., Nuthall, G. A., & Patrick, J. (1993). Reframing classroom research: A lesson from the private world of children. *Harvard Educational Review, 63*(1), 50–84.

Amosa, W., Ladwig, J., Griffiths, T., & Gore J. (2007, November). *Equity effects of quality teaching: Closing the gap.* Paper prepared for the Australian Association for Research in Education Conference, Fremantle, Australia.

Anthony, G., & Walshaw, M. (2007). *Effective pedagogy in mathematics/pangarau: Best evidence synthesis iteration.* Wellington, New Zealand: Ministry of Education. Available from http://educationcounts.edcentre.govt.nz/goto/BES

Baker, S., & Smith, S. (1999). Starting off on the right foot: The influence of four principles of professional development in improving literacy instruction in two kindergarten programs. *Learning Disabilities Research & Practice, 14*(4), 239–253.

Ball, D. (1988). Unlearning to teach mathematics. *For the Learning of Mathematics, 8*(1), 40–48.

Beecher, B., & Arthur, L. (2001). *Play and literacy in children's worlds.* Newtown, Australia: Primary English Teaching Association.

Benton, R. (1986). Now fades the glimmering: Research in classrooms in New Zealand. *SET: Research Information for Teachers, 2*, Item 12.

Biddulph, F., Biddulph, J., & Biddulph, C. (2003). *The complexity of community and family influences on children's achievement in New Zealand: Best evidence synthesis.* Wellington, New Zealand: Ministry of Education. Available from http://educationcounts.edcentre.govt .nz/goto/BES

Bishop, R., Berryman, M., Powell, A., & Teddy, L. (2005). *Te Kotahitanga: Improving the educational achievement of Maori students in mainstream education: Phase 2. Towards a whole school approach* [Progress report and planning document]. Wellington, New Zealand: Ministry of Education.

Bishop, R., & Glynn, T. (1998). Achieving cultural integrity in education in New Zealand. In K. Cushner (Ed.), *International perspectives on intercultural education* (pp. 38–70). New York: Lawrence Erlbaum.

Black, P., & Wiliam, D. (1998). Assessment and classroom learning. *Assessment in Education. 5*(1), 7–74.

Borman, G. D., Slavin, R. E., Cheung, A., Chamberlain, A. M., Madden, N. A., & Chambers, B. (2005). Success for all: First-year results from the national randomized field trial. *Educational Evaluation and Policy Analysis, 27*(1), 1–22.

Boruch, B., & Herman, R. (in press). What Works Clearinghouse (US). In *Evidence in education: Linking research and policy.* Paris: Organisation for Economic Co-operation and Development, Centre for Educational Research and Innovation. Available from http://www .oecd.org/edu/rd/ebpr

Bossert, S. (1979). *Tasks and social relationships in classrooms: A study of instructional organisation and its consequences.* London: Cambridge University Press.

Bowles, S., & Gintis, H. (1976). *Schooling in capitalist America.* London: Routledge/Kegan Paul.

Bransford, J. D., Brown, A. L., & Cocking, R. R. (2000). *How people learn: Brain, mind, experience, and school.* Washington, DC: National Academies Press.

Bransford, J., Darling-Hammond, L., & LePage, P. (2005). Introduction. In L. Darling-Hammond & J. Bransford (Eds.), *Preparing teachers for a changing world: What teachers should learn and be able to do* (pp 1–39). San Francisco: Jossey-Bass.

Britzman, D. P. (1995). Is there a queer pedagogy? Or, stop reading straight. *Educational Theory, 45*(2), 151–165.

Brophy, J. (Ed.). (2001). *Subject-specific instructional methods and activities* (Advances in Research on Teaching, Vol. 8). New York: Elsevier.

Butler, D. L., & Winne, P. H. (1995). Feedback and self-regulated learning: A theoretical synthesis. *Review of Educational Research, 65*(3), 245–274.

Camburn, E. (1997). *The impact of professional community on teacher learning and instructional practice.* Unpublished doctoral dissertation, University of Chicago.

Cardelle-Elawar, M. (1995). Effects of metacognitive instruction on low achievers in mathematics problems. *Teaching and Teacher Education, 11*(1), 81–95.

Carkeek, L., Davies, L., & Irwin, K. (1994). *What happens to Maori girls at school? Final report.* Wellington, New Zealand: Ministry of Education.

Carpenter, T. P., Fennema, E., Peterson, P. L., Chiang, C.-P., & Loef, M. (1989). Using knowledge of children's mathematics thinking in classroom teaching: An experimental study. *American Educational Research Journal, 26*(4), 499–553.

Cazden, C. B. (1990). Differential treatment in New Zealand: Reflections on research in minority education. *Teaching and Teacher Education, 6*(4), 291–303.

Clay, M. (1985). Engaging with the school system: A study of interactions in New Zealand classrooms. *New Zealand Journal of Educational Studies, 20*(1), 20–38.

Cobb, P., Wood, T., Yackel, D., Nicolls, J., Wheatley, G., Trigatti, B., et al. (1991). Assessment of a problem-centered second-grade mathematics project. *Journal for Research in Mathematics Education, 22*, 13–29.

Coburn, C. E. (2001). Collective sensemaking about reading: How teachers mediate reading policy in their professional communities. *Educational Evaluation and Policy Analysis, 23*(2), 145–170.

Coburn, C. E. (2003). Rethinking scale: Moving beyond numbers to deep and lasting change. *Educational Researcher, 32*(6), 3–12.

Cochran-Smith, M., & Lytle, S. L. (1999). The teacher research movement: A decade later. *Educational Research, 28*(7), 15–25.

Cochrane-Smith, M., & Zeichner, K. M. (Eds.). (2005). *Studying teacher education: The report of the AERA Panel on Research and Teacher Education.* Mahwah, NJ: Lawrence Erlbaum.

Cohen, E. (1994). Restructuring the classroom: Conditions for productive small groups. *Review of Educational Research, 64*(1), 1–35.

Cohen, J. (1988). *Statistical power analysis for the behavioral sciences* (2nd ed.). Hillsdale, NJ: Lawrence Erlbaum.

Coleman, J. S., Campbell, E., Hobson, C., McPartland, J., Mod, A., Weinfeld, F., et al. (1966). *Equality of opportunity.* Washington, DC: U.S. Government Printing Office.

Colwell, R. (1999). The arts. In G. Cawelti (Ed.), *Handbook of research on improving student achievement* (2nd ed., pp. 39–85). Alexandria, VA: Educational Research Service.

Confrey, J., Castro-Filho, J., & Wilhelm, J. (2000). Implementation research as a means to link systemic reform and applied psychology in mathematics education. *Educational Psychologist, 35*(3), 179–191.

Cuttance, P. (1998). Quality assurance reviews as a catalyst for school improvement in Australia. In A. Hargreaves, A. Lieberman, M. Fullan, & D. Hopkins (Eds.), *International handbook of educational change* (Part 2, pp. 1135–1162). Dordrecht, Netherlands: Kluwer.

Darling-Hammond, L. (2000). Teacher quality and student achievement: A review of state policy evidence. *Education Policy Analysis Archives, 8*(1). Retrieved May 30, 2007, from http://epaa.asu.edu/epaa/vol8.html

Darling-Hammond, L., & Bransford, J. (Eds.). (2005). *Preparing teachers for a changing world: What teachers should learn and be able to do.* San Francisco: Jossey-Bass.

Datnow, A., Borman, G. D., Stringfield, S., Overman, L. T., & Castellano, M. (2003). Comprehensive school reform in culturally and linguistically diverse contexts: Implementation and outcomes from a four-year study. *Educational Evaluation and Policy Analysis, 25*(2), 143–170.

Dilworth, M., & Brown, C. (2001). Consider the difference: Teaching and learning in culturally rich schools. In V. Richardson (Ed.), *Handbook of research on teaching* (4th ed., pp. 643–667). Washington, DC: American Educational Research Association.

Donovan, S. M., Bransford, J. D., & Pellegrino, J. W. (Eds.). (1999). *How people learn: Bridging research and practise.* Washington, DC: National Academy Press.

Doyle, C. S. (1992). *Outcome measures for information literacy within the national education goals of 1990: Final report to National Forum on Information Literacy. Summary of findings.* (ERIC Document Reproduction Service No. ED351033)

Doyle, W. (1983). Academic work. *Review of Educational Research, 53,* 159–199.

Doyle, W. (1990). Themes in teacher education research. In W. Houston (Ed.), *Handbook of research on teacher education* (pp. 3–24). New York: Macmillan.

Earl, L., & Katz, S. (2006). *Rethinking classroom assessment with purpose in mind: Assessment for learning, assessment as learning and assessment of learning.* Winnipeg, MB, Canada: Minister of Education, Citizenship and Youth.

English, C., & Bareta, L. (2006). *Literacy professional development milestone report.* Wellington, New Zealand: Learning Media.

Evertson, C. M., & Weinstein, C. S. (Eds.). (2006). *The handbook of classroom management: Research, practice, and contemporary issues.* Mahwah, NJ: Lawrence Erlbaum.

Farquhar, S. (2003). *Quality teaching: Early foundations. Best evidence synthesis iteration.* Wellington, New Zealand: Ministry of Education. Available from http://educationcounts .edcentre.govt.nz/goto/BES

Fennema, E., Franke, M., Carpenter, T. P., & Carey, D. (1993). Using children's mathematical knowledge in instruction. *American Educational Research Journal, 30*(3), 555–583.

Firestone, W. A., Schorr, R. Y., & Monfils, L. F. (2004). *The ambiguity of teaching to the test: Standards, assessments, and education reform.* Mahwah, NJ: Lawrence Erlbaum.

Fishman, B. J., Marx, R. W., Best, S., & Tal, R. T. (2003). Linking teacher and student learning to improve professional development in systemic reform. *Teaching and Teacher Education, 19*(6), 643–658.

Froumin, I. (2007, July). *Assessing learning outcomes: What works.* Invited keynote to the 31st annual conference of the Pacific Circle Consortium, Honolulu, Hawaii. Available from http://hisii.hawaii.edu/pcc2007/program.htm

Ginsburg, M., & Gorostiaga, J. (2003). Dialogue about educational research, policy, and practice: To what extent is it possible and who should be involved? In M. Ginsburg & J. Gorostiaga (Eds.), *Limitations and possibilities of dialogue among researchers, policymakers and practitioners: International perspectives on the field of education* (pp.1–36). New York: Falmer.

Gore, J., Ladwig, J., Griffiths, T., & Amosa, W. (2007, November). *Data-driven guidelines for high quality teacher education.* Paper prepared for the Australian Association for Research in Education Conference, Fremantle, Australia.

Gough, D. (2007). The Evidence for Policy and Practice Information and Co-ordinating (EPPI) Centre, United Kingdom. In *Evidence in education: Linking research and policy.* Paris: Organisation for Economic Co-operation and Development, Centre for Educational Research and Innovation. Available from http://www.oecd.org/edu/rd/ebpr

Guskey, T. R. (2000). *Evaluating professional development.* Thousand Oaks, CA: Corwin.

Hammerness, K., Darling-Hammond, L., Bransford, J., Berliner, D., Cochran-Smith, M., McDonald, M., et al. (2005). How teachers learn and develop. In L. Darling-Hammond & J. Bransford (Eds.), *Preparing teachers for a changing world: What teachers should learn and be able to do* (pp. 358–389). San Francisco: Jossey-Bass.

Hanushek, E. (2005). *Economic outcomes and school quality. Education Policy Series.* International Academy of Education and International Institute for Educational Planning, UNESCO. Available from http://www.smec.curtin.edu.au/iae/

Hattie, J. (1990). Performance indicators in education. *Australian Journal of Education, 34*(3), 249–276.

Hattie, J. (1992). Measuring the effects of schooling. *Australian Journal of Education, 36*(1), 5–13.

Heath, S. B. (1982). What no bedtime story means: Narrative skills at home and school. *Language in Society, 1*, 49–76.

Heath, S. B. (1993). The madness(es) of reading and writing ethnography. *Anthropology & Education Quarterly, 24*(3), 256–268.

Higgins, J. (2001). *Developing numeracy: Understanding place value. Report to the Ministry of Education.* Wellington, New Zealand: Ministry of Education.

Higgins, J., Irwin, K., Thomas, G., Trinick, T., & Young Loveridge, J. (2005). *Findings from the New Zealand Numeracy Development Project 2004.* Wellington, New Zealand: Ministry of Education.

Hill, P. W., & Rowe, K. J. (1996). Multilevel modelling in school effectiveness research. *School Effectiveness and School Improvement, 7*(1), 1–34.

Hohepa, M., Hingaroa Smith, G., Tuhiwai Smith, L., & McNaughton, S. (1992). Te Kohanga Reo hei Tikanga ako I te Reo Maori: Te Kohanga Reo as a context for language learning. *Educational Psychology, 12*(3/4), 333–346.

Irvine, J. J., & York, D. E. (1995). Learning styles and culturally diverse students: A literature review. In J. Banks & C. McGee (Eds.), *Handbook of research on multicultural education* (pp. 484–497). New York: Macmillan.

Jencks, C., Smith, M. S., Ackland, H., Bane, J. J., Cohen, D., Grintlis, H., et al. (1972). *Inequality: A reassessment of the effects of families and schools in America.* New York: Basic Books.

Kahle, J., Meece, J., & Scantlebury, K. (2000). Urban African-American middle school science students: Does standards-based teaching make a difference? *Journal of Research in Science Teaching, 37*(9), 1019–1041.

Kennedy, M. M. (1999). The role of preservice teacher education. In L. Darling-Hammond & G. Sykes (Eds.), *Teaching as the learning profession: Handbook of teaching and policy* (pp. 54–86). San Francisco: Jossey-Bass.

Kerman, S., Kimball, T., & Martin, M. (1980). *Teacher expectations and student achievement: Coordinator manual.* Bloomington, IN: Phi Delta Kappa.

Knapp, M. S. (2003). Professional development as a policy pathway. *Review of Research in Education, 27,* 109–157.

Lipman, P. (1997). Restructuring in context: A case study of teacher participation and the dynamics of ideology, race and power. *American Educational Research Journal, 34*(1), 3–37.

Lipsey, M. W., & Wilson, D. B. (1993). The efficacy of psychological, educational, and behavioral treatment: Confirmation from meta-analysis. *American Psychologist, 48*(12), 1181–1209.

Luke, A., & Hogan, D. (2006). Redesigning what counts as evidence in educational policy: The Singapore model. In J. Ozga, T. Seddon, & T. Popkewitz (Eds.), *World yearbook of education. Educational research and policy: Steering the knowledge-based economy* (pp. 173–174). London: Routledge.

Marzano, R. J., Pickering, D. J., & Pollock, J. E. (2001). *Classroom instruction that works: Research-based strategies for increasing student achievement.* Alexandria, VA: Association for Supervision and Curriculum Development.

Mayer, S. E. (2002). *The influence of parental income on children's outcomes.* Wellington, New Zealand: Ministry of Social Development. Available from http://www.msp.govt.nz/publications/influence_parental_income/index.html

McClain, K., & Cobb, P. (2001). An analysis of development of sociomathematical norms in one first-grade classroom. *Journal for Research in Mathematics Education, 32*(3), 236–266.

McNaughton, S. (2002). *Meeting of minds.* Wellington, New Zealand: Learning Media.

McNaughton, S., Lai, M. K., MacDonald, S., & Farry, S. (2004). Designing more effective teaching of comprehension in culturally and linguistically diverse classrooms in New Zealand. *Australian Journal of Language and Literacy, 27*(3), 184–197.

McNulty, R., & Daggett, W. (2007). *Preparing students for their future. Successful schools: From research to action plans.* Invited keynote to the 31st annual conference of the Pacific Circle Consortium, Honolulu, Hawaii.

Millward, P., Neal, R., Kofoed, W., Parr, J., Kuin Lai, M., & Robinson, V. (2001). Schools learning journeys: Evaluating a literacy intervention at Dawson Road Primary School. *SET Research Information for Teachers, 2,* 39–42.

Ministry of Education & the University of Auckland. (2001). *Assessment Tools for Teaching and Learning: Project asTTle.* Wellington, New Zealand: Author.

Mitchell, M., & Cubey, P. (2003). *Characteristics of professional development linked to enhanced pedagogy and children's learning in early childhood settings: Best evidence synthesis.* Wellington, New Zealand: Ministry of Education. Available from http://educationcounts.edcentre.govt.nz/goto/BES

Moll, L. (2001). Through the mediation of others: Vygotskian research on teaching. In V. Richardson (Ed.), *Handbook of research on teaching* (4th ed., pp. 111–129). Washington, DC: American Educational Research Association.

Muijs, D., & Reynolds, D. (2001). *Effective teaching: Evidence and practice.* London: Paul Chapman.

Murray, S. (2006). *Achievement at Maori immersion and bilingual schools 2005.* Wellington, New Zealand: Ministry of Education. Available from http://educationcounts.edcentre.govt.nz/themes/maori/achieve-maori-immersion-2005.html

National Staff Development Council. (2001). *National Staff Development Council's standards for staff development* (Rev. ed.). Oxford, OH: Author. Available from http://www.nsdc.org/library/standards2001.html

New Zealand Education Review Office. (2003). *Maori students in mainstream schools. Evaluation Report*. Wellington, New Zealand: Author.

Newmann, F. (1994). *School-wide professional community: Issues in restructuring schools* (Issue Report No. 6). Madison: University of Wisconsin, Center on Organization and Restructuring of Schools.

Niemi, H. (2007). Life as learning: A Finnish national research programme. In *Evidence in education: Linking research and policy* (pp. 117–124). Paris: Organisation for Economic Co-operation and Development, Centre for Educational Research and Innovation. Available from http://www.oecd.org/edu/rd/ebpr

Nuthall, G. (1999). Learning how to learn: The evolution of students' minds through the social processes and culture of the classroom. *International Journal of Educational Research, 31*, 1–256.

Nuthall, G. (2004). Relating classroom teaching to student learning: A critical analysis of why research has failed to bridge the theory-practice gap. *Harvard Educational Review, 74*(3), 273–306.

Nye, B., Konstantanopoulos, S., & Hedges, L. V. (2004). How large are teacher effects? *Educational Evaluation and Policy Analysis, 26*(3), 237–257.

Oakley, C., Moore, D., Burford, D., Fahrenwald, R., & Woodward, K. (2005). The Montana model: Integrated primary care and behavioral health in a family practice residency program. *Journal of Rural Health, 21*(4), 351–354.

Organisation for Economic Co-operation and Development. (2001). *Knowledge and skills for life: First results from the OECD Programme for International Student Assessment (PISA) 2000*. Paris: Author.

Organisation for Economic Co-operation and Development. (2003). *Knowledge management: New challenges for educational research*. Paris: Author.

Organisation for Economic Co-operation and Development. (2005a). *Education at a glance: OECD indicators 2005*. Paris: Author.

Organisation for Economic Co-operation and Development. (2005b). *Teachers matter: Attracting, developing and retaining effective teachers*. Paris: Author.

Organisation for Economic Co-operation and Development. (2007). *Understanding the social outcomes of learning. Centre for Research and Innovation*. Paris: Author.

Palincsar, A. S., & Brown, A. L. (1984). Reciprocal teaching of comprehension fostering and comprehension monitoring activities. *Cognition and Instruction, 1*(2), 117–175.

Palincsar, A. S., Magnusson, S. J., Marano, N., Ford, D., & Brown, N. (1998). Designing a community of practice: Principles and practices of the GIsML community. *Teaching and Teacher Education, 14*(1), 5–19.

Parke, H. M., & Coble, C. R. (1997). Teachers designing curriculum as professional development: A model for transformational science teaching. *Journal of Research in Science Teaching, 34*(8), 773–789.

Parr, J., Timperley, H., Reddish, P., Jesson, R., & Adams, R. (2006). *Literacy Professional Development Project: Identifying effective teaching and professional development practices for enhanced student learning. Milestone 5* [Final report]. Wellington, New Zealand: Learning Media.

Pawson, R. (2002). Evidence-based policy: The promise of realist synthesis. *Evaluation, 8*(3), 340–358.

Phillips, G., McNaughton, S., & MacDonald, S. (2004). Managing the mismatch: Enhancing early literacy progress for children with diverse language and cultural identities in mainstream urban schools in New Zealand. *Journal of Educational Psychology, 96*(2), 309–323.

Phillips, J. (2003). Powerful learning: Creating learning communities in urban school reform. *Journal of Curriculum and Supervision, 18*(3), 240–258.

Post Primary Teachers' Association. (2007). *Adding value to society: Your guide to the Secondary Teachers' Collective Agreement Claim 2007*. Wellington, New Zealand: Author.

Plato (1968). *The republic: Book III* (B. Jowett, Trans.). New York: Airmont.

Putman, R. T., & Borko, H. (2000). What do new views of knowledge and thinking have to say about research on teacher learning? *Educational Researcher, 29*(1), 4–15.

Raghavan, K., Cohen-Regev, S., & Strobel, S. A. (2001). Student outcomes in a local systemic change project. *School Science and Mathematics, 101*(8), 417–426.

Reaney, M. J. (1911). Educational research: Who is to undertake it? The place and value of experimental psychology in a training college course. *Journal of Experimental Pedagogy and Training College Record, 2,* 382–384.

Rex, L., Green, J. & Dixon, C. (1997). Constructing opportunities for learning academic literacy practices. *Interpretations, 30*(2), 78–104.

Reyes, P., Scribner, J. D., & Scribner, A. P. (Eds.). (1999). *Lessons from high-performing Hispanic schools: Creating learning communities.* New York: Teachers College Press.

Reynolds, D., & Teddlie, C. (2000). The processes of school effectiveness. In C. Teddlie & D. Reynolds (Eds.), *The international handbook of school effectiveness research* (pp. 134–159). London: Falmer.

Richardson, V. (Ed.). (2001). *Handbook of research on teaching* (4th ed.). Washington, DC: American Educational Research Association.

Robbins, P., & Wolfe, P. (1987). Reflections on a Hunter-based staff development project. *Educational Leadership, 44*(5), 56–61.

Robinson, V., Hohepa, M., & Lloyd, C. (in press). *Educational leadership: Schooling. Best evidence synthesis iteration.* Wellington, New Zealand: Ministry of Education.

Robinson, V. M. J. (1993). *Problem-based methodology: Research for the improvement of practice.* Oxford, UK: Pergamon.

Rowe, K. J., & Hill, P. W. (1998). Modelling educational effectiveness in classrooms: The use of multilevel structural equations to model students' progress. *Educational Research and Evaluation, 4*(4), 307–347.

St. George, A. (1983). Teacher expectations and perceptions of Polynesian and Pakeha pupils and the relationship to classroom behaviour and school achievement. *British Journal of Educational Psychology, 53*(1), 48–59.

Saxe, G. B., Gearhart, M., & Nasir, N. (2001). Enhancing students' understanding of mathematics: A study of three contrasting approaches to professional support. *Journal of Mathematics Teacher Education, 4,* 55–79.

Scheerens, J, Vermeulen, C., & Pelgrum, W. J. (1989). Generalizability of instructional and school effectiveness indicators across nations. *International Journal of Educational Research, 13*(7), 789–799.

Schorr, R. Y. (2000). Impact at the student level: A study of the effects of a teacher development intervention on students' mathematical thinking. *Journal of Mathematical Behavior, 19,* 209–231.

Seixas, P. (2001). Beyond "content" and "pedagogy": In search of a way to talk about history education. *Journal of Curriculum Studies, 31*(3), 317–337.

Shulman, L. S. (1986). Those who understand: A conception of teacher knowledge. *American Educator, 10*(1), 9–15.

Shulman, L. S. (1987). Knowledge and teaching: Foundations of the new reform. *Harvard Educational Review, 57*(1), 1–22.

Smith, L. T. (1999). *Decolonising methodologies: Research and indigenous peoples.* London and New York: Zed.

Sparks, D. (2004). Focusing staff development on improving the learning of all students. In G. Cawelti (Ed.), *Handbook of research on improving student achievement* (3rd ed., pp. 245–255). Arlington, VA: Educational Research Service.

Spillane, J. P. (2000). Cognition and policy implementation: District policy-makers and the reform of mathematics education. *Cognition and Instruction, 18*(2), 141–179.

Spillane, J. P., Reiser, B. J., & Reimer, T. (2002). Policy implementation and cognition: Reframing and refocusing implementation research. *Review of Educational Research, 72*(3), 387–431.

Stallings, J., & Krasavage, E. M. (1986). Program implementation and student achievement in a four-year Madeline Hunter follow-through project. *Elementary School Journal, 87*(2), 117–137.

Tallmadge, G. (1977). *The Joint Dissemination Review Panel idea book.* Washington, DC: National Institute of Education and the U.S. Office of Education.

Thomas, D. (Ed.). (1984). *Patterns of social behaviour: New Zealand and the South Pacific* (Psychology Research Series No. 17). Hamilton, New Zealand: University of Waikato.

Timperley, H., & Parr, J. (2006). Theory competition and the process of change. *Journal of Educational Change, 6*(3), 227–252.

Timperley, H., & Phillips, G. (2003). Changing and sustaining teachers' expectations through professional development in literacy. *Teaching and Teacher Education, 19*, 627–641.

Timperley, H., Wilson, A., Barrar, H., & Fung, I. (in press). *Teacher professional learning and development: Best evidence synthesis iteration.* Wellington, New Zealand: Ministry of Education. Available from http://www.minedu.govt.nz/goto/bestevidencesynthesis

Timperley, H. S. (2005). Distributed leadership: Developing theory from practice. *Journal of Curriculum Studies, 37*(6), 395–420.

Town, S. J. H. (1998). *Is it safe to come out yet? The impact of secondary schooling on the positive identity of ten young gay men, or that's a queer way to behave.* Unpublished doctoral dissertation, Victoria University, Wellington, New Zealand.

Trinick, A. (2005). Poutama Tau. In J. Higgins, K. Irwin, G. Thomas, T. Trinick, & J. Young Loveridge. (Eds.), *Findings from the New Zealand Numeracy Development Project 2004* (pp. 103–114). Wellington, New Zealand: Ministry of Education.

University of Hawaii Curriculum Research and Development Group. (2002). Foundational approaches in science teaching (FAST). In J. Killion (Ed.), *What works in the middle: Results-based staff development* (pp. 114–117). National Staff Development Council. Available from http://www.nsdc.org/connect/projects/resultsbased.cfm

Van Der Sijde, P. C. (1989). The effect of a brief teacher training on student achievement. *Teaching and Teacher Education, 5*(4), 303–314.

Walter, I., Nutley, S., & Davies, H. (2005). What works to promote evidence-based practice? A cross-sector review. *Evidence and Policy, 1*(3), 335–363.

Wilson, S., & Berne, J. (1999). Teacher learning and the acquisition of professional knowledge: An examination of research on contemporary professional development. In A. Iran-Nejad & P. D. Pearson (Eds.), *Review of Research in Education* (Vol. 24, pp. 173–209). Washington, DC: American Educational Research Association.

Winch, W. H. (1911). The place and value of experimental psychology in a training college course. *Journal of Experimental Pedagogy and Training College Record, 2*, 375–382.

Wood, T., & Sellers, P. (1996). Assessment of a problem-centered mathematics program: Third grade. *Journal for Research in Mathematics Education, 27*, 337–353.

Wright, S. P., Horn, S. P., & Sanders, W. L. (1997). Teacher and classroom context effects on student achievement: Implications for teacher evaluation. *Journal of Personnel Evaluation in Education, 11*, 57–67.

Zimmerman, B. (2001). Theories of self-regulated learning and academic achievement: An overview and analysis. In E. Zimmerman & D. Schunk (Eds.), *Self-regulated learning and academic achievement* (pp.1–38). Mahwah, NJ: Lawrence Erlbaum.

About the Editors

Judith Green is currently a professor and emphasis leader for teaching and learning in the Department of Education in the Gevirtz Graduate School of Education at the University of California, Santa Barbara. She is also director of the Center for Literacy and Inquiry in Networking Communities. She obtained her PhD in education from the University of California, Berkeley, in 1977. Her research interests include the social construction of disciplinary knowledge in class rooms; literacy as a social process; and ethnography, discourse, and video analysis of factors that support and constrain equity of access to disciplinary knowledge, identity potentials, and literacy as a social process in classrooms and other social contexts. Her published books include *Handbook of Complimentary Methods in Education Research* (Green, Camilli, & Elmore, 2006), *Multiple Perspective Analyses of Classroom Discourse* (Green & Harker, 1988), and *Multidisciplinary Perspectives on Literacy Research* (Beach, Green, Kamil, & Shanahan, 2005).

Gregory J. Kelly is currently a professor of science education and head of the Department of Curriculum and Instruction at the Pennsylvania State University. He is a former Peace Corps Volunteer and physics teacher. He received his PhD from Cornell University in 1994. His research focuses on classroom discourse, epistemology, and science learning and has been supported by grants from Spencer Foundation, National Science Foundation, and the National Academy of Education. His recently published chapter, "Epistemology and Educational Research," appears in J. Green, G. Camilli, and P. Elmore (Eds.), *Handbook of Complementary Methods in Education Research*. He teaches courses in science education and qualitative research methods. He serves as editor for the journal *Science Education*.

Allan Luke is a professor of education at Queensland University of Technology. He is a Canadian-trained primary teacher who did his PhD at Simon Fraser University. He led state and national curriculum reform as deputy director general and chief ministerial advisor for Queensland's schools from 1999 to 2002. He is currently a coeditor of *Pedagogies, Asia Pacific Journal of Education, and Teaching Education*. He is currently working on Australian Research Council projects on early literacy pedagogy and on the spread of transnational secondary school curriculum, and on a Queensland state government project redesigning state curriculum. His most recent book, with James Albright, *is Pierre Bourdieu and Literacy Education* (Lawrence Erlbaum).

Review of Research in Education
February 2008, Vol. 32, pp. 370–370
DOI: 10.3102/0091732X07313906
© 2008 AERA. http://rre.aera.net

About the Contributors

Adrienne Alton-Lee is the chief education adviser for the New Zealand Ministry of Education's Iterative Best Evidence Synthesis Programme. Her role is to strengthen the evidence-base informing policy and practice in education and to provide medium-term strategic advice to government. She is a fellow of the International Academy of Education. She was formerly a teacher, classroom researcher, professor of teacher education, and associate editor of *Teaching and Teacher Education*. She collaborated with Graham Nuthall on a series of replications of her doctoral study tracing and explaining student long-term learning from their experiences in classrooms. She has published in a range of leading educational journals, including *Harvard Educational Review, Elementary School Journal, International Journal of Inclusive Education*, and *American Educational Research Journal*. Her work has been reviewed in recent editions of the *Handbook for Research on Teaching* and the *Handbook of Research on Classroom Management: Research, Practice and Contemporary Issues*. She is author of the New Zealand Ministry of Education's *Quality Teaching for Diverse Students in Schooling: Best Evidence Synthesis Iteration*.

Anne DiPardo is a professor of language, literacy, and culture at the University of Iowa, where she works with preservice English language arts teachers and teaches graduate courses in literacy theory and research. From 2003 to 2008, she was a coeditor (along with Melanie Sperling) of the empirical journal of the National Council of Teachers of English (NCTE), *Research in the Teaching of English*. She has served NCTE in a number of other capacities, cochairing its Assembly for Research and serving on its Standing Committee for Research and Research Forum; currently, she is a member of the Executive Committee of the NCTE Conference on English Education (CEE) and of the NCTE College Forum. She is a fellow of the National Conference on Research in Language and Literacy and a past recipient of the NCTE/CEE Meade Award for outstanding English education research, the Conference on English Leadership/NCTE *English Leadership Quarterly* Article of the Year Award, the National Writing Centers Association Outstanding Scholarship Award, the NCTE Promising Researcher Award, and an NAE/Spencer postdoctoral fellowship. Her current research focuses on how teachers construct implications from research across sites and professional communities.

Review of Research in Education
February 2008, Vol. 32, pp. 371–375
DOI: 10.3102/0091732X07313907
© 2008 AERA. http://rre.aera.net

Richard Durán is a professor at the Gevirtz Graduate School of Education at the University of California, Santa Barbara. Prior to joining the university in 1984, he served as a research scientist at Educational Testing Service, where he conducted studies on the validity of the SAT for use with Latino/a students and the validity of the Test of English as a Foreign Language from a communicative competence perspective. His specialty areas include assessment and education policy, and education strategies serving English language learners. He has served as a member of the National Research Council Board on Testing and Assessment and as a member of its Committee on Appropriate Test Use, which authored a congressionally mandated report on high-stakes assessment. He also has served as a member of assessment technical advisory committees for California, New York, Oregon, Texas, and Washington and as a member of the National Assessment of Education Progress Validity Studies Panel.

Richard A. Duschl (PhD, 1983, University of Maryland-College Park) is a professor of science education in the Graduate School of Education at Rutgers University and executive member of the Rutgers Center for Cognitive Studies. Prior to joining Rutgers, he held the chair of science education at King's College London. He recently served as chair of the National Research Council research synthesis report *Taking Science to School: Learning and Teaching Science in Grades K-8* (National Academies Press, 2007). His research focuses on establishing epistemic learning environments and on the role of students' inquiry and argumentation processes. Twice, he has received the JRST Award (1989, 2003) for the outstanding research article published in the *Journal of Research in Science Teaching*. He also served for more than a decade as editor of the research journal *Science Education* and editor for TC Press's *Ways of Knowing in Science and Math* book series.

Donald Freeman is an associate professor of education and director of teacher education at the School of Education, University of Michigan, Ann Arbor. He is also a senior faculty fellow at the School for International Training, Brattleboro, Vermont. His research interests focus on teacher learning in the context of organizational and systemic reform and its influence on student learning. His books include *Teacher Learning in Language Teaching* (coedited with Jack C. Richards; Cambridge University Press, 1996) and *Doing Teacher-Research: From Inquiry to Understanding* (Thomson, 1998). He was series editor of the *TeacherSource* professional development series published by Thomson Learning. He serves on the editorial board of the *Modern Language Journal* and previously served on the boards of *Educational Researcher* and *TESOL Journal.* He is a past president of Teachers of English to Speakers of Other Languages and a member of the University of Cambridge ESOL Advisory Council.

Vivian L. Gadsden is the William T. Carter Professor of Education and Child Development and the director of the National Center on Fathers and Families in the Graduate School of Education at the University of Pennsylvania. She received her doctorate from the University of Michigan in child development and education. Her research interests focus on cultural and social factors affecting learning, literacy, and language across the life course and within families, particularly, those at the greatest risk for academic and social vulnerability. Her current research studies, including a federally funded study of early childhood and a study on children of incarcerated parents, examine the intergenerational and cross-cultural nature of learning and identity formation among children, issues of persistence and resilience, and youth cultures. Her conceptual framework, family cultures, focuses on the interconnectedness between families' political, cultural, and social histories and racialized identities.

Victoria M. Hand is an assistant professor of mathematics education at the University of Colorado at Boulder. She is concerned with the interplay of culture, race, power, resistance, and learning in elementary and middle school mathematics classrooms in perpetuating what she calls the participation gap. Her work examines how classroom activity systems perpetuate or disrupt broader discourses about culture and mathematics learning in the production of hybrid versus polarized classroom participation structures. In her most recent research in an urban middle school, she studied opportunities for mathematical engagement in a low-track classroom and the construction of opposition by the students and teacher. She has been affiliated with the Diversity in Mathematics Education (DiME) center, a National Science Foundation (NSF)–funded Center for Learning and Teaching geared toward knowledge and capacity building for research and teaching on issues of equity in mathematics.

Carey Jewitt is currently a reader in the area of education and technology in the London Knowledge Lab at the Institute of Education, University of London. She is a coeditor of the journal *Visual Communication* and the director of research at the Centre for Multimodal Research at the Institute of Education. Her research interests include visual and multimodal research method and theory, representations of knowledge, and technology-mediated teaching and learning. She has written several books on multimodal and visual research, most recently *Technology, Literacy and Learning: A Multimodal Approach* (2006, Routledge) and *English in Urban Classrooms* (2005, RoutledgeFalmer) with Gunther Kress, Ken Jones, and colleagues. She is currently editing the *Routledge Handbook of Multimodal Analysis*.

Diane Larsen-Freeman is a professor of education, professor of linguistics, and director of the English Language Institute at the University of Michigan, Ann Arbor. She is also a distinguished senior faculty fellow at the School for International Training in Brattleboro, Vermont. Her research interests revolve around second-language acquisition, English linguistics, language teaching, and language-teacher education. Her books include *An Introduction to Second Language Acquisition Research* (coauthored with Michael Long; Longman, 1991), *The Grammar Book: An ESL/EFL Teacher's Course* (with Marianne Celce-Murcia; Thomson Publishing, 1999, second edition), *Techniques and Principles in Language Teaching* (Oxford University Press, 2000, second edition), *Teaching Language: From Grammar to Grammaring* (Thomson Publishing, 2003), and *Complex Systems and Applied Linguistics* (with Lynne Cameron; Oxford University Press, in press). From 1980 to 1985, she was editor of the journal *Language Learning*. In 1997, she was inducted into the Vermont Academy of Arts and Sciences. In 1999, she was selected by *ESL Magazine* as one of "the ESL pioneers." In 2000, she received the lifetime achievement award from Heinle and Heinle Publishers.

Na'ilah Suad Nasir is an assistant professor in the Stanford University School of Education. She obtained her PhD in psychological studies in education at the University of California, Los Angeles, in 2000. Her research interests center on exploring the relation between learning and culture, particularly in relation to youth in urban communities. One line of research has examined the relation between the in-school and out-of-school mathematics learning of African American children in urban schools and describes the complex cognitive strategies that some children employ in out-of-school practices such as basketball and dominoes. Another line of research examines the nature of students' racial–ethnic identities, how they are negotiated in school and classroom contexts, and how they are related to academic identity and schooling outcomes. She is a coeditor (with Paul Cobb) of *Improving Access to Mathematics: Diversity and Equity in the Classroom*, published by Teacher's College Press.

Melanie Sperling is an associate professor of education at the University of California, Riverside, where she teaches graduate courses in teaching and learning, discourse analysis, and literacy theory and research. From 2003 to 2008, she was a coeditor (along with Anne DiPardo) of the empirical journal of the National Council of Teachers of English (NCTE), *Research in the Teaching of English*. She has served the American Educational Research Association (AERA) as chair of the Writing and Literacies SIG and has served NCTE as chair of its Assembly for Research, director of its Commission on Composition, and member of its Standing Committee for Research and its Research Forum. She is a fellow of the National Conference on Research in Language and Literacy and is a past recipient of the NCTE Promising Researcher Award; the University of California, Berkeley, School of Education's Outstanding Dissertation Award; the AERA Writing and Literacies SIG Steve Cahir Award, and a National Academy of Education (NAE)/Spencer postdoctoral fellowship. She has served as a consultant for the National Writing Project (NWP) for a number of years and is a past editor of the NWP *Quarterly*. Her current research focuses on teachers' theories of teaching and learning in the context of secondary school reading and writing.

Edd V. Taylor is an assistant professor of learning sciences at Northwestern University. He obtained his PhD at the School of Education at the University of California, Berkeley. His research focuses on issues of equity in mathematics education as they relate to understanding the relationship between culture and mathematical cognition. Previous work utilized mixed methods to examine the ways students develop mathematical understandings while making purchases in corner stores. He is currently examining religious practices related to mathematical thinking, specifically, tithing. In other work, he studied an NSF-sponsored professional development program administered through the DiME Center for Learning and Teaching examining the ways teachers draw on their students' informal mathematical knowledge, the ways children engage curriculum that considers out-of-school knowledge, and the supports and constraints of drawing on children's everyday practices in classroom instruction.

Helen Timperley is currently a professor of education in the Faculty of Education at the University of Auckland, New Zealand. Her research interests include promoting the organizational and professional learning of policymakers, school leaders, and teachers in ways that affect student outcomes. She has been involved in several major projects that have been successful in developing improved outcomes for some of the country's most underserved students and has worked with policymakers to develop system levers to create the conditions to sustain those conditions. This chapter is drawn from a best-evidence synthesis iteration on professional learning and development commissioned by the New Zealand Ministry of Education. She has published four books in her specialty areas and written numerous articles published in journals such as *Journal of Curriculum Studies, Review of Educational Research, Journal of Educational Change,* and *Leadership and Policy in Schools.*

Bruce VanSledright is a professor and head of the History/Social Studies Education Program in the Department of Curriculum and Instruction at the University of Maryland, College Park. He has written extensively about the teaching and learning of history in elementary and secondary schools in the United States. Currently, he is engaged in research on ways of teaching history that rely primarily on extended investigations of the past as a means of deepening and enriching students' understandings. He can be reached at bvansled@umd.edu.

Michael Young is a professor of education at the Institute of Education and at the University of Bath. He holds degrees from the universities of Cambridge, Essex, and London, and in 1989, he was awarded an honorary doctorate by the University of Joensuu, Finland. He is a fellow of the City and Guilds of London Institute. He is an extraordinary professor at the University of Pretoria, South Africa, and Capital Normal University, Beijing. His research interests are in the sociology of knowledge and its relationship to the curriculum, vocational education, and the role of qualifications. His new book, *Bringing Knowledge Back In,* as published by Routledge in November 2007.